Comparative Approaches to Law and Religion

Comparative Approaches to Law and Religion examines the methodological challenges of studying the interplay between law and religion across diverse jurisdictions. This volume fills a critical gap in the literature by focusing on "how" to conduct comparative research, offering both theoretical foundations and practical applications. Scholars from varied legal and cultural backgrounds contributed chapters that showcase innovative methodologies tailored to specific issues in law and religion.

The book is divided into three parts. Part I explores the foundational theories, methods, and frameworks of comparative research in law and religion, addressing state-religion models, legal pluralism, and the inclusion of minors in research. Part II applies these approaches through comparative case studies, tackling topics such as medical treatment for minors, religious freedom in the EU, and judicial populism in religion-related cases. Part III provides a critical evaluation of the methodologies employed, encouraging reflection and dialogue on their strengths, limitations, and broader applicability.

This volume is an essential resource for scholars of law and religion and comparative law. By offering a blend of theoretical insights and practical examples, it equips researchers with the tools to navigate the complexities of interdisciplinary and comparative legal studies across varied jurisdictions and traditions.

Renae Barker is a senior lecturer at the School of Law in University of Western Australia and Honorary Research Fellow at the Centre for Muslim States and Societies.

Camilla Baasch Andersen is a professor at the School of Law in University of Western Australia.

Mohammad Rasmi Alumari is an assistant professor in comparative private international law and head of the private law department at the Faculty of Law -Mutah University, Jordan.

Comparative Approaches to Law and Religion

Methods and Epistemologies of Comparative Legal Analysis

Edited by Renae Barker, Camilla Baasch Andersen and Mohammad Rasmi Alumari

Routledge
Taylor & Francis Group
LONDON AND NEW YORK

First published 2025
by Routledge
4 Park Square, Milton Park, Abingdon, Oxon OX14 4RN

and by Routledge
605 Third Avenue, New York, NY 10158

Routledge is an imprint of the Taylor & Francis Group, an informa business

British Library Cataloguing-in-Publication Data
A catalogue record for this book is available from the British Library

Library of Congress Cataloging-in-Publication Data
Names: Barker, Renae, editor. | Andersen, Camilla Baasch, editor. | Alumari, Mohammad Rasmi, editor.
Title: Comparative approaches to law and religion: methods and epistemologies of comparative legal analysis / edited by Renae Barker, Camilla Baasch Andersen, Mohammad Rasmi Alumari.
Description: 1. | New York: Routledge, 2025. |
Includes bibliographical references and index.
Identifiers: LCCN 2024060150 |
Subjects: LCSH: Comparative law. | Religion and law. | Ecclesiastical law. | Legal research. | Law–Methodology.
Classification: LCC KB197 .C66 2025 | DDC 340/.2–dc23/eng/20250102
LC record available at https://lccn.loc.gov/2024060150

ISBN: 978-1-032-47888-3 (hbk)
ISBN: 978-1-032-47891-3 (pbk)
ISBN: 978-1-003-39731-1 (ebk)

DOI: 10.4324/9781003397311

Typeset in Galliard
by Deanta Global Publishing Services, Chennai, India

Contents

Illustrations

Figures

Tables

Contributors

Amin Al-Astewani focuses on the role played by religious tribunals in Western legal systems. Over the past few years, he has led cutting-edge research on a novel type of religious tribunal in the UK, namely Islamic Shariah tribunals. After conducting fieldwork research at four of the most prominent of these tribunals, Dr Al-Astewani submitted written evidence to Parliament on the legal status of their decisions and practices, as part of the government's first public review of Shariah councils in the UK. His evidence was subsequently cited by over 20 media outlets, including internationally. As part of his engagement with communal organisations and bodies, Dr Al-Astewani has also advised the UK Board of Shariah Councils on the legal status of Islamic Tribunals. He continues to offer his expertise and advice to both policymakers and Shariah councils on the legal status and role of Islamic tribunals in the modern English legal system.

Mohammad Rasmi Alumari is an assistant professor in comparative private international law and head of the private law department at the faculty of law, Mutah University, Jordan (PhD UWA Australia, 2020). His research interests include conflict of laws, property law, law and religion, contractual liability, and the theory of obligations.

Camilla Baasch Andersen is a professor at the School of Law at the University of Western Australia. Throughout her career, she has served at numerous universities worldwide, including the University of Leicester in the United Kingdom, Centre for Commercial Law Studies, University of London, and University of Copenhagen in her native Denmark. She is the founding co-editor of *The Journal of Comparative Law* and has been the National Reporter for the United Kingdom for the International Academy of Comparative Law. She works closely with business, government, and academia in pursuit of Commercial Law facilitating trade and has written extensively on the CISG, international commerce, visual law and legal design, comparative method, dispute resolution, and proactive approaches to law. She founded and leads the Comic Book Contract project at UWA (see www.comicbookcontracts.com). For more information, and an overview of her extensive publications, see: https://research-repository.uwa.edu.au/en/persons/camilla-andersen

P T Babie is Bonython Chair in Law and Professor of Law and Associate Dean of Law (International) at Adelaide Law School, The University of Adelaide, Australia. His research interests include property law, property theory, the history of property, and law and religion.

Renae Barker is a senior lecturer in the Law School at the University of Western Australia and an honorary research fellow at the Centre for Muslim States and Societies. In 2024, she was a visiting professor at Università degli Studi di Milano – Bicocca, Dipartimento di Giurisprudenza, where she conducted research on state and religion modelling. She is an alumni of the International Centre for Law and Religion Studies Young Scholars Fellowship on Religion and the Rule and Law and regularly presents master classes in the fellowship on state and religion. She has published widely on a range of law and religion issues both domestically and internationally. She is the author of *State and Religion: The Australian Story* (Routledge 2019) and the lead editor of *Law and Religion in the Commonwealth: The Evolution of Case Law* (Hart 2022).

Arvind P Bhanu has worked in the field of law for over two decades, holding various positions at different institutes. He ascended from assistant professor to principal and head. Additionally, he served as a professor of law with a deep interest in legal research and acting director of Amity School of Law, Delhi (ALSD) – India's top five law schools. Currently, Dr Bhanu works as a professor of law and additional director/joint head, overseeing law research at ALSN, Amity University, Noida. His research interests span comparative constitutional law, law of crimes, human rights law, and law and religion. Dr Bhanu earned his doctoral degree in his area of research interest from Aligarh Muslim University, Aligarh, India. Notably, he serves as the editor of the prestigious *Amity Law Review* (ALR), and his work has been featured in flagship *US Law Reviews* as well as numerous publications in journals indexed by SCOPUS, WoS, UGC-listed journals etc.

Georgina Clarke graduated with a *Juris Doctor* from the University of Western Australia in 2022. She was a judge's associate for the Federal Court of Australia before moving to Clifford Chance, Perth, Western Australia.

Esther Erlings is a senior lecturer in law at Macquarie University (Sydney, AU). She has previously held positions at Flinders University and The Chinese University of Hong Kong, where she also completed her PhD following prior degrees from Utrecht and Maastricht Universities. Esther's research concentrates on family, health, and tort law, in combination with human rights. She is particularly interested in decision-making ability, expressed as both internal ability (capacity or competence) and external ability, including the impact of substitute decision-making regimes, and access to dispute resolution processes. Esther is the author of *Religious Rights within the Family: From Coerced Manifestation to Dispute Resolution in*

France, England and Hong Kong (Routledge UK, 2020), and has published widely on aspects of parental responsibility and children's education in journals such as the *Asian Journal of Law* and Society and the *Child and Family Law Quarterly*. As a socio-legal researcher, Esther is a lifetime member of the Asian Law and Society Association (ALSA) and the current president of the Law and Society Association of Australia and New Zealand (LSAANZ). She is the skills coordinator for Macquarie Law School's research degrees and a member of the University's Human Research Ethics Committee.

Sarah Moulds is an associate professor in law at the University of South Australia, editor of the *Australasian Parliamentary Review*, and co-founder and director of the Rights Resource Network SA. She is passionate about parliaments and connecting citizens and communities with lawmakers. In 2022, Dr Moulds was awarded a Churchill Fellowship to explore how to empower young people to engage effectively with Australian parliaments. Her publications explore the important role that parliamentary committees play in rights protection in Australia and the role parliaments can and should play in holding governments to account. Dr Moulds is also the Deputy Chair of the International Parliamentary Engagement Network, a group that helps connect people to parliaments all around the world. Dr Moulds' career has a strong law reform focus and includes seven years at the Law Council of Australia, including as Director of Criminal Law and Human Rights. She also served as a senior project officer at the South Australian Law Reform Institute where she helped deliver a wide range of legislative reforms that promote equality and protect human rights.

Tania Pagotto is a postdoctoral research fellow in Law and Religion at the School of Law, University of Milan-Bicocca, where she teaches courses on the Law of Religions. Her current research focuses on civil religion and national-religious symbols. She served as an editor for *Security, Religion, and the Rule of Law: International Perspectives* (Routledge) and has published extensively on topics such as religious symbols and reasonable accommodation.

Jeremy Patrick is a senior lecturer at the University of Southern Queensland School of Law and Justice. He has law degrees from the University of Nebraska (JD), University of Toronto (LLM), and York University (PhD). He specialises in law and religion and constitutional law and has published in American, Canadian, and Australian journals. He is the author of *Faith or Fraud? Fortune-Telling, Spirituality, and the Law* (UBC Press, 2020) and founding co-editor of the *Australian Journal of Law and Religion*.

Neville Rochow KC is an Australian barrister and an associate professor (Adj.) at the Adelaide Law School. He holds the following degrees: Bachelor of Laws (with Honours); Master of Laws; a Doctor of Philosophy (each from the University of Adelaide); and Master of Laws in Competition and Consumer Law and Policy (from Deakin University). His practice as a barrister has been at trial and at all appellate levels in a diversity of areas that include competition, consumer, commercial, constitutional law, and human rights. Dr Rochow has held honorary professorships and international fellowships at various universities in Australia and abroad. In 2019, he was awarded the Hans-Jürgen and Marianne Ohff Research Grant, to take up a position as Gastwissenschaftler at the University of Mannheim Law School. During his broad and long career, he has presented on legal and policy topics in the United Kingdom, Europe, Asia, the United States, New Zealand, and Australia. He has appeared before the English Law Commission on reform of marriage law; he has also spoken in Australian state and federal parliaments and parliamentary inquiries, in the European Parliament in Brussels, at the European Court of Human Rights in Strasbourg, and in the House of Lords at Westminster. Since joining the Bar, Dr Rochow has endeavoured to maintain an interest in the theoretical operations of the law. He has written dozens of articles, book chapters, and professional papers on a variety of legal subjects. He accepted invitations to present the research underlying the chapter in this volume to conferences held in May 2014 in Athens, Greece, and in Palermo (Sicily), Italy.

Ronen Shoval is the Dean of the Argaman Institute in Jerusalem and the head of the Herzl Advanced Program for Philosophy and Culture Studies. He has served as a research fellow and lecturer in political philosophy at Princeton University. Dr Shoval is a distinguished philosopher and the author of *Herzl's Vision* 2.0 (Mass 2013), which explores the political philosophy of Zionism. His second book, *Holiness and Society: A Socio-Political Exploration of the Mosaic Tradition* (Routledge 2024), delves into the subtle political philosophy within the Biblical narrative.

Sonia Sthapak is an associate professor, Department of Education, University of Allahabad, India. Her research interests lie in higher education and legal education. She has several books/book chapters, research articles, and funded projects to her credit.

Matt Watson is a senior lecturer in the TC Beirne School of Law, The University of Queensland. His research interests lie primarily in the fields of legal and political philosophy. Dr Watson's core research areas include multiculturalism and minority rights (with an emphasis on minority language rights and language policy), constitutionalism, law and religion, and all aspects of the philosophy of law.

Gerhard van der Schyff is an associate professor in the Department of Public Law and Governance at the Law School of Tilburg University in the Netherlands. His research interests include constitutional law and fundamental rights, especially from a comparative and European perspective.

In 2015, he held a Humboldt Fellowship at the Chair of Professor Christian Calliess at the Freie Universität Berlin in Germany on the topic of constitutional identity in the European Union. Together, they edited *Constitutional Identity in a Europe of Multilevel Constitutionalism* (Cambridge University Press, 2020).

Flavia Bellieni Zimmermann is a lecturer in Public Policy in the School of Social and Political Sciences at the University of Melbourne. She is also an adjunct research fellow in the School of Social Sciences at the University of Western Australia. Flavia was a visiting fellow at Western Sydney University and a member of the University of Western Australia Centre for Muslim States and Societies, where she conducted a comparative study with migrant Brazilians and Pakistanis in Australia, exploring lived experiences of honour, religion, and gender. She has published widely on Brazilian politics, policy, and international relations, both internationally and domestically. She is the author of the forthcoming book *Honour Consciousness, Religion and Gender: Brazilian and Pakistani Lived Experiences in Australia* (Brill 2024).

Introduction

Camilla Baasch Andersen, Mohammad Rasmi Alumari, and Renae Barker

Introduction: Comparative Approaches

Under various labels and guises, "comparative law" and "comparative legal methodology" has been used for hundreds of years for various purposes in legal and socio-legal sciences. Although the term is a relatively modern one, first used in the 19th century when it became clear that a systematic comparison of legal institutions served the understanding of foreign cultures and legal progress, the origins of modern Comparative Law can actually be traced back as far as 1667 to Gottfried Wilhelm Leibniz in *Nova Methodus Discendae Docendaeque Iurisprudentiae.*[1] So, it is far from new. What IS perhaps more contemporary is the more serious pragmatic analysis it has been undergoing for the last few decades, as its complexity and potential are nurtured and better embraced in law.[2]

As it has grown in application and popularity, the concept of what the comparative method is and how it can be used has become increasingly confusing. One of the most challenging questions over the past few decades has thus been "How do you conduct a comparative legal study?", and that challenge applies across all areas of law where comparative analysis could function as a valuable tool. This is not a unique challenge for the emerging area of law and religion. However, we are seizing the opportunity to showcase the difficulties of the comparative method in this discipline for two reasons. First, to help grow the tool of comparing in this field of law directly, but also to showcase what comparative method/epistemology and approaches can look like and how they

1 Gottfried Wilhelm Leibniz, *Nova Methodus Discendae Docendaeque Jurisprudentiae* (Frankfurt, 1667).

2 See, for instance, Pierre Legrand 'How to Compare Now' (1996) 16(2) *Legal Studies* 157–274; Geoffrey Samuels 'Taking Method Seriously' (Part One) (2007) 2(2) *Journal of Comparative Law* 94–119; and Geoffrey Samuels 'Taking Method Seriously' (Part Two) (2007) 2(1) *Journal of Comparative Law 210–237.* The latter two by Geoffrey Samuels published in a (then) newly launched law journal dedicated entirely to comparative method, The Journal of Comparative Law (launched in 2006).

DOI: 10.4324/9781003397311-1

function to influence any area of law that needs inspiration for how this tool can apply and what it can do.

So – how CAN it apply? There is no simple answer to that question, and we project that there never will be, nor should there be. As will become clear to the novice in comparative method while reading this book, and is already known to the intermediary reader, there is no set method for comparative analysis. It is more an epistemology of establishing a variety of protocols or approaches to design a method which works for the purpose of the study. For this reason, this book seeks to create a mosaic image of the understanding of the comparative methodology in law and religion, which reflects a wide variety of beliefs, experiences, and cultural backgrounds of the authors of this book's chapters. Those aspects make this book original because they reflect the "real" world from different dimensions.

Since this book focuses on comparative methodology for studying law and religion, it is worth mentioning that its contents, as a whole, do not necessarily reflect the views of the participating researchers or its editors. In other words, this book is not intended to present the religious or legal opinions contained herein, as they necessarily express the views of the authors, which are derived from their scientific convictions, experience, and culture; and therefore, may differ from what others believe. Rather, this book aims to describe and demonstrate the methodology adopted by researchers as a theoretical foundation for designing comparative methodologies in law and religion studies.

Introduction: Law and Religion

Law and religion is a vast and multifaceted field, intersecting across jurisdictions, cultures, and epochs. Just as comparative legal approaches involve diverse methods and epistemologies, so too does law and religion. There is no universally agreed-upon definition of what constitutes the study of law and religion. As Sandberg notes in his recent work, *Rethinking Law and Religion*, there is a tendency for academic study as well as advocacy in the sphere of law and religion to focus primarily on freedom of religion rights' analysis.[3] This is perhaps due to the dominance of human rights discourse over the past few decades. However, the field of law and religion is much more.

Law and religion can be practical, focusing on the day-to-day interactions between the state and religious individuals, institutions, and groups operating within the chosen jurisdiction(s). It can also take a theoretical approach, attempting to understand the theoretical underpinnings of those interactions. The discipline encompasses almost any conceivable aspect of secular law. As Latham CJ observed in the Australian High Court case *Adelaide Company of Jehovah's Witnesses v Commonwealth*, religion can touch upon almost any aspect of a person's life:

3 Russell Sandberg, *Rethinking Law and Religion* (Edward Elgar Publishing, 2024).

> It may influence what they eat and drink, what they wear, whom they associate with, how they raise their children, when they wake up and when they go to sleep, which day they work and which they rest … It can even influence how they interact within civil society and, in a democracy, whom they vote for.[4] (references omitted)

Law and religion also go beyond the study of secular law – including religious law such as Sharia, Rabbinical, or Canon law. It includes both the study of how religious legal systems intersect with the secular law as well as the study of religious law in its own context. This field can appear relatively modern in some jurisdictions, while being deeply rooted in ancient traditions in others.

In this volume, the various chapters illustrate the diversity of perspectives within the study of law and religion. However, this perspective does not capture the entire scope of the field. While the scope of this volume reflects a broad approach to the study of law and religion, it is important to acknowledge that certain areas are under-represented. Much of the focus in this volume is on Western jurisdictions with predominantly Christian traditions, although there are notable exceptions, which means that other religious and cultural frameworks, such as Islamic, Hindu, or Indigenous legal systems, receive less attention. This is not a limitation of the field itself but rather of the scope of this particular volume. Just as comparative legal methodologies are numerous, so too are the potential avenues for exploring the intersections between law and religion.

We hope that this contribution to the study of law and religion will spark further exploration, encouraging the systematic application of comparative approaches to a wider range of jurisdictions and faith traditions. Ultimately, the study of law and religion, like comparative law, is not a static or monolithic field but one that evolves with the legal, social, and religious landscapes it seeks to understand.

Structure of This Book

This book is divided into three main parts. Part I discusses the comparative methodology in law and religion from various aspects. It explores how methodologies in law and religion could be designed, spanning five individual chapters that offer different perspectives in specific areas.

Part II consists of nine chapters, where the authors have moved from the theoretical perspective to practical application. Instead of dealing with the theoretical issues of comparative methodology, the authors in this part have developed and employed their methodologies to fit their research questions. Finally, Part III includes only two chapters, but is the heart of this book. These

4 Renae Barker, 'Rejecting Security' in Tania Pagotto, Joshua M Roose and GP Marcar (eds) *Security, Religion, and the Rule of Law* (Routledge, 2024) 151, 153.

chapters "un"-critically analyse and respond to the comparative approaches employed in the proceeding chapters with a particular focus on the chapters from Part II of the book.

Part I: Comparative Theories, Approaches, and Methods

Part I consists of five chapters focusing on specific issues for comparative approaches in law and religion. It begins with Patrick (Chapter 1) "How to Do Comparative Law and Religion", which builds on established comparative law methodologies, particularly John Reitz's principles.[5] Patrick contributes to the general understanding of comparative methodology by justifying the application of Reitz's principles to law and religion studies. Barker and Clarke (Chapter 2), in "Understanding Models of State-Religion Relationships", aim to sort state-religion relationships into categories to aid researchers in navigating this complex area, offering a way to navigate this aspect of research. Al-Astewani (Chapter 3), in "The Utility of Legal Pluralism as a Conceptual Approach in the Field of Law and Religion", analyses the utility of legal pluralism as a conceptual approach to law and religion studies, arguably clarifying that this may be a tool itself in the contexts of comparative approaches. Erlings' (Chapter 4) chapter, "Minors in Comparative Law and Religion Research", focuses on establishing a theoretical framework for comparative law and religion studies involving children, not only highlighting the need to consider this as a separate yardstick but also to be sensitive to pragmatic functional aspects of society in all law and religion comparisons. Finally, Shoval (Chapter 5), in "Studies in the Sociological Method of Biblical Scholarship", utilises and suggests methods on how Biblical interpretation can be conducted as part of law and religion studies. The chapter introduces social science tools to the comparativist and addresses the complexity of understanding religious texts as teachings and cultural constructs, not merely words.

Part II: Comparative Case Studies in Law and Religion

Part II consists of nine chapters and will be the most familiar to scholars of law and religion. Each chapter conducts a comparative analysis focusing on a specific law and religion topic across two or, in some cases, more jurisdictions. As we discussed earlier and highlight in Chapter 15 of the book, the authors employ a range of different comparative methods and approaches and provide concrete examples of how these approaches can be used in the context of comparative law and religion analysis.

5 John C Reitz, 'How to Do Comparative Law (Symposium: New Directions in Comparative Law)' (Pt American Journal of Comparative Law) (1998) 46(4) *American Journal of Comparative Law* 617.

The first two chapters, Watson (Chapter 6), "A Socio-Legal Explication of the Divergent Legal Approaches to State Funding of Religious Schools in Canada and the United States", and Babie (Chapter 7), "American Constitutional Experience and the Interpretation of the Australian Religion Guarantees", both consider the issue of state funding of religion. We therefore invited the authors to reply to one another – these replies have been included as Chapters 6.1 and 7.1. This legal dialogue illustrates the aspects that a comparatist should be aware of and know how legal systems may differ significantly upon closer look even while appearing similar from afar.

Barker and Andersen (Chapter 8), "Refusal of Life Saving Medical Treatment by Mature Minors – A Comparative Analysis of Australia, Canada, and the United Kingdom" represents an example of the diversity of methodology that this book advances: the bespoke intermediary jurisprudence. Perhaps unsurprisingly given that the authors are two of the editors of this book! The chapter highlights how different comparative approaches can be combined, in this case in the context of a transplant study considering the translatability of laws regulating the consent and refusal of medical treatment by mature minors from the United Kingdom and Canada to Australia.

In "Interpreting the Right to Freedom of Religion in the EU Charter of Fundamental Rights: Outlining and Analysing the Function of the European Convention on Human Rights According to Art 52(3) CFR", van der Schyff (Chapter 9) also looks at this issue of transplants and offers an example of employing the theory of legal transplants to establish relationships between the legal systems being compared.

Pagotto (Chapter 10), "The *Kirpan* Case Law in Italy and Canada: Comparing Law and Religion Judgments in the Rise of Judicial Populism", is a good example of how to utilise the methods of comparative law to establish a reliable argument regarding complicated issues in law and religion. By employing the analytical method to define the kirpan,[6] the author opens the discussion and paves the way to illustrating the conflict between two laws within the same legal system regarding the same issue. Likewise, Rochow (Chapter 11) utilises the analytical method to define a central term in "Of Missiles and Wedding Cakes: Utilising Human Dignity to Hold a Hohfeldian Lens in Comparative Jurisprudence". These two chapters will be useful for future

6 The kirpan is a ceremonial sword that is one of the five articles of faith required to be worn by baptized Sikhs, known as Khalsa Sikhs. It represents a Sikh's duty to protect the weak and uphold justice and righteousness. The wearing of the kirpan is a mandatory religious obligation and is deeply intertwined with the Sikh principles of compassion, honour, and the fight against oppression. See Renae Barker, 'Rejecting Security: A Comparative Analysis of the Rejection of Security, Public Safety, and Public Order Concerns as a Ground for Restricting Freedom of Religion in Religious Dress Cases' in Tania Pagotto et al. (eds), *Security, Religion, and the Rule of Law: International Perspectives* (Taylor & Francis, 2023) 156–159. See also *Multani v Commission Scolaire Marguerite-Bourgeoys* [2006] 1 SCR 256.

researchers dealing with legal issues, the complexities of which are attributed to the terminology used in their area of research.

In "Listening to the People? A Comparative Analysis of Parliamentary Committee Inquiries Concerning Freedom of Religious Belief in Australia and Scotland", Moulds (Chapter 12) offers an example of legal studies that take methods seriously. Moulds explains and clearly outlines her methodology providing a practical example of how intermediary jurisprudence can be developed and employed in a comparative study. To this end, Moulds dedicates a significant part of her introduction to explaining how she designed the methodology, including the steps and their importance. She highlights the considered factors and their indicators and continues to explain how the methodology will be applied to her study. This approach helps readers not only to understand her methodology but also the underlying logic, which makes it adjustable and transplantable.

Bhanu and Sthapak (Chapter 13), in their chapter, "Religion as Individual Affair and Constitutional Permissions in India – Gathering Comparative Perspectives of Practicing It and Religious Mark on the Body in Public Domain", provide an example of how to employ comparative methodology in law and religion without ignoring the uniqueness of each legal system. They focus on cultural and political contexts, which play a vital role not only in shaping the law but also in its interpretations by the court. The methodology adopted by the authors highlights the importance of social and academic dialogue surrounding a legal issue to approach it from a comparative perspective, ie, how material other than academic work might enhance the researcher's understanding of a legal issue and its roots.

Last but not least, Bellieni Zimmermann (Chapter 14) offers in her chapter, "Grounded Theory in the Study of Religion: A Critical Appraisal to Socio-Cultural Factors and Gender-based Legislation in Brazil and Pakistan", an example of an interdisciplinary study, using social science methods to understand the impact of law and its religious context on the chosen societies. To achieve this, Bellieni Zimmermann spends a significant amount of time on the cultural and legal landscape in Brazil and Pakistan. The aim is not to compare those two jurisdictions as such but rather to use that as cultural context to explain the views on honour held by (Australian) migrant women from these two countries. This work bridges comparative law to its nearby disciplines, particularly social science.

Part III: Critiquing Comparative Approaches

Part III includes only one chapter but is very much at the core of this book. Indeed, as outlined, those who are new to comparative methodology and analysis might like to begin here. In this chapter, we as the editors; Rasmi Alumari, Andersen, and Barker (Chapter 15) – engage directly with the extensive debate on how to conduct a comparative study. It offers an explanation of the different methods that have been suggested by comparative law scholars and evaluates them in a manner that makes them easier to use, before proceeding with applying these methods to the work of the authors in Part II. This chapter does not aim to evaluate the methodologies used by the authors; it simply aims to label their methods to create a mosaic image of comparative methodologies for the benefit of future researchers.

In bringing together this volume, we hope to create a dialogue between the authors and editors on the question of methodology and approach to comparative analysis in the field of law and religion. To that end, the chapter authors were invited to provide a rejoinder to our analyses of their approaches. While we received several responses, most responded to the project as a whole rather than to our specific critiques of the methods employed in their charters. We have, therefore, chosen to include these responses, unabridged, in Appendix I.

Final Reflections from the Editors: How to Use This Book

As mentioned, this book is not only intended to be a handbook for comparatists working on issues involving law and religion, but also a showcase of the applications and utilities of various comparative legal methodologies. The use of the book will thus depend on what the reader hopes to accomplish and their level of familiarity with both with comparative approaches and law and religion.

We recommend that the reader first become familiar with the structure of this book as set out earlier. A novice in comparative law might then want to read Chapter 15, Sections I–III, which set out our theories of comparative methods and how we believe they should be understood and contextualised. Those who are new to the study of law and religion might like to begin with Chapters 1 and 2, which set out some foundational issues in law and religion and how they might be used in comparative studies before diving into the meatier topics in later chapters.

The reader interested in the theoretical debate on comparative methodology and how it should be designed might then move to Part I of the book and its commentary in Chapter 15, where selected toolsets specific to law and religion, but exemplary of comparative method protocols, are set out. For those with an active interest in law and religion, reading the book from start to finish will work well to get across all the messages in the book. Of course, if you have a specific interest in the topics of any of the individual chapters, you are welcome to start there too!

When reading any of the chapters in Part II of the book, we recommend that the reader have a look at the analysis of that chapter in Chapter 15, Section III, followed by the author's response in the Appendix. To facilitate this approach, we have added cross-referencing boxes at the conclusion of each chapter in Parts I and II of the book.

However you read it, we hope you enjoy it and feel inspired by it. And we hope it helps to spark debate and further development of one of law's most significant epistemologies: comparative method.

Part I

Comparative Theories, Approaches, and Methods

1 How to Do Comparative Law and Religion

Jeremy Patrick[1]

I Introduction

Scholars of law and scholars of religion work in fields that share deep similarities because both subjects are "normative structures which govern communal life … and are both concerned with the interpretation of age-old texts".[2] In an important essay, Harold Berman noted that:

> Like religions, law everywhere communicates its values (a) through *ritual*, that is, formal procedures of legislation, adjudication, and administrative regulation that symbolise its objectivity, (b) through *tradition*, that is, distinctive legal language and practices handed down over generations and centuries that symbolise its continuity with the past and its continuation into the future, (c) through *authority*, that is, reliance upon written or spoken sources that effectively symbolise its binding power, and (d) through *universality*, that is, justification of itself in axiomatic terms as the embodiment of universally valid principles and concepts … These characters of law tend to give it a sacred quality.[3]

These similarities might make doing comparative work in law and religion seem natural and appealing. Indeed, as the present volume indicates, there is no shortage of examples in the scholarly literature. But doing comparative law and religion and doing comparative law and religion *well* are two different things – because as much as they have similarities, there are crucial distinctions

1 Senior Lecturer, University of Southern Queensland. The author would like to acknowledge Professor Reid Mortensen, Dr Rena MacLeod, and Dr Renae Barker for their extremely helpful feedback.

2 Joshua Neoh, 'Text, Doctrine and Tradition in Law and Religion' (2013) 2(1) *Oxford Journal of Law and Religion* 175, 176.

3 Harold J Berman, 'Comparative Law and Religion' in Mathias Reimann and Reinhard Zimmerman (eds), *The Oxford Handbook of Comparative Law* (Oxford University Press, 2006) 746.

DOI: 10.4324/9781003397311-3

between them that are easy for a specialist in just one or the other field to overlook. Comparative law is a well-established and theoretically advanced subset of legal studies, just as comparative religion is a well-established and theoretically advanced subset of anthropology. But scholarly literature on the methodology of "comparative law and religion" as an independent interdisciplinary subject is scarce.[4]

The goal of this chapter is to provide a concise, practical guide for improving the quality of comparative research in law and religion. It is inspired by John Reitz's classic article "How to Do Comparative Law",[5] a clearly-written and approachable statement of nine principles for the comparative legal scholar to remember. Similarly, this chapter will cover some initial considerations and challenges that a researcher in the specific area of comparative law and religion may face. If successful, it will provide the reader some useful advice and reminders in a straightforward, non-theory-heavy format. As Reitz says, "[m]ost of us who teach and write in the field of comparative law … were not taught formally how to *do* comparative law".[6] The same is surely even more true for doing comparative law and religion, and so the only way most of us can gain proficiency and improve is to read widely and share what we have learned through experience.

II Initial Considerations

Although there are certainly exceptions, most people working in comparative law and religion are lawyers by training, not sociologists of religion or cultural anthropologists.[7] Expertise in law is not the same as expertise in religion, and, unfortunately, the old adage that "legal training sharpens the mind by narrowing it" can be an obstacle to good work in comparative law and religion. The goal of this section is to discuss three general considerations about the interaction of law and religion that may provide a useful conceptual backdrop for a scholar's work in the field. Specifically, this section discusses how law and religion recognise each other in different ways, how both law and religion can blur into general cultural norms, and why it is valuable to distinguish between form and substance in both fields.

A Mutual Disparate Recognition

When it comes to religion, law must try to do the impossible: define it. In law, whether something is or is not a "religion" is not merely an interesting academic, philosophical, or intellectual exercise; it is a label that carries with

4 See ibid 739–40.

5 John C Reitz, 'How to Do Comparative Law' (1998) 46 *American Journal of Comparative Law* 617.

6 Ibid 617 (emphasis added).

7 Cf Berman (n 2) 741 ('Students of comparative law have typically been lawyers – jurists by profession, not theologians or religious scholars'.).

it concrete advantages (and, occasionally, disadvantages). A group of people legally classified as religious may be able to gain tax benefits, discriminate against protected categories of minorities, or be entitled to have representatives ("chaplains") in public institutions like schools and hospitals. On the other hand, at least in some countries, a group of people once legally classified as religious may be forbidden from meeting under laws banning "extremism",[8] while in other countries "conspicuous religious garb" may lead to exclusion of individuals from school or the public service.[9] As Barker says,

> [t]he way in which the State defines religion is itself an important interaction between the State and religion. The State's definition of religion has the power to exclude and include; to make legitimate or illegitimate religions which fall inside or outside its definition.[10]

However, a key reminder is that we need not take law's recognition that something is "religious" or "not religious" as gospel (pardon the pun). Although Voltaire said "[i]f you wish to converse with me, define your terms",[11] a conversation is a two-way street, and law does not get the final say except within its own domain. In other words, a scholar remains perfectly free to argue that Scientology is not a religion despite the High Court of Australia's decision in *Church of the New Faith*,[12] or that Psychic Sophie's idiosyncratic blend of Christianity, New Age, and pseudoscience should be considered equivalent to a religion despite the Fourth Circuit Court of Appeals in the United States.[13] A *legal* definition of religion is relevant in a *legal* context in a particular jurisdiction, but does not exhaust the possibilities beyond that – and many other disciplines have grappled with those possibilities.[14]

Law recognises religion through definitions, rules, and policies, but religion has its own ways of recognising law. Some religions are happy to be enmeshed in the state and cede some practical control for the additional influence, funding, and opportunities it brings.[15] Others see law as a brooding background presence that demarcates only what cannot be done while leaving everything

8 See, eg, Emily B Baran, 'Life Under Ban: Jehovah's Witnesses in Russia Since 2017' (2021) 41(2) *Occasional Papers on Religion in Eastern Europe* 35.

9 See, eg, Isabelle Rorive, 'Religious Symbols in the Public Space: In Search of a European Answer' (2009) 30 *Cardozo Law Review* 2669.

10 Renae Barker, *State and Religion: The Australian Story* (Routledge, 2019) 15.

11 Will Durant, *The Story of Philosophy* (Time Incorporated, rev ed 1962) 58.

12 See *Church of the New Faith v Commissioner of Pay-roll Tax (Victoria)* [1983] HCA 40.

13 See *Moore-King v Chesterfield*, 708 F.3d 560 (4th Cir. 2013).

14 See, eg, Inger Furset and Pal Repstad, *An Introduction to the Sociology of Religion* (Taylor & Francis, 2007) 15–28 (discussing various sociological approaches to defining religion); Morton Klass, *Ordered Universes: Approaches to the Anthropology of Religion* (Boulder: Westview Press, 1995) 8 (noting enormous disagreement in the field of anthropology on how to define religion).

15 Formally established religions, like the Church of England, are good examples of this category.

else within the autonomy of the religious group.[16] But importantly, "law" itself may have a different (or additional) meaning to a religious individual. Beyond law as representing the public civil and criminal justice system of a nation-state, some religious groups have centuries-old and elaborate systems of internal regulation. Guilt, shame, and various forms of social ostracism can create enormously coercive psychological pressure on a person to conform to the standards of their religious community. Secular authorities might think of such religious codes of conduct as simply "private", "optional", or "self-imposed" and of no *real* concern, but, to the person of faith, the consequences of being found to have violated religious law may be far more impactful and traumatic than an encounter with secular law.[17] This holds weight for both how much allowance the law makes for conscientiously-motivated behaviour by religious persons, but also potentially complicates the traditional liberal notion that "the right of exit" is a complete answer to the problematic internal decision-making of some religious groups.

As law and religion recognise each other in mutually disparate ways, it is important for a scholar to understand and be able to work within these shifting perspectives.

B Cultural Blurring

From an external point of view, law and religion are (at least to a degree) artefacts of culture. When it comes to law, we know that "legal rules and legal texts are typically deeply rooted within a specific economic, political, moral, and cultural background, … [and therefore] the comparative lawyer … must be 'culturally fluent' in another legal language".[18] Similarly, a student of religion will quickly glean just how much religious beliefs and traditions are influenced by a specific geographical, historical, and cultural matrix at its founding and throughout its subsequent evolution. This is not to say that law or religion are *identical* with culture (especially when recent transplants are considered), but that they are certainly not completely independent and self-generated institutions. Law and religion can blur into a society's background culture in such a way that it is difficult, or perhaps at times impossible, to extricate strands of influence and causality.

Why does this matter? Barker explains one reason, writing that:

> There is a fine line between religion and culture, particularly in relation to religious practice. It is not uncommon for there to be debate

16 Good examples of this approach include Mennonites and the Amish.

17 See Farrah Ahmed, 'Personal Autonomy and the Option of Religious Law' (2010) 22 *International Journal of Law, Policy, and Family* 222, 227, 230.

18 Nils Jansen, 'Comparative Law and Comparative Knowledge' in Mathias Reimann and Reinhard Zimmerman (eds), *The Oxford Handbook of Comparative Law* (Oxford University Press, 2006) 306–307.

> around whether a particular practice is religious or cultural. This has particular relevance in relation to arguments relating to freedom of religion. If a practice is cultural rather than religious, then it will not attract the protection of human rights instruments that guarantee freedom of religion.[19]

Debates over whether a practice is religious or cultural have arisen, for example, in the context of legislation in some jurisdictions regulating clitoral circumcision or the wearing of head scarves and veils. Framing a cultural practice as a religious practice is sometimes essential for legal accommodation, but that does not mean the practice is necessarily motivated by distinct religious beliefs even if a post hoc justification can always be found. Similarly, a particular set of laws in a jurisdiction may be attributed to the religious beliefs of its people, when a plausible argument can be made that culture, in the form of political ideology, may be just as much to blame. Some would point to the incredibly disparate regulation of abortion across different parts of the United States as an example where tribalism and partisan political manoeuvring is at least as important as religion when it comes to explanatory power.

The takeaway is that we should avoid a simplistic understanding that Religious Belief X *causes* Law Y in a country. Religion is a product of, and an influence on, culture. Law is a product of, and an influence on, culture. There may indeed be a relationship between religion and law, but it is equally possible that their shared background culture holds more explanatory power than anything else.

C A Masquerade of Form and Substance

One of the commonalities between law and religion that Berman identified is their shared predilection for ritual:[20] formal and symbolic practices that lend a sense of sacred reverence to their decrees. Ritual can mask reality, and in both law and religion, form can misrepresent fact.

If a Martian were to read the *Australian Constitution*, they would naturally get the impression that the King of England reigns supreme, deeply involved in government, and fully capable of refusing assent to legislation passed by Parliament, or to even change their mind and cancel it afterward. There's no mention of the Prime Minister, the fact that the King's representative in Australia always does what the Prime Minister tells them to, or that in all actual fact, the monarch frankly has little routine care or concern about what happens in the domestic political affairs of a former colony a thousand miles away. In a more mundane context, we could all scour the statute books and come up with laws that would seem deeply problematic – if they were ever enforced.

19 Barker (n 9) 6.
20 See Berman (n 2).

Formal legal rules as reflected in statutes and casebooks provide us only a small window into how the legal system actually operates in a community: there is a distinction between "law in books" and "law in action"[21] or as Grace Davie writes, "[l]aw is one thing; everyday life quite another".[22]

That same Martian could read the Bible from cover to cover, memorise the Church of England's 39 Articles of Religion, and study English ecclesiastical law in great detail, and emerge with limited practical insight into what it means to be Anglican in England today. In *Protestant-Catholic-Jew*, his classic study of religion in mid-20th-century America, Will Herberg wrote that "[n] owhere are surface appearances more deceptive, nowhere it is more necessary to try to penetrate beyond mere assertions of belief than in such ultimate matters as religion".[23] Indeed, if we were to separate out four distinct facets of one's relationship to religion – self-identity, beliefs, practices, and formal affiliation – we should not be surprised to find seeming inconsistencies just within one individual, much less an entire group. A formal statement of tenets, whether institutional or individual, should not be taken as a reliable guide to actual practice. For the Martian, sociology would be as valuable as theology in understanding a religion.

For the comparative scholar in law and religion, the problem is that it is these formal statements that are the easiest to find. In law, appellate decisions and national statute collections are much easier to discover and peruse than deep socio-legal analyses of how particular common law rules or statutory regimes work in practice. For religion, a catechism or statement of doctrine can be Googled in seconds, but understanding the complex interplay behind belief, behaviour, and identity can take years (and is likely an ongoing process). There is no easy and instant solution to this problem, but nonetheless a good faith effort should be made to look behind form in order to find substance.[24] Formal statements, whether in law or in religion, should be taken as only one piece of the overall puzzle. "For you, meanwhile, the task of setting yourself so far as in you lies to question always, as you go, what lies beyond;

21 Richard Ingleby and Richard Johnstone, 'Invocation and Enforcement of Legal Rules' in Rosemary Hunter, et al., (eds), *Thinking About Law* (Allen & Unwin, 1995) 157–158.

22 Grace Davie, 'Law, Society, and Religion: An Awkward Threesome' (2012) 1(1) *Oxford Journal of Law and Religion* 1, 5.

23 Will Herberg, *Protestant-Catholic-Jew: An Essay in American Religious Sociology* (Anchor Books, rev ed, 1960) 72. Or as the great Saki put it, '[i]t is the golden rule of all religions that no one should really live up to their precepts; when a man observes the principles of his religion too exactly he is in the immediate danger of founding a new sect'. Hector Hugh Munro, 'When William Came' in *The Complete Stories of Saki* (Wordsworth, 1993) 548.

24 From this starting point, those open to theory may find that valuable insights could be gleaned from the proponents and opponents of functionalism in (separately) comparative law and in comparative religion. See, eg, Jansen (n 17) 328; Ralf Michaels, 'The Functional Method of Comparative Law' in Mathias Reimann and Reinhard Zimmerman (eds), *The Oxford Handbook of Comparative Law* (Oxford University Press, 2006) 340; Reitz (n 4) 620.

to *whom* does this rule mean anything at all? And *how much*, even to that man, does it mean?"[25]

III Challenges

Research in comparative law and religion involves all of the challenges of comparative law (eg, access to resources, language barriers, cultural barriers) plus additional challenges from the specifically religious subject matter. In what follows, three potential challenges of comparative work in law and religion are discussed.

A Religion Should Be a Plural Noun

A reader should wince if they ever see a sentence begin with something like "Christianity says ..." or "Muslims believe ..." because, unless that sentence ends with the most basic common denominator of the religion ("Jesus is the messiah" or "Muhammad is the Prophet of God"), it is almost certainly wrong. Under one grouping falls a nearly infinite array of variations in doctrine. The same holds true for practices, and even groups with outwardly similar practices may attach different levels of importance to them: both Protestants and Catholics read the Bible and attend church, but reading scripture is more important for Protestants and attending Mass is more important for Catholics.[26] No religion is monolithic, and the larger and older a religion becomes, the more sects, denominations, heresies, orthodoxies, and variations it will have.[27] From a sociological perspective, all must be treated as equally valid representations of the religion.[28] Generalising about a religion is impossible because its sheer scope and diversity make everything said about it both true and false at the same time.[29]

If over-generalising about a religion is a problem, so too is the opposite: cherry-picking a particular sect's tenet or practice from some place in the world or some time in history and using it as a stand in to represent the entirety of

25 Karl Llewellyn, *The Bramble Bush* (Ocean Publications, 1981) 91.

26 In other words, not all religious groups will attach equal (or any) *religious* significance to particular practices they share with other religious groups.

27 See, eg, Yasuko Hassall Kobayashi, 'Debunking negative representations of Muslim minorities to overcome the binary between white Australia and minorities' (2017) 30 *Journal of Australian Studies* 17, 26 ('[O]ften Muslims are represented as one monolithic group in the media. However ... [this] does not reflect reality. Linguistic, ethnic and cultural diversity is also quite wide ... In addition to this diversity, their religious practices also have vast difference. Even within Islamic religion, there exist varieties'.)

28 Though for the purpose of analysis, it is rational to pay more attention to views with more adherents.

29 Cf James T Farrell, 'Introduction' in H L Mencken (ed) *Prejudices: A Selection* (John Hopkins University Press, 1996) xiii ('America is so vast that almost everything said about it is likely to be true, and the opposite is probably equally true'.).

the faith. Even if all else were held constant, even a slight change of geographical or chronological frame can provide a vastly different picture of the relationship between law and religion in a given context. Both are American, but being a Christian in Manhattan is likely a very different experience than being a Christian in Wyoming. What the Catholic Church represented in Quebec in 1950 is completely different than what it represented in 1970 after the Quiet Revolution. We all know that a change in jurisdiction can mean a change in law, but for religion, some scholars have an unfortunate picture of singularity and unchangeability that can easily lead readers into error.

Another common fault is privileging believers labelled as "Orthodox" over other members of the faith, as if the former were somehow more "really religious" than the latter.

> Just because orthodox adherents of a particular faith do not engage in a particular practice does not necessarily mean the practice is not a manifestation of a religious belief by another adherent. Nor does the fact that orthodox adherents of a faith manifest their belief in a particular way mean that all people who engage in that behaviour are necessarily doing so for religious reasons.[30]

A final risk, and one worth emphasising now more than ever, is that a foreign reader will stumble into self-serving statements about the relationship between law and religion in a country and assume they are the scholarly consensus. Whether it is Christian nationalism in the United States, Hindu nationalism in India, or Muslim nationalism in Indonesia, there are partisans who will use the guise of scholarship to proclaim that history or culture or demographics or law or something else "means" that country *really* belongs to a particular faith (while probably attributing everything good in that country to that faith, and everything bad in that country to "straying" from that faith). Always read widely from across the spectrum of religious, political, and ideological currents in a society so that these claims can be put into context and the full scope of academic debates in an area can be engaged with. "Read not to contradict and confute; not to believe and take for granted; nor to find talk and discourse; but to weigh and consider".[31]

B Problematic Terms

Terminology must be handled delicately in scholarship involving comparative law and religion because it can be both crucial and misleading. Incorrect use of terminology in law will reveal the scholar to be an outsider to the system, while choices about terminology in religion can be seen as intentionally

30 Barker (n 9) 7.
31 Francis Bacon, 'Of Studies' in Francis Bacon (ed), *The Essays* (Penguin, 1985) 208.

exclusivist. For example, referring to the 'Old Testament' positions oneself within a Christian framework (because there is also a "New" Testament), whereas referring to it as the "Hebrew Bible" is preferred by many scholars as a more neutral descriptor. When a sociologist of religion uses the term "cult", they may define it in morally non-judgemental terms, as "a culturally innovative cohesive group oriented to supernatural concerns", for example.[32] On the other hand, the term "cult" when used by the popular media has a definitely negative connotation that can make small and new religious groups into pariahs for doing the same things that larger, mainstream religious groups do. Older, and especially American, scholars may refer to constitutional anti-establishment provisions as guaranteeing "the separation of *church* and state" when it would be more apt (and more inclusive) to discuss the relationship between "religion and the state". Many more examples could be adduced.

From a methodological perspective, one of the insights of the functionalist approach in comparative law is that the precise terminology of a legal rule may be exactly the same, but what it actually *does* may differ dramatically between the two jurisdictions under comparison.[33] Likewise, in comparative religion, two different religions may use the exact same terminology to mean very different things. For example, the "Sabbath" ("Shabat") will be observed in distinctly different ways by Orthodox Jews compared to liberal Protestants, and valuable information can be gleaned from each religion by observing the similarities and differences. But a functionalist approach (despite whatever sociological insights it may yield) could also be viewed as reductive and even offensive to believers.[34] A researcher in comparative law and religion should be precise and careful with their choice of words and, where possible, draw upon external readers from both within and outside the faith for feedback prior to publication.

C The Limits of Immersion

Total immersion is one of the most effective ways to learn something, whether it be a language, a legal system, or a culture. As Clifford Geertz once said about scholars like himself, "We had to make ourselves parochial in order

32 See the excellent discussion in William Sims Bainbridge, *The Sociology of Religious Movements* (Routledge, 1997) 21–25 (also discussing the term 'sects').

33 See Michaels (n 23) 342 ('functionalist comparative law is factual, it focuses not on rules but on their effects, not on doctrinal structures and arguments but on events'); Mark Tushnet, 'The Possibilities of Comparative Constitutional Law' (1999) 108 *Yale Law Journal* 1225, 1235 ('functional inquiries are inherently empirical …[t]hey prompt the courts to make some assessment of the way institutions work in the real world').

34 See Jansen (n 17) 328 ('Seeing the Lord's commands and Christ's resurrection as functional solutions to our mundane problems would be a ridiculous misunderstanding').

to make ourselves cosmopolitan".[35] Many legal comparativists have practiced or taught law in the jurisdictions they are comparing, giving them firsthand experience with each. As an undergraduate, I had a sociology professor who wrote a book on homelessness after voluntarily living on the street for a year. But when it comes to religion, total immersion hits a wall. Conceivably, with permission, a scholar could embed themself within a religious institution for a set period of time to learn more about the faith, but this type of "immersion" will only ever be partial because without a true conversion and inner change of belief, only some aspects of the religion and its followers' mindsets could be learned.

This problem intensifies when the religion intends some of its sacred doctrines and texts to be accessible only to selected individuals or groups. The Church of Scientology, for example, limits access to certain material to members (or members who have reached certain thresholds within the organisation).[36] In Australia, some Aboriginal cultures separate spiritual knowledge into "men's business" and "women's business", limiting access accordingly.[37] Even if an outsider scholar *could* access this information, serious thought would have to be given to the ethical considerations involved in writing about it publicly.[38]

But what about the scholar who *has* been immersed – perhaps for a lifetime – in a particular religion? Here, the challenge is the uncritical assumption that one's particular experience in a religion is representative of everyone else's, or that it automatically lends insight into the "essence" of the religion. A childhood filled with supportive and encouraging priests of integrity and virtue should not lead to the conclusion that the entire institution is free of abusers and their enablers ("they would never do that!"), just as bad experiences with one megachurch or televangelist should not be taken as "proof" that all preachers in that faith are greedily fuelling their private wealth through donations ("they're all crooks!"). Anecdotes and personal "lived experience" may be interesting and illustrative, but they are not sufficient by themselves to warrant general conclusions about something as complex as a religion. The limits of immersion when it comes to comparative religion necessitates that findings are articulated as limited, tentative, and modest rather than as definitive and conclusive.

IV Conclusion

In "How to Do Comparative Law", Reitz concluded:

35 Quoted in Lawrence Rosen, 'Beyond Compare' in Pierre Legrand and Roderick Munday (eds), *Comparative Legal Studies: Traditions and Transitions* (Cambridge University Press, 2003) 508.

36 See generally, Douglas E Cowan, 'Researching Scientology: Perceptions, Premises, Promises, and Problematics' in James R Lewis (ed), *Scientology* (Oxford University Press, 2009).

37 See, eg, *Kartinyeri v Commonwealth*, (1998) 195 CLR 337.

38 I am indebted to Dr Renae Barker for this point and these examples.

> [W]hile the comparative method is simple to describe, it is difficult to apply because satisfactory results can be obtained only if the one making the comparisons has command of a large amount of information about the legal systems under comparison as well as the broader societies in which the legal systems exist. This factor may explain at least some of the general disappointment with comparative law: It is difficult to do well. Nevertheless, it is ever more indispensable in our interconnected and shrinking world.[39]

If it is difficult to do comparative law well, how much more challenging must it be to do comparative law and religion well? Not only must the researcher have deep knowledge of multiple legal systems and the societies that contain them, but the researcher also needs an understanding of multiple religions as well – an enormous and perhaps daunting task. As discussed throughout, challenges and pitfalls abound. Poor comparative law and religion scholarship can be myopic, culturally imperialist, insensitive, or just plain unhelpful.

But if it is so hard, why do it at all? The answer is similar to the one the comparative law scholar must make to the question "but what about the price of rutabagas in Zimbabwe?" If one had unlimited time, resources, and expertise, there would always be more and better comparisons to make; but one has to start somewhere to get anywhere, and this means the perfect cannot be the enemy of the good. Despite its challenges, comparative scholarship in law and religion holds tremendous potential for the insight (even tentative and partial) it can provide us in understanding the rules that govern us, in matters both worldly and heavenly.

Further Reading:

For analysis of the methods used in this chapter, see Chapter 15 – Section II – subsection A *Gandalf and Subjectivity* and subsection B *Multivalence and Superman*; Section IV – subsection A *The Doctrinal Method*.

For a discussion about problems associated with pluralism in the context of methodological approaches to law and religion, see Chapter 3.

39 Reitz (n 4) 635.

2 Understanding Models of State-Religion Relationships

Renae Barker[1] *and Georgina Clarke*[2]

I Introduction

A common comparative approach in the study of the interaction between the state and religion is to classify jurisdictions according to their state-religion relationship.[3] Numerous models, also sometimes referred to as typologies or taxonomies, have been suggested to describe and classify these relationships.[4]

1 Senior Lecturer University of Western Australia Law School, Honorary Research Fellow Centre Muslim States and Societies. Part of this research was conducted as a Visiting Professor at Università degli Studi di Milano-Bicoccca.

2 Graduate of the Juris Doctor of Law at the University of Western Australia, current practicing lawyer.

3 Sometimes referred to as the state-religion interaction or interaction of church and state.

4 See for example Shimon Shetreet, 'The Model of State and Church Relations and Its Impact on the Protection of Freedom of Conscience and Religion: A Comparative Analysis and a Case Study of Israel' in Winfried Brugger and Michael Karayanni (eds), *Religion in the Public Sphere: A Comparative Analysis of German, Israeli, American and International Law* (Springer, 2007) 87, 87–93; Winfried Brugger, 'On the Relationship Between Structural Norms and Constitutional Rights in Church-State Relations' in Winfried Brugger and Michael Karayanni (eds), *Religion in the Public Sphere: A Comparative Analysis of German, Israeli, American and International Law* (Springer, 2007) 21, 31–48; Viet Bader, 'Religions and States: A New Typology and a Plea for Non-Constitutional Pluralism' (2003) 6(1) *Ethical Theory and Moral Practice* 55, 65–72; Carl Esbeck, 'A Typology of Church-State Relations in Current American Thought' (1998) 15(1) *Religion & Public Education* 43; Jeroen Temperman, *State-Religion Relationships and Human Rights Law: Towards a Right to Religiously Neutral Governance* (Brill, 2010); W Cole Durham, 'Perspectives on Religious Liberty: A Comparative Framework' in John Witte Jr and Johan D van der Vyver (eds), *Religious Human Rights in Global Perspective* (Martinus Nijhoff Publishers, 1996) bk 2, 1, 20–23; Rex Ahdar and Ian Leigh, *Religious Freedom in the Liberal State* (Oxford University Press, 2013) 88–124; Michel Rosenfeld, 'Introduction: Can Constitutionalism, Secularism and Religion Be Reconciled in an Era of Globalisation and Religion Review' (2009) 30(6) *Cardoza Law Review* 2349–2351; Cécile Laborde, 'Political Liberalism and Religion: On Separation and Establishment' (2013) 21(1) *Journal of Political Philosophy* 67, 68; Richard Albert, 'The Separation of Higher Powers' (2012) 65(1) *Southern Methodist University Law Review* 3, 3–69; Renae Barker, *State and Religion: The Australian Story* (Routledge, 2019) 21–9 ('*State and Religion*'); Darryn Jensen, 'Classifying Church-State Arrangements: Beyond Religious versus Secular' in Nadirsyah Hosen and Richard Mohr (eds), *Law and Religion in Public Life: The Contemporary Debate*

DOI: 10.4324/9781003397311-4

While there is significant overlap and similarities between these models, they also have significant differences. These differences often stem from the purpose for which the model is derived. For example, the model outlined by Esbeck in *A Typology of Church-State Relations in Current American Thought*[5] is inevitably narrower in focus than many others, in that its primary purpose is to describe and categorise state-religion relationships which either exist, or are argued for, in the United States of America. By contrast, the model outlined by Temperman in his book *State Religion Relationships and Human Rights Law*[6] includes a full spectrum of possible state-religion relationships, from the complete fusion of state and religion at one extreme, through to states that seek to abolish religion and impose an alternative ideology at the other. The primary difference between these two approaches is whether the model is intended to analyse, explain, or compare different state-religion relationships within a single or small number of jurisdictions or whether it is intended to be theoretically applicable to all states. In the case of the former, the relatively narrow application means that the range of possible state-religion relationships used in the model can be customised and limited to those that are most plausible in the jurisdictions under consideration. As a result, they usually exclude extremes and can be much deeper in their analysis. By contrast, comprehensive models are broader and inevitably not as deep in their analysis. They include all possible state-religion relationships, even those which are rare or extreme. Both approaches can be useful to better understand state-religion dynamics and can act as a yardstick for comparison both between and within jurisdictions.

The purpose of this chapter is to examine the strengths and weaknesses of comprehensive models of state-religion relationships and outline some uses of these types of models in better understanding and comparing the interaction between state and religion. Models focused on one jurisdiction, or a small number of jurisdictions, must by their very nature be bespoke; developed specifically for the jurisdictions which are the subject of the comparative analysis. By contrast, the comprehensive models examined in this chapter can be developed in the abstract – although knowledge of state-religion relationships

(Routledge, 2011) 15; Julian Rivers, 'Irretrievable Breakdown? Disestablishment and the Church of England' (1994) 3 *Cambridge Papers* 2–4; Adrian Hastings, *The Faces of God Reflections on Church and Society* (Orbis Books, 1976) 47–67; Renae Barker, 'Pluralism versus Separation: Tension in the Australian Church-State Relationship' (2021) 16(1) *Religion and Human Rights* 1, 1–40 ('Pluralism versus Separation'); Alex Deagon, *A Principled Framework for the Autonomy of Religious Communities* (Hart Publishing 2023); J Christopher Soper *et al*, *The Challenge of Pluralism Church and State in Six Democracies* (Lanham, Maryland: Rowman & Littlefield, 2017); R Hirschl, *Constitutional Theocracy* (Harvard University Press, 2012) 26–40; Paul Babie, 'Religion and Constitutionalism: Oscillations Along a Continuum' (2015) 39 (1) *Journal of Religious History* 123.

5 Esbeck (n 2) 3.

6 Temperman (n 2).

in practice is obviously helpful in developing these models, and the models should be grounded in analysis of existing and historical examples. This chapter begins with an outline and categorisation of some of the types of state-religion relationships which are common in comprehensive models. . It then outlines four comprehensive models of state-religion relationships which have been proposed by Babie,[7] Temperman,[8] Ahdar and Leigh,[9] and Durham and Scharffs.[10] Finally, the chapter outlines three examples of how models can be used to answer a question not often asked in relation to models of state-religion relationships: "so what"?

II Categories of State-Religion Relationship

As outlined in the Introduction, this chapter will focus primarily on four comprehensive models of state-religion relationship. However, there are numerous other such models which have been proposed. Each have their own, often unique, categorisations and classifications for the various state-religion relationships they describe, with differing degrees of granularity and generality. It is beyond the scope of this chapter to provide a detailed description of each potential category of state-religion relationship. Instead, what Section II of this chapter seeks to do is to acknowledge the full range of categories used in models of a state-religion relationship, noting that there may be convergence, overlap and divergence in the names of the categories used in the various models, as well as in the types of state-religion relationships these different categories describe. These categories or classifications can be divided into four broad groupings: (1) positive identification; (2) positive interaction; (3) separation; and (4) negative identification/suppression. In naming these categories, the use of the terms "positive" and "negative" are not intended as a normative statement as to which state-religion categories are to be preferred. Rather, they are intended to reflect the view of the relevant state towards religion, or in the case of more exclusive identifications, at least the chosen religions, sects, or denominations.

The state-religion relationships within each broad category are not fixed. At the margins of each broad category there are classifications which, depending on how they are carried out in practice, may exist in an area of overlap between the broad categories. Our broad categories are not intended to be prescriptive, but rather to provide a way to compare and classify categories of state-religion relationships which may be called different things or divided in different ways

7 Babie (n 2) 123.
8 Temperman (n 2).
9 Adhar and Leigh (n 2).
10 W C Durhamn and B G Scharffs, *Law and Religion: National, International, and Comparative Perspectives* (Aspen Publishing, 2nd ed, 2019).

in the models but which, in fact, have much in common or may simply be a different way of understanding the same phenomenon.

It is also important to note that individual states may also exhibit characteristics of more than one category. As observed by Babie, "most nations" constitutional approach to religion "oscillates" around a number of points along a "zone" of the continuum.[11]

A "Positive" Identification

The primary feature in states with a "positive identification" between the state and religion is a choice by the state to identify with one religion, narrowly or broadly defined. States that adopt a "positive" state-religion relationship would be considered "confessional" states.[12] The classical examples of state-religion relationships in this broad category include theocracies[13] and jurisdictions with a state or established Church.[14] In a theocracy, there is a complete fusion of state and religion, with religion dominant over the state. The purpose of the state is to further the religion. Often there is no separation between civic and religious rulers and, where there are, the civic leaders are subject to religious rulers.[15] By contrast, in states with an established or state religion, the state identifies one religion, sect, or denomination (or sometimes a small number of religions) for formal recognition and support.[16] There is a high level of interaction between the state and the established or recognised religion, sect, or denomination.[17] This is usually accompanied with some form of official recognition of the religion's status; however, unlike a theocracy, there is usually separation between the civic and religious rulers. Some states with established religions, such as the United Kingdom, may even arguably be described as secular where the privileging of the established religion does not come with active discrimination against religious institutions and individuals belonging to other religions, or no religion.[18] Other state-religion relationships in this

11 Babie (n 2) 125.

12 Temperman (n 2) 12.

13 Barker, *State and Religion* (n 2) 23; Durham and Scharffs (n 8) 125; Ahdar and Leigh (n 2) 90–11; Durham (n 2) 19; Aernout J Nieuwenhuis, 'State and Religion, a Multidimensional Relationship: Some Comparative Law Remarks' (2012) 10(1) *International Journal of Constitutional Law* 156; Ahmet Alibašić, 'Models of State-Church Relations in Europe and the USA and Their Consequences' (2008) 2(1) *Archers Quarterly* 42; Jensen (n 2) 15.

14 *State and Religion* (n 2) 24; Durham and Scharffs (n 8) 125–126; Ahdar and Leigh (n 2) 100–99; Temperman (n 2) 31–63; Jensen (n 2) 16 and 21; Alibašić (n 13) 42–3; Durham (n 2) 20; Nieuwenhuis (n 13) 156; Bader (n 2) 59.

15 Ahdar and Leigh (n 2) 90; Durham and Scharffs (n 8) 18; Temperman (n 2) 12–3.

16 Ahdar and Leigh (n 2) 91, Durham and Scharffs (n 8) 125–6.

17 Soper et al (n 2).

18 Barry A Kosmin and Ariela Keysar (eds), *Secularism & Secularity: Contemporary International Perspectives* (ICCC, 2007) 9; see also W S Holdsworth, 'The State and Religious Non-

broad category include Erastianism, also referred to as Caesaropapism,[19] as well as Islamic states,[20] Christian states,[21] religious jurisdictional enclaves,[22] and secular jurisdictional enclaves.[23]

State-religion relationships such as plural establishment,[24] preferred set of religions,[25] religious status systems,[26] endorsed religions[27] mild/modest establishment,[28] millet systems[29] and selective accommodation[30] fall between the "positive identification" and "positive interaction" broad categories. These states have the identification or endorsement of the state of specific religions but lack exclusivity. Where a specific jurisdiction belongs will depend on how narrow the list of religions is drawn – the longer the list, the more likely the state is to move from "positive identification" to "positive interaction".

Compare, for example, Belgium and India. Belgium currently recognises seven religions or world views for state support: Roman Catholicism, Protestantism, Judaism, the Anglican Church, Islam, Orthodox Christianity, and non-confessional (secular) Humanism.[31] The remuneration of both recognised religious leaders and "equivalent" secular leaders are financed by the state, along with both religious education and "non-denominational moral teaching".[32] Given the broad and inclusive nature of the list in Belgium, and the nature of the support given, it is arguable that this form of plural establishment/preferred set of religions better fits within the "positive interaction" category. By contrast in India, in addition to Hinduism,[33] India formally

conformity: An Historical Retrospect' (1920) 26 *Law Quarterly Review* 339, 340; Vernon Bogdanor, *The Monarchy and the Constitution* (Clarendon Press, 1995), 228; See also *Aston Cantlow Parochial Church Council v Wallbank* [2004] 1 AC 546, 555 (per Lord Nicholls).

19 Ahdar and Leigh (n 2) 91; *State and Religion* (n 2) 23; see also Ian A McFarland et al, *The Cambridge Dictionary of Christian Theology* (2011 Cambridge University Press) 77, 167–8.

20 Temperman (n 2) 19–25.

21 Temperman (n 2) 13–9.

22 Babie (n 2) 131; Hirschl (n 2) 32.

23 Babie (n 2) 131; Hirschl (n 2) 33.

24 See Renae Barker, 'Under Most Peculiar Circumstances: The Church Acts in the Australian Colonies as a Study of Plural Establishment' (2016) 3 *Law & History* 28.

25 Durham and Scharffs (n 8) 126.

26 Ibid.

27 Ibid.

28 Laborde (n 2) 72; Deagon (n 2) 165–73; Babie (n 2) 131.

29 Bader (n 2) 80; Rosenfeld (n 2) 2349.

30 Babie (n 2) 131.

31 Leni Franken, 'State Support for Religion in Belgium: A Critical Evaluation', 59 *Journal of Church and State* (2017) 67–8.

32 Temperman (n 2) 96; see also ibid 59.

33 Which is deemed to include, for the purpose of constitutional and personal law, Sikhs, Buddhists, Baha'is, and Jains.

recognises six minority faiths: Muslims, Sikhs, Christians, Parsis, Jains, and Buddhists.[34] Importantly, in contrast to Belgium, in India:

> Personal status laws establish civil codes for members of certain religious communities in matters of marriage, divorce, adoption, and inheritance based on religion, faith, and culture. Hindu, Christian, Parsi, Jewish, and Islamic personal-status laws are legally recognized and judicially enforceable.[35]

While the Belgian list is smaller than the Indian one, arguably the consequences of inclusion or exclusion are less far-reaching. In Belgium, the focus is on state financial support of the relevant institutions; while in India, state support includes enforceability of religious law on individuals as determined by their religious identity. As a result, India arguably fits within the religious status system or millet system and is better positioned within the "positive identification" broad category.

B "Positive" Interaction

Jurisdictions with a "positive interaction" between the state and religion lack the high level of identification with single, or a narrow range of, religions, while maintaining a positive association between the state and religion. In these categories of state-religion relationship, the states, and the religions themselves, see the interaction between the two as a net positive. Space is made for religion in both private and public spaces.

As discussed earlier, some categorisations could fall into either the "positive identification" or "positive interaction" broad groupings. As Temperman has observed, in practice:

> the number of states which genuinely accommodate and support religion *in abstracto* is fairly small. Constitutional accommodation of religion in practice, more often than not, translates into practices of cooperation and support from which some (but not all) religions and beliefs benefit.[36]

The further the state moves away from supporting religion in the abstract and towards supporting specific religions, sects, or denominations, the more likely they will fall into the "positive identification" category.

34 US Department of State Office of International Religious Freedom, *2022 Report on International Religious Freedom: India* (Web Page, 2022) https://www.state.gov/reports/2022-report-on-international-religious-freedom/india/#:~:text=Federal%20law%20provides%20official%20minority,minorities%20in%20a%20particular%20region

35 Ibid.

36 Temperman (n 2) 94.

However, such abstract support of religion is not impossible. Within the category of "positive interaction" are categorisations where the state positively interacts with religion broadly defined, often in a non-discriminatory way. In doing so, the state does not attempt to fully separate itself from religion, instead choosing to work with and alongside religion. However, there may be an element of separation or non-establishment. State-religion relationships in this category include pluralism,[37] be it pragmatic or principled,[38] state support,[39] acknowledgment[40] and accommodation of religion,[41] weak religious establishment,[42] as well as cooperation with religion.[43] The difference between these categories of state-religion relationship is often a matter of degree or nomenclature rather than substantive. Alibašić, for example, refers to many of these categories as various forms of separation or anti-church regimes. Notably, Alibašić equates separation with neutrality[44] and pluralism with being anti-church,[45] explaining that in this context anti-church does not mean anti-religion and might be better thought of as anti-establishment or non-identification.

C Separation

The broad category of "separation" contains categorisations such as non-identification,[46] non-establishment,[47] separation,[48] secularism/secular states,[49] neutrality,[50] *laïcité*,[51] competitive market of religions,[52] and various forms of separation including transvaluing,[53] structural,[54] assertive, and formal separation.[55] As with some of the categories discussed previously, the difference between these categories is often a matter of degree and nomenclature.

37 Soper et al (n 2); Barker, *State and Religion* (n 2) 24–5; Bader (n 2); Alibašić (n 13) 45.
38 Ahdar and Leigh (n 2) 109–12.
39 Temperman (n 2) 65–72.
40 Ibid 72–90.
41 Durham and Scharffs (n 8) 127; Temperman (n 2) 94–103.
42 Babie (n 2) 131.
43 Durham and Scharffs (n 8) 126–7.
44 Alibašić (n 13) 44–5.
45 Ibid 45–6.
46 Temperman (n 2) 103–9, 115–21; Durham (n 2) 16.
47 Barker, *Pluralism v Separation* (n 2) 25–7; Bader (n 2); Durham (n 2) 17; Alibašić (n 13) 45; Laborde (n 2) 70.
48 Temperman (n 2) 121–5; Durham and Scharffs (n 8) 127–8; Ahdar and Leigh (n 2) 93–4.
49 Temperman (n 2) 115; Ahdar and Leigh (n 2) 94–100.
50 Temperman (n 2) 11–5; Ahdar and Leigh (n 2) 112–9; Alibašić (n 13) 44–5.
51 *State and Religion* (n 2) 27; Rosenfield (n 2) 2349; Jensen (n 2) 16; Laborde (n 2) 70.
52 Ahdar and Leigh (n 2) 119–22.
53 Alibašić (n 13) 44.
54 Ibid 434.
55 Babie (n 2) 130.

There is less opportunity for overlap between "separation" as a broad grouping and "positive interaction" than there is between "positive identification" and "positive interaction". This is due to the key feature of these categories of state-religion relationship, which is a deliberate choice to separate the state and religion. This does not necessarily mean a negative reaction by the state towards religion, but does usually include some form of removal of religion from the public sphere, even if this is no more than formal in nature. However, categories such as neutrality and accommodation, depending on how they are carried out in practice, could arguably fit into either category. Formal neutrality requires a state to be "religion blind".[56] As Ahdar and Leigh explain, "[r]eligion is to be treated no differently than anything else".[57] In practice, such an approach could lead to a relatively high level of state interaction with religion by, for example, funding religious service providers alongside secular ones, which looks in practice much like cooperation. Similarly, as Durham and Scharffs observe, accommodationist regimes "may incline towards separation of religion and state yet retain a posture of benevolent neutrality towards religion".[58] Again, depending on the nature and extent of the accommodation, this may look in practice very similar to non-establishment. 'Separation' does not necessarily mean a hostility towards religion. Categories such as non-establishment and formal neutrality, therefore, sit at one end of the spectrum of this broad category. These categories merely require that the state refrain from formally establishing any religion, and in the case of formal neutrality, treating religions like equivalent secular organisations or world views, leaving significant scope for state-religion interaction.

Further along the spectrum are categorisations such as *laïcité*, transvaluing separation, and substantive neutrality, which require a more substantive separation of state and religion, effectively removing religion from the public sphere. While a negative view of religion is not required, the greater the separation the easier it is for inadvertent, and perhaps even deliberate, insensitivity, and hostility to creep in. The high level of separation may, in some cases, be motivated by a negative attitude towards religion.

D "Negative" Identification/Suppression

The final broad category is "negative identification/suppression" of religion. Categorisations of state-religion relationship in this broad category have moved beyond mere separation of religion to view religion negatively, and implement laws and policies to remove religion, not only from the most obvious places in the public sphere, but also to reduce the influence of, or even to suppress, religion in the private realm. As Babie has observed, there is some

56 Ahdar and Leigh (n 2) 113.
57 Ibid.
58 Durham and Scharffs (n 8) 127.

overlap with restrictive political regimes noting: "communist or totalitarian regimes would be found here".[59]

Categorisations such as secular control regimes,[60] states with a secular ideology,[61] abolitionist states,[62] and atheist and proactive elimination regimes[63] would all fit within this broad category. As with all the broad categories, there is some overlap between categorisations in the broad category of "separation" with the most extreme forms of removal of religion from the public sphere and the broad category of "negative identification/suppression". *Laïcité* and transvaluing separation, for example, could fall into this crossover, depending upon how the separation is carried out in practice, and the level of hostility towards religion.

The least has been written about categorisations falling into this broad category. True abolitionist states are rare. Historical examples include Albania during the Soviet era and Nazi Germany during the Holocaust – although in the latter case, and more generally, as Durham and Scharffs observed, the state has not attempted to abolish all religions and instead "[subjects] predominant religions to control while seeking to eliminate or drive minority religions from the country".[64] More common are secular control regimes and secular states which adopt an alternative ideology such as secularism or Marxism in a similar way that states with established religions adopt and support the beliefs and practices of the chosen faith. Arguably, Erastianism (Caesaropapism) and secular control regimes have much in common, and the difference between them may well be a matter of degree and emphasis.

Ultimately, all state-religion categories exist on a spectrum, and states may exhibit features of more than one category, oscillating along a particular zone of the continuum.[65] How big of a zone will depend on many factors and, as discussed in more detail in following sections, measuring that zone is one of the ways in which models of state-religion relationships can be used. We have categorised these state-religion relationships into four broad categories based around the level of positive or negative interaction (from the perspective of the state) with religion. However, if we focus on control, then theocracies and Erastianism have much in common with abolitionist states. In the most extreme forms of theocracies, the state seeks to abolish religion and non-religious beliefs and practices which do not conform to the state-sanctioned faith. Indeed, even those who belong to the sanctioned religion may face significant restrictions and control in how they practice their faith.

59 Babie (n 2) 130.
60 Durham and Scharffs (n 8) 128.
61 Temperman (n 2) 140–3.
62 Barker, *State and Religion* (n 2) 28; Durham and Scharffs (n 8) 128.
63 Babie (n 2) 130.
64 Durham and Scharffs (n 8) 128.
65 See Babie (n 2) 123.

III Introducing Four Models

As canvassed earlier, states identify with, and relate to, religion in a myriad of different ways. These relationships may then be classified into broader categories of state-religion relationships. Having explored the categorisation of state-religion relationships, it is useful to expand outwards to consider existing models of state-religion relationships. These models bring together the different categories in order to explain and explore interrelationships between and across categories. They serve as comparative frameworks, or yardsticks, through which the diverse configurations between states and religion can be analysed. The purpose of Section III is to explain four existing models of state-religion relationship primarily drawn upon in Section II: Paul Babie, *Religion and Constitutionalism: Oscillation Along a Continuum*;[66] Rex Ahdar and Ian Leigh in *Religious Freedom in the Liberal State*;[67] Jeroen Temperman in *State-Religion Relationships and Human Rights Law*[68] and W Cole Durham and Brett G Scharffs in *Law and Religion: National, International, and Comparative Perspectives*.[69] It goes beyond the scope of this chapter to provide a comprehensive analysis of these models. Instead, the following discussion will summarise the models to inform the question of how they may be employed.

A Oscillation Model – Babie

Building upon Hirschl's taxonomy of state-religion relationships outlined in *Constitutional Theocracy*,[70] Babie's model seeks to explore inconsistencies in state-religion relationships. The model is set out in a traditional continuum with categories stretching from atheism and proactive elimination on the far left, through various forms of separation and cooperation with, and establishment of, religion, to mixed systems of religious law and general legal principles on the far right of the model.

In building upon Hirschl's model, Babie observed it was often difficult to precisely plot states into a single slot along the continuum of state-religion relationships. Instead, a state may "approximate several, perhaps many points along the continuum, depending upon the issue and one's perspective".[71] As a result, states exist along "zones" of the continuum.

As shown in Figure 2.1, the categories of state-religion relationships are therefore grouped into three "zones": (1) secular/separation zone; (2)

66 See ibid.
67 Ahdar and Leigh (n 2).
68 Temperman (n 2).
69 Durham and Scarffs (n 8) 113–122; Durham and Scharffs' model draws heavily on that presented in Durham (n 2) 1 and Ahdar and Leigh (n 2) 5.
70 Hirschl (n 2) 26–40.
71 Babie (n 2) 131.

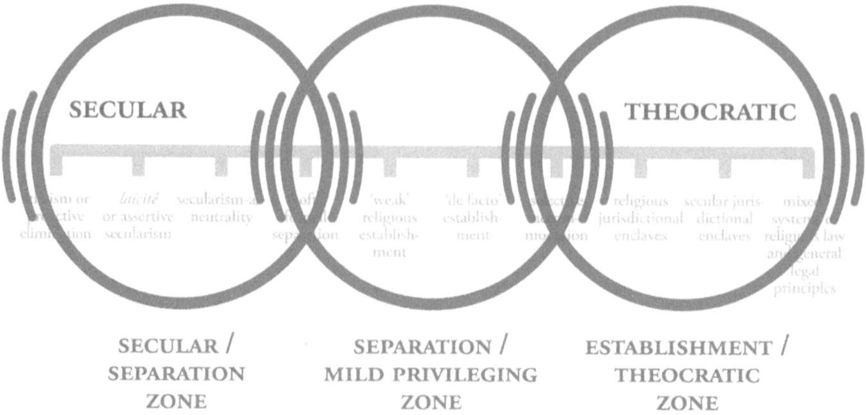

Figure 2.1 Oscillation Model.

Babie (n 2) 135.

separation/mild privileging zone; and (3) establishment/theocratic zone. This is similar to the four broad categories outlined in Section II. These circles or "zones" overlap, demonstrating that even these categorisations are not fixed.

Babie argues that in plotting the location of individual states along the continuum, a certain level of oscillation should be expected. Many states do not exist in a single category but may oscillate across multiple categories, exhibiting features of all of them. Babie's model is, therefore, particularly helpful in understanding the very complex nature of state-religion relationships in practice. However, the model does not relate the nature of the state-religion relationship to other factors, such as freedom of religion, equality and inclusion, security, or human rights. Its application is, therefore, limited to understanding state-religion dynamics on their own terms.

B Grid Model – Ahdar and Leigh

Another well-known model of state-religion relationships is that offered by Ahdar and Leigh. Similar to Babie's model described previously, Ahdar and Leigh's model differentiates between states along a continuum spanning the polar extremes or "ideal types" of complete unity between state and religion at one end, and their complete separation at the other. Accordingly, relationships whereby the state is conflated with religion, including theocracies and Erastianism, are located at one extreme. Conversely, relationships defined by a rejection of religion, such as hostile separationism, are found at the opposite extreme. Intermediate relationships that represent varying degrees of cooperation between the state and religion are found between these extremes.

This model is based on a grid as shown in Table 2.1. Ahdar and Leigh's model serves to examine the legal and constitutional issues relating to the protection and limits of religious states. As a result, their analysis of systems for structuring the relationship between state and religion orients itself around the question of which structure can adequately protect religious freedom. For this reason, economic labels are included in the grid to capture the insight that economic models have provided in social sciences' scholarship more broadly.[72] Ultimately, they conclude that arrangements recognising a measure of interaction and cooperation between governments and religious communities, including mild establishment, pluralism, and substantive neutrality, confer the best protection of religious freedom. It is these arrangements that are considered to fall within the parameters of a liberal society.[73]

Ahdar and Leigh's emphasis on freedom of religion of the state-religion dynamic is notable insofar that it recognises that liberalism does not necessitate an absence of religion. However, it also presents a weakness of the model that limits its potential application and use. Further, the model assumes a level of similarity between states' legal structures that hinders jurisdictional comparison.

C Temperman

Similarly, Temperman's model of state-religion relationships takes the form of a continuum spanning across two polarities, starting from a high level of religious interaction and identification and finishing with a hostile state position towards religion. Further, like Ahdar and Leigh's model, Temperman's model is driven by a precise research question: how does the manner in which a particular state identifies with religion affect its compliance with human rights?[74] However, unlike the other four models discussed in Section III, Temperman's model has no visual element, such as the line, grid, or loop, but instead provides a comprehensive comparative legal analysis of the diverse ways by which states can relate to religion.

Indeed, the high level of detail of Temperman's analysis illustrates, with unique clarity, the broad spectrum of state-religion identifications. The comparative legal framework examines wide-ranging systems from unequivocal positive state identification with religion, through to various forms of state support and state acknowledgement of religion, neutral forms of religious accommodation, secularism and separationism, and negative state-religion identification or anti-religious regimes.[75] In positing this continuum, Temperman recognises a continual circle, whereby the most extreme forms

72 Ibid.
73 Ahdar and Leigh (n 2) 124.
74 Temperman (n 2) 4.
75 Temperman (n 2) ch 2–6.

Table 2.1 State-Religion Identification as a Grid

	Unity (monism)		*Hybrid (cooperation)*		*Separation*	
Structural/ Institutional	Theocracy	Erastianism	De jure Establishment Single v multiple Comprehensive v partial Symbolic v substantive		Strict (no aid) Separation	
Beliefs			De facto Establishment			De facto Secularism Hostile Separation Irreligion
Legal Stance			Non-preferentialism (assistance for all religions vis-à-vis secular entities/ activities)	Substantive neutrality Equal treatment (of religious and secular groups) Accommodation	Formal neutrality No assistance (for any religion) No accommodation	
Regulation	Monopoly		Partial regulation	Competition Deregulation		Partial regulation

1 Ahdar and Leigh (n 2) 89.

of non-identification with religion by a state actually constitute ideologies themselves, in a comparable manner to strongly religious states.[76]

Of particular note in Temperman's analysis is its focus on the formal state-religion relationship outlined in a country's constitution and other formal documents of state. Temperman proposes numerous distinctions based on these legal instruments. Notably, Temperman observes that a state can be ***constitutionally secular*** if it declares in its formal documents of state that it is not religious, is non-denominational, is not linked to any ideology or religious belief, or if it does not invoke religious justifications for its authority.[77] This legal declaration may be combined with the promotion of secularism as an atheist ideology, but not necessarily so, and is clearly distinguishable.[78] Accordingly, Temperman's model recognises the distinction between the formal legal commitments of a state and state practice. This clarification of what laws and public policies were contemplated in constructing Temperman's model is its primary distinguishing factor. However, Temperman's legal analysis does not allow for a more nuanced understanding of the way in which the constitutional provisions have been interpreted by national or local courts, nor of the ways in which different laws operating at a lower level than the constitution may impact the state-religion relationship.[79] Further, the model does not account for the internal differentiation that can occur within a given jurisdiction with respect to its interaction with religion, including the experience of majority and minority faiths, as well as in federations where matters relating to religion are devolved to the local level.[80]

D Loop Model – Durham and Scharffs

Finally, Durham and Scharffs' model of state-religion interactions portrays the broad array of identities that a state can adopt in relation to religion on a continuum curved into a horseshoe loop.[81] This loop significantly departs from traditional schemas, which present state-religion relationships on a straight-line continuum spanning between two polarities, starting from a hostile state position towards religion on the left and finishing with a high level of religious interaction and identification on the right. The degree of religious freedom in any given jurisdiction has been presented on a straight-line continuum from total religious freedom to the complete absence of religious freedom as shown in Figure 2.2.

76 Temperman (n 2) 140–3; Rivers (n 2) 316–8.
77 Temperman (n 2) 112.
78 Ibid 140–3.
79 Renae Barker, Law and Religion in the Classroom (2022) 1 *Australian Journal of Law and Religion*, 4 ('Law and Religion in the Classroom').
80 Gila Stopler, Religion-State Relations and Their Effects on Human Rights: Nationalization, Authorization, and Privatization (2017) 6 *Oxford Journal of Law and Religion* 474, 478.
81 Or as some of our students have called it, the light bulb model.

Figure 2.2 Continuum of Religious Freedom.
Durham and Scarffs (n 8) 122.

However, as first identified by George Ryskamp, "[e]xamination of the relationship between a country's position on the identification line versus its position on the religious freedom line yields no clear pattern".[82] The two continuums are two separate models of two different phenomena. While they are usually drawn together, doing so is not necessary, and does not reveal any link between the two phenomena they depict. As a result, while these models are useful to demonstrate the range of potential state-religion relationships, they do not adequately grapple with the relationship between state and religion models and freedom of religion. The solution, posited by Ryskamp in 1980,[83] refined by Durham in 1996[84] and later re-canvassed by Durham and Scharffs in 2010,[85] is to redraw the state-religion identification continuum as a loop, as depicted in Figure 2.3.

Durham and Scharffs explain that such a solution

> … lies in reconceptualizing the religious-state identification continuum in two respects. First, it is important to recognize that the range of possible relationships run not merely from complete identification to non-identification. In fact, the possibilities run from complete (and positive) identification through non-identification to outright hostility and persecution (ie, negative identification). Second, in order for the correlations

82 Ibid.
83 Ibid 652–3.
84 Durham (n 2) 1–44.
85 Durham and Scharffs (n 8) 122–9.

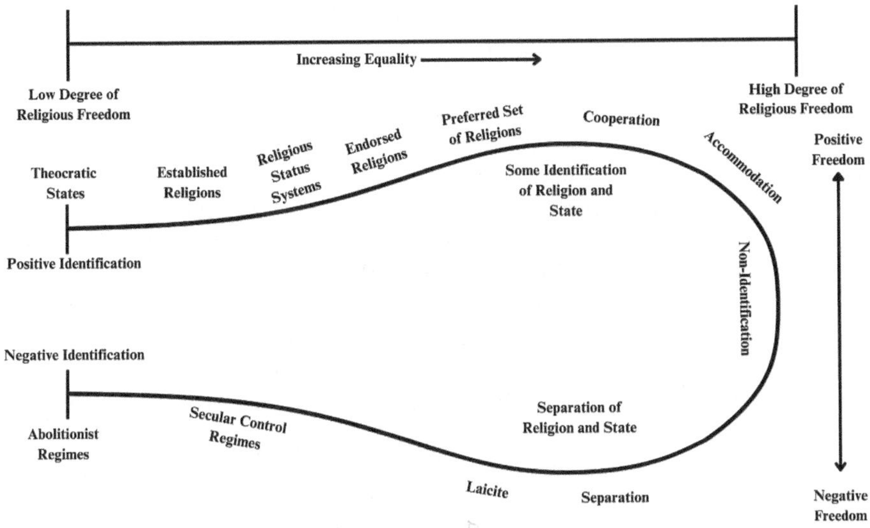

Figure 2.3 Simplified State-Religion Identification as a Loop.

This is a simplified version of the model presented by Durham and Scharffs, see Durham and Scharffs (n 8) 123.

> between institutional configurations and the religious freedom continuum to become clear, the identification continuum needs to be laid out as a loop, … [w]hat this schematization suggests is that a lack of religious freedom correlates with a high degree of *either* positive *or* negative identification of the state with religion.[86]

Accordingly, Durham and Scharffs' model in Figure 2.3 reconceives the traditional straight-line continuum into a horseshoe loop configuration, stretching from regimes with positive and absolute state identification with religion, to states with negative identification with religion, for example, those with an anti-religious ideology. The significance of the curvature of the loop lies in its reflection of religious freedom. The two far ends of the spectrum correlate with an absence of religious freedom, while the middle zone of the loop corresponds with a variety of state systems that optimise religion. The inner and outer bands of the identification continuum also have a distinct meaning. The inner band portrays the attitude of the relevant state towards religion. Conversely, the outer band concentrates on the structural features of specific types of state-religion relationships, including theocratic states, established religions, religious status systems, and so forth. The separation of the outer

86 Ibid (emphasis in original). A full explanation of the model is beyond the scope of this paper. For more details of the model and how it operates, including definitions of the various state-religion relationship categories, see Durham and Scharffs (n 8) 122–9.

and inner bands is notable because it recognises that although there is often a correlation between the institutional structure of a given state and its religious posture, there equally exists a high degree of flexibility between the two. The outer loop thus maintains a detached position and can move independently around the inner loop, which elucidates the elasticity of institutional structures in relation to a state's particular attitude towards religion.

The shape of the loop is also important: the end (far left) depicting a high degree of identification (positive or negative) with religion is notably closer than the middle or far end of the model. When first developing the model Ryskamp observed, in the context of Spanish history that "[h]igh positive identification of the church with the state and negative identification are very close, which allows for relative ease of transition from one to the other".[87] The loop consequently narrows at this point, bringing the two ends of the loop together. However, unlike the opposite end (far right), there is not a smooth transition from one categorisation to the other. The shape of the model remains a loop with disconnected ends rather than a circle. This indicates that while it may be easier for a state to flip between strong positive and strong negative association than between other positions opposite each other on the loop, there cannot be a smooth transition. Such a shift will be radical in nature, even if the overall freedom of religion in the given state changes very little.[88]

The advantages of Durham and Scharffs' model lies in its uniquely visual depiction,[89] as well as its elaboration of the implications of a particular state's relationship with religion upon societal and institutional conceptions of freedom and equality. Indeed, it is the elaboration of these implications that has led the schema to be used for such analyses as how a country's state-religion identification affects state compliance with human rights law[90] and understanding state reactions to minority religions.[91] However, a limitation of the model is that it is largely descriptive and does not clarify what laws and public policies were contemplated in constructing the model's composite categories. This complicates the process of determining where particular jurisdictions fit within the model.[92] Finally, the model assumes a certain degree of similarity between the laws of any given jurisdiction, such that states in transition, and regional differences in the role of religion within states, are difficult to locate within it.[93]

87 George R Ryskamp, 'The Spanish Experience in Church-State Relations: A Comparative Study of the Interrelationship between Church-State Identification and Religious Liberty' [1980] 1980(3) *Brigham Young University Law Review* 616, 635.
88 Durham and Scharffs (n 8) 124.
89 Barker, Law and Religion in the Classroom (n 79) 4.
90 Temperman (n 2).
91 Stopler (n 80) 474.
92 Barker, Law and Religion in the Classroom (n 79) 5–6.
93 Ibid; Stopler (n 80) 478.

IV So What? – Comparing and Using the Models

While the creation of models of state-religion relationships appears to be a common pastime of academics working on matters related to law and religion, the sheer volume of such models fails to answer the fundamental question of "so what" – what do these models contribute and how can they be used? If they are mere taxonomies, listing jurisdictions according to a set of categories, they contribute little to our understanding. However, if they are used as a yardstick to compare across and within jurisdictions, they may offer something of real value. Yet, before looking at how these models can be used, it is important to acknowledge their weaknesses and limitations.

A Limitations

We have already outlined some of the specific weaknesses in the models presented by Babie, Durham and Scharffs, Ahdar and Leigh, and Temperman. In this section we outline some further weaknesses common to many models of state-religion relationship: (1) reliance on tautologies; (2) inconsistencies; (3) lack of clarity in laws considered; and (4) they are often Western or Eurocentric.

First, models of state-religion relationship have a tendency to rely on tautologies. This is best demonstrated by the way the French state-religion relationship is generally described. Temperman,[94] Ahdar and Leigh,[95] and Durham and Scharffs[96] all describe the French state-religion relationship as *laïcité* (literally, governance by laymen). This is the official French policy on state-religion relationships. *Laïcité* and France are so synonymous that you cannot have one without the other. This approach means that the content of *laïcité* changes as French policy and law does. As a result, its usefulness as a category of state-religion relationship is arguably limited, as it has effectively come to mean a state-religion dynamic "like France". Something similar also tends to occur with the United States and the United Kingdom. The United States is often described as having a "wall of separation"[97] between church and state, a reference to comments by Thomas Jefferson in a letter to the Danbury Baptist Association in 1802.[98] The phrase was given its modern meaning by the United States Supreme Court in *Reynolds v United States*[99] in 1879 and *Everson v Board of Education*[100] in 1947. However, relying on this "wall of separation" ignores many realities of the state-religion relationship including, inter alia, the motto

94 Temperman (n 2) 113.
95 Ahdar and Leigh (n 2) 93–5.
96 Durham and Scharffs (n 8) 160–9.
97 Brugger (n 2) 21, 23, 26; Esbeck (n 2) 7–8; Rosenfeld (n 2) 2349–50; Rivers (n 2) 2–3.
98 *Reynolds v United States*, 98 US 145, 168 (1878).
99 98 US 145 (1878).
100 330 US 1 (1947).

on USA bank notes and coins "In God We Trust".[101] Similarly, models often include the United Kingdom as an example of an established church. While it is true that the Church of England is the established church of England and the Church of Scotland is the established church of Scotland, as Durham and Scharffs point out, there is also a form of "reasonably robust secularism"[102] which contributes to the overall state-religion relationship.

Second, as previously outlined, the models focus on different aspects of the state-religion relationship and have different objectives. This results in inconsistencies. While the literature is consistent in the way it describes the French state-religion relationship, this is not the case for other jurisdictions. For example, Durham and Scharffs describe India as having a "religious status system",[103] while Temperman describes it as secularism.[104] Similarly, Ahdar and Leigh describe Belgium's state-religion relationship as "establishment"[105] while Temperman describes it as "accommodation".[106] While some of these differences may be no more than a matter of degree or nomenclature, they still make it difficult to reconcile the conclusions of the different models. It is also important to remember that in most cases the aim of these comprehensive models, as presented, is not to classify particular states but rather to outline particular categories. States are, therefore, included as examples rather than as part of a detailed analysis of the state-religion relationship in that specific jurisdiction. Where different models use the same state to illustrate different points, this may highlight different facets of the state-religion relationship and end up placing them in seemingly contradictory categories.

Third, the models are not always clear which laws, public policies, and social settings were considered in constructing the categories within the model and how these should be applied. This makes it difficult to repeat the analysis and apply the models. As outlined earlier, Temperman's model is an exception. However, his model primarily focuses on the relationship as outlined in formal documents of state, which ignores other laws, public policies, and social settings which impact upon the state-religion relationship.[107] While not discussed, Hasting's model is at the other extreme. It is comprehensive, yet imprecise in exactly which laws, for example, should be considered when ascribing a state to a particular state-religion category. In his model outlined in *The Faces of God: Reflecting on Church and Society*, Hastings identified six factors which are relevant to the state-religion relationship:

101 Temperman (n 2) 86.
102 Durham and Scharffs (n 8) 124.
103 Ibid 126.
104 Temperman (n 2) 90.
105 Ahdar and Leigh (n 2) 106.
106 Temperman (n 2) 989 (see footnotes).
107 Barker, Law and Religion in the Classroom (n 79) 1.

> The first is the various basic patterns of relationship possible; the second, an analysis of types of church in relation to the state; the third, types of state in relation to the church; the fourth, deeper elements in the shape of society which can influence both state and church; the fifth, the grounds of cooperation; the sixth, the grounds of conflict.[108]

The model then goes on to examine each factor in some detail, yet fails to outline specific laws or public policies which should be considered.

The challenges presented by the existence of multiple different models of state-religion relationships which focus on different aspects of the state-religion dynamic and are opaque in which laws and policies were included in the analysis can best be demonstrated by comparing the classification of jurisdictions by three of the models considered in this chapter.Table 2.2 provides a sample of jurisdictions classified by Temperman, Ahdar and Leigh, and Durham and Scharffs. For the purpose of illustration, we have selected 14 jurisdictions which are discussed in all three models.

As Table 2.2 demonstrates, there is significant difference in how the state-religion relationship in each jurisdiction is described. In some cases, this is due to a different nomenclature used by authors (see, for example, Finland). In others, this may be due to the models being published at different points in time and the state-religion relationship undergoing significant changes in the interim. For example, the Lutheran Church of Norway was disestablished and renamed the People's Church in 2012.[109] However, Temperman's model was published in 2010, and while Ahdar and Leigh's was published in 2013 owing to the nature of lags in publishing, it is likely the analysis of Norway as a de jure establishment was finalised prior to the church's disestablishment.[110] This highlights the need to ensure, when using models and analysis of state-religion relationships, that the analysis is up to date and that no significant changes have taken place since the analysis was conducted. There are also cases where the different models have assigned the state to fundamentally different categories. This can be seen in the case of Australia, which is categorised as establishment,[111] non-establishment,[112] cooperation, and secularism.[113] In the wider literature on Australian state-religion relationships, Australia has also been categorised as pragmatic pluralism,[114] liberal separation,[115] and

108 Hastings (n 2) 49. The author writing in 1976 used the older language of church and state.
109 Durham and Scharffs (n 8) 123.
110 Ahdar and Leigh (n 2) 103–4.
111 Ibid 104.
112 Temperman (n 2) 118; Durham and Scharffs (n 8) 139.
113 Durham and Scharffs (n 8) 124.
114 Soper et al (n 2) 121.
115 Stephen McLeish, 'Making Sense of Religion and the Constitution: A Fresh Start for Section 116' 18 *Monash University Law Review* (1992) 221–222; Babie (n 2) 52–6.

Table 2.2 Comparison of Three Models of State-Religion Relationship

	Ahdar and Leigh	*Temperman*	*Durham and Scharffs*
Australia	Establishment (symbolic formal)	Non-establishment	Non-establishment Cooperation–Secularism
Canada	Establishment (symbolic formal)	State support and acknowledgement of religion; Constitutional reference	State neutrality
China	Erastianism	Secular state ideology: Socialist state, governmental atheism	Secular control regime
Finland	Establishment (formal, de jure)	National churches: Evangelical Lutheran Church and Orthodox Church of Finland (establishment)	Established church
France	*Laïcité* (structural separation); Secularism (benevolent/soft/procedural)	Secular state; Separation of state and religion	*Laïcité* (secular republic)
Germany	Quasi-establishment (formal, de jure)	Non-establishment; Separation of state and religion; Accommodation of religion	Cooperationist regime
Great Britain	Establishment (formal, de jure and informal, de facto)	Established state churches	Established church
India	Secularism	Secular state; Separation of state and religion; Parallel religious laws	Religious status system
Iran	Theocracy (Islamic)	State religion: Islam	Extreme positive identification
Norway	Establishment (formal, de jure)	State religion: Evangelical Lutheranism	Disestablishment
Spain	Separation between church and state	Non-establishment	Cooperationist regime
Sweden	Disestablishment	Disestablishment; Separation	Disestablishment
Turkey	Secularism (structural separation)	Secular state; Separation of state and religion	Secularism
United States of America	Secularism	Non-establishment	Non-establishment Separationist; Accommodationist tensions

non-establishment pluralism.[116] What this perhaps indicates is that different aspects of the Australian state-religion relationship exhibit characteristics of different categories, and therefore, an attempt to categorise states into just one category, no matter how widely defined, may be an extreme oversimplification of a dynamic and complex interrelationship. This complexity can be seen in some of the states in Table 2.2 where they have been assigned to more than one category, most often by Temperman. Inevitably, models are an oversimplification of the real world, unable to capture all aspects of reality.

Finally, the models tend to be Eurocentric and Western in their focus. Of the 21 countries discussed in Durham and Scharffs' model, 11 (52%) are in Europe.[117] Of the remaining ten, three, Australia, Canada, and the United States, are all usually considered Western. Ahdar and Leigh discuss 24 countries in their model, of which 17 (71%) are European.[118] As with Durham and Scharffs' model, Australia and the United States are included in the remaining seven. Babie's model is more diverse. Of the eight states specifically considered, the only European jurisdiction considered is Spain. His analysis focuses on the USA, but also includes China, Nepal, Israel, Morocco, Tunisia, and Algeria. Interestingly, both Durham and Scharffs and Babie group together Latin American states in their analyses.[119] While there may be good reasons that European and Western countries feature heavily as examples in these models, the focus on Europe misses the rich diversity of state-religion dynamics in Africa, Asia, South America, and Oceania. It also leaves open the very real possibility that these models are only models of state-religion relationships in European/Western contexts. More work needs to be done to ensure the models better represent and include a wider range of jurisdictions.

B Using the Models

As long as their limitations are kept in mind, the models of state-religion relationships discussed can be used to further our understanding of the dynamic interrelation between the state and the religious beliefs and practices, institutions, and individuals, which operate within them. Using these models as mere taxonomies is not enough. One of the most common uses of these models is to understand the interrelationship between state-religion relationships and freedom of religion. Indeed, as outlined earlier, Durham and Scharffs' model was originally developed by Ryskamp,[120] and later refined by Durham[121] to

116 Barker, *Pluralism v Separation* (n 2).
117 Albania, Finland, France, Germany, United Kingdom, Italy, Norway, Poland, Spain, Sweden and Turkey.
118 Belgium, Denmark, Finland, France, Germany, United Kingdom, Greece, Iceland, Ireland, Luxembourg, Malta, Netherland, Norway, Portugal, Spain, Sweden and Turkey.
119 Babie (n 2) 138–9; Durham and Scharffs (n 8) 126.
120 Ryskamp (n 89) 616.
121 Durham (n 2) 1.

better explain that interaction. Similarly, Ahdar and Leigh's aim was to determine which state-religion relationship advanced religious freedom in a liberal state and which were incompatible with freedom of religion. Temperman's model was developed in order to better understand the extent to which different categories of, what he termed, state-religion identification was consistent with and facilitated compliance with international human rights norms.

Both Temperman and Ahdar and Leigh's models enter the normative debate about the best state-religion relationship to facilitate compliance with human rights norms in the case of the former and freedom of religion in the case of the latter. While Durham and Scharffs' model does not explicitly enter this debate, there is an implicit underlying assumption that greater freedom of religion is normatively to be preferred. However, this assumes that greater freedom and greater compliance with international human rights norms is a normative objective good. There are, arguably, other goals which a state might legitimately pursue in their state-religion relationship. For example, Singapore actively pursues social harmony, which inevitably comes with restrictions of the freedom of religion of individuals where this threatens social harmony.[122] Nigeria is another example where the need to balance the competing needs of diverse religious groups, as well the very real threat of violence if their religious needs are not met, justifies restrictions on freedom of religion in the form of blasphemy laws, which are usually seen as antithetical to freedom of religion.[123] Another social good which could be pursued is inclusion or equality, which may manifest in a number of ways, including religious pluralism, an emphasis on anti-discrimination law, and social inclusion of traditionally marginalised groups such as women and the LGBTQI+ community. Social harmony, security, and equality are all legitimate normative goods which a state may choose to pursue, and which may at times conflict with, or require the curtailment of, freedom of religion. Therefore, in using models of state-religion relationships, it is necessary to keep in mind that states may be pursuing different legitimate ends and that maximising freedom of religion is not the only goal.

Next, we have outlined three additional ways in which the Durham and Scharffs' loop typology could be used: (1) measuring change over time; (2) understanding tension; and (3) mapping range. All of these are aimed at using the model within a single jurisdiction. We have chosen to use Australia for illustrative purposes as this is the home jurisdiction of both authors. However,

122 Singapore Ministry of Home Affairs, *Maintaining Racial and Religious Harmony* (Web Page) https://www.mha.gov.sg/what-we-do/managing-security-threats/maintaining-racial-and-religious-harmony; see also Jaclyn Neo, 'Regulating Pluralism: Laws on Religious Harmony and Possibilities for Robust Pluralism in Singapore' (2020) 18(3) *The Review of Faith and International Affairs* 1–15.

123 See Azizat O Amoloye-Adebayo and Muhammad Kamaldeen Imam-Tamim, 'Shalla v State: Is Blasphemy a Religious or Criminal Offence in Nigeria under Islamic Law?' in Renae Barker, Paul Babie, and Neil Foster (eds), *Law and Religion in the Commonwealth: The Evolution of Case Law* (Hart Publishing, 2022) 95–103.

in each case, repeating the analysis across multiple jurisdictions could prove enlightening as a way of better understanding differences and similarities across jurisdictions. The other models outlined earlier could also be used in similar ways. The Durham and Scharffs' model has been chosen due to its visual nature which renders it particularly advantageous for demonstrating the uses we propose.

C Measuring Change over Time

Ryskamp originally developed the loop typology to better understand the apparent dramatic shifts in the interaction between the state and religion in Spain. Beginning in 1800, Ryskamp traced this interaction from the early constitutional period (1800 to 1869) through multiple changes in the relationship, ending his analysis in 1978.[124] Using models to trace changes in the relationship between the state and religion over time can provide both historical insights as well as insight into potential future shifts in that relationship.

Australia is typically considered to have moved through four periods of state-religion relationship: (1) de jure or de facto establishment; (2) plural establishment; (3) liberal separation; and (4) pragmatic pluralism.[125] While these categories do not all appear on the Durham and Scharffs' model, they can be equated with categories/positions on that model as shown in Figure 2.4.

As shown in Figure 2.4, the Australian state-religion relationship has undergone significant changes since European colonisation in 1788. Presenting these changes as part of a comprehensive model allows the consequences of those changes to become more readily apparent. For example, in plotting these shifts on the loop model, the consequential shifts in freedom of religion, particularly in the move from plural establishment (endorsed religions) to liberal separation (separation). At the same time, it is also clearer that while there may be significant differences between pragmatic pluralism (cooperation) and liberal separation (separation), the consequential impact on freedom of religion would not have been as stark.

D Tension between More Than Two Categories

While the current Australian state-religion relationship is often considered to fall with in the category of cooperation[126] or pragmatic pluralism,[127] there is, in fact, significant disagreement within the literature.[128] This is a split between

124 Ryskamp (n 89).
125 Soper et al (n 2) 121.
126 Durham and Scharffs (n 8) 124.
127 Soper et al (n 2) ch 5.
128 *Pluralism v Separation* (n 2) 6–8.

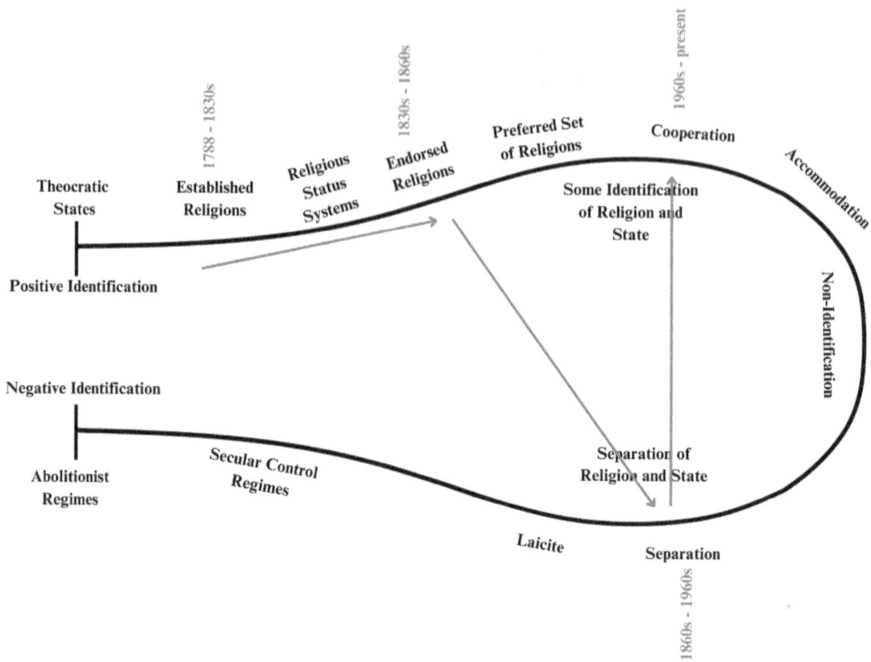

Figure 2.4 Changes in Australian State-Religion Relationship over Time.

those who argue for a relationship of cooperation/pluralism and those who argue for some form of separation. A closer examination of the relationship, taking into account the myriad of laws and public policy settings that contribute to the Australian state-religion relationship, in fact, has elements of both pluralism and separation.[129] Barker has described this as non-establishment pluralism, a term which attempts to "acknowledge[…] the reality of the Australian state-religion relationship by recognising the role of both section 116 of the *Australian Constitution* and the reality of the high level of cooperation between the state and religion".[130] It is non-establishment in that the *Australian Constitution* both prohibits the establishment of a state church or religion, while at the same time prohibiting the establishment of pluralism itself. "Pluralism in Australia is, therefore, a product of ordinary law, political will, and policy. As a result, pluralism is precarious".[131] This can be plotted onto the loop model as shown in Figure 2.5.

In outlining their model, Durham and Scharffs noted that some jurisdictions may exist in a state of tension between two categories of a state-religion

129 Ibid 32.
130 Ibid 34.
131 Ibid 35.

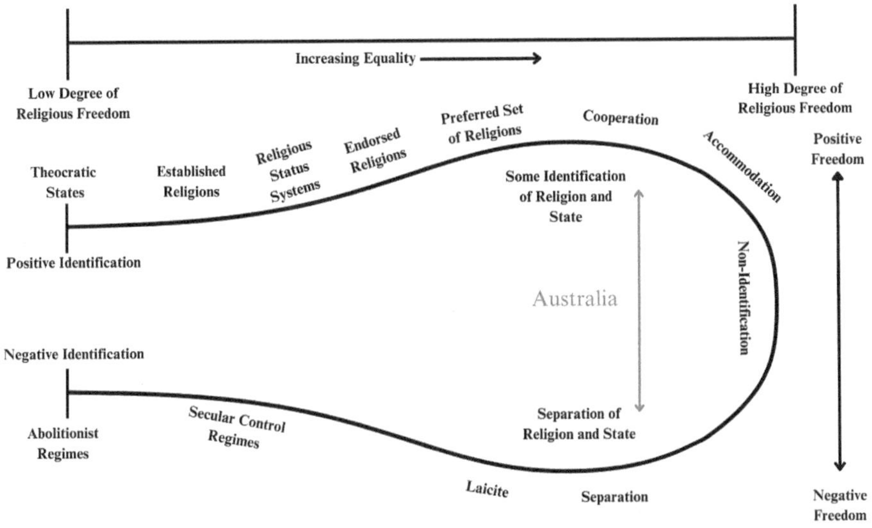

Figure 2.5 Tension in the Australian State-Religion Relationship.

relationship. They noted that both in Australia and the United Kingdom "there is a vacillation between cooperation and a reasonably robust secularism" noting that "such shifts back and forth between radically contrasting religious and secular ideologies may not be wide pendulum swings but vacillating shifts of control between highly polarised political groupings that, in fact, closely resemble each other in their drive for power".[132] We would suggest that this analysis can be taken a step further to recognise that in some jurisdictions the underlying features of the state-religion relationship have resulted dynamically with features of more than one category. This can result in an ongoing tension and, while the expression of the relationship may change, as power shifts the underlying tension remains.

E Range and Scope of Potential Relationships

Another way to use the loop model is to map the range and scope of all potential state-religion relationships within a given jurisdiction. This may be helpful, for example, in jurisdictions which, as outlined previously, have an underlying tension in the state-religion relationship, to help better understand the full range of state-religion relationships which could manifest as power shifts.

Further, it is easy to assume that the current state-religion relationship in a given jurisdiction is the "correct" one, or the only one possible given the current laws and public policy settings. Similarly, it is tempting to assume that

132 Durham and Scharffs (n 8) 124.

a new law which does not appear to "fit" within the accepted state-religion relation is a radical departure or a sign of a shift in the state-religion relationship. However, examining the potential range and scope of the state-religion relationship challenges these assumptions. Using the model in this way has two steps: (1) identifying any anchors for the state-religion relationship, and (2) analysing the full range of possible state-religion relationships permitted by the anchor.

In many states, there will be a fundamental law or structural element which is at the heart of the state-religion relationship. It is this that forms the foundation or anchor for that relationship. Other laws, state practices, and policies build upon the anchor, giving the state-religion relationship form and detail. In many jurisdictions, this anchor will be found in the constitution. Such provisions may enshrine freedom of religion, prohibit the establishment of a state church, or mandate a secular state. In others, the constitution recognises a particular religion, establishes a state church or provides that the laws of the state must confirm with the doctrine of a particular religion.

While the anchor to the state-religion relationship will often be found in a constitution, it may also be found in other fundamental legal documents and in state conventions and practice. For example, the guarantee of religious freedom in Article 9 of the *European Convention on Human Rights* forms part of the anchor for all state parties to that convention. The anchor may also be found in more than one legal text and may be a combination of laws, state conventions, and practice. For example, in England the establishment of the Church of England does not rest in a written constitution. At its heart, the establishment of the Church of England is based on section VIII of *Act of Supremacy 1558*, which states that "all spiritual jurisdiction" is "united to the Crown" and "shall for ever by authority of this present Parliament be united and annexed to the Imperial Crown of this Realm".[133] Beyond this, Ahdar and Leigh identify three key elements of the establishment of the Church of England.

> First, is the position of the sovereign as head of state and Supreme Governor of the Church of England. Second, there is state involvement in church procedures, whether the requirement of parliamentary approval for church legislation or the Crown's role in senior ecclesiastical appointments. Third, there is church involvement in state processes, such as the coronation of the new monarch and the representation of senior bishops in the House of Lords.[134]

133 *Act of Supremacy* 1558 (UK) s 8.
134 Adhar and Leigh (n 2) 101.

These elements, along with Article 9 of the *European Convention on Human Rights* form the anchor to the English state-religion relationship.[135] The exact location of the law is not as important as the role it plays and its stability.

In Australia the anchor can be found in section 116 of the Australian Constitution, which states:

> The Commonwealth shall not make any law for establishing any religion, or for imposing any religious observance, or for prohibiting the free exercise of any religion, and no religious test shall be required as a qualification for any office or public trust under the Commonwealth.

Once the anchor has been identified, the next step is to determine the potential range of state-religion relationships permitted by the anchoring law. This is the full range of potential interpretations of the anchor. The range is not limited to the current interpretation or application of the anchoring law, nor to the historical range of interpretations given to this law, although the history of its interpretation is important. Nor is it limited to the probable or likely interpretations – rather, the full range of all possible interpretations reasonably open on the law must be considered.

In examining the full range of potential state-religion relationships, it is important to distinguish between laws or public policy which are possible and permitted by the anchoring law, and those which have, in fact, been enacted. For example, a state's anchoring laws may permit state funding of religious schools, but that does not necessarily mean that the government will choose to fund religious schools.[136]

As shown in Figure 2.6, the full range of state-religion relationships in Australia stretches from cooperation through to *laïcité*. Dissenting judgements, such as Murphy J in the *DOGS* case,[137] as well as the work of Australian scholars such as Beck,[138] point to an interpretation of section 116 of the *Australian Constitution* with a more American, or even French, style; separation of state and religion. As the anchor of the Australian state-religion relationship, section 116 does not require the state to cooperate with religion in the public sphere. Removing prayers in Parliament, tax exemptions, and even charitable status for purely religious activities would all be permissible under section 116, so long as they did not unduly infringe upon and/or have the purpose of restricting freedom of religion. Indeed, at a sub-national level, there would be nothing prohibiting Australian states and territories from enacting

135 The *European Convention on Human Rights* is incorporated into United Kingdom domestic law via *Human Rights Act 1998* (UK).

136 Prior to 1968 the Australian federal government provided no funding to non-government schools including those that are operated by religious organisations.

137 *Attorney General (Vic) (Ex rel Black) v Commonwealth* [1980] 146 CLR 559, 619–35.

138 See Luke Beck, *Religious Freedom and the Australian Constitution: Origins and Future* (Routledge 2018).

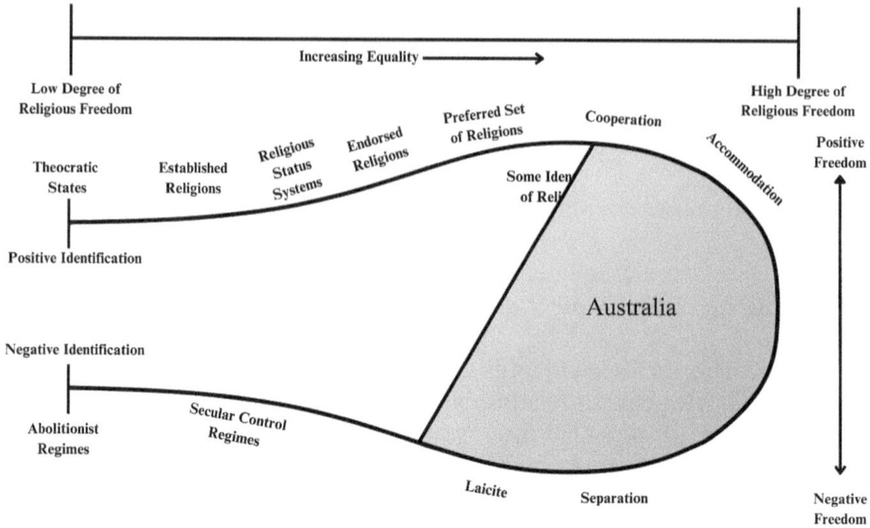

Figure 2.6 Range of the Australian State-Religion Relationship.

laws prohibiting the wearing of religious clothing in public, and at the federal level, such laws may be permissible if they pursued a legitimate purpose other than prohibiting the free exercise of religion.[139] A French style "burqa" ban could, at least theoretically, be enacted in Australia.

At the other end, section 116 would prohibit the 'establishment' of multiple religions. As a result, the creation of a preferred set of religions to receive government support, such as in Belgium, would be impermissible. However, as demonstrated in the *DOGS* case, the Australian Federal Government can fund religious schools and could arguably fund other religious institutions directly, so long as it did so on a non-discriminatory basis.[140] Deagon has gone so far as to argue that a form of 'mild establishment' of Christianity would be permissible under section 116 of the Australian Constitution.[141]

Once the full range of state-religion relationships has been identified, historical or proposed changes in the state-religion relationship can be analysed in light of that range. Shifts in the relationship which occurred within the range are likely to be the work of ordinary political processes. While laws, policies, or their application may have been changed, the anchoring law, and therefore the bedrock of the state-religion relationship, is likely to have remained the same. However, where a proposed or historical change takes the state-religion

139 See Anthony Gray, 'Religious Freedom and Section 116 of the Australian Constitution: Would a Banning of the Hijab or Burqa Be Constitutionally Valid?' (2011) 2 *Forum on Public Policy* 1.

140 Barker, *State and Religion* (n 2) 89.

141 Deagon (n 2) 153–182.

relationship outside the identified range, it will likely have required a change in the laws which anchor the state relationship, and therefore, a much more fundamental shift in the state-religion relationship.

V Conclusion

The purpose of this chapter was to examine comprehensive models of state-religion relationships. Such models can be useful both in understanding the relationship within a given jurisdiction as well as comparing different jurisdictions. However, as models, they are inevitably simplifications of reality. As a result, such models have several weaknesses, including that nuances and detail can be glossed over if the models are applied uncritically. More development is needed in a number of areas. For example, the existing models need be further developed with clearer articulation of the laws, public policies, and social settings relied upon in developing and applying these models. This is essential to enable these models to be applied successfully in both single jurisdiction and comparative analysis. Like all "scientific" methods, it must be repeatable by others seeking to replicate the results. Without further development and clarification this is not always possible. More work is also needed to develop models to better understand and explain the relationship between state-religion relationships and other normative goods, such as social harmony, security, and equality. Freedom of religion is not necessarily the only objective.

Despite the limitations outlined in the chapter, state-religion models remain a useful tool and yardstick for better understanding state-religion relationships in comparative perspectives, so long as their limitations and need for further refinement is kept in mind when applying them. They have potential to be used both as yardsticks in comparative analysis, as well as to provide additional depth in our understanding of the development of state-religion relationships in specific jurisdictions.

Further Reading:

For analysis of the methods used in this chapter, see Chapter 15 – Section III – subsection B *The Historical Method*.

For a discussion and application of state-religion relationships, see Chapters 6, 7, and 13.

3 The Utility of Legal Pluralism as a Conceptual Approach in the Field of Law and Religion

Amin Al-Astewani[1]

I Introduction

Despite its radical premises, the concept of legal pluralism in academic discourse does not show any signs of abating. On the contrary, it seems only to be gaining momentum and has now been extended across many legal disciplines.[2] The modern legal pluralism movement currently pays much of its attention to the multiplicity of legal orders found in today's newly globalised world. Examples which are cited in this regard include international conventions which regulate transnational commercial transactions, regional laws such as European law which have been incorporated by member states into their domestic laws, and private arbitration tribunals which function on a transnational level and offer litigants an alternative to national state courts.

In the field of law and religion, legal pluralism has been consistently invoked in the literature as a conceptual framework to assess the legal status of religious tribunals. Indeed, one of the earliest legal studies of Shariah tribunals in Britain invoked legal pluralism for this purpose.[3] Menskis renowned construction of the term "*angrezi shariat*" to describe the legal activities of British Muslims was, in fact, based on the work of the prominent legal pluralist Masaji Chiba. Legal pluralism thus had a major impact on Menski's analysis of Shariah tribunals, as well as on subsequent analyses by other authors.[4]

This chapter will explore the particular case study of British Shariah tribunals within law and religion literature as a microcosm to reflect upon and assess the utility of legal pluralism as a conceptual approach for researchers working in the

1 Lecturer in Law, Lancaster University Law School.

2 B Tamanaha, *Legal Pluralism Explained: History, Theory, Consequences* (Oxford University Press, 2021) ('*Legal Pluralism Explained*').

3 D Pearl and W Menski, *Muslim Family Law* (Sweet & Maxwell, 1998).

4 See, eg, Samia Bano, 'Complexity, Difference and 'Muslim Personal Law': Rethinking the Relationship between Shariah Councils and South Asian Muslim Women in Britain' (DPhil Thesis, University of Warwick, 2004); Rajnaara Akhtar, 'British Muslims and Transformative Processes of the Islamic Legal Traditions: Negotiating Law, Culture and Religion with Specific Reference to Islamic Family Law and Faith Based Alternative Dispute Resolution' (DPhil Thesis, University of Warwick, 2013).

DOI: 10.4324/9781003397311-5

field of law and religion. The chapter will begin by assessing the political and legal setting in which legal pluralism was born as a conceptual framework. An in-depth methodological analysis of the modern concept of legal pluralism will then be undertaken. The utility of legal pluralism in determining the legal status of religious tribunals, and consequently its broader utility as a conceptual approach to law and religion, will then finally be evaluated. During this final evaluation, the broader concept of normative pluralism will also be considered as a potentially suitable candidate for the purposes of analysing religious systems of law.

II The Political and Legal Setting in Which Legal Pluralism Was Developed as a Conceptual Framework

Legal pluralism emerged as a novel conceptual framework within legal academic discourse in the latter half of the 20th century. As with any novel phenomenon, it was shaped by the particular legal and political setting within which it was developed. Before undertaking a methodological analysis of legal pluralism, it is thus most appropriate to begin with a contextual overview of this particular setting.

A The Political Setting

Western nations in the modern era generally underwent a fundamental political transition from absolute monarchy and the empire state to parliamentary democracy and the nation state, with the Treaty of Westphalia serving a crucial historical turning point. England was no exception in this regard, although its transition was peculiar to its own unique setting.[5] This political shift affected major changes in the way modern society was organised. In pre-modern monarchies and empires, localised communities were usually recognised as bearers of collective rights and thus left free to follow their customs and practices as well as manage their own affairs. The modern nation-state, however, developed a very different conception of social organisation, attaching great importance to physical territory. It only recognised the individual members of society as bearers of rights and sought to create a unified legal, economic, and political space for the whole of society confined within a demarcated physical territory. This required it to dismantle long-established communities and reunite individuals on the basis of a homogenous culture. Identities such as religion, ethnicity, and social status were all subdued under the dominating territorial or national identity.[6]

5 For a detailed account, see C Andrews, *A Short History of England* (Allyn and Bacon, 1921) 71–424.

6 For a detailed account of the modern nation-state, see Q Skinner, *The Foundations of Modern Political Thought* (Cambridge University Press, 1978) vol 2.

B The Legal Setting

Within the shifting political currents of the modern era, the medieval systems of law that had existed in pre-modern Western societies were transformed.[7] The case of the English legal system is illustrative in this regard. Up until the 19th century, isolated systems of law administered by members of local communities or distinctive social groupings were a norm in England.[8] In his famous speech on law reform in 1828, Lord Brougham referred to customary law being applied "in a thousand manors, all different from the Common Law that regulates free-hold estates, most of them differing from each other".[9] This vast body of local and special courts that "largely comprised the English legal system in 1830" was replaced by the county courts in 1846 and was fully incorporated within the centralised common law system from the 1850s onwards.[10] That such a narrative will raise the eyelids of many a reader today is informative of how accustomed society has become to the fully centralised and uniform character of the modern English legal system.

Bearing this context in mind, it comes as no surprise that a formal positivist jurisprudence of law was developed in this period, according with the legal and political developments that were actually occurring in society. In the second half of the 19th century, British jurist John Austin set out his renowned exposition of law as the command of the sovereign.[11] Albert Dicey followed Austin's exposition in the beginning of the 20th century with his classic modern exposition of the "rule of law".[12] Austin and Dicey succeeded in establishing their positivist exposition of law as the generally accepted exposition which prevailed over all others. Law thereafter was understood to refer to rules enacted by parliament and expounded by the superior courts. Only Parliament enjoyed sovereignty to create law and, in the words of Dicey, "no person or body is recognised by the law of England as having a right to override or set aside the legislation of Parliament".[13] All citizens were subject to the same law. Any isolated enclaves of special or customary law must be made subject to the central legal system; in the emphatic words of Lord Justice Scrutton, "there must be no Alsatia in England where the King's writ does not run".[14] Rules enacted by any other body must not be termed law for analytical purposes.

7 For a brief survey of such systems, see B Tamanaha, 'Understanding Legal Pluralism: Past to Present, Local to Global' (2008) 30 *Sydney Law Review* 377–81.

8 W Holdsworth, *History of English Law* (Methuen and Boston, Little, Brown, 1923–66) 182 vol 14.

9 H Brougham, *Present State of the Law* (Carey, Lea & Carey, 1828) 51.

10 H Arthurs, *Without the Law* (University of Toronto Press, 1985) 15.

11 J Austin, *Lectures on Jurisprudence* (R Campbell ed, John Murray, 1885) 263.

12 A Dicey, *Introduction to the Study of the Law of the Constitution* (Liberty Classics, 1915) 114.

13 Ibid 3–4.

14 *Czarnikow Ltd v Roth Schmidt & Co* [1922] 2 KB 478, 488.

Doing so would be, in the words of Austin, "one most prolific source of jargon, darkness, and perplexity".[15]

It must be noted that this positivist exposition of law did not become established without opposition.[16] One of the prominent opponents of the positivist school of law was the sociological school of law. The sociological school challenged the positivist proposition that law can only exist when attached to and emanating from a state authority. This challenge was strongly supported by new anthropological discoveries at the time which proved that savage stateless societies did, in fact, adhere to a primitive set of legal norms.[17] Despite failing to dismantle the authority of the positivist school of law, the sociological school of law's opposition became the intellectual basis for the modern "legal pluralism" movement.

III A Methodological Analysis of the Modern Conception of Legal Pluralism

The modern legal pluralism movement may be traced back to a paper first presented at a conference in 1979, and eventually published in 1986, by John Griffiths with the title, "What is Legal Pluralism?"[18] In this paper, Griffiths successfully established legal pluralism as a concept which was functional for a descriptive theory of law.[19] This is evidenced by the large number of legal studies which adopted the concept thereafter.[20] Griffiths' paper contains the central tenets of the modern legal pluralism movement and is thus the

15 J Austin, *The Province of Jurisprudence Determined* (Weidenfeld & Nicholson ed, Hackett Publishing Company, 1998) 371.

16 For a concise survey of the various oppositions made to the positivist school of law, see C Allen, *Law in the Making* (7th ed, Oxford University Press, 1964) 1–66.

17 Such studies included B Malinowski, *Crime and Custom in Savage Society* (Rowman and Littlefield, 1926); I Hogbin, *Law and Order in Polynesia: A Study of Primitive Legal Institutions* (Harcourt Brace and Company, 1934); A Hoebel, *The Law of Primitive Man: A Study in Comparative Legal Dynamics* (Harvard University Press, 1954).

18 J Griffiths, 'What is Legal Pluralism?' (1986) 24 *Journal of Legal Pluralism* 1.

19 A paper published in 1981 by Galanter may seem to precede Griffiths in providing a comprehensive account of legal pluralism as a concept suitable for a descriptive theory of law. Nevertheless, Galanter acknowledges in footnote 18 of his paper that he is relying on Griffiths for the concept of 'legal centralism': see M Galanter, 'Justice in Many Rooms: Courts, Private Ordering, and Indigenous Law' (1981) *Journal of Legal Pluralism* 1. Galanter's paper can still be seen as a pioneering attempt at establishing the concept of legal pluralism in the formative years of the modern legal pluralism movement, something which Griffiths himself acknowledges, see ibid 39.

20 See, eg, B Santos, 'Law: A Map of Misreading: Toward a Postmodern Conception of Law' (1987) 14 *Journal of Law & Society* 279; S Merry, 'Legal Pluralism' (1988) 22 *Law & Society Review* 869; F Benda-Beckmann, 'Who's Afraid of Legal Pluralism?' (2002) 47 *Journal of Legal Pluralism & Unofficial Law* 37; G Woodman, 'Ideological Combat and Social Observation: Recent Debate about Legal Pluralism' (1998) 42 *Journal of Legal Pluralism* 21; G Teubner, 'The Two Faces of Janus: Rethinking Legal Pluralism' (1992) 13 *Cardozo Law Review* 1443.

most appropriate focal point for analysing and evaluating the concept of legal pluralism.

Griffiths' article is split into three parts. In the first part, Griffiths deals with the positivist exposition of law. Griffiths acknowledges this as the "dominant position in legal thought" and thus the major obstacle for establishing legal pluralism as a superior exposition of law.[21] It becomes clear from the very beginning of the paper that Griffiths is not simply interested in challenging the positivist exposition of law as a legal theory found in books of jurisprudence. Rather, his more pressing concern is challenging the positivist exposition of law as an ideological framework adopted by the modern nation-state to justify its "moral and political claims" and thus reflected in the actual political and legal structures of modern society.[22] In this regard, Griffiths chooses to describe the positivist exposition of law as "the ideology of legal centralism":

> According to what I shall call the ideology of legal centralism, law is and should be the law of the state, uniform for all persons, exclusive of all other law, and administered by a single set of institutions. To the extent that other, lesser normative orderings, such as the church, the family, the voluntary association, and the economic organisation exist, they ought to be and in fact are hierarchically subordinate to the law and the institutions of the state.[23]

Griffiths' main contention with the positivist school of law is that it simply serves and is built upon the "hegemonic claim of the modern nation state" rather than objectively seeking to derive an empirical theory of law:

> Precisely because it is an ideology, a mixture of assertions about how the world ought to be … the consequence has been a series of attempts to build an empirical theory of law directed not toward a phenomenon conceived of in general terms but rather one defined directly or indirectly in terms of the hegemonic claim of the modern state. Conceptions of what law *is* have reflected a particular idea of what law *ought to be*.[24]

Once Griffiths establishes the weaknesses which he portrays as inherent in the positivist exposition of law, he uses the rest of part one to discuss what he labels "weak" legal pluralism. "Weak" legal pluralism is used by Griffiths to describe the legal situation first found but not limited to colonised and post-colonised societies, in which the state either recognises or incorporates the legal norms and institutions of a particular religious or ethnic community

21 Griffiths (n 17) 1.
22 Ibid.
23 Ibid 3.
24 Ibid.

alongside its own set of legal norms and institutions. Such a situation leads to a plurality of legal norms and institutions within the central legal system.[25] Legal pluralism in this sense is described by Griffiths as a "fixture" of the Western colonial experience that:

> ... has persisted beyond the moment of formal "independence" proving one of the most enduring legacies of European expansion and characterising at the present day the larger part of all the world's national legal systems.[26]

Griffiths' main objective in formulating the concept of "weak" legal pluralism is to argue that this does not constitute "real" legal pluralism, but rather is simply a form of "legal diversity".[27] This is because it is a plurality of legal norms controlled by and dependent upon the state legal system, and thus, in reality, is another form of legal centralism. Griffiths goes further in claiming that the eventual ambition of the modern state in such a situation is always unification of its own legal system, to be enacted "as soon as circumstances permit".[28] Thus, weak legal pluralism is "merely a particular arrangement in a system whose basic ideology is centralist". Griffiths contrasts "weak" legal pluralism to 'strong' legal pluralism, in which law functions outside the parameters of the legal system and thus constitutes a "designation of an empirical state of affairs in society".[29] Strong legal pluralism is the concept that Griffiths ultimately depends upon and advocates as the concept most suitable for a descriptive theory of law.

Griffiths devotes part two of his paper to a critique of three legal studies that first attempted to provide a descriptive concept of legal pluralism, namely those undertaken by Hooker, Gilissen, and Vanderlinden. Although Griffiths credits these authors with attempting to formulate the concept of legal pluralism as an alternative to legal centralism, he criticises them for confusing legal diversity and legal pluralism. In other words, Griffiths dismisses their studies as a discussion of "weak" legal pluralism as opposed to a discussion of "strong" legal pluralism. He thus concludes that such studies do not provide an appropriate alternative to legal centralism as a descriptive theory of law.

The final part of Griffiths' paper focuses on four legal studies which do rely on and advocate a "strong" concept of legal pluralism as a descriptive theory of law.[30] It is these four studies that Griffiths decides to rely upon for his own

25 Ibid 5–6.
26 Ibid 6.
27 Ibid 11.
28 Ibid 8.
29 Ibid.
30 It is clear from the beginning of part three that Griffiths has confused anthropology with sociology. He describes the four studies in part three as attempts by 'anthropologists' to define law, however the four studies are, in fact, sociological studies of law since they are attempting

formulation of legal pluralism presented at the very end of the paper. The four studies by Pospisil, Smith, Moore, and Ehrlich, respectively, are all praised by Griffiths for recognising legal pluralism "as a feature of the social groups with which they are concerned". In other words, these studies argued that social groups such as the family, school, church, and corporation contain inner regulatory orders that should properly be described as "law" just as the state's set of regulations are described as "law".[31] Such an argument nullifies the legal centralist notion of law, which includes only state legal norms and institutions and does not recognise the regulatory orders of social groups as "law" in the proper sense of the term. Out of the four studies, the study which serves as the original foundation for this argument is that of Ehrlich, a point that Griffiths fails to note. The other three studies (Pospisil, Smith, and Moore) are simply reformulations or refinements of Ehrlich's theory of "living law". A close analysis of Griffiths' own conception of legal pluralism reveals that it is also a reformulation of Ehrlich's theory of "living law". This is despite Griffiths' insistence that Ehrlich's theory contains certain inadequacies that he claims his own concept of legal pluralism overcomes.

Ehrlich's magnum opus "Fundamental Principles of the Sociology of Law", originally published in 1913, offered the first comprehensive sociological theory of law which challenged the positivist theory of law prevalent in his time. In the forward to his 1913 publication Ehrlich stated:

> It is often said that a book must be written in a manner which permits of summing up its content in a single sentence. If the present volume were to be subjected to this test, the sentence might be the following: At the present as well as any other time, the centre of gravity of legal development lies not in legislation, nor in juristic science, nor in judicial decision, but in society itself. This sentence, perhaps, contains the substance of every attempt to state the fundamental principles of the sociology of law.[32]

Ehrlich was thus keen to establish that positivist legal theories that recognise law simply as a sum of statutes and judgements failed to give an adequate view of the legal reality of a community or, as Griffiths chose to describe it

to identify legal norms in domestic civilised society. One major distinction between the sciences of anthropology and sociology is that the former focuses on foreign, non-Western societies whereas the latter focuses on domestic society: see B Tamanaha, 'The Folly of the 'Social Scientific' Concept of Legal Pluralism' (1993) 20(2) *Journal of Law and Society* 203. ('The Folly of the 'Social Scientific' Concept of Legal Pluralism'); Thus Hooker's study of colonised societies cited in part two of the paper is, in fact, more appropriately described as the work of an anthropologist as opposed to the work of a 'lawyer' as Griffiths describes.

31 Griffiths (n 17) 14.

32 E Ehrlich, *Fundamental Principles of the Sociology of Law* (W Moll translation, Harvard University Press, 1936) xiv.

in his paper, the "empirical state of affairs in society".[33] Building on Gierke's conception of social groups as "associations", Ehrlich's main argument was that the inner regulatory orders of social groups govern the life of society and sometimes attract far greater social authority than the legal norms of the state legal system. For this reason, such "living law" should not be excluded from a descriptive theory of law:

> It is not an essential element of the concept of law that it be created by the state, nor that it constitute the basis for the decisions of the courts or other tribunals, nor that it be the basis of a legal compulsion consequent on such a decision. A fourth element remains, and that will have to be the point of departure, i.e. the law is an ordering ... The inner order of the association of human beings is not only the original, but also down to the present, the basic form of law.[34]

The main criticism of Ehrlich's theory by his contemporaries was that including social regulatory orders within the definition of law rendered the concept so vague and broad that it could no longer be distinguished from social life itself:

> Ehrlich's attempts to define the nature and scope of the 'facts of law', or to frame any clear conception of the 'inner order' of associational functions, cannot be regarded as successful; and this is not surprising, when we remember that the 'facts of law' are really the facts of the whole of life itself. It is for this reason that Ehrlich found the greatest difficulty in setting any boundaries to his subject, and ended by setting none whatsoever.[35]

Turning now to Griffiths' formulation of legal pluralism at the very end of his paper, it becomes patently clear that it is simply a reformulation of Ehrlich's theory of living law:

> ... it follows that law is the self-regulation of a "semi-autonomous social field"..."Legal pluralism" refers to the normative heterogeneity attendant upon the fact that social action always takes place in the context of multiple, overlapping "semi-autonomous social fields"...A situation of legal pluralism – the omnipresent, normal situation in society – is one in which law and legal institutions are not all subsumable within one

33 Griffiths (n 17) 8.
34 Ehrlich (n 31) 24, 37.
35 Allen (n 15) 30. See also W Friedmann, *Legal Theory* (Stevens & Sons, 1967) 251–252.

> "system" but have their sources in the self-regulatory activities of all the multifarious social fields present.[36]

The modern concept of legal pluralism in this regard is nothing but a reformulation of the sociological conception of law, and thus attracts the same criticisms that were aimed at Ehrlich's theory.

There are two points of distinction, however, with Griffiths' formulation. The first is that it reduces Ehrlich's theory into a much more simplistic conception by arguing that state law cannot be distinguished from "living law". In the words of Griffiths, "the state is an association like all others: it has no special attribute requiring a distinct descriptive treatment".[37] Ehrlich, on the other hand, insisted that distinctions do exist between traditional legal norms adopted by state institutions and social norms.[38] The second point of distinction is that Ehrlich's theory was more concerned with opposing the positivist conception of law as a theory of jurisprudence, rather than as an ideological framework adopted by the modern nation-state. Griffiths' conception is, on the other hand, a direct challenge to the positivist conception of law as an ideology used to support the moral and political claims of the modern nation-state. This is why Griffiths expressed dissatisfaction with Ehrlich's theory as a descriptive theory of law. A close study of Griffiths' paper reveals that the driving force behind his promotion of legal pluralism as a legal theory is his own personal reservations regarding the policies and aspirations of the modern-nation state. This becomes particularly clear in his discussion of "weak" legal pluralism, in which he heavily criticises the colonialist policies of Western states.[39] Indeed, as Tamanaha notes, two politically infused motivations are implicit in the modern theory of legal pluralism.[40] The first is to reduce the stature of state law by questioning the legitimacy of its legal monopoly, as well as questioning the moral and political motivations behind its claims to such a monopoly. The second is to establish more authority for the social regulatory orders found within society with the insistence that they should also be termed "law", particularly because they exert more social influence than the state legal system.

In summary, then, the modern legal pluralism movement must be seen in its correct historical context. It is a simplistic reformulation of the sociological theory of law infused with a particular political agenda.

36 Griffiths (n 17) 38–39.
37 Ibid 27.
38 See Tamanaha, 'The Folly of the 'Social Scientific' Concept of Legal Pluralism' (n 29) 209 for a detailed discussion.
39 Griffiths (n 17) 6–8.
40 Tamanaha, 'The Folly of the 'Social Scientific' Concept of Legal Pluralism' (n 29) 205.

IV An Overview of the History, Function, and Legal Status of British Shariah Tribunals

Before critically analysing the way in which the concept of legal pluralism has been applied to the discourse on Shariah tribunals, it is necessary, first, to understand how these tribunals have emerged and the way in which they function. The Islamic Sharia Council currently based in the London district of Leyton was the first Sharia tribunal to be established in Britain.[41] It was formed in 1982 after the representatives of ten Islamic community centres from across the country met in Birmingham in order to discuss the formation of such a body.[42] The reason that triggered such a meeting was an urgent dilemma being faced by a number of Muslim women living in Britain.

These women had, for various reasons, separated from their husbands, however their husbands were refusing to give them an Islamic divorce. In Islamic Law, a woman is unable to remarry until her husband pronounces the formula of divorce. If she enters a new relationship without obtaining a divorce from her husband, the relationship will be considered an adulterous one. This acted as a barrier for British Muslim women from entering new relationships, not only because they did not want to engage in the sinful act of adultery, but also because of the negative way their families and communities would respond to such a relationship. These women were thus effectively left "chained" in a limping marriage, unable to remarry and move on with their lives. While an English judge could issue them with a civil divorce, he was helpless in obtaining an Islamic divorce for them. The only individual empowered by Islamic Law to unilaterally annul an Islamic marriage against the wishes of the husband is an Islamic judge. Thus, the Islamic Sharia Council was set up to resolve this issue by giving British Muslim women access to Islamic scholars who, acting as judges, could issue them with an Islamic divorce after assessing their cases.[43]

41 A Al-Astewani, 'Loci of Leadership: The Quasi-Judicial Authority of Shariah Tribunals in the British Muslim Community' (2019) 10(7) *Religions* 406.

42 The ten centres are listed on the Islamic Sharia Council's website, https://www.islamic-sharia.org/ accessed 1 September 2023. It should be noted that some religious scholars resident in the UK, such as Zaki Badawi, were resolving disputes within the Muslim community on an informal basis even earlier than the establishment of the Islamic Shariah council in 1982. Indeed, it is arguable that Zaki Badawi was one of the first pioneers in seeking to establish an institution which could offer the Muslim community Islamic dispute resolution services. He eventually went on to set up the Muslim Law Shariah Council in London (MLSC) at a conference attended by over 250 British Muslim scholars and community leaders. The MLSC ranks alongside the Islamic Shariah council as one of the pioneering attempts to establish a British Shariah tribunal, which other tribunals later looked up to as a model to follow. See, in this regard, M King, *God's Law v State Law* (Grey Seal Books 1995) 73.

43 Jewish Beth Din tribunals, which have been established in Britain for a much longer period than Shariah tribunals, also deal with the same issue faced by Jewish women: see A Barnett, 'Getting a 'Get': The Limits of the Law's Authority? *N v N (Jurisdiction: Pre-Nuptial Agreement)* [1999] 2 F.L.R. 745' (2000) 8 *Feminist Legal Studies* 243; G Douglas et al, *Social*

The work of Shariah tribunals slowly expanded as they developed. They began to resolve other personal disputes between members of the Muslim community, such as commercial and inheritance disputes. They also offered advice to the community on religious matters whenever this was sought, again by giving members of the community access to the Islamic scholars employed at the tribunal. Nevertheless, these additional areas of work only ever formed a small part of their caseload. The vast majority of their cases were always related to the particular issue of limping marriages, a fact which is still true today.[44]

The Islamic Sharia Council was envisaged as a central umbrella body when it was first set up, overlooking smaller branches which could be set up to suit the needs of the British Muslim community in any urban location. However, once the success of the model was witnessed by other Islamic centres, they decided to set up their own independent tribunals. Moreover, Birmingham Central Mosque, which was originally one of the ten founding members, split off from the group and decided to form its own independent tribunal. For this reason, several tribunals now exist in various cities, some of which are branches of the Islamic Sharia Council in Leyton, and some of which are independently formed tribunals. The exact number of Shariah tribunals that currently exist in Britain has not yet been established, however a report funded by the Ministry of Justice and published by the University of Reading in 2012 managed to identify at least 30 tribunals in England.[45]

Contrary to common perceptions, the English legal system has not been turning a blind eye to the emergence of Shariah tribunals. Religious groups other than the Church of England have been allowed by law to practice their religion and perform religious activities with certain qualifications since the *Toleration Act 1689* prompted a new era of religious freedom.[46] Shariah tribunals are no exception in this regard. Communal bodies such as Shariah tribunals that have been established to perform religious services and engage in religious activities are usually treated by law as voluntary associations.[47] Their

---

Cohesion and Civil Law: Marriage, Divorce and Religious Courts (Report of a Research Study Funded by the AHRC, Cardiff Law School 2011) 14.

44 J Bowen, *On British Islam: Religion, Law, and Everyday Practice in Sharia Councils* (Princeton University Press, 2016).

45 S Bano, 'An Exploratory Study of Shariah Councils in England with Respect to Family Law' (University of Reading, 2012) 15. It has often been reported by media outlets that 85 Shariah courts currently exist in Britain. This inflated figure is taken from a Civitas report in 2009, which counted Islamic websites which issued legal rulings online in response to questions posed by internet users as 'Shariah courts': see D MacEoin, 'Sharia Law or "One Law for All"' (Civitas Institute for the Study of Civil Society 2009) 69–70.

46 R Sandberg, 'Islam and English Law' (2010) 164 *Law and Justice Christian Law Review* 29; M Hill, R Sandberg, and N Doe, *Religion and the Law in the United Kingdom* (Kluwer Law International 2011) 24–25.

47 A Al-Astewani, 'The Legal Framework for Regulating Shariah Councils in the UK: A Potential Model for Ireland?' in Kathryn O'Sullivan (eds), *Minority Religions under Irish Law* (Brill 2019).

authority to rule on religious matters such as religious divorce is thus derived entirely from the community and does not derive from the state. Their decisions on Islamic divorce have no legal status or authority. Clients who approach them for a religious divorce do so voluntarily and cannot be summoned to do so. In this respect, the jurisdiction of these tribunals relies completely on the members of the community themselves, who voluntarily decide to accept the religious jurisdiction of such an institution by virtue of the service it is able to provide. English law does, however, provide two avenues for the decisions of Shariah tribunals to accrue legal status and thus become enforceable by the civil courts.

The first avenue is provided by contract law. If a decision of a Shariah tribunal relates to financial matters, then such a decision will be given legal effect for the purposes of contract law. The main qualification, however is that both parties must have consented to have their original dispute resolved by the Shariah tribunal. This qualification was established by Rix J in *Al-Midani v Al-Midani*, the first case to consider the legal status of a decision issued by a British Shariah tribunal.[48] The Islamic Shariah Council in London had in this case issued a decision on the division and distribution of assets in an inheritance dispute between Muslim litigants. Rix J decided that the decision had no legal effect because one of the parties had not consented to having the dispute adjudicated by the Shariah Council. The case includes an important account of the nature and function of the Islamic Shariah Council by an English judge:

> The Shari'a Council was, as explained in its own brochure, established in 1982 by scholars representing a number of mosques in the UK ... Some 1,500 cases, most of them divorce cases, had been referred to it by 1995 ... It acknowledges that it 'is not yet legally recognised by the authorities in the UK', but represents itself as gaining recognition and confidence among the Islamic community and at large. It would seem that Islamic divorce and matrimonial questions in general are the focus of its advisory and judicial work ... It can grant Islamic divorce, but it emphasises that such divorce nullifies only the Islamic marriage and has nothing to do with the civil contract ... The bench of the Shari'a Council would seem to provide a welcome facility to the Muslim community of the UK to render decisions on Islamic law, particularly in the matrimonial and family sphere. Its authority appears to rest largely on consent, in as much as it responds to the needs of the community it serves, but it may be that under Shari'a law it has autonomous power, as a religious court, to promulgate decisions in favour of a claimant even against the will of a respondent ... I am unable, however, to see how Its judgement can be binding on the heirs or any of them without their consent. Certainly

48 *Al-Midani and another v Al-Midani and others* [1999] CLC 904.

> Myrna and Omar never gave their consent to the Shari'a Council's jurisdiction, unless the arbitration agreement bound them to do so.[49]

Two more significant cases have appeared since *Al-Midani* that clarify the law on this matter, namely *Choudhury v Choudhury* and *Uddin v Choudhury*.[50] In *Choudhury v Choudhury*, a decision was also issued in an inheritance dispute by an Islamic scholar. The agreement which was drafted as a result of this decision was deemed to have legal effect by the judge.[51] The crucial factor in this case that distinguishes it from *Al-Midani* was that the parties to the dispute had consented to having their dispute resolved by an Islamic judge.[52] The more recent case of *Uddin* v *Choudhury* involved a financial dispute between two spouses who had their marriage dissolved by the Islamic Shariah Council in Leyton at the request of the wife in 2004. The couple had conducted an Islamic marriage ceremony in 2003 with the intention of conducting a civil ceremony later, but this never occurred. Mummery LJ decided on appeal that the marriage was "validly dissolved by decree of the Islamic Shariah Council" and thus activated the obligation of the husband to pay his wife the financial gifts which had been stipulated in the Islamic marriage contract:

> On this point it seems to me that, on the basis of the evidence given by Mr Saddiqui and the findings of fact by the judge, it was a valid marriage under Sharia law and that it was then validly dissolved by decree of the Islamic Sharia council. This was not a matter of English law. There was no ceremony was recognised by English law, but it was a valid ceremony so far as the parties were agreed and it was valid for the purposes of giving legal effect to the agreement which had been made about gifts and dowry ... Looking to the evidence of Mr Saddiqui as summarised by the judge in his judgement, it is not correct to say, as Mr Uddin does, that those gifts should be deducted from the dowry or that there is no legal right to enforce the dowry in the circumstances in which this marriage was dissolved. As a matter of contract, arising out of the agreement which the parties had made, I think that the judge was entitled in law to say that this was an enforceable agreement, and therefore he was right to grant judgement on the counterclaim.[53]

49 Ibid, 911, 912, 913.

50 *Choudhury v Choudhury* [2006] EWHC 1837 (Ch); *Uddin v Choudhury* [2009] EWCA Civ 1205.

51 *Choudhury v Choudhury* [2006] EWHC 1837 (Ch), 203.

52 The decision in this dispute was issued by the head scholar of Bury Park Mosque in a meeting held at the family home of the litigants, and not by a formal Shariah tribunal. Nevertheless, the scholar was acting as an Islamic judge in considering the case before him, just like an Islamic scholar employed by a formal Shariah council. His decision can thus be treated by analogy, like a decision issued by a formal Shariah tribunal.

53 *Uddin v Choudhury* [2009] EWCA Civ 120511, 13.

Uddin v Choudhury thus confirms that English judges are willing to recognise an Islamic decree of divorce issued by a Shariah tribunal in a financial dispute for the purposes of contract law.[54]

The second avenue for the decisions of Shariah tribunals to accrue legal status is provided by the *Arbitration Act 1996*. As Sandberg notes, the *Arbitration Act* is a facilitative piece of legislation that focusses on people rather than on dispute-resolution bodies.[55] It allows citizens to refer their disputes to private arbitrators rather than civil courts.[56] More crucially, it allows the parties themselves to decide what law the arbitrators will use to resolve the dispute, including religious law such as Jewish or Islamic Law.[57] Once the parties choose to be bound by an arbitration agreement, then the decision of the arbitrator will become legally binding and will be enforced by the civil courts under the law of contract. Recent cases such as *Kohn v Wagschal & Ors*[58] and *AI v MT*[59] affirm that the civil courts will enforce arbitration decisions made according to religious law. Limitations do, however, exist on arbitration. Criminal and civil divorce proceedings are beyond its jurisdiction. English law retains a complete monopoly over these two legal areas. Thus, if a Shariah tribunal sought to enforce a punishment, they would be liable under English criminal law for assault or false imprisonment. Likewise, if a Shariah tribunal sought to rule on ancillary matters in a divorce settlement such as child custody or financial assets, their decision would contain no legal authority and would not be recognised by the courts. Any attempt to enforce such a decision would again make them liable under English criminal law.[60] Arbitration decisions that do not comply with minimal standards of fairness, or which fall foul of public policy, can also be quashed by the courts via section 68 of the *Arbitration Act* or via the *Human Rights Act 1998*.[61]

Interviews conducted with case-workers and judges at Shariah tribunals have confirmed that Shariah tribunals are very aware of their legal status, as well as the rights and obligations afforded to and imposed upon them by the English legal system.[62] In the case of Islamic divorce, which constitutes the vast

54 Mummery L J's reasoning in Uddin has been criticised for failing to take into account several important factors in the dispute, including the basis for the Shariah tribunal's decision to issue the decree of divorce: see J Bowen, 'How Could English Courts Recognise Shariah?' (2010) 7(3) *University of St Thomas Law Journal* 422–435.

55 Sandberg (n 45) 33.

56 *Arbitration Act 1996* s 1.

57 Ibid s 46; R Blacklett, 'The Status of Religious 'Courts' in English Law' (2009) *Disputes and International Arbitration Newsletter* 11–14.

58 *Kohn v Wagschal & Ors* [2007] EWCA Civ 1022.

59 *AI v MT* [2013] EWHC 100 (Fam).

60 Ibid.

61 Sandberg (n 45) 33–38.

62 A Al-Astewani, 'Shariah Tribunals in Britain: A Law in Context Study of Their Role as Religious Institutions which Serve the Needs of the British Muslim Community' (DPhil Thesis, University of Manchester, 2016) ('Shariah Tribunals in Britain'); Bowen (n 43).

majority of their work, they understand that their ruling has no effect upon the status of a legally registered civil marriage. Furthermore, they understand that ancillary matters, such as child custody and financial settlement, belong exclusively to the jurisdiction of the civil courts. If the client they are dealing with has legally registered their marriage, they advise the client to apply to the civil courts to obtain a civil divorce.

In relation to civil disputes such as commercial disputes, the Shariah tribunals are also aware of the powers given to them by the *Arbitration Act* as well as the limits of such powers. Indeed, the Muslim Arbitration Tribunal, the first of its kind in Britain, was formed in 2008 with the aim of focusing specifically on resolving disputes as an arbitration tribunal functioning under the *Arbitration Act*. They also clearly demonstrate an awareness of their legal status under arbitration law, stating that:

> MAT operates within the legal framework of England and Wales thereby ensuring that any determination reached by MAT can be enforced through existing means of enforcement open to normal litigants. All areas of civil and personal religious law can be dealt with by MAT. The only areas of law that MAT cannot deal with are divorce proceedings (other than a religious divorce), child custody and criminal matters, as MAT does not have jurisdiction to deal with such matters. In such instances, the applicants will be referred to the civil courts and/or any other appropriate body.[63]

In general, Shariah tribunals repeatedly emphasise that they have no desire to challenge the jurisdiction of the state legal system, nor act in derogation of it. On the contrary, they insist that their work simply complements the work of the civil courts by providing a much-needed religious service to the community. The founder and chief arbitrator of the Muslim Arbitration Tribunal, Mr Siddiqui, has stated in this regard:

> With MAT, we are not establishing a parallel legal system, rather we are establishing an alternative legal system, its ADR, its alternative dispute resolution mechanism, and that is welcomed by English law, any form of ADR is welcome by English law, because it takes the heat from the English legal system, and ADR is part of English law. The Beth Din courts have been established in many secular countries, they have never threatened the secular fabric of those countries, they are merely providing a service to the Jewish community, and that's how we looked at it, we merely want to provide a service to the Muslim community ... it is purely to provide a service to the Muslim community, third and fourth generation people, who have no affiliation with back home, Sudan, Somalia,

63 A Al-Astewani, 'Shariah Tribunals in Britain' (n 61).

Pakistan, India, Bangladesh, Arabia, rather they are British Muslims. They need servicing in this country, and that's how we looked at it.[64]

From this brief survey it can be seen that the Shariah tribunals actually play a very limited and particular role. The vast majority of their work is related to providing a religious service to members of the community which has no relation with the civil legal system. In this regard, they affirm that they have no interest in challenging the civil jurisdiction of the state legal system. It can also be seen that the tribunals are functioning very much within the ambit of the law. They are fully aware of their rights and obligations, as bestowed and imposed upon them by the law of the land.

V The Problem with Analysing Shariah Tribunals via the Lens of Legal Pluralism

In 2008, the (then) Archbishop of Canterbury, Rowan Williams, delivered an infamous speech regarding the accommodation of religious tribunals in Britain that caused a media uproar and attracted a lot of public attention.[65] This speech prompted several academic commentators to apply the concept of legal pluralism to Shariah tribunals.[66] This is interesting to note considering the Archbishop himself did not explicitly refer to legal pluralism. On the contrary, he made clear that his speech was concerned simply with the degree of accommodation that the law of the land should offer to religious tribunals and that he was not suggesting any form of parallel legal system: "I want to say very firmly that I am not talking about parallel systems, but about how the law of the land most fruitfully, least conflictually, accommodates (religious) practice".[67] Nevertheless, his endorsement of Shachar's model of transformative accommodation as an ideal model to positively accommodate religious tribunals in Britain did echo the sentiments of the legal pluralism movement. Shachar's model of transformative accommodation depicts religious tribunals as competitors of the state legal system who battle with the state to win over citizens and thus gain authority.[68] This resonates with the legal pluralism discourse,

64 Ibid.

65 A Al-Astewani, 'Religion and Legal Pluralism', ed, Russel Sandberg' (2016) *Journal of Law, Religion and State* 4(2).

66 J Chaplin, 'Legal Monism and Religious Pluralism: Rowan Williams on Religion, Loyalty and Law' (2008) 2 *International Journal of Public Theology* 418; A Tucker, 'The Archbishop's Unsatisfactory Legal Pluralism' (2008) 4 *Public Law Journal* 463; R Hill, 'Legal Pluralism in the Liberal State: A Defence of the Archbishop of Canterbury or a Human Rights Impasse?' (2010) 165 *Law and Justice Christian Law Review* 124; B Turner, 'Legal Pluralism, State Sovereignty and Citizenship' (2011) 7(4) *Democracy and Security* 317.

67 R Williams, 'Civil and Religious Law in England: A Religious Perspective' (2008) 10(3) *Ecclesiastical Law Journal* 276.

68 For an excellent analysis of Shachar's overall thesis regarding state accommodation of communal practices, see R Sandberg et al, 'Britain's Religious Tribunals: 'Joint Governance' in Practice' (2013) 33(2) *Oxford Journal of Legal Studies* 263.

which frames social institutions as rivals and competitors of the state legal system which often enjoy more authority over members of society.[69] Moreover, the archbishop's use of terms such as "supplementary jurisdiction" in relation to religious tribunals and "unqualified secular legal monopoly" in relation to the state legal system further clouded the message he was trying to convey.[70]

It was this unfortunate lack of clarity in the Archbishop's speech which helped to instigate a media frenzy and which even led one legal commentator to believe that the Archbishop was suggesting criminal jurisdiction should be delegated to religious tribunals.[71] More relevantly for this discussion, it was these indications in the Archbishop's speech that led to a series of articles adopting legal pluralism as a paradigm within which to analyse the emergence of Shariah tribunals. One of these articles in particular demonstrates the problem with analysing the case of Shariah tribunals via the lens of legal pluralism, and thus deserves a closer study.[72]

In a critical evaluation of the Archbishop's speech, Hill uses the concept of legal pluralism as a framework to shed light on the case of Shariah tribunals in Britain. In this regard, he refers to the Griffiths' concepts of "strong" and "weak" legal pluralism.[73] Hill defines "strong" legal pluralism as a state of affairs where:

> … "unofficial" legal systems, although not bearing legal strength within the official legal system, challenge the official system through the real strength they have for certain groups of society, even to the point of usurping official law.[74]

He then adopts the view that Shariah tribunals in Britain are a case of "strong" legal pluralism. To justify such a position, he refers to Shariah tribunals as an "unofficial parallel 'legal' system" and a "lacuna in the legal sphere" which "challenges the very notion of the absolute sovereignty of the law" and that the state cannot simply "ignore". Shariah tribunals are thus depicted via the lens of legal pluralism as a fully-fledged parallel legal system which has developed outside the parameters of the law, and which directly challenges the civil jurisdiction of the state legal system. Hill further amplifies this depiction of Shariah tribunals by noting the supremacy of religious law when there is a "clash of legal orders" and the fact that "to abandon Islamic law for a Muslim would appear a non-option".[75]

69 Galanter (n 18) 17.
70 Williams (n 66) 262, 268, 273 and 274.
71 Tucker (n 65) 463–6.
72 Hill (n 65).
73 Ibid 128–9, 132.
74 Ibid 132.
75 Ibid 128.

Hill's article amply demonstrates the problem with using legal pluralism as a framework for analysing the case of Shariah tribunals in Britain. It led the author in this case to draw an inaccurate and misleading picture of Shariah tribunals and their relationship with the state legal system. Such a picture contributes to the general public panic being stirred by the media, and public reports which portray the emergence of Shariah tribunals as the beginnings of a fanatical attempt to impose the Shariah and Islamic rule upon the entire British population, as well as being directly opposed to equality and "one law for al".[76]

Hill's inaccurate depiction of Shariah tribunals was, of course, only possible in the first place due to an ignorance of the way Shariah tribunals are actually functioning on the ground as well as an ignorance of their legal status. Indeed, other commentators such as Chaplin, Tucker and, to a lesser extent, Turner offered a more sophisticated analysis of Shariah tribunals despite insisting on using the framework of legal pluralism.[77] This was because they were more aware of the way Shariah tribunals are actually functioning and their relationship with the state legal system. Nevertheless, even in their case, the attempt to relate legal pluralism to the discourse on Shariah tribunals should have been avoided due to its problematic premises as well as the particular political motivations that underlie its central tenets. These factors meant that it clouded rather than illuminated the discourse on Shariah tribunals and provided an unsuitable paradigm within which to analyse such tribunals.

VI Legal Pluralism as a Conceptual Approach in the Field of Law and Religion: Some Reflections

Despite its problematic premises, the concept of legal pluralism in academic discourse does not show any signs of abating. On the contrary, it seems only to be gaining momentum and has now been extended across many legal disciplines.[78] Indeed, in a review of Berman's recent publication on legal pluralism, it was boldly stated:

> The book is a landmark contribution to legal pluralist theory, amassing a near comprehensive survey of the range of situations of overlapping and conflicting legal orders. The range of phenomena identified alone ought to settle beyond doubt the falsity of any view which holds that such conflicts and non-state legal phenomena exist only at the margins and under rare conditions and so are safely ignored by general theories of law.[79]

76 MacEoin (n 44); M Namazie, 'Shariah Law in Britain: A Threat to One Law for All and Equal Rights' (One Law for All, 2010).
77 Chapman (n 65); Tucker (n 65); Turner (n 65).
78 Tamanaha, '*Legal Pluralism Explained*' (n 1) 375–6.
79 M Giudice, 'Global Legal Pluralism: What's Law Got to Do with It?' (2014) 34(3) *Oxford Journal of Legal Studies* 591.

The modern legal pluralism movement currently pays much of its attention to the multiplicity of legal orders found in today's newly globalised world. Examples which are cited in this regard include international conventions which regulate transnational commercial transactions, regional laws such as European law which have been incorporated by member states into their domestic laws, and private arbitration tribunals which function on a transnational level and offer litigants an alternative to national state courts.[80] Nevertheless, legal pluralism advocates are yet to provide an adequate justification for using the term "legal pluralism" to describe such a state of affairs. The English common law, from its very inception, involved the incorporation and formalisation of religion and custom.[81] It was, in fact, this process of formalisation which led to the formation of a "common" law, administered by the King's courts, and applicable on a national scale.[82] English judges historically had no qualms with benefiting from foreign laws in their decisions.[83] To this day, English judges regularly agree to apply the provisions of foreign laws in the context of private international law. Moreover, the English legal system has historically never had an issue with delegating its legal functions to private institutions and still does so via the *Arbitration Act 1996*. As for the multiplicity of social regulatory orders in society, everyone agrees that this is not a novel phenomenon.

Why then, should legal pluralists reframe this diversity and multiplicity of legal norms and institutions as a "rediscovery" of legal pluralism?[84] Why can they not simply refer to the diversity of legal norms within the law or to the multiplicity of social regulatory orders which exist in society as a case of normative pluralism, as Tamanaha and An-Na'im both suggest?[85] Normative pluralism is a broader concept than legal pluralism, and simply refers to the

80 Tamanaha, '*Legal Pluralism Explained*' (n 1), 386–8.

81 Religious norms and local social customs were two foundational legal sources that influenced the development of English law early on in the history of its development, with Christianity in particular having a dominating influence on English laws' use of religious norms as a legal basis for legislation and case law. For further details regarding this historical process, see S F C Milsom *Historical Foundations of the Common Law* (London: Butterworths, 1981) and H Baker *An Introduction to English Legal History* (London: Butterworths, 2002).

82 Theodore Plucknett, *A Concise History of the Common Law* (Butterworth 1956) 342; W Robson, *Civilisation and the Growth of Law* (Macmillan and Company, 1935) 57.

83 See, eg, *Acton v Blundell* [1843] 12 M&W 353, in which Tindal CJ declared the authority of Marcellus in the Digest as 'decisive'. See also *Manton v Brocklebank* [1923] 2 KB 212, in which Lord Sterndale stated 'I think he began as some of the cases did with the book of Exodus, and one of the cases on this subject, *Card v. Case* discusses the Mosaic law, the Athenian, the Roman, and the Code Civil. It must not be forgotten, however, that we are dealing with the English common law, and that these other systems of jurisprudence are relevant only so far as they throw light on our law'.

84 Galanter (n 18) 20.

85 Tamanaha, '*Legal Pluralism Explained*' (n 1); A An-Na'im 'Religious Norms and Family Law: Is it Legal or Normative Pluralism?' (2011) 25 *Emory International Law Review* 791–94.

coexistence of multiple systems of norms or rules in society.[86] Normative pluralism allows for a distinction to be drawn between the state legal system and other social regulatory orders. Both can be described as normative systems, but they can still be distinguished as each having distinctive characteristics. An-Na'im argues that normative pluralism in this sense would be more conducive to the purpose of legal pluralism:

> The purpose and rationale of legal pluralism are better served through the concept and methodology of normative pluralism than through the ambiguous idea of legal pluralism. As noted earlier, a distinction, not dichotomy, between state law and religious normativity is necessary for mediating competing claims of religious and customary norms and state law. Conversely, insisting on an expansive and unrestrained use of the terms 'law' and 'legal' to include all norms that are religiously or culturally binding will be counterproductive to the purpose of legal pluralism. This does not mean that state law is superior or more effective than other normative systems. Rather, the point is that because the source and authority of state law are different from that of religious normative systems, it is confusing to use the term 'law' for both types of normative systems.[87]

This distinction would affirm the existence of a multiplicity of social regulatory orders in society which may very well enjoy more social influence than the state legal system without blurring the distinction between the two.

However, the more pertinent issue with legal pluralism, in this author's view, is the doubts that it raises regarding the authority and sanction of state law. The authority of the state legal system is constantly questioned and challenged in the legal pluralism literature, with the implication that its jurisdiction is not exclusive or absolute. This belies reality, a fact which can be amply illustrated by the English legal system and the case of Shariah tribunals. If the English legal system wished, it could decide to end the jurisdiction of any Shariah tribunals from functioning at any point it chooses, just as it decided to end the jurisdiction of local and special courts in 1846 via the *County Courts Act*. This absolute authority was demonstrated in 2013 when a group of British Muslim men tried to enforce a Sharia zone in East London, by confronting members of the public and demanding that they conform to Sharia law. The men were duly arrested and were eventually issued with jail sentences for criminal offences after their case was heard at the Old Bailey.[88] The English

86 W Twining, 'Normative and Legal Pluralism: A Global Perspective' (2009) 20 *Duke J. Comp. & Int'l L* 476.

87 Ibid 797.

88 Sam Jones, 'Muslim Vigilantes Jailed for "Sharia Law" Attacks in London' *The Guardian* (6 December 2013) http://www.theguardian.com/uk-news/2013/dec/06/muslim-vigilantes-jailed-sharia-law-attacks-london accessed 1 September 2023.

legal system could also decide to repeal or amend the *Arbitration Act 1996* to limit the power that religious tribunals have under arbitration law. This has already been done by the Canadian province of Ontario after a controversial debate over the applicability of the Shariah consumed the province. The debate arose after a group of Muslims from Toronto announced their intention to make use of the *Arbitration Act 1991* by establishing Islamic Arbitration Tribunals.[89] The Ontario legislature responded by passing the *Family Statute Law Amendment Act 2005*, which amended the *Arbitration Act* and required for family law arbitration to be "conducted exclusively in accordance with the law of Ontario or of another Canadian jurisdiction".[90] There have also been similar parliamentary attempts in the UK to limit the power of British Shariah tribunals, although they have not as of yet proved to be successful.[91]

It is this ultimate jurisdiction over law which distinguishes state law from other regulatory orders within society. Such regulatory orders enjoy neither the same absolute jurisdiction nor the same absolute powers of enforcement as the state legal system. One of Griffiths' fundamental errors was blurring this distinction. Moreover, a multiplicity of legal norms may exist within the ambits of the state legal system, but their authority derives from, and is ultimately dependant on, the state legal system, as Griffiths himself noted in his discussion of "weak" legal pluralism. Thus, European Law may be an example of legal diversity within the English law, but its authority derives from and is dependent upon the acts of Parliament which initially granted it legal jurisdiction. The severe consequences that can flow from obscuring this reality have been illustrated in this chapter by the application of legal pluralism to the discourse on Shariah tribunals. Any discourse on the multiplicity or diversity of legal norms and institutions in society, whether it takes the name "legal pluralism" or any other name, must be very clear from the outset on the jurisdiction of the state legal system in this regard. This will prevent such discourses from drawing false analogies and misleading conclusions.

On a separate note, this chapter has also demonstrated the importance of having an intimate knowledge of the legal and empirical reality on the ground in such discourses. The current academic discourse on Shariah tribunals is particularly lacking in this regard and has thus been the victim of largely theoretical discussions which are divorced from reality. An intimate knowledge of the actual work of Shariah tribunals as well as their legal status would

89 It should be re-emphasised here that such tribunals would have functioned within the limits and restrictions imposed by the Arbitration Act 1991, which includes a prohibition of engaging in arbitration of matrimonial and criminal cases. In this sense, these Islamic arbitration tribunals would not have had the freedom to apply Islamic law in an unqualified and unrestricted way during arbitration proceedings.

90 N Bakht, 'Were Muslim Barbarians Really Knocking On the Gates of Ontario?: The Religious Arbitration Controversy – Another Perspective' (2006) 40 *Ottawa Law Review* 80.

91 A Al-Astewani, 'Reflections on the Rise and Fall of the Arbitration and Mediation Services (Equality) Bill' (2017) *Public Law* 4.

allow academic discourse to focus on more important discussions regarding the tribunals, such as the benefits, if any, that flow from the state's decision to delegate legal functions to private institutions such as religious arbitration tribunals. This would consequently help to reframe the wider public debate on Shariah tribunals, which is currently filled with much rhetoric and little substance. Such rhetoric not only encourages negative stigmatisation of the British Muslim community, but also takes the focus away from more serious and pragmatic questions related to the procedures of these tribunals and whether they are treating their clients with the justice and fairness that such clients would receive in the English courts.

Further Reading:

For analysis of the methods used in this chapter, see Chapter 15 – Section IV – subsection A *The Doctrinal Method.*

For a comparative analysis involving legal institutions, see Chapter 12.

4 Minors in Comparative Law and Religion Research

Esther Erlings[1]

I Introduction

Despite children's central place in most religions, comparative law and religion research with minors remains rare. Research considering children in multiple jurisdictions often focuses on a comparative study of international jurisdictions[2] or involves a simple collection of studies on children's religious rights in various countries.[3] Such research is also normally doctrinal, rather than socio-legal with involvement of the minors concerned.[4] Yet children are increasingly recognised as agents in their own right, instead of objects of adult concern,[5] and if the field of law and religion is to keep up with this development, it should turn its focus to children themselves. Bringing together comparison, law, religion, and minors, however, is not an easy task! It requires significant preparation and a multitude of considerations. Some of these form the subject of this chapter, which aims at providing the legal researcher with an initial lead into comparative law and religion research with minors by discussing a number of key considerations within the comparative context: whether the value system at play is, indeed, a religion (Section II); whether children can be seen as independent believers (Section III); how children's religiosity might be approached (Section IV), and; what issues arise when setting up research with minors as participants, including matters of consent (Section V).

1 Senior Lecturer in Law, Macquarie University.

2 See, eg, Sylvie Langlaude, *The Right of the Child to Freedom of Religion in International Law* (Brill, 2007).

3 See, eg, Martha Albertson Fineman and Karen Worthington, *What Is Right for Children? The Competing Paradigms of Religion and Human Rights* (Ashgate, 2009).

4 A study which (imperfectly) seeks to do the latter is the author's work: Esther Erlings, *Religious Rights within the Family: From Coerced Manifestation to Dispute Resolution in France, England and Hong Kong* (Routledge, 2020).

5 Committee on the Rights of the Child ('CmRC'), *General Comment No. 7 (2005) Implementing Rights in Early Childhood*, 40th sess, UN Doc CRC/C/GC/7.Rev1 (20 September 2006) [17].

DOI: 10.4324/9781003397311-6

II Religion and (Cultural) Value Systems

The first thing to consider when conducting law and religion research concerning minors is whether the object of investigation is, indeed, part of religion and/or perceived as such. This is an issue that affects all law and religion research, and the children's context may simply be an area in which it plays out. For example, in *Lautsi v Italy*, the European Court of Human Rights case on the display of crucifixes in Italian classrooms, opinions diverged between States as to whether the crucifix was an expression of religion or merely a cultural artefact and part of a tradition with which children should be acquainted.[6] Similarly, the matter of what counts as religion in Japan, where people who do not form part of congregational religion would normally describe themselves as non-religious ('*Mushūkyō*'),[7] has had its reflection on children, their education, and their societal status.[8] However, Italian and Japanese adults also have to contend with these traditions and definitions of (non-)religion.

By contrast, from the perspective of research with minors, the issue can be more pertinent where the focus regarding the suggested religion comprises not merely objects and rituals, but also covers intergenerational value systems with specific expectations in respect of children. For example, the African notion of *Ubuntu* may strike many as bearing some of the hallmarks of religion; a moral view on life, principles, and values for communities, and intergenerational transmission.[9] Moreover, academic literature on *Ubuntu* is often published in religion or theology journals.[10] Yet, whilst spiritual aspects of *Ubuntu* may be recognised, the system itself is not normally regarded as a religion.[11] Perhaps even more controversial, but also more common, is the designation of Confucianism as a form of religion. Some major historical designations of the religious nature of Confucianism were the work of Westerners, rather than Confucians themselves.[12] Despite, inter alia, its value systems and clear

6 *Lautsi and Others v Italy* (European Court of Human Rights, Grant Chamber, Application No 30814/06, 18 March 2011).

7 Mitsutoshi Horii, 'Problems of 'Religion' in Japan: Part 1' (2020) 14(11) *Religion Compass* e12376, 8.

8 See, eg, Alec R LeMay, 'Mushūkyō Identification and the Fragile Existence of Catholic Children in Japan' (2019) 10(7) *Religions* 414.

9 Robert K Chigangaidze, 'An Exposition of Humanistic-Existential Social Work in Light of Ubuntu Philosophy: Towards Theorizing Ubuntu in Social Work Practice (2021) 40(2) *Journal of Religion & Spirituality in Social Work* 146, 148–158; Lesley Le Grange, 'Ubuntu, Ukama, Environment and Moral Education' (2012) 41(3) *Journal of Moral Education* 329, 331–5; Marta Bonn 'Children's Understanding of 'Ubuntu'" (2007) 177(8) *Early Child Development and Care* 863, 864–6.

10 See article and footnotes, Rev Jacob Mokhutso, 'Ubuntu: A Countermeasure for Challenges in Child-Rearing' (2022) 103 *Pharos Journal of Theology* (online); Chigangaidze (n 8).

11 See Chigangaidze (n 8) 157.

12 Anna Sun, *Confucianism as a World Religion: Contested Histories and Contemporary Realities* (Princeton University Press, 2013) 47; Max Weber, *The Religion of China: Confucianism and Taoism*, tr Hans H Gerth (Free Press, 1951).

rules for social/intra-family interaction based on filial piety, rituals including the veneration of ancestors (often translated as "ancestor worship"), and the existence of authoritative books (notably the Analects),[13] Confucianism is not normally regarded as a religion by those who practice it.[14] However, the presence of Confucianism and adherence to its values, whether within a societal or religious community, educational or other institution, or family, can have a significant impact on minors, the regulation of their lives, the application of legal concepts, and the exercise of their rights.[15] Since Confucianism is not always an aspect of the whole-of-society context, and will not come out in questions around, for example, ethnic background, this places researchers in a bind. Noting in empirical research that a minor's Confucian parents are 'non-religious' may be correct, but it might introduce bias if a number of non-religious parents do, in fact, ascribe to a tightly regulated value and belief system with spiritual aspects.

At the same time, calling a system religious when it is not so regarded by its adherents is disrespectful. Horii, for example, criticises especially Western scholars' "tendency to try to find what they call 'religion' where [local] people say that there is not such a thing".[16] Moreover, researchers can cause substantial misunderstanding amongst their research subjects when the connection with religion is not apparent to participants. This may be all the more true in case the participants are minors who may not reason by analogy. There is no easy answer to the question of religion itself, but it is one that should be carefully considered in research on law, religion, and minors, quite apart from the issue of whether children should themselves be seen as independent believers.

III Children as Independent Believers

There is a historical inclination in academic research to refer to "religious children" and "religious families" on the basis of parental religion, even where research questions are aimed at children's own agency.[17] This tendency can be linked with the debate around existing rights for parents and children in the matter of children's freedom of religion and their upbringing in alignment

13 See Tu Weiming, 'Confucianism', *Encyclopedia Brittanica* (17 August 2023) https://www.britannica.com/topic/Confucianism; Yong Chen, *Confucianism as a World Religion: Controversies and Consequences* (Brill, 2013); Sun (n 11); Rodney L Taylor, 'The Religious Character of the Confucian Tradition' (1998) 48(1) *Philosophy East and West* 80.

14 Sun (n 11) 1.

15 See eg Juha Hämäläinen, Shih-Yun Wu and Fang Zhao, 'The Chinese View of the Rights of the Child: An Analysis of the Law of the Protection of Minors' (2023) 31(1) *The International Journal of Children's Rights* 167.

16 See Horii (n 6) 8.

17 See, eg, Betsy Hughes Barrow, David C Dollahite and Loren D Marks, 'How Parents Balance Desire for Religious Continuity with Honouring Children's Religious Agency' (2021) 13(2) *Psychology of Religion and Spirituality* 222.

with parental preferences.[18] Whether children can, indeed, be regarded as independent believers, separate from their parents and family, is a crucial premise for law and religion research. It takes on even further significance in the case of comparative research, which may base itself on either a human rights approach or the *lex localis* – legal frameworks that can differ very significantly and influence the way in which research can be conducted and understood.

The point considered here is a legal one. This is quite separate from the question whether particular religions would consider children to be religious from the moment they are born or conceived or only following a specific ritual, oath, or passing of a certain age – and whether this manifestation is a confirmation or an active choice.[19] In this respect, it is important to be mindful of the fact that many religions have an age of religious majority or maturity,[20] sometimes referred to as "the age of reason",[21] but that it is not necessarily true that children under that age would *not* be regarded as religious. If the question of children as independent believers is considered from the perspective of a particular community, then the focus should turn to the specific rules, perspectives, and understandings of that religious community. These are best discovered through active interaction with the community, if not already known to the researcher(s) – and if they are not known to the researcher, the question may need to be asked whether a greater emphasis on co-design or collaboration would be suitable.[22] A fuller discussion of children as independent believers within particular religions is beyond the scope of this section, which will instead focus on legal aspects and the identified human rights and *lex localis* approaches.

A The Human Rights Approach

For a significant period of time following the adoption of key human rights instruments, debate continued on whether children should be seen as having

18 See Heiner Bielefeldt, Nazila Ghanea and Michael Wiener, *Freedom of Religion or Belief; and International Law Commentary* (Oxford, 2016) 205 ff; Langlaude (n 1) chs 1, 2.

19 Rituals often coincide with the taking of religious responsibility in addition to acceptance: Munider Kaur Ahluwalia, Tyce Nadrich and Ikbal Singh Ahluwalia, 'Sikh Youth Coming of Age: Reflections on the Decision to Tie a Turban' (2019) 64(1) *Counselling and Values* 20, 23–4.

20 Robert Roseby, 'Why Are There Coming of Age Ceremonies at the Onset of Adolescence?' (2020) 56(12) *Journal of Paediatrics and Child Health* 1982, 1982.

21 'Benedict XVI Affirms First Communion for Children at Age of Reason', *Catholic News Agency* (News Release, 10 August 2010) https://www.catholicnewsagency.com/news/20595/benedict-xvi-affirms-first-communion-for-children-at-age-of-reason.

22 Inspiration can be derived from community-based research with Indigenous Peoples: Ray Lovett, Laimena Muwadda and Vanessa Lee, 'Aboriginal and Torres Strait Islander Community-Based Research' in Maggie Walter (ed), *Social Research Methods* (Oxford University Press, 4th ed, 2019) 410–429. See also: Jo Howard and Mariz Tadros (eds), *Using Participatory Methods to Explore Freedom of Religion and Belief* (Bristol University Press, 2023).

independent rights to freedom of religion at the international level or whether parental rights and preferences should prevail.[23] The matter was so unclear and controversial by the time the 1989 *Convention on the Rights of the Child* ('*CRC*')[24] was adopted, that its provision on the child's right to freedom of religion (Article 14) attracted declarations and reservations from all sides of the debate.[25] States who prioritised parental rights *and* States who gave prevalence to children's rights both felt the need to specify their interpretations of, and limitations on Article 14 of the CRC.[26] At present, the situation is clearer, and it is now safe to say that the human rights approach is one that rests on children's independent rights and agency, with an accessory role (but not rights) for parents. In a large research study, the current author has, for example, surveyed the *travaux préparatoires*, comments and cases of various human rights regimes to conclude that the often-suggested parental rights to determine and impose children's religion and manifestation were never intended and are not enforced,[27] and that by bringing their own cases, children have identified themselves as independent rights-holders.[28] Parents have primary responsibility for their children's upbringing and this role should be respected, but not to the extent of violations of children's independent rights.[29] In 2016, the Committee on the Rights of the Child issued a conclusive interpretation of Article 14 that (should have)[30] ended the debate in its General Comment on rights in adolescence (emphasis added):

> *[I]t is the child who exercises the right to freedom of religion, not the parent,* and the *parental role* necessarily diminishes as the child acquires an increasingly active role in exercising choice throughout adolescence.[31]

23 Erlings (n 3) ch 2, see especially 20; Eva Brems, 'Article 14: The Right to Freedom of Thought, Conscience and Religion' in A Alen et al (eds), *A Commentary on the United Nations Convention on the Rights of the Child* (Martinus Nijhoff, 2006) 25–31.

24 *Convention on the Rights of the Child,* opened for signature 20 November 1989, 1577 UNTS 3 (entered into force 2 September 1990).

25 Langlaude (n 1) 118–20.

26 Sharon Detrick, *A Commentary on the United Nations Convention on the Rights of the Child* (Martinus Nijhoff, 1999) 248–9.

27 Erlings (n 3) ch 2.

28 Ibid 33–4. See, eg, Human Rights Committee ('HRC'), *Views: Communication No 1852/2008*, 106th sess, UN Doc. CCPR/C/106/D/1852/2008 (4 February 2013) ('*Singh v France*').

29 See the overview of cases and resolutions in Erlings (n 3) ch 2. See also Marc J Bossuyt, *Guide to the 'Travaux Préparatoires' of the International Covenant on Civil and Political Rights* (Martinus Nijhoff Publishers, 1987) 368, 369.

30 But see on continued questioning: Wouter Vandenhole, Gamze Erdem Türkelli and Sara Lembrechts, *Children's Rights: A Commentary on the Convention on the Rights of the Child and Its Protocols* (Edward Elgar, 2019) 170–2.

31 CmRC, *General Comment No. 20 (2016) on the Implementation of the Rights of the Child during Adolescence*, UN Doc CRC/C/GC/20 (6 December 2016) [43] (emphasis added).

This statement builds on a previous General Comment on rights in early childhood in which the Committee noted that the CRC's general article on parental direction and guidance in children's exercise of their rights (Article 5):

> ... contains the principle that parents (and others) have the responsibility to continually adjust the levels of support and guidance they offer to a child [as children's capacities evolve]. ... Evolving capacities should be seen as a positive and enabling process ... Parents (and others) should be encouraged to offer "direction and guidance" in a child-centred way, through dialogue and example, in ways that enhance young children's capacities to exercise their rights, including their right to participation (art. 12) and their right to freedom of thought, conscience and religion (art. 14).[32]

The human rights approach is thus one centred on children's independent rights to freedom of religion. This means that labels such as "religious" cannot be assigned without understanding a child's individual situation and that consideration must be given to who speaks for a child (see following sections).

However, the statement does not take away the fact that multiple States (and the Holy See as a distinct member) have explicitly rejected this approach through prior reservations and declarations in respect of Article 14. Many Islamic States in particular included reservations to Article 14 with a view to preserving the application of Shariah law and preventing children from obtaining rights to potentially change their religion (apostacy).[33] For example, Bangladesh has entered a general reservation to the whole of Article 14(1); Iraq accepted the *Convention* "subject to a reservation ..., concerning the child's freedom of religion, as allowing a child to change his or her religion runs counter to the provisions of the *Islamic Shariah*"; and Algeria issued an interpretative declaration to state that it will interpret Article 14 in line with provisions in its constitution and family code that specify Islam as the State religion and require children to be educated in the religion of their fathers.[34] Consequently, applying a human rights approach to these countries is not straightforward and could potentially be considered unfair where application of rights has been explicitly excluded in favour of the *lex localis.*

32 CmRC (n 4) [17].

33 Shaheen Sardar Ali and Sajila Sohail Khan, 'Evolving Conceptions of Children's Rights: Some Reflections on Muslim States' Engagement with the UN Convention on the Rights of the Child' in Nadjma Yassari, Lena-Maria Möller and Imen Gallala-Arndt, *Parental Care and the Best Interests of the Child in Muslim Countries* (Springer, 2017) 285–324; International Commission of Jurists, *Reservations to the Convention on the Rights of the Child: A Look at the Reservations of Asian State Parties* (Paper, 01 February 1994) 9–10, 28–32.

34 'Status of Treaties: 11. Convention on the Rights of the Child', *United Nations Treaty Collection* (Web Page, 12 September 2023) https://treaties.un.org/pages/ViewDetails.aspx?src=IND&mtdsg_no=IV-11&chapter=4&clang=_en#EndDec.

B Lex Localis

A second approach to the status of children as independent believers and holders of rights is that of the *lex localis*, or the law that applies to a particular constituency. As noted earlier, at a national level, very particular rules may apply to minors, their parents, and third parties in respect of religion, and these can differ substantially from human rights. It may make perfect sense to research "religious families" or "religious children" based on parental religion in contexts where there is an expectation or legal fact that citizens follow a particular religion and that children take on their parents' (or a parent's) religion. Notably, *lex localis* considerations are not reserved for non-Western States like the Islamic States referred to in the previous section. For example, under the principle of parental responsibility such as that applies in England and Wales and in Australia, parents are responsible for their child's religion, and this "duty" arguably comes with a concomitant right to determine their child's religion and religious upbringing until a child has become *Gillick* competent (see Section V).[35] Whilst the United Kingdom and some Australian States and Territories have adopted human rights legislation, this legislation does not apply horizontally between family members.[36] Instead, parental impositions of religion and manifestation can only be limited by the child protection threshold, which in England and Wales requires that the religion in question is "immoral or socially obnoxious", "pernicious", or otherwise not "legally and socially acceptable",[37] or the practices and/or their imposition cause "significant harm".[38] This is unlikely to be the case where parents exercise their parental responsibility rights,[39] and thus considerable interference with children's human rights – and practical absence of their independent rights-holding – can be a legally acceptable situation under national law leading to de facto "religious families". Conversely, States such as France uphold radical forms of secularism that have a chilling effect on children's religious rights.[40]

35 For England & Wales see Esther Erlings, 'Is Anything Left of Children's Rights? How Parental Responsibility Erodes Children's Rights under English Law (2016) 24(3) *International Journal of Children's Rights* 624; for Australia see Grant RiethMuller and Robin Smith, *Family Law* (Thomson Reuters, 7th ed, 2022) 306–9.

36 Dominic McGoldrick, 'The United Kingdom's Human Rights Act 1998 in Theory and Practice' (2001) 50(5) *International and Comparative Law Quarterly* 901, 936; Louis Schetzer, 'Voluntarily 'Opting In' – The Australian Approach to Seeking Human Rights Compliance from Non-Government Entities' (2021) 27(3) *Australian Journal of Human Rights* 402, 405–8.

37 *Re G (Children)* [2012] EWCA Civ 1233 (4 October 2012) [36].

38 *Children Act 1989* (UK) c 41, s 31(2)(a) – the harm must be the result of failure to provide the care that can be reasonably expected of a parent, s 31(2)(b).

39 *Newcastle City Council v Z* [2005] EWHC 1490 (Fam) (11 July 2005) [56]: a parent 'faithfully striving to follow the teachings of one of the great religions' is unlikely to act unreasonably.

40 Committee on the Rights of the Child, *Concluding Observations of the Committee on the Rights of the Child: France*, 51st sess, CRC/C/FRA/CO/4 (11 June 2009) paras 28, 30, 45, 46.

In these countries, children may be posited as autonomous from their parents and families in matters of religion (especially in schools), but the State curtails the human rights they would ordinarily enjoy on the basis of national laws and constitutional provisions.[41] This means that children are seen as independent in their beliefs, but at the same time not fully rights-holders in the way expected under a human rights approach.[42] Hence, application of a *lex localis* approach requires a deep understanding of local law-in-context, and thorough consideration of the real comparableness of jurisdictions (unless the very idea is to include jurisdictions that are fundamentally different).

Overall, when conducting comparative law and religion research with minors, it is of central importance to consider and clearly stipulate the approach or approaches adopted. In most cases, at least some reference to *lex localis* is unavoidable, and the question is primarily whether the research commences from a local or human rights premise in respect of children's status (eg, whether the research at all contemplates that children can be independent believers with individual rights or whether a family unity approach is to be preferred). Research with immigrant children can add an extra layer of complexity, where, for example, the country of origin has a clear State religion with reservation to the CRC, and the host country is secular, having also lodged objections to religion-based CRC reservations – or where both countries are legally secular, but one is socially religious.[43] Separately, the research method may determine the approach. For example, law and religion research, such as that aimed at law reform, may be based on data derived from population surveys, like household surveys and other existing datasets. These may simply list the whole family as religious without disaggregating between members or fail to record minors' religion separately.[44] In the case of jurisdictions that favour a familial approach, this would be justified – in jurisdictions that do not, this would be a significant limitation. Such data excludes a human rights approach. Where a human rights approach *is* adopted, the next question becomes at which point children can practically become (non-)believers, that is, when religiosity or religious capacity arises. An understanding of religious

41 Erlings (n 3) 106–25.

42 The matter is further complicated by the fact that French children can legally have rights, but cannot exercise them because they do not have legal capacity or standing, ibid; Philippe Bonfils and Adeline Gouttenoire, *Droit des Mineurs* (Dalloz, 3rd ed, 2021) 266–287, 488–94; Marie-Philomène Gil-Rosado, *Les libertés de l'esprit de l'enfant dans les rapports familiaux* (Défrenois 2006) 46–83.

43 The latter is the case for Turkish minors in Germany. Olivia Spiegler, Derya Güngör and Birgit Leyendecker, 'Muslim Immigrant Parents' Social Status Moderates the Link between Religious Parenting and Children's Identification with the Heritage and Host Culture' (2016) 47(9) *Journal of Cross-Cultural Psychology* 1159.

44 See Barry R Chiswick and Donka M Mirtcheva, 'Religion and Child Health: Religious Affiliation, Importance, and Attendance and Health Status among American Youth' (2013) 34(1) *Journal of Family and Economic Issues* 120, 124 (use of parental religion as a proxy).

cognition in children is nonetheless important for all law and religion research with minors.

IV Children's Religiosity

Children's religiosity as here used refers to children's actual religious cognition, that is, their functional capacity in relation to religious belief and manifestation. For example, it would be incongruous to regard a four-year-old as having the capacity for fully autonomous religious choice as understood by the CRC, but a child this age will be able to understand a particular ritual or information as belonging within the sphere of religion.[45] Religious understanding matters, for example, in determining when certain types of state-sponsored religious education may (not) be appropriate,[46] or when children can legally refuse life-saving medical treatment on the basis of religious belief.[47]

Children's religiosity has long been the subject of study in the social sciences and today comprises a large research area commonly referred to as "religious cognition".[48] Historically, understandings of children's religiosity, including in law, were heavily influenced by "stage theories" of development.[49] These theories focus on broad concepts, like children's moral reasoning,[50] rather than specific aspects of religion in context, such as the way children understand prayer as communication with a supernatural or the universe.[51] The most well-known stage theory of development is that proposed by Piaget, often complemented by insights from Kohlberg's moral reasoning and/or Fowler's faith

45 Compare Larry P Nucci, *Education in the Moral Domain* (Cambridge University Press, 2001) 21; Charles C Helwig and Elliott Turiel 'Children's Social and Moral Reasoning' in Peter K Smith and Craig H Hart (eds), *The Wiley-Blackwell Handbook of Childhood Social Development* (2nd ed, Wiley-Blackwell, 2011) 569–76.

46 Eg, a likelihood to 'influence the minds of young children' was important in the finding that the religious education classes amounted to indoctrination in *Hasam and Eylem Zengin v Turkey* no. 1448/04 (03 March 2009) ECtHR [64].

47 Irrespective of whether courts can override that refusal despite capacity: *X v The Sydney Children's Hospitals Network* (2013) 85 NSWLR 294.

48 Rebekah A Richert and Kathleen H Corriveau, 'Development of Religious Cognition' (2022) 4 *Annual Review of Developmental Psychology* 185, 186.

49 See Barabara Bennett Woodhouse, 'Religion and Children's Rights' in John Witte Jr and M Christian Green, *Religion & Human Rights: An Introduction* (Oxford University Press, 2012) 299–315, 306; Charles C Helwig and Urszula Jasiobedzka, 'The Relation between Law and Morality: Children's Reasoning about Socially Beneficial and Unjust Laws (2001) 72(5) *Child Development* 1382, 1382–3, 1390.

50 See Jeremy I M Carpendale, 'Kohlberg and Piaget on Stages and Moral Reasoning' (2000) 20(2) *Developmental Review* 181.

51 See Jonathan D Lane, 'Probabilistic Reasoning in Context: Socio-Cultural Differences in Children's and Adult's Predictions about the Fulfillment of Prayers and Wishes' (2020) 21(2) *Journal of Cognition and Development* 240.

development.[52] Stage theories suggest that children develop religious capacity around age seven,[53] though development towards genuine autonomy continues into adolescence. Yet, as Fortin notes, whilst it cannot be denied that children have evolving capacities, stage theories have been largely discredited, or at least become subject to critique, due to their broadness and inability to fully account for children's individual development, which may be influenced by the time and culture in which they are brought up.[54] Whilst the concept of a "theory" may resonate with lawyers, stage theories are too abstract and general (and Western-focused) to be of significant help to a comparative lawyer of law and religion research with minors.

In response to generalist stage theories, social scientists developed research programmes that considered specific aspects of religion and/or specific religious situations to examine children's capacity at different ages.[55] For example, in a research project with Canadian minors that looked at children's fundamental rights, Helwig found that the majority of participating six-year-olds judged "restrictions on [prayer] as wrong and outside the scope of governmental, school, and familial authority in both Canada and other countries",[56] thereby suggesting a contextual understanding of religious manifestation. In the same vein, research found that children around the age of four to six distinguished religious rules and manifestations on the basis of their morality and imperativeness,[57] and evaluated the effectiveness of rituals of their own and others' religions.[58] Despite being a reaction against stage theories, this new(er)

52 Linda L Barnes et al, 'Spirituality, Religion and Pediatrics: Intersecting Worlds of Healing' (2000) 104(6) *Pediatrics* 899, 900.

53 Starting from the concrete operation stage (7–11) in Piaget's theory, and the conventional stage (7–13) in Kohlberg's theory. Fowler did not attach specific ages to his stages. See also Ralph W Hood Jr, Peter C Hill and Bernard Spilka, *The Psychology of Religion: An Empirical Approach* (Gilford Press, 4th ed, 2009) 77 ff.

54 Jane Fortin, *Children's Rights and the Developing Law* (3rd ed, Cambridge University Press, 2009) 83. See also Willem Koops, 'Developmental Psychology in Cultural Historical Context – Overview and Further Reflections' (2023) 11(2) *Current Issues in Personality Psychology* 130, 132; Liesbeth van Beemen, *Ontwikkelingspsychologie* [Developmental Psychology] (Noordhoff, 2020) ch 6; Usha Goswami, 'Cognitive Development: No Stages Please – We're British' (2001) 92(1) *British Journal of Psychology* 257, 261. This is not to say that stage theorists made no allowance at all for non-linear development; see ibid 260. For similar commentary on other developmental theories – specifically from the perspective of the best interests of the child, see, eg, Nancy E Dowd, 'A Developmental Equality Model for the Best Interests of Children' in Elaine S Sutherland and Lesley-Anne Barnes Macfarlane (eds), *Implementing Article 3 of the United Nations Convention on the Rights of the Child: Best Interests, Welfare and Well-Being* (Cambridge University Press, 2016) 112–130.

55 Parts of this paragraph are based on Erlings (n 3) 51.

56 Charles C Helwig, 'The Role of Agent and Social Context in Judgments of Freedom of Speech and Religion' (1997) 68(3) *Child Development* 484, 492.

57 Nucci (n 44) 21; Helwig & Turiel (n 44) 569–76.

58 See Rebekah A Richert and Pehr Granqvist, 'Religious and Spiritual Development in Childhood' in Raymond F Paloutzian and Crystal L Park (eds), *Handbook of the Psychology of Religion and Spirituality* (2nd ed, Guilford Press, 2015) 165–182, 169.

research has often found religious cognition in respect of manifestations to arise around age four to six,[59] with early adolescence a transition point for more abstract thinking and autonomy.[60] Yet, whilst convincing for its demographic, the second research wave had important limitations; studies were almost exclusively conducted in North America and remained monotheism-focused.[61]

In a 2022 comprehensive review of religious cognition research, Richert and Corriveau highlight a more recent understanding of "the mutually constituted relationship between cognition and culture".[62] Providing an analysis based on over 120 research studies from across the globe, the review suggests that religious cognitive development, religious understanding, and religiosity are highly dependent on national and cultural context, as well as the particular faith in which children have been raised.[63] For example, confidence in aspects of religion can be affected by knowing that there is no consensus on the religion or its practice within a certain society,[64] whereas children's essentialism is lessened by exposure to religious diversity.[65] This means that religious cognition will develop very differently in jurisdictions where a State religion (or strict secularity) is enforced, from jurisdictions where a melting pot of different faiths is present and accessible to children. Culture adds a further layer. For example, in relation to matters of death and conceptions of afterlife, significant differences exist in the (spiritual) understanding of minors raised in cultures where they are actively involved in death rituals like some Asian societies or Mexico with its symbols of death and *Día de Muertos*,[66] and minors raised in European-American cultures where they are deliberately shielded from death and have less opportunity to develop experiential capacity in the matter.[67] These newer insights have important implications for the comparative researcher of law and religion in respect of minors. If minors are directly involved in research, their responses may be influenced by their religious cognition, and this in turn may be linked to culture and community in

59 Erlings (n 3) 52. See also Richert and Corriveau (n 47) who note capacities arising around age five throughout their paper.

60 Emily Nakkawita and Larissa Heiphetz, 'The Cognitive Science of Religion: A Case for the Importance of Adolescence' (2021) 6(3) *Adolescent Research Review* 309; Hood, Hill and Spilka (n 52) ch 5.

61 Richert and Corriveau (n 47) 198. See also Erlings (n 3) 51.

62 Richert and Corriveau (n 47) 185.

63 Ibid 198.

64 See overview at ibid 196–7.

65 Ibid 195.

66 See ibid 192, citing Liqi Zhu, 'Do Chinese Children Believe in an Afterlife?' in Ryan G Hornbeck, Justin L Barrett and Madeleine Kang (eds), *Religious Cognition in China: 'Homo Religiosus' and the Dragon* (Springer, 2017) 151–158; Isabel T. Gutiérrez et al, 'Embracing Death: Mexican Parent and Child Perspectives on Death' (2020) 91(2) *Child Development* 491.

67 Richert and Corriveau (n 47) 192, citing Karl S Rosengren et al (eds.), *Children's Understanding of Death: Toward a Contextualized and Integrated Account* (Wiley-Blackwell, 2014).

ways not captured by the legal considerations outlined earlier. It is also possible that the human rights approach aligns with Western conceptions of religious cognition.[68] Hence, if this approach is used, particular attention should be paid to anything that might point towards different cognitive development. Whilst it is likely that children's religiosity arises well before most legal systems would be comfortable in recognising and accommodating capacity,[69] comparative research should further contend with non-homogenous religious development. This may affect considerations in respect of both theory and method.

V Research Method

This section is first and foremost concerned with socio-legal research; research that employs methods from the social sciences, such as surveys (questionnaires), interviews, focus groups, or observation. It is presumed that readers will be quite familiar with a doctrinal legal method, but less so with what will be collectively called 'empirical research'. Whilst the chapter so far has a bearing on both types of research, the following principally considers the latter, empirical research.

A Legal Boundaries

When working on a sensitive topic like law and religion, the primary method-related consideration should be that the research will not result in either researchers or participants engaging in conduct that is illegal or places them at risk. Researchers may be quite attuned to the more obvious situations, but care is required in respect of many countries. For example, French law prohibits the collection of data on religious affiliation or conviction, unless an express exemption is granted by its (equivalent of a) privacy commission.[70] The law was adopted in response to the singling out of Jews on the basis of their religion during the Second World War.[71] Combined with the general background of *laïcité*, this means that it may be regarded as highly inappropriate (and perchance illegal) to pose questions pertaining to religious affiliation in general,

68 Though the debate around the potential Western sources of religious rights is contentious, as suggested by Bielefeldt, who later became the Special Rapporteur on Freedom of Religion or Belief; Heiner Bielefeldt, ''Western' versus 'Islamic' Human Rights Conceptions?: A Critique of Cultural Essentialism in the Discussion on Human Rights' (2000) 28(1) *Political Theory* 1.

69 Erlings (n 3) 52; Noam Peleg, 'Reconceptualising the Child's Right to Development: Children and the Capability Approach' (2013) 21(3) *International Journal of Children's Rights* 523, 534.

70 Loi n° 78-17 du 6 janvier 1978 *relative à l'informatique, aux fichiers et aux libertés*, art 6.

71 For an English source, see Rick Noak, 'Some French Wanted to Find Out How Racist Their Country Is. They Might Get Sued for It', *The Washington Post* (online, 4 February 2016) https://www.washingtonpost.com/news/worldviews/wp/2016/02/04/why-it-can-be-illegal-to-ask-people-about-their-religion-or-ethnicity-in-france/.

but especially in settings such as schools.[72] Research instruments may thus need to be amended accordingly, unless the mentioned exemption is sought. Even where the obtaining of religion-related data is not problematic per se, in many jurisdictions, including, for example Nigeria, Brazil, Australia, and the European Union, religious affiliation and/or belief is considered sensitive data,[73] and these jurisdictions often also have specific data rules in relation to children.[74] This means that data protection may need to be keenly considered, if the data is to be collected, exported and/or stored at all. Comparative researchers will especially need to invest time in fully understanding restrictions on the exportation of data out of a jurisdiction, which is characteristic of most comparative research.

Beyond data protection, special consideration should be paid to the existence of apostacy and blasphemy laws in combination with age of criminal responsibility, parental responsibility (including potential loss of custody), and (lack of) privilege attaching to research data, as well as any other laws that regulate religion-related communications. For example, in 2014 the Maldives implemented a regulation under which the death penalty can now be (re-) imposed for apostacy.[75] As a *hadd*, or *hudud* offence, the lower age of criminal responsibility applies, meaning that children aged seven and over are now liable to prosecution.[76] This has made it crucial that research with children, if any, should not provide probes for answers that could be seen as potentially signalling apostacy. Furthermore, the position of (foreign, comparative) researchers themselves is complicated in the Maldives, as the law also prohibits the explaining of religious principles without a permit (relating mostly to sermons, but can be interpreted broadly to, eg, cover explanations included in a Participant Information Sheet); openly expressing religious beliefs; holding public congregations for religious activities and involving Maldivians in such activities (if the emphasis is placed on "activities" over "congregation", this may capture research); bringing any item, including religious literature, into the country that the Ministry of Islam Affairs consider contrary to Islam; and, most importantly, "disrupting religious unity, and having discussions or

72 See, eg, Erlings (n 3) 105. Teachers objected to questions directly probing religious affiliation in a survey distributed at schools, though it was possible (albeit perhaps pushing the boundaries of the law) to ask *if* children were religious, but not what that religion was.

73 Respectively, *Nigeria Data Protection Act 2023*, s 65 'sensitive personal data'; *Lei Geral de Proteção de Dados*, Federal Law No. 13,709/2018, Art 5 II; *Privacy Act 1988* (Cth) s 6 'sensitive information'; *Regulation (EU) 2016/679 of the European Parliament and of the Council of 27 April 2016 on the protection of natural persons with regard to the processing of personal data and on the free movement of such data, and repealing Directive 95/46/EC (General Data Protection Regulation,* GDPR*)* [2016] OJ L119/1, Art 9 (GDRP).

74 Eg, GDRP (n 72) Art 8, Recitals 38, 58, 65.

75 UN News, 'Maldives Should Repeal New Regulation Providing for Death Penalty, Says UN Rights Office' (Press Release, 29 April 2014) https://news.un.org/en/story/2014/04/467162.

76 Ibid.

committing acts that promote religious differences".[77] The latter is a provision easily enlivened by probing research questions, and especially pertinent for (comparative) law and religion research with minors, because such research often has a tendency to consider the existence of religious dissonance between parents and children.

To add to that, around the world, evidentiary privilege for researchers is normally limited or non-existent, meaning that courts and tribunals can force researchers to provide their research data to a requesting party and/or within the context of a legal case.[78] Moreover, in some instances authorities may seize research material without court involvement, despite such practices being increasingly challenged, including, for example, in India at the time of this writing.[79] Even in countries with a strong research culture such as Canada, researchers have faced contempt of court charges for not producing subpoenaed research material that was promised to be confidential to participants.[80] In addition, researchers may be subject to mandatory reporting obligations in respect of children who have been maltreated or are at risk of harm, either because they are staff at a tertiary educational institution or because general provisions apply.[81] This could make research on matters like religiously motivated corporal punishment, onerous forms of religious fasting, or rituals impacting children's health a delicate affair.[82] Mandatory reporting sometimes allows for research exceptions, but these are not always broad enough to cover all research and may not provide adequate legal certainty. For example, the Australian state of New South Wales (NSW) has legislation that makes a failure to report when a reasonable suspicion arises that a "child abuse offence" has been committed a generally applicable offence, subject to reasonable excuse

77 See United States Department of State, *Maldives 2022 International Religious Freedom Report* (Report, 2022) 3–5 (quote at p 3).

78 A handful of jurisdictions have what have been called 'shield laws', but these can be patchy and subject to conditions. See Ted Palys and John Lowman, 'Anticipating Law: Research Methods, Ethics and the Law of Privilege' (2002) 32(1) *Sociological Methodology* 1, 3–4.

79 'SC to Hear on Nov 2 Plea Seeking Guidelines on Seizure of Electronic Devices by Police', *Economic Times: Legal World* (online, 13 October 2023) https://legal.economictimes.indiatimes.com/news/litigation/sc-to-hear-on-nov-2-plea-seeking-guidelines-on-seizure-of-electronic-devices-by-police/104403489.

80 See for an overview: Ted Palys and John Lowman, 'Eight Challenges to Research Confidentiality in Canada: Invoking and Protecting Research-Participant Privilege' in Christopher D L Hunt (ed), *Perspectives on Evidentiary Privileges* (Thomson Reuters, 2019) 213–237.

81 This is an area in flux. See Robert D Lytle et al, 'Do I Report This? Understanding Variation in the Content of State Mandatory Reporting Laws' (2021) 10(2) *Journal of Qualitative Criminal Justice & Criminology* DOI: 10.21428/88de04a1.a323769a.

82 Perhaps as a result, most comparative accounts are doctrinal. See, eg, Bernadette Saunders, Pernilla Leviner and Bronwyn Naylor (eds), *Corporal Punishment of Children: Comparative Legal and Social Developments Towards Prohibition and Beyond* (Brill, 2018) Part 2 Culture, Law and Religion; Tamar Morag, 'Religious Tradition and Corporal Punishment of Children: A Comparison of the American and Israeli Legal Systems' (2011) 25(3) *International Journal of Law, Policy and the Family* 338.

(mostly belief the situation is already known or fear of endangering a person).[83] The definition of a child abuse offence covers a wide range of matters from grievous bodily harm to failure to provide necessities of life.[84] Researchers are eligible for an exemption, but this translates to a discretion for the Director of Public Prosecutions ('DPP') to withhold approval to prosecute.[85] Although Matthews argues that proper statutory interpretation would mean that the DPP is not to grant approval especially in cases where the research is *aimed at* investigating maltreatment (though civil liability may warrant reporting),[86] the situation for researchers of law and religion is characterised by a much higher level of uncertainty. This means that careful thought must be given to both the research inquiry and any explanations regarding confidentiality provided to participants, whether they be parents, other adults involved in children's lives, or children themselves.

B Ethics

Data protection legislation is not the only research-related place where the special position of children and the sensitive nature of religion-related data are recognised. The same is true in respect of ethics applications, with ethics approval being a requirement for engaging in empirical research.[87] The type of ethics approval to be obtained depends on the type of research; normally a form of human research ethics is sufficient, but if research is conducted within certain settings, eg, health sites such as hospital premises, a specialised ethics committee may be in charge of the application.[88] On the whole, ethics schemes normally consider children to be part of a vulnerable population,[89] and religion a sensitive topic,[90] thus inviting greater justification for the research and increased attention to matters such as mitigation of potential disadvantage or harm and assurances around anonymity and confidentiality. These issues are exacerbated where the proposal is to (also) conduct research abroad as part of a comparative project, with further questions around cultural competence

83 *Crimes Act 1900* (NSW) s 316A.
84 Ibid s 43B(3).
85 Ibid s 316A(6)–(7) jo *Crimes Regulation 2020* (NSW) reg 4(g).
86 Ben Matthews, 'Legal Duties of Researchers to Protect Participants in Child Maltreatment Surveys: Advancing Legal Epidemiology' (2022) 45(2) *University of New South Wales Law Journal* 722, 737, 741–2.
87 See Susan Banks, 'Ethics and Social Research' in Walter (n 21) 83–118.
88 See, eg, 'Ethics & Governance', *NSW Health* (Web Page, nd) https://www.medicalresearch.nsw.gov.au/ethical-scientific-review/.
89 See, eg, National Health and Medical Research Council, Australian Research Council and Universities Australia (NHMRC/ARC/UA), *National Statement on Ethical Conduct in Human Research* (2007 (Updated 2018)) 65–7 (*National Ethics Statement*).
90 NHMRC/ARC/UA, *Management of Data and Information in Research: A Guide Supporting the Australian Code for the Responsible Conduct of Research* (2019) 7.

and the overcoming of language barriers to be expected.[91] This is quite apart from the fact that proposed research in foreign countries will normally trigger a host of further procedures, including, for example, a risk mitigation plan for the researcher(s) themselves.[92] Whilst it is not possible here to discuss ethics applications for law and religion research with minors in depth, researchers should keep the three golden rules of ethics in mind: honesty, mitigation, justification.

First, honesty. There is arguably a tendency for researchers to take a political approach to ethics by talking around issues, rather than explicitly and honestly recognising them.[93] This is counterproductive for two reasons. The first is that part of the goal of an ethics procedure is for the researcher to show that they have ethical insight, so that the ethics committee can be assured that also unexpected ethical dilemmas will be recognised as such by researchers and handled sensibly.[94] Failing to address ethical barriers suggests that this insight might be lacking. The second is that ethics reviewers normally "have seen it all".[95] There is no advantage to beating around the bush because reviewers will likely see through this and all that will be "gained" is a delay in approval until the issue has been addressed to the reviewers' satisfaction via re-submission. Honesty from the start is a far more helpful approach for all parties involved, but especially the researcher.

Second, mitigation. Once an ethical barrier is revealed, the next step is to consider ways in which it might be mitigated.[96] In the case of comparative law and religion research with minors, this often involves considerations around institutional consent (see upcoming Section C) and employing people on the project who can help overcome the barriers related to working with minors and/or in foreign jurisdictions. This could, for example, include arranging for someone who is trained in working with children to conduct the actual research (eg, the in-person interaction with children), or engaging a research assistant from a relevant background for insights on whether research instruments are culturally sensitive and how certain responses may be understood

91 *National Ethics Statement* (n 88) 80–2.

92 An interactive risk map is available at 'Overseas Research Roadmap' *University College London* (Web Page, May 2023) https://www.ucl.ac.uk/research/integrity/overseas-research-roadmap.

93 This may correlate with the increased effort required if ethical barriers are revealed. Compare findings in Julia J Lee et al, 'Lay Theories of Effortful Dishonesty: Does the Dishonesty-Effort Association Justify Making Dishonest Decisions?' (2019) 104(5) *Journal of Applied Psychology* 659.

94 Reid et al refer to 'ethical reflexivity'; Anne-Marie Reid et al, 'Ethical Dilemmas and Reflexivity in Qualitative Research' (2018) 7(2) *Perspectives in Medical Education* 69, 70.

95 Quite similar to academics who grade student papers of differing quality and integrity.

96 See *mutatis mutandis*, Sara Shaw and Geraldine Barrett, 'Research Governance: Regulating Risk and Reducing Harm?' (2006) 99(1) *Journal of the Royal Society of Medicine* 14. See also supra note 91; *National Ethics Statement* (n 88).

for the purposes of analysis.[97] However, mitigation is not always possible. For example, if questions are asked about religious accommodation in public schools under non-discrimination legislation – or vice versa, the experience of LGBTQI+ students in religious schools under discrimination exemption, there will likely be participants who have distressing stories and may relive some of the trauma experienced.[98] Whilst these participants may be guided to support services, some harm and distress is inevitable and cannot be mitigated.

This brings us to the third rule, justification. Where mitigation is unavailable, reliance should be placed on justification.[99] That means explaining why, despite the risks, it is still important that the research is conducted. Many researchers are afraid to reach this last stage, but it is important to keep in mind that ethics approval can be obtained for drug trials with risks of unknown and potentially debilitating side effects,[100] and it is thus not true that the existence of risks will always undermine potential approval.[101] What comparative law and religion researchers will have to contend with is the more intangible benefit for society that may arise out of the research. The legal aspect can be important here. Research may be valuable because it could, for example, lead to recommendations for law or policy reform that can improve the situation of children within a certain jurisdiction.[102] This provides a clear societal benefit that may justify some short-term distress. Even so, there may be situations where neither mitigation nor justification outweigh the risks, and this can prompt researchers to consider who should be the direct participant in their research. Can minors speak for themselves or should someone speak for them?

C Who Speaks for Children?

The ideal situation for comparative law and religion research with minors is to involve minors themselves in the research. As already explained earlier, this involves a variety of ethical considerations – in addition to regard for what level of religious cognition children may be at the time. One particular matter that needs addressing is whether research with minors is at all allowed in a particular jurisdiction and from whom consent would need to be obtained for

97 Janet Boddy, 'Research Across Cultures, Within Countries: Hidden Ethics Tensions in Research with Children and Families?' (2014) 14(1) *Progress in Development Studies* 91, 97–8.

98 See respectively, Bérengère Massignon, 'Laïcité in Practice: The Representations of French Teenagers' (2011) 33(2) *British Journal of Religious Education* 159; Tiffany Jones, 'Religious Freedom and LGBTIQA+ Students' (2023) 20(3) *Sexuality Research & Social Policy* 1133.

99 These two often go hand in hand, see Hayda Alves et al, 'Children and Adolescents' Voices and the Implications for Ethical Research' (2022) 29(1) *Childhood* 126, 127.

100 Michael O S Afolabi and Lauren E Kelly, 'Non-static Framework for Understanding Adaptive Designs: An Ethical Justification in Paediatric Trials' (2022) 48(11) *Journal of Medical Ethics* 825, 829.

101 See also *National Ethics Statement* (n 88) ch 2.1 (Risk and Benefit).

102 Wendy Larcombe et al, 'Making Good Law: Research and Law Reform', *Melbourne School of Government* (Research Paper Series, August 2015) 4–5.

a minor's direct participation.[103] Under virtually all national legal frameworks, minors are subject to parental responsibility, authority, or rights, even if they may gain autonomy on the basis of legislated exceptions or concepts such as *Gillick* competence (a common law concept under which a minor who has reached a very high-threshold level of competence is able to take their own decisions, at which point parental rights and powers are extinguished).[104] In many cases, this means that parental consent must be obtained, whether or not in combination with consent from the minors themselves.[105] The exact rules are not always included in legislation and will most often need to be obtained from whichever national agency is in charge of research regulation and/or through application by analogy. For example, the Dutch law on medical scientific research[106] has established the Central Committee on Research Involving Human Subjects (*Centrale Commissie Mensgebonden Onderzoek*),[107] which in turn has adopted rules on minors' participation in medical scientific research. The rules state that for children under the age of 12, parents need to consent; for children over 12 but under 16, both parents and the minor need to consent; and for minors over 16, the young person can consent themselves.[108] As noted, these rules were made for medical and not general research; the Netherlands does not have any legislation-based rules for non-medical research. Yet, it now seems generally accepted that the rules apply across the board to research with minors and they have been included in national research codes of conduct.[109] However, if the research is to be conducted via schools, these types of consent alone are not enough. Dutch privacy legislation requires that parents are at least informed of the potential data that may be obtained from minors, even if they are able to consent to research themselves.[110] Moreover, whether in the Netherlands or elsewhere, involving institutions in, for example, the distribution of research materials like surveys and research invitations, or using an institution's premises for the conduct of research, may mean that further

103 Alves et al (n 98) 128–9.

104 Derived from *Gillick v West Norfolk & Wisbeck Area Health Authority* [1986] AC 112; Fortin (n 53) 89–103.

105 Alves et al (n 98) 128–9.

106 *Wet medisch-wetenschappelijk onderzoek*, *Stb* 2022, 99.

107 Ibid art 14.

108 'Kinderen en Jongeren', *Centrale Commissie Mensgebonden Onderzoek* (nd) https://www.ccmo.nl/proefpersonen/toestemming-geven/kinderen-en-jongeren.

109 See, eg, MOA Center for Information Based Decision Making and Marketing Research, Vereniging voor Beleidsonderzoek and Vereniging voor Statistiek en Onderzoek, *Gedragscode voor Statistisch Onderzoek 2022* (9 June 2022) 28, 41; and academic requirements, eg, 'Hoe Regel Ik Toestemming van Respondenten (Informed Consent)? *Tilburg University* (2023) https://www.tilburguniversity.edu/nl/over/gedrag-integriteit/privacy-en-security/onderzoeksdata/toestemming.

110 S J C Höfte, 'Juridische Notitie: Toestemming Jongere Niet Medisch Wetenschappelijk Onderzoek' https://www.hsleiden.nl/binaries/content/assets/hsl/lectoraten/residentiele-jeugdzorg/onderzoek/notitie-toestemming-jongere.pdf .

consent needs to be obtained.[111] This normally involves institutional consent from the relevant holders of authority to provide such consent (eg, a school principal, religious governing body, director of a service, or an executive committee of a charity or other organisation), but a green light from other representative bodies within the institution may also need to be obtained. For example, approval from the parents' council may be required in the case of educational institutions.[112] Institutional consent will need to be determined on a case-by-case basis, as it may be a condition for participation set by the institution on an ad hoc basis, rather than a policy rule.[113] In that respect, it is also important for the researcher to consider carefully what conditions of entrance are compatible with independent research and what requirements set by the proposed facilitating institution could ultimately undermine the project.

In all of the noted situations, a related question is how to phrase the invitations, participant information sheets,[114] and consent forms. In the case of minors themselves, the concern is to ensure that all information is understandable to the relevant age group so that informed consent can truly be obtained.[115] In the case of consent forms for especially parents, different considerations arise. The first is to ask who qualifies as parent (or carer) and whether more than one parent/carer needs to consent. Given the nature of both religion and research participation, it may be that, in the case that a child's parents are divorced, consent needs to be obtained from both parents, whether as a legal, ethical, or institutionally agreed condition for participation in research.[116] Moreover, given the sensitivities that might surround law and religion research, there is a tension between full disclosure of the plans and goals to parents and ensuring an acceptable response rate.[117] This is especially true if the research, for example, contains inquiries into religious dissonance between parents and children, non-mainstream practices/manifestations of religion, or religion-based forms of upbringing that do not correspond with

111 Alves et al (n 98) 135.

112 See Erlings (n 3) 105.

113 Conditional access or consent may constitute potentially problematic gate-keeping. See Sue Heath et al, 'Informed Consent, Gatekeepers and Go-betweens: Negotiating Consent in Child- and Youth-Oriented Institutions' (2007) 33(3) *British Educational Research Journal* 403.

114 Most ethics procedures will require a plain language statement of the goals and aspects of research, storage of data and contact information, written in a manner understandable to the relevant research subject.

115 *National Ethics Statement* (n 88) 65–6. This includes information on research and consent itself: Boddy (n 96) 100.

116 See generally David Shumaker and David Medoff, 'Ethical and Legal Considerations When Obtaining Informed Consent for Treating Minors of High-Conflict Divorced or Separated Parents' (2013) 21(3) *The Family Journal* 318.

117 See Paula Fomby and Narayan Sastry, 'Data Collection on Sensitive Topics with Adolescents Using Interactive Voice Response Technology' (2019) 13(1) *Methoden, Daten, Analysen* 91, 103.

societal expectations. In these situations, researchers may feel tempted to resort to elusion and deliberate creation of misunderstanding in order not to "give the game away", either for the purposes of obtaining authentic research data or not to risk low participation. In a limited number of circumstances, this may be acceptable from an ethics perspective but it would need to be justified at a high threshold as a form of deception.[118] In general, the level of information researchers give to parents should be the same they would give to an adult participant, since parents essentially stand as an adult in their children's shoes. If that means that consent for participation is unlikely to be obtained, the researcher will need to consider a different approach. The same is true where it is generally unlikely that ethics or institutional approval can be obtained for research with minors directly.

In cases where directly approaching children is either not possible or not suitable, a solution is to turn to "young persons".[119] The United Nations define a young person, or "youth", as someone aged 15–24.[120] For the purposes of research, the targeted category would be 18–24; young persons who have just become adults and can, therefore, make their own decisions on research participation. The advantage of working with young persons is that the ethical conundrums relevant to children do not apply, but that at least the later years of childhood are still considered to be fresh in mind.[121] However, the latter idea is perhaps somewhat optimistic and drives the main argument against research with young adults rather than minors themselves; most people cannot remember what last week was like, but research with young persons may ask them to remember events and emotions from years before.[122] There is, thus, the risk that memories have disappeared or become distorted over time, although it can also be said that very strong sentiments and issues that impressed will be remembered, so that time works as a filter to leave participants with a stronger sense of what matters affected them.[123] Either way, it is likely that some nuance will be lost, quite apart from the fact that the comparative researcher must be aware of cultural impact on memory.[124] In comparative research with 18–24-year-olds from Thailand and Australia, for example,

118 *National Ethics Statement* (n 88) 20.

119 College/University students are often targeted, eg, Pehr Granqvist and Lee A Kirkpatrick, 'Religious Conversion and Perceived Childhood Attachment' (2004) 14(4) *The International Journal for the Psychology of Religion* 223, 229–31.

120 'Global Issues: Youth', *United Nations* (Web Page, nd) https://www.un.org/en/global-issues/youth.

121 Erlings (n 3) 137.

122 See, eg, Angie L Dahl and Renee V Galliher, 'LGBTQ Young Adult Experiences of Religious and Sexual Identity Integration' (2009) 3(2) *Journal of LGBT Issues in Counselling* 92, 98–9.

123 See D Stephen Lindsay et al, 'Adults' Memories of Childhood: Affect, Knowing and Remembering' (2004) 12(1) *Memory* 27, esp. 31, 37.

124 See overview in Nattakarn Somhom, 'Autobiographical Memory in Thai and Australian Emerging Adults: A Cross-Cultural Study' (Master Thesis, Macquarie University, 2021).

Somhom found important cultural differences in autobiographical memory.[125] This signals a challenge for comparative research with young adults as participants may not remember similar aspects of their memories.

A second option where directly approaching minors may not be feasible is by engaging parents as participants in research instead, and asking them about their children's practices and ways, or even perceived sentiments. Whilst this may be appropriate for children who do not yet have the capacity to participate in research, caution is required in all other situations. Parents are notoriously unreliable informants on their children's lives (although this may vary across societies)[126] and they may be particularly tempted to resort to socially acceptable answering (whether the relevant social group is the jurisdiction generally, their religious community – if any, or their family with a view to establishing family unity). Such answers lead to what is known as "social desirability bias".[127] For example, in survey research by the current author with both minors and their parents in Hong Kong, the minors were willing to note they belonged to a number of different religions.[128] By contrast, all parents willing to indicate their child's religion (if any) stated that their child was Christian, which was the religious affiliation of the participating school their children attended.[129] This is not to suggest that these parents were incorrect about their child's religion (anonymity prevented matching), but that parental responses clearly took context into account in a way minors' responses did not.

Finally, adults other than parents may be engaged to report on children's experiences. Research can, for example, be conducted with teachers, religious leaders, youth workers, and other staff of community-based organisations.[130] These adults can work as "key adult informants" on the experiences of children in their care, children for whom they are otherwise responsible or with whom they are in other ways in contact.[131] Adult informants may have deep knowledge of children's situations and/or views, especially if they, for example, are a

125 Ibid 47–8.

126 See Leslie A Rescorla et al, 'Cross-Informant Agreement between Parent-Reported and Adolescent Self-Reported Problems in 25 Societies' (2013) 42(2) *Journal of Clinical Child & Adolescent Psychology* 262.

127 Konrad Hackett, 'Seven Things to Consider When Measuring Religious Identity' (2014) 44(3) *Religion* 396, 404–5; Ivar Krumpal, 'Determinants of Social Desirability Bias in Sensitive Surveys: A Literature Review' (2013) 47(4) *Quality & Quantity* 2025, 2030.

128 Erlings (n 3) 174.

129 Ibid 173–174.

130 I would like to thank the reviewers for suggesting this addition.

131 Quarshie, Waterman and House, for example, used key adult informants in a study on self-harm amongst adolescents in Ghana, where such practices are religiously seen as a sin: Emmanuel N-B Quarshie, Mitch G Waterman and Allan O House, 'Adolescents at Risk of Self-Harm in Ghana: A Qualitative Interview Study Exploring the Views and Experiences of Key Adult Informants' (2020) 20(1) *BMC Psychiatry* 310.

child's designated case worker,[132] homeroom teacher, or, eg, perform a mentoring role. Depending on the case, key adult informants may also offer less biased views than parents as a result of their relative emotional distance from the child, commonly referred to as their "professional distance".[133] However, there are often very important limitations on this kind of research, because as a general rule, those working with children are subject to duties of confidentiality as a result of legislation, professional regulation, or workplace policy.[134] This means that key adult informants may be able to provide general insights and experiences, and perhaps some anonymised case examples, but only insofar as no identifying information about the child – or other confidential knowledge – is shared. As a result, a heavy burden is also placed on the researcher who should at all times be ready to intervene when a participant is on the point to divulge confidential information: promising to interrupt will be a minimal ethics requirement in these circumstances. These considerations also make it important that significant thought is given to how data is obtained and which questions are asked, which brings us to the matter of research methods.

D Research Methods

A full exploration of potential research methods is outside the scope of this chapter – and, given that empirical research relies on social research methods, better explained by social scientists who work with them daily.[135] This section only very briefly introduced the four key methods that lawyers may be comfortable with.

132 See, eg, the Finnish 'Five Years in Care' study, asking social workers to report on cases in their files: Tarja Pösö and Tuija Eronen, 'Care Orders as Successful Interventions: The Social Workers' Point of View' (2014) 20(2) *Child Care in Practice* 207, 210–12.

133 For an overview of the different aspects of professional distance, see Mike W Martin, *Meaningful Work: Rethinking Professional Ethics* (Oxford University Press, 2000) ch 6 'Professional Distance'. The concept itself is contentious, see, eg, Rosemary Green, Raeleene Gregory and Robyn Mason, 'Professional Distance and Social Work: Stretching the Elastic?' (2006) 59(4) *Australian Social Work* 449.

134 For example, the Code of Conduct for Australian social workers notes that 'Social workers will ensure service users' anonymity and remove identifying details when permitted to use confidential information for … research'. This suggests that there needs to be (1) a research project (with ethics review), (2) permission to use confidential information (though it is unclear who should provide that permission – possibly both an ethics committee and those responsible for the service), and (3) anonymisation (including of contextual identifiers) even in the case there is permission for the use of confidential information for research. See Australian Association of Social Workers, *Australian Association of Social Workers Code of Ethics 2020* (November 2020, updated February 2021) r 5.4.9.

135 Useful books include Alan Bryman et al, *Social Research Methods* (Oxford University Press, 6th ed, 2021); Steven Engler and Michael Strausberg (eds), *The Routledge Handbook of Research Methods in the Study of Religion* (Routledge, 2nd ed, 2021); Earl Babbie, *The Practice of Social Research* (Cengage, 15th ed, 2020); Walter (n 21). See also Howard and Tadros (n 21).

First, observation research, which, as the name suggests, relies on observing participants, sometimes in combination with fieldwork and/or as a direct participant in peoples' or communities' religious lives and rituals.[136] An example of less-involved observational research could be to observe instances of minors putting on religious attire upon exiting an educational establishment in a country that prohibits the wearing of religious symbols at schools.[137] This type of research is normally unobtrusive, but, if conducted in (semi-)public, generally means that there will not be opportunities to obtain explicit consent.[138] That means there is a very high ethics barrier to overcome (and care should be taken not to violate local laws that, for example, question the apparent spying on minors). For observation research in semi-private settings, such as classrooms, childcare centres, or gatherings in houses of worship, consent would normally need to be obtained from (the parents of) all parties present,[139] though this can potentially be done via opt-out consent where consent is presumed unless explicitly rejected by a participant (and/or their parent[s]).

Second, survey research, which would typically include distribution of a questionnaire.[140] Today, this is often done online – and doing so assists the crossing of geographical boundaries in comparative research.[141] However, there is little opportunity to obtain any required parental consent online.[142] More personal distribution, often via schools or other social or religious organisations/entities that provide information and/or consent forms to parents, makes obtaining consent more feasible, especially when ethics approval for carefully considered parental opt-out consent is obtained.[143] Questionnaires are a way to reach many participants and they tend to be anonymous,[144] which assists with data protection. Whether questionnaires invite (because no one can check if a participant's best representation of themselves is true)[145] or pre-

136 See Graham Harvey, 'Field Research and Participant Observation' in Engler and Strausberg (n 129) 273–299.

137 This situation is widespread in France. See, eg, Julie Kleinman, 'All Daughters and Sons of the Republic'? Producing Difference in French Education' (2016) 22(2) *The Journal of the Royal Anthropological Institute* 261, 273–4.

138 Compare Harvey (n 135) 291.

139 See, Christine Robinson, 'Young Children's Spirituality: A Focus on Engaging with Nature' (2019) 44(4) *Australasian Journal of Early Childhood* 339, 344.

140 See Michael Strausberg, 'Surveys and Questionnaires' in Engler and Strausberg (n 134) 461–482, 461.

141 Ibid 466.

142 Harris and Porcellato consider best practice in Jane Harris and Lorna Porcellato, 'Opt-out Parental Consent in Online Surveys: Ethical Considerations' (2018) 13(3) *Journal of Empirical Research on Human Research Ethics* 223.

143 This arguably also reduces bias: Thérèse Shaw et al, 'Bias in Student Survey Findings from Active Parental Consent Procedures' (2015) 41(2) *British Educational Research Journal* 229, 240.

144 Which may mean that an opt-out from one parent means that an entire segment (eg, a full class) may need to be excluded in order not to single a child out.

145 Strausberg (n 139) 463.

vent (because anonymity inspires honesty)[146] social desirability bias is a matter of contention,[147] and may differ per country. It is nonetheless noteworthy that distribution via a religious organisation or individual churches, temples, mosques etc. could have an effect on social desirability bias, since, even if the entity has no access to the data, participants may perceive the survey as an activity of the religious entity and keep this in mind when answering questions in ways similar to the Hong Kong school example mentioned previously. Extra attention should thus be paid to potential impacts on authenticity in these circumstances, as well as voluntariness, because potential participants may feel pressured into participating when the survey reaches them via their house of worship or other faith-based organisation. In the case of comparative research there is, moreover, another issue to consider. Unless personally administered, questionnaire items cannot be explained. This means that research participants from different jurisdictions may interpret concepts differently from researchers, even if brief explanations are provided.[148] A further issue is the potential effect of translation, especially between yes/no and correct/incorrect languages. For example, if a child would not mind attending a place of worship of another religion, and the survey requires yes/no for "I would not mind attending a place of worship of another religion", an English-speaking participant will tick "no" (no, I would not mind that), but a Chinese participant may choose "yes" (*dui*, correct, I would not mind that). This could be remedied by verification or engaging a researcher from the relevant cultural and linguistic background to help with the survey.[149]

Third, interviews, which would involve a looser form of questioning – in the case of minors normally in person – with possibilities to explore issues in-depth and follow-up on answers.[150] Here, the previously raised matter of ensuring competent staff comes in at full force, as well as power dynamics (which work both ways in intercultural contexts).[151] There will also be considerations around suitable, private spaces to meet with children and the presence of family members.[152] As for surveys, the application of social desirability bias is disputed: on the one hand, interviewers have opportunities to fact-check

146 Maggie Walter, 'Surveys' in Walter (n 21) 146 176, 158.

147 Mark D Regnerus and Jeremy E Uecker, 'Religious Influences on Sensitive Self-Reported Behaviour: The Product of Social Desirability, Deceit, or Embarrassment?' (2007) 68(2) *Sociology of Religion* 145, 146–7.

148 See Strausberg (n 139) 472–4.

149 Boddy (n 96) 97–8. See also 'back translation' in Tanya Marie Luhrmann, 'Interview Methods' in Engler and Strausberg (n 134) 345–364, 360.

150 For different forms see Luhrman (n 148) 347–54.

151 See Imane Kostet, 'Shifting Power Dynamics in Interviews with Children: A Minority Ethnic Working-Class Researcher's Reflections' (2023) 23(2) *Qualitative Research* 451.

152 Naomi Bushin, 'Interviewing Children in Their Homes: Putting Ethical Principles into Practice and Developing Flexible Techniques' (2007) 5(3) *Children's Geographies* 235, 242–8.

what minors say in interviews;[153] but on the other hand, interviewees may be tempted to provide socially acceptable answers because they feel a cultural compulsion to tell the interviewer what they think the latter wants to hear or because they do not want to lose face in the interpersonal relationship.[154] There may, like for surveys, also be a potential element of pressure for both participation and answers provided if interviews are facilitated with the help of the participant's religious organisation or community. In all circumstances a key consideration is rapport, of which there can be too little or too much, depending on the cultural situation.[155] Healthy rapport is difficult to build if a participant does not feel the interviewer is on their side or neutral.[156] This may be particularly relevant where religion is involved – though not necessarily meaning that the interviewer should be of the same (non)-religion, especially where a minor's adherence is in question.

Fourth, focus groups, which work like a round-table conversation by the minors (normally around six to eight per focus group) into which a researcher–facilitator feeds discussion topics.[157] Focus groups can be conducted with children of all ages, including teenagers and very young children aged four to five.[158] However, focus groups have an aspect that potentially makes them less appropriate for law and religion research with minors; there is no guarantee of confidentiality between participants.[159] Even if the importance of confidentiality of what was said during discussions is impressed upon participants, it would be naïve to think that especially younger minors would not share aspects of the discussion with their parent(s), carers, or even friends. This means that potentially very sensitive information on other children or families could find its way into the community. Hence, focus groups with children may not be ideal for the kind of research contemplated in this chapter, though it could be beneficial if the participants are parents, who could, for example, find recognition in the stories of others or if participants are older minors able to appreciate the importance of confidentiality.[160]

153 On adult religious attendance: Philip S Brenner, 'Narratives of Response Error from Cognitive Interviews of Survey Questions about Normative Behaviour' (2017) 46(3) *Sociological Methods and Research* 540.

154 See Bryan S K Kim et al, 'A Qualitative Study of Adaptation Experiences of 1.5-Generation Asian Americans' (2003) 9(2) *Cultural Diversity & Ethnic Minority Psychology* 156, 160.

155 See Justina Agula, Jennifer B Barrett and Hilde Tobi, 'The Other Side of Rapport: Data Collection Mode and Interviewer Gender Effects on Sexual Health Reporting in Ghana' (2015) 19(3) *African Journal of Reproductive Health* 111, 112, 115.

156 Luhrmann (n 148) 346.

157 Kristin Adler, Sanna Salanterä and Maya Zumstein-Shaha, 'Focus Group Interviews in Child, Youth and Parent Research: An Integrative Literature Review' (2019) 18 *International Journal of Qualitative Methods*, DOI: 10.1177/1609406919887274.

158 Ibid.

159 See Emily Winter and Linda Woodhead, 'Focus Groups' in Engler and Strausberg (n 134) 542–553, 546.

160 See example in ibid 544–5.

As comparative research frequently teaches us; one size very often does not fit all. This is certainly the case for research methods, which should be carefully tailored to the specific research situation to allow for both research sensitivity and success.

VI Conclusion

Conducting comparative law and religion research with minors is an incredibly valuable activity and one that is likely to gain increasing attention. Practically, this may be the result of academic research grants often prompting empirical components with affected parties. More important, however, are principled reasons to include minors in comparative law and religion research. Not only is there a largely untapped wealth of knowledge that speaks directly to the experience of a large section of society, today children are recognised as legal subjects with agency in, and views on, matters of law and religion that nonetheless remain shaped by their particular environments. Involving minors as actors in comparative law and religion research is only the next logical step.

Further Reading:

For the author's rejoinder and reflection, see Appendix Section I.
For a comparative analysis involving children, see Chapter 8.

5 Studies in the Sociological Method of Biblical Scholarship[1]

Ronen Shoval[2]

I Introduction

There are two central approaches to studying the Bible.[3] One was developed by Biblical criticism, by which the Bible should be treated as any other ancient text. This approach discusses the language in which the Bible was written, its historical context, the text and its subjects based on internal comparisons, errors creeping into the text as it was copied through to its final form, and the literary sources serving its development into a complete corpus. This perspective seeks to understand the philological, paleographic, and archaeological development of the text from start to finish.[4] At the other end of the spectrum is ideological reading of the Bible, which seeks to learn how to act from the text, sometimes by firing the arrow, then painting the target, and enlisting the text's sacred status for its own needs. Thus, as opposed to the critical approach

1 This article is based on an chapter, 'Theoretical Introduction', from t, *Holiness and Society: A Socio-Political Exploration of the Mosaic Tradition*, by Ronen Shoval. (Routledge, 2024). https://www.routledge.com/Holiness-and-Society-A-Socio-Political-Exploration-of-the-Mosaic-Tradition/Shoval/p/book/9781032751610

2 Dean of the Argaman Institute in Jerusalem and the head of the Herzl Advanced Program for Philosophy and Culture Studies.

3 Another approach not noted here is 'literary' reading of the Bible. This approach views the Bible as a static text, but which the reader necessarily interprets when engaging the text. Every reader is planted in a time and place, every interpreter is a product of cultural context. Literary reading is based on examining the plain sense of the Biblical text, seeking to understand the Bible based on a careful reading of the details comprising the work as a whole. The assumption underlying this reading is that all the textual portions relate to one another in a single fabric, so the context is what grants meaning to the details. This reading figures out what is written, how it is expressed, and why it says it. For a discussion of this approach, see Yair Zakovitch, 'Al Matzav Hameckhar: Skirah al Hamechkar Hasifruti shel Hamikra Beyisra'el', (1982) 20; *Yedi'on Ha'Igud Ha'Olami Lemada'ei Hayahadut* 17–29; Uriel Simon and Bakesh Shalom Veradfehu, *She'elot Hasha'ah Be'Or Hamikra* (Tel Aviv, Yediot Acharonot, 2002) 18–21.

4 Yitzhak Julius Gutman, *Dat Umada* (Hebrew University Magnes Press, 1979) 259–64; Yaakov Yehoshua Ross, 'Spinoza Upeirush Hamikra Beyameinu', in Menachem Brinker, Marcello Daskal and Dan Nesher (eds), *Baruch Spinoza Kovetz Ma'amarim al Mishnato* (Mifalim Universitayim Publishing, 1979) 116–27; Michael Walzer, *In God's Shadow: Politics in the Hebrew Bible* (Yale University Press, 2012) xiv–xv.

DOI: 10.4324/9781003397311-7

that moves from present to past, the ideological reading seeks to make the Biblical text prominent in the present.[5]

These two trends are rounded out by the sociological approach to studying the Bible. According to this methodology, the Bible is not seen as a text of divine revelation but rather one written by authors and editors. The subject of this sociological research is not God, but the actions of men, as it is interested in the way human beings present God and their relationship with Him. Sociological study of the Bible thus presents a method for philosophical inquiry into the narrative of the authors and editors of the Bible.[6] The sociological method creates an important tool for such inquiry. It offers a systematic method for discussing a human text, presenting the actions of human beings in relation to social structures and their function, which themselves embody complex human conceptions and philosophical ideas.

The sociological method argues that the authors and editors of the Bible were real people, subjects with ideas and thoughts we need to understand. In this sense, the sociological method does not seek to understand what actually happened in the Bible, as pursuit of historical truth is not its aim.[7] Sociological study of the Bible assumes that the work of the Biblical authors and editors reflected a narrative to be studied. In this sense, Biblical criticism differs from the sociological method, while the former seeks to break down the Bible into all its composite parts and understand them as such, the latter is uninterested in such a reading, since the Biblical author and editor, the subject of the sociological method, clearly did not intend their work to be read this way.[8] Sociological studies ask not who wrote the Bible but whether they had something important to say. In order to answer this question, they read the text as a whole and ask what it is trying to teach. They assume the Biblical narrative advances ideas embodied in the text, even though those ideas are clearly not articulated in the classic philosophical style. The ideas are presented as a narra-

5 Writing of this sort is common among thinkers who seek to find inspiration for their work in a Biblical source, and can be found among the Founders of the United States and among Jewish and Israeli thinkers. See, eg, Anita Shapira, 'Hatanach Vehazehut Hayisra'elit' in Anita Shapira (ed), *Hatanach Vehazehut Hayisra'elit* (Magness, 2006) 1–33; Simon and Veradfehu (n 1); Gershon Greenberg, *The Holy Land in American Religious Thought, 1620–1948: The Symbiosis of American Religious Approaches to Scripture's Sacred Territory* (University Press of America, 1994) 2–9; Moshe Davis, *With Eyes Towards Zion, II*, (Arno Press, 1977) 152–642.

6 Yoram Hazony, 'Does the Bible Have a Political Teaching?' (2006) 1(2) *Hebraic Political Studies* 139.

7 Ahad Ha'am, *Kol Kitvei Ahad Ha'am*, (Dvir, 1947) 342–347; see also cf Yaira Amit, 'Ktiva Ideologit Kemekor Histori', (1998) 10 *Hed Hachinuch* 14–17; Micha Goodman, *Historiographiya Vehistoriosofiya Behagutam shel Ha-Rambam veha-Ramban*, (PhD Thesis, Jerusalem: Hebrew University, 2005) 3; Yehoshua Arielly, *Historiya Vemeta-Historiya* (David Ohana ed, Mossad Bialik, 2003) 79; Isaiah Berlin, *Liberty: Incorporating Four Essays on Liberty*, (Oxford University Press, 2002) 94–165; Itamar Zinger, 'Ha-Tanach Ke-Historiya?' in Anita Shapira (ed), *Ha-Tanach Vehazhut Hayisra'elit*, (Magness, 2006) 159–69.

8 Aaron Wildavsky, *Moses as Political Leader* (Shalem Press, 1984) 19.

tive, so in order to uncover their insights, one must assume that a conception of truth can be articulated in narrative form. These scholars argue that the Biblical narrative is sensitive to developments, moral approaches, and changes in historical circumstances and power relations.

Although sociological study is not historical, it has historical meaning. The sociological reality that the Bible seeks to describe is a historical one, and if it does not reliably describe the past per se, it does describe the ideas of the authors and editors of the past. Historiographic works whose reliability can be questioned can have great importance in understanding the era of their writing, as these can be used to understand the social and cultural forces which operated within the society that birthed and shaped these works.

Biblical scholarship with sociological tools is not new.[9] In fact, the Bible has been studied with sociological methods since the discipline first formed.[10] Sociology provides another tool for analysing historical events and theories regarding the development of society. Sociology provides pathways allowing us to address the source, transmission, and meaning of the text in the context of social laws, groups, and structures. Sociology provides the scholar with emphases on what ancient Israel considered holy and how the group, society, and individuals were perceived.[11] It allows us to understand the role of the different worldviews, pointing to the way in which different interests shaped them and how these were expressed in the text. The Biblical text as viewed through the lens of sociology embodies social situations; it is a collection of cultural activities which can be analysed. The sociological approach argues that religious phenomena have a structure and pattern which influences social function.[12] Analysing the Bible with these tools can, therefore, contribute to an understanding of the Biblical faith, as some of its theological assumptions can be reflected in the structure of social activity.

9 On trends in sociology, see Shmuel Noah Eisenstadt and Miriam Korelro, *Hasotziologiya Paradigmot Umashberim*, (Magness, 1982) 94–136; see also John W Rogerson, *Anthroplogy and the Old Testament* (Basil Balckwell, 1978); Bernhard Lang (ed), *Anthropological Approaches to the Old Testament: Issues in Religion and Theology* (Fortress Press and SPCK, 1985); Ronald E Clements, (ed), *The World of Ancient Israel: Sociological, Anthropological and Political Perspective* (Cambridge University Press, 1989); Thomas W Overholt, *Cultural Anthropology and the Old Testament (Guides to Biblical Scholarship)* (Fortress Press, 1996); Charles E Carter, 'A Discipline in Transition: The Contribution of the Social Sciences to the Study of the Hebrew Bible' in Charles E Carter and Carol L Meyeres (eds), *Community, Identity, and Ideology: Social Science Approaches to the Hebrew Bible* (Eisenbrauns, 1996) 3–36; David J Chalcraft (ed), *Social Scientific Old Testament Criticism: A Sheffield Reader* (Sheffield Academic Press, 1997).

10 Robert R Wilson, *Sociological Approach to the Old Testament* (Fortress Press, 1984) 1–3.

11 Ibid 5–9.

12 In this sense, the sociological approach complements the historical one. While the former deals with the sequential unfolding of events in ancient Israel, the latter deals with the structures and the roles of relational patterns, both at a given moment and as history changes: see Norman K Gottwald, 'Sociological Method in the Study of Ancient Israel' in M J Buss (ed), *Encounter with the Text: From History in Hebrew Bible* (Fortress Press, 1979) 69; Edwin Yamauchi, 'Sociology, Scripture and the Supernatural' (1984) 27(2) *JETS* 176.

The sociological approach assumes that observations and calculations of processes have importance only if we decipher the ideas which give them direction and meaning. Social facts acquire meaning through a theoretical framework that can provide perspective for social events. Sociological study of the Bible, therefore, also seeks the raw data and the traces of the idea behind it. It seeks a theoretical concept it can use to create a model which will reflect processes such that the information and its manner of arrangement are comprehensible, and will thus contribute to an understanding of the social evolution of ancient Israel.[13]

II Trends in the Sociological Study of the Bible

The sociological tradition of the study of religion was developed by Max Weber and Emile Durkheim,[14] with the two offering differing explanations for this social phenomenon. Durkheim argued that one cannot base the socio-religious phenomenon solely at the level of the individual, and therefore sought to explain this social activity through collective rather than individual forces. By contrast, Weber emphasised the intentions and actions of the individual. Weber argued that causal explanations are needed for behaviour, which is why religion exists, as it grants meaning to a range of unclear aspects of human existence. Both rejected the positivistic view that religion is simply primitive, and both viewed religion as a system of beliefs and actions that can be scientifically explained.[15]

The sociological study of the Bible is comprised of a number of schools of thought. One school directly approaches the Biblical world, examining it chronologically and describing the sociological ideas underlying the historical, religious, and social developments it details.[16] An opposing school approaches the study of the Bible from the world of sociological research, to seek how sociological concepts are expressed in the text.[17] The former approach has been criticised for being insufficiently analytical, due to the lack of a sufficiently broad sociological framework and for being insufficiently systematic, which prevents it from providing comprehensive theoretical sociological

13 Andrew Mayes, *The Old Testament in Sociological Perspective* (Marshall Pickering, 1989) 2–3.

14 Emile Durkheim, *The Elementary Forms of the Religious Life* (Courier Corporation, 2008); Max Weber, *Ancient Judaism* (The Free Press, 1952) (*Weber 1952*); Max Weber, *The Protestant Ethic and the Spirit of Capitalism: And Other Writings* (Penguin, 2002) (*Weber 2002*).

15 Weber and Durkheim relied on Tonnies' distinctions between 'community' and 'society'. These fundamental distinctions greatly influenced Biblical scholarship: see, eg, Mayes (n 11) 11–7. For Tonnies' work, see Ferdinand Tonnies, *Community and Society* (C P Loomis [trans], Harper & Row, 1963).

16 For an example of this school, see Herbert F Hahn, *The Old Testament in Modern Research* (Fortress Press, 1966).

17 Robert Nisbet was among those who took this approach, studying sociological concepts like community, authority, status, holiness, and alienation: Robert A Nisbet, *The Sociological Tradition* (Heinemann, 1967).

explanations. The latter approach has been criticised for losing sight of the necessary historical context and perspective needed to avoid anachronistic thinking. A common third way seeks to integrate the two.[18]

We should also take note of the sociological-anthropological approaches to studying the Bible.[19] Prominent examples of this approach include the work of Mary Douglas, Edmund Leach, and others.[20] Other works have focused on the study of ritual, since theories about rituals help us to understand the social structure and the decisions individuals make.[21] Another direction scholarship has taken is the study of prophecy. Overholt's work examined prophecy in ancient Israel in comparison to other religions. He created a comparative methodology for examining the integration of prophet, God, and the prophecy's target audience. His models examine the relationship between the three and try to determine the function of the prophetic authority.[22] Other studies used sociological tools to examine the phenomenon of ecstatic prophecy.[23]

18 For works that take an integrative approach, see, eg, Philip F Esler (ed), *Ancient Israel: The Old Testament in Its Social Context* (Fortress Press, 2006); Bruce J Malina, 'The Social Sciences and Biblical Interpretation', (1982) 37 *Interpretation* 229–42; Louis Wallis, *The Sociological Study of the Bible* (University of Chicago Press, 1912); Louis Wallis, *God and the Social Process* (University of Chicago Press, 1935); Louis Wallis, *The Bible in Human* (Columbia University Press, 1942); Herbert Gordon May, 'A Sociological Approach to Hebrew Religion', (1944) 12 *Journal of Bible and Religion* 98–106; Jack M Sasson, 'On Choosing Models for Recreating Israelite Pre-Monarchic History' (1981) 21 *Journal for the Study of the Old Testament* 3–24; Norman K Gottwald, *The Tribes of Jahweh: A Sociology of the Religion of Liberated Israel 1250–1050 B.C.E* (Orbis, 1979); Mayes (n 11) 128–41; Wilson (n 8) 81–3; Philip F Esler and Anselm C Hagedorn, 'Social-Scientific Analysis of the Old Testament' in Philip F Esler (ed), *Ancient Israel: The Old Testament in Its Social Context* (Fortress Press, 2006) 31–2.

19 Rogerson (n 7).

20 Mary Douglas, *Purity and Danger: An Analysis of Concepts of Pollution and Taboo* (Routledge & Kegan Paul, 1966); Mary Douglas, *Leviticus and Literature* (Oxford University Press, 1999); Mary Douglas, *Jacob's Tears: The Priestly Work of Reconciliation* (Oxford University Press, 2004); Edmund R Leach, 'The Legitimacy of Solomon', in Edmund R Leach, *Genesis as Myth and Other Essays* (Jonathan Cape, 1969) 25–83; Edmund R Leach and D Alan Aycock, *Structuralist Interpretations of Biblical Myth* (Cambridge University Press, 1983); Pinchas Karni, *Achen Ru'ach Hi Be'Enosh: Iyunim Ba'antropologiya shel Hamikra* (Tel Aviv University, 1970); Chaim Zeev Reiness, *Yachid Vetzibur Bayahadut: Mavo Lephilosophiya Ulesotziologiya Shel Hayahadut* (Shlesinger Brothers, 1940).

21 Arnold Van Gennep, *The Rites of Passage* (University of Chicago Press, 1960); Alfred R Radcliffe-Brown, *Structure and Function in Primitive Society: Essays and Addresses* (Free Press, 1952); Clifford Geertz, *The Interpretation of Cultures* (Basic Books, 1973); Victor Turner, *The Forest of Symbols: Aspects of Ndembu Ritual* (Cornell University Press, 1967); Esler and Hagedorn (n 16) 23–4.

22 Thomas W Overholt, 'Prophecy: The Problem of Cross-Cultural Comparison' in R C Culley and T W Overholt (eds), *Anthropological Perspectives on Old Testament Prophecy* (Scholars Press, 1982) 55–78; Thomas W Overholt, 'Prophecy in Cross-Cultural Perspective: A Sourcebook for Biblical Researchers' (Scholars Press, 1986); Thomas W Overholt, *Channels of Prophecy: The Social Dynamics of Prophetic Activity* (Fortress Press, 1989).

23 Robert R Wilson, 'Prophecy and Ecstasy: A Reexamination' (JBL, 1979) 321–37; Robert R Wilson, *Prophecy and Society in Ancient Israel* (Fortress Press, 1980).

Sociological-anthropological study of the Bible also deals in the study of the law. Traditionally, Biblical scholars compared Biblical law to law codes common in the region and sought the sources of the laws that were written in the Bible.[24] The direction of sociological-anthropological research in studying the law devoted much time to the socioeconomic conditions which led to the development of Biblical law, specifically in the internal context of Biblical society, with an emphasis on legal practice rather than just written legal instructions.[25]

A series of studies on ancient Israel emphasised the place of political thought therein. These sociological interpreters looked at the Biblical text as embodying social situations and social structures from which a political philosophy reflecting the Biblical faith can be extracted. Some of these studies also sought to create theoretical models for understanding processes and ideas in ancient Israel. The effort to create a systematic study of the Jewish political tradition, which includes the Bible as a political text, began with the work of Elazar and was later expanded by Wildavsky, Walzer, and Trigano.[26] These works created a vital opening for analysing the Biblical text through a sociological-political lens.[27]

24 Dale Patrick, *Old Testament Law: An Introduction* (SCM Press/John Knox, 1985).

25 Frank Crusemann, *The Torah: Theology and Social History of Old Treatment Law* (Fortress Press, 1996); Esler & Hagedorn (n 16) 29–30; Meir Malul, *Hevra, Mishpat Veminhag Beyisra'el Betkufat Hamikra Ubetarbuyot Hamizrah Hakadum* (Bar-Ilan, 2006) 7–12.

26 Elazar argued that Jewish philosophy also deals with the essence of power and justice. As opposed to the question asked by general political philosophy – the good government – the overarching question asked by the Bible regarding political philosophy deals with the proper relations regarding the conception of collective identity, including the relationship between ruler and ruled and between justice and power: see Daniel J Elazar, 'Hakdama – Giluyah Mechadash shel Hapolitica al yedei Ha'Am Hayehudi – Hatofa'ah Vehashlachotehah' in Daniel J Elazar (ed), *Am Ve'Edah* (Reuven Mass, 1992) 13; Daniel J Elazar & Stuart A Cohen, *The Jewish Polity: From Biblical Times to the Present* (Indiana University Press, 1985); Wildavsky (n 6); Aaron Wildavsky, *Assimilation versus Separation: Joseph the Administrator and the Politics of Religion in Biblical Israel* (Transaction Publishers, 1993); Michael Walzer, *Exodus and Revolution* (Basic Books, 1986); Walzer (n 2); Michael Walzer (ed), *Law, Politics and Morality in Judaism* (Princeton University Press, 2006); Shmuel Trigano, *Philosophy of the Law: the Political in the Torah* (Shalem Press, 2011).

27 See, eg, William Safire, *The First Dissident: The Book of Job in Today's Politics* (Random House Publishing Group, 2011); Yoram Hazony, *The Dawn: Political Teachings of the Book of Esther* (Shalem Press, 2000); Alan Mittleman, *The Scepter Shall not Pass from Judah: Perspectives on the Persistence of the Political in Judaism* (Lexington, 2000); Norman Podhoretz, *The Prophets: Who They Were, What They Are* (The Free Press, 2002); Leon R Kass, *The Beginning of Wisdom: Reading Genesis* (The Free Press, 2003); Michael Walzer, Menachem Loberboim and Noam J Zohar (eds), *The Jewish Political Tradition* (Yale University Press, three vols, 2000–2018).

III The Sociology of Knowledge

The discipline of the sociology of knowledge seeks to figure out how thought and action connect and correspond with each other, and it offers a range of stances regarding the conditions that allow us to understand reality. The discipline's central insight is that concepts and worldviews must be understood via the context in which they appear. Max Scheler argued that relations between ideal factors and real factors should be viewed as a social framework for the appearance of knowledge but not as its specific context.[28] As he argues, material factors only create the opportunity for certain historical ideas to be expressed. The power of the base structure is limited to the existence of the phenomenon; it does not shape the phenomenon's actual content. Therefore, Scheler argues the sociology of knowledge has to do with understanding the context in which knowledge is created. This context is that knowledge a person considers a priori, granting him a field of meaning in which he exists. This is the worldview the person considers to be "natural".

Karl Mannheim sought to follow up on this and study ideology as a way of thought for the group as well as the individual. Mannheim thus sought to turn the Marxist foundation on its head, as he not only identified existence as shaping consciousness but also how collective consciousness shapes individual consciousness.[29] Mannheim thus considers individual consciousness to be subordinate to both existence and to collective consciousness. He argues that knowledge has different meanings: what we believe and what we consider a given are a function which changes depending on community, class, culture, and the generation we are born into. He says that epistemology can only analyse knowledge that was already available before.[30]

According to Mannheim, assumptions about reality are built as a religious structure, expressed in collective consciousness, but it does not exist only in the mind of individuals as it has a "life of its own" and develops according to its own internal rules.[31] A different collective consciousness distinguishes between human societies; every society has unique dominant ideas expressed in a specific way.[32]

Like language, the dominant cultural code expresses the subordination of a wide range of phenomena to a fundamental characteristic of a way of

28 Max Scheler, *Problems of a Sociology of Knowledge (Routledge Revivals)* (Routledge, 2012).
29 Karl Mannheim, *Ideology and Utopia* (Routledge, 2013).
30 Gunter W Remmling, *The Sociology of Karl Mannheim: With a Bibliographical Guide to the Sociology of Knowledge, Ideological Analysis, and Social Planning* (Routledge, 2020) 23.
31 Raymond Aron, Daniel J Mahoney and Brian C Anderson, *Main Currents in Sociological Thought: Volume Two — Durkheim, Pareto, Weber* (Routledge, 2018).
32 John E Smith, *Quasi-Religions: Humanism, Marxism and Nationalism* (Macmillan, 1994); Robert N Bellah, *The Broken Covenant: American Civil Religion in Time of Trial* (University of Chicago Press, 1992).

thinking.[33] The differences between the religions lie in their different holistic perspective, hence the different values expressed by each religion and the interpretation given the roles of these values.

Werner Stark continued this trend and offered an analysis of social structure as forming a worldview, arguing that all knowledge depends on the group thinking it and on the social conditions themselves.[34] In their classical study, Berger and Luckmann sought to ask a series of deliberately unphilosophical questions in order to understand the consequences of the sociology of knowledge for daily life.[35] By understanding the way knowledge is perceived, they tried to discern how the collective construction of reality is formed and how society itself is created.

IV Culture as Collective Consciousness

In recent decades, the focus of the sociology of knowledge has tended towards the influence of culture on collective and individual consciousness.[36] Its central claim is that reference to reality depends on bedrock objects such as God, time, space; and individual objects such as emotions, assessments, judgements – all of which are trapped within a web of cultural context. The field's central question is, therefore: what sort of knowledge enables the social order and how do its different elements create meaning?[37] Culture is understood as a structure of a collective sense, expressed in a range of products: movies, books, series, advertisements, games, sports, food, fashion, and so on. All these products bear significance for people living within a particular culture. However, a culture also bears unknowing baggage with it, values and beliefs on which society is based that are expressed in stories, myths, and sounds that grant meaning to participants. Through mutual communication regarding the objects of culture, we can grant meaning and position ourselves vis-à-vis society. Thus is the structure created that shapes our thought and grants meaning to our actions, dreams, and beliefs. This is what "religion" is for the sociology of knowledge.[38]

33 Frederic Jameson, *Postmodernism, or, the Cultural Logic of Late Capitalism* (Duke University Press, 1991).

34 Werner Stark and E Doyle McCarthy, *The Sociology of Knowledge: Toward a Deeper Understanding of the History of Ideas* (Routledge, 2020).

35 Peter L Berger and Thomas Luckmann, *The Social Construction of Reality: A Treatise in the Sociology of Knowledge* (Doubleday, 1967).

36 E Doyle McCarthy, *Knowledge as Culture: The New Sociology of Knowledge* (Routledge, 2005).

37 Ann Swidler and Jorge Arditi, 'The New Sociology of Knowledge' (1994) *Annual Review of Sociology* 305–29; Reiner Keller, *Analysing Discourse: An Approach from the Sociology of Knowledge* (Historical Social Research/Historische Sozialforschung, 2006) 223–42; Reiner Keller, Anna-Katharina Hornidge and Wolf J Schünemann (eds), *The Sociology of Knowledge Approach to Discourse: Investigating the Politics of Knowledge and Meaning-Making* (Routledge, 2018).

38 Gordon Lynch, *Understanding Theology and Popular Culture* (Blackwell, 2004).

The collective consciousness is the social context into which the individual is born and what he interprets as a priori reality.[39] The individual's belonging to a collective consciousness allows him to decipher subtle cultural symbols, understand principles and beliefs, notice subtext, sense implicit and explicit emotional dynamics, and pick up on silences and humour. From the moment of birth, man forms the world through human concepts which his consciousness participates in.[40] The individual shapes his identity and absorbs values through social interactions within the different collectives he is part of: family, community, nation, and global humanity.[41] Processes of group identification create a sense of self for him and his private interest is bound up with the interest of the collective.[42] The individual has no existence without the context in which he is placed. In other words, we are individuals only through our connection to collective identities. Our individual consciousness is social in its origin, nature, and purpose.

Social, collective identity penetrates into our private sense of self. In fact, most of our life experiences are influenced by our collective consciousness until we cannot isolate our individual consciousness as being separate from it. Our experience as members of a group grants us meaning as individuals: "I am his son", "I am his father", "I am Jewish", "I am American", "I am a bus driver", and so on.[43] In accordance with this tradition of thought, every choice we must make in life – from the clothes we wear to the subjects we study – is subordinate to the collective identity and consciousness in which the individual takes part.[44] In no instance can the individual simply shed his cultural identity and remain without one.

Collective consciousness drives human behaviour while bearing its collective memory and serving as a collective conscience. This consciousness leads to adherence to customs, norms, and values, and even creates solidarity. However, this does not mean that collective consciousness is the same as uniformity or wholesale obedience; rather, it means collective tendencies towards ideas and behaviours which operate differently depending on the society in question. These tendencies are expressed in the products society creates: culture, education, politics.[45] Collective consciousness has a vitality beyond the collection of individuals comprising it, and it therefore continues to exist even

39 C Geertz, *The Interpretation of Cultures* (Basic Books, vol 5019, 1973).

40 Jean Piaget, *Six études de psychologie* (Gallimard, 1987).

41 George Herbert Mead and Cornelius Schubert, *Mind, Self and Society* (University of Chicago Press, 1934).

42 E Tory Higgins, 'Accessibility Theory' in Paul A M van Lange, E Tory Higgins and Arie W Kruglanski (eds), *Handbook of Theories of Social Psychology* (Sage Publications, 2011) vol 1, 84.

43 Alexandra Walker, *Collective Consciousness and Gender* (Springer, 2018) 1–7.

44 Naomi Ellemers, 'The Group Self' (2012) 6083 *Science* 336, 849.

45 Tom R Burns and Erik Engdahl, 'The Social Construction of Consciousness — Part 1: Collective Consciousness and Its Socio-Cultural Foundations' (1998) 5(1) *Journal of Consciousness Studies* 67–85.

when these individuals are replaced. Nations continue to exist even as generations change, and societies continue to exist even after the founders pass on.[46] But collective consciousness can also have a life cycle: it is formed, it changes, and it can even disappear.[47]

V Religion and Law as Viewed by the Sociology of Knowledge

In general, sociology has two central approaches to analysing the religious phenomenon: the substantive-phenomenological and the functionalist.[48] The substantive-phenomenological approach tries to define a religion in reference to questions of faith, rituals, and institutions presenting certain truth claims and values.[49] Scholars that take a more substantive line will emphasise the formative social structure in symbolic time and space, while scholars who adopt a more phenomenological approach will consider the question of how truth claims are identifiable as such, as well as the experiential dimension of the truth.[50]

As opposed to the substantive-phenomenological approach, the functionalist approach does not try to define religion, but rather tries to understand what religion does.[51] According to Durkheim, religion binds people through values and beliefs; for Clifford Geertz, religion is a framework of symbols that serves as a source of meaning. The functionalist definition expands the meaning of "religion" beyond its content to include social action. When we observe it via the prism of social function, it turns out that religion need not be limited to faith or mystical claims in its definition.[52]

Robert Merton proposed a method for integrating the sociology of knowledge with Durkheim's functionalist theory.[53] It is at this junction that religion is described as a social function: it has a structure organising norms, guiding towards goals, creating means, and generating conditions and categories for action. In this sense, religion is a system of beliefs and actions that connects people to each other, expressing the ideas of society regarding collective moral character, and it is a fundamental condition expressed in institutions and ceremonies. Religion is a condition for the formation of society because societies

46 Walker (n 41).
47 Arnold J Toynbee, *A Study of History: Volume I* (Oxford Paperbacks, 1987).
48 Gordon Lynch, *What Is This 'Religion' in the Study of Religion and Popular Culture?* (I B Tauris & Co, 2007): 125–142.
49 Edward Burnett Tylor, *Primitive Culture: Researches into the Development of Mythology, Philosophy, Religion, Art and Custom* (J Murray, 1871).
50 Mircea Eliade, *Patterns in Comparative Religion* (University of Nebraska Press, 2022).
51 Emile Durkheim, 'The Elementary Forms of Religious Life' in Emile Durkheim, *Social Theory Re-Wired* (Routledge, 2016) 52–67.
52 Thomas Luckmann, *The Invisible Religion: The Problem of Religion in Modern Society* (Taylor & Francis, 2022).
53 Robert King Merton and Robert C Merton. *Social Theory and Social Structure* (Simon and Schuster, 1968).

need to act based on agreement over the shared moral basis generating the social solidarity.[54]

The assumption of the sociology of knowledge is that every social and political action requires justification and legitimacy transcending it.[55] "Religion" should, therefore, be understood more broadly: religion is the social framework which appears when there is a need to justify actions that unite individuals into a moral community.[56] If so – is everything religion? This is precisely the conclusion Berger and Luckman reached in their classical work, stating that "a sociology of knowledge without a sociology of religion is impossible (and vice versa)".[57] In my view, this is too sweeping. True, in functionalist terms, religion is a holistic and totalising phenomenon which organises an absolute structure of meaning. However, not every sociological action claims to operate within such a holistic and totalising mode of thought. In other words, every religious phenomenon is a sociological phenomenon but not every sociological phenomenon is a religious phenomenon, since there are sociological phenomena which do not bear such deep and broad meaning as the religious sociological phenomenon does.

Religion is a system of symbols and interactions which requires a certain type of behaviour and ethics. This system is expressed through a range of social functions, ceremonies, institutions, and laws creating a sense of partnership and uniqueness for the member of the community. Religions sanctify things, generate taboos, and create a hierarchy in reality in order to justify the moral action created by human community. This shared system, formed by repeated interactions, creates norms, manifested in the law. For instance, people do not want children to be sexual objects because they are not biologically and socially mature enough, which is why the community will regulate sexual behaviour and determine that certain kinds of sexual activity – paedophilia and the like – are taboo, and therefore, illegitimate. By contrast, sexual activity in social conditions arranged and approved by society – the institution of marriage – is legitimised through the blessing of the religious priest or the city clerk. Thus, do beliefs and ceremonies have a moral function serving the good of society.

Social institutions contain ideas within them regarding cultural morality, including the positive moral dogma and set of values members should strive for. These create social stratification and grant believers with social status, power, privileges, and prestige. Through social stratification, the believer's reference group is formed, through which he generates his opinions, beliefs, and directs his activities. On the other hand, the negative moral dogma and the

54 Victor Lidz, 'The Functional Theory of Religion' in Bryan S Turner (ed), *The New Blackwell Companion to the Sociology of Religion* (Wiley, 2010) 76, 76–9.

55 Claude Lefort, *The Permanence of the Theologico-Political?* (Fordham University Press, 2006); John A Saliba, '*Homo Religiosus*' in Mircea Eliade (ed), *An Anthropological Evaluation* (Brill Archive, 1976).

56 Paul Tillich, *Dynamics of Faith* (Zondervan, 2001).

57 Berger and Luckmann (n 33) 185.

values to be avoided generate mechanisms of social surveillance whose function is to punish the deviant. Social surveillance includes common mechanisms of coercion: from organised violence via police power, to bureaucracies whose role is to damage economic or professional capital, to sanctions expressed as mockery, condemnation, and excommunication. These mechanisms of social control reach to the level of the family unit – "the personal is political".[58] Religions are, therefore, never an entirely private affair – to the contrary, they are always a public matter penetrating into the world of the individual. The individual unwillingly operates within a cultural context inside a social structure sanctifying, desecrating, and secularising rites, actions, and places.

Based on this encounter between the sociology of knowledge and sociological functionalism, we can state the religion, broadly understood, and the Biblical world in particular, express a social function. In the terms of this chapter, the term "religion" should not be understood in the narrow sense but rather more like the common usage of the term "culture". Religion is a social structure organising norms, guiding towards goals, generating means, and creating conditions and categories for action. As such, religion is a system of beliefs and actions which connects individuals to each other. We can, therefore, determine that the Bible generates symbols that form a religious relationship, and that the unique collective consciousness embodied in the Bible expresses ideas regarding the collective moral character expressed in institutions and ceremonies.[59]

This methodological framework allows us to examine the collective consciousness invested in the Bible and to extract the social norms, ethical conceptions, and social structures that this text seeks to establish. Through this prism, we can reveal the web of meaning by which the Bible sought to organise the world.

Further Reading:

For another example of a chapter that does not take a legal approach, see Chapter 14.

For another example of a chapter with Biblical references, see Chapter 11.

58 Kristin A Kelly, 'Private Family, Private Individual: John Locke's Distinction between Paternal and Political Power' 2002 28(3) *Social Theory and Practice* 361–80.

59 Lidz (n 52) 76–9.

Part II

Comparative Case Studies in Law and Religion

6 A Socio-Legal Explication of the Divergent Legal Approaches to State Funding of Religious Schools in Canada and the United States

Matt Watson[1]

I Introduction

In the United States, government provision of funding or other aid to private religious schools is a hugely controversial issue, and one which has spawned a voluminous and complex jurisprudence. In Canada, by contrast, the debate is much more muted and generally does not find its way into the courtroom. What exactly are the legal differences between the two countries when it comes to state aid for religious schools? And what accounts for these differences? This chapter will be organised around these two questions. After an outline of the paper's methodological approach in Section II, Section III compares and contrasts the legal doctrines relating to state aid for religious education on both sides of the 49th parallel. Section IV then provides an argument, drawing on historical, social, and philosophical differences between the two countries, as to why the American and Canadian law in this area differ so markedly. It is contended that the Canadian acceptance and the American rejection of direct state funding of religious schools can be explained with reference to differences that exist between the two countries along five dimensions: the countries' respective founding moments; demographic realities; perspectives on how best to achieve unity; fears of religious tyranny; and concerns over protecting religion from the state.

II Methodology

The methodology employed in this chapter revolves around a comparative analysis and explanation of the legal frameworks governing state aid for religious schools in the United States and Canada. The central questions guiding

1 Senior Lecturer, T C Beirne School of Law, University of Queensland. I am grateful to Professor Stephen Ross and Geneviève Murray for their helpful comments on an earlier draft. Much of this chapter originally appeared in (2015) 34(2) *University of Queensland Law Journal* 319–340, and those portions are reprinted with permission.

DOI: 10.4324/9781003397311-9

this exploration are twofold: what are the relevant legal distinctions between the two countries regarding state support for religious education, and what factors underpin these distinctions? The chapter is structured to address these queries through a systematic approach that is, in turns, doctrinal and socio-legal.

First, a doctrinal comparative analysis is undertaken, which explains and contrasts the legal doctrines governing state support for religious education in the United States and Canada. This section forms the empirical foundation of the chapter, highlighting the significant disparities in legal approaches between the two nations.

Section IV synthesises the findings from Section III and advances an explanatory argument for the observed differences. Integrating historical narratives, philosophical underpinnings, and societal dynamics and demographics, the chapter proposes a multifaceted, interdisciplinary explanation for why American and Canadian legal doctrines around state funding for religious schools diverge so substantially.

By systematically explicating the doctrinal differences through the lens of historical, demographic, social, political, and philosophical differences, the chapter provides a robust explanation for the divergent legal landscapes. This methodological framework enables a holistic and multidimensional understanding of the path-dependent nature of the current state of the law in the two countries, and sheds light on the origins and intricacies of a complex and often contentious issue on both sides of their shared border.

III The Legal Differences

A United States

In the United States, state funding of religious schools is governed by the Establishment Clause of the First Amendment of the United States Constitution, which states that "Congress shall make no law respecting an establishment of religion".[2] While the First Amendment on its face only applies to the federal government, the United States Supreme Court in *Everson v Board of Education*[3] employed the incorporation doctrine and ruled that its protections apply also to the states through the Due Process Clause of the Fourteenth Amendment.[4] Making sense of the Establishment Clause jurisprudence relating to the public funding of religious schools since *Everson* is not an easy task. As one apparently exasperated legal scholar described First Amendment cases at the turn of the new millennium:

2 United States Constitution, Amendment I.

3 *Everson v Board of Education* 330 US 1 (1947) ('*Everson*').

4 The Court in *Everson* declared, that is, that the right to be free from governmental establishment of religion was a liberty protected from state infringement under the Fourteenth Amendment.

> Few areas of law today are so riven with wild generalizations and hair-splitting distinctions, so given to grand statements of principle and petty applications of precept, so rife with selective readings of history and inventive applications of precedent. Few areas of law hold such a massive jumble of juxtaposed doctrines and rules.[5]

Amidst the complex and often contradictory case law, however, we can clearly see some distinct strands of thought in the courts' handling of Establishment Clause cases. Many of these strands are brought to light in the seminal case of *Everson*, which held that a New Jersey statute compensating students who rode public buses to their private, mainly Catholic, schools was constitutionally permissible. According to law and religion scholar John Witte Jr, the majority opinion of Justice Black in *Everson* can be read as highlighting four principles that animate the Establishment Clause: liberty of conscience, religious equality, religious pluralism, and separation of church and state.[6]

However, the majority decision clearly focused on the last of these principles, the separation of church and state. For example, while the Court found that reimbursing the students for their transportation costs did not, in fact, aid religion, it concluded that any such aid would constitute an unconstitutional establishment of religion and declared that the state cannot pass any laws "which aid one religion, aid all religions, or prefer one religion over another".[7] As Justice Black elaborated,"[no] tax in any amount, large or small, can be levied to support any religious activities or institutions".[8] The majority explicitly linked this "no aid" interpretation to the Establishment Clause, finding that "the clause against establishment of religion by law was intended to erect a wall of separation between church and state".[9]

As Professor Witte notes, this emphasis on separation between the state and religion "set the tone" for much of the Establishment Clause case law that followed, with the result that "[t]he other founding principles of disestablishment were increasingly lost in the Court's opinions for the next forty years".[10] However, as the disjuncture between the majority's language in *Everson* and its actual holding in the case would indicate, "no aid" didn't really mean no aid. Justice Black's decision explicitly acknowledges, for instance, that the state's provision of basic necessities such as police and fire services to religious institutions does not violate the Constitution.[11] Thus, it is clear that this approach still "begs the question of where to draw the line between what aid

5 John Witte Jr, *Religion and the American Constitutional Experiment: Essential Rights and Liberties* (Westview Press, 2000) 182.
6 Ibid 164.
7 *Everson* (n 2) 15.
8 Ibid 16.
9 Ibid, quoting *Reynolds v United States* 98 US 145 (1878).
10 Witte (n 4) 165.
11 *Everson* (n 2) 25–26.

is allowed and what is not".[12] American courts have struggled mightily with this challenge.

One of the ways in which the Supreme Court has attempted to perform this exercise in line-drawing is by distinguishing between the religious and the secular missions of religious institutions. On this ground, for example, the Court has upheld the provision of secular textbooks to religious institutions,[13] but not the provision of other aid, such as money, that is easily diverted to furthering the religious mission of the institution.[14] Another important consideration in the Court's analysis has been the route the aid takes to get to the religious school. Even amidst Justice Black's separationist language in *Everson*, for instance, the "Court seemed impressed with the argument that the aid ... went not to the religious school but directly to the parent, thus benefiting the individual instead of the religious entity".[15] In contrast, in *Committee for Public Education v Nyquist*,[16] the Court struck down aid programs for (predominantly Catholic) private schools that gave tuition reimbursements and tax relief for low income parents. The Court seemed little concerned with the path the aid took in reaching the parochial schools, or even whether it reached them at all:

> ... if the grants are offered as an incentive to parents to send their children to sectarian schools by making unrestricted cash payments to them, the Establishment Clause is violated whether or not the actual dollars given eventually find their way into the sectarian institutions.[17]

Another, and the most infamous, tool the Court has employed to decide establishment cases is the *Lemon* test, so called because it was first articulated in the 1971 Supreme Court case of *Lemon v Kurtzman*.[18] The test – which appears to have been unceremoniously killed off by a majority of the US Supreme Court in the 2022 case of *Kennedy v Bremerton School District*[19] – required that in order to be constitutionally valid, an impugned law must: 1) have a

12 John E Ferguson Jr, 'Public Funds and Religious Schools: the Next Prayer Debate?' in David Odell-Scott (ed), *Democracy and Religion: Free Exercise and Diverse Visions* (2004) 48, 57.

13 *Board of Education v Allen* 392 US 236 (1968).

14 See, eg, *Committee for Public Education v Nyquist* 413 US 756 (1973) ('*Nyquist*'), which held that state grants linked to the maintenance of – and tuition paid to – sectarian schools violated the Establishment Clause because they advanced religion and/or fostered excessive entanglement. Of course, this whole approach is problematic given that, as Ferguson puts it, 'simple economics dictates that if funds are not needed in one place, then they can be used in another' (Ferguson (n 11) 57.

15 Ferguson (n 11) 58.

16 *Nyquist* (n 13).

17 Ibid 786.

18 *Lemon v Kurtzman* 403 US 602 (1971) ('*Lemon*').

19 *Kennedy v Bremerton School District* 597 US 507 (2022) ('*Kennedy*').

secular purpose; 2) have a primary effect that neither hinders nor advances religion; and 3) not foster an excessive entanglement between church and state.

Under the first prong of the test, "what is relevant is the legislative *purpose* of the statute, not the possible religious *motivations* of the legislators who enacted the law".[20] However, the purpose itself must be bona fide, as "the Court is more than willing to review an action to make sure that it is not merely a cover for unconstitutional purposes".[21]

In the end, however, little government action will fail to meet the hurdle set by the first branch of the test.[22] The real substance of the test is the second branch, under which most cases fell to be decided. It is usually at this stage in the analysis, for instance, that the Court addresses the issue of whether the aid flows directly to the religious institutions or is mediated by the choices of private individuals. The third prong, excessive entanglement, involves asking "whether there is a discernible line of demarcation between government and religion".[23] Deciding what counts as "excessive" entanglement in any particular case is so contestable that adjudication of the matter may, to paraphrase Justice Scalia's language from a different establishment context, make interior decorating look like a rock-hard science.[24] It can safely be said, however, that "where government regulation or oversight is so extensive that the religious enterprise is subsumed into it, excessive entanglement has occurred".[25]

Far from settling the law in the area of public funding for religious schools, the *Lemon* test "left ample room for interpretation" and can be interpreted as either allowing significant accommodation of religion or as requiring strict separation.[26] However, the decision in *Lemon* itself infused the test with the logic of separation. *Lemon* held that a state policy of reimbursing (primarily Catholic) private schools for some of the costs of textbooks on secular subjects, and for portions of the salaries of teachers who taught only secular subjects, violated the Constitution by causing an excessive entanglement between state and church. Specifically, the Court was of the view that the level of bureaucratic surveillance required to ensure that the teachers at private

20 Witte (n 4) 181, quoting *Board of Education of the Westside Community Schools v Mergens*, 496 US 226 (1990), 249 (per O'Connor, J).

21 Ferguson (n 11) 84 (n 143).

22 See *McCreary County v ACLU* 545 US 844 (2005), 859: 'We have found government action motivated by an illegitimate purpose only four times since *Lemon'*, and 'the secular purpose requirement alone may rarely be determinative …' (per Souter J, quoting from *Wallace v Jaffree* 472 US 38 (1985), 75).

23 Ferguson (n 11) 61.

24 *Lee v Weisman* 505 US 577 (1992) ('*Lee*').

25 Ferguson (n 11) 61. The *Lemon* test was modified somewhat by the Supreme Court in *Agostini v Felton* 521 US 203 (1997). There the Court reduced the number of prongs in the *Lemon* test to two: purpose and effect. The question of excessive entanglement was said to be, rather than a separate prong of the test, a factor to be considered in determining whether the relevant government action has the effect of hindering or promoting religion.

26 Witte (n 4) 157.

religious schools for whom compensation was given would remain “religiously neutral” in the classroom[27] was “precisely the kind of excessive entanglement between church and state that the disestablishment clause outlaws”.[28] This interpretive approach, emphasising separation, “guided most of the Court’s disestablishment cases for the next 15 years”.[29]

Since it was first articulated, the *Lemon* test has been roundly criticised as ad hoc, amorphous, and even incoherent.[30] In 1984, in a concurring judgement in *Lynch v Donnelly*,[31] Justice Sandra Day O’Connor sought to “clarify”[32] the *Lemon* test. In so doing, she articulated what has come to be known as the “endorsement test”. According to O’Connor J in *Lynch*, the Establishment Clause prohibits governmental action that is intended to endorse or disapprove of religion, as well as governmental action that has the effect of sending a message to a reasonable observer that the state endorses or disapproves of religion.[33] There has been a considerable lack of clarity in Establishment Clause jurisprudence as to the precise relationship between the endorsement test and the *Lemon* test. Generally, the endorsement test has been understood to be a further articulation of what the first and second prongs of the *Lemon* test forbid. According to O’Connor J, for instance:

> The purpose prong of the *Lemon* test asks whether government’s actual purpose is to endorse or disapprove of religion. The effect prong asks whether, irrespective of government’s actual purpose, the practice under review in fact conveys a message of endorsement or disapproval.[34] The endorsement test is therefore often understood to be subsumed within the *Lemon* test in such a way that state endorsement of religion will be sufficient to show that the impugned action fails the *Lemon* test.[35]

27 *Lemon* (n 17) 619.
28 As quoted in Witte (n 4) 158.
29 Ibid.
30 Jesse H Choper, ‘The Endorsement Test: Its Status and Desirability’ (2002) 18 *Journal of Law and Policy* 499, 499–504.
31 *Lynch v Donnelly* 465 US 668 (1984) (‘*Lynch*’).
32 ‘Focusing on institutional entanglement and on endorsement or disapproval of religion clarifies the *Lemon* test as an analytical device’ (689 [O’Connor J]). See, however, Joel S Jacobs, “Endorsement as ‘Adoptive Action’: A Suggested Definition of, and an Argument for, Justice O’Connor’s Establishment Clause Test” (1994) 22 *Hastings Constitutional Law Quarterly* 29, 35: ‘Yet if it were a clarification, it would simply be a more detailed explanation of the *Lemon* test and not alter the basic direction of *Lemon’s* inquiry. Instead, the endorsement test replaces the foci of the *Lemon* test with foci of its own, thereby altering the test considerably; how state action affects religion is no longer important. Rather, the endorsement test focuses on how people perceive the relationship between the state and religion’.
33 *Lynch* (n 30) 687–93.
34 Ibid 691.
35 See, eg, *Doe v Elmbrook School District* 687 F 3d 840 (2012), 849–50 (per Flaum J) (‘*Elmbrook*’). See also *DeStefano v Emergency Housing Group, Inc* 247 F 3d 397 (2001), 410–11: ‘In recent Supreme Court decisions, the ‘endorsement’ inquiry has been subsumed under

A third test that has been employed by the Supreme Court in Establishment Clause cases is referred to as the "coercion test". This test emerges from the dissent of Justice Kennedy in *County of Allegheny v ACLU*.[36] There, Justice Kennedy argued that whether state action amounts to an establishment of religion should turn on the question of whether the relevant action "coerce[s] anyone to support or participate in any religion or its exercise".[37] The coercion test has found favour in more recent years, particularly in cases involving "passive" state action concerning religion, such as displays of religion on public property.[38] As for the relationship between the coercion test and the other tests for Establishment Clause violations, Justice Blackmun in *Lee*, in a concurring judgement that was joined by Justices Stevens and O'Connor, wrote that:

> Although our precedents make clear that proof of government coercion is not necessary to prove an Establishment Clause violation, it is sufficient. Government pressure to participate in a religious activity is an obvious indication that the government is endorsing or promoting religion.[39]

Further, it has for some time also been possible, when looking at the jumble that is the Court's Establishment Clause jurisprudence, to identify a fourth approach that has been used.[40] In *Marsh v Chambers*,[41] for instance, in which the Supreme Court held that paying a chaplain for religious services with tax-

the *Lemon-Agostini* framework such that analysis of the criteria for determining a practice's primary effect also resolves any endorsement challenge'.

36 *County of Allegheny v ACLU* 492 US 573 (1989), 655: 'In keeping with the usual fashion of recent years, the majority applies the *Lemon* test to judge the constitutionality of the holiday displays here in question. I am content for present purposes to remain within the *Lemon* framework, but do not wish to be seen as advocating, let alone adopting, that test as our primary guide in this difficult area' (per Kennedy J) ('*Allegheny*').

37 Ibid 659.

38 See, eg, *Lee* (n 23); *Santa Fe Independent School District v Doe*, 530 US 290 (2000), and the concurring opinions of Thomas and Scalia JJ in *Town of Greece v Galloway* 572 US 565 (2014).

39 Ibid 604. In *Elmbrook* (n 34) 850, the Court of Appeals for the Seventh Circuit expressly noted its uncertainty as to 'Where the coercion test belongs in relation to the *Lemon* test', before quoting from the judgement of Blackmun J in *Lee* in support of the proposition that coercion is sufficient but not necessary to prove a violation of the Establishment Clause. (It is arguable, however, that Justice Kennedy's judgement in *Allegheny* 'appears to argue that a showing of either direct or indirect state coercion should be both necessary and sufficient to prove an Establishment Clause violation' (Cynthia V Ward, 'Coercion and Choice Under the Establishment Clause' [2006]) 39 *UC Davis Law Review* 1621, 1632, n 37).

40 In addition to the three jurisprudential approaches discussed earlier, there is even case law to suggest that it is appropriate to apply all three of the *Lemon*, endorsement, and coercion tests to the facts of the alleged Establishment Clause violation. (See *Doe by Doe v Beaumont Independent School District* 173 F 3d 274 [1999]).

41 *Marsh v Chambers* 463 U.S. 783 (1983).

payer money did not violate the Constitution, the Court appears not to have employed any of the three established tests, focusing instead on the question of whether the impugned governmental action has been historically permitted.[42] This history-based approach was also followed in the 2015 Supreme Court case of *Town of Greece v Galloway*,[43] which held that it was constitutionally permissible for the Town of Greece, New York, to open board meetings with a prayer led by volunteer chaplains. This historical approach appears to be combined at times with an application of the coercion test. According to Justice Kennedy in *Allegheny*, for example:

> Noncoercive government action within the realm of flexible accommodation or passive acknowledgement of existing symbols does not violate the Establishment Clause unless it benefits religion in a way more direct and more substantial than practices that are accepted in our national heritage.[44]

On the whole, it can be said of this particularly muddled area of constitutional jurisprudence, that the law had for many decades been in a state of flux,[45] if not disarray.[46] The *Lemon* test long clung to life, at least in the context of school funding cases, but only in modified form. Following *Lynch*, for instance, virtually all leading cases that purported to apply the *Lemon* test have asked not only whether the action was intended to, or has the effect of, "advancing or inhibiting" religion, but also whether that action was intended to endorse or disapprove of, or has had the effect of endorsing or disapproving of, religion.

Indeed, the tenacity of the *Lemon* test in the face of pointed criticism was vividly attested to as far back as the early 1990s by Justice Scalia (who would himself have been very happy to see it put to rest).[47] Scalia J, for instance,

42 Justice Brennan, joined in dissent by Marshall J, remarked: 'The Court makes no pretense of subjecting Nebraska's practice of legislative prayer to any of the formal 'tests' that have traditionally structured our inquiry under the Establishment Clause' (796).

43 See n 37. Justice Scalia starkly declared that '*Town of Greece* abandoned the antiquated 'endorsement test'. (See *Elmbrook School District v Doe*, 134 S. Ct. 2283 at 2284 (2014) (Scalia, J, dissenting from the denial of certiorari).

44 *Allegheny* (n 35) 663.

45 This was the conclusion of Charles Warren in 2003 (Charles G Warren, 'No Need to Stand on Ceremony: The Corruptive Influence of Ceremonial Deism and the Need for a Separationist Reconfiguration of the Supreme Court's Establishment Clause Jurisprudence' (2003) 54 *Mercer Law Review* 1669, 1670), and it would appear to remain an accurate description today.

46 *Rosenberger v Rector and Visitors of the University of Virginia* 515 US 819 (1995), 861 (Thomas J, concurring): '[O]ur Establishment Clause jurisprudence is in hopeless disarray'.

47 *Lee* (n 23) 644: 'The Court today demonstrates the irrelevance of *Lemon* by essentially ignoring it … and the interment of that case may be the one happy byproduct of the Court's otherwise lamentable decision'. See also Scalia J's concurring judgement in *Lamb's Chapel et al v Center Moriches Union Free School District et al* 508 US 384 (1993), 399: 'For my part, I agree with the long list of constitutional scholars who have criticized *Lemon* and bemoaned

floridly described the test as akin to "some ghoul in a late-night horror movie that repeatedly sits up in its grave and shuffles abroad, after being repeatedly killed and buried".[48]

By 2005, the Supreme Court's decision in *Van Orden v Perry*[49] not to apply an endorsement analysis, and to expressly declare that the *Lemon* test is not applicable in certain Establishment Clause contexts, might have seemed to presage an end to the zombie-like existence of the *Lemon* and endorsement tests.[50] However, these rumours of the *Lemon* test's demise proved also to be exaggerated, with the Court of Appeals for the Tenth Circuit summarising the prevailing view as to the weight of authority when it wrote in *Weinbaum v City of Las Cruces New Mexico* – just a few years after *Van Orden* – that "the touchstone for Establishment Clause analysis remains the tripartite test set out in *Lemon*".[51] As it happened, the coup de grace did not arrive until more than 15 years later, with the conservative super-majority's recent decision in *Kennedy v Bremerton*.[52]

The case of *Kennedy*, which did not relate directly to the constitutionality of state funding for religious schools, involved a high school football coach whose employment contract was not renewed by the school board after he insisted on praying in the middle of the school football field after games. The court held that the Free Exercise clause of the First Amendment protected Kennedy's right to pray in the manner that he did, and in the process rejected the argument that the Establishment Clause precluded the exercise of that right: "No historically sound understanding of the Establishment Clause begins to 'mak[e] it necessary for government to be hostile to religion in this way'", the six majority justices reasoned.[53] The majority seemed to take some relish, moreover, in pronouncing that "given the apparent 'shortcomings' associated with Lemon's 'ambitiou[s]', abstract, and ahistorical approach to the Establishment Clause [...] this Court long ago abandoned *Lemon* and its endorsement test offshoot".[54] In terms of the various approaches to

the strange Establishment Clause geometry of crooked lines and wavering shapes its intermittent use has produced'.

48 Ibid 398.

49 *Van Orden v Perry* 545 US 677 (2005) ('*Van Orden*').

50 Rehnquist CJ, in his opinion for the majority in *Van Orden*, for example, wrote that 'Many of our recent cases simply have not applied the *Lemon* test' (686). He went on to add that 'Others have applied it only after concluding that the challenged practice was invalid under a different Establishment Clause test' (686). (Breyer J, concurring in the judgement, also clarified that 'in reaching the conclusion that the Texas display falls on the permissible side of the constitutional line, I rely less upon a literal application of any particular test than upon consideration of the basic purposes of the First Amendment's Religion Clauses themselves' [703–04]).

51 *Weinbaum v City of Las Cruces New Mexico* 541 F 3d 1017 (2008), 1030.

52 *Kennedy* (n 18).

53 Ibid 5, citing *Zorach v Clauson* 343 US 306 (1952), 24–30.

54 *Kennedy* (n 18) 22 (citing to *American Legion v American Humanist Assn* 588 US [(2009]).

interpreting the Establishment Clause laid out here, *Kennedy* appears to be the apotheosis – at the time of writing, at least – of an approach that combines a focus on history with a concern for coercion.[55]

Despite the ongoing confusion over which test, if any, ought to be applied to Establishment Clause cases, it can safely be said that since the latter part of the 1980s, the general trend in cases involving public aid for parochial schools appears to have been a retreat from the strict separationist flavour given to the *Lemon* test at its inception, and an increasing willingness to allow some indirect aid to flow to religious schools.[56] In Witte's opinion, "in this process of retreat, the Court has issued a number of blatantly contradictory opinions".[57]

However, a clear trend has emerged in which the Court will countenance the provision of public aid to private religious schools if its path to the institution is mediated by genuine individual choice. By way of illustration, in the important 2002 school voucher case of *Zelman v Simon-Harris*,[58] the Court found that the relevant Ohio program was animated by the secular purpose of "providing educational assistance to poor children in a demonstrably failing public school system".[59] Further, since no surveillance of day-to-day operations such as that required in the *Lemon* context would be necessary, the program did not generate excessive entanglement. What is more, the Court held that because the vouchers could be used by parents to send their children to either public or private religious schools, the parents had a "true private choice"[60] as to whether to use the voucher credit at a secular or religious school. As such, the Court found that the government was not violating the Establishment Clause by favouring religion; rather, it was acting in a neutral manner. Accordingly, as measured against the *Lemon* test, the primary effect of the program neither hindered nor advanced religion. Moreover, any "*incidental* advancement of a religious mission, or the perceived endorsement of a religious message, was reasonably attributable *to the individual aid recipients, not the government*, whose role ends with the disbursement of benefits".[61]

55 Ibid 11, 22–24, 25.
56 See Witte (n 4) 174.
57 Ibid 175.
58 *Zelman v Simon-Harris* 536 US 639 (2002).
59 Ibid 649 (per Rehnquist J).
60 Ibid.
61 Ibid 652 (emphasis added). Whether the relevant governmental scheme involves genuine private choice was also held to be a crucial factor arguing in favour of the constitutionality of the program in the earlier Supreme Court case of *Mitchell v Helms* 530 US 793 (2000), 795: 'If aid to schools, even "direct aid", is neutrally available and, before reaching or benefiting any religious school, first passes through the hands (literally or figuratively) of numerous private citizens who are free to direct the aid elsewhere, the government has not provided any "support of religion"' (per Thomas J), as well as the decision in *Locke v Davey* 540 US 712 (2004), 719: 'Under our Establishment Clause precedent, the link between government funds and religious training is broken by the independent and private choice of recipients' (per Rehnquist J).

The extent to which this trend, and a host of legal precedents in the freedom of religion sphere more broadly, might be challenged by the Supreme Court's recent repudiation of the *Lemon* test and its embrace of an approach that interprets the Establishment Clause by "reference to historical practices and understandings",[62] remains to be seen.[63]

B Canada

In Canada, the legal landscape with regard to public funding of religious schools is markedly different from that of the US. Section 2(a) of the *Charter of Rights and Freedoms* protects "freedom of conscience and religion" in much the same way that the Free Exercise Clause, by proscribing any law prohibiting the free exercise of religion, protects religious freedom in America.[64] However, there is no equivalent to the Establishment Clause within the Canadian Constitution.[65] Indeed, not only is direct funding of religious schools by the Canadian provinces constitutionally permitted, section 93(1) of the *Constitution Act 1867* actually mandates provincial funding for denominational schools in order to preserve any "right or privilege" accorded by law to any "class of persons" in respect of such schools at the time the province joined Confederation.[66] This means, for example, that the provincial government of Ontario not only *may* provide funding to Roman Catholic schools, but is actually *required* to do so, since the failure to provide such funding would prejudicially affect the

62 *Town of Greece* (n 37) 576, cited with approval in *Kennedy* (n 18) 4, 22, 23.

63 See, eg, Daniel L Chen, 'Kennedy v Bremerton School District: The Final Demise of Lemon and the Future of the Establishment Clause' [2022] 2022 Harvard Journal of Law & Public Policy Per Curiam 1; Stephanie H Barclay, 'The Religion Clauses After *Kennedy v Bremerton School District*' 108(5) Iowa Law Review 2097.

64 For scholarship which notes the substantially similar jurisprudence created by religious freedom cases in both countries, see, eg, Robert Sedler, 'The Constitutional Protection of Freedom of Religion, Expression, and Association in Canada and the United States: A Comparative Analysis' (1988) 20(2) *Case Western Reserve Journal of International Law* 577; Christopher Manfredi, *Judicial Power and the Charter: Canada and the Paradox of Liberal Constitutionalism* (2000); Donald Beschle, 'Does the Establishment Clause Really Matter? Non-Establishment Principles in the United States and Canada' (2002) 4(3) *University of Pennsylvania Journal of Constitutional Law* 451.

65 For the suggestion that in spite of this Canada's freedom of religion case law suggests Canada possesses a 'hidden establishment clause', see Jeremy Patrick, 'Church, State, and Charter: Canada's Hidden Establishment Clause' (2006) 14(1) *Tulsa Journal of Comparative and International Law* 25.

66 Bruce Ryder, 'State Neutrality and Freedom of Conscience and Religion' (2005) 29 *Supreme Court Law Review* (2nd) 169, 178–79. Section 93(1) of the *Constitution Act 1867* reads as follows:

> In and for each Province the Legislature may exclusively make Laws in relation to Education, subject and according to the following Provisions:
>
> (1.) Nothing in any such Law shall prejudicially affect any Right or Privilege with respect to Denominational Schools which any Class of Persons have by Law in the Province at the Union.

right to publicly funded separate Catholic schools that was obtained when that province joined Confederation in 1867. Moreover, section 29 of the *Charter* provides that none of the rights in the *Charter* – such as section 2(a)'s guarantee of freedom of religion – can be used to "abrogate or derogate" from any of the rights or privileges in respect of denominational schools guaranteed by section 93(1).

The Supreme Court of Canada, in *Re An Act to Amend the Education Act (Ontario)*,[67] (hereafter *Reference re Bill 30*), has also made it clear that the provinces are free to use their "plenary power" over education given by the opening words of section 93 to extend funding to other religious schools, such as Jewish or Islamic institutions, provided this funding does not prejudicially affect the denominational school rights set out by s. 93(1).[68] In Canada, such funding may be direct and it may be total or partial; there is no *Lemon* test, for example, to be applied. Further, in obiter dicta that was later seized upon by a majority of the Canadian Supreme Court in the leading case of *Adler*,[69] Wilson J in *Reference re Bill 30* argued that since section 93(3) specifically contemplates provincial legislative action to augment the denominational school rights protected by section 93(1),[70] such legislative action would be immune from *Charter* review, notwithstanding that section 29 would be inapplicable.[71] As Justice Wilson wrote for the majority:

> The Confederation compromise in relation to education is found in the whole of s. 93, not in its individual parts. The section 93(3) rights and privileges are not guaranteed in the sense that the s. 93(1) rights and privileges are guaranteed, ie, in the sense that the legislature which gave them cannot later pass laws which prejudically [*sic*] affect them. But they are insulated from *Charter* attack as legislation enacted pursuant to the plenary power in relation to education granted to the provincial legislatures as part of the Confederation compromise. Their protection from *Charter* review lies not in the guaranteed nature of the rights and

67 *Re An Act to Amend the Education Act (Ontario)* (1987) 1 S.C.R. 1148 ('*Reference re Bill 30*').

68 Ibid 1174 (per Wilson J); at 1202 (per Estey J). See also *Adler v Ontario* (1996) 3 SCR 609, 648–49 (per Iacobucci J); at 636 (per Sopinka J) ('*Adler*').

69 Ibid 62.

70 Sub-section 93(3) reads: 'Where in any Province a System of Separate or Dissentient Schools exists by Law at the Union or is thereafter established by the Legislature of the Province, an Appeal shall lie to the Governor General in Council from any Act or Decision of any Provincial Authority affecting any Right or Privilege of the Protestant or Roman Catholic Minority of the Queen's Subjects in relation to Education'.

71 Section 29 is inapplicable in light of the fact that the additional rights or privileges created pursuant to s. 93(3), in contrast to the rights and privileges contemplated by s. 93(1), would not be, in the language of s. 29, 'rights or privileges *guaranteed* by or under the Constitution of Canada in respect of denominational, separate or dissentient schools' (emphasis added).

privileges conferred by the legislation but in the guaranteed nature of the province's plenary power to enact that legislation.[72]

What remained unclear after *Reference re Bill 30* was whether the provinces might be *required* to provide funding to private religious schools in light of the fact that public funding was provided to both the public school system and to the denominational (or "separate") schools protected by section 93. This question was answered in the negative in *Adler*. In that case, a group of parents who sent their children to private Jewish and Protestant schools in Ontario made two *Charter* arguments. Firstly, they claimed that section 2(a) required the province to fund independent religious schools. The majority of the Court disposed of this claim by finding that section 93 represents a "comprehensive code" of denominational school rights'.[73] As such, while section 93 guarantees the denominational rights enjoyed at the time of union, section 2(a) "cannot be used to enlarge this comprehensive code".[74] Thus while a province could choose to extend denominational school rights to additional religious groups not covered by section 93(1),[75] section 2(a) does not compel it to do so.[76]

The Supreme Court based its conclusion on the finding that section 93 was the "product of an historical compromise" that "provide[s] the province[s] with the jurisdiction to legislate in a prima facie selective and distinguishing manner".[77] Consequently, the majority rejected the proposition that section 2(a) required an extension of funding to additional religious groups, as such a finding would, in their opinion, amount to "hold[ing] one section of the Constitution violative of another".[78] In doing so, the majority expressly cautioned that although section 93(1)'s conferring of a "privileged status on those religious minorities which, at the time of Confederation, enjoyed legal rights with respect to denominational schools … may sit uncomfortably with the concept of equality embodied in the *Charter*",[79] it "must nonetheless be respected".[80]

The claimants' second argument in *Adler*, as characterised by the Supreme Court, was that "by funding Roman Catholic separate schools and secular public schools at the same time as it denie[d] funding to independent

72 *Reference re Bill 30* (n 66) 1198.

73 *Adler* (n 67) 639.

74 Ibid 642 (per Iacobucci J).

75 Ibid 648–49 (per Iacobucci J); 636 (per Sopinka J).

76 As the majority emphasised: 'an ability to pass such legislation does not amount to an obligation to do so': *Adler* (n 67) 648–49 (underlining in original).

77 Ibid 641–42 (per Iacobucci J) quoting with approval *Reference re Bill 30* (n 66) 1206.

78 Ibid 642. As Wilson J wrote in *Reference re Bill 30* (n 66) at 1197: 'It was never intended … that the *Charter* could be used to invalidate other provisions of the Constitution'.

79 Ibid 641–42.

80 Ibid.

religious schools, the province [was] discriminating against the appellants on the basis of religion contrary to [the equality guarantees of] section 15(1) [of the *Charter*]".[81] In response, the Court held that as the province's funding of Catholic schools was mandated by section 93(1), section 29 of the *Charter* "explicitly exempts" such funding from *Charter* challenge.[82] In addition, the majority found that the public schools too, were "impliedly but nonetheless clearly within the terms of the regime set up by s. 93".[83] It did this by examining the last piece of legislation relating to denominational schools pre-Confederation, which it found defined the rights of Ontario's Catholic schools with reference to those of the public schools.[84] This brought the public schools within the special purview of section 93, rendering the public school system "an integral part of the Confederation compromise" and one which, "consequently, receives a protection against constitutional or *Charter* attack".[85]

The veneration of the provinces' plenary power over education that occurred in *Reference re Bill 30* and *Adler* does not, however, mean that all legislation regarding public schooling is immune from *Charter* review. The majority in *Adler* was careful to make this clear:

> [I]t should be pointed out that all of this is not to say that no legislation in respect of public schools is subject to *Charter* scrutiny, just as this court's ruling in *Reference Re Bill 30* did not hold that no legislation in respect of separate schools was subject to *Charter* scrutiny. Rather, it is merely the fact of their existence ... that is immune from *Charter* challenge. Whenever the government decides to go beyond the confines of this special mandate, the *Charter* could be successfully invoked to strike down the legislation in question.[86]

To summarise, section 93 of the *Constitution Act 1867* requires provinces to fund denominational schools wherever a class of persons in the province enjoyed a legal right or privilege to such funding at the time the province joined Confederation. However, the rights and privileges relating to denominational schools at the time of union varied by province.[87] There was, as one commentator puts it, a "patchwork quilt of standards for public funding" of education in Canada after 1867, as the number of Canadian provinces gradu-

81 Ibid 639.
82 All the justices in *Adler* took this position, even the four who rejected the majority's view that section 93 is a complete code in respect of denominational schools that could not be enlarged by any part of the *Charter*.
83 Ibid 646.
84 Ibid 645.
85 Ibid 647–48.
86 Ibid 649.
87 As might be expected, given that the ten provinces did not join Confederation at the same time. Newfoundland, for instance, the last province to join, did not do so until 1949.

ally expanded.[88] In four provinces – British Columbia, New Brunswick, Nova Scotia, and Prince Edward Island – there were no denominational school rights or privileges at the time of union. As a result, these provinces have never funded "separate schools" of the kind given constitutional protection by section 93.[89] Further, while denominational schools were provided for by law in Quebec and Newfoundland at their respective dates of union, neither province is currently bound to fund denominational schools under section 93, since the application of that section to the two provinces has been ousted by constitutional amendment.[90] Consequently, there are presently only three provinces that are required under section 93 to fund denominational schools: Ontario, Saskatchewan, and Alberta. In addition, five provinces have chosen to give at least partial funding to private religious schools of any faith,[91] while one – Alberta – also fully funds a number of previously independent religious schools, which it has folded into the public system. Four others – New Brunswick, Nova Scotia, Prince Edward Island, and Newfoundland – do not fund religious schools of any kind.[92] Ontario is in the remarkable position of providing full funding to Catholic separate schools but no funding of any kind to any other religious schools.[93]

In sum, then, the differences between the American and Canadian law relating to state funding of religious schools can be reduced to two main points. First, while Canada has a parallel to the Free Exercise Clause in the form of section 2(a) of the *Charter*, it lacks an equivalent to the Establishment Clause. Secondly, whereas the provision of state aid directly to religious schools for the purpose of furthering their religious mission is constitutionally prohibited in America, not only is such aid permissible in Canada, section 93(1) *requires* Canadian provinces to fund minority religious schools where failing to do

88 John Young, 'Religious Education in Canada' in Derek Davis and Elena Miroshnikova (eds), *The Routledge International Handbook of Religious Education* (2013), 71.

89 David Seljak, 'Education, Multiculturalism, and Religion' in Lori Beaman (ed), *Religion and Canadian Society: Contexts, Identities, and Strategies* (2012), 314.

90 In Quebec, this occurred in 1997; in Newfoundland, in 1998. In both cases the amendment required merely the consent of the legislative assembly of each province and the consent of the federal Parliament, pursuant to the amending formula laid out in section 43 of the *Constitution Act 1982.*

91 These provinces are: British Columbia, Alberta, Saskatchewan, Manitoba, and Quebec. They provide funding to schools of any religious affiliation, provided they fulfil certain criteria, such as adhering to the provincial curriculum and hiring provincially certified teachers (see Gregory M Dickinson and Nora M Findlay, 'From "Common Christianity" to "Equal Concern and Respect": Working Out a New Understanding of Religion's Place in Canada's Schools' in Charles Russo [ed], *International Perspectives on Education, Religion and Law* [201]) 111, 111–13).

92 Ibid 112.

93 In *Waldman v Canada (Communication No 694/1996)*, the United Nations Human Rights Committee condemned Ontario's policy of funding only Catholic religious schools as discriminatory and found that it violates the *International Covenant on Civil and Political Rights.*

so would prejudicially affect rights to denominational schools that existed at Confederation.

IV Explaining the Differences

What explains the stark differences between the two countries when it comes to the constitutionality of public funding of religious schools? I will discuss five explanatory factors: divergent motivations behind the push for union, significantly different demographic realities, opposing perspectives on how best to achieve political and social unity, Americans' more acute concerns over the risk of religious tyranny, and their greater fear that religion will be debased by a close affiliation with the state.

A The Founding Moment

Canada and the United States, and their constitutions, were born out of divergent circumstances. America became a republic after it went to war for its ideals and overthrew British colonial rule. Confederation, on the other hand, was through and through a pragmatic political decision. Focusing on the American context, it is crucial to note that the Revolutionary War "was fought for religious liberty no less than political liberty".[94] Indeed, from its colonial beginnings America was viewed as a refuge for the religiously persecuted. As one historian puts it, "[m]any of the people who settled British North America in the seventeenth century came for religious reasons, for the opportunity to worship God in ways that were unacceptable in Europe".[95] This was as true of the Puritan settlers who left England to escape what they viewed as the tainting of the Church of England by Roman Catholicism, as it was of later groups, including Presbyterians, Mennonites, Catholics, and Jews.

In contrast, the provision of asylum to the religiously persecuted was not, historically speaking, central to Canada's self-conception, despite the fact that the colonies of what is now Canada were also populated by their fair share of religious dissenters and misfits from Europe. Further, Canada, despite attempts by the Continental Congress to enlist its support, did not join in the Americans' revolution, with religious concerns, in fact, playing an important role in keeping at least French Canada out of the fight. Catholicism, for example, was expressly protected by the *Quebec Act* of 1774,[96] and the Catholic francophone population had little hope of receiving comparable protections

94 Edwin S Gaustad, *Church and State in America* (2nd ed, 2003) 31.
95 James H Hutson, *Religion and the Founding of the American Republic* (1998) 3.
96 *An Act for Making More Effectual Provision for the Government of the Province of Quebec in North America,* 14 Geo III ch 83 (1774) [*Quebec Act*].

from the Americans, given their broad disinclination to support religion, and given their anti-Catholic sentiment more particularly.[97]

Further, whereas the inclusion of the First Amendment in the Bill of Rights was the result of a deep commitment among the American founders to the fundamental importance of liberty of conscience, the raw politics of religious compromise was a reality of the Canadian state from the very beginning. For the French in Upper (English-speaking) Canada, as well as for the minority (and predominantly Protestant) English in Lower Canada, it was unacceptable that the protection of their religion be left in the hands of the unsympathetic majority.[98]

Against this backdrop, then, it is not surprising that a political compromise over denominational schools was struck. As one of the fathers of Confederation, Charles Tupper, put it, "without this guarantee for the rights of minorities being embodied in that new constitution, we should have been unable to obtain any confederation whatever".[99] Justice Iacobucci, penning the majority decision in *Adler*, was of the same opinion, noting that section 93 was "a crucial step along the road leading to Confederation", which represented a "solemn pact" and a "cardinal term" of Union, without which "there would have been no Confederation".[100] Interestingly, whereas for Thomas Jefferson and many of the other American founders, religious freedom "was and would always be the foundation on which all other freedoms rested",[101] the Supreme Court of Canada in *Adler* found that the section 93 "pact" "is a child born of historical exigency, … [and] does not represent a guarantee of fundamental freedoms".[102] We have in all of this, then, a clear answer to the question of why Canada does not have an Establishment Clause. Since a necessary ingredient in the birth of the country was constitutionally guaranteed government support for denominational schools, Canada could not very well have precluded any laws "respecting an establishment of religion".

Thus, whereas the Establishment Clause was drafted with the aim of preserving the fundamental value of religious freedom, the controlling constitutional provision in Canada in respect of religious schooling – section 93 – was motivated by, as it were, more parochial concerns. Its purpose was not to

97 See, eg, Vernon P Creviston, 'No King Unless It Be a Constitutional King: Rethinking the Place of the Quebec Act in the Coming of the American Revolution' (2011) 73(3) *The Historian* 463.

98 *Adler* (n 67) 690–93 (per Sopinka, J).

99 As quoted in ibid 690.

100 Ibid 640.

101 As quoted in Gaustad (n 93) 42.

102 *Adler* (n 67) 640. Moreover, the concurring judgements of Sopinka and Major JJ and McLachlin J, and the dissenting opinion of L'Heureux-Dube J, all rejected the notion that freedom of religion requires funding for religious education. As Justice McLachlin (as she then was) wrote, borrowing from the lower court judgement of Dubin CJ, 'Never … has it been suggested that freedom of religion entitles one to state support for one's religion' (713).

ensure religious freedom. (The Supreme Court's decision in *Reference re Bill 30* conceded, for instance, that "It is axiomatic … that if the Charter has any application to Bill 30, this Bill would be found discriminatory and in violation of s. 2[a] and s. 15 of the *Charter of Rights*".)[103] Rather, its purpose was to sufficiently appease the two dominant religious groups such that a workable, enduring political union could be fashioned.

B Demographics

We have seen that whereas Canadian Confederation would not have occurred but for a guarantee of continued support for minority religious schools, the American founders deliberately sought to create a republic committed to the ideal of religious freedom. However, this observation, on its own, does not have all that much explanatory power. We should go further and ask *why* the section 93 compromise was a necessary condition of Confederation in Canada. Likewise, we should seek to understand why, in the name of religious freedom, the American founders chose to prohibit the establishment of any religion, as opposed to requiring instead that all government support for religion occur in an even-handed manner.

On the latter score, it is clear that the American founders were deeply hostile to the British establishment of the Anglican Church.[104] Based on this model, and on the adaptations of it employed in the American colonies themselves, the founders came to view the "essential characteristic" of establishment as "support for a preferred church through government coercion".[105] However, while banning support for *any* religion would see that this evil was avoided, so too would requiring *even-handed* support for *all* religions. Moreover, the First Amendment itself can be read as neutral as to "whether disestablishment of religion outlaws all government support for religion or only preferential support for some religions".[106] As such, and given that there was no consensus among the founders on this issue,[107] why did the Supreme Court not adopt this latter non-preferentialist approach?

Demographics provide much of the answer to these questions. On the issue of why the United States chose to adopt a "support none" as opposed to a "support all" model, it is instructive to note that the even-handed approach is most feasible where the number of groups receiving state support is few. This was the case in Canada, where there existed two main religious groups, Catholics and Protestants, with the latter a relatively cohesive community.

103 *Reference re Bill 30* (n 66) 1205–06.

104 See, eg, William W Sweet, 'The Role of the Anglicans in the American Revolution' (1947) 11(1) *Huntington Library Quarterly* 51, 69–70.

105 Arlin M Adams and Charles J Emmerich, *A Nation Dedicated to Religious Liberty: The Constitutional Heritage of the Religion Clauses* (1990) 55.

106 Witte (n 4) 53.

107 Ibid.

In the United States, by contrast, "[w]hile it is true that the vast majority of denominations were Christian, the sense of difference among them was profound".[108] Thus in the eighteenth century and well after the founding of the American republic:

> There were Anglicans, Congregationalists, Methodists, Deists, Dutch Reformed, Baptists, Presbyterians, Quakers, and Catholics, as well as Jews. Protestants, taken as a whole, extended a strong influence, but the category, 'Protestant', hides a wide array of religious beliefs and institutions – none of which ever held sole power over all of the colonies or states.[109]

In addition to the large number of discrete Protestant sects in America, the proportion of the total population belonging to a Protestant denomination also goes a long way to explaining why the United States opted against a non-preferentialist model of state support for religion. Indeed, not only were Protestants a significantly higher proportion of the population of the American republic in 1776 compared to their numbers within the population of Canada in 1867, but the individualist ethos that prevailed across Protestant creeds inclined these early Americans against giving government an active role in supporting religion. As Samuel Huntington observed:

> The Protestant emphasis on the individual conscience and the responsibility of individuals to learn God's truths directly from the Bible promoted the American commitment to individualism, equality, and the rights to freedom of religion and opinion. ... With its congregational forms of church organization, Protestantism fostered opposition to hierarchy and the assumption that similar democratic forms should be employed in government.[110]

Relatedly, as Huntington also notes, "Protestantism stressed the work ethic and the responsibility of the individual for his own success or failure in life".[111] Such a viewpoint links up with the Millian conviction, historically much in vogue in America, that if left to her own devices, the truth will win out. This strand of thought clearly pervades American free speech jurisprudence, for instance, and sets it in sharp relief from the Canadian law in this area, which is informed by a much more pessimistic view of the ability of truth to conquer

108 Marci Hamilton, 'The Religious Origins of Disestablishment Principles' (2006) 81:5 *Notre Dame Law Review* 755, 755.

109 Ibid.

110 Samuel Huntington, *Who Are We?: The Challenges to America's National Identity* (2004) 68.

111 Ibid.

falsity.[112] As it relates to religion, the American sentiment is best summed up by Thomas Jefferson in the preamble to his Virginia Statute of Religious Freedom. For Jefferson, religious liberty was crucially about letting various religious doctrines compete, on an equal footing, for the individual's intellectual assent. Consequently, he prefaced his guarantee of religious freedom by declaring unequivocally that "truth is great and will prevail if left to herself", and that

> ... she is the proper and sufficient antagonist to error, and has nothing to fear from the conflict, unless by human interposition disarmed of her natural weapons, free argument and debate; errors ceasing to be dangerous when it is permitted freely to contradict them.[113]

As such, if a particular religious sect were unable to survive or thrive under conditions of religious freedom, this would be suggestive merely of some defect in dogma.

In Canada, by contrast, Catholic minorities in Upper Canada (now Ontario) and Protestant minorities in Lower Canada (now Quebec) entertained real fears that their communities would not survive without governmental protection.[114] Added to a strongly held belief that a religious education was crucial to the moral upbringing of children, these early Canadians were keenly aware of the assimilative pressures they would have to endure in the absence of government support for parochial schools. They took little comfort in the notion that the truth of their creed might guarantee the continued survival of the faith. Likewise, those in Lower Canada were not nearly as taken with Protestant anti-hierarchical ideals of the sort that held sway in America; instead, they were comfortably familiar with the corporatism of the Catholic Church.

Indeed, Catholics in Lower Canada had gotten rather used to state support for their religion by the time of Confederation. For example, in the wake of the English victory over New France at the Plains of Abraham in 1759, the British government initially planned to "establish the Anglican Church and to apply, in Canada, the anti-Catholic measures that were in force in Great Britain and in other British colonies".[115] However, given the growing American uprising

112 Compare especially the contrasting free speech cases of *R v Keegstra* (1990) 3 SCR 697 and *Collin v Smith* 439 US 916 (1978).

113 *Act for Establishing Religious Freedom* (Laws of Va, 1 Rev Code 1819, p 77) (*Virginia Statute for Religious Freedom*, 16 January 1786).

114 As Justice Wilson noted in *Reference re Bill 30* (n 66) 1173 '[t]he protection of minority religious rights was a major preoccupation during the negotiations leading to Confederation because of the perceived danger of leaving the religious minorities in both Canada East [Lower Canada] and Canada West [Upper Canada] at the mercy of overwhelming majorities'.

115 Rosalie Jukier and José Woehrling, 'Religion and the Secular State in Canada', in Javier Martinez-Torron and W Cole Durham (eds), *National Reports* (2010) 155, 159.

in the years that followed, "the British government was rapidly impelled to guarantee freedom of worship to its new Catholic subjects in order to ensure their loyalty and dissuade them from joining the American colonists in their anti-British activities".[116] This it did via the Royal Proclamation of 1763. Further, the *Quebec Act* of 1774 "confirmed this conciliatory policy by authorising the Catholic Church to collect tithes".[117] French Catholics were more than content to continue with such arrangements in place. The alternative of embracing high-flown commitments to religious liberty like those prevailing in the American colonies, and fighting against linguistic and religious assimilation in an environment of total disestablishment, was decidedly unappealing.

In addition, the demographic reality that Catholics made up a huge proportion of the Canadian population but a very small proportion of the American population was sustained by migration patterns in the late eighteenth century.[118] A significant trend in this regard was the migration to Quebec of French priests, many of them fleeing France in the wake of the French Revolution and its anti-clerical elements.[119]

In sum, the large numbers, territorial concentration, and enormous political clout wielded by the Catholic French-speaking population of Lower Canada made them unique compared to any religious minority group in the American colonies.[120] The Catholic demand for a constitutional guarantee of denominational school rights, therefore, was not one that predominately Protestant English Canada could ignore.

Demographics also explain a lot when it comes to the further question of why public funding for religious schools varies across the Canadian provinces. Since 1867, Canada has, of course, become a much more multicultural country. Its provinces are home to vastly greater proportions of non-Christians than was true at the time of Confederation.[121] In light of this, it is quite clear that had the fathers of Confederation not included the section 93 compromise, no province today would adopt a similar scheme guaranteeing public

116 Ibid.

117 Ibid.

118 See, eg, James T Fisher, *A History of Catholics in America* (Oxford University Press, 2002) 10.

119 See, eg, Michel Tetu, 'Quebec and the French Revolution' (1989) 12(3) *Canadian Parliamentary Review* 1, 5: '51 carefully chosen French priests ... came to Quebec between 1792 and 1815. ... They settled around Lac St-Pierre, near Trois-Rivières; in fact, the area would even be called "La Petite France". At the time there were only 140 priests in all of Quebec, so the arrival of 51 more marked the second foundation of the Church in Canada'. See also Robert Choquette, *Canada's Religions: An Historical Introduction* (2004) 198.

120 Indeed, the term 'religious minority' is somewhat inapt in the early American context, as in most colonies and later states, as well as federally, there was no one religious sect that was a 'majority', in the sense of representing over 50% of the population. (This largely remains the case in the United States to this day.)

121 *Canada's Changing Religious Landscape* (27 June 2013) Pew Research Centre http://www.pewforum.org/2013/06/27/canadas-changing-religious-landscape at 6 November 2015.

funding to only Catholic and Protestant minority groups.[122] As noted earlier, even the Supreme Court, in upholding the preferential treatment guaranteed under section 93, conceded that it "sits uncomfortably with the concept of equality embodied in the *Charter*".[123]

The fact that Canada has become a much more pluralistic nation, and has enshrined equality rights in the *Charter*, thus provides an explanation for why Quebec[124] and Newfoundland chose to oust the application of section 93 to their education legislation via constitutional amendment.[125] Why then, we might ask, have Alberta, Saskatchewan, and, most notably, Ontario not done likewise? Here again we must take note of the demographic realities, as well as the political realities that tend to flow on from them. For instance, the demographic situation in all three provinces is such that Catholics today represent the largest unified religious group.[126] No individual Protestant sect is anywhere near the size of the Catholic "minority".[127] Indeed, the fact that Catholics are no longer a true minority in any of these provinces "is seen by some as straining the characterization of s. 93 guarantees as a form of minority protection".[128] With regard to Ontario in particular, "[t]he fact that Quebec has turned its back on s. 93 has also brought into question its continued existence in Ontario, given the original purpose of the provision as a compromise between these two provinces".[129] The sheer number of Catholic Ontarians today – they have represented a larger proportion of that province's population

122 As one editorial in a leading Ontario newspaper noted in 2007, 'public funding for Roman Catholic schools is bizarre'. It then went on to ask, very much rhetorically, 'If such a system did not exist, would we invent it now?' (G Gardner, 'A Tough Sell for the Premier', *Ottawa Citizen* [Ottawa, Canada] [(28 July 2007]). For a likeminded analysis of how 'odd' this arrangement would 'appear to someone steeped in the modern U.S. constitutional tradition', see Christopher L Eisgruber and Mariah Zeisberg, 'Religious Freedom in Canada and the United States' (2006) 4(2) *International Journal of Constitutional Law* 244, 256.

123 *Reference re Bill 30* (n 66) 1198 (per Wilson J).

124 In the case of Quebec, the vastly greater social salience of *linguistic*, as opposed to religious, difference in the modern-day life of that province – itself, of course, the result of a demographic change – is also a huge part of the story.

125 These demographic changes probably also go some way to explaining why five provinces currently fund religious schools without discrimination on the basis of creed. However, the same sort of multiculturalist argument that can be made against privileging Catholic and Protestant schools is often invoked to defend the claim that the provinces should fund only the secular public schools. The rationale here is that restricting funding to the public schools will encourage children from all religious traditions to learn together, rather than be siloed in private religious schools.

126 Statistics Canada, *Religion by gender and age: Canada, provinces and territories (2021 Census)*, https://www150.statcan.gc.ca/t1/tbl1/en/tv.action?pid=9810035301 at 30 August 2023.

127 Ibid.

128 Zoe Oxaal, 'Second-Guessing the Bishop: Section 93, the Charter, and the Religious Government Actor in the Gay Prom Date Case' (2003) 66:2 *Saskatchewan Law Review* 455, 484.

129 Ibid.

than the total Protestant population since 2011[130] – thus makes the guarantee of Catholic school rights in that province appear particularly anachronistic. But it also explains why altering the status quo has proved so contentious.[131] Those benefiting from the funding of Catholic schools in Ontario have a vested interest in seeing that the arrangement endures. Further, "Catholic education in Ontario is supported by a strong infrastructure of organizations"[132] whose combined political power means that reforming the status quo on education funding would risk "a great backlash".[133]

C Response to the Fear of Internal Division

Another important difference between Canada and the United States that goes some way to explaining the doctrinal differences we have canvassed derives from a fear, common in fact among both nations, that religious differences could lead to conflict and divisiveness. In 1771, for example, Virginia politician Richard Bland, drawing on the recent history of Europe, stated that "a religious dispute is the most fierce and destructive of all others to the peace and happiness of government".[134] Canada's fathers of Confederation would not likely have quarrelled with this characterisation. Where the two countries parted company dramatically, however, was in the solutions they proposed to the problem of religious strife.

For the American founders, the real cause of religious conflict within states was the state itself establishing one religion as the true path and hindering the free pursuit of other creeds. It was this practice that had lit the flame of the religious wars that had engulfed Europe, and it was this that the British government wished to continue in America. A firm separation between church and state, however, would ensure the unity and peace of the community. As Justice Frankfurter put it one year after *Everson*, "the great American principle of eternal separation … is one of the vital reliances of our Constitutional system for assuring unities among our people stronger than our diversities".[135]

130 Statistics Canada, *Immigration and Ethnocultural Diversity* (*2011 National Household Survey*), https://www150.statcan.gc.ca/n1/en/catalogue/99-010-X2011032 at 30 August 2023.

131 See, eg, 'Funding for Faith-based Schools Defines Ontario Election', CBC Digital Archives http://www.cbc.ca/player/play/2129427378 at 6 November 2015.

132 Andrew Chung, 'Newfoundland offers religious school lessons', *Toronto Star* (Toronto, Canada), 16 September 2007 http://www.thestar.com/news/2007/09/16/newfoundland_offers_religious_school_lessons.htm at 6 November 2015. (This infrastructure 'includes the Institute for Catholic Education, the Ontario Conference of Catholic Bishops, Catholic parents' groups, Catholic teachers' unions, and the Catholic trustees association').

133 Ibid. See also *Policy on Public Financing of Religious Schools* (2009) Canadian Secular Alliance 2 http://secularalliance.ca/wp-content/uploads/2009/10/csa-policy-on-public-financing-of-religious-schools.pdf at 6 November 2015.

134 As quoted in Gaustad (n 93) 33.

135 Witte (n 4) 167, quoting *McCollum v Board of Education* 333 US 203 (1948).

Justice Frankfurter's emphasis on unification deserves special attention, since it draws out another important difference between Canada and the United States. In America, for instance, the founders appear to have been much more enthralled with the Enlightenment notion that all people are fundamentally equal. This view finds a privileged place, for example, within the Declaration of Independence, which declares that "all men are created equal". And this idea has led American courts to be sceptical about the constitutional validity of government action that seeks to categorise individuals on the basis of personal characteristics.[136] In the minds of many Americans – and in much of the US Supreme Court's Equal Protection jurisprudence – such action, even when it is designed to redress the historical disadvantages faced by particular groups, is inherently suspect, since it emphasises what separates Americans, as opposed to what unites them. Further, there is a deep concern that this type of redress does not truly respect individuals *qua* individuals, but rather treats them merely as members of a particular class.[137]

In Canada the situation is very different. Canada has historically been much more willing to embrace, and even give governmental protection to, religious and linguistic differences. Whereas Canada by 1867 had an established history of allowing the French minority to seek to preserve its language by insularising itself, Americans actively sought to ensure that children from all backgrounds entered the melting pot that was the public school system. Thus Canadians – who have always lived with the fact of a large linguistic (and, historically, religious) minority in its midst, and since 1971 have lived with an official multiculturalism policy that is given constitutional protection through section 27 of the *Charter* – have long been considerably less likely than Americans to view the protection of such differences as manifesting a lack of regard for the individual, or as, per se, divisive.

Canadian courts, for example, have embraced the notion that governmental recognition of difference may be *necessary* in order to treat individuals equally.[138] Section 15(2) of the *Charter*, for example, in stark contrast (and indeed in direct response),[139] to the American equal protection jurisprudence, explicitly sanctions government actions that make distinctions on the basis of select personal characteristics where these actions are designed to ameliorate the conditions faced by disadvantaged groups.

Further, conventional wisdom in Canada has it that treating all groups in an identical fashion will tend to undermine, rather than promote, national

136 See, eg, Cass R Sunstein, 'Public Values, Private Interests, and the Equal Protection Clause' (1982) *Supreme Court Review*, 127–166 (explaining the degrees of scrutiny applied in American jurisprudence to cases arising under the Equal Protection Clause of the 14th Amendment).

137 See, eg, *Regents of the University of California v Bakke* 438 US 265 (1978).

138 See, eg, *R v Kapp* 2008 SCC 41; *Lovelace v Ontario* (2000) 1 SCR 950.

139 Jena McGill, 'Section 15(2), Ameliorative Programs and Proportionality Review' (2013) *Supreme Court Law Review* 521, 524–525.

unity.[140] The universalist impulse, which is at the heart of the American melting pot ideal, is in tension with the mosaic model of Canadian multiculturalism. It is axiomatic in Canadian politics, for example, that due to the unique cultural circumstances of Quebec, it would never have joined Confederation had it not been able, through a federal division of powers, to administer its own unique civil code relating to property and civil rights. Similarly, as we have seen, the unification of Quebec with the three other founding provinces would not have occurred but for the special recognition afforded to the Catholic minority schools in Ontario by section 93.[141] Thus, while constitutional protection for denominational schools set apart the religious minorities in Ontario and Quebec, it helped to bring the solitudes together as well, as it assured Catholic Francophones that their views and their faith would be given voice and protection within the new Canada.

From the foregoing, it should be evident that in America the central concern was to avoid religious tensions by way of a separation of church and state that would unite the populace together as one people. In Canada, by contrast, unity meant something a little different. The political compromise in section 93 was aimed at the formation not of a unified, culturally cohesive people, but rather a governable whole that would protect the religious (and linguistic) differences of its constituent parts. The Confederation compromise around religious schools was a means to this more modest end.

D Fear of Religious Tyranny

Not only were the American founding fathers, as we have seen, more enamoured with the ideal of religious liberty than were their Canadian counterparts, they also harboured considerably greater concerns over the possibility of a descent into religious tyranny. Compulsory public funding of religious institutions, in particular, was seen to be the thin edge of the wedge. As John Adams put it with reference to the government in London, "if Parliament could tax us, they could establish the Church of England with all its creeds, articles, tests, ceremonies, and tithes".[142] James Madison, too, shared the fear that the merest establishment could lead to religious tyranny. "Who does not see", Madison asked his compatriots rhetorically, "that the same authority which can force a citizen to contribute three pence only of his property for

140 See, eg, Will Kymlicka, *Multicultural Citizenship* (Oxford University Press, 1995) 173–192.

141 Lest there be any doubt that special recognition is indeed what section 93 provides, we see the majority judgement of the Supreme Court in *Reference re Bill 30* quote with approval from the previous decision of the Ontario Court of Appeal: 'These educational rights, granted specifically to the Protestants in Quebec and the Roman Catholics in Ontario, make it impossible to treat all Canadians equally. The country was founded upon the recognition of special or unequal educational rights for specific religious groups in Ontario and Quebec' (n 66, 1198).

142 As quoted in Gaustad (n 93) 33.

the support of any one establishment, may force him to conform to any other establishment in all cases whatsoever".[143]

Why has America been so taken by this slippery slope argument in favour of separating church and state, whereas Canada seems to have been little bothered by it? The answer again lies in the divergent histories and political cultures of the two nations. Specifically, the American state, at its founding and ever since, has nursed a fundamental suspicion of governmental power.[144] This distrust is more or less absent in the Canadian context. As Wilson J explained in dissent in *McKinney v University of Guelph*:

> Unhappy with the injustices the Americans perceived were perpetrated against them by the British, the American people were left with a deep distrust of powerful states. The United States Constitution enshrines the belief of the American people that unless the state is strictly controlled it poses a great danger to individual liberty. Its primary focus, articulated in the bulk of its provisions, is against 'state action'. *Canada does not share this history.*[145]

Further, as one expert in comparative Canadian and American constitutional law puts the point:

> [T]he decision by Canadian colonists not to join the American revolution, coupled by the mass migration of United Empire Loyalists from the American colonies, meant that the Province of Canada, from its inception, had as its core value a trust of the very government from which Americans rebelled.[146]

E Fear of Degrading Religion

The fifth and final factor to mention by way of explaining the differences in American and Canadian law relating to the funding of religious schools involves the concern that without a clear separation of church and state, religion will suffer. We have seen herein that the American founders feared, and the US Supreme Court continues to fear, that religious tyranny may follow on from religious establishment. The concern, as one commentator characterises it, is that "[r]eligion is … too powerful … and too greedy to permit

143 Ibid 69.

144 This quintessentially American fear of centralised authority explains much of the founders' preoccupation with creating a strong federal union in which the states could act as a check on the federal government.

145 *McKinney v University of Guelph* (1990) 3 SCR 229, 343. (emphasis added).

146 Stephen Ross, *Comparative Constitutional Law (US/Canada/Australia) 2009*, ch 8–20 https://pennstatelaw.psu.edu/_file/Ross/Chapter_Eight.pdf (accessed 25 June 2024).

its unhindered pervasion of a civil magistracy".[147] Inversely, however, prevailing views in the United States on the greed and menace of the *state* (such as those canvassed in the previous section) also explain why America has long been preoccupied with keeping government's hands off religion. This concern for protecting not the state from religion but rather religion from the state is evident in the writings of such seventeenth century American figures as Roger Williams and William Penn. Williams, for example, created the "wall of separation" metaphor, 150 years before Jefferson co-opted the phrase, to describe what was necessary to protect the purity of religious belief.[148]

This concern to protect religion from the state continues to inform the US Supreme Court's interpretation of the Establishment Clause, especially in the case of those justices who have clung to a strict separationist approach.[149] The words of Justice Black in *Engel v Vitale* succinctly present the dual dangers the Establishment Clause protects against: "a union of government and religion tends to destroy government and degrade religion".[150]

In contrast, and as we have seen, Canadians' historical faith in government and relative distrust of majorities has long made them more willing to abide a connection between religion and the state. From this vantage, the American concern that any such connection would undermine the broadly liberal nature of the state or the purity of religion (or both) seems exaggerated.[151]

V Conclusion

The American and Canadian freedom of religion jurisprudence is broadly similar. There are, however, important and marked differences when it comes to the law in the two countries surrounding the public funding of religious schools. Specifically, Canada has no constitutional bar on the establishment of religion, as is found in the US Establishment Clause. Moreover, whereas direct state funding of religious schools is constitutionally impermissible in the United States, it is not only permissible in Canada but even, in certain provinces, constitutionally required.

147 Witte (n 4) 145 (paraphrasing the judgement of Black J in *Engel v Vitale* 370 US 421 [1962], 430–32).

148 Adams and Emmerich (n 104) 5.

149 See especially the dissenting opinion of Justice Souter (joined by Stevens J and Ginsburg J) in *Mitchell v Helms* (n 60) 871–72 .

150 *Engel* (n 146) 431.

151 This is not to say, of course, that one cannot find this type of argument in Canada today. The Canadian Secular Alliance, for instance, makes an argument of this sort when it claims that 'Refusing financial subsidy from the state may actually be in the best interests of private religious schools, since they will inevitably come under public pressure to change any anti-liberal-democratic practices as a pre-condition of receiving public money. Declining public funding would eliminate this source of leverage and free religious groups to practice their beliefs without interference by the government or the courts' (Canadian Secular Alliance, [n 132]).

In order to understand why these legal differences exist, this chapter explored five notable contrasts between the American and Canadian experiences. Firstly, whereas a commitment to the ideal of religious freedom was central to the founding of the American republic, Canadian Confederation was through and through a pragmatic political compromise. Secondly, whereas Canada was composed of a large and powerful Catholic minority, the United States was overwhelmingly Protestant, but historically comprised Protestant sects who saw themselves as being as different from one another as they were from Catholics. Thirdly, whereas the United States responded to the fear that religious difference could lead to internal division by attempting to forge a common identity in conditions of religious disestablishment, the Canadian state addressed the same concern by specifically recognising and protecting its religious minority communities. Fourthly, whereas the United States, in keeping with its historical distrust of governmental authority, has long harboured a deep-seated fear of state-led religious tyranny, Canadians have been much less troubled by this concern. Lastly, whereas the fear that a close relationship between church and state would degrade religion was, and remains, a common concern in the United States, it has never been as worrying for Canadians. Together, this combination of historical, demographic, social, political, and philosophical differences helps explain why the law relating to state funding of religious schools is the way it is on either side of the border.

Further Reading:

For analysis of the methods used in this chapter, see Chapter 15 – Section IV – subsection A *The Doctrinal Method*; B *The Historical* Method; E *The Cultural* Method; F *The Yardstick Method*.

For the author's rejoinder and reflection, see Appendix Section II.

For a response to this chapter, see Chapter 6.1.

For an analysis involving the United States, see Chapters 7, 11, and 13.

6.1 Response to Matt Watson, "A Socio-legal Explication of the Divergent Legal Approaches to State Funding of Religious Schools in Canada and the United States"

P T Babie[1]

Although Canada and the United States share a physical border, the same cannot be said of the constitutional treatment of the metaphysical boundary between church and state. As Matt Watson so ably shows in Chapter 6, as they arise in relation to public funding for religious schools, and in the absence in Canada of a constitutional bar to such funding, the legal differences between the two nations represent the product of divergent constitutional histories. In revealing these dual histories, Watson:

> advances an explanatory argument … [that] … [i]ntegrat[es] historical narratives, philosophical underpinnings, and societal dynamics and demographics, … propos[ing] a multifaceted, interdisciplinary explanation for why American and Canadian legal doctrines around state funding for religious schools diverge so substantially.[2]

Watson identifies five key differences:

1. Unlike the American founding, in which religious freedom played a key role, the Canadian founding represented a pragmatic political compromise;
2. The Canadian experience involved a large and powerful Catholic minority, whereas in the United States there existed a large number of Protestant sects;
3. Canada specifically recognised its religious minority communities in the constitutional settlement, while the United States attempted to secure a common identity through religious disestablishment;

1 Bonython Chair in Law and Professor of Law, Adelaide Law School, The University of Adelaide.

2 Matt Watson, A socio-Legal Explication of the Divergent Legal Approaches to State Funding of Religious Schools in Canada and the United States in Renae Barker, Camilla Baasch Andersen and Mohammad Alumari (eds) Comparative Approaches to law and Religion (Routledge, 2025) 116.

DOI: 10.4324/9781003397311-10

4. Canadians have been largely untroubled by the fear of religious tyranny that has characterised the course of American history; and
5. The fear of religious degradation in the United States, which comes from a close relationship between church and state, has never been as worrying for Canadians.[3]

Watson concludes that "[t]ogether, this combination of historical, demographic, social, political, and philosophical differences helps explain why the law relating to state funding of religious schools is the way it is on either side of the border".[4]

Watson presents a novel methodology, helpful not only to those engaged in research into Canadian and American constitutional law, but also to those engaged in comparative constitutional analysis generally. Indeed, applying Watson's heuristic to the Australian experience, as I have done in my chapter in this volume, could yield similar results to those that I found: the Australian religion clauses, being broadly similar to, and historically based upon, the American, might provide sage guidance for the interpretation of the former. If only the judges would allow it. As they have not, to date, done so, means that Australia loses an opportunity for a wider, substantive understanding of those clauses, one which might admit of social science evidence in assessing violations, and the application of a judicially-crafted limitations analysis for assessing when a legitimate state objective might mean that the individual right must give way to the community interest.

Yet, perhaps Watson's conclusions can give Australians comfort that all is not lost in the narrow approach which the High Court has taken to its religion clauses. For allowing for state support of religious education is so well and widely accepted in Canada that, to the extent that it concerns Canadians at all, it is a "debate [that] is much more muted and generally does not find its way into the courtroom".[5] So ingrained has that acceptance become that when a case *does* reach the courts, it gains widespread attention. When, in 2021, the Supreme Court of Canada dismissed the application for leave to appeal in *Good Spirit School Division No 204 v Government of Saskatchewan* ('*Good Spirit*'), it brought to an end litigation which had challenged publicly-funded Catholic schools which had wound its way through Saskatchewan's courts for almost 20 years.[6] In doing so, without the need even to hear the appeal on its merits,

3 Ibid 116–130.

4 Ibid 142.

5 Ibid 115.

6 *Good Spirit School Division No 204 v Christ the Teacher Roman Catholic School Division No 212*, 2017 SKQB 109 (Layh J); *Good Spirit School Division No 204 v Saskatchewan*, 2020 SKCA 34; *Good Spirit School Division No 204 v Government of Saskatchewan* (2021-02-25) (39212) (SCC, application for leave to appeal dismissed). See Edward R (Ted) Lewis, 'A School Divided: A Historicist Legal Analysis of *Good Spirit School Division No 204 v Christ Teacher Roman Catholic Separate School Division No 212*' (2019) 28 *Dalhousie Journal of Legal Studies*

the Supreme Court of Canada affirmed the long-standing and well-accepted relationship of state involvement in religious schools: such funding, part of Canada's constitutional 1867 settlement, was constitutional.

The converse is true in the United States. So frequent *are* disputes involving the Establishment Clause that they hardly warrant mention. Further, until 2022, when the Supreme Court in *Kennedy v Bremerton* ('*Kennedy*') found that it had long been abandoned,[7] nothing like the accommodation of publicly-funded religious education found in Canada could even be countenanced under *Lemon v Kurtzman* ("the *Lemon* test") orthodoxy which barred any "entanglement" between state and church whatsoever.[8] Keen to test the borders of the post-*Lemon* landscape, hardly had *Kennedy* been decided when, in 2023, Oklahoma announced that it would establish a publicly-funded Catholic faith-based charter school.[9] Unsurprisingly, in less than a year, the challenges to that school have already reached the Oklahoma Supreme Court,[10] in what is no doubt merely a staging post on the way to the inevitable hearing in the Supreme Court of the United States. Yet the challenge to the Oklahoma school is just one of myriad Establishment Clause cases involving publicly-funded education facing American courts every year.

Watson's clear and cogent analysis shows that, ironically, the very thing that so worries Americans about a collapse of the "wall of separation" and consequential "entanglement" of state with church is not only a fact of life for Canadians, but has also resulted in little, if any, discernible controversy or conflict. So ingrained has "entanglement" become that Canadians scarcely think of it; indeed, it is cases like *Good Spirit*, and its unexpected challenge to the status quo, that seem anomalous. Some "entanglement" results in little, if any, discernible effect on the way in which most Canadians live their lives, and perhaps, in its own way, Australia has come to the same place: *Attorney-General (Vic) (Ex rel Black) v Commonwealth*[11] and *Williams v Commonwealth*,[12] notwithstanding the narrow view taken of the religion clauses, constitutionalise interaction and cooperation between the state and religious schools, establishing not an impenetrable barrier, but a "semi-permeable membrane" or

1; Beth Bilson, Michelle Biddulph, Bryce C Tingle, Jonathan Milani, Firuz Rahimi, 'We Don't Need No (Catholic) Education – But Why Can't It Be Saved by Section 1: A Comment on *Good Spirit School Division No. 204*' (2017) 80 *Saskatchewan Law Review* 359.

7 *Kennedy v Bremerton School District*, 597 US 507 (2022).

8 *Lemon v Kurtzman*, 403 US 602 (1971).

9 Nuria Martinez-Keel, 'Nation's first religious charter school receives green light to open in Oklahoma next year', *Oklahoma Voice* (9 October 2023) https://oklahomavoice.com/2023/10/09/nations-first-religious-charter-school-receives-green-light-to-open-in-oklahoma-next-year/.

10 Laura Meckler, 'Oklahoma Supreme Court considers nation's first religious charter school', *The Washington Post* (2 April 2024) https://www.washingtonpost.com/education/2024/04/02/oklahoma-religious-charter-school-supreme-court-hearing/.

11 *Attorney-General (Vic) (Ex rel Black) v Commonwealth* (1981) 146 CLR 559.

12 *Williams v Commonwealth* (2012) 248 CLR 156.

"imaginary wall" between church and state in which, "metaphorically, the flow of Commonwealth largesse to religious institutions is permitted; what is blocked is the reverse passage of religious entanglement with Commonwealth affairs".[13]

Thus, far from degrading religion or imposing a religious hegemony, the Canadian and Australian approach results, broadly, in a secular public square accepting of religion as one among many voices welcome there. All that without the heat generated by the more aggressive application of the religion clauses by the American judiciary.

13 Tom Frame, *Church and State: Australia's Imaginary Wall* (UNSW Press, 2006) 7–9, and 103-104; Peter Macfarlane & Simon Fisher, *Churches, Clergy and the Law* (Federation Press, 1996) 32 (citing *Lemon v. Kurtzman*, 403 U.S. 602, 613 [1971]).

7 American Constitutional Experience and the Interpretation of the Australian Religion Guarantees

P T Babie[1]

I Introduction

Controversy attends the use of foreign legal materials in the interpretation of a domestic national constitution.[2] But what if the words found in the provisions of two constitutions are very similar, if not identical? Consider these clauses, the first, an amalgam of the First Amendment and Article VI, cl 3, § 2, of the *United States Constitution* and, immediately following, s 116 of the *Australian Constitution*:

> Congress shall make no law respecting an establishment of religion,
> or prohibiting the free exercise thereof;
> but no religious Test shall ever be required as a Qualification to any
> Office or public Trust under the United States.
> The Commonwealth shall not make any law for establishing any religion,
> {or for imposing any religious observance,}[3]
> or for prohibiting the free exercise of any religion,
> and no religious test shall be required as a qualification for any office or
> public trust under the Commonwealth.

And what if the framers of the second text (the newer text) were not only great admirers of the work of those of the first text (the older text),[4] but also expressly adverted to that work in drafting the new constitution?[5] Then, one might reasonably conclude, it would be appropriate for those charged with

1 Bonython Chair in Law and Professor of Law, Adelaide Law School, The University of Adelaide, Australia.

2 See Ganesh Sitaraman, 'The Use and Abuse of Foreign Law in Constitutional Interpretation' (2009) 32 *Harvard Journal of Law & Public Policy* 653; Tania Groppi and Marie-Clair Ponthoreau, *The Use of Foreign Precedents by Constitutional Judges* (Hart Publishing, 2013).

3 This guarantee has no counterpart in the *United States Constitution*.

4 J A La Nauze, *The Making of the Australian Constitution* (Melbourne University Press, 1972) 13.

5 Kathleen Morris and James Allsop, 'The United States and the Australian Constitution: Influence of US Constitutional Model on Development and Interpretation of the Australian Constitution' (2015) 89 *Australian Law Journal* 309.

DOI: 10.4324/9781003397311-11

interpreting the newer of the two constitutions to draw upon not only the background and text of the older, but also on the authoritative interpretations of that text. One might indeed expect that that would happen. But it is not always so, and certainly not in Australia.[6] This chapter, however, mounts an argument for a methodology in the use of the American constitutional text, experience, and interpretation in the application of s 116.

The chapter contains five sections. The first briefly recounts the American antecedents to the framing of the *Australian Constitution*. The second examines the use made by Australian judges of American experience, text, and interpretations of the *United States Constitution*. The third considers the use of the American religion clauses (the first text noted earlier) by Australian judges in interpreting the Australian counterparts (the second text). My claim is that making explicit use of American materials would allow the High Court of Australia to find its way out of the dead end it has created for itself with the interpretation of s 116 – treating it as no more than a limitation on legislative power – by recognising it for what it is: the protection of a fundamental freedom. For that reason, the fourth part suggests that American materials ought to be used in the interpretation of the Australian religion clauses; but more than that, if that use were to be made, it would both rejuvenate s 116, paying important dividends in relation to the substance of the protections it contains, the type of evidence that might be used to determine violations of those protections, and how such violations might nonetheless be justifiable in certain circumstances. The final part offers brief concluding reflections on the methodological approach advocated.

II American Antecedents in the Framing

As we have seen, the religion guarantees in the *Australian Constitution* bear striking similarity to those found in the *United States Constitution*. For good reason. Although well-versed in the operation of the three great federations of the day – the American, Canadian, and Swiss[7] – the framers of the *Australian Constitution* were clearly enamoured of the American constitutional experience. Sir Henry Parkes, the Australian "father of federation", said that "it is, indeed, quite apparent that time, and thought, and philosophy, and the knowledge of what other nations have done, have settled this question in that great country to which we must constantly look, the United States of America"[8] and Andrew Inglis Clark, the most influential of the Australian framers,

6 See ibid.
7 Ibid 313.
8 *Official Record of the Debates of the Australasian Federal Convention*, Sydney, 4 March 1891, 23 (Sir Henry Parkes).

> profoundly admired American institutions from his youth. … He was a federalist, as in more or less vague sense [the framers] all were; … he had closely studied, in scholarly literature and in the judgments of the United States Supreme Court, the growth and operation of the Constitution of the greatest of all federations.[9]

Drafting their constitution in the late nineteenth century, then, the Australian framers drew heavily on almost a century of American experience with the *United States Constitution*, including Article VI and the First Amendment. The framers completed their work in two conventions, the first held in Sydney in 1891, and the second held in stages in 1897 and 1898 in Adelaide, Sydney, and Melbourne. Throughout both, the framers adverted to a wide variety of materials and texts, a great many of which made extensive and favourable reference to American constitutional history.[10] This, of course, means that the intellectual antecedents of the American founders made its way into the *Australian Constitution* – those antecedents include early liberalism[11] and the classical thought of Greece and Rome.[12] Early drafts of the *Australian Constitution*, therefore, relied heavily on American experience.[13]

The *Constitution* inaugurated the Australian federal republic on 1 January 1901,[14] its text revealing that:

> where the wording of the American Constitution was found to fit exactly with the needs of the Australian people and had been demonstrated to be effective during its century of use, those provisions were adopted and incorporated. Where they were found to require alteration – either because of the different conditions in Australia or because history had shown them to be vague or inadequate – they were modified or discarded. And where they failed to provide for circumstances unique to Australia, to accord with the preferences of the Australian polity and public, or were inconsistent with modern modes of thinking, new provisions were created, most particularly in relation to the list of enumerated legislative powers of the Commonwealth Government and those provisions introducing the British systems of responsible government

9 La Nauze (n 3), 13. See also Richard Ely, *Unto God and Caesar: Religious Issues in the Emerging Commonwealth 1891–1906* (Melbourne University Press, 1976).

10 Morris and Allsop (n 4), 313–4.

11 Andreas Kalyvas and Ira Katznelson, *Liberal Beginnings: Making a Republic for the Moderns* (Cambridge University Press, 2008); Suzanna Sherry, 'The Intellectual Origins of the Constitution: A Lawyers' Guide to Contemporary Historical Scholarship' (1988) 5 *Constitutional Commentary* 323.

12 Thomas E Ricks, *First Principles: What America's Founders Learned from the Greeks and Romans and How That Shaped Our Country* (Harper, 2020).

13 Morris and Allsop (n 4), 314.

14 See generally La Nauze (n 3).

> and constitutional monarchy. In addition, the framers were well aware of the different historical circumstances in America – in particular, the background of revolutionary war and declaration of independence from Britain, the failure of the Articles of Confederation, the centrality of notions of nationhood, and the lack of trust in the judicial powers of the States – and were mindful to take those differences into account. As such, while it is true that the Australian Constitution borrowed heavily from the American model, it was not a slavish copy of it.[15]

This is clearly so in the case of free exercise – as we have already seen, the Australian text of s 116 is very similar, although not identical, to the guarantee found in the First Amendment. Andrew Inglis Clark, the strongest advocate for borrowing from the American model, "was bound to appropriate or adapt such an admirable provision and indeed he went further, to make sure that neither believers nor unbelievers should have power to enforce their views on others".[16]

In addition to the text of the American religion clauses, between the adoption of the *United States Constitution* in 1788 and the Bill of Rights in 1792, the Supreme Court of the United States had interpreted those clauses in at least three cases, all of which were decided before the adoption of the *Australian Constitution*. Most notably, *Reynolds v United States*, in 1878, decided that a religious duty – here, bigamy and polygamy – was no defence to a criminal indictment;[17] in *Church of the Holy Trinity v United States*,[18] decided in 1892, Justice Brewer famously wrote that "[t]hese, and many other matters which might be noticed, add a volume of unofficial declarations to the mass of organic utterances that this is a Christian nation";[19] and, in 1899, in *Bradfield v Roberts*, the Court held that a government appropriation of money to a Roman Catholic hospital was not a law respecting an establishment of religion.[20] Australia's framers clearly knew about, and made reference to, these interpretations during the debates concerning the adoption of s 116.[21] It has been widely assumed, then, that they form part of the historical background to the meaning ascribed to the Australian religion guarantees.

Differences in the history of the two nations, along with the very subtle differences in textual language of the two constitutions, however, have influenced the way in which the modern High Court of Australia views the use of

15 Morris and Allsop (n 4), 317 (footnotes omitted).

16 La Nauze (n 3) 228. And see also John Quick & Robert Randolph Garran, *The Annotated Constitution of the Australian Commonwealth* (1901; LexisNexis Butterworths, 2015 [revd ed]) § 462, 1160-2; Ely (n 8), 52, 78–9.

17 *Reynolds v United States*, 98 US 145 (1878).

18 *Church of the Holy Trinity v United States*, 143 US 457 (1892).

19 Ibid 471 (Brewer J).

20 *Bradfield v Roberts*, 175 US 291 (1899).

21 Quick & Garran (n 15), § 462, 1160–2; Ely (n 8), 83.

the history, text, and interpretation of the American religion clauses as aids to the interpretation of the Australian counterparts.[22] Before turning to the way in which Australian courts have used the American materials in relation to the religion clauses specifically, however, the next section briefly outlines how the Australian judiciary makes use of those materials in constitutional interpretation generally. This will provide the context within which the use of those materials is understood when applied to s 116's religion guarantees.

III American Precedent in General Interpretation

In a recent study of the relationship between the American and Australian constitutions,[23] Kathleen Morris and James Allsop consider the use of judicial authority of the former by judges of the latter.[24] They find a variable willingness of Australian judges to consider American precedent, with an increase in such citations since the late 1970s. This is also reflected in the methodological approach taken by the High Court to the use of American precedent, of which Morris and Allsop discern three dominant approaches, each corresponding to a discrete historical-jurisprudential period: (i) from the inauguration of the High Court in 1903 until 1919, (ii) from the decision in *Amalgamated Society of Engineers v Adelaide Steamship Co Ltd* ('*Engineers' Case*')[25] in 1920 until 1970, and, (iii) following the decision in *Victoria v Commonwealth* ('*Payroll Tax Case*')[26] in 1971.[27] This section briefly recounts each, providing a background to the way in which those approaches have been deployed in respect of the religion guarantees over the course of Australia's federal history.

During the first period, led by Sir Samuel Griffith, both a framer of the *Australian Constitution* and the High Court's first Chief Justice, the High Court made frequent use of foreign precedent in interpreting the *Australian Constitution*, "plac[ing] particular emphasis on the views and intentions of the framers and on American authorities, even adopting American doctrines such as 'reserved State powers' and 'implied instrumentalities' and 'turn[ing] to American authorities where they were considered to offer guidance or

22 Morris and Allsop (n 4), 324–9.

23 Ibid.

24 See also Geoffrey Sawer, 'The Supreme Court and the High Court of Australia' (1957) 6 *Journal of Public Law* 482, 484; Paul von Nessen, 'The Use of American Precedents by the High Court of Australia, 1901–1987' (1992) 14 *Adelaide Law Review* 181, 194–6; Cheryl Saunders and Adrienne Stone, 'Reference to Foreign Precedents by the Australian High Court' in Tanya Groppi and Marie-Claire Ponthoreau, *The Use of Foreign Precedents by Constitutional Judges* (Hart Publishing, 2013) 31–8.

25 *Amalgamated Society of Engineers v Adelaide Steamship Co Ltd* (1920) 28 CLR 129 (*Engineers' Case*).

26 *Victoria v Commonwealth* (1971) 122 CLR 353 (*Payroll Tax Case*).

27 Morris and Allsop (n 4), 324–9.

like interpretation'".[28] In *D'Emden v Pedder*,[29] decided in 1904, the High Court legitimated the use of American authorities in order to interpret the *Australian Constitution* as part of a "historic and constructionist approach", although such precedents were neither binding nor infallible.[30]

The *Engineers' Case* marked a watershed moment in the High Court's approach to interpreting the *Australian Constitution*, characterising, at least formally, all subsequent interpretative methodological approaches. Unlike the earlier bench, dominated by Griffith CJ, the Court now

> ... favoured a broad view of Commonwealth legislative powers and utilised a method of constitutional interpretation which focused on the literalist, ordinary, and natural meaning of the text. They also considered that the *Constitution* should, for the purposes of interpretation and construction, be treated as an ordinary British statute, subject to the usual methods of legal construction which had developed over the centuries in British jurisprudence. In particular the *Constitution* was to be interpreted based on its explicit terms and its 'plain and natural meaning', and not from its history of enactment or via implications from its structure.[31]

The High Court was therefore "bound to follow 'the course of judicial investigation which those two august tribunals of the Empire [House of Lords and Judicial Committee of the Privy Council] have marked out as required by law'".[32] Upon taking the oath of office of Chief Justice in 1952, Sir Owen Dixon characterised the new approach this way:

> Close adherence to legal reasoning is the only way to maintain the confidence of all parties in federal conflicts. It may be that the Court is thought to be excessively legalistic. I should be sorry to think that it is anything else. There is no other safe guide to judicial decisions in great conflicts than a *strict and complete legalism*.[33]

Unsurprisingly, American precedent bore little relevance to an interpretation of the constitutional text for a court whose "chief and special duty [is] faithfully to expound and give effect to [the *Constitution*] according to its own

28 Ibid 324.
29 *D'Emden v Pedder* (1904) 1 CLR 91, 111–3 (Griffith CJ).
30 Morris and Allsop (n 4), 324–5.
31 Ibid (footnotes omitted).
32 Ibid 324–5, citing *Amalgamated Society of Engineers v Adelaide Steamship Co Ltd* (1920) 28 CLR 129, 150 (Knox CJ, Isaacs, Rich, and Starke JJ).
33 Sir Owen Dixon, 'Address upon taking the oath of office in Sydney as Chief Justice of the High Court of Australia on 21 April, 1952' in Cazimir Woinarski (ed), *Jesting Pilate and Other Papers and Addresses* (Lawbook, 1965) 247 (emphasis added). And see Philip Ayres, 'Federalism and Sir Owen Dixon' (1999) 11 *Upholding the Australian Constitution* 139.

terms, finding the intention from the words of the compact, and upholding it throughout precisely as framed".[34] Citation of American precedent dropped precipitately following the *Engineers' Case*.

Paradoxically, however, it was Justice, and later Chief Justice, Dixon who "propound[ed] the use of foreign law for the purpose of determining the 'true principle or doctrine' and making numerous references to American case law during his tenure on the High Court from the 1930s to the 1960s". Thus, in *The Queen v Kirby; Ex parte Boilermakers' Society of Australia* (*Boilermakers' Society of Australia*), in 1956, the Court declared that "the Australian *Constitution* was framed so as closely to correspond with its American model in the classical division of powers between the three organs of government";[35] and in a number of lectures, Dixon suggested that Australia is "a federal Commonwealth indebted for its constitutional structure to the United States" and, for that reason, judges ought "to draw upon the resources supplied by the constitutional law and theory of [America] for concepts, principles and examples that may be applied to the solution of our own Australian problems".[36]

Beginning with Justice Windeyer's 1971 judgement in *Victoria v Commonwealth*, the High Court began to soften its ostensibly strict and complete legalist approach to constitutional interpretation, suggesting that perhaps there were implications to be found in the text, which might be found using a constructionist-purposive approach to interpretation.[37] In recognising an implied freedom of political communication in 1992,[38] the Court "made explicit reference to the existence of such freedoms in other jurisdictions (England, Canada, and the United States)"[39] expressing a short-lived enthusiasm for American precedent in support. It would not last; five years after recognising the freedom, the Court "once again [...] asserted the primacy and exclusivity of the text and structure of the *Constitution* in undertaking constitutional interpretation. This in turn rejected the influence which American precedents had once again briefly held".[40]

34 *Amalgamated Society of Engineers v Adelaide Steamship Co Ltd* (1920) 28 CLR 129, 142 (Knox CJ, Isaacs, Rich and Starke JJ).

35 *The Queen v Kirby, Dunphy, Ashburner and Metal Trades Employers Association; Ex parte Boilermakers' Society of Australia* (1956) 94 CLR 254, 276, and 297 (Dixon CJ, McTiernan, Fullagar and Kitto JJ). See also *Melbourne Corporation v Commonwealth* (1947) 74 CLR 31, 74–5 (Dixon J), 81–2 (Starke J).

36 Sir Owen Dixon, 'Concerning Judicial Method' (1956) 29 *Australian Law Journal* 468, 468.

37 Morris and Allsop (n 4), 327–8.

38 *Australian Capital Television v Commonwealth* (1992) 177 CLR 106, 138 (Mason CJ); *Nationwide News Pty Ltd v Wills* (1992) 177 CLR 1, 48–51 (Brennan J), 72–5 (Deane and Toohey JJ); *Theophanous v Herald & Weekly Times Ltd* (1994) 182 CLR 104; *Cunliffe v Commonwealth* (1994) 182 CLR 272; *Stephens v West Australian Newspapers Ltd* (1994) 182 CLR 211.

39 Morris and Allsop (n 4), 328.

40 Ibid.

IV American Precedent and the Religion Guarantees

The three historical approaches to the use of American precedent identified by Morris and Allsop are evident in the interpretation of the religion clauses. That said, though, in the federal history of Australia, only five cases have directly considered the application of s 116: *Krygger v Williams*,[41] *Adelaide Company of Jehovah's Witnesses Inc v The Commonwealth* (*ACJW*),[42] and *Kruger v the Commonwealth* (the *Stolen Generations Case*)[43] in relation to free exercise; *Attorney-General (Vict); Ex rel Black v The Commonwealth* (the *DOGS Case*)[44] as concerns establishment, and *Williams v The Commonwealth* (*School Chaplains*)[45] on the religious test component. In the last of these cases, *School Chaplains*, Gummow and Bell JJ wrote that "the similar terms in which the 'religious test clause' is expressed in Art VI, cl 3 of the United States Constitution was emphasised by the plaintiff but there is no clear stream of United States authority on this provision".[46] This suggests that if such a stream of United States authority existed, it would be relevant to the interpretation of s 116; but because it did not exist, Gummow and Bell JJ said no more on the matter. Ultimately, then, the case provides no guidance as to the use of American precedent in the interpretation of s 116.

Only *ACJW* and *DOGS* contain a thoroughgoing analysis of the approach to be followed in the use of American precedent in s 116 litigation. The former falls into the second period identified by Morris and Allsop – that of a waning use of American precedent – while the latter occurred during the third, a period of cautious waxing. This section considers both cases, bearing in mind that the focus is not definition of the rights found in those s 116 guarantees – free exercise and establishment, respectively – but the use of American materials in the relevant analysis.

A Adelaide Company of Jehovah's Witnesses Inc v The Commonwealth

Adelaide Co of Jehovah's Witnesses v The Commonwealth (*ACJW*) contains a sustained treatment of American precedent in the interpretation of the free exercise guarantee of s 116. Chief Justice Latham wrote:

> There is, therefore, full legal justification for adopting in Australia an interpretation of s. 116 which had, before the enactment of the Commonwealth Constitution, already been given to similar words in

41 *Krygger v Williams* (1912) 15 CLR 366.

42 *Adelaide Company of Jehovah's Witnesses Inc v The Commonwealth* (*ACJW*) (1943) 67 CLR 116.

43 *Kruger v The Commonwealth* (*Stolen Generations*) (1997) 190 CLR 1.

44 *Attorney-General (Vict); Ex rel Black v The Commonwealth* (*DOGS*) (1981) 146 CLR 559.

45 *Williams v The Commonwealth* (*School Chaplains*) (2012) 248 CLR 156.

46 Ibid 223 (Gummow and Bell JJ).

> the United States. This interpretation leaves it to the court to determine whether a particular law is an undue infringement of religious freedom.[47]

On this basis, those Supreme Court decisions decided prior to 1900 were taken to be known to the framers, and so could operate as guidance to judicial officers interpreting s 116 about what might have been in the minds of the framers in drafting that provision, while post-1900 American decisions would not have been known and so would not apply to interpretations of the Australian text.[48] Justice Starke, however, wrote this:

> The Constitution of the United States of America contains a provision substantially the same as that contained in s. 116 of the Constitution. But I shall not go through the American cases which may be found at large in *Willoughby on the Constitution of the United States* ... and in *Willis on Constitutional Law* ... and in the late cases of *Minersville School District v Gobitis*, already mentioned, *Jones v Opelika* [and since this judgment was delivered *West Virginia Board of Education v [Barnette]*, where the main American decisions may be found.[49]

This suggests, without expressly saying so, that even decisions decided after 1900 bear relevance to the interpretation of s 116. Indeed, such a conclusion is supported by Starke J's citation of *Minersville School District v Gobitis*,[50] in which:

> The present Chief Justice of the Supreme Court of the United States [Harlan Fiske Stone] observed in his dissenting judgement in the case of *Minersville School District v Gobitis*: 'Concededly the constitutional guarantees of personal liberty are not always absolutes. Government has a right to survive and powers conferred upon it are not necessarily set at naught by the express prohibitions of the Bill of Rights. It may make war and raise armies. To that end it may compel citizens to give military service, ... and subject them to military training despite their religious objections ... It may suppress religious practices dangerous to morals, and presumably those also which are inimical to public safety, health and good order'.[51]

47 *ACJW* (n 41), 131 (Latham CJ).

48 Ibid 127–31 (Latham CJ), 154–5 (Starke J).

49 Ibid 154–5 (Starke J) (internal citations omitted), citing *Minersville School District v Gobitis* (1940) 310 US 586; *Jones v Opelika* (1942) 316 US 584; *West Virginia State Board of Education v Barnette*, 319 US 624 (1943).

50 *Minersville School District v Gobitis* (1940) 310 US 586.

51 *ACJW* (n 41), 154–5 (Starke J), citing *Minersville School District v Gobitis* (1940) 310 US 586, 602, 603 (Stone CJ).

In developing the approach to the free exercise guarantee, therefore, both Latham CJ and Starke J drew heavily on American free exercise jurisprudence developed both before and after the coming into force of the *Australian Constitution*. For Latham CJ, the American experience provided significant guidance for the principle "according to which it is left to the court to determine whether the freedom of religion has been *unduly* infringed by some particular legislative provision. This view makes it possible to accord a real measure of practical protection to religion without involving the community in anarchy".[52] More importantly, it is decidedly the judiciary, both in the United States and in Australia, which is tasked with interpreting the meaning of "free".[53]

B Attorney-General (Vict); Ex rel Black v The Commonwealth

Six justices wrote separate judgements in *Attorney-General (Vict)*; *Ex rel Black v The Commonwealth* (*DOGS*).[54] Of those, only five directly addressed the use of American precedent in interpreting the establishment guarantee. In the first, Barwick CJ concluded that because the text of the *Australian Constitution* controls, similar or even identical language in the American text or its construction by the American judiciary is rarely, if ever, helpful; moreover, any relevance weakens when the texts begin to diverge.[55] Yet:

> [i]n the case of ambiguous language in [the Australian] text, language reasonably capable of bearing more than one meaning, a consideration of the American text and of its judicial interpretation, particularly that which preceded the expression of the Australian text, may assist to determine which of those meanings the language of our text should bear.[56]

For Barwick CJ, the difference between the word "respecting" in the First Amendment and "for" in s 116 meant that there was no ambiguity: "what the former may fairly embrace, quite clearly the latter cannot".[57] As such, "s. 116 … [is] quite unambiguous and [so there is] no need to attempt to give it meaning by analogy of, or by derivation from, that of the [American] Bill of Rights or from the interpretations it had received".[58]

Justice Gibbs considered the plaintiffs' argument that because it was modelled closely on the First Amendment, the framers must have intended s 116 to hold the same meaning applied to the First Amendment by the Supreme

52 Ibid 131 (Latham CJ) (emphasis in the original).
53 Ibid 126, 128 (Latham CJ).
54 *DOGS* (n 43).
55 Ibid 578 (Barwick CJ).
56 Ibid.
57 Ibid 579.
58 Ibid.

Court of the United States prior to Australian federation in 1900 and, more importantly, that "United States' decisions since that date provide a useful guide to the meaning of the section".[59] Federation, therefore, demarcates when it is appropriate to make use of American precedent from when it is not: any American judicial interpretations pre-1900 could be assumed to have been in the minds of the Australian framers, and so form part of what was meant by the words of s 116, while anything after that date clearly was not, and so potentially carries limited value in interpreting the Australian text.

The problem, however, was that before 1900, the Supreme Court of the United States had yet to find that the First Amendment prohibited "Congress to give aid, financial or otherwise, to one or more religious bodies"[60] – the central issue in *DOGS* – and nor had American commentators treated the Establishment Clause as containing that prohibition.[61] In fact, it was not until *Everson v Board of Education*,[62] in 1947, and well after Federation, that the Supreme Court reached that conclusion, and it was not until *Lemon v Kurtzman*, in 1971, that the Court formulated a test for applying the American Establishment Clause.[63] So, could *Everson* and *Lemon* be used to interpret s 116? For Gibbs J, the answer was no, concluding that the different words used in the two texts and the divergent histories of development between the two nations "provide reasons why the American decisions as to the meaning of the First Amendment do not necessarily provide any safe guide to the meaning of s. 116".[64]

Justice Stephen, in a short judgement reviewing Australia's colonial history, concluded, as did Gibbs J, that pre-Federation the colonies provided support for religion, with no strict wall of separation.[65] For Justice Stephen, nothing in the pre-1900 American experience subverted that conclusion.[66] While that presumably left open the possibility that in relation to other factual matrices, pre-1900 American experience may be relevant, Stephen J said nothing about that.

Justice Mason found that it was the pre-1900 "interpretation which the framers of our Constitution would have had in mind when they framed s. 116".[67] Because the meaning of the Establishment Clause pre-1900 was,

59 Ibid.

60 Ibid 599, citing *Reynolds v United States*, 98 US 145 (1878); *Bradfield v Roberts*, 175 US 291 (1899).

61 *DOGS* (n 43), 601 (Gibbs J), citing Thomas M Cooley, *General Principles of Constitutional Law in United States of America* (Little, Brown, and Company, 3rd ed Andrew C McLaughlin [ed], 1898) 24–5.

62 *Everson v Board of Education*, 330 US 1, 16 (1947) (Black J).

63 *DOGS* (n 43), 600 (Gibbs J).

64 Ibid 599 (Gibbs J).

65 Ibid 609 (Stephen J).

66 Ibid.

67 Ibid 614 (Mason J).

therefore, easily ascertainable, there was no reason to expand upon a limitation of legislative power which might be found in the post-1900 American materials, which in any case were interpretations of similar but not identical wording – as had Barwick CJ and Gibbs J, Mason J also pointed to the difference between "respecting" and "for":[68]

> [c]onsequently, the content of the prohibition against establishment of religion should not be expanded by reference to a more extensive interpretation given to similar words in the First Amendment by judicial decisions pronounced since 1900, assuming, without deciding, that those decisions have such an effect.[69]

In other words, Mason J considered the Australian establishment guarantee to be narrower than that found in the First Amendment,[70] which in turn meant that post-1900 American experience was of little value in interpreting s 116.[71]

The principal point of difference between the majority judgements and Murphy J's dissent centres on the use of American experience – for Justice Murphy, because the two main provisions of s 116, the establishment and the free exercise guarantees, are individual rights rather than limitations on legislative power, the Australian and the American establishment clauses were the same.[72] From that, it follows that American text and interpretation is expressly relevant to interpreting the *Australian Constitution*. Following a lengthy review of the language used in the American and Australian provisions and of the history of Supreme Court interpretations pre-1900, Justice Murphy concluded that American authority supported separation as the meaning of s 116.[73] Excoriating the other members of the Court, Justice Murphy wrote that

> ... the United States' decisions on the Establishment Clause should be followed. The arguments for departing from them (based on the trifles of differences in wording between the United States and the Australian establishment clauses) are hair-splitting, and not consistent with the broad approach which should be taken to constitutional guarantees of freedom. Even if the United States' decisions were set aside, the considerations to which I have referred show that the same interpretation is reached by applying ordinary constitutional principles of interpretation.[74]

68 Ibid 616.
69 Ibid 615.
70 Ibid 616.
71 Ibid.
72 Ibid.
73 Ibid 620–31 (Murphy J).
74 Ibid 632.

Justice Murphy concluded with the strongest statement possible on the nexus between the American experience and Australian interpretation, and what that might mean for the protection afforded by the Australian version of the Establishment Clause:

> A reading of s. 116 that the prohibition against 'any law for establishing any religion' does not prohibit a law which sponsors or supports religions, but prohibits only laws for the setting up of a national church or religion, or alternatively prohibits only preferential sponsorship or support of one or more religions, makes a mockery of s. 116. [Thomas] Jefferson warned against this tendency. 'Our peculiar security is the possession of a written Constitution. Let us not make it a blank paper by construction'. We should heed his warning.[75]

For Murphy J, all five justices of the majority failed to heed this warning, adopting the view that if American experience is relevant at all, the boundary line is 1900, that between pre- and post-Australian federation. The majority made clear that both the text of the *United States Constitution* and its interpretations pre-1900 would have been in the minds of the Australian framers, but that any changes or interpretations after that date would not form part of that background meaning to the Australian text. Justice Murphy characterised the majority's concerns with the difference between the words "respecting" and "for" as hair-splitting trifles. For Murphy J, all American precedent, both pre- and post-1900, is relevant to an interpretation of s 116.

Still for both the majority and Murphy J, *DOGS* establishes a general methodological principle for the use of American experience in interpreting s 116. For the majority, that principle allows for a limited acceptance of American precedent; for Murphy J, that methodological scope could have been greatly expanded. While the majority position remains the approach to American precedent in the interpretation of s 116,[76] the next section presents what, if one adopted Murphy's approach, an expanded approach to American materials could look like for the development of s 116.

V Methodology Proposed and Its Dividends

The steps of the methodological approach proposed here is three-fold, each step representing the way in which American constitutional materials could be used in the interpretation of s 116. Thus, Australian courts could make use of American judicial materials to: (i) interpret and so develop the substantive meaning of those s 116 guarantees that have American correlates, namely free exercise, establishment, and no religious tests for public office; (ii) accept

75 Ibid 633, citing Thomas Jefferson, *Writings* (Washington ed., 1859) 506.
76 See *Kruger v Commonwealth* (1997) 190 CLR 1 (Gaudron J).

social science evidence as part of assessing whether there has been a violation of the relevant s 116 guarantees; and, (iii) establish an approach to assessing whether any infringements of the relevant s 116 guarantees are, nonetheless, justifiable due to the government's pursuit of a legitimate objective.

A Substance: Entanglement and History

One of the difficulties for the use of the guarantees enshrined in s 116 is the fact that extant High Court interpretation treats it as a limitation on the legislative and executive power of the Commonwealth, as opposed to a broad protection of an individual right.[77] That limitation notwithstanding, what if one were to make use of American precedent in the way proposed by Murphy J? In the American jurisprudence, all three protections – the establishment and free exercise clauses of the First Amendment and the religious tests clause of Article VI, cl 3, § 2 – have received considerable Supreme Court attention, forming a complex body of case law.[78] And a radical shift in free exercise

77 *DOGS* (n 43), 605 (Gibbs J).

78 On the Establishment Clause of the First Amendment, see: *Kennedy v Bremerton School District*, 597 US 507 (2022); *Carson v Makin*, 596 US 767 (2022); *Shurtleff v City of Boston*, 596 US 243 (2022); *American Legion v American Humanist Ass'n*, 588 US 29 (2019); *Espinoza v Montana Department of Revenue*, 591 US 464 (2018); *Town of Greece v Galloway*, 572 US 565 (2014); *Hosanna-Tabor Evangelical Lutheran Church and School v EEOC*, 565 US 171 (2012); *Van Orden v Perry*, 545 US 677 (2005); *McCreary County v ACLU of Kentucky*, 545 US 844 (2005); *Zelman v Simmons-Harris*, 536 US 639 (2002); *Santa Fe Independent School District v Doe*, 530 US 290 (2000); *Rosenberger v Rector and Visitors of the University of Virginia*, 515 US 819 (1995); *Zobrest v Catalina Foothills School District*, 509 US 1 (1993); *Lee v Weisman*, 505 US 577 (1992); *Allegheny County v ACLU*, 492 US 573 (1989); *Edwards v Aguillard*, 482 US 578 (1987); *Estate of Thornton v Caldor, Inc*, 472 US 703 (1985); *Wallace v Jaffree*, 472 US 38 (1985); *Lynch v Donnelly*, 465 US 668 (1984); *Marsh v Chambers*, 463 US 783 (1983); *Mueller v Allen*, 463 US 388 (1983); *Widmar v Vincent*, 454 US 263 (1981); *Stone v Graham*, 449 US 39 (1980); *Lemon v Kurtzman*, 403 US 602 (1971); *Walz v Tax Commission of City of New York*, 397 US 664 (1970); *Epperson v Arkansas*, 393 US 97 (1968); *McCollum v Board of Education*, 333 US 203 (1948); *Everson v Board of Education*, 330 US 1 (1947).

On the free exercise clause of the First Amendment, see: *Groff v DeJoy*, 600 US 447 (2023); *303 Creative LLC v Elenis*, 600 US 570 (2023); *Kennedy v Bremerton School District*, 597 US 507 (2022); *Carson v Makin*, 596 US 767 (2022); *Fulton v Philadelphia*, 593 US 522 (2021); *Trinity Lutheran Church of Columbia, Inc v Comer*, 582 US ___ (2017); *Burwell v Hobby Lobby Stores, Inc*, 573 US 682 (2014); *Hosanna-Tabor Evangelical Lutheran Church and School v EEOC*, 565 US 171 (2012); *Gonzales v O Centro Espirita Beneficente Uniao do Vegetal*, 546 US 418 (2006); *Locke v Davey*, 540 US 712 (2004); *City of Boerne v Flores*, 521 US 507 (1997); *Church of the Lukumi Babalu Aye, Inc v City of Hialeah*, 508 US 520 (1993); *Employment Division v Smith*, 494 US 872 (1990); *Lyng v Northwest Indian Cemetery Protective Ass'n*, 485 US 439 (1988); *Bowen v Roy*, 476 US 693 (1986); *Goldman v Weinberger*, 475 US 503 (1986); *Thomas v Review Board of the Indiana Employment Security Division*, 450 US 707 (1981); *Wisconsin v Yoder*, 406 US 205 (1972); *Abington School District v Schempp*, 374 US 203 (1963); *Sherbert v Verner*, 374 US 398 (1963); *Engel v Vitale*, 370 US 421 (1962); *Torcaso v Watkins*, 367 US 488 (1961); *McGowan v Maryland*, 366 US

jurisprudence looms – on 31 July 2023, ten plaintiffs filed a lawsuit against the State of Oklahoma challenging the proposed establishment of a publicly-funded religious school.[79] Until now, a wall of separation, admittedly shaky over the last decade, would have prevented such outright public funding of a religious school. But the Supreme Court decision in *Kennedy v Bremerton*[80] that allowed for accommodation of prayer in publicly-funded schools signalled that a new majority of that Court might be willing to consider a broader accommodation along the lines proposed by Oklahoma. The Oklahoma challenge will no doubt end in the Supreme Court.[81] There is no need, though, for present purposes, to examine the entirety of the Supreme Court jurisprudence in detail. Instead, because it is very likely that in *DOGS*, the High Court has already, at least partially, made use of American case law in relation to the establishment guarantee,[82] it is enough to examine its treatment in the Supreme Court in order to demonstrate what American precedent offers in relation to s 116.

The most important Supreme Court decision interpreting the Establishment Clause was, and likely remains, the 1971 case of *Lemon v Kurtzman*,[83] in which Chief Justice Burger enunciated what has come to be known as the "entanglement" or "*Lemon*" test. The test has three prongs, synthesised by Chief Justice Burger from the Court's earlier Establishment Clause jurisprudence: "First, the statute must have a secular legislative purpose; second, its principal or primary effect must be one that neither advances nor inhibits religion …; finally, the statute must not foster an excessive government

420 (1961); *Braunfeld v Brown*, 366 US 599 (1961); *Zorach v Clauson*, 343 US 306 (1952); *Girouard v United States*, 328 US 61 (1946); *West Virginia State Board of Education v Barnette*, 319 US 624 (1943); *Minersville School District v Gobitis*, 310 US 586 (1940); *Reynolds v United States*, 98 US 145 (1878).

On Article VI, cl 3, § 2, see: *Board of Education v Grumet*, 512 US 687 (1994); *Torcaso v Watkins*, 367 US 488 (Black J); *American Communications Association v Douds*, 339 US 382 (1950); *Girouard v United States*, 328 US 61 (1946); *Bridges v California*, 314 US 252 (1941); *Cantwell v Connecticut*, 310 US 296 (1940); *Church of the Holy Trinity v United States*, 143 US 457 (1892).

79 *Okplac Inc et al v Statewide Virtual Charter School Board et al* (District Court of Oklahoma County, State of Oklahoma (filed July 31, 2023) https://ffrf.org/uploads/legal/OkComplFinSigned.pdf. See also Adam Kemp, 'In Oklahoma, a New Test of Religion in Public Schools', *PBS NewsHour* (4 August 2023) https://www.pbs.org/newshour/nation/a-new-lawsuit-is-trying-to-block-the-nations-first-religious-public-charter-school; Charles J Russo, 'Faith-based Charter Schools: An Emerging and Contentious Legal Frontier', *The Catholic World Report* (8 August 2023) https://www.catholicworldreport.com/2023/08/08/faith-based-charter-schools-an-emerging-and-contentious-legal-frontier/.

80 *Kennedy v Bremerton School District*, 142 SCt 2407 (2022).

81 Kemp (n 78); Russo (n 78).

82 See Paul T Babie, 'What Happened When *DOGS* Tasted *Lemon*: Australian Reflections on the Contemporary Relevance of Chief Justice Burger's Opinion in *Lemon v Kurtzman* (2022) 49 *Rutgers Law Record* 155.

83 *Lemon v Kurtzman*, 403 US 602 (1971).

entanglement with religion".[84] The test has since been widely recognised as adopting a "separation thesis" in the interpretation of the First Amendment, an approach requiring "that to the greatest extent possible government and religion should be separated. The government should be, as much as possible, secular; religion should be entirely in the private realm of society".[85] The adoption of entanglement as a means of ensuring strict separation represents the lasting, and recently, controversial significance of *Lemon*. It is also this entanglement standard, although used as part of allowing for some accommodation of religion in the public sphere, that has been adopted by the High Court in *DOGS*.[86]

American controversy has swirled around *Lemon* for some time; it came to a head in the Supreme Court's 2022 term, when Justice Gorsuch, in *Shurtleff v Boston* and *Kennedy v Bremerton*, characterising it as grand unified theory, wrote that "*Lemon* ignored the original meaning of the Establishment Clause, … disregarded mountains of precedent, and … substituted a serious constitutional inquiry with a guessing game".[87] As such, "*Lemon* has long since been exposed as an anomaly and a mistake,"[88] an "ahistoric alternative [that] quickly proved both unworkable in practice and unsound in its results",[89] the "'shortcomings' associated with this 'ambitiou[s]', abstract, and ahistorical approach to the Establishment Clause … so 'apparent' that this Court long ago abandoned *Lemon* and its endorsement test offshoot".[90] As such, the Court rejected "the policy outcomes *Lemon* can be manipulated to produce"[91] in favour of a test based upon original meaning, in which one finds a "more humble jurisprudence".[92] The Court turned to "history and tradition",[93] a test that makes "reference to historical practices and understandings",[94] and which "contains some helpful hallmarks that localities and lower courts can rely on".[95] Justice Gorsuch, and a majority of the Court, proposed a "line" that courts and governments "must draw between the permissible and the impermissible", which must "accor[d] with history and faithfully reflec[t] the

84 Ibid 612–3 (Burger CJ) citing *Walz v Tax Commission of City of New York*, 397 US 664, 674 (1970) (Burger CJ) (other internal citations omitted).
85 Howard Gillman & Erwin Chemerinsky, *The Religion Clauses: The Case for Separating Church and State* (Oxford University Press, 2020) 46.
86 See Babie (n 81).
87 *Shurtleff v City of Boston*, 142 SCt 1583, 1610 (2022) (Gorsuch J).
88 Ibid 1606.
89 Ibid 1606–07.
90 *Kennedy v Bremerton School District*, 142 SCt 2407, 2427 (2022) (Sotomayor J) (citation omitted).
91 *Shurtleff v City of Boston*, 142 SCt 1583, 1608 (Gorsuch J).
92 Ibid 1604.
93 *Kennedy v Bremerton School District*, 142 SCt 2407, 2434 (Sotomayor J).
94 Ibid 2428 (citation omitted).
95 *Shurtleff v City of Boston*, 142 SCt 1583, 1609 (Gorsuch J, concurring).

understanding of the Founding Fathers".[96] An analysis focused on original meaning and history, Justice Gorsuch suggested, "has long represented the rule rather than some 'exception' within the Court's Establishment Clause jurisprudence".[97]

It seems possible, though, that *both* entanglement and history and tradition may not only be an acceptable test, but also the relevant standard applied by the Supreme Court. Justice Sotomayor, for the minority in *Kennedy*, wrote that the "historical practices and understandings" test is one in which "this Court's settled precedents offer guidance to assist courts, governments, and the public in navigating [Establishment Clause] tensions".[98] Yet, it cannot be a general test, nor one that should be the exclusive focus of a court,[99] because it "offers essentially no guidance" for government officials who must ensure that church and state remain separate.[100] As such, history and tradition cannot be the sole test, but it can undoubtedly work in concert with entanglement, providing historical examples of government involvement with religion that falls on either side of excessive entanglement. And, in fact, the High Court may already have taken that very approach. In *DOGS*, Justice Gibbs demonstrated that by looking at prior case law – history – one can determine which side of the line of the entanglement test a given set of facts falls.[101]

B Violations: Social Science Evidence

The use of social science evidence in constitutional human rights litigation undoubtedly faces difficulties.[102] Jonathan Yovel and Elizabeth Mertz write that:

> there are pervasive tensions impeding a direct translation between social science and law. The two fields have vastly different epistemologies, metadiscursive rules, and social purposes. On the one hand, social science stands poised to provide useful and incisive critiques of legal systems and assumptions. Social science is also a promising source of information and critical questioning when the law attempts to interpret and understand aspects of society that social scientists are trained to analyse.[103]

96 *Kennedy v Bremerton School District*, 142 SCt 2407, 2428 (Gorsuch J).
97 Ibid (citation omitted).
98 *Kennedy v. Bremerton School District*, 142 SCt 2407, 2445 (Sotomayor J).
99 Ibid 2450.
100 Ibid.
101 *DOGS* (n 43), 602 (Gibbs J) citing *Tilton v Richardson*, 403 US 672 (1971); *Hunt v McNair*, 413 US 734 (1973); *Roemer v Maryland Board of Public Works*, 426 US 736 (1976); *Committee for Public Education and Religious Liberty v Regan*, 444 US 646 (1980).
102 Jonathan Yovel and Elizabeth Mertz, 'The Role of Social Science in Legal Decisions' in Austin Sarat (ed), *The Blackwell Companion to Law and Society* (Blackwell, 2004) 410–31.
103 Ibid 427–8.

Those authors "urge[...] caution in attempting to translate between the two",[104] recognising that "[d]ata are used in the courtroom in a manner consistent with the standards of the legal community, not the social sciences community".[105] Still, while attended by difficulties, there is also little doubt that much in social science evidence can be useful in the judicial determination of human rights violations. As Yovel and Mertz write, "[i]t is to be hoped that future progress in this dialogue will involve more of a compromise, enabling the legal system to bring to fuller fruition the promise of social science as a source of critique and information".[106]

The United States pioneered the use of social science evidence as a means of establishing rights violations. Prior to 1908, the history of the American constitutional jurisprudence was marked by "legal formalism" or "classical legal thought", which viewed "law [...] as a 'science' that could be separate from politics and that legal reasoning could be sharply distinguished from moral or political reasoning".[107] In 1908, however, the Supreme Court accepted a "Brandeis brief" (named for the first lawyer – and later Supreme Court Justice – to use it: Louis D Brandeis),[108] in *Muller v Oregon*,[109] a document that "contain[ed] two pages of legal argument and ninety-five pages of sociological and economic data about the conditions of working women's lives in factories ... highlighting social and economic reality, suggest[ing] that the trouble with the existing law was that it was out of touch with that reality". This "legal 'realism' sought to undermine the claim of the old order that its legal categories and modes of legal reasoning were natural, neutral, and necessary".[110]

While critics pointed to the questionable objectivity of the social science evidence presented in such briefs,[111] Rustad & Koenig write that the Brandeis brief "was one of the first instances where an advocate emphasized the law-in-action over the formalistic pronouncements of the law-in-the-books". It came to be utilised in order to marshal social science evidence demonstrating violations of the rights contained in the Bill of Rights. Today, "[t]he term 'Brandeis brief' has come to refer to any use of policy-oriented extra-legal arguments in briefs. Frequently, constitutional litigators employ the Brandeis brief to bring facts to the Court that do not appear in the record below".[112]

104 Ibid 428.

105 Rosemary J Erickson and Rita J Simon, *The Use of Social Science Data in Supreme Court Decisions* (University of Illinois Press, 1998) 149.

106 Yovel and Mertz (n 101), 429.

107 Morton J Horwitz, *The Transformation of American Law 1870–1960* (Oxford University Press, 1992) 6.

108 Noga Morag-Levine, 'Facts, Formalism, and the Brandeis Brief: The Origins of a Myth' 2013(1) *University of Illinois Law Review* 59.

109 Muller v Oregon, 208 US 412, 423 (1908) (Brewer J).

110 Horwitz (n 106), 209. See also Morag-Levine (n 107).

111 Morag-Levine (n 107), 99.

112 Michael Rustad & Thomas Koenig, 'The Supreme Court and Junk Social Science: Selective Distortion in Amicus Briefs' (1993) 72 *North Carolina Law Review* 91, 93, n 5 (footnotes omitted).

They are frequently used by amicus curiae or "friends of the court"[113] (which allows "organizations deeply interested in an area of constitutional law … [to] petition for and be granted permission to participate" in the litigation, especially in the Supreme Court),[114] and as a result "[t]he United States Supreme Court has used social science evidence for many decades. Social science data is now routinely injected into the Court's decision-making through litigant briefs, expert social scientific testimony, Brandeis briefs, and judicial notice".[115] "Today … many amici are lobbyists or representatives of private interests with a direct or indirect stake in the outcome of the litigation. The number of amici filing in United States Supreme Court cases has increased in recent years".[116]

There is little doubt that "[t]hird-party amici providing social science data can be an important check against governmental abuse of power". Rustad & Koenig argue that:

> The alternative to admitting social science data is to return to nineteenth century legal formalism, according to which justices or other powerful groups substitute their own normative beliefs for scientific findings. *Korematsu v United States* illustrates the hazard of exclusive reliance on abstract doctrinal reasoning. There, the Court sanctioned a civilian exclusion order requiring the wholesale removal of Japanese-Americans from the west coast. The Court's decision was based on the government's untested assertion that substantial numbers of Japanese-Americans were likely to engage in treasonous activities. Even famous civil libertarians like Justice Hugo Black accepted the claim of Japanese-American disloyalty without a scintilla of social scientific data. Justice Murphy dissented from the majority opinion, arguing that the removal order was based upon 'misinformation, half-truths and insinuations'. … Sociological surveys, focus groups, anthropological studies, or any accepted empirical research would have shown the questionable grounds for the Court's decision in *Korematsu*.[117]

Assuming that the s 116 guarantees are individual rights – taking Murphy J's American-inspired view, as opposed to the current limitation on legislative power view – a litigant remains faced with the need to demonstrate that the governmental conduct in question resulted in a violation of the relevant guarantee in s 116. While an approach founded on strict and complete legalism would go no further than relevant legal materials – cases and legislation

113 See Paul M Collins, *Friends of the Supreme Court: Interest Groups and Judicial Decision Making* (Oxford University Press, 2008) 37–74.

114 Arthur A Leff, 'The Leff Dictionary of Law: A Fragment' (1985) 94 *Yale Law Journal* 1855, 2012.

115 Rustad & Koenig (n 111), 93.

116 Ibid 96–7 (footnotes omitted).

117 Ibid 161–2, citing *Korematsu v United States*, 323 US 214, 218–9 and 223 (1944) (Black J).

– a wider use of extrinsic materials, including social science evidence of the type used in Brandeis briefs, would allow the court to examine the effect of impugned legislation on the s 116 guarantees. And the High Court itself may already countenance the use of extrinsic materials, most notably those that reveal "the relevance of a historical approach to assist in understanding the meaning of words used or the reconstruction of the purposes embodied in or behind the text of the Constitution".[118] But what about social science evidence?

If the High Court were to use American materials as part of the interpretative process in assessing violations of s 116, that would open the possibility of making use of social science evidence as a means of determining whether a claimed infringement constitutes an excess of legislative power. Indeed, it is the very exercise of legislative power that may, itself, rely upon social science evidence as background to the enactment of statutes. That being so, social science evidence may provide important insights into the operation of such legislation during constitutional litigation; as such, "some courts will invite, and able counsel will know to prepare and submit, 'Brandeis briefs', in which social science and other evidence is compiled and presented on the justice and rights compliance of the measure in dispute" and that would "assist in putting more information before the court".[119]

Assuming, then, that a violation animating the operation of s 116 has been found – those guarantees encompassing a broader substantive protection than a limitation on legislative power – what might American constitutional materials tell us about the justifiability of that infringement? The next section turns to that question.

C Limitations: Levels of Scrutiny

No right is absolute, and there will certainly be cases in which a claimed government infringement of a guaranteed right will be treated by a court as legitimate, or justifiable, for some pressing reason – public safety, public health, public order, national defence, and so on. Balancing the competing individual and community interests, or proportionality analysis, characterises this stage of the judicial function. And, as with assessing the violation itself, social science evidence proves useful, as part of "evaluati[ing] … the necessity of measures and the comparable efficacy of unchosen alternative measures, as well as

118 Morris and Allsop (n 4), 328. See *Cole v Whitfield* (1988) 165 CLR 360, 385 (Mason CJ, Wilson, Brennan, Deane, Dawson, Toohey, and Gaudron JJ); *A-G (Cth) (Ex rel McKinlay) v Commonwealth* (1975) 135 CLR 1; *McGinty v Western Australia* (1996) 186 CLR 140; *R v Trade Practices Tribunal; Ex parte St George County Council* (1974) 130 CLR 533; *Ng v The Queen* (2003) 217 CLR 521, 526 [9] (Gleeson CJ, Gummow, Hayne, Callinan and Heydon JJ).

119 Grégoire Webber, 'Judicial Power and Judicial Responsibility' (2017) 36(2) *University of Queensland Law Journal* 205, 218, 219.

evaluations of benefits and burdens in determinations of overall balance".[120] But what is the standard that is applied to such proportionality testing?

American experience provides insight into how the judiciary may develop a standard when one is not expressly provided by the constitutional text. What seems clear from First Amendment jurisprudence is that a court must engage sequentially in two inquiries. The first assesses whether the conduct is protected and has been infringed by government action. If it is, a court must apply a standard in order to determine whether that infringement can be justified because of a pressing government concern or objective. It is probably impossible to identify with any precision the precise standard that American courts apply; rather, the tests of vagueness[121] and overbreadth,[122] as well as the standards of scrutiny[123] have been applied in cases depending on the circumstances. The most that can be said about these tests is that *some* standard must be applied. One of those tests, however, predominates in relation to the religion clauses: strict scrutiny.

The various levels of American constitutional scrutiny – rational basis, intermediate, and strict[124] – developed from the famous footnote 4 of *United States v Carolene Products Co.*[125] Crafted by judicial interpretation, levels of scrutiny analysis establishes the standard by which limitations imposed upon the rights of a religious group must take the least restrictive or narrowest means possible.[126] Such limitations must either demonstrate (i) a rational relationship to a legitimate governmental purpose[127] with a strong, but rebuttable, presumption of treating legislative limitations as constitutional,[128] or (ii) a compelling state interest,[129] in which case limits must be drawn as narrowly as possible. Strict scrutiny appears to be the level of analysis most frequently applied to violations of a protected category of free exercise.[130] As applied to free exercise,

120 Ibid 218.
121 Johnny H Killian & George A Costello (eds), *The Constitution of the United States of America: Analysis and Interpretation – Annotations of Cases Decided by the Supreme Court of the United States* (United States Government Printing Office, 1992) 1164–70.
122 Ibid.
123 Ibid.
124 See Mario Barnes & Erwin Chemerinsky, 'The Once & Future Equal Protection Doctrine?' (2011) 43 *Connecticut Law Review* 1059, 1076–90; Ashutosh Bhagwat, 'Hard Cases and the (D)evolution of Constitutional Doctrine' (1998) 30 *Connecticut Law Review* 961, 963.
125 *United States v Carolene Products Company*, 304 US 144, 152, n 4 (1938) (Stone J).
126 *Sherbert v Verner*, 374 US 398 (1963). See also Richard H Fallon, Jr, 'Strict Judicial Scrutiny' (2007) 54 *UCLA Law Review* 1267; Eugene Volokh, 'Freedom of Speech, Permissible Tailoring, and Transcending Strict Scrutiny' (1996) 144 *University of Pennsylvania Law Review* 2417.
127 *City of Cleburne v Cleburne Living Centre*, 473 US 432 (1985).
128 See *Hazelwood School District v Kuhlmeier*, 484 US 260 (1988).
129 *Korematsu v United States*, 323 US 214 (1944).
130 Adam Winkler, 'Fatal in Theory and Strict in Fact: An Empirical Analysis of Strict Scrutiny in the Federal Courts' (2019) 59 *Vanderbilt Law Review* 793; Fallon (n 125); Volokh (n 125); Killian & Costello (n 120) 1142–69; Kenneth R Thomas & Larry M Eig (eds), *The*

strict scrutiny appears to result in an outcome that is "strict in theory and fatal in fact".[131]

It is important to bear in mind that the levels of scrutiny are judicially crafted standards – they appear nowhere in the constitutional text. That is significant, for it means that if such standards can be created in the American setting, the same is possible in Australia. And the judicial crafting of a limitations or proportionality standard for use in Australian constitutional litigation is not far-fetched. One finds its seeds in Latham CJ's judgement in *ACJW*:[132]

> The interpretation and application of the guarantee cannot, under our Constitution, be left to Parliament. If the guarantee is to have any real significance it must be left to the courts of justice to determine its meaning and to give effect to it by declaring the invalidity of laws which infringe it and by declining to enforce them. The courts will therefore have the responsibility of determining whether a particular law can fairly be regarded as a law to protect the existence of the community, or whether, on the other hand, it is a law 'for prohibiting the free exercise of any religion'.[133]

But even if what Latham CJ said is nothing more than *obiter* – which it very likely was not – more recently the High Court has shown itself quite willing to engage in this sort of craftsmanship in relation to the implied freedom of political communication, defining a three-step standard by which to test the justifiability of limitations that may be placed upon the implied freedom by either the Commonwealth or the states.[134] Taking Latham CJ's entrée, and using American experience with the levels of scrutiny, and especially strict scrutiny, the High Court could do the same for s 116.

VI Conclusion: Methodology Summarised

A constitution, by its very nature, uses open-ended and vague language, especially in relation to the protection of human rights, leaving it to later generations and other institutions of government, to determine the precise meaning of its words in specific circumstances. If it were not, it would fail as a living document responsive to the changing needs and demands of the people for

---

Constitution of the United States of America: Analysis and Interpretation – Annotations of Cases Decided by the Supreme Court of the United States (United States Government Printing Office, Centennial ed, 2014) 1142–69.

131 Winkler (n 198).

132 *ACJW* (n 41), 126–7, 131–2 (Latham CJ), and see 159–60 (Williams J), 148–9 (Rich J), 154–5 (Starke J).

133 Ibid 131–2 (Latham CJ).

134 *McCloy v New South Wales* (2015) 257 CLR 178, 193–5 [2] (French CJ, Kiefel, Bell and Keane JJ) (citations omitted). And see also *Brown v Tasmania* (2017) 261 CLR 328.

whom it constitutes a government. But that open-endedness and vagueness comes at a cost, and that is the inability of the judiciary, the principal body charged with interpretation and adaptation, to locate within the text itself a means of undertaking those dual tasks. In other words, a constitution, and especially protections of rights, come with no user's manual to guide judges in the application of its protections to new conditions. The judges must develop those techniques themselves, as part of the response to changing context.

When a constitutional text bears a striking resemblance to an already existing constitution, indeed, when it is clear that the later text was expressly designed by its framers to adopt and adapt the provisions of an earlier text, then judges are provided with the rare opportunity to look to that earlier text and its history and the experience of judges in interpreting it as at least providing the rudiments of a user's guide. That is the case with the *Australian Constitution* generally, and s 116 specifically. And yet the Australian judges, and most notably, the High Court, have failed to seize that opportunity. Not only have the judges failed to seize that opportunity; they have actively eschewed it.

Why does it matter? It is an odd stance for Australia's judiciary to take, and one that rejects, at least implicitly, the historical reality that the *Australian Constitution*, in more than a superficial way, draws upon American experience. While not every reader will agree with the arguments advanced in this chapter, there are clear benefits that would derive from the use of American experience in the interpretation of s 116. At the very least, the possible dividends that would follow a methodology that employs American precedent – a means of interpreting the substance of s 116's guarantees, the use of a wider class of extrinsic materials in determining whether those guarantees have been violated, and the guidance provided in assessing whether a claimed governmental intrusion is nonetheless justified – would at least provide a place from which to start, and a set of standards for the judges either to accept or reject. And that would, in turn, allow s 116 to play a role in Australian political life that its current interpretation denies it.

Further Reading:

For analysis of the methods used in this chapter, see Chapter 15 – Section IV – subsection A *The Doctrinal Method*; B *The Historical* Method; C *The Functionalist Method*; D *The Analytical Method*; F *The Yardstick Method*.

For the author's rejoinder and reflection, see Appendix Section III.

For a response to this chapter, see Chapter 7.1.

For an analysis involving Australia, see Chapters 8, 11, 13, and 14.

7.1 Response to P T Babie, "American Constitutional Experience and the Interpretation of the Australian Religion Guarantees"

Matt Watson[1]

P T Babie's excellent chapter argues that were Australian judges, in interpreting s 116 of the Australian Constitution, to make "explicit use of American materials"[2] relating to the religion clauses found within that country's Constitution, this would "rejuvenate" s 116.[3] Specifically, it is claimed that such consideration of American precedent holds the promise of allowing Australian judges to better appreciate the substance of s 116's protections, to "use a wider class of extrinsic materials in determining whether those guarantees have been violated",[4] and to benefit from American jurisprudential guidance on the circumstances in which "a claimed governmental intrusion [on freedom of religion guarantees] is nonetheless justified".[5]

Babie remarks, uncontroversially, that "a constitution, and especially protections of rights, come with no user's manual to guide judges in the application of its protections to new conditions".[6] However, Babie notes that in fact – given that s 116 is not just strikingly similar to the religion clauses contained within the American Constitution, but is the product of a constitutional drafting process that "expressly adverted"[7] to those provisions – the American "text and its history and the experience of judges in interpreting it" can be seen to "at least provid[e] the rudiments of a user's guide" for Australian judges.[8]

In reflecting on methodology, as we are doing in this section of the book, it is worth noting that Babie's core claim is simultaneously substantive and methodological – ie, it is a substantive, normative claim about the appropriate

1 Senior Lecturer, TC Beirne School of Law, University of Queensland.
2 P T Babie, 'American Constitutional Experience and the Interpretation of the Australian Religion Guarantees' in Renae Barker, Camilla Baasch Andersen and Mohammad Rasmi Alumari (eds) Comparative Approaches to Law and Religion (Routledge 2025) 148.
3 Ibid.
4 Ibid 169.
5 Ibid.
6 Ibid.
7 Ibid 147.
8 Ibid 961.

DOI: 10.4324/9781003397311-12

methodology that Australian jurists ought to employ in adjudicating s 116 cases. Further, it is somewhat striking to me that the methodology Babie employs to make this claim about judicial methodology overlaps significantly with that of my own chapter – notwithstanding that whereas Babie's chapter aims to advance what is (again) an ultimately normative claim, mine self-consciously aims at explicating doctrinal differences without explicit comment on the virtues or vices of the divergent approaches that have been adopted.

Straightforwardly, both of our chapters combine a descriptive, comparative analysis of judicial interpretation with an appeal to history. But more than this, I see a special affinity between our methodologies in that I want to insist that we can't fully understand the state of the law in Canada or America (or Australia, of course, for that matter) when it comes to the permissibility of state funding for religious schools without an appreciation of the wider socio-historical context. Babie appears similarly committed to the importance of paying due regard to history as his argument unfolds –the relevant historical picture for his purposes being not just the history of how s 116 of the Australian Constitution came to be, but also the historical evolution of the High Court of Australia's propensity to consult American case law in its interpretation of the Constitution generally.[9]

Babie also insightfully points out that owing to the reticence of Australian judges to consider American freedom of religion jurisprudence in their interpretations of s 116, the Australian legal community has missed out on a chance to gain "a wider, substantive understanding of those clauses"[10]– precisely the sort of wide-lens understanding I endeavoured to provide in my analysis of the socio-historical factors that have shaped American and Canadian law around public funding for religious schools.

Finally, I agree with Babie that a greater willingness to make explicit use of American judicial materials holds out the appealing prospect of allowing the Australian judiciary to more fully appreciate s 116 "for what it is: the protection of a fundamental freedom" and not merely a "limitation on legislative power".[11] Indeed, this more full-blooded interpretation of s 116 is what properly reckoning with history – both Australia's and America's – appears to demand.

9 Ibid, Section III of Chapter 7 'American Precedent in General Interpretation'].
10 Ibid.
11 Ibid 166.

8 Refusal of Life Saving Medical Treatment by Mature Minors – A Comparative Analysis of Australia, Canada, and the United Kingdom

Renae Barker[1] *and Camilla Baasch Andersen*[2]

I Introduction

As Abella J has observed, "The tension between autonomy and child protection is real, often dramatic, and always painful".[3]

In January 1959, baby Stephen Jehu died after his father, Alvin Jehu, refused to consent to a blood transfusion.[4] In the wake of baby Stephen's death, the subsequent coronial inquest, and the murder trial of Mr Jehu, all Australian states and territories introduced legislation permitting medical practitioners to administer blood transfusions to minors without the consent of their parents.[5] Legislation regulating the provision of medical treatment to minors continues in Australia, stemming from these so-called "blood laws" introduced beginning in the 1950s. The focus of the legislation is on authorising medical practitioners to provide medical treatment to minors without parental consent where such treatment is likely to be lifesaving and, at the same time, on protecting the medical practitioners from legal claims for battery brought by the child or their parents. However, since these laws were introduced over half a century ago societal attitudes to the decision-making capacity of mature minors has changed. Parents are no longer automatically regarded by the medical profession as the sole proxy consent givers for children. Instead, mature minors are recognised as having increased autonomy and rights over their own bodily integrity, including in the provision of medical treatment. This increased

1 Senior Lecturer, Law School, University of Western Australia, Honorary Research Fellow Centre for Muslim States and Societies.

2 Professor, Law School, University of Western Australia.

3 *A.C. v Manitoba (Director of Child and Family Services)* [2009] 2 SCR 181, [83] ('*AC*').

4 Renae Barker, *State and Religion: The Australian Story* (Routledge, 2009), 212–213. (State and Religion).

5 Ibid 213.

DOI: 10.4324/9781003397311-13

autonomy exists on a sliding scale commensurate with the developing capacity of the child.[6]

This shift in societal attitude has been reflected in common law decisions such as *Gillick v West Norfolk and Wisbesh Area Health Authority* and *Department of Health and Community Services* v *JWB* ('*Marion's Case*'). It is also reflected in the articles of the *United Nations Convention on the Rights of the Child* ('*CRC*'). For example, under Articles 5 and 14 of the CRC, States must respect parents' rights and duties to provide direction to their child in exercising their rights under the CRC "in a manner consistent with the evolving capacities of the child". Similarly, Article 12 provides for "a child who is capable of forming his or her own view the right to express those views in all matters affecting the child, the views of the child being given due weight in accordance with the age and maturity of the child".[7]

With the arguable exception of South Australia,[8] the shift in attitudes towards the medical decision-making capability of children has not been reflected in Australian legislation. Australian legislation remains paternalistic, handing decision-making over to medical practitioners without requiring them to consider the views of the child nor, in most cases, the child's best interests. In some cases, the only consideration is whether the proposed medical treatment is potentially lifesaving.[9] Given the shift in the international and common law understandings of the decision-making capacity of minors, it is time to reconsider the Australian "blood laws" and look for alternative mechanisms for promoting the best interests of children and respecting their evolving capacities in medical decision-making.

In January 2021, the High Court of the United Kingdom (UK) in *Re X (a child) (No 2) An NHS Trust v X* ('*Re X*') handed down a detailed judgement determining that a 16-year-old could be compelled to undergo blood transfusions against her wishes while at the same time refusing to make a "rolling order" for future blood transfusions should her ongoing medical condition require them.[10] In 2009, the Supreme Court of Canada in *AC v Manitoba (Director of Child and Family Services)* ('*AC*') handed down an equally detailed decision in the case of a 14-year-old upholding the constitutional validity of laws authorising courts to order medical treatment against the wishes of a child under the age of 16 by defining the best interest of the child to include taking into account their evolving capacity to make medical decisions.[11] Unlike many cases concerning lifesaving medical treatment for minors, the children's

6 Jane Fortin, *Children's Rights and the Developing Law* (Cambridge University Press, 2009) 146–147.
7 See AC (n 2) [93].
8 See *Consent to Medical Treatment and Palliative Care Act 1995* s6 and s12(b).
9 See *Human Tissue and Transplant Act 1982* (WA) and *Children and Young Persons (Care and Protection) Act 1998* (NSW).
10 *Re X (a child) (No 2) An NHS Trust v X* [2021] EWHC 65 (fam) ('Re X').
11 *AC* (n 1).

lives were not in imminent danger at the time these courts heard their cases. In *Re X*, the imminent medial emergency had been resolved via a previous order that X receive a blood transfusion and the main issue was whether a pre-emptive order for future blood transfusions should be made. AC was an appeal against previous decisions ordering that AC undergo a blood transfusion. The required blood transfusion having already taken place, the issues in the case were primarily a matter of principle.[12]

In both cases, the Courts were able to take the necessary time to carefully weigh all of the arguments and provide detailed reasons for their conclusions. This presents a unique opportunity to compare the approaches of these two common law jurisdictions to the important issue of the state-ordered medical treatment of mature minors who refuse treatment. While the outcomes of these two cases was functionally the same, the underlying legislative frameworks are different. Both legislative frameworks also differ markedly from those in Australia, with perhaps the exception of South Australia, presenting an opportunity to compare holistically the approaches of these three jurisdictions to the refusal of lifesaving medical treatment by mature minors and assess the suitability of the English and Welsh, and Manitoban approaches for Australia.

This chapter is divided into six sections. Section I sets out the background and premise of this analysis. Section II outlines our methodological approach and key methodology decisions and challenges. Sections III and IV provide a comparative analysis of the law with Section III focusing on the legislative and human rights frameworks while Section IV analyses five cases drawn from the UK, Canada, and Australia. Section V contains a discussion drawing on that analysis before offering some conclusions and discussion of the viability of a transplant of the English and Welsh, and Manitoban approaches to Australia. Finally, the chapter concludes in Section VI by summarising transplant thinking as it applies to the analysis outlined in this chapter and the conclusion reached in Section V.

II Methodology

One of the trickier aspects of comparative legal methodology is that it is not one approach or one method, but rather an elaborate pick-and-mix of different approaches from different disciplines and perspectives combined to support the holistic interpretation of a specific idea or goal which the relevant comparison pursues. As von Hoecke puts it: "There is no agreement on the kind of methodology to be followed, nor even on the methodologies that could be

12 Ibid [120]–[121]; AC was also no longer under the age of 16, meaning the future medical treatment would be governed by different legislative provisions.

followed".[13] Palmer has expressed this as a "sliding scale" of approaches,[14] and others characterise it as an epistemology of varying methods designed to clarify the cultural position of a legal phenomenon.[15] However defined, it raises the thorny issue that any approach can be critiqued and viewed as significant, for the simple reason that any perspective can have cultural significance on a legal aspect of a society. For the present chapter, that raises the ever-perplexing challenge of how best to compose a method that can measure how different societies with different legal systems address the challenge of children's blood transfusions and their legitimate refusal. This, in turn, raises the questions: What do we include? What do we not include? And – importantly – how do we justify it?

When we initially began composing this chapter in April 2021, we wanted to take a very functionalist approach to defining and measuring the rights of a child and their interests as represented within and outside the scope of their legal guardians. As part of the process, which we label our "intermediary jurisprudence", in developing a bespoke methodology for a comparative project, we began to look for data from previous legal comparisons on the significance of children's ages in different legal systems, and we found very little comparative work had been done. Thus, to establish a yardstick for comparing the rights of children in relation to medical needs and blood transfusion, we first needed to develop a method for defining children and their relative legal rights in other jurisdictions. Consequently, we had to put this research on hold while completing the necessary functional building block for how to measure the relative legal attitudes to children in differing legal jurisdictions. The results of this, initially developed for a multi-jurisdictional, seven-state society within Australia, was published in 2024. In the paper, we set up a very law-centred analytical yardstick for measuring children's relative rights in law, using a traffic light system for measuring how much autonomy children are given in different societies based solely on legislative instruments: measuring attitudes to law regarding children.[16] This yardstick has limitations, as the paper describes, which are inherently carried over into this chapter: A) it is highly functional, looking solely at law, and risks looking at legal instruments outside their cultural interpretational context and so may be inaccurate in places, and B) it faces the challenge that age is just a number, and the actual maturity of children is

13 Mark Van Hoecke, 'Methodology of Comparative Legal Research' (2015) 12 *Law and Method* 1.

14 Vernon Valentine Palmer, 'From Lerotholi to Lando: Some Examples of Comparative Law Methodology (2005) 53(1) *The American Journal of Comparative Law* 261–290.

15 Mohammad Rasmi Alumari, Camilla Andersen and Jeanette Høj Jensen, 'A New Understanding of Comparative Methodology – An Exploration of the Intermediary Jurisprudence of Comparative Legal Studies' [2025] *The Journal of Comparative Law* [forthcoming].

16 Renae Barker and Camilla Andersen, 'The Methodology of Measuring the Rights of the Child: The Australian Model Advancing an International Study' (2023) 49(2) *Monash University Law Review* 191–224.

not always accurately measured by the ages represented in legislation, which is, in turn, sometimes dealt with by flexible applications and interpretations or complex mechanisms in some societies for the emancipation of children. In that paper, and here, we acknowledge our awareness of these inaccuracies; however, our objective is to present a broad-brush snapshot of the law in this area in different jurisdictions before looking at some of the specific nuances for the jurisdictions chosen. To that end, this chapter draws not only on functional comparison of the legal age of maturity of a child but also examines the compatibilities of other aspects of the legal system and societies, including relevant human rights frameworks and religious demographics. It also includes a content analysis extracting the key themes from five cases chosen as representative of their relevant jurisdictions to determine the thematic focus of the judiciary when determining these challenging cases. We have, therefore, employed a multiplicity of methods to provide a more holistic answer to our initial questions of whether the English and Welsh, or Manitoban approaches could be employed in Australia to provide better recognition of the evolving capacities of the child, and to better consider the child's bests interests and views in a holistic way.

A Jurisdiction and Case Law Selection

In selecting jurisdictions and case law, we were guided by an approach advocated by Seawright and Gerring,[17] based on the aim of the paper. Since our main goal is to consider the viability of any alternative legislative frameworks that Australia (and, hence, all Australian States) could adopt for dealing with adolescents who refuse lifesaving medical treatment, we needed to ensure compatibility across the most disparate of Australian States in this area, taking a functionalist, pragmatic approach to the viability of shared transplantations. As identified by Barker in *State and Religion,* laws regulating the refusal of lifesaving medical treatment are state-based and fall into two broad categories:

> First, those that specifically deal with blood transfusions to minors and second those that are more general in their application, dealing with lifesaving medical procedures carried out on a minor.[18]

The Australian Capital Territory, Queensland, Tasmania, Victoria, and Western Australia fall into the first category; while the Northern Territory, New South Wales, and South Australia fall into the second. Considering legislation and case law from all seven jurisdictions is beyond the range of this

17 Jason Seawright and John Gerring, 'Case Selection Techniques in Case Study Research: A Menu of Qualitative and Quantitative Options' (2008) 61(2) *Political Research Quarterly* 294, 301–302.

18 Barker, 'State and Religion' (n 2) 210.

chapter, which is intended as a scoping exercise to determine the feasibility of legal transplant, rather than the specificity of its implementation.[19] We therefore decided to select one jurisdiction from each category, along with South Australia. South Australia was selected due to the existence of section 6 of the *Consent to Medical Treatment and Palliative Care Act 1995* ('*SA Act*'), which, as will be discussed in more detail in following sections, is relatively unique.[20]

In order to select the other two Australian jurisdictions, we first selected the three cases for analysis as case studies of the Australian law. Cases considered for selection were drawn from the Australian literature on the refusal of medical treatment by adolescents.[21] The cases selected were chosen on the basis of their relative importance and prominence in the literature, the age of the children (over 15), the medical procedure refused, and which of the two categories of laws operate in that jurisdiction. We chose to focus on cases involving blood transfusions specifically because (1) the so called "blood laws" in some Australian jurisdictions only deal with this type of medical procedure, and (2) as this brings in the element of religion, as a common reason for refusal of blood transfusions is religious belief, necessitating a careful consideration of the religious compatibility of the jurisdictions under consideration. In the case of South Australia, we were unable to identify a relevant case involving a mature minor. Recent South Australian cases involve children aged three,[22]

19 For an comparative analysis of the legal maturity of the child in all seven Australian jurisdiction see Barker and Andersen (n 14).

20 See Seawright and Gerring (n 15): 'Influential Case' and 'Deviant Case' categories.

21 See for example Nicholas Lennings, 'Children and Refusal of Medical Treatment: In Urgent Need of Reform' (2013) 21(1) *Journal of Law and Medicine* 122–141; S Woolley, 'Children of Jehovah's Witnesses and Adolescent Jehovah's Witnesses: What Are Their Rights?' (2005) 90 *Archives of Disease in Childhood* 715–719; Thomas Humphrey, 'Children, Medical Treatment and Religion: Defining the Limits of Parental Responsibility' (2008) 14(1) *Australian Journal of Human Rights* 141–169; Michaela Okninski, 'Determining a Child's Best Interests When Parents Refuse Medical Treatment – *CAHS v Kiszko & Anor* [2016] FCWA 19 (2016) 13 *Bioethical Inquiry* 365–368; Davis Ranson, 'Managing Patients Who Refuse Blood Transfusion' (1999) 6 *Journal of Law and Medicine* 222–225; Linda Starr, 'Minors and Refusal of Treatment: Who Decides on the Best Interests of the Child?' (2012) 21(1) *Australian Nursing Journal* 31; Joanna Manning, 'Parental Refusal of Life-Prolonging Medical Treatment for Children: A Report from New Zealand' (2011) 8 *Journal of Law and Medicine* 263–285; Angela J Alessandri, 'Parents Know Best: Or Do They? Treatment Refusal in Paediatric Oncology' (2011) 47 *Journal of Paediatric Child Health* 628–631; Pip Trowse, 'Refusal of Medical Treatment – A Child's Prerogative?' (2010) 10(2) *Queensland University of Technology Law and Justice Journal* 191–212; Ian Freckelton and Simon McGregor, 'Refusal of Potentially Life-Saving Treatment for Minors: The Emerging International Consensus by Courts' (2016) 23(4) *Journal of Law and Medicine* 813–834; Pei-Teing Kee, 'Refusal to Consent to Treatment on Religious Grounds' (1995) 2(2) *Murdoch University Electronic Journal of Law*; Meredith Blake, 'Religious Beliefs and Medical Treatment: The Challenge of Patient Consent' (2007) 19(1) *Bond Law Review* 26–60.

22 *Women and Children's Health Network Inc v M, CN* [2013] SASC 16.

four,[23] and ten.[24] Cases involving younger children do not normally include an inquiry regarding the maturity of the child and may, therefore, weigh factors such as the child's views differently. However, for the purposes of this study, we have included *Children, Youth & Women's Health Services Inc v YJL, MHL and TL* ('*YJL*'),[25] which was decided under the relevant South Australian legislation. The relatively young age of the children in the South Australian case law should be kept in mind in relation to the analysis to come.

Another factor in determining which Australian jurisdictions and cases to consider is the existence of human rights legislation. As is discussed in more detail further on, Australia does not have a national bill or charter of rights. However, the Australian Capital Territory,[26] Queensland,[27] and Victoria,[28] do have local human rights laws which apply to those jurisdictions. During case selection, the Victorian case of *Mercy Hospital Victoria v D1& Anor*[29] ('*Mercy*') was considered for inclusion, and had it been selected would have enabled comparison between jurisdictions with and without a legislative human rights framework. However in *Mercy* Macaulay J noted that "it is difficult to be confident that D1's presently expressed choices are the product of an independently formed, carefully considered, and long-held adherence to tenets of the Jehovah's Witness faith",[30] ultimately concluding

> I am not satisfied D1 does have a sufficient understanding of the consequence of her choice. I am not convinced she has based her choice on a maturely formed and entrenched religious conviction. … In summary, I do not consider that allowing her, in effect, to choose to die or only survive with serious injuries is in her best interests taking into account a holistic view of her welfare.[31]

As a result, the case was ultimately not selected for analysis.[32]

Again, Manitoba and the UK were chosen as comparisons for the Australian jurisdictions due to the two cases which provided an unusually detailed analysis of the relevant principles, legislative and human rights framework, and

23 *Women and Children's Health Network Inc v JC* [2012] SASC 104.
24 *Children, Youth & Women's Health Services Inc v YJL, MHL and TL* [2010] SASC 175 (YJL).
25 [2010] SASC 175.
26 See *Human Rights Act 2004* (ACT).
27 See *Human Rights Act 2019* (Qld).
28 See Charter of Human Rights and Responsibilities Act 2006 *(Vic).*
29 *Mercy Hospitals Victoria v D1 & Anor* [2018] VSC 519 (31 August 2018).
30 Ibid [44].
31 Ibid [76].
32 Our decision not to include the case took into account the fact that a case from Western Australia, where the so-called 'blood laws' apply only to blood transfusions, in a similar way to Victoria, was included as well as the inclusion of a South Australian case involving a child who was similarly not classified as a mature. We were consciouse of not = skewing the analysis by the inclusion of multiple cases where the minor was considered to lack the requisite maturity.

relevant case law in these jurisdictions. These jurisdictions also offered two alternative legislative frameworks that could be adopted in Australia. In the case of the UK, due to the unique legal framework in place, the relevant laws considered apply primarily to England and Wales, rather than more broadly across the whole of the UK. References to the UK should be read as references to England and Wales unless otherwise specified.

The cases selected for analysis were *Re X* (England and Wales),[33] *AC* (Manitoba), *Minister for Health v AS* ('*AS*')[34] (Western Australia), *Sydney Children's Hospital Network v X and Other* ('*X and Other*')(New South Wales)[35] and *YJL* (South Australia).

B What Is a Mature Minor?

This chapter considers whether the laws applicable to mature minors in relation to the consent to, or refusal of, lifesaving medical treatment in either the UK or Canada can be transplanted to Australia. A threshold question, therefore, is what is a mature minor, and is the concept of a mature minor the same in Australia, Canada, and the UK?

The Committee on the Rights of the Child (CRC Committee), which is responsible for monitoring the implementation of the CRC, has not indicated a firm test for when a child may be considered mature enough to make medical decisions. How this is to be determined is, therefore, within the discretion of States.[36] In many common law jurisdictions, the assessment of the competence of a minor to consent to medical treatment is based on *Gillick v West Norfolk and Wisbesh Area Health Authority*[37] ('*Gillick*'). The doctrine, stemming from this case, which supports the medical decision-making capacity of competent minors is variously described as "Gillick-competence" or the "mature minor" doctrine.[38]

In *Gillick*, the primary issue for the court was "whether a doctor can lawfully prescribe contraception for a girl under 16 years of age without the consent of her parents".[39] The majority (Lords Fraser, Scarman and Bridge) held that it was. As Lord Scarman explained:

> ... I would hold that as a matter of law the parental right to determine whether or not their minor child below the age of 16 will have medical

33 The case selection process took place in mid-2021, prior to the handing down of *E & F (Minors: Blood Transfusions)* [2021] EWCA Civ 1888.

34 *Minister for Health v AS* (2004) 33 Fam LR 223; WASC 286; WAR 517 (AS).

35 *Sydney Children's Hospital Network v X and Other* [2013] NSWSC 368 (X and Other).

36 John Tobin, 'Article 24 the Right to Health' in John Tobin (ed) *The UN Convention on the Rights of the Child: A Commentary* (Oxford University Press, 2019) 902–969, 917.

37 *Gillick v West Norfolk and Wisbesh Area Health Authority* [1986] AC 112 (Gillick).

38 *JSC v Wren* (1986) 76 ALR 115, [57]–[58] (JSC).

39 Gillick (n 33).

> treatment terminates if and when the child achieves a sufficient understanding and intelligence to enable him or her to understand fully what is proposed.[40]

The Gillick-competence doctrine was adopted by the Australian High Court in *Marion's Case*,[41] and by the Canadian Supreme Court in *JSC v Wren*.[42] While the concept of Gillick-competence supports the ability of a mature minor to *consent to* medical treatment, it is less clear whether it supports a mature minor's ability to *refuse* the same treatment. The ability of Gillick-competence to support the refusal of medical treatment is even more doubtful where the child's life is at stake.[43]

Gillick-competence, however, is not the only way in which the law measures a child's maturity. Another way to measure how the law and, to a certain extent, the society more generally, view children and their decision-making capacity is to examine the legal minimum age for participation in various activities, or the accumulation of various rights and responsibilities.[44] This is, of course, not the only measure of how a particular jurisdiction or society views the decision-making ability and autonomy of children, however, for our purposes, it stands as a useful proxy for measuring the jurisdiction under consideration's understanding of the maturity, decision-making capacity, and autonomy of children.

As outlined by McLachlin CJ in *Gosselin v Quebec*, "age-based distinctions are a common and necessary way of ordering … society".[45] As Abella J observed "[t]hey are currently employed to determine when a person can marry, vote, drive, consent to sexual intercourse and sell property".[46]

They provide an indication of when a particular society considers a child mature enough to take on certain rights and responsibilities. Biological age is, however, a blunt tool for assessing maturity. Various factors can influence an individual child's maturity and development. Best practice would, as the CRC suggests, consider the "evolving capacities of the child" on a case-by-case basis.[47] Such an approach is, however, in most cases impractical. An electoral officer cannot practically ascertain a child's maturity when they present at the ballot box. Such an assessment both requires expertise and time, which the official does not have. As a result, 18 is generally selected as a proxy for sufficient maturity to participate in the electoral process. However, there are situ-

40 Ibid.
41 *Department of Health and Community Services* v *JWB* (1992) 175 CLR 218.
42 *JSC* (n 34).
43 See Lisa Young, Mary Anne Kenny and Geoggrey Monahan, *Children and Law in Australia* (2017 2nd edition LexisNexis Butterworths) 489–491.
44 Barker and Andersen (n 14).
45 *Gosselin v Quebe (Attorney General)* [2002] 4 SCR 429.
46 *AC* (n 1) [110].
47 See, eg, CRC Articles 5, 14, and 12, all of which talk about the maturity of the child.

ations, such as consent to medical treatment, where a more nuanced approach can be taken. In such cases, the child "is already presenting before a medical practitioner when they seek treatment".[48]

Set out in Table 8.1 is a representative sample of the minimum age at which certain activities, rights, and responsibilities are permitted under the laws of New South Wales, Western Australia, South Australia, England and Wales, and Manitoba. The legal age limits selected are those included in the 1991[49] and 1996[50] guidelines issued by the CRC Committee as to the reporting on minimum ages it wished to see in States' Party Reports. Where a jurisdiction has a range which may be dependent on certain factors, such as, for example, parental consent, the full range has been indicated, with the youngest age used for the purposes of benchmarking. Given that New South Wales, Western Australia, and South Australia are all state jurisdictions within the Australian federal system, there is significant overlap in legal minimum ages, especially where the relevant legal minimum age limit is set by federal law. However, there are a few notable deviations and, as such, they have been included separately.

As Table 8.1 shows, there is a relatively high level of consistency between the minimum ages in New South Wales, Western Australia, South Australia, England, Wales, and Manitoba. This would suggest similar attitudes about the age that children attain sufficient maturity to engage in these activities. The similarities in terms of the minimum age of criminal responsibility is particularly striking. While the minimum age in Manitoba is two years higher than in the Australian and UK jurisdictions, all are notably much lower than the international standard. While the CRC does not set a minimum age of criminal responsibility under Article 40(1)(c), States' Parties are required to account for a child's age and are, in effect, required to establish a minimum age for criminal responsibility.[51] In its 2007 General Comment on *Children's Rights in Juvenile Justice*, the CRC committee commented that 12 was "the absolute minimum age",[52] and encouraged States to set a high minimum age of criminal responsibility at 14, or even 16.[53] In its 2019 General Comment

48 David Archer and John Tobin, 'Article 1: The Definition of a Child' in John Tobin (ed) *The UN Convention on the Rights of the Child* (Oxford University Press, 2019) 21–40, 30.

49 Committee on the Rights of the Child, *General Guidelines regarding the For and Content of Initial Reports to Be Submitted by State Parties under Article 44, paragraph 1(a) of the Convention*, UN doc CRC/C/5 (30 October 1991), 3.

50 Committee on the Rights of the Child, *General Comment No 20* (2016) *on the Implementation of the Rights of the Child during Adolescence*, UN doc CRC/C/GC/20, [40].

51 John Tobin with Cate Read 'Article 40: The Rights of the Child in the Juvenile Justice System' in John Tobin (ed) *The UN Convention on the Rights of the Child* (Oxford University Press, 2019) 1596–1665, 1652.

52 Committee on the Rights of the Child, *General Comment No 10 (2007) Children's Rights in Juvenile Justice*, UN doc CRC/C/GC/10, [32].

53 John Tobin with Cate Read 'Article 40: The Rights of the Child in the Juvenile Justice System' in John Tobin (ed) *The UN Convention on the Rights of the Child* (Oxford University

Table 8.1 Minimum Ages of Participation in Australia, England and Wales, and Manitoba

	International Norms	*Australia*			*England and Wales*	*Manitoba*
		New South Wales	*Western Australia*	*South Australia*		
Consent to Sexual Interactions	15[1]	16[2]		17[3]	16[4]	16[5]
Vote	18[6]	18[7]			16–18[8]	18[9]
Purchase and Consumption of Alcohol	18	18[10]			16–18[11]	18[12]
End of Compulsory Education	15	15–17[13]	17–18[14]	16–17[15]	16–18[16]	18[17]
Marriage	18	16[18]–18[19]			16[20]	16[21]
Minimum Age of Criminal Responsibility	14[22]	10–14[23]			10[24]	12[25]
Recruitment into the Armed Forces	18	16–17[26]			16[27]	16–17[28]
Employment	15[29]	No min–15	15[30]	No min[31]	13[32]	13[33]

[1] Article 34 of the CRC provides for the protection of children from 'all forms of sexual exploitation and sexual abuse'. However, there is no internationally recognised standard for the age of consent for sexual interactions. In some countries there is no minimum age, others prohibit sexual interactions before marriage, while others set the minimum age at a variety of ages up to the age of majority. See Michael Richards, 'Why the Age of Sexual Consent Continues to Be a Worldwide Challenge', *the Conversation* (online, 4 April 2018) https://theconversation.com/why-the-age-of-sexual-consent-continues-to-be-a-worldwide-challenge-94334.

[2] *Crimes Act 1900* (NSW) s. 66C; *Criminal Code Act Compilation Act 1913* (WA) s. 321.

[3] *Criminal Law Consolidation Act 1935* (SA) s 49.

[4] *Sexual Offences Act 2003* (UK) s 9.

[5] *Criminal Code*, RSC 1985, c C-46, s 150.1 (1).

[6] While the CRC has recommended that the age of voting be set at 18, the CRC recognises that the minimum age may be set lower, see Committee on the Rights of the Child, *General Comment No 20* (2016) *on the Implementation of the Rights of the Child during Adolescence*, UN doc CRC/C/GC/20, [24].

[7] *Commonwealth Electoral Act 1918* (Cth) s. 93(1)(a) and (2); *Electoral Act 2017* (NSW) s *Electoral Act 1907* (WA) s. 17(1).

[8] UK Parliament, *Voting Age* (19 November 2020) https://commonslibrary.parliament.uk/research-briefings/sn01747/.

[9] *Canada Elections Act*, S.C. 2000, c. 9, s. 3.

[10] *Liquor Control Act 1988* (NSW) ss. 117–118; *Liquor Control Act 1997* (WA) s121; *Liquor Licensing Act 1997* (SA) s 110A.

[11] Drinkaware, *The Law on Alcohol and Under-18s* (accessed 2 September 2024) https://www.drinkaware.co.uk/facts/alcohol-and-the-law/the-law-on-alcohol-and-under-18s#:~:text=It%20is%20against%20the%20law1%202%3A&text=For%20someone%20under%2018%20to,and%20accompanied%20by%20an%20adult.

[12] Manitoba, Resources for Residents: Legal Drinking Age (accessed 2 September 2024) https://residents.gov.mb.ca/reference.html?d=details&program_id=388#:~:text=In%20Canada%2C%20there%20is %20no,must%20show%20valid%20photo%20ID.

[13] *Education Act 1990 No 8* (NSW), s. 21B(2).

[14] *School Education Act 1999* (WA) s. 6.

[15] *Education and Children's Services Act 2019* (SA) ss 3 & 61.

[16] Gov.UK, *School Leaving Age* (accessed 2 September 2024) https://www.gov.uk/know-when-you-can-leave-school#:~:text=England,for%20example%20at%20a%20college.

[17] Manitoba, *Education and Early Learning* (accessed 2 September 2024) https://www.edu.gov.mb.ca/k12/schools/gts.html.

[18] *Marriage Act 1961* (Cth) s. 12.

[19] *Marriage Act 1961* (Cth) s. 11.

[20] *Marriage Act 1949* (UK) s. 2.

[21] *Civil Marriage Act*, SC 2006, c. 33, s. 2.2.

[22] The CRC recommends that State Parties set the minimum age of criminal responsibility at no lower than 14. See Committee on the Rights of the Child, *General Comment No 24 (2019) on Children's Rights in the Child Justice System*, [32].

[23] *Criminal Code Compilation Act 1913* (WA) s. 29; *Young Offenders Act 1993* (SA) s. 5. Australia has been urged to increase the minimum age of Criminal Responsibility. While several states have committed to doing so, the three under consideration in this analysis have not yet done so. See *Criminal Code Amendment* (*Age of Criminal Responsibility*) *Bill* 2022 (NT); see Shane Rattenbury, Rachel Stephen-Smith and Emma Davidson, 'Raising the Age of Criminal Responsibility' (Joint Media Release, 3 November 2022) https://www.cmtedd.act.gov.au/open_government/inform/act_government_media_releases/davidson/2022/raising-the-minimum-age-of-criminal-responsibility#:~:text=%E2%80%9CIn%202023%2C%20the%20ACT%20Government,%2C%E2%80%9D%20said%20the%20Attorney%20General; Roger Jaensch, 'Raising the Minimum Age of Detention' (Media Release, 8 June 2022) https://www.premier.tas.gov.au/site_resources_2015/additional_releases/raising_the_minimum_age_of_detention; see also Kershlin Krishna and Sarah Moulds, 'Old Enough to Know Better? Reform Options for South Australia's Age of Criminality Law' (2020) 41(1) *Adelaide Law Review* 313–323.

[24] CPS, *Youth Crime* (accessed 2 September 2024) https://www.cps.gov.uk/crime-info/youth-crime#:~:text=The%20age%20of%20criminal%20responsibility,10%20who%20break%20the%20law.

[25] *Youth Criminal Justice Act* (S.C. 2002, C. 1), s. 2(1).

[26] ADS Careers, *Eligibility Requirements* (accessed 2 September 2024) https://www.defencejobs.gov.au/joining/can-i-join/age-and-gender; *Combined Fifth and Sixth Periodic Reports Submitted by Australia under Article 44 of the Convention, Due in 2018*, UN doc CRC/C/AUS/5-6 (22 November 2018), 41.

[27] ForcesWatch, *The Recruitment of under 18s into Then UK Armed Forces* (February 2011) https://www.parliament.uk/globalassets/documents/joint-committees/human-rights/Briefing_from_Forces_Watch_age_of_recruitment.pdf

[28] *Combined Fifth and Sixth Reports Submitted by Canada under Article 44 of the Convention, Due in 2018*, UN doc CRC/C/CAN/5-6 (3 March 2020), 29.

[29] The International Labour Organisation recommends that the minimum age for any employment should not be set lower than the age of completion of compulsory education, and in any event, not less than 15; see International Labour Organisation, *Minimum Age Convention, 1973 (No. 138)* Article 2(3); see also Article 7 which permits 'light work' for those aged 13–15 years and which permits these ages and the age outlined in Article 2 to be lowered by one year where the 'economy and educational facilities are insufficiently developed'. See Article 2(4).

[30] *Children and Community Services Act 2004* (WA) s 190.

[31] *Education and Children's Services Act 2019* (SA) s 74.

[32] Children and Young Persons Act 1993 (UK) s 18(2)(a)(i).

[33] QFIB, *What You Need to Know When Hiring Someone under 18 in Manitoba* (accessed 2 September 2024) https://www.cfib-fcei.ca/en/tools-resources/health-safety/what-you-need-know-when-hiring-someone-under-18-manitoba#:~:text=Under%2012%20years%3A,for%20employment%20is%2013%20years.

on *Children's Rights in the Child Justice System*, the CRC committee reiterated that 12 was "still too low", and enjoined States' Parties to set a minimum age of criminal responsibility of at least 14 years.[54] It further commended "[S] tates' [P]arties that have a higher minimum age".[55]

Another notable similarity, which is out of step with international norms, is the minimum age for joining the military. The United Kingdom has been criticised as the only country in Europe to permit those under the age of 18 to join their armed forces.[56] While Australia and Canada have the higher minimum age of 17 (although 16-year-olds can begin the application process) this is still lower than the standard of 18 set by the CRC Committee.[57] Similarly, all jurisdictions permit marriage of 16-year-olds, two years younger than the minimum recommended by the CRC committee.[58]

While there are significant similarities, there are also some differences. While Manitoba and England and Wales set 13 as the minimum age of employment,[59] the situation in Australia is different. In Western Australia, the minimum age is 15, consistent with the international benchmark and two years higher than England and Wales and Manitoba. However, New South Wales and South Australia do not set a minimum age, opting instead to impose restrictions and conditions.[60] Similar variation can be seen across the jurisdictions in relation to the end of compulsory education. However, despite these variations, we are confident that there are sufficient similarities in how the law determines the maturity, decision-making capacity, and autonomy of children to enable comparisons to be made for the purposes of this study. We do not believe the differences in the way in which England and Wales and Manitoba view the legal maturity of the child as compared to Australia would act as a bar to the transplantation of either the England and Wales or Manitoban approach to Australia.

Press, 2019) 1596–1665, 1653; Committee on the Rights of the Child, *General Comment No 10 (2007) Children's Rights in Juvenile Justice*, UN doc CRC/C/GC/10, [32]–[33].

54 Committee on the Rights of the Child, *General Comment No 24 (2019) on children's rights in the child justice system*, [32].

55 Ibid.

56 ForcesWatch (n 75).

57 Committee on the Rights of the Child, *General Comment No 20 (2016) on the Implementation of the Rights of the Child during Aadolescence*, UN doc CRC/C/GC/20, [40]; however, the text of the CRC itself does not take a 'straight' 18 approach. See Mark A Drumbl and John Tobin, 'The Optional Protocol on Children and Armed Conflict' in John Tobin (ed) *The UN Convention on the Rights of the Child* (Oxford University Press, 2019) 1666–1711.

58 Committee on the Elimination of Discrimination against Women and Committee on the Rights of the Child, *Joint General Recommendation No. 31 of the Committee on the Elimination of Discrimination against Women / general comment No. 18 of the Committee on the Rights of the Child on Harmful Practices*, UN doc. CEDAW/C/GC31 – CRC/C/GC18, 7–8.

59 For the purposes of this analysis, employment includes both part- and full-time employment. This includes employment that must be undertaken under certain condition or within certain hours, such as outside of normal school hours.

60 Barker and Andersen (n 14).

C Religion and Refusal

The reasons for refusal of lifesaving medical treatment are complex, and often specific to a particular case and individual. One of the more well-known examples of the refusal of lifesaving medical treatment by both adults and minors is the refusal of blood transfusions by Jehovah's Witnesses. All five cases considered in this study involved children who belonged to the Jehovah Witness faith and, as outlined earlier, it was the death of a Jehovah's Witness child that acted as the catalyst for the creation of the so-called 'blood laws' in Australia.

Jehovah's Witnesses' refusal of medical treatment involving the use of blood products, even where doing so is life-threatening, is well documented. The refusal is based on their interpretation of various passages of the Bible, such as Genesis 9:3–4, Leviticus 17:13–14, and Acts 15:28–29, which prohibit the consumption of blood.[61] Jehovah's Witnesses interpret this injunction to include the 'consumption' of blood, including their own blood via medical procedures including blood transfusions.[62]

The religious element of cases concerning refusal of medical treatment by children, or on their behalf by parents or guardians, comes through in the language used by judges in the case law. For example, in the often-quoted passage from the US case *Prince v Massachusetts*:

> [P]arents may be free to become martyrs themselves. But it does not follow they are free, in identical circumstances, to make martyrs of their children before they have reached the age of full and legal discretion when they can make that choice for themselves.[63]

Similarly in *Re E (A Minor) (Wardship: Medical Treatment)*, Ward J commented:

> There is compelling and overwhelming force in the submission of the Official Solicitor that this court, exercising its prerogative of protection, should be very slow to allow an infant to martyr himself.[64]

This is a sentiment with which Justice Munby agreed in *Re X*.[65]

While all five cases concern Jehovah's Witnesses, it should not be assumed that the religious and cultural landscapes of all five jurisdictions are the same or necessarily comparable. It is, therefore, necessary to carefully examine this key

61 Barker, 'State and Religion' (n 2) 211.

62 Watch Tower Bible and Tract Society of Australia – Hospital Information Services, '*Family Care and Medical Management for Jehovah's Witnesses*' (Watchtower Bible and Tract Society of Australia, 1995) 3–4.

63 US Supreme Court, *Prince v Massachusetts*, 321 USA 158 (1944).

64 *Re E (A Minor) (Wardship: Medical Treatment)* [1993] 1 FLR 386.

65 *Re X* (n 8) [50].

Table 8.2 Religious Demographics in Australia, England and Wales, and Canada

	Australia	*England and Wales*	*Canada*
Majority Religion/s (> 50%)	N/A	N/A	Christian (53.3%)
Significant Minorities (> 10%)	Christian (43.9%)[1] No religion (38.9%)	Christian (46.2%)[2] No religion (37.2%)	No religion (34.6%)
Other Minorities (> 2%)	Muslim (3.2%) Hinduism (2.7%) Buddhism (2.4%) No answer (6.9%)[3]	Muslim (6.5%) No answer (6%)[4]	Muslim (4.9%) Hinduism (2.3%) Sikhs (2.1%)
Jehovah's Witnesses	0.26%[5]	0.21%[6]	0.31%[7]

1 Australian Bureau of Statistics, *Religious Affiliation in Australia* (4 July 2022) https://www.abs.gov.au/articles/religious-affiliation-australia
2 Office for National Statistics, *Religion, England and Wales: Census 2021* (29 November 2022) https://www.ons.gov.uk/peoplepopulationandcommunity/culturalidentity/religion/bulletins/religionenglandandwales/census2021.
3 The question on the census is optional.
4 The question on the census is optional.
5 JW.ORG, *Australia* (accessed 2 September 2024) https://www.jw.org/en/jehovahs-witnesses/worldwide/AU/.
6 JW.ORG, *Britain* (accessed 2 September 2024) https://www.jw.org/en/jehovahs-witnesses/worldwide/GB/; note this is the percentage for Great Britain which includes England, Scotland, Wales and Northern Ireland.
7 JW.ORG, *Canada* (accessed 2 September 2024) https://www.jw.org/en/jehovahs-witnesses/worldwide/CA/.

aspect of culture in each jurisdiction before determining if a legal transplant would be successful or appropriate.

Table 8.2 sets out the religious demographics of Australia, England and Wales, and Canada, as the most recent census which was in 2021 for all three jurisdictions. We note that the specific religious demographics of Manitoba, Western Australia, South Australia, and New South Wales may deviate from the national statistics represented here. We argue, however, that the national statistics provide a useful starting point to understand if there is sufficient convergence to make a transplant of either the Manitoban or English and Welsh approaches to Australia appropriate.

As the table demonstrates, all three jurisdictions' dominant religion is Christianity, though Canada is the only one where Christians still account for the majority of the population. The loss of majority status for Christianity in both England and Wales and Australia is relatively recent. In the 2016

Australian census, Christians made up 52.1% of the population.[66] Christians made up 59.3% of the population in the 2011 census in England and Wales.[67] All three have large proportions of the population that reported themselves as having no religion in the 2021 censuses.

Australia and Canada are more religiously diverse with significant (> 2%) Hindu (Aust. and Canada), Buddhist (Aust.), and Sikh (Canada) populations. By contrast, England and Wales' only significant minority religion is Islam. Canada and Australia also have significant Muslim populations.

While these differences are arguably important in helping to explain key cultural differences between the jurisdictions under consideration, we are satisfied that they are not such as to make implausible the transplant of either of the Manitoban or English and Welsh approaches to Australia. All three have a large Christian population, which either is, or was until recently, the majority. All three also have a large proportion of the population that identify as not having a religion. Finally, all three have a small but significant proportion of the population that identify with minority faiths – although which faiths varies.

While the religious demographics are an important factor in considering the compatibility of the three jurisdictions for analysis, other factors such as the interaction or relationship between the state and religion and laws regulating religious practice should also be considered. While the religious demographics of the three jurisdictions are relatively similar, their state-religion relationships diverge. Australia's state-religion relationship has been described in a variety of ways, including pragmatic pluralism,[68] liberal separation,[69] non-establishment,[70] cooperation,[71] symbolic establishment,[72] and non-establishment pluralism.[73] In his analysis, Temperman placed Canada in his discussion of (mono)theist States,[74] and states with constitutional acknowledgement of God,[75] due to the acknowledgement of God in the *Canadian Constitution*. Ahdar and

66 Australian Bureau of Statistics (n 97).

67 Office for National Statistics (n 98).

68 J Christopher Soper et al, *The Challenge of Pluralism Church and State in Six Democracies* (Lanham, Maryland: Rowman & Littlefield, 2017) 121.

69 Stephen McLeish, 'Making Sense of Religion and the Constitution: A Fresh Start for Section 116' 18 *Monash University Law Review* (1992) 221–222; Paul Babie et al., *Religion and Law in Australia*, 2nd ed. (Netherlands: Kluwer Law International, 2019) 52–56.

70 W C Durham and B G Scharffs, *Law and Religion: National, International, and Comparative Perspectives* (Aspen Publishing, 2nd ed, 2019) 208; Jeroen Temperman, *State-Religion Relationships and Human Rights Law: Towards a Right to Religiously Neutral Governance* (Brill, 2010) 118.

71 Durham and Scharffs (n 108) 193.

72 Rex Ahdar and Ian Leigh, *Religious Freedom in the Liberal State* (Oxford University Press, 2013) 104.

73 Renae Barker, 'Pluralism versus Separation: Tension in the Australian Church-State Relationship'(2021) 16(1) *Religion and Human Rights* 1–40.

74 Temperman (n 108) 30–3.

75 Ibid 77–79

Leigh similarly place Canada in their symbolic establishment category,[76] while Durham and Scharffs suggest the appropriate description of the state-religion relationship is neutrality.[77] In England and Wales, the Church of England is the officially established church, with most analysis placing it in the establishment (*de jure* or de facto) category.[78] Given the inherent complexities of state-religion relationships and the focus of different scholars, some deviation in categorisation is normal and to be expected[79] – however, it does pose significant challenges for researchers seeking to undertake a comparative analysis, as there is no clear agreement on the state-religion relationship in each individual jurisdiction, let alone how these ought to be compared. A full analysis of the state-religion relationship in each jurisdiction is beyond the scope of this chapter. What can be seen from the analysis, however, is that while there is divergence, there is also some element of pluralism or accommodation of different faiths in the state-religion relationship along with a generally positive attitude towards religion, as opposed to separation from religion in the public sphere, in all three jurisdictions. This tends to suggest that approaches to laws regulating the refusal of blood transfusions by minors on the grounds of religion that accommodate religious diversity would be compatible with the state-religion relationship of all three. As mentioned in Section II, we have necessarily had to take a relatively "broad-brush" approach to the methodology developed for this study. We acknowledge that the above brief insight into religion in these jurisdictions is somewhat simplified, but it enables that admittedly blurry snapshot of the compatibility of the different jurisdictions with a view to projecting the feasibility of a transplant.

Given the very particular beliefs of Jehovah's Witnesses in relation to blood transfusions and the fact Jehovah's Witnesses make up less than one half of one percentage of the population in all three jurisdiction, some consideration must be given of how this tiny minority has been treated both culturally and legally. A full analysis of the treatment of Jehovah's Witnesses is beyond the scope of this chapter. We would note, however, that, for example, Jehovah's Witnesses faced persecution in the UK, Canada, and Australia during WWII due to, inter alia, their objection to military service and objections to involvement in the war effort more generally.[80]

76 Ahdar and Leigh (110) 104.
77 Durham and Scharffs (n 108) 155.
78 Durham and Scharffs (n 108) 95; Ahdar and Leigh (n 110) 101, 104 and 106; Temperman (n 108) 44 and 47.
79 Renae Barker, 'Law and Religion in the Classroom: Teaching Church-State Relationships' (2022) 1 (1) *Australian Journal of Law and Religion* 12–14.
80 For the treatment of Jehovah's Witnesses by the law, see for example Barker, 'State and Religion' (n 2) 196–201; Tony Brace, 'Jehovah's Witnesses and the Law: "Caesar's Things to Caesar, but God's Things to God"' in Eileen Barker and James T Richardson (eds) *Reactions to the Law by Minority Religions* (Routledge 2021) 37–57; William Kaplan, 'The World War Two Ban on the Jehovah's Witnesses in Canada: A Study in the Development of Civil Rights'

III Domestic Legal Framework

Generally speaking in Australia, Canada, and the UK, a competent adult has full authority to consent to or refuse medical treatment. In many instances, consent can be given or refused in anticipation of future medical treatment in circumstances where the adult in question cannot consent via advanced health care directives. By contrast, the law presumes that children are unable to consent to, or refuse consent to, medical treatment. Instead, their parent or other legal guardian provides substituted consent on their behalf. As outlined previously, this general presumption is modified in the case of mature minors. Mature minors may rebut the presumption as to their lack of competence if they can demonstrate that they have sufficient maturity. However, as outlined, doubt remains as to the effectiveness of a refusal of consent by a mature minor.

The common law presumption that children under the age of majority (18 years) lack the competency to consent or refuse medical treatment has, in some cases, been modified via legislation. Legislation has also, in some cases, modified parents' and guardians' ability to consent or refuse consent on behalf of their minor children. Legislation of this type can be divided into two categories: (1) legislation specifically dealing with the ability of minors to consent, and (2) legislation specifically abrogating parental or guardians' authority to consent or refuse consent. Further in Australia, the UK, and Canada, the courts have an inherent jurisdiction, referred to as the *parens patriae* or welfare jurisdiction, enabling them to make orders for the "best interest" of a minor.

This section outlines the position in Australia (Western Australia, New South Wales, and South Australia), the United Kingdom (England and Wales) and Canada (Manitoba).

A Legislating for the Consent of Minors

As shown in Table 8.3, New South Wales, South Australia, the United Kingdom, and Manitoba all have legislation specifically dealing with the first category identified, the ability of minors to consent. Western Australia does not have any equivalent legislation and, as such, relies on the common law.

"As Table 8.3 outlines, there are broadly two legislative approaches as to modifying the common law position regarding the consent of minors. The first is to expressly give minors under the age of 18 the ability to consent to medical treatment or veto consent given by others on their behalf. The United

(PhD Thesis, Stanford University, 1988); James T Richardson, 'In Defence of Religious Rights: Jehovah's Witness Legal Cases Around the World' in Stephen J Hunt (ed) *Handbook of Global Christianity: Themes and Developments in Culture, Politics and Society* (Brill 2015); William Kaplan, 'The World War Two Bans on the Jehovah's Witnesses in Canada and Australia: Do Constitutional Protections Really Work?' (1991) 9 *Australian Canadian* Studies 5; Jayne Persian, 'A National Nuisance: The Banning of the Jehovah's Witnesses in Australia in 1941' (2008) 25 *Flinders Journal of History and Politics* 4–16.

Table 8.3 Legislation Regulating Ability of Minors to Consent to Medical Treatment

		Defence for Medical Practitioners	*Right to Consent*
		Australia	
New South Wales	Minors (Property and Contracts) Act 1970	s. 49(1) < 16 Defence for assault or battery if consent given by parent or guardian s. 49(2) > 14 defence for assault or battery if consent given by child	
South Australia	Consent to Medical Treatment and Palliative Care Act 1995		s. 12(b) If medical practitioner believes child "capable of understanding consequences and risks of treatment" and "treatment is in best interest of child" and has concurring written opinion of another medical practitioner s. 6 > 16 Decisions about medical treatment as valid and effective as an adult
		United Kingdom	
England and Wales	Family Law Reform Act 1968		S. 8(1) < 16 Consent as effective as if of full age
		Canada	
Manitoba	Manitoba Child and Family Services Act		S25(2) > 16 Medical or dental treatment requires the consent of the child (apprehended child) S25(8) > 16 Consent of child required for court-ordered medical treatment unless child is unable to understand relevant information or unable to appreciate foreseeable consequences of refusal of consent

Kingdom, Manitoba, and South Australia take this approach. In the United Kingdom, Section 8(1) of the *Family Law Reform Act 1968* (UK) provides that the consent of a minor aged 16 years or older to surgical, medical, or dental treatment "shall be as effective as it would be if he were of full age". The section specifically references the common law position that providing such treatment without consent "would constitute a trespass to his person" and confirms that where consent has been obtained from a minor aged 16 years or above, "it shall not be necessary to obtain any consent for it from his parent or guardian". The courts have held that Section 8(1) does not abrogate the ability of parents or guardians from giving consent on behalf of a child aged 16 or 17 years, nor does it oust the court's *parens patriae* jurisdiction.[81]

Manitoba's *Manitoba Child and Family Services Act*, like the *Family Law Reform Act 1968* (UK), focuses on the ability of children to consent. Sections 25(2) and 25(8) preclude the relevant authority from providing consent to medical treatment on behalf of a child 16 years or over without their consent unless it can be shown that the child lacks "the maturity to understand the decision or appreciate its consequences".[82] In effect, the Manitoba law presumes that in the case of a child 16 years or over, their best interest will be served by respecting their medical decisions.[83] The effect is to oust the courts' and, presumably, the parents' ability to consent on behalf of children 16 years or over unless it can be shown the child lacks the requisite maturity.

Like England and Wales, and Manitoba, South Australia's *Consent to Medical Treatment and Palliative Care Act 1995* (SA) explicitly provides that children can consent to medical treatment. In the case of children over the age of 16, Section 6 provides that a minor "may make decisions about his or her own medical treatment as validly and effectively as an adult". The effect of the provision in relation to the refusal of consent for medical treatment is unclear, as it has not been specifically considered by the courts. However, given the similarity in wording to the English and Welsh provision discussed earlier, it is likely that Australian courts would find that this provision does not entirely oust the *parens patriae* jurisdiction of the court.[84] For children under 16, a medical practitioner may rely on a child's consent if the medical practitioner is of the opinion that the child "is capable of understanding the nature, consequences and risk" of the proposed treatment, and the medical practitioner is of the opinion that the proposed treatment is in the child's best interests.[85] They must also obtain a concurring written opinion from another medical

81 Fortin (n 4) 155.
82 AC (n 1), [24].
83 Ibid [24].
84 See for example *Re Jamie* (2013) 560 Fam LR 396. [131]–[133] where the Family Court of Australian refers to section 6 of the *Consent to Medical Treatment and Palliative Care Act 1995* (SA) alongside section 8 of the *Family Law Reform Act 1969* (UK) and section 36(1) of the *Care of Children Act 2004* (NZ).
85 *Consent to Medical Treatment and Palliative Care Act 1995* (SA) s. 12(b)(i).

practitioner.[86] Section 12(a), however, provides that a parent or guardian may provide consent for a child, suggesting that in the event a child refuses consent, a medical practitioner may nonetheless rely on the consent of the parent or guardian.

New South Wales takes a different approach. Instead of focusing on the ability of the minor to consent, Section 49 of the *Minors (Property and Contracts) Act 1970* (NSW) focuses on the consequences for medical practitioners if they fail to obtain consent. Section 49(1) protects medical practitioners providing medical or dental treatment from a claim in assault or battery by a minor where the minor is under 16 and the minor's parents or guardians provide consent. Section 49(2) provides similar protection where a minor aged 14 years or older provides consent to medical or dental treatment. The effect is that there is a default age of consent of 14, with a two-year overlap where both the child and their parent or guardian can provide the requisite consent. Once a minor obtains the age of 16, consent must be given by the minor.[87] As with the provisions of the *Family Law Reform Act 1968* (UK), the courts have held that Section 49 of the *Minors (Property and Contracts) Act 1970* (NSW) does not "provide an answer to the whole of the law's concern with the quality of the child's consent, or the parental consent on his or her behalf".[88] Given the way in which the provision is worded, it is a defence for medical practitioners where consent is given. It does not override the common law or other statutory provisions where consent is withheld.

B Administration of Medical Treatment without Consent

The second category of legislation modifying the common law position regarding the consent of minors are those specifically authorising medical treatment without the consent of the minor or their parents or guardians. New South Wales, Western Australia, South Australia, and Manitoba all have legislative provisions specifically outlining the circumstances in which this may take place. England and Wales does not have any legislation to this effect, and instead relies on the common law *parens patriae* jurisdiction.

In the Australian jurisdictions, the focus of the legislation is on the medical practitioner and the medical nature of the procedure. The nature of the medical procedures authorised by the legislation varies. Western Australia's is the narrowest, applying only to blood transfusions, while New South Wales is the broadest, applying to both medical and dental treatment. However, in all three Australian jurisdictions, the decision-maker is a medical practitioner who

86 Ibid s. 12(b)(ii).

87 Section 49(1) and (2) both refer to consent being valid 'as if, at the time when the consent is given, he or she were aged twenty-one years or upwards'.

88 *Re Kevin* (2017) 351 ALR 329, [81], Thackray, Strickland and Murphy JJ quoting with approval the submissions of the Attorney General.

Table 8.4 legislation Authorising Medical Treatment without the Consent of Minors of Their Parents/Guardians

	Legislation	*Blood Transfusions*	*Medical Treatment*	*Dental Treatment*	*Criteria*	*Decision-Maker*
			Australia			
New South Wales	Children and Young Persons (Care and Protection) Act 1998 (NSW)		✓	✓	Necessary Matter of urgency Save life or prevent serious damage to health	Medical practitioner Registered dentist
South Australia	Consent to Medical Treatment and Palliative Care Act 1995		✓		Best interests of child's health and well-being	Medical practitioner
Western Australia	Human Tissue and Transplant Act 1982 (WA)	✓			Reasonable and proper treatment for the condition Likely to die	Medical practitioner
			Canada			
Manitoba	Child and Family Services Act		✓	✓	Best interests	Court

must base their decision on medical well-being criteria. In New South Wales and Western Australia, the relevant medical practitioner is not required to specifically consider the child's best interests – instead, they may administer the relevant medical procedure without consent where, respectively, it is necessary to "save life or prevent serious damage to health"[89] or where the child is "likely to die" without the relevant medical treatment.[90] In South Australia, the decision-maker may act where the medical treatment is in the "best interests of the child's health and well-being".[91] However, this is narrower than "the child's best interests", which would require a more holistic analysis, including, for example, the child's views of the matter. The Australian approach can be contrasted with the Manitoban approach, which places the decision in the hands of the court as well as requiring the court to consider the child's best interests. This places the focus on the child, rather than on the medical practitioner and the medical decision-making.

C Human Rights Framework

Before turning to an analysis of the case law, it is important to consider the domestic and international human rights frameworks within which the domestic legislative frameworks outlined earlier operate. Australia is (in)famous as being the only Western liberal democracy without a national bill or charter of human rights.[92] However, this does not mean that there are no protections for human rights or the rights of the child. Protection is instead provided via what has often been described as a 'patchwork' of federal and state legislation, including narrow rights contained in the *Australian Constitution*, anti-discrimination laws at both the national and state levels, and state-based human rights charters.[93] This approach has also been referred to as an "ethos" of rights.[94] The Australian jurisdictions considered in this chapter do not have legislative bills or charters of rights.[95]

By contrast, both the UK and Canada have robust human rights frameworks with a well-established jurisprudence. Canada has constitutional protection for human rights under the *Canadian Charter of Rights and Freedoms* ('*Charter*') contained in the *Constitution Act 1982*. In *AC*, AC challenged the

89 *Children and Young Persons (Care and Protection) Act 1998* (NSW) ss 174(1)(b) and 174(2)(b).
90 *Human Tissue and Transplant Act 1982* (WA) s21(1)(b) and (3)(d).
91 *Consent to Medical Treatment and Palliative Care Act 1995* (SA) s13(5).
92 Louise Chappell, John Chesterman and Lisa Hill, *The Politics of Human Rights in Australia* (Cambridge University Press, 2009) 27–29.
93 Barker, 'State and Religion' (n 2) 105–109.
94 See Paul T Babie, 'The Ethos of Protection for Freedom of Religion or Belief in Australian Law' (2010) 47 *University of Western Australia Law Review* 64–91.
95 The Australian states with legislative charters of rights are Victoria, Australian Capital Territory and Queensland.

constitutional validity of Sections 25(8) and 25(9) of the *Child and Family Services Act* under Sections 2(a), 7, and 15 of the *Charter*. The UK has taken a non-constitutional approach to protection of equality and human rights via the *Human Rights Act 1998* (UK), implementing the *European Convention on Human Rights*, and the *Equality Act* 2010 (UK), which consolidated various anti-discrimination laws. Where a party has exhausted their domestic remedies, they may also take a complaint about a violation of human rights to the European Court of Human Rights. The Respondent in *Re X* argued that the imposition of a blood transfusion against the wishes of a mature 15-year-old, as well as the request for a "rolling order" until their 18th birthday was a breach of Sections 3, 5, 8, and 9 when taken in conjunction with Article 14 of the *European Convention on Human Rights*.

Also relevant to the analysis is the international human rights framework. All three jurisdictions are signatories of the *ICCPR* which protects, inter alia, freedom of religion and belief in Article 18. In relation to children specifically, the CRC outlines the rights of children and young people. Australia, Canada, and the UK are all signatories to the CRC.

A number of articles of the CRC are relevant to the issues of the refusal of consent for blood transfusions by children, mature minors, and their parents. Most relevant are Article 3 (best interests),[96] Article 14 (freedom of religion and belief),[97] and Article 24 (health).[98] Other articles which are relevant include Article 5 (evolving capacity), Article 12 (right to be heard), and Article 6 (right to life). The position under the CRC is not settled. The CRC Committee has not directly commented on the issue of the refusal of medical treatment by mature minors. However, tacit support for respecting the refusal of consent by sufficiently mature minors may be implied from the CRC committee's comments relating to consent for euthanasia for children aged 12 and over in the Netherlands.[99] Yet, the position of domestic courts has, almost unanimously, been to override the express views of mature children where they have refused lifesaving medical treatment.[100] Nonetheless, as Langlaude Doné and Tobin have observed, "there is growing support for an alternative approach whereby once a child reaches sufficient maturity, there can be no

96 For a discussion of the application of Article 3, see John Eekelaar and John Tobin, 'Article 3: The Best Interests of the Child' in John Tobin (ed) *The UN Convention on the Rights of the Child: A Commentary* (Oxford University Press, 2019) 73–107, 86–87.

97 For a discussion of the application of Article 14 see Sylvie Langlaude Doné and John Tobin, 'Article 14: The Right to Freedom of Thought, Conscience, and Religion' in John Tobin (ed) *The UN Convention on the Rights of the Child: A Commentary* (Oxford University Press, 2019) 475–516, 514.

98 For a discussion of the application of Article 14 see John Tobin, 'Article 24: The Right to Health' in John Tobin (ed) *The UN Convention on the Rights of the Child: A Commentary* (Oxford University Press, 2019) 902–969, 917–918.

99 John Tobin, 'Article 24: The Right to Health' in John Tobin (ed) *The UN Convention on the Rights of the Child: A Commentary* (Oxford University Press, 2019) 902–969, 917–918.

100 Langlaude Doné and Tobin, (n 137) 514.

justification for a state adopting protective measures that would interfere with the child's autonomy".[101] Munby J was critical of this approach when argued before him in *Re X* commenting 'I do not criticise counsel for taking the point, but I have to say that it is the kind of point which probably has more traction amongst the dreaming spires of the Academy than in the robust and ultimately pragmatic world of the court room[102]

IV Analysis of Case Law

The previously mentioned analysis outlined the legislative frameworks governing the refusal of medical treatment by mature minors. However, the jurisdictions under consideration are all common law, which means that a significant portion of the relevant law is found in the interpretations of these legislative provisions by judges, as well as in standalone common law principles such as *parens patriae*. Further, to understand if a transplant would be successful, it is necessary to first understand how the transplanted legislative provisions might be interpreted in Australia. Obviously, it is impossible to know for certain how a law will be interpreted until it is, in fact, implemented; however, by analysing the key themes that emerge in similar cases, in this case the refusal of blood transfusions by mature minors, we hope to gain some insight.

As can be seen in Table 8.5, while all five cases concerned blood transfusions for minors from the Jehovah Witness faith, the specific circumstances of each case varied. The children ranged in age from ten to 17. The level of urgency of the particular medical treatment also varied from low to high. The nature of the underlying medical treatment also varied. In the three Australian cases, *AS*, *YJL*, and *X and Other*, the underlying condition was various forms of cancer. By contrasts in the UK case, *Re X*, and the Canadian case, *AC*, the underlying conditions were lifelong and likely to involve multiple blood transfusions across the child's life. Indeed, in *Re X*, medical practitioners were seeking a rolling order for ongoing blood transfusions as needed due to the ongoing life-threatening nature of the child's condition.

As outlined in Table 8.5, we analysed five cases drawn from our five jurisdictions to identify key themes emerging from the judicial analysis. Each case was read three times. First each case was read in totality to enable the researcher to gain on overall impression of the case.[103] During the second detailed reading, key emergent themes were noted for further analysis. Each case was then read a third time and coded using Nvivo software using the key themes that emerged from the second reading. This enabled cross-checking of themes that emerged in one case with the other cases in this study to determine if the same, similar, and analogous themes emerged in all, some, or only one of the cases.

101 Ibid.
102 *Re X* (n 8) [60].
103 The researcher was generally familiar with all five cases from previous research projects.

Table 8.5 Summary of Case Law Analysed in This Study

Case	*Year*	*Age*	*Mature Minor*	*Religion*	*Medical Treatment*	*Urgency*
Minister for Health v AS	2004	15	Yes	Jehovah's Witness	Blood transfusion – Cancertreatment	Moderate
A.C. v Manitoba (Director of Child and Family Services)	2009	14	N/A	Jehovah's Witness	Blood transfusion – Crohn's disease	Low
Children, Youth & Women's Health Services Inc v YJL, MHL and TL (by His Next Friend)	2010	10	No	Jehovah's Witness	Blood transfusion – Cancer	Moderate to High
Sydney Children's Hospital Network v X and Other	2013	17	Yes	Jehovah's Witness	Blood Transfusion – Cancertreatment	Moderate
Re X (a child) (No 2) An NHS Trust v X	2021	15	Yes	Jehovah's Witness	Blood Transfusion – Sickle Cell syndrome	Low

We identified a number of key themes across the cases, including the jurisdiction's scope and content of the *parens patriae* jurisdiction, the intersection of the child's views, and the child's best interests, rights including the rights of the child, the rights of the parent, and broader concepts of human rights as well as, unsurprisingly, religion. While not all themes were present in every case, in the context of a transplant study, the absence of themes found in one jurisdiction but not another may be an indicator of the likely success of a transplant.

A Parens Patriae Jurisdiction

All five cases referred to the inherent *parens patriae* or welfare jurisdiction of the court. All three of the Australian cases,[104] as well as *Re X*,[105] relied upon the *parens patriae* jurisdiction for the necessary legal authority to make the orders

104 *JJL* (n 22) [35], *X and Other* (n 33), *AS* (n 32) [23].
105 *Re X* (n 8).

authorising the giving of a blood transfusion without the consent of the child or their parents. Indeed, while *Re X* considered the case of a child under 16, in obiter Munby J noted that had the respondent been over 16, and therefore the rolling order sought would have applied until she turned 18, *parens patriae* would have been the only jurisdiction under which the requested orders could have been sought as a result of the operation of Section 8 of the *Family Law Reform Act 1968* (UK).[106] The jurisdiction of the court was not ousted by the operation of the *Family Law Reform Act 1968* (UK). *YJL*,[107] *X and Other*,[108] and *AS*[109] also noted that the court's *parens patriae* jurisdiction had not been ousted by statute. For example, White J in *YJL* commented that "[i]n order to displace the court's supervisory jurisdiction with respect to Guardians and the welfare of children, Parliament must do so in unambiguous language".[110]

Similarly, in reaching his conclusion that even a Gillick-competent child can be ordered to undergo a medical procedure without their consent, Munby J noted that "[t]he changes for which [the Respondent] contends is a matter for Parliament, not the courts".[111]

By contrast, while *AC* refers to the *parens patriae* jurisdiction, it does not rely on or apply it.[112] The references to *parens patriae* are primarily in relation to the historical development of case law and statutes relating to the welfare of children, or contained in quotes from other cases. Instead of relying on the *parens patriae* jurisdictions, courts in Manitoba rely on the provisions of the *Child and Family Services Act*, which the court in *AC* found to be constitutionally valid.

B Child's Best Interests and Child's Views

All five cases referred extensively to the best interest or welfare of the child as the court's primary or paramount consideration.[113] In the three Australian cases, the child's bests interests and the child's views, including their religious beliefs, were considered as separate factors. Where there was a conflict, the child's best interests inevitably outweighed these other factors. As White J explained in *YJL*:

> The welfare of the child is the court's first and paramount consideration and the court must make its own independent judgment on any question which involves the interests of the child. While proper respect is paid

106 Ibid [33] see also [2].
107 *YJL* (n 22) [35].
108 *X and Other* (n 33) [50].
109 *AS* (n 32) [18].
110 *YJL* (n 22) [35].
111 *Re X* (n 8) [162].
112 *AC* (n 1) [54]–[57], [68], [104].
113 In AC (n 1) this was mandated by section 2(1) of the *Family and Children Services Act*.

> to the views of the parents or of the child in question, where there is a conflict it is for the court to decide what should occur.[114]

Similarly, in *AS*, Pullin J commented:

> … the fact that the child refusing to consent to medical treatment may be of sufficient maturity and intelligence to understand the nature and implications of the proposed treatment, so as to be '*Gillick* competent', while relevant and important does not prevent the court from authorising medical treatment where the best interests of the child require. … The guiding principle upon which the exercise of the *parens patriae* jurisdiction is based is that the welfare of the child is paramount. Protection of the child should be elevated above all other interests, although those other interests are not completely disregarded. … When faced with the stark reality that the child will die if lifesaving treatment is not performed … , it is beyond doubt that it is in the child's best interests to receive that treatment.[115]

By contrast, in *AC* and *Re X*, the court interpreted the best interest to include taking into account the child's wishes. As Abella J put it, this involved a "blending" of these two factors.[116] As a result of this blending:

> [t]he more a court is satisfied that a child is capable of making a mature, independent decision on his or her own behalf, the greater the weight that will be given to his or her views when a court is exercising its discretion … In some cases, courts will inevitably be so convinced of a child's maturity that the principles of welfare and autonomy will collapse altogether and the child's wishes will become the controlling factor. If, after a careful and sophisticated analysis of the young person's ability to exercise mature, independent judgment, the court is persuaded that the necessary level of maturity exists, it seems to me necessarily to follow that the adolescent's views ought to be respected. Such an approach clarifies that in the context of medical treatment, young people under 16 should be permitted to attempt to demonstrate that their views about a particular medical treatment decision reflect a sufficient degree of independence of thought and maturity.[117]

114 *YJL* (n 22) [32].
115 *AS* (n 32) [20]–[21].
116 *AC* (n 1) [90].
117 Ibid [87].

Re X considered extensively the reasoning in *AC*,[118] reaching a similar conclusion regarding the blending of the child's best interests and the child's wishes. Earlier in his judgement, Munby J quoted with approval from Balcombe LJ's judgement in *R (A Minor) (Wardship Consent to Treatment*:[119]

> Accordingly the older the child concerned the greater the weight the court should give to its wishes, certainly in the field of medical treatment. In a sense this is merely one aspect of the application of the test that the welfare of the child is the paramount consideration. It will normally be in the best interests of a child of sufficient age and understanding to make an informed decision that the court should respect its integrity as a human being and not lightly override its decision on such a personal matter as medical treatment, all the more so if that medical treatment is invasive.[120]

However, in both cases the court ultimately concluded that even in the case of a mature or Gillick-competent minor, the court retained the discretion to order medical treatment despite the child's objections where doing so was in the child's best interests.[121]

C Human Rights Framework

Both *AC* and *Re X* make extensive reference to the applicable human rights framework in Canada and the UK, respectively. In *AC*, the appeal was grounded in an argument that Sections 25(8) and 29(9) of the *Child and Family Services Act* were unconstitutional because they breached Sections 7, 15, and 2(a) of the *Charter*.[122] Indeed, in this case, the primary question was not whether the child should receive a blood transfusion, having already received one as a result of the original court order,[123] but, in effect, whether the original order and the legislation under which that order was authorised was constitutionally valid. While this was, in many ways, an appeal based on a matter of principle, it also had long-term consequences given the lifelong nature of the child's condition. Similarly, in *Re X*, the court makes extensive reference to the *Human Rights Act 1998* and the *European Convention on Human Rights* with particular reference to Articles 2, 3, 5, 8, and 9 of the *European Convention on Human Rights*.[124]

118 *Re X* (n 8) [85]–[104].
119 [1992] Fam11.
120 *Re X* (n 8) [50] quoting *R (A Minor) (Wardship Consent to Treatment) at* [1992] Fam11, 88.
121 *Re X* (n 8) [104].
122 AC (n 1) [97]–[121].
123 Ibid [13].
124 *Re X* (n 8) [105]–[158].

By contrast, there is no discussion of a human rights framework in the three Australian cases. While the three Australian cases, in contrast to the Canadian and UK cases, all involved an element of emergency necessitating shorter judgements, the lack of discussion of a human rights framework in the Australian cases is striking when compared with the extensive discussion in both *AC* and *Re X*. In the Canadian and UK cases, the judgements carefully address each section or clause from the human rights framework relevant to the decision. There is no such discussion in the Australian cases, owing the absence of such a framework. As outlined previously, Australia does not have a national bill or charter of rights, and the three States selected for this analysis do not have state-based charters of rights. As such, the court is not required to apply a human rights framework. However, this is not to say that rights in the broader sense are not discussed at all in the Australian cases. For example, in *X and Other*, after noting the need to balance rights in the Canadian cases, Basten AJ noted "[m]any of these ideas are succinctly captured by the concepts of 'sanctity of life' and 'best interests' of a young person",[125] going on to note "the jurisdiction requires the reconciliation of fundamental, but potentially conflicting, principles of constitutional significance inherent in the common law, absent any written bill of rights".[126]

As discussed earlier, the child's best interests is a theme present in all five cases. Similarly, the concept of the right to life or the sanctity of life is discussed in four of the five cases.[127] This is often coupled with a discussion of the right to autonomy. The only case not to discuss the sanctity or right to life, even briefly, is *YJL*. However, given this case did not concern the refusal of treatment by a mature minor, but rather the refusal of treatment on behalf of a child by their parents, the issues in question were subtly different, which may account for this apparent discrepancy. Where the sanctity or right to life is discussed, it is often contrasted with the right to the autonomy of the individual, and although not made explicit, there is an implied suggestion of a right for a child to reach the age of majority. For example, in *AS*, Pullin J noted "[w]here faced with the stark reality that the child will die if lifesaving treatment is not performed which has a good prospect of a long-term cure, it is beyond doubt that it is in the child's best interests to receive that treatment".[128] This view can be contrasted with that of Binnie J in dissent in *AC*:

> Individuals who do not subscribe to the beliefs of Jehovah's Witnesses find it difficult to understand their objection to the potentially lifesaving effects of a blood transfusion. It is entirely understandable that judges,

125 *X and Other* (m 33) [62].
126 Ibid [67].
127 See for example *AC* (n 1) [16] and [191]–[192]; *AS* (n 32) [21]; *Re X* (n 8) [52] and [143]; *X and Other* (n 33) [57].
128 *AS* (n 32) [21].

as in this case, would instinctively give priority to the sanctity of life. Religious convictions may change. Death is irreversible. Even where death is avoided, damage to internal organs caused by loss of blood may have serious and long-lasting effects.

Yet, strong as is society's belief in the sanctity of life, it is equally fundamental that every competent individual is entitled to autonomy to choose or not to choose medical treatment except as that autonomy may be limited or prescribed within the framework of the Constitution. The rights under s. 2(a) of the Charter (religious freedom) and s. 7 (liberty and security of the person) are given to everyone, including individuals under 16 years old.[129]

D Religion

Given that all five cases involved refusal of blood transfusions due to the religious beliefs, it is perhaps unsurprising that all five judgements considered religion to some extent. All five, for example, mention the religious beliefs of the child and/or parents.[130] The court in all cases accepts, explicitly or implicitly, that the religious beliefs are sincerely held. However, this is not the focus of the judgements in any of the cases. Even in the UK and Canada, where the right to freedom of religion and belief is considered as part of the relevant human rights framework, the focus of the judgement is on the best interests of the child. These "best interests" inquiries primarily revolve around resolving the tension between autonomy and life, focusing on physical best interests as opposed to spiritual.

V Discussion

In *Re X*, the court refused to make an anticipatory or rolling order for the child to receive blood transfusions as and when they became necessary, even though it found it had the jurisdiction to do so.[131] The court agreed with submissions by counsel representing the child that such an order risks privileging "medical paternalism" over "judicial protection".[132] However, this is exactly the effect of the "blood laws" in Australia. Born out of the tragic death of an infant, these laws place decision-making in the hands of medical practitioners, rather than the courts. In effect, they make medical practitioners the default guardians of all children in Australia, able to overrule not only the refusal of consent of young children and mature minors, but also of parents and guard-

129 *AC* (n 1) [191]–[192].
130 See for example *AC* (n 1) [5]; *YJL* (n 22) [1] and [20]; *AS* (n 32) [2]; *Re X* (n 8) [6] and [16]; *X and Other* (n 33) [4].
131 Re X (n 8) [165].
132 Ibid [168].

ians. By contrast, in England and Wales and Manitoba, it is the court that has this ultimate authority, placing the onus on medical practitioners and the state to establish that the proposed medical procedure is not only potentially lifesaving, but also in the child's best interest.

Further, as our analysis has demonstrated, where the decision to overrule the refusal of consent of mature minors is left to the courts, not only is the child's best interests explicitly considered, but the courts are willing to consider the child's views and maturity as part of their analysis of the child's best interests. Indeed, in this kind of analysis, the twin concept of "welfare and autonomy" will inevitably "collapse altogether" as the maturity of the child increases such that eventually the "child's wishes will become the controlling factor".[133] By contrast, in the three Australian cases, while the best interests of the child are discussed, this is seen as being in conflict with the autonomy of the child, with the best interest defined almost exclusively as ongoing life, "winning" in any contest between the two.

However, the mere existence of the "blood laws" in Australia cannot fully explain the different approaches of England and Wales, and Manitoban courts, as opposed to the Australian ones, to the best interests of the child. The three Australian cases analysed did not apply the 'blood law' legislation, as that only applies to medical practitioners making decisions in an emergency or lifesaving context. Where medical practitioners wish to carry out blood transfusions, or other medical procedures, against or without parental consent or the consent of a mature minor, they must still apply to the courts under the court's inherent *parens patriae* jurisdiction. The difference in approach, therefore, must be found elsewhere.

Our analysis would suggest that one factor in this difference lies in the existence of a human rights framework in the UK and Canada, and its absence in the Australian jurisdictions considered in this analysis. The existence of this framework forces the courts to interpret the best interests of the child in a way consistent with the human rights framework including, inter alia, the right to autonomy. While the three cases considered in this analysis occurred in jurisdictions without a human rights framework, in *Mercy* the court noted that the *Charter of Human Rights and Responsibilities* 2006 (Vic), and in particular s 14, "did not directly impact the Court's exercise of its *parens patriae* jurisdiction".[134] This would seem to suggest that it is not the existence of the human rights framework alone but its interaction with the relevant legislative provisions and the *parens patriae* jurisdiction which may be relevant to the transplantability of the Manitoban or English and Welsh to Australia. However, it is interesting to note that in *Mercy*, Macaulay J found that the "welfare of the child travels beyond a concern only for physical survival",

133 AC (n 1) [87].
134 *Mercy Hospitals Victoria v D1 & Anor* [2018] VSC 519 (31 August 2018) [52].

explicitly rejecting the reasoning of Pullin J in *AS*.[135] Despite finding that D1 did not have sufficient maturity, Macaulay J went on to consider the impact of making an order against D1's wishes on her psychological and spiritual welfare.[136] While this is different from the blending of the child's best interests and the child's wishes in the international cases, it is also different from a clash between the two interests seen in the Australian judgements analysed in this chapter. It is unclear if this difference is due to the existence of the *Charter of Human Rights and Responsibilities* 2006 (Vic) in Victoria.

Leaving aside the issue of the absence of a human rights framework in most Australian jurisdictions, adopting the English and Welsh approach would be the less radical. The Manitoban legislation has the effect of ousting the *parens patriae* jurisdiction, while the English and Welsh approach preserves it. Given the reliance on this jurisdiction in the Australian context, this would be a more natural fit. However, based on the earlier analysis, despite the similarities of approach in understanding the legal autonomy and maturity of the child and the similarities in terms of religious demographics, we do not believe transplanting the English and Welsh or Manitoban approach to Australia absent a human rights regime would be effective in promoting greater consideration of the child's wishes and autonomy in decision-making in the context of the refusal of life-saving medical treatment by mature minors. The best approach may be for other Australian jurisdictions to adopt South Australia's approach, which combines specific legislation regarding the ability of minors to consent with laws that require medical practitioners to take into account the "best interests of child's health and well-being".[137] This could be strengthened by removing the focus on health and insisting on a more holistic understanding of the child's best interest, as argued for by Macaulay J in *Mercy*, which may, we can hope, include a consideration of the child's maturity and wishes in the matter.

VI Conclusion: Transplant Thinking in a Nutshell …

This chapter has sought to compare the different approaches in various jurisdictions addressing the problem of what to do where medical transfusion needs clash with children's rights. In doing so, we invariably became tempted to look at whether any existing frameworks were sufficiently effective and functioned in sufficiently similar frameworks, systems, and societies to enable a so-called legal transplant. The term "legal transplant", as first popularised by Watson in 1974,[138] describes the phenomenon of one legal jurisdiction (the "host")

135 Ibid [61]–[63].
136 Ibid [77].
137 *Consent to Medical Treatment and Palliative Care Act 1995* (SA) s13(5).
138 Alan Watson, *Legal Transplants: An Approach to Comparative Law* (Scottish Academic Press, 1974), 18.

changing its laws to become more like those of another jurisdiction ("the donor") in an attempt to meet a legal/societal need for addressing a problem or achieving a similar result as that of the donor jurisdiction. Undeniably, while it is tempting to explore the idea of transplanting legislation to meet this growing societal need, it is a complex piece of legislation to transplant, for a variety of reasons.

Any thorough transplant study will look at the need for a transplant (ie, is there something here that needs fixing?), and then proceed to identifying a culturally relevant donor jurisdiction whose approach may function similarly, before proceeding to identify any obstacles to allowing the transplanted laws to function to achieve the desired outcome. Many of such identified obstacles may well be found outside what is traditionally considered law, in the social or economic norms and culture of a given society. In our case, we identified the need to take greater account of the wishes and autonomous decision-making of mature minors in medical decision-making, in line with shifts in international norms since the original introduction of the Australian "blood laws". We then identified England and Wales and Manitoba as potential donor jurisdictions. But in looking more loosely at these two jurisdictions which may offer functioning solutions to this legal issue, we find too many obstacles to recommend transplantation.

We do not believe that we have identified any significant issues neo-functionally concerning the cultural or theoretical transplantability of the English and Welsh or Manitoban model into Australia more broadly. However, in taking a structuralist approach to the transplant, we have identified a serious issue in the lack of constitutional support, in the form of a human rights framework, for such legislation, and, consequently, the South Australian approach might be best advocated.

Ultimately, from a functional perspective, the outcome for the children in all five cases considered in this analysis were the same. The child was required to undergo a blood transfusion despite their religious objections and their (or their parent's) refusal of consent. Our analysis does not suggest that adopting the approach of one or other of the legislative regimes analysed would lead to a different outcome. However it does, we argue, in conjunction with a human rights regime, lead to a difference in reasoning – one we would submit is material to the recognition, or otherwise, of the increasing autonomy of children as they age. This is more than paying lip service to the idea of the evolving capacity of the child outlined in international law. Rather, it is a fundamentally different understanding of a child's best interest – one that includes the child's wishes and autonomy within the concept of best interest, rather than as opposing it.

As expressed in the Manitoban case, from which the opening quote to this chapter also stems:

> One of the most sensitive decisions a judge can make in family law is in connection with the authorization of medical treatment for children. It engages the most intensely complicated constellation of considerations and its consequences are inevitably profound.[139]

The same is true for medical practitioners, yet as the Australian "blood laws" are currently written, they are not required to take into account the child's best interests, let alone their wishes and right to autonomy.

In conclusion, based on our analysis, we do not believe that a straight transplant of either the Manitoban or English and Welsh approach to Western Australia, New South Wales, or South Australia would produce the change in reasoning that we have identified as necessary, or be suited for transplantation as is.

In a nutshell – despite similar societal goals in balancing children's rights and medical needs, there simply isn't sufficient similarity amongst the jurisdictions when it comes to the protection of children's interests, and how their rights are balanced and are enshrined in law to recommend transplantation of existing frameworks.

More research is needed in those Australian jurisdictions that have legislative bills or charters of rights of the impact of those bills and charters on judicial reasoning, and how that might apply in the context of judicial decision-making about refusal of life-saving medical treatment of a mature minor.

Further Reading:

For analysis of the methods used in this chapter, see Chapter 15 – Section IV – subsection F *The Yardstick Method*.

For the author's rejoinder and reflection, see Appendix Section IV.

For another example of the yardstick method, see Chapter 12.

For a discussion about methodological and ethics issues in comparative law and religion research involving children, see Chapter 4.

139 AC (n 1) [1] (Abella J).

9 Interpreting the Right to Freedom of Religion in the EU Charter of Fundamental Rights: Outlining and Analysing the Function of the European Convention on Human Rights According to Art 52(3) CFR

*Gerhard van der Schyff**

I Introduction: Setting the Scene

The right to freedom of religion in article 10(1) of the *Charter of Fundamental Rights of the European Union* ('*CFR*'), which was proclaimed in 2000 and came into force in 2009, is a topic that is gaining increased attention in the case law of the Court of Justice of the European Union ('CJEU').[1] Central to the interpretation of this right is article 52(3) *CFR*. According to this provision, the "meaning and scope" of rights which 'correspond' to the *European Convention on Human Rights* ('*ECHR*') shall be the same as those laid down in the *ECHR*.[2] Article 10(1) *CFR* is a prime example of such a right, as it corresponds with the right to freedom of religion in article 9 *ECHR*. The impact of article 52(3) *CFR* is vast, given that it also covers many other rights in the *CFR*. This is compounded by the fact that the *CFR* is addressed to the organs of the European Union ('EU') and its Member States when implementing EU law according to article 51(1) *CFR*. The effect is that the *CFR* applies whenever EU law is applied.[3] This means that the *CFR* affects the EU level as

1 Associate Professor, Department of Public Law and Governance, Law School, Tilburg University, The Netherlands.

Charter of Fundamental Rights of the European Union 2000 [2012] OJ C 326, 391 ('*CFR*'). See, eg, *Centraal Israëlitisch Consistorie van België and Others v Vlaamse Regering* (Court of Justice of the European Union, C-336/19, ECLI:EU:C:2020:1031, 17 December 2020) ('*Centraal Israëlitisch Consistorie*').

2 *Convention for the Protection of Human Rights and Fundamental Freedoms*, 4 November 1950, 213 UNTS 221.

3 See *Åklagaren v Hans Åkerberg Fransson* (Court of Justice of the European Union, C-617/10, ECLI:EU:C:2013:105, 26 February 2013), [20], [23].

DOI: 10.4324/9781003397311-14

well as the 27 Member States in the multilevel framework which makes up the EU legal system.[4]

Given the relative novelty and importance of article 52(3) *CFR*, the purpose of this contribution is to outline and analyse the provision as an interpretative method. In particular, attention will be paid to its effect on the right to freedom of religion in article 10(1) *CFR*. Reference will be made to the most appropriate and illustrative judgements in studying freedom of religion and article 52(3) *CFR*, instead of attempting to treat them all. In addressing this issue, the contribution will first provide the necessary background to EU and *ECHR* law, with particular reference to the position of the CJEU and the European Court of Human Rights ('ECtHR') in each legal system (Section II). The interconnection between the EU and *ECHR* will then be explored in the context of fundamental rights protection (Section III). The attention will then turn to outlining article 52(3) *CFR* (Section IV), after which its application to the right to freedom of religion in article 10(1) *CFR* will be investigated regarding the interpretation of the right's protective scope and the limitation of that protection (Sections V–VIII). Taking into account the preceding analysis, the contribution will conclude with seven inter-related observations regarding the application and function of article 52(3) *CFR* as a method of interpretation (Section IX).

II Two European Legal Orders and Their Courts

What today comprises the EU, established by the Maastricht Treaty of 1992 but whose origins can be traced to the 1957 European Economic Community ('EEC'), along with the Council of Europe founded in 1949 and whose signatory treaty is the *ECHR*, were both created after the Second World War to chart a new future for the European continent. Whereas the EU, and especially its forerunner the EEC, traditionally pursued European integration through the creation of a customs union and a common or internal market between the Member States, the Council of Europe fostered greater unity between its Member States by pursuing "the maintenance and further realisation of human rights and fundamental freedoms".[5] The main purpose of the *ECHR*, dating from 1950, was to protect typical classical rights, derived from the *Universal Declaration of Human Rights*, through collective enforcement in ensuring "effective political democracy" according to its preamble. Both the EU and the Council of Europe, which each has a distinct legal order,

4 On the multilevel framework, see Ingolf Pernice, 'Multilevel Constitutionalism in the European Union' (2002) 27(5) *European Law Review* 511.

5 The quote is taken from the preamble to the *ECHR*. On European integration, see Paul Craig and Gráinne de Búrca, *EU Law: Text, Cases, and Materials* (Oxford University Press, 7th ed, 2020) 1–31; Roel de Lange, 'The European Public Order, Constitutional Principles and Fundamental Rights', (2007) 1(1) *Erasmus Law Review* 1, 12–15.

therefore, pursue European integration or unity, but depart from different objectives in doing so.

The treaties governing the EU are interpreted and applied by the CJEU in Luxemburg, while the ECtHR in Strasbourg ensures observance of the *ECHR* and its protocols.[6] There are key differences between the enforcement mechanisms of the EU and *ECHR*. EU law operates in the legal orders of Member States according to the conditions set out by EU law itself. In this regard, EU law can take direct effect in national orders and national institutions must accord it primacy over countervailing national law, including the country's constitution.[7] The final word on EU law, and its primacy over countervailing national law, is spoken by the CJEU.[8] The primary route to the CJEU is that of preliminary references made by Member State courts, including tribunals, concerning a question of EU law.[9] This means that when a question of EU law arises before a national court, a judge may, and in some instances must, refer the matter to the CJEU and await its ruling before concluding the case. EU law, it should be noted, is a broad category, which covers primary law, in other words, EU treaties; and secondary law, which includes EU legislation such as regulations and directives.

The ECtHR, in contrast to the CJEU, does not give preliminary rulings during national proceedings. Instead, applicants may bring a case before the ECtHR against a Member State after having exhausted all domestic remedies according to article 35(1) *ECHR*.[10] This means that the ECtHR functions at the *end* of national proceedings and not *next to* such proceedings as does the CJEU. In this regard, article 34 *ECHR* explains that applicants can be "any person, non-governmental organisation or group of individuals" claiming to be a "victim" of an *ECHR* rights violation. According to article 33 *ECHR*, the ECtHR can also hear inter-state cases, although the vast majority of cases concern individual applicants against Member States. It is not possible for a non-state applicant to bring a case against another non-state applicant. The *ECHR* system does not require Member States to accord direct effect and primacy to its guarantees, as does EU law. Instead, each Member State decides

6 Art 19(1) *Treaty on European Union* 2009 (Lisbon Treaty) [2012] OJ C 326, 13 ('*TEU*'); art 19 *ECHR*.

7 The countervailing law is not nullified, according to the doctrine of primacy, but simply not applied in a given case, thereby affording primacy of application to EU law.

8 The primacy of EU law is not guaranteed in the EU treaties as such, but referred to in *Declaration 17* concerning primacy.

9 Art 19(3) *TEU*; *Treaty on the Functioning of the European Union 2009* (Lisbon Treaty) [2012] OJ C 326, 13) art 267 ('TFEU').

10 Art 35(2)–(4) outline the other admissibility requirements. Judgements are passed by Chambers, with some cases being reheard by the Grand Chamber after which the matter is closed (arts 42–4 *ECHR*).

on the basis of its constitutional law how to give effect to its commitments under the *ECHR*.[11]

Comparing the two systems and their courts, it is clear that the ECtHR acts as an international fundamental rights court of last resort which exercises jurisdiction in cases where a Member State fails to protect *ECHR* rights. While the ECtHR's jurisdiction is limited to deciding whether a Member State violated a right under the *ECHR*, the CJEU's jurisdiction is broader by comparison.[12] In this regard, the CJEU can best be described as an international supreme court, constitutional court and, increasingly, a fundamental rights court.[13] The supreme court function is the CJEU's mainstay as it covers all the material competences conferred on the EU according to article 5 *Treaty on European Union* ('*TEU*').[14] This includes the exercise of the EU's wide-ranging federal-like exclusive competences, such as the customs union and Eurozone monetary policy; the competences it shares with the Member States, such as the internal market and the environment; and the EU's competence to support Member States in fields such as industry and tourism.[15] The CJEU also adjudicates typical constitutional matters, such as the validity of EU legislation in the light of the EU treaties and the limits of the federal-like competences conferred on the EU.[16] Added to this is the function of the CJEU as a fundamental rights court, which decides, for example, whether fundamental rights have been respected in the exercise of the EU's competences.

11 This can entail direct effect and primacy such as in the Netherlands, where courts must refuse to apply national law that conflicts with the *ECHR*, or it can entail the incorporation of the *ECHR* into national law before courts may apply it, such as in the United Kingdom, where courts are to give effect to selected *ECHR* rights according to the terms of the *Human Rights Act* of 1998. For these examples, see Elisa Bertolini and Graziella Romeo, 'The Dutch System and the Supranational Law: The Application of the ECHR in a Comparative Perspective' in Giuseppe Franco Ferrari, Reijer Passchier and Wim Voermans (eds), *The Dutch Constitution beyond 200 Years: Tradition and Innovation in a Multilevel Legal Order* (Eleven International Publishing, 2018) 83, 87–90; Gerhard van der Schyff, *Judicial Review of Legislation: A Comparative Study of the United Kingdom, the Netherlands and South Africa* (Springer, 2010) 17–20.

12 See also Ronan McCrea, 'Singing from the Same Hymn Sheet? What the Differences between the Strasbourg and Luxembourg Courts Tell Us about Religious Freedom, Non-Discrimination, and the Secular State' 2016 5(2) *Oxford Journal of Law and Religion* (2016) 183, 192–3.

13 See also Monica Claes and Maartje de Visser, 'The Court of Justice as a Federal Constitutional Court: A Comparative Perspective' in Elke Cloots, Geert De Baere and Stefan Sottiaux, (eds) *Federalism in the European Union* (Hart Publishing, 2012) 83, 98–104.

14 On art 5 *TEU*, see Albrecht Weber, 'Article 5. [Principles on the Distribution and Limits of Competences]' in Hermann-Josef Blanke and Stelio Mangiameli (eds) *The Treaty on European Union (TEU). A Commentary* (Springer, 2013) 255–86.

15 These competences are listed in arts 3, 4 and 6 *TFEU*.

16 See Claes and De Visser (n 13) 98–100.

III Two Interconnected Legal Orders

Although the EU and Council of Europe represent two separate legal orders in Europe, they are closely connected to each other in the field of fundamental rights. The interconnection between the *CFR* and *ECHR* becomes especially vivid when a right such as that to freedom of religion is considered. Article 10(1) *CFR* reads that:

> Everyone has the right to freedom of thought, conscience and religion. This right includes freedom to change religion or belief and freedom, either alone or in community with others and in public or in private, to manifest religion or belief, in worship, teaching, practice and observance.

Apart from some style differences, this wording is nearly identical to the right as stated in article 9(1) *ECHR* and it is no coincidence.[17] This close coupling can be traced through the overlap in membership between the EU and the Council of Europe, and through article 6 *TEU*, which provides the key to understanding the architecture of fundamental rights protection in the EU by listing the various sources.[18]

Although distinct legal orders in the European continent, all 27 Member States of the EU also belong to the *ECHR*, whose parent body, the Council of Europe, counts 46 Member States.[19] This overlap in membership is used by the EU to expand and protect fundamental rights in its legal system. In this regard, article 6(2) *TEU* requires that the EU accedes to the *ECHR* as a non-state party, thereby becoming its 47th member.[20] To date, accession has not yet taken place, which means that the *ECHR* cannot be relied on directly before the CJEU.[21] This turns the focus to article 6(3) *TEU*.[22] Article 6(3) *TEU* recognises the fundamental rights in the *ECHR* and those resulting from the constitutional traditions common to the Member States as "general principles" of EU law. This reflects a long-standing practice of the CJEU, which

17 Art 9(1) *ECHR* provides that: 'Everyone has the right to freedom of thought, conscience and religion; this right includes freedom to change his religion or belief and freedom, either alone or in community with others and in public or private, to manifest his religion or belief, in worship, teaching, practice and observance'.

18 On art 6 *TEU*, see Christoph Grabenwarter and Katharina Pabel, 'Article 6. [Fundamental Rights – The Charter and the ECHR]' in Hermann-Josef Blanke and Stelio Mangiameli (eds), *The Treaty on European Union (TEU). A Commentary* (Springer, 2013) 287–348.

19 Regarding membership, it can be noted that the United Kingdom ceased to be an EU member on 31 January 2020 and the Russian Federation ceased to be an *ECHR* member on 16 September 2022.

20 See in general, Grabenwarter and Pabel (n 18) 308–32.

21 See the opinion of Advocate General Wahl in *Liga van Moskeeën en Islamitische Organisaties Provincie Antwerpen and Others v Vlaams Gewest* (Court of Justice of the European Union, C-426/16, ECLI:EU:C:2017:926, 30 November 2017), [45]–[47].

22 See in general, Grabenwarter and Pabel (n 18) 333–7.

for many years used such principles to compensate for the lack of an EU bill of rights before the adoption and enforcement of the *CFR* in the 2000s.[23]

When the *CFR* was eventually adopted, it was decided to affirm the existing connection with the *ECHR* by copying a number of its provisions, such as article 9(1) *ECHR*. This link was cemented by the requirement in article 52(3) *CFR* that the new rights be interpreted in the same way as the rights they copy. In this way, the "necessary consistency" between *ECHR* rights and the corresponding rights in the *CFR* was achieved, as noted in the Explanations to the *CFR* in 2007.[24] Also noteworthy is that the adoption of the *CFR*, which is recognised as a source of fundamental rights in article 6(1) *CFR*, did not replace the existing sources of fundamental rights protection in place in EU, international, and national law as and where applicable to the EU and its Member States.[25] Instead, the *CFR*, according to article 53 *CFR*, provides a minimum level of protection that other applicable sources may exceed, as long as "the primacy, unity, and effectiveness of EU law are not thereby compromised".[26] However, article 53 *CFR* seems to be redundant as regards the *ECHR* in the context of article 52(3) *CFR*. This is because the latter provision requires that EU law must comply with the *ECHR*, which precludes the application of a higher *ECHR* standard than in EU law.[27]

IV Article 52(3) *CFR* on Corresponding Rights

As article 52(3) *CFR* is clearly intended to serve as a pivot in consolidating the interconnection between the *CFR* and the *ECHR*, it calls for a closer examination. The provision states in full that:

> In so far as this Charter contains rights which correspond to rights guaranteed by the Convention for the Protection of Human Rights and Fundamental Freedoms, the meaning and scope of those rights shall be the same as those laid down by the said Convention. This provision shall not prevent Union law providing more extensive protection.

23 See *Nold v Commission* (Court of Justice of the European Union, Case 4/73, ECLI:EU:C:1974:51, 14 May 1974), [12]–[13].

24 *Explanations Relating to the Charter of Fundamental Rights of the European* Union [2007] OJ C 303, 17, 33.

25 See also Bruno De Witte, 'Article 53' in Steve Peers, Tamara Hervey, Jeff Kenner and Angela Ward (eds), *The EU Charter of Fundamental Rights: A Commentary* (Hart Publishing, 2021) 1675, 1676.

26 *Stefano Melloni v Ministerio Fiscal* (Court of Justice of the European Union, C-399/11, ECLI:EU:C:2013:107, 26 February 2013), [60]. Compare De Witte (n 25) 1683.

27 See Paul Lemmens, 'The Relation between the Charter of Fundamental Rights of the European Union and the European Convention on Human Rights – Substantive Aspects', 8(1) *Maastricht Journal of European and Comparative Law* (2001) 49, 55.

The nexus between the *CFR* and *ECHR* is determined by the verb "correspond", as it is only when a *CFR* provision corresponds to one in the *ECHR* that article 52(3) *CFR* applies. In this context, the Explanations to the *CFR*, previously mentioned, play an important role in listing the provisions which correspond. The weight of the Explanations is also confirmed by article 6(1) *TEU*, which requires that the *CFR* be interpreted "with due regard to the explanations referred to in the Charter, that set out the sources of those provisions". The case law of the CJEU confirms the importance of the Explanations in this regard. For instance, in *Achbita*, the Explanations were referred to explicitly in finding that "Article 10(1) of the Charter corresponds to the right guaranteed in Article 9 of the ECHR and, in accordance with Article 52(3) of the Charter, has the same meaning and scope".[28] Although the wording of article 10(1) *CFR* is nearly identical to article 9(1) *ECHR*, this is not a general requirement for rights to "correspond". It is also sufficient if a provision in the *CFR* covers a similar guarantee to that found in the *ECHR* without copying the exact wording, such as the second and third paragraphs of article 47 *CFR* on the right to a fair trial and article 6(1) *ECHR*.[29] In such cases, as gathered from the Explanations, the meaning corresponds but the scope of the *CFR* right is broader than that in the *ECHR*.[30]

If a right in the *CFR* is confirmed to correspond with a right in the *ECHR*, its "meaning and scope" will be the same as in the *ECHR*. This is the essence of article 52(3) *CFR* and raises the question what it entails. Again, the Explanations provide a number of guidelines. In this context, it should be noted that the reference to the *ECHR* includes not only the treaty as such, but also its protocols.[31] The "meaning and scope" of a right is understood broadly to include "authorised limitations".[32] Also, the content of a corresponding right is to be determined by reference to the text of the *ECHR* and the case law of the ECtHR and the CJEU.[33] This means that the meaning and scope of such a right is ultimately decided by the CJEU, which in turn has to base itself on the *ECHR* text as interpreted by the ECtHR. For example, the CJEU in the *WABE* case, referring to article 52(3) *CFR*, relied on the ECtHR's judgement in *Dahlab* to conclude that the right to freedom of religion "represents one of the foundations of a 'democratic society".[34] In this way, the

28 *Samira Achbita and Centrum voor gelijkheid van kansen en voor racismebestrijding v G4S Secure Solutions NV* (CJEU, C-157/15, EU:C:2017:203, 14 March 2017), [26]–[27] ('*Achbita*'). See also *IX v WABE eV and MH Müller Handels GmbH v MJ* (Court of Justice of the European Union, C-804/18, ECLI:EU:C:2021:594, 15 July 2021), [81] ('*WABE*').

29 Explanations (n 24) 15.

30 Ibid 19.

31 Ibid 18.

32 Ibid.

33 Ibid.

34 *WABE* (n 28) [48]; 15; *Dahlab v Switzerland* (European Court of Human Rights, Application No 42393/98, 15 February 2001) ('*Dahlab*').

Explanations recognise that the CJEU is entrusted with the definitive interpretation of the EU treaties, which includes the *CFR*, under article 19(1) *TEU*.

In addition, it is it important to take in account that article 52(3) *CFR*, according to the Explanations, cannot be applied in a way that adversely affects the autonomy of EU law and that of the CJEU itself.[35] In other words, the purpose of a corresponding right is to set a level of protection under the *CFR*, and not to compromise the logic and operation of EU law as an autonomous legal system. The CJEU has also been at pains, such as in *Centraal Israëlitisch Consistorie*, to stress this point.[36] The last sentence of article 52(3) *CFR* should also be read in the light of the autonomy of EU law, as the *ECHR* is not meant as an upper limit for corresponding rights, but as a minimum level of protection that can be exceeded by EU law.[37] For example, the EU legislator, when adopting a regulation or directive, may choose to protect a corresponding right, such as that to freedom of religion, in a more extensive manner than that required by the *ECHR*.[38]

V Freedom of Religion as a Corresponding Right

Two general remarks can be made in turning the attention to outlining freedom of religion as a corresponding right in accordance with article 52(3) *CFR*. The first remark to make is that the CJEU uses article 9(1) *ECHR* to answer questions not only for preliminary rulings which expressly require the interpretation of article 10(1) *CFR*, such as in *Liga van Moskeeën* and *Centraal Israëlitisch Consistorie*, but also to answer questions that require the interpretation of other provisions of EU law, such secondary law in *Achbita*, *Bougnaoui*, and *Jehovan todistajat*.[39] This wide approach by the CJEU is to be welcomed, as it ensures legal certainty and unity by relying on article 9(1)

35 Explanations (n 24) 18.

36 Eg *Centraal Israëlitisch Consistorie* (n 1) [56].

37 See Steve Peers and Sacha Prechal, 'Article 52', in Steve Peers, Tamara Hervey, Jeff Kenner and Angela Ward, eds, *The EU Charter of Fundamental Rights: A Commentary* (Hart Publishing, 2021) 1611, 1651.

38 For example, according to the opinion of Advocate General Hogan in *Centraal Israëlitisch Consistorie van België and Others v Vlaamse Regering* (Court of Justice of the European Union, C-336/19, ECLI:EU:C:2020:695, 10 September), [86] ('*Centraal Israëlitisch Consistorie van België*') the EU regulation in question provided 'a more specific protection to the freedom of religion than that which may have been required by Article 9' *ECHR*. This seemed to indicate that EU secondary law provided more extensive protection than required under the *ECHR*. The judgement did not follow the opinion, though. See also McCrea (n 12) 209–10 who discusses differences in protecting the right to freedom of religion under *ECHR* and EU law.

39 *Liga van Moskeeën en Islamitische Organisaties Provincie Antwerpen and Others v Vlaams Gewest* (Court of Justice of the European Union, C-426/16, ECLI:EU:C:2018:335, 29 May 2019), [26] ('*Liga van Moskeeën*'); *Centraal Israëlitisch Consistorie* (n 1) [32]; *Asma Bougnaoui and Association de défense des droits de l'homme (ADDH) v Micropole SA* (Court of Justice of the European Union, C-188/15, ECLI:EU:C:2017:204, 14 March 2017), [19]

ECHR whenever a question regarding freedom of religion requires attention in EU law.

Secondly, it is important to consider the architecture of the right to freedom of religion in both the *CFR* and the *ECHR*. Fundamental rights guarantees distinguishing between rights that allow limitations and those that do not allow limitations.[40] This distinction is also made in the *CFR* and the *ECHR*. In this regard, article 9(2) *ECHR* contains a specific limitation clause that applies solely to the right to freedom of religion in article 9(1) *ECHR*.[41] The *CFR*, on the other hand, does not attach a specific limitation clause to the right to freedom of religion in article 10(1) *CFR*, but contains a general limitation clause in article 52(1) which covers multiple provisions. The effect in both instances is the same, as the right can be divided into a scope and a limitation clause which can be applied to that scope. In following this distinction, the analysis of freedom of religion in article 10(1) *CFR* will first outline its scope and then consider how that may be limited by considering what amounts to an interference with the scope and when that may be justified.

VI Scope of Protection

It is a standard practice for the CJEU to refer to, and rely on, article 9(1) *ECHR* when interpreting the scope of the right to freedom of religion in article 10(1) *CFR*. For instance, in the cases of *Achbita* and *Bougnaoui*, which related to the wearing of religious symbols by employees, the CJEU noted that article 10(1) *CFR* corresponded with article 9(1) *ECHR*.[42] The CJEU then defined the concept of "religion" by reference to the *ECHR* and noted that the term had to be understood in a "broad sense" as including the freedom of people to manifest their religion.[43] According to the CJEU, the EU legislature must be presumed to have intended the same meaning for the term "religion" in article 1 of *Directive 2000/78/EC*, which intended to establish a general framework for equal treatment in employment and occupation by combatting discrimination on a number of grounds.[44] This meant that the term "religion" had to be interpreted as encompassing the distinction, well known in *ECHR* law, between the *forum internum*, understood as "the fact of having a belief" and the *forum externum*, understood as "the manifestation of religious faith

('*Bougnaoui*'); *Achbita* (n 28) [21]; *Jehovan todistajat* (Court of Justice of the European Union, C-25/17, ECLI:EU:C:2018:551, 10 July 2018), [24].

40 On this distinction, see Gerhard van der Schyff, *Limitation of Rights: A Study of the European Convention and the South African Bill of Rights* (Wolf Legal Publishers, 2005) 11–14.

41 Compare art 3 *ECHR* which does not contain a limitation clause.

42 *Achbita* (n 28) [27]; *Bougnaoui* (n 39) [29].

43 *Achbita* (n 28) [28]; *Bougnaoui* (n 39) [30].

44 *Council Directive 2000/78/EC of 27 November 2000 Establishing a General Framework for Equal Treatment in Employment and Occupation* [2000] OJ L 303, 2 December 2000, 16. This directive is no longer in force.

in public".[45] This was significant, as article 1 of the *Directive* simply referred to the term "religion", which raised the question whether discrimination on account of manifesting one's religion was covered by the *Directive*, or simply discrimination on account of belonging to a particular religion. As Advocate General Sharpston explained in her opinion in the *Bougnaoui* case, the applicant was dismissed because she manifested her belief and not because of her religious membership as such.[46] Although the CJEU could very well have taken the same view on its own, applying the case law of the ECtHR settled the matter in an authoritative manner.

Apart from establishing that the right to freedom of religion in article 10(1) *CFR* protects one's membership of a religion and its subsequent expression, the CJEU has also used *ECHR* case law to decide which manifestations are to be protected. In this regard, it can be noted that article 10(1) *CFR* is interpreted in conformity with the ECHR as protecting theistic and non-theistic beliefs, as well as atheistic beliefs, equally.[47] When it comes to deciding which religious manifestations qualify for protection under article 10(1) *CFR*, Advocate General Mengozzi adopted the *ECHR* line that "Article 9(1) ECHR does not, however, protect every act motivated or inspired by a religion or belief", as explained by the ECtHR in *Larissis*, for example.[48] In interpreting article 10(1) *CFR* in *Jehovan todistajat*, the Advocate General referred to the *Larissis* judgement and made a distinction between article 9(1) *ECHR* protecting proselytism, as a manifestation of "teaching" religion, while not protecting "improper proselytism", which included applying "improper pressure with a view to gaining new members for a Church".[49] The CJEU also referred to ECtHR case law in the matter, and agreed with the Advocate General that "door-to-door preaching activities of the member of a religious community is thereby protected by Article 10(1)" *CFR*.[50] This was relevant in the case in addressing the main issue of whether *Directive 95/46/EC* on the

45 *Achbita* (n 28) [28]; *Bougnaoui* (n 39) [30].

46 Opinion of Advocate General Sharpston in *Samira Achbita and Centrum voor gelijkheid van kansen en voor racismebestrijding v G4S Secure Solutions NV* (Court of Justice of the European Union, C-188/15, ECLI:EU:C:2016:553, 13 July 2016), [85]–[87] ('*Bougnaoui*').

47 See Ronan McCrea, 'Article 10' in Steve Peers, Tamara Hervey, Jeff Kenner and Angela Ward (eds), *The EU Charter of Fundamental Rights: A Commentary* (Hart Publishing, 2021) 313, 315, 327. And also *Kokkinakis v Greece* (European Court of Human Rights, Application No 14307/88, 25 May 1993), [31].

48 Opinion of Advocate General Mengozzi in *Jehovan todistajat* (Court of Justice of the European Union, C-25/17, ECLI:EU:C:2018:57, 1 February 2018) [49], fn 51 quoting *Larissis and Others v Greece* (European Court of Human Rights, Application No 23372/94, 24 February 1998), [45] ('*Larissis*').

49 Ibid. See also fn 50.

50 *Jehovan todistajat* (n 39) [49].

protection of individuals with regard to the processing of personal data and on the free movement of such data, applied to door-to-door proselytism.[51]

Mention can also be made of article 10(2) *CFR*, which recognises the right to conscientious objection "in accordance with the national laws governing the exercise of this right". This provision was probably included in the *CFR* because until the *Bayatyan* case in 2011, the ECtHR did not recognise conscientious objection as a right under article 9(1) *ECHR*.[52] The effect of article 52(3) *CFR* on article 10(1) *CFR* would have been that such a right would not be protected under article 10(1) *CFR* either. The drafters of the *CFR* apparently wanted to avoid this situation by including article 10(2) *CFR*. Although article 9(1) *ECHR* is now understood by the ECtHR to protect a right to conscientious objection, article 52(3) *CFR* seemingly does not apply to such objection as it is governed under article 10(2), which is not mentioned as a corresponding right in the Explanations.[53] This would be the case unless the CJEU interpreted article 10 *CFR* as a corresponding right as such and not only article 10(1) *CFR*.[54]

VII Interference with the Scope

As the Explanations also include "authorised limitations" under article 52(3) *CFR*, notice should also be taken of what constitutes an interference with the right to freedom of religion under article 9(1) *ECHR*, as any interference with its scope would require limitation analysis.[55] The finding of an interference with the right to freedom of religion often proves to be straightforward.[56] However, two examples, both concerning ritual slaughter, illustrate the importance of considering this step more closely when applying the right to religious freedom in the context of article 52(3) *CFR*.

51 Ibid [1], [76]. *Directive 95/46/EC of the European Parliament and of the Council of 24 October 1995, on the Protection of Individuals with Regard to the Processing of Personal Data and on the Free Movement of Such Data* [1995] OJ L 281, 31.

52 *Bayatyan v Armenia* (European Court of Human Rights, Grand Chamber, Application No 23459/03, 7 July 2011), [110].

53 Only art 10(1) *CFR* is mentioned as corresponding to art 9 *ECHR* by the Explanations (n 24) 6, 18. The Explanations reveal that art 10(2) *CFR* 'corresponds to national constitutional traditions and to the development of national legislation on this issue' (6).

54 McCrea (n 47) 326 remarks that in practice the impact of art 10(2) *CFR* might be limited, as EU law generally does not concern issues such as national defence. However, questions regarding conscientious objection can be much broader, as illustrated by the COVID-19 pandemic and discussions related to vaccinations and travel restrictions. To the extent that this concerns EU law, it would be advisable to ensure consistency with *ECHR* standards (such as in *Vavřička and Others v the Czech Republic* [European Court of Human Rights, Grand Chamber, Application Nos 47621/13 and 5 others, 8 April 2021]) for the sake of a common approach on such important questions.

55 Explanations (n 24) 18.

56 Eg *Leyla Şahin v Turkey* (European Court of Human Rights, Grand Chamber, Application No 44774/98, 10 November 2005), [76]–[78].

Although the CJEU, like the ECtHR, considers that the right to freedom of religion protects ritual slaughter, the CJEU probably departed from the ECtHR when identifying an interference with this right in the past. This can be argued in the light of the ECtHR's case law in *Cha'are Shalom* and before its recent judgement in *Executief van de Moslims.*[57] According to *Cha'are Shalom*, "there would be interference with the freedom to manifest one's religion only if the illegality of performing ritual slaughter made it impossible" for religious adherents "to eat meat from animals slaughtered in accordance with the religious prescriptions they considered applicable".[58] This position differs from the routes taken by the CJEU in *Liga van Moskeeën* and *Centraal Israëlitisch Consistorie*. Both these cases concerned Flanders, a Belgian region, and its implementation of *Regulation No 1099/2009* on the protection of animals at the time of killing.[59] Article 4(4) of the *Regulation* allows the Jewish and Muslim faiths' exemptions from the rule in article 4(1) that animals must always be stunned when slaughtered, provided that the slaughter takes place in an approved slaughterhouse.

In *Liga van Moskeeën*, the CJEU had to decide whether article 4(4) of the *Regulation* interfered with the right to freedom of religion in article 10(1) *CFR*.[60] This was because during the Muslim Feast of Sacrifice, the approved slaughterhouses in Flanders did not have sufficient capacity to meet the demand for ritual slaughter, while temporary slaughterhouses were not allowed for failing to meet the requirements of approved slaughterhouses.[61] The CJEU ruled that article 4(4) of the *Regulation* did not "restrict" the right to freedom of religion in article 10(1) *CFR* even though not all Muslims could exercise the right.[62] This was because article 4(4) applied in a "general and neutral manner" and the applicable "technical framework is not in itself of such a nature as to place a restriction on the right to freedom of religion of practising Muslims".[63] However, on account of article 52(3) *CFR*, the CJEU should probably have used the ECtHR's rule outlined earlier. Although in this case the outcome might probably have been the same if the *ECHR* approach had

57 *Cha'are Shalom Ve Tsedek v France* (European Court of Human Rights, Grand Chamber, Application No 27417/95, 27 June 2000) ('*Cha'are Shalom*'); *Executief van de Moslims van België v Belgium* (European Court of Human Rights, Application Nos 16760/22 and ten others, 13 February 2024) ('*Executief van de Moslims*'). The latter judgement was only handed down after this contribution was largely completed, references to the judgement should, therefore, be understood as preliminary remarks on the case.

58 *Cha'are Shalom Ve Tsedek* (n 57) [80].

59 *Council Regulation (EC) No 1099/2009 of 24 September 2009 on the Protection of Animals at the Time of Killing* [2009] OJ L 303, 1.

60 *Liga van Moskeeën* (n 39) [26], [52].

61 Ibid [17]–[18], [70].

62 Ibid [68].

63 Ibid [59], [61].

been followed, it could have been different in other cases.[64] This possibility emphasises the need to follow the *ECHR* approach unless the EU approach leads to more extensive protection of the right to freedom of religion.

The *Centraal Israëlitisch Consistorie* judgement is arguably an example where the EU approach provided more extensive protection than the *ECHR* one. In this case, the CJEU had to decide whether Flanders could derogate from the religious exemptions in article 4(4) of the *Regulation* to require that animals must always be stunned when slaughtered, interfered with the right to freedom of religion in article 10(1) *CFR*. If the CJEU had applied the ECtHR rule, there would have been no interference with the right as qualifying meat could be accessed from Brussels, a different Belgian region or imported from other countries where ritual slaughter could be practised more freely.[65] However, the CJEU found that the Flemish derogation did, indeed, interfere with believers' rights to freedom of religion, as it stipulated, contrary to their religious precepts, that ritual slaughter could not be carried out without stunning.[66] In finding that a factual interference with the scope of the right warranted limitation analysis, the CJEU departed from the high threshold set by the ECtHR in *Cha'are Shalom*. The effect of lowering the threshold is to make it easier for believers to call the state to account for interfering with ritual slaughter, thereby increasing the protection afforded them under article 10(1) *CFR*. It is noteworthy that in the recent *Executief van de Moslims* ruling, the ECtHR took a similar approach to the *Centraal Israëlitisch Consistorie* ruling, by also requiring a lower threshold.[67]

These two examples show how the approach by the CJEU can differ between comparable cases while also deviating from the *ECHR* approach in finding an interference with the right to freedom of religion in article 10(1) *CFR*. In this regard, it would be advisable for the CJEU to adopt an approach that is more consistent with the case law of the ECtHR, unless it chooses to go further in protecting the right to freedom of religion. Also, the CJEU has to keep abreast of the ongoing developments in the case law of the ECtHR, as illustrated by the *Executief van de Moslims* judgement.

64 The outcome would probably have been the same, as the lack of capacity did not make it impossible to access ritually slaughtered meat, especially on a fixed basis.

65 See the opinion of Advocate General Hogan (n 38) [85].

66 *Centraal Israëlitisch Consistorie* (n 1) [53]–[55]. In [55], the judgement explains that the derogation entailed a 'limitation' on the exercise of the right, while later in the judgement the derogation is referred to as an 'interference' with the right ([72], [75]. In this context, the terms interference and limitation are used as synonyms, denoting that the scope of the right cannot be exercised freely.

67 *Executief van de Moslims* (n 57) [82]–[83], [88]. The ECtHR distinguished the facts (in effect prohibiting ritual slaughter if animals are not stunned first) from those in *Cha'are Shalom* (n 57) [58] (granting permission to one organisation to conduct ritual slaughter, but not to another). However, this distinction does not appear to explain the difference in the threshold for finding an interference with religious freedom. It seems more likely that the ECtHR has developed its jurisprudence on this point by lowering the threshold.

VIII Limitation of the Scope

As remarked previously, the *CFR* contains a general limitation clause in article 52(1) *CFR* which covers multiple guarantees. This provision provides that:

> Any limitation on the exercise of the rights and freedoms recognised by this Charter must be provided for by law and respect the essence of those rights and freedoms. Subject to the principle of proportionality, limitations may be made only if they are necessary and genuinely meet objectives of general interest recognised by the Union or the need to protect the rights and freedoms of others.[68]

In comparison, the *ECHR* does not contain a general limitation clause, but attaches a specific limitation clause to each right which may be limited. The rights in articles 8 to 11 *ECHR*, including freedom of religion in article 9(1) *ECHR*, each has a specific limitation provision. In respect of freedom of religion, article 9(2) *ECHR* provides that:

> Freedom to manifest one's religion or beliefs shall be subject only to such limitations as are prescribed by law and are necessary in a democratic society in the interests of public safety, for the protection of public order, health or morals, or for the protection of the rights and freedoms of others.

There is an ongoing debate on whether article 52(3) *CFR* precludes the application of the general limitation clause in article 52(1) *CFR*.[69] In the context of article 52(3) *CFR*, the Explanations reveal that as a corresponding right, limitations of article 10(1) *CFR* 'must therefore respect Article 9(2)' *ECHR*.[70] With regard to similar corresponding rights, such as articles 6, 11, 12, and 17 *CFR*, the Explanations state that their limitation "may not exceed" what is provided for in the *ECHR*.[71] On a more general note about corresponding rights, the Explanations add that "the legislator, in laying down limitations to those rights, must comply with the same standards as are fixed by the detailed limitation arrangements laid down in the ECHR (...), without thereby adversely affecting the autonomy" of EU law and the CJEU.[72] Looking at the quoted passages together, it seems reasonable to contend that the Explanations do not

68 Although the clause is formulated in general terms, it is accepted that it does not apply to some rights, such as the right to human dignity, which is 'inviolable' according to art 1 *CFR*. See in this regard Koen Lenaerts, 'Exploring the Limits of the EU Charter of Fundamental Rights' (2012) 8(3) *European Constitutional Law Review* 375, 388.

69 Peers and Prechal (n 37) 1648–9, 1651, 1670.

70 Explanations (n 24) 6.

71 Ibid 4, 7, 8.

72 Ibid 18.

exclude the application of the general limitation clause in article 52(1) *CFR* to the right to freedom of religion in article 10(1) *CFR*, provided that the standards of the *ECHR* are met as a minimum. Meeting and not exceeding the "same standards" as provided under article 9(2) *ECHR* is not the same as requiring that the provision be applied as such.

The CJEU adopted a comparable approach in *Centraal Israëlitisch Consistorie* where it applied article 52(1) *CFR*, while noting that the provision had "the same effect" as article 9(2) *ECHR*.[73] This approach is logical as it allows the CJEU to comply with the wording of article 52(1) *CFR*, according to which it applies to "any limitation", while simultaneously taking due account of the importance of article 9(2) *ECHR*. Also, by applying its own limitation criteria, EU law can more easily provide a higher level of protection than the *ECHR*. An example of this can be found in the opinion of Advocate General Sharpston in the earlier mentioned *Bougnaoui* case on religious discrimination. The Advocate General explained that article 9 *ECHR*, read together with the prohibition on discrimination in article 14 *ECHR*, allowed for unequal treatment, provided such treatment pursued a legitimate aim and was proportionate.[74] In other words, the rights to freedom of religion and equality could be limited upon satisfying these limitation criteria. This "restrictions-based approach", according to the Advocate General, mirrored the prohibitions based on discrimination in *Directive 2000/78* concerning indirect discrimination, but not direct discrimination.[75] Direct discrimination, in EU law, was only permissible when specifically provided for by the relevant EU legislation, such as *Directive 2000/78*.[76] Although articles 10(1) and 21 *CFR* on non-discrimination corresponded with articles 9 and 14 *ECHR*, the EU limitation regime was stricter in some respects, which the Advocate General deemed acceptable with regard to article 52(3) *CFR*.[77]

The challenge for the CJEU in applying the general limitation clause in article 52(1) *CFR*, or a specific limitation regime related to it, such as the prohibition on discrimination in *Directive 2000/78*, is to properly reconcile such criteria with article 9(2) *ECHR*. In this context, a number of observations can be made when comparing article 52(1) *CFR*, which provides the ultimate EU legal basis for reviewing a limitation of freedom of religion, with the benchmark of article 9(2) *ECHR*. Overall, although worded differently, both limitation clauses require that a limitation of the right (i) is prescribed by law and (ii) pursues a legitimate aim in (iii) a proportionate manner, while the main textual difference is that under article 52(1) *CFR*, the essence of the

73 *Centraal Israëlitisch Consistorie* (n 1) [57]–[58].
74 Advocate General Sharpston (n 46) [55], [58]–[60].
75 Ibid [60], [63].
76 Ibid [63].
77 Ibid [64].

right must also be respected.[78] In what follows, the various limitations requirements will be considered more closely, in particular with regard to *Centraal Israëlitisch Consistorie* given the detailed attention paid to the requirements in that judgement.

A Prescribed by Law

Article 9(2) *ECHR* requires that a limitation be "prescribed by law". This means, according to the ECtHR, that the limitation must be based on a legal rule from the applicable jurisdiction and that the rule must be accessible and the consequences of its application foreseeable to the bearer of the right.[79] This requirement can be matched with article 52(1) *CFR*, which calls for a limitation to be "provided by law". The latter provision, as understood with reference to article 9(2) *ECHR*, can be applied to EU law and its implementation by Member States without difficulty. This was illustrated in *Centraal Israëlitisch Consistorie*. The CJEU noted that the requirement in article 9(2) *ECHR* that a limitation must be "prescribed by law" and the requirement in article 52(1) *CFR* that a limitation must be 'provided by law" were of the "same effect", after which it concluded that the national legislation at issue satisfied the latter requirement.[80] This meant that the limitation analysis could proceed to the next stage of the inquiry.

B Legitimate Aim

The requirement in article 9(2) *ECHR* that a limitation must pursue a legitimate aim can also be reconciled with the requirement in article 52(1) *CFR* that a limitation must "genuinely meet objectives of general interest recognised by the Union or the need to protect the rights and freedoms of others". In this regard, it should be kept in mind that the list of legitimate aims in article 9(2) *ECHR* is exhaustive, while their formulation in article 52(1) *ECHR* is more open-ended.[81] In practice, however, the objectives in the *ECHR*'s limitation clauses are interpreted broadly, which minimises the risk that an objective under article 52(1) *CFR* would not correspond with any of the listed aims.[82] This was illustrated in *Centraal Israëlitisch Consistorie* where the CJEU

78 Compare Jürgen Kühling, 'Fundamental Rights' in Armin von Bogdandy and Jürgen Bast (eds), *Principles of European Constitutional Law* (Hart Publishing/CH Beck, 2009) 479, 503 regarding these three limitation requirements.

79 See *Sunday Times v The United Kingdom* (European Court of Human Rights, Application No 6538/74, 27 April 1979), [48]–[49].

80 *Centraal Israëlitisch Consistorie* (n 1) [57]–[58], [60].

81 The list is exhaustive as art 18 *ECHR* provides that: 'The restrictions permitted under this Convention to the said rights and freedoms shall not be applied for any purpose other than those for which they have been prescribed'.

82 See also Van der Schyff (n 40) 186–96.

found that the limitation of freedom of religion was in the interest of "animal welfare".[83] Although this aim is not included under article 9(2) *ECHR* as such, the ECtHR has recognised that animal welfare is a legitimate aim for limiting rights in the context of the protection of morals.[84]

C Proportionality

The proportionality of a limitation in relation to the objective pursued is often the crux of the matter in determining whether a limitation is justified. The approaches under EU law and *ECHR* law are broadly similar upon inspection. In contrast to article 52(1) *CFR*, article 9(2) *ECHR* does not mention proportionality as such. However, the proportionality test is deduced by the ECtHR from the requirement in article 9(2) *ECHR* that a limitation must be "necessary in a democratic society", as in *Leyla Şahin*.[85] At first glance, the argument might be made that the proportionality test in article 9(2) *ECHR* is more stringent than that under article 52(1) *CFR* because the latter only requires a limitation to be proportional in relation to the EU's objectives, as opposed to necessary in a democratic society. This literal interpretation of the textual difference between the two limitation clauses is contradicted by case law and to be avoided. The CJEU has, on a number of occasions, relied on ECtHR case law to describe the right to freedom of religion as one of the foundations of a democratic society, as in the *WABE* judgement mentioned earlier and also in the opinion in *Bougnaoui*.[86] This position was reaffirmed in *Centraal Israëlitisch Consistorie* and taken a step further by linking the term "necessary in a democratic society" in the limitation clause in article 9(2) *ECHR* to the limitation clause in article 52(1) *CFR*.[87] As a consequence, the requirement of proportionality in article 52(1) *CFR* should be read in conjunction with the ECtHR's case law on determining whether a limitation is necessary in a democratic society.

In this regard, it is important to take note of the *ECHR* doctrine on the margin of appreciation, which entails a less stringent proportionality test and more discretion for the state in limiting a right such as that to freedom of religion.[88] The doctrine applies in cases where the state authorities are better placed than

83 *Centraal Israëlitisch Consistorie* (n 1) [62]–[63].

84 This was recognised in *ECHR*, *Friend and Others v United Kingdom* (European Court of Human Rights, Application Nos 16072/06 and 27809/08, 24 November 2009), [18] in the context of art 11(2) *ECHR* and recently in *Executief van de Moslims* (n 57) [95]–[102] in the context of art 9(2) *ECHR*.

85 *Leyla Şahin* (n 56) [117] where it was explained that: 'The Court must now determine whether in the instant case there was a reasonable relationship of proportionality between the means employed and the legitimate objectives pursued by the interference'.

86 *WABE* (n 28) [48]. See also Advocate General Sharpston (n 46) [45].

87 *Centraal Israëlitisch Consistorie* (n 1) [57]–[58].

88 On this doctrine, see Yutaka Arai-Takahashi, *The Margin of Appreciation Doctrine and the Principle of Proportionality in the Jurisprudence of the ECHR* (Intersentia, 2002).

the ECtHR in Strasbourg to judge the necessity of an interference, while not allowing the authorities a free hand either.[89] This is the case, for example, when there is no European consensus on a particular issue, which means that the ECtHR will be reluctant to substitute its view for that of the Member States.[90] When copying the "meaning and scope" of the right to freedom of religion, as required under article 52(3) *CFR*, the presence or absence of a margin of appreciation should be factored in accordingly under EU law. This should not prove to be particularly difficult, as a comparable doctrine exists in the case law of the CJEU to give Member States more leeway in complying with EU law than would otherwise be the case.[91] In *Centraal Israëlitisch Consistorie*, for example, the CJEU noted that under article 9 *ECHR*, the state should, in principle, be afforded a "wide margin of appreciation", as opinions on the relationship between the state and religions may reasonably differ widely in a democratic society.[92] The CJEU saw no reason to deviate from this margin, as there was no consensus on the issue in question at EU level.[93] However, if there had been an EU consensus that the right to freedom of religion in article 10(1) *CFR* required more extensive protection than that provided for under the *ECHR*, article 52(3) *CFR* would have allowed the CJEU to require, for example, a stricter proportionality test. If, on the other hand, *ECHR* law gave Member States little or no discretion on how to protect freedom of religion in a particular case, article 52(3) *CFR* would preclude EU law from giving states a discretion that would compromise the *ECHR* level of protection.

The final point in dealing with proportionality review relates to the rule in article 52(1) *CFR* that a limitation must respect the "essence" of a right such as that to freedom of religion. The CJEU interprets this requirement independent of the proportionality test, as illustrated in *Centraal Israëlitisch Consistorie*.[94]

89 *Handyside v The United Kingdom* (European Court of Human Rights, Application No 5493/72, 7 December 1976), [48]–[49].

90 See the example in *Kiyutin v Russia* (European Court of Human Rights, Application No 2700/10, 10 March 2011), [65] regarding arts 8 and 14 *ECHR*.

91 See, eg, *Omega* (Court of Justice of the European Union, C-36/02, ECLI:EU:C:2004:614, 14 October 2004) [31] it was explained that: 'The fact remains, however, that the specific circumstances which may justify recourse to the concept of public policy may vary from one country to another and from one era to another. The competent national authorities must therefore be allowed a margin of discretion within the limits imposed by the Treaty (…)'. See generally Janneke Gerards, 'Pluralism, Deference and the Margin of Appreciation', (2011) 17(1) *European Law Journal* 80.

92 *Centraal Israëlitisch Consistorie* (n 1) [67]. Particular reference was made to *SAS v France* (European Court of Human Rights, Grand Chamber, Application No 43835/11, 1 July 2014) [129], [131].

93 Ibid [67]–[68]. The 'EU level' refers to *Regulation No 1099/2009* of 24 September 2009, which, as secondary law, harmonised Member States' approaches to animal welfare at the time of killing.

94 Ibid [61], [64]. See generally Peers and Prechal (n 37) 1632; Koen Lenaerts, 'Limits on Limitations: The Essence of Fundamental Rights in the EU' (2019) 20(6) *German Law Journal* 779, 787–8.

While the proportionality test examines whether the right to freedom of religion was limited to an acceptable degree, the essence test examines whether the right as such was prohibited. In the case cited, the CJEU explained that the requirement that animals be stunned when they were slaughtered limited only one aspect of the religious rite, as opposed to the rite as a whole, thereby preserving the essence of the right.[95] This allowed the CJEU to assess the proportionality of the interference under article 52(1) *CFR*. By comparison, the ECtHR, as illustrated in *Cha'are Shalom* and *Executief van de Moslims*, does not require a similar test in addition to the proportionality test.[96] This raises the question whether the essence test can be applied to the right to freedom of religion in article 10(1) *CFR* in the context of article 52(3) *CFR*. In principle, there is no objection to applying the essence test in article 52(1) *CFR* to freedom of religion, provided that here too, care is taken not to diminish the level of protection provided for under article 9 *ECHR*. In practice, a finding that the essence of the right was violated by its prohibition as such will probably also correspond to a violation of the proportionality test under the *ECHR* and, if not, lead to a higher level of protection under EU law.[97]

IX Seven Observations to Conclude

This contribution has shed light on the interpretation of the right to freedom of religion in article 10(1) *CFR* as a corresponding right in the context of article 52(3) *CFR*. Based on the analysis and further to it, seven interrelated concluding observations can be made about this method of interpreting a right such as that to freedom of religion.

The first observation to be made is that a common language implicitly aids the implementation of an interpretation method such as article 52(3) *CFR*. A common language dispenses with the need for translation and the complications this may cause in determining a provision's meaning.[98] In this regard, it can be noted that article 10(1) *CFR* was adopted in the official languages of the EU, which include English and French. Both English and French are the official languages of the Council of Europe, which explains why the *ECHR* is written in both these languages, as well as the judgements of the ECtHR. Common languages are beneficial when modelling the interpretation of one provision on the meaning of another provision.

The second observation to be made is that the method of interpretation in article 52(3) *CFR* is aided by the fact that article 10(1) *CFR* essentially copies the wording of article 9(1) *ECHR*. This avoids the need to compare and

95 *Centraal Israëlitisch Consistorie* (n 1) [61].

96 Compare *Cha'are Shalom* (n 57) [84]; *Executief van de Moslims* (n 57) [103].

97 As far as art 52(1) *CFR* is concerned, Lenaerts (n 94) 786 explains that a violation of a right's essence will also amount to a disproportional violation of the right.

98 See generally Mark Tushnet, *Advanced Introduction to Comparative Constitutional Law* (Edward Elgar, 2nd ed, 2018) 6 on language as a method in constitutional law.

discuss textual differences, and shifts the attention to determining the "meaning and scope" of the right as determined by the ECtHR. Simultaneously, textual differences do not rule out the proper functioning of a provision such as article 52(3) *CFR* either. This is reflected in the textual differences between the limitation clauses in article 52(1) *CFR* and article 9(2) *ECHR*, which the CJEU compensates for by using the "same effect" approach, as in the case of *Centraal Israëlitisch Consistorie*.[99] On a related note, it is also not necessary that both jurisdictions use the same judicial enforcement mechanisms, as illustrated by the CJEU's preliminary reference approach compared with the ECtHR's exhaustion of domestic remedies approach.

The third observation to be made is that the method of interpretation in article 52(3) *CFR* is not a discretionary exercise. When interpreting article 10(1) *CFR*, the CJEU and other EU institutions are bound to follow the example set by the *ECHR*, as interpreted by the ECtHR. The view of Advocate General Wahl in *Liga van Moskeeën* that article 52(3) *CFR* means that the interpretation of article 9 *ECHR* by the ECtHR "may therefore have some relevance for, or at least be a source of inspiration for the interpretation of Article 10 of the Charter" cannot be supported.[100] Article 52(3) *CFR* establishes a far-reaching duty to factor in the "meaning and scope" of article 9 *ECHR* when interpreting article 10(1) *CFR*, as evidenced by the careful approach adopted by the CJEU in *Centraal Israëlitisch Consistorie*. The function of article 52(3) *CFR* is to go beyond providing a source of inspiration, which may only have some relevance to interpreting article 10(1) *CFR*.

The fourth observation to be made is that although the duty in article 52(3) *CFR* is particularly far-reaching, it also has its limits. In other words, the duty is not absolute in all respects. As the provision notes, the 'meaning and scope' of article 9 *ECHR* serves only as a lower limit and not as an upper limit. EU law can, therefore, provide more protection to the right to freedom of religion, as illustrated in *Centraal Israëlitisch Consistorie* in relation to *Cha'are Shalom*, thereby respecting the autonomy of EU law. An additional limit is that article 52(3) *CFR* does not replace the workings of the general limitation clause in article 52(1) *CFR*, provided that the 'same effect' is achieved as would have been the case under article 9(2) *ECHR*.[101] Article 52(3) *CFR*, therefore, establishes a relationship between article 10(1) *CFR* and article 9 *ECHR* without the latter replacing or displacing the former. Instead, article 9 *ECHR* informs the interpretation of article 10(1) *CFR*.

The fifth observation to be made is that the method of interpretation established by article 52(3) *CFR* can best be described as a normative institutional relationship between article 10(1) *CFR*, as interpreted by the CJEU, and article 9 *ECHR*, as interpreted by the ECtHR. The method does not fit the

99 *Centraal Israëlitisch Consistorie* (n 1) [58].
100 Opinion of Advocate General Wahl (n 21) [48].
101 *Centraal Israëlitisch Consistorie* (n 1) [58].

general description of an institutional dialogue, hence this sui generis classification. This is because a dialogue assumes that "two or more persons, recognized as equal partners, exchange words, ideas, opinions, feelings, emotions, intentions, desires, judgements, and experiences together within a shared space of intersubjective meanings".[102] The dialogical exchange can be in the form of a "conversation", which is more informal and has no specific practical purpose, or a "deliberation", which is more formal and aims to address matters of "mutual practical purpose" through taking decisions in common or solving problems collectively.[103] On the terms of article 52(3) *CFR*, the CJEU and ECtHR are not entirely equal partners, as the CJEU is required to follow the 'meaning and scope' given to article 9 *ECHR* by the ECtHR. In addition, the relationship is a formal one with a specific purpose in mind, namely, interpreting article 10(1) *CFR*, which rules out dialogue as conversation. Deliberation as dialogue is also excluded, as the process is not aimed at joint action in arriving at a common solution. This is because the interpretation of the 'meaning and scope' of article 9 *ECHR* does not depend on the cooperation of the CJEU, whereas the CJEU is bound by the interpretation of the ECtHR. Article 52(3) *CFR* legitimises the interpretation of article 10(1) *CFR*, not by way of dialogue, but as the result of a normative relationship in which the position of the ECtHR is decisive in order to ensure a minimum level of protection in EU law.

The sixth observation to be made is that the effect of article 52(3) *CFR* is comparable to the effect if the EU had been a member of the *ECHR*. This is because article 53 *ECHR* allows Member States to provide more, but not less protection than that foreseen under the *ECHR*.[104] In practice, the ECtHR must give priority to the laws of Member States that offer more protection to a right such as that to freedom of religion, while states must adopt *ECHR* standards as minimum thresholds. While not being obligated to do so by the *ECHR*, article 52(3) *CFR* requires of the EU to adopt *ECHR* minimum thresholds. This diminishes the likelihood that the ECtHR will find one of its Member States in violation of the *ECHR* for implementing EU law, as the latter is presumed to meet *ECHR* standards.[105] In this way, the EU takes into

102 Luc B Tremblay, 'The Legitimacy of Judicial Review: The Limits of Dialogue between Courts and Legislatures' (2005) 3(4) *International Journal of Constitutional Law* 617, 630.
103 Ibid 631.
104 See generally Janneke Gerards, 'Article 53 ECHR and Minimum Protection by the European Court of Human Rights', (2022) 3(4) *European Convention on Human Rights Law Review* 451, 452–4.
105 See, eg, in *Executief van de Moslims* (n 57) [124], the ECtHR found that the contested Belgian legislation did not violate the right to the freedom of religion in art 9(1) *ECHR*, similarly to the *CJEU* ruling regarding the right to freedom of religion in art 10(1) *CFR* in *Centraal Israëlitisch Consistorie* (n 1) [96]. The ECtHR, [112]–[115], also referred to the review undertaken by the CJEU. See also *Bosphorus Hava Yollari Turizm ve Ticaret Anonim Şirketi v Ireland* (European Court of Human Rights, Grand Chamber, Application

account the fact that all its 27 Member States are also members of the *ECHR*, and prevents them from having to implement EU laws that conflict with the standards of the *ECHR*. Additionally, it may also be recalled that the EU is destined to become a member of the *ECHR*, according to article 6(2) *TEU*. In this respect, article 52(3) *CFR* paves the way for accession by aligning the standard of fundamental rights protection in the EU with that required under the *ECHR*. Following accession, article 52(3) *CFR* could be read as confirming the EU's new international legal duty to recognise *ECHR* standards as minimum thresholds according to article 53 *ECHR*.

The seventh observation to be made is that a provision such as article 52(3) *CFR* is a useful method to ensure consistency in the protection of a right such as freedom of religion in different jurisdictions, thereby promoting greater legal integration. Such an interpretation method, in which one system unilaterally binds itself to another system without being part of that system, is workable only in an environment where the other system is sufficiently trusted. In this respect, article 52(3) *CFR* is the result of a long-standing and close relationship between the EU and the Council of Europe regarding the protection of corresponding rights. More to the point, the recognition of this method by the *CFR* can be seen as the logical conclusion of the CJEU's traditional dependence on the ECtHR in setting human rights standards in EU law. Finally, as explained in the previous observation, this dependence will become even stronger when the EU becomes a non-state member of the *ECHR* in the future.

Further Reading:

For analysis of the methods used in this chapter, see Chapter 15 – Section IV – subsection A *The Doctrinal Method*; C *The Functionalist Method*; D *The Analytical Method*; F *The Yardstick Method*.

For another example of the Functionalist and Analytical Method, see Chapter 11.

No 45036/98, 30 June 2005), [155]–[156], [165] on the relationship between *ECHR* and EU law.

10 The *Kirpan* Case Law in Italy and Canada

Comparing Law and Religion Judgements in the Rise of Judicial Populism

Tania Pagotto[1]

I Introduction: Judicial Populism and Religious Symbols

In an era marked by the rise of popular movements and the resurgence of authoritarian regimes, religious symbols have gained heightened sensitivity. A prevalent political strategy has long been leveraging religion and freedom of religion to gather support, establish credibility, and wield influence. Endorsing narratives rooted in the dominant religion, national history, cultural symbols, and shared interests are tools to mobilise collective identities and religious affiliations.

Central to the spectrum of these movements is the cultivation of an "us-versus-them" narrative,[2] fostering a stark contrast between "the people" – depicted as a homogenous, uncomplicated entity – and "the other" – identified as either corrupt elites or religious minority groups.[3] Amidst this landscape, religious symbols straddle a delicate line, transitioning from embodiments of spiritual significance to markers of distinct identity. Many leaders of these movements leverage religious symbols by oversimplifying the complex spectrum of religious beliefs, lacking nuance and critical thinking.[4] From Modi's emphasis on Hindu pride in India to Bolsonaro's alignment with conservative Christian values in Brazil, populist leaders worldwide resonate with religious symbols to solidify power and engage their political base.[5]

1 Post-doctoral research fellow in Law and Religion, School of Law, University of Milan-Bicocca.

2 On identity politics, see, among many others, Luca Pietro Vanoni and Benedetta Vimercati, 'dall'Identità alle Identity Politics: La Rinascita dei Nazionalismi nel Sistema Costituzionale Europeo' (2020) 40(1) *Quaderni costituzionali* 31.

3 See, among many, Andrew Arato and Jean L Cohen, 'Civil Society, Populism, and Religion' (2017) 24(3) *Contellations* 283; Jeffrey Haynes, 'Right-Wing Populism and Religion in Europe and the USA' (2020) 11(10) *Religions* 490; Jose Pedro Zúquete, 'Populism and Religion' in Cristóbal Rovira Kaltwasser et al (eds), *The Oxford Handbook of Populism* (Oxford University Press, 2017) 445.

4 Alessandro Morelli, ''Valori Occidentali' e Principi Costituzionali: Il Tema Identitario nella Giurisprudenza in Materia di Simboli Religiosi' [2017] (2) *Democrazia e sicurezza* 15, 19.

5 Daniel Nilsson DeHanas and Marat Shterin, *Religion and the Rise of Populism* (Routledge, 2020).

DOI: 10.4324/9781003397311-15

The entwining of populist narratives with religious symbols poses significant risks across various contexts. When employed in politics, this fusion may result in the targeting of religious minority groups.[6] Furthermore, in adjudicating cases related to religious symbols, judicial reasoning may intertwine with populist rhetoric, jeopardising the constitutionally protected rights of religious minorities.

An often-overlooked variant of populism, known as judicial populism, emerges in the judiciary. The understanding of judicial populism has been significantly enriched within the realm of Italian legal scholarship, particularly in the context of criminal law, and has led to a lively and extensive debate surrounding the phenomenon.

In instances dealing with religious symbols, both populism and judicial populism tend to reject the nuanced aspects of pluralist democracy. Populist leaders present themselves as direct spokespersons for the thoughts, grievances, fears, and hopes of "the people", while judicial decisions influenced by judicial populism attempt to interpret the "the true interests and expectations of justice of the people [...] beyond the formal mediation of the law".[7]

Judicial populism, prevalent in courts, "insists that there are clear, correct answers to complex, debatable problems".[8] Grounding decisions in a rationale marked by both judicial populism and populist rhetoric "simplifies the issues legal institutions address and claims special access to a true, single meaning of the law".[9] Consequently, these narratives pose a threat to religious diversity by challenging the values of religious pluralism and hindering dialogue among different religious groups within the same political community.[10]

II Research Questions and Methodology Adopted

This chapter investigates the correlation between religious symbols, conceived as a manifestation of freedom of religion or belief, and judicial populism. It focuses on the case study of the carrying of the ***kirpan***, the ritual dagger worn by Amritdhari (initiated) Sikhs, and by juxtaposing two judgements delivered by state secular courts: the Supreme Court of Cassation in Italy[11] and the

6 Susanna Mancini and Michel Rosenfeld, 'Nationalism, Populism, Religion, and the Quest to Reframe Fundamental Rights' (2020) 101–169 *Cardozo Law Review* 463.

7 Giovanni Fiandaca, 'Populismo Politico e Populismo Giudiziario' [2013] *Criminalia* 95, 105.

8 Anya Bernstein and Glen Staszewski, 'Judicial Populism' (2021) 106(1) *Minnesota Law Review* 283, 284.

9 Ibid.

10 Vincenzo Pacillo, 'Sovranismo e Libertà Religiosa Individuale' in Pierluigi Consorti (ed), *Costituzione, Religione e Cambiamenti nel Diritto e nella Società* (Pisa University Press, 2019) 173.

11 The Italian Supreme Court of Cassation is the highest court of the Italian system and acts as the ultimate appellate body. It oversees and decides on appeals from lower courts and guarantees the uniform interpretation of the law within the Italian jurisdiction. It does not deliver judgements on the constitutionality of laws, since the judicial review of legislation is an exclusive competence of the Italian Constitutional Court.

Supreme Court of Canada.[12] These two jurisdictions are vastly different. Italy is a civil law jurisdiction, belonging to the legal landscape of Mediterranean Europe, while Canada is mostly a common law jurisdiction, with elements of civil law (especially in Québec), exposed to the legal culture of North America, and with a history as a former British colony.[13]

The juxtaposition of the two rulings provides an insightful process of legal comparison. It allows for the contrasting (with due caution) of two factually similar cases but two exceptionally different *judicial rationales* (in terms of the reasoning behind one court's decisions).[14] The investigation does not focus primarily on comparing the institutional elements characterising Italian and Canadian legal orders – rather, it scrutinises similarities and differences of two judicial orientations and approaches, drawing findings from the judgements' rationales.

On one side, religious law regulates the rights, duties, and statuses of individuals and communities, irrespective of different states' secular norms. The diaspora of religious groups in different state jurisdictions has given rise to similar demands for religious accommodations and requests for courts' interventions. This offers a reliable baseline for comparing how secular court judgements approach issues stemming from the application of, and the adherence to, religious law, and respond to the quest for religious accommodation.[15]

On the other side, the wearing of the *kirpan* represents the ideal case study via which to explore two main research aims:

(i) to verify the presence of manifestations of judicial populism and their potential impact on decisions related to religious symbols; and
(ii) to investigate strategies for formulating judgements on religious symbols that can counteract the surge of judicial populism.

The first aim will be addressed through the study of the Italian case-law, while the second will be explored through the illustration of the Canadian case-law.

12 The Supreme Court of Canada serves as the highest court in the country, providing final decisions on appeals from provincial and federal courts; it also interprets the Constitution, resolving legal disputes of national importance.

13 Canada still has the English monarch as its head of state: see Richard Albert and David R Cameron (eds), *Canada in the World: Comparative Perspectives on the Canadian Constitution* (Cambridge University Press, 2017); Nathan Tidridge, *Canada's Constitutional Monarchy* (Dundurn, 2011).

14 'Eclatante': Alessandro Ferrari, 'L'ospitalità del Diritto o dell'Impervio Cammino della Dignità Umana' [2020] (22) *Stato, Chiese e Pluralismo Confessionale* 44, 60.

15 Religious law can be considered as the 'independent variable' of the comparison, a factor the legal scholar can control to see how it affects secular courts' responses to requests for religious accommodations. See Ran Hirschl, *Comparative Matters: The Renaissance of Comparative Constitutional Law* (Oxford University Press, 2014).

III Navigating Judicial Populism: The *Kirpan* as a Legal Conundrum

The *kirpan* epitomises a microcosm of contradictions and anxieties situated at the intersection between religious pluralism, judicial populism, and public security.[16] It is a ritual dagger imbued with symbolic and religious significance for those practicing Sikhism, representing resistance to evil, commitment to justice, and protection of the vulnerable. Male and female initiated Sikhs must carry a *kirpan*, alongside the other sacred "articles of faith", known as the "five Ks".[17] *Kirpans* come in various sizes, ranging from small blades to knives that exceed 20 centimetres in length, and even larger, more conspicuous swords.[18] The removal of articles of faith is prohibited, and their abandonment involves a set of rituals to symbolise remorse and repentance, including specific prayers and community involvement.[19]

From a legal perspective, carrying a *kirpan* is a manifestation of the right to religious freedom by observance, often in public, either alone or in community with others. Yet, at the same time, it raises complex legal issues related to the permissibility of this religious practice because of its resemblance to a weapon.[20] The ability of a *kirpan* to cause harm or threat presents a challenge to criminal laws aimed at restricting the possession of weapons to ensure public safety.[21] This means that the right to carry a *kirpan* results in very different

16 The interaction between religious belonging in a multicultural society has been developed, among many others, Pierluigi Consorti (ed), *Costituzione, Religione e Cambiamenti nel Diritto e nella Società* (Pisa University Press, 2019); Maria D'Arienzo, 'Le Sfide della Multiculturalità e la Dimensione Religiosa' in Fulvia Abbondante and Salvatore Prisco (eds), *Diritto e Pluralismo Culturale: I Mille Volti Della Convivenza* (Editoriale Scientifica, 2015) 45. See also Antonio Fuccillo and Paolo Palumbo, *Pluralismo Confessionale e dinamiche interculturali: Le Best Practices per una Società Inclusiva* (Editoriale Scientifica, 2023).

17 In 1699, Gobind Singh mandated that all Sikh believers shall carry five objects: The kesh – uncut hair, symbolising nature; the kangha – a wooden comb, symbolising discipline; a kara – an iron-made bracelet, symbolising unity; a kachera – cotton undergarments, symbolising purity; and the *kirpan* – a ritual knife or sword, symbolising resistance to evil: Satvinder Singh Juss, 'Kirpans, Law, and Religious Symbols in Schools' (2013) 55(4) *Journal of Church and State* 758. See also Shauna Van Praagh, *Hijab et* Kirpan: *Une Histoire de Cape et d'Epée* (Presses Université Laval, 2006).

18 Jasjit Singh, 'Symbols (Sikhism)' in Arvind-Pal Singh Mandair (ed), *Sikhism* (Springer Netherlands, 2017) 422.

19 Ibid.

20 On the interpretation of the *kirpan* and its semantic transfiguration/transmigration see Mario Ricca, 'Il Tradimento delle Immagini Tra Kirpan e Transazioni Interculturali. Cultura vs Competenza Culturale nel Mondo Del Diritto' [2013] *E/C, Rivista dell'Associazione Italiana di Studi Semiotici* 1.

21 Many other religious symbols and practices are perceived in terms of public security, such as the wearing of the Islamic headscarf or the use of psychoactive substances for religious rites (peyote or ayahuasca). For the first aspect, see Renae Barker, 'Rejecting Security: A Comparative Analysis of the Rejection of Security, Public Safety and Public Order Concerns as a Ground for Restricting Freedom of Religion in Religious Dress Cases' in Tania Pagotto, Joshua M Roose and G P Marcar (eds), *Security, Religion, and the Rule of Law: International*

decisions across the globe. In certain jurisdictions, carrying *kirpans* is consistent with constitutional protections for religious freedom;[22] in many others, it is subject to various restrictions, or even prohibition, often accompanied by criminal sanctions.[23] The misalignment between a state's criminal laws within secular jurisdiction and religious laws and duties is generally framed as a culturally motivated offense.[24] This arises when religious and cultural background significantly influences an individual's behaviour, causing the ultimate violation of criminal laws.[25] In the case of the *kirpan* in particular, carrying a religious symbol that could potentially be harmful constitutes an act steeped in religious and cultural significance. Simultaneously, it breaches those secular criminal laws prohibiting the possession of weapons, resulting in the typical scenario of a dual allegiance dilemma.[26]

The resurgence of religious fervour and the rise of populism further complicate the delicate balance between safeguarding religious observance and ensuring public safety.[27] Illiberal agendas frequently adopt a securitisation approach

---

Perspectives (Taylor & Francis Limited, 2023). For the second aspect, see Charlotte Walsh, 'Beyond Religious Freedom: Psychedelics and Cognitive Liberty' in Beatriz Caiuby Labate and Clancy Cavnar (eds), *Prohibition, Religious Freedom, and Human Rights: Regulating Traditional Drug Use* (Springer, 2014) 211.

22 Constitution of India, Art. 25, explanation I: 'The wearing and carrying of *kirpans* shall be deemed to be included in the profession of the Sikh religion': www.constitutionofindia.net See, generally, Mohammad Naseem and Saman Naseem, *Religion and Law in India* (Kluwer Law International, 2nd ed, 2020).

23 In 2006, a member of the Danish Sikh minority faced legal consequences for wearing a *kirpan* in public. The court's decision concluded that the exercise of religious freedom cannot exempt an individual from being punished, for the fact of carrying a weapon in public: see Conviction number U 2007.316 (Eastern High Court of Denmark, 2007).

24 On culturally motivated crimes, see Fabio Basile, 'I Reati Cd. 'Culturalmente Motivati' Commessi dagli Immigrati: (Possibili) Soluzioni Giurisprudenziali' (2017) 2017(1) *Questione Giustizia* 126; Alessandro Bernardi, *Il 'Fattore Culturale' nel Sistema Penale* (Giappichelli, 2010); Pierluigi Consorti, 'Reati 'Culturali' e Reati 'Religiosi': Un Fenomeno di Glocalismo Giuridico'. (2016) 22(2) *Diritto e Religioni* 353; Cristina De Maglie, *I Reati Culturalmente Motivati: Ideologie e Modelli Penali* (ETS, 2010); Elisa Olivito, 'Giudici e Legislatori di Fronte alla Multiculturalità' [2011] *Stato, Chiese e Pluralismo Confessionale, Rivista Telematica* (www.statoechiese.it).

25 Alessandro Bernardi, 'Populismo Giudiziario? L'evoluzione della Giurisprudenza Penale sul Kirpan' (2017) 60(2) *Rivista Italiana di Diritto e Procedura Penale* 671, 706.

26 See Angelo Licastro, 'Il Motivo Religioso non Giustifica il Porto Fuori dell'Abitazione del Kirpan da Parte del Fedele Sikh (Considerazioni in Margine alle Sentenze n. 24739 e n. 25163 del 2016 della Cassazione Penale)' [2017] (1) *Stato, Chiese e Pluralismo Confessionale, Rivista Telematica* (www.statoechiese.it) 1, 5.

27 On the relation between freedom of religion and security, see Natascia Marchei and Daniela Milani (eds), *Freedom of Religion, Security and the Law: Key Challenges for a Pluralistic Society* (Routledge–Giappichelli, 2023); Marco Parisi, 'Diritto alla Sicurezza e Libertà Democratiche: Quale (Possibile) Bilanciamento?' (2022) 53(2) *Politica del Diritto* 165; Roberto Mazzola, *La Convivenza delle Regole: Diritto, Sicurezza e Organizzazioni Religiose* (Giuffrè, 2005). On populism in Italy, see Giuseppe Martinico, *Filtering Populist Claims to Fight Populism: The Italian Case in a Comparative Perspective* (Cambridge University Press, 2021) 15. On pop-

towards freedom of religion, depicting minority religious practices as immediate threats to national unity.[28] Tribunal decisions sometimes prioritise public safety over the spiritual importance of *kirpans*, as seen in Italian case law, potentially overshadowing the protection of fundamental rights to freedom of religion or belief.[29]

The following section will explore how courts may prioritise constitutional concerns for public safety, influenced by arguments rooted in judicial populism.

IV The Italian Legal Landscape on *Kirpans*: Judicial Populism in Action

Italian jurisprudence on *kirpans* is a noteworthy, albeit not extensive, body of case law. Courts and tribunals have been called upon to rule on issues related to the wearing of *kirpan* symbols since the late 2000s.[30] The decision that generated significant public discourse was judgement no. 24084, delivered by the Supreme Court of Cassation in 2017.[31]

The debate over the carrying of the *kirpan* in Italy stemmed from two key factors. First, the 2017 judgement marked a shift from previously established Italian jurisprudence.[32] Prior to 2016, a consistent case law carefully balanced the religious freedom of Sikh adherents to carry the *kirpan* with the need for public safety. This typically resulted in no sanctions for Sikh individuals who unfortunately found themselves embroiled in legal proceedings involving the carrying of the sacred knife.[33] In particular, prior case law acknowledged the act of carrying the *kirpan* as an expression of the right to religious freedom and excused criminal responsibility, recognising the legal defence commonly referred to as *"scriminante"*.[34] In addition, scholars challenged a specific aspect

---

ulism and *laicità* see Pierluigi Consorti, 'Accezioni della Laicità in Tempi di Populismo Trionfante' [2017] (CXXVIII) *Diritto Ecclesiastico* https://doi.org/10.19272/201730802008. On *laicità*, religion and culture see Mario Ferrante, 'Diritto, Religione, Cultura: Verso una Laicità Inclusiva' [2016] *Diritto Ecclesiastico: CXXVII, 3/4, 2016* 425 ('*Diritto, Religione, Cultura*').

28 Antonello De Oto, 'Pratiche di Culto ed Esigenze di Europeizzazione del Diritto Penale: Tra Bisogno di Libertà e Pretese di Sicurezza' [2007] *La Chiesa e l'Europa* 287.

29 Francesco Alicino, 'I Reati Culturalmente Motivati fra Assimilazionismo e Relativismo Multiculturale' [2022] *Stato, Chiese e Pluralismo Confessionale* 26. 'At the intertwine of criminal law and cultural diversity, [...] it is equally important to never lose sight of the main objective: an effective and efficient guarantee of fundamental rights and freedoms'.

30 See, for example, *Sentenza n 15* [2009] Tribunal of Cremona (Criminal Section).

31 *Sentenza n 24084* (Sezione Prima Penale) [2017] Corte Suprema di Cassazione 24084.

32 The case law moved from being 'indulgent', to 'rigorous' to 'intransigent': Bernardi (n 24).

33 Cristiana Cianitto, 'Le Minoranze Religiose in Italia. Nuovi Problemi(?)' [2021] *Stato, Chiese e Pluralismo Confessionale* 62.

34 See Bernardi (n 24).

of the Court's reasoning as being ambiguous and imprecise,[35] and, as we will see, for offering a regrettable example of judicial populism.[36]

The circumstances leading to the 2017 judgement were straightforward. A Sikh practitioner was convicted for carrying a *kirpan* in a public place. Local police officers found the man with the *kirpan* attached to his belt and requested he surrender the object. The man refused, referring to his identity as a Sikh believer of Indian origin and his religious duty to carry the sacred dagger.[37] He also alleged that the *kirpan* was a religious symbol, and carrying it amounted to a manifestation of the right to freedom of religion or belief, protected by the Italian Constitution.[38]

To understand the rationale of the judgement, it is important to contextualise the legal framework regulating the control of weapons, ammunition, and explosives. Italian legislation draws a clear distinction between two categories of weapons.[39] It prohibits the possession of weapons naturally designed for causing injuries or death, such as firearms or rifles.[40] Prohibition is absolute unless a valid firearm certificate has been issued by competent authorities.[41] The law also establishes a more nuanced framework for the possession

35 Morelli defined the formula employed as 'exemplary in its vagueness and ambiguity': Morelli (n 3) 24.

36 'The risk of judicial populism seems, therefore, to have really materialized in this decision': Fabio Basile, 'Reati Culturalmente Motivati' (2019) 2019(1) *Diritto Penale Contemporaneo* 98, 201.

Italian scholarship has extensively commented on the judgement. Beyond the scholarship quoted and relied on throughput this chapter, see in addition: Roberto Bin, 'Il Problema non è il Kirpan ma la Stampa', *laCostituzione.info* (16 May 2017) https://www.lacostituzione.info/index.php/2017/05/16/il-problema-non-e-il-kirpan-ma-la-stampa/; S Carmignani Caridi, 'Ostentazione di Simboli Religiosi e Porto di Armi od Oggetti Atti ad Offendere. Il Problema del Kirpan dei Fedeli Sikh' [2009] *Diritto Ecclesiastico* 739; Marta Cartabia, 'The Many and the Few: Clash of Values of Reasonable Accommodation Lectures' (2017) 33(4) *American University International Law Review* 667; Gianfranco Macrì, 'Cosa Minaccia la Società Pluralista? C'è Ben Altro Oltre il Kirpan', *laCostituzione.info* (20 May 2017) https://www.lacostituzione.info/index.php/2017/05/20/cosa-minaccia-la-societa-pluralista-ce-ben-altro-oltre-il-kirpan/; Anna Maria Nico, 'Ordine Pubblico e Libertà di Religione in ana Società Multiculturale (Osservazioni a Margine di una Recente Sentenza Della Cassazione Sul Kirpan)' [2017] (2) *Osservatorio AIC* 1; Giovanni Poggeschi, 'Quel Pugnale Vietato a Mantova e Permesso a Montreal', *laCostituzione.info* (19 May 2017) https://www.lacostituzione.info/index.php/2017/05/19/quel-pugnale-vietato-a-mantova-e-permesso-a-montreal/; Michele Madonna, 'Simboli e Segni Religiosi nella Giurisprudenza della Corte di Cassazione, in Dialogo Con le Altre Giurisdizioni' [2012] *Diritto ecclesiastic : CXXIII, 3/4, 2012* 609.

37 Paras 1–3 of *Sentenza n. 24084 (Sezione Prima Penale)* (n 31).

38 Article 19 of the Italian Constitution states that: 'Anyone is entitled to freely profess their religious belief in any form, individually or with others, and to promote them and celebrate rites in public or in private, provided they are not offensive to public morality'.

39 See Legge 18 aprile 1975, n. 110, 'Norme Integrative della Disciplina Vigente per il Controllo delle Armi, delle Munizioni e degli Esplosivi'.

40 They can be defined as 'proper weapons' (in Italian, '*armi proprie*').

41 Art. 4, para 1, of Legge 18 aprile 1975, n. 110 (n 38).

of objects that are not inherently aimed at causing physical harm or threats, but may still have the potential to do so. These include items such as sticks, iron-made objects, chains and, potentially, *kirpans*.[42] In this second scenario, prohibition is not absolute: Article 4, para 2, of Law no. 110 of 1975 punishes the carrying of such objects outside one's private residence with criminal sanctions, unless a justifiable reason for carrying such objects exists.[43]

Despite the defendant's consideration that his *kirpan* represented a meaningful religious symbol deserving constitutional protection, the Supreme Court of Cassation classified it as a weapon subject to Article 4, para 2, of Law no. 110. Therefore, the Court confirmed the lower court's decision and convicted the defendant for the crime of carrying a weapon without valid justification. In the Court's view, religious freedom cannot trump public safety, and religious grounds are not able to exempt a defendant's conduct from criminal liability.[44]

It must be emphasised that criminal law is a complex and jurisdiction-specific field. Justifying conduct prohibited by criminal law on religious grounds has limited acceptance within the Italian criminal legal system, and extensive scholarly attention was dedicated to analysing the technical complexities of the case at hand.[45] In addressing the first research aim of the present chapter, which focuses on how decisions influenced by judicial populism may approach religious symbols, it is important to acknowledge that the Italian Supreme Court of Cassation held that:

> It is not acceptable that the adherence to one's own values, even if lawful in accordance with the laws of the country of origin, lead to the conscious violation of those of the host society. A multi-ethnic society is a necessity, but it cannot lead to the creation of conflicting cultural enclaves, stemming from the ethnic groups that compose it. The *unity of our country's cultural and legal fabric* would oppose it, since it identifies

42 They can be defined as 'improper' or 'unconventional weapons' (in Italian '*armi improprie*').

43 Art. 4, paras 2 and 3, of the Legge 18 aprile 1975, n. 110 (n 38): 'Without a justifiable reason, no person shall carry, outside of their dwelling or its appurtenances, items such pointed or sharp-edged sticks, cutting implements capable of causing harm, clubs, pipes, chains, slingshots, bolts, metal balls, or any other item not explicitly categorized as a pointed or sharp-edged implement. [...] Those who violate this prohibition shall be subject to criminal sanctions, including imprisonment for a period of one month to one year and a fine [...]'.

44 For a summary and a comment of the decision in English, see Sophie Charlotte Monachini, 'Culturally Motivated Crimes: The Cultural Test in the Italian Jurisprudence: A Comparative Study' [2020] (17) *Stato, Chiese e Pluralismo Confessionale* 135, 137–138.

45 Beyond the literature quoted in this chapter, see also Andrea Chibelli, 'La Cassazione e La (Ir) Rilevanza Penale del Fattore Multiculturale: Su Kirpan e Dintorni' [2017] *La Cassazione e la (ir)Rilevanza Penale del Fattore Multiculturale: Su Kirpan e Dintorni* 695; De Oto (n 27); Gianfranco Martiello, 'Fattore Religioso e 'Giustificato Motivo' del Porto di un Coltello: La Vicenda del 'Kirpan' Approda in Cassazione' [2017] (3) *L'Indice Penale* 839.

> public safety as a good to be protected and, for that, prohibits the carrying of weapons and objects intended to cause harm.[46]

This passage has been criticised on many grounds for being "unnecessary, inappropriate, and ill-considered".[47] First, it shows bias against minoritarian religious beliefs and cultures. Deeming some religious symbols as prima facie incompatible with the Italian pluralist constitutional project amounts to an abstract curtailment of the right to religious freedom.[48] Instead, a delicate and nuanced approach to balancing religious freedom with concerns over public safety would have been preferable.[49] Second, the rationale behind the passage is conceptually rooted in an assimilationist approach that does not align with the foundational principles of the 1948 Italian Constitution.[50] The protection of pluralism underpinning the Italian Constitution is anchored in many constitutional provisions, including those recognising and protecting communities, guaranteeing linguistic and cultural diversity, and securing the autonomy of local and regional level of governments. By contrast, conceiving the cultural fabric of the country as uniform, as the Supreme Court of Cassation suggests, severely constrains the space for religious pluralism.[51]

The Court further affirmed that:

> In a multi-ethnic society, coexistence between people of different ethnicities necessarily requires the identification of a common core in which immigrants and host society must recognize each other. While integration does not impose the abandonment of the culture of origin, in consonance with the provision of Article 2 of the [Italian] Constitution, which values social pluralism, the insurmountable limit is constituted by respect for human rights and the legal civilization of the host society. It is therefore essential for the immigrant *to align his or her values to those of the Western world*, in which he has willingly chosen to integrate.[52]

46 *Sentenza n. 24084 (Sezione Prima Penale)* (n 31), para 2.3 (emphasis added).

47 Edoardo Mazzanti, 'Porto Non Autorizzato di Kirpan e Conformazione ai Valori Occidentali: Un Caso di Diritto Penale 'Dalla Parte del Manico'' [2017] (12) *Cassazione Penale* 4474, 4481 ('Porto non Autorizzato di Kirpan e Conformazione ai Valori Occidentali').

48 Cianitto (n 32) 62.

49 Mazzanti (n 46) 4481.

50 Morelli (n 3) 17. Bernardi described this passage as 'particularly marked by the populist assimilationist ideology that has now fully taken root among large swathes of public opinion': Bernardi (n 24) 684.

51 Giovanni Cavaggion, 'Diritto alla Libertà Religiosa, Pubblica Sicurezza e 'Valori Occidentali': Le Implicazioni della Sentenza della Cassazione nel 'Caso Kirpan' per il Modello di Integrazione Italiano' [2017] (12) *federalismi.it* 1, 9.

52 *Sentenza n. 24084 (Sezione Prima Penale)* (n 31), para 2.3 (emphasis added). Article 2 of the Italian Constitution reads: 'The Republic recognizes and guarantees the inviolable rights of the person, both as an individual and in the social groups where human personality is

The statement constitutes another point of criticism because the notion of "indefinite and arbitrarily identifiable Western values",[53] to which 'the immigrant' is expected to adhere, is legally tenuous from several points of view.[54] First, mandating adherence to specific values, rather than mere compliance with established rules, runs counter to the democratic principles upheld by the Italian constitutional legal order. The law should focus on regulating external behaviours and actions, rather than delving into the internal beliefs or values of those subject to the law itself. Such imposition infringes upon personal freedoms and autonomy, potentially encroaching upon constitutional rights and freedoms, including religious freedom itself.[55] Second, the reference to "the West" does not meet any valid legal definition.[56] It overlooks a significant body of case law arising from jurisdictions traditionally considered as 'Western' stabilised democracies. In contrast to the Italian scenario, many jurisdictions, including the United States,[57] the Netherlands,[58] the United Kingdom,[59] and Belgium,[60] have managed to accommodate the wearing of the ***kirpan*** within the right to freedom of religion or belief.

The Supreme Court of Canada adopted a rather different reasoning to the Italian position. In the following section, we will see how the Canadian Court reflected an appreciation for religious diversity and an inclusive pluralist perspective that, at the same time, did not disregard constitutional interest to public safety.

---

expressed. The Republic expects that the fundamental duties of political, economic and social solidarity be fulfilled'.

53 Alessandro Negri, 'Religious Freedom and Inviolable Lines in Pluralist Societies: The Case of Cultural Crimes' (30) 186.

54 On a recent and comprehensive study on migration, human rights and ways to build welcoming communities see Carmela Ventrella (ed), *La Gestione dei Flussi Migratori. Diritti Umani, Dinamiche dell'Accoglienza e Circuiti Confessionali* (Cacucci, 2022).

55 This holds significant relevance within the Italian constitutional framework. Consider that Article 19 of the Italian Constitution, which regulates freedom of religion, foresees only one explicit limit to the manifestation of religious freedom: religious rites shall not violate public morality (see fn 37). By contrast, earlier legislation, entered into force under the fascist regime, included also that religious principles shall not violate immaterial public order. The framers of the Italian Constitution deliberately opted to discard references to religious principles and immaterial public order, aiming at maximising the scope of the religious freedom, while minimising restrictions on the right to engage in religious actions, specifically religious rites. See Giuseppe Casuscelli (ed), *Nozioni di Diritto Ecclesiastico* (Giappichelli, 5th ed, 2015) 105 ff.

56 Antonio Gusmai, "'Giustificato Motivo' e (in)Giustificate Motivazioni sul Porto del Kirpan: A Margine di Cass. Pen., Sez. I, Sent. n. 24084/2017" [2017] (1) *Dirittifondamentali.it* 1, 14.

57 *People v Singh*, 135 Misc 2d 701, 516 NYS.2d 412 (NY Crim Ct 1987); *Cheema v Thompson*, 67 F 3d 883 (9th Cir 1995); *State v Singh*, 117 Ohio App 3d 381, 690 NE 2d 917 (Ohio Ct App 1996).

58 Decision no. 1997–24 (The Netherlands Equal Treatment Commission 1997).

59 Criminal Justice Act of 1988, art 139, para 5, and art 139A (England and Wales); Criminal Law (Consolidation) (Scotland) Act 1995, art. 49.

60 Decisions nos. 1204 P 2007 and 1205 P 2007 (Court of Appeal of Antwerp 2009).

V Lessons from the Canadian Case Law on *Kirpans*: Precautions against Judicial Populism

Gurbaj Singh Multani was playing at his school in Montreal when his *kirpan* accidentally fell onto the school yard. He was a twelve-year-old student who identified as an orthodox Khalsa Sikh, obliged by his faith to wear a *kirpan* anywhere, any time. After the incident, his family sought to negotiate with the school principal to secure an accommodation of his religious practice. The school board, citing safety concerns, ultimately opted to enforce the school's code of conduct, which prohibited the possession of weapons (including *kirpans*) on school premises. In a spirit of compromise, the school administrators proposed carrying a symbolic *kirpan*, made from safe materials such as plastic or wood.[61]

The Multani family's case reached the Supreme Court of Canada, whose judgement diverged significantly from the Italian case, both in terms of outcome and legal rationale.[62] The Italian case was focused on whether there was a valid justification for carrying the *kirpan* in public places, with the aim of verifying if it was possible to exempt the defendant from criminal liability. In contrast, the Canadian Court addressed two primary legal issues.[63] First, it considered whether the school's zero-tolerance policy regarding *kirpans* infringed Multani's freedom of religion, protected under section 2(a) of the Canadian Charter of Rights and Freedoms.[64] Second, it evaluated whether the restriction imposed on the claimant's manifestation of freedom of religion or

61 *Multani v Commission Scolaire Marguerite-Bourgeoys* [2006] Supreme Court of Canada [2006] 1 SCR. 256, 2006 SCC 6. For comments, beyond the ones quoted throughout this chapter, see in addition: Santiago Canamares Arribas, 'Religious Liberty and Public Security in the Canadian Juridical Experience Section 2: Studies' (2007) 47(94) *Ius Canonicum* 527; Lori G Beaman, 'Just Work It out amongst Yourselves: The Implications of the Private Mediation of Religious Freedom' (2012) 16(2) *Citizenship Studies* 255; Claudia Bianca Ceffa, 'Sensibilità Costituzionale e Salvaguardia dei Valori Giuridici Interni nella Giurisprudenza Italiana in Tema Di Diversità Religiosa nel Contesto della Società Multiculturale' (2017) 4(2017) *Rivista AIC* 1; Bryce Chandler, 'Freedom of Religion: The Supreme Court and the Kirpan' (2006) 46(3) *Education in Canada* 33; Gregory M Dickinson, 'Balanced on a Knife's Edge: School Safety Meets Religious Freedom at the Supreme Court of Canada' (2006) 2006(3) *Education Law Journal* 171; Mark Witten, 'Rationalist Influences in the Adjudication of Religious Freedoms in Canada Discussion Pieces' (2012) 32 *Windsor Review of Legal and Social Issues* 91; Howard Kislowicz, 'Law, Religion, and Feeling Included/Excluded: Case Studies in Canadian Religious Freedom Litigation' (2015) 30(03) *Canadian Journal of Law and Society/Revue Canadienne Droit et Société* 365; Cinzia Piciocchi, 'L'interculturalismo nel Diritto Costituzionale: Una Storia di Parole' (2019) 39(2) *DPCE Online*; C Darius Stonebanks, 'Secularism and Securitisation: The Imaginary Threat of Religious Minorities in Canadian Public Spaces' (2019) 40(3) *Journal of Beliefs & Values* 303.

62 *Multani v Commission Scolaire Marguerite-Bourgeoys* (n 61).

63 Ibid 13.

64 *Canadian Charter of Rights and Freedoms* art 2(a) ('*Canadian Charter of Rights and Freedoms*'): 'Everyone has the following fundamental freedoms: (a) freedom of conscience and religion'.

belief was reasonable and demonstrably justifiable in a free and democratic society, in accordance with section 1 of the Canadian Charter.[65]

The Court observed that the school's code of conduct, which prohibited all potential weapons on school grounds, was driven by a legitimate concern for safety. However, it assessed the limitation imposed on Multani's religious freedom through the criteria outlined by the so-called "*Oakes*" test.[66] Under this test, any restriction of a constitutional right is considered legitimate only if (1) it serves a pressing and substantial objective; (2) if there is rational connection between the restriction and its objective; (3) if the restriction minimally interferes with the right or freedom protected by the Charter; and (4) if there is a proportional balance between benefits achieved by the government's measure and its negative impact.[67] Within the context of this legal framework, the Court recognised that safeguarding public safety is a legitimate aim worthy of legal protection. Nevertheless, the blanket ban on wearing a *kirpan* at school was deemed as a disproportionate and unreasonable limitation of the constitutionally guaranteed right to religious freedom. The Court emphasised that the religious accommodation, initially designed and accepted by Multani but later withdrawn by the school principal, was not unconditional, but subject to strict conditions. The *kirpan* had to be concealed beneath clothing, placed within its sheath, securely wrapped and sewn securely in a safe envelope, and affixed to the *guthra*, the traditional turban worn by Sikh men.[68]

According to the Court, this approach represented a practical accommodation that effectively balanced the right to religious freedom with the need to ensure safety. In addition, it stood as the sole means to avert an outcome characterised by religious intolerance:

> A total prohibition against wearing a *kirpan* to school undermines the value of this religious symbol and sends students the message that some religious practices do not merit the same protection as others. On the other hand, *accommodating* Gurbaj Singh and allowing him to wear his *kirpan* under certain conditions demonstrates the importance that our society attaches to protecting freedom of religion and to showing respect

65 Ibid art 1: 'The Canadian Charter of Rights and Freedoms guarantees the rights and freedoms set out in it subject only to such reasonable limits prescribed by law as can be demonstrably justified in a free and democratic society'.

66 *R v Oakes* [1986] Supreme Court of Canada 1986 CanLII 46 (SCC).

67 See for comments Rafael Tedrus Bento, 'Oakes Test and Proportionality Test: Balance between the Practical Costs of Limiting Rights and the Benefits Arising from the Law' (2021) 15(5) *International Journal of Law and Political Sciences* 558; Moshe Cohen-Eliya and Iddo Porat, 'Proportionality and the Culture of Justification' (2011) 59(2) *The American Journal of Comparative Law* 463; Tania Groppi, *Canada* (Il Mulino, 2006); W P M Kennedy, *The Constitution of Canada: An Introduction to Its Development and Law – Introduction by Martin Friedland* (Oxford University Press, 2014); Peter W Hogg, *Constitutional Law of Canada* (Carswell, 2nd ed, 1985).

68 *Multani v Commission Scolaire Marguerite-Bourgeoys* (n 61) 8.

> for its minorities. The deleterious effects of a total prohibition thus outweigh its salutary effects.[69]

The decision rendered by the Supreme Court is particularly relevant to the context of education and is less dependent on the technicalities of criminal law that were specific to the Italian case. In Canada, schools are notably conceived as a reflection of society and of the larger multicultural community. This perspective encourages parents, students, and educators to design an educational environment that mirrors the multifaceted constitutional implications of diversity and pluralism.[70] Apart from these context- and country-specific distinctions, there was a clearly notable difference between the two judgements. *Multani* is often lauded as "an inspiring example of multiculturalism, cultural and legal tolerance in Canada"[71] for two crucial facets emerging from the judgement: the Court's comprehension of religious identities and its judicial rationale. First, the *Multani* bench made a conscious effort to construct its reasoning while understanding the interplay of the student's multiple identities as both a Sikh believer and as an individual belonging to a secular community.[72] In doing so, the Court aligned with contemporary constitutional systems by acknowledging that the applicant viewed carrying the *kirpan* as a deeply held religious obligation.[73] While the Italian bench asserted that a person belonging to a religious minority should comply with "the legal civilisation of the host society",[74] the Canadian Court conveyed a nuanced and sensible understanding of the *kirpan*, defining it as a religious symbol rather than as a weapon.[75] Second, the Canadian Court was significantly influenced by factual arguments and contextual analysis, as opposed to relying on the abstract approach taken

69 Ibid 79 (emphasis added).

70 Allison N Crawford, 'Learning Lessons from Multani: Considering Canada's Response to Religious Garb Issues in Public Schools Notes' (2007) 36(1) *Georgia Journal of International and Comparative Law* 159, 179. See also Eleonora Ceccherini, 'Cittadinanza, Immigrazione e Integrazione: L'approccio Multiculturale Canadese in Bilico' in Ginevra Cerrina Feroni and Veronica Federico (eds), *Strumenti, Percorsi e Strategie dell'Integrazione nelle Società Multiculturali* (Edizioni Scientifiche Italiane, 2018) 345. For an Italian perspective about education environment see Enrica Martinelli, 'From Foreigners to Citizens: Freedom of Religion, Education and Policies of Social Integration for Muslim Minors' in Mark Hill and Lina Papadopoulou (eds), *Islam, Religious Liberty and Constitutionalism in Europe* (Hart Publishing, 2024).

71 Monachini (n 43) 139.

72 Ayelet Shachar, *Multicultural Jurisdictions: Cultural Differences and Women's Rights* (Cambridge University Press, 2001).

73 Francesco Alicino, 'The Collaborations-Relations between Western (Secular) Law and Religious Nomoi Groups in Today's Multicultural Context: The Cases of France and Canada' (2011) 18(2) *Transition Studies Review* 430, 441.

74 *Sentenza n. 24084 (Sezione Prima Penale)* (n 31), para 2.3.

75 Howard Kislowicz, 'Sacred Laws in Earthly Courts: Legal Pluralism in Canadian Religious Freedom Litigation' (2013) 39(1) *Queen's Law Journal* 175, 411.

in the Italian case.[76] While the Italian Court concluded that it is "essential for the immigrant to align his or her values to those of the Western world",[77] the Canadian Court ascertained that not only did Mr Multani have no prior history of displaying violent behaviour at school, but also that "over the 100 years since Sikhs have been attending schools in Canada, not a single violent incident related to the presence of *kirpans* in schools had been reported".[78]

The Court finally emphasised that even if the *kirpan* were worn by Multani under the conditions set forth by the school's administrators, its potential for causing harm would be exceptionally limited. As the Court put it, "a student who wanted to commit an act of violence could find another way to obtain a weapon, such as bringing one in from outside the school" or obtaining one easily at school "such as scissors, pencils, and baseball bats".[79]

VI Conclusion: Countering Judicial Populism in Legal Practice

In jurisprudence, certain rulings, while focusing on a specific and technical legal issue, like the wearing of the *kirpan*, resonate with the foundational principles embedded in a legal system and may have a long-term and unexpected impact.[80] It may be sufficient to note that in 2023, the administrative tribunal of Lazio confirmed, in two different decisions, the denial of applications for Italian citizenship from two third-country nationals.[81] The applications were rejected on the grounds of the applicants' previous criminal convictions for carrying a *kirpan*. According to the tribunal's perspective, a breach of Italian criminal law indicated a lack of integration of the individual into the social fabric, deemed a prerequisite for acquiring citizenship.[82] What is most concerning is that the decisions relied on the 2017 Supreme Court of Cassation judgement, quoting it as a landmark precedent and as an influencing legal authority.[83]

76 François Crepéau, 'Canadian Multiculturalism in Question: Diversity or Citizenship?' in Isabelle Rorive, Djordje Sredanovic and Andrea Rea (eds), *Governing Diversity: Migrant Integration and Multiculturalism in North America and Europe* (Editions de l'Université de Bruxelles, 2019) 107, 113.

77 *Sentenza n. 24084 (Sezione Prima Penale)* (n 31), para 2.3.

78 *Multani v Commission Scolaire Marguerite-Bourgeoys* (n 61) 59; see also Elisabetta Palici di Suni, 'Simboli Religiosi e Laicità: Aperture e Chiusure in Alcune Recenti Pronunce' [2017] (1) *Rivista di Diritti Comparati* 1, 8.

79 *Multani v Commission Scolaire Marguerite-Bourgeoys* (n 61) 58.

80 Antonio Ruggeri, 'La Questione del Kirpan Quale Banco di Prova del Possibile Incontro (e Non dell'Inevitabile Scontro) Tra le Culture, nella Cornice del Pluralismo Costituzionale (a Margine di Cass., I Sez. Pen., n. 24084 del 2017)' [2017] (2) *Consulta on line* 316, 310.

81 See Art. 9, letter 'f' of the Italian Citizenship Law, Legge 5 febbraio 1992, n. 91, 'Nuove Norme sulla Cittadinanza'.

82 *Sentenza* [2023] TAR Lazio–Roma (sez V) 13511; and also (in the same light) *Sentenza* [2023] TAR Lazio–Roma (sez V) 6967.

83 The two judgements define the 2017 judgement as 'a fixed point'.

The comparative inquiry on the carrying of the *kirpan*, offered in the present chapter, has demonstrated how matters regarding religious symbols might be influenced by manifestations of judicial populism. As the Italian case shows, such an approach not only undermines the constitutionally protected values of religious pluralism and marginalises minority religious groups, but also jeopardises judicial independence, impartiality, and public trust in the judiciary, reinforcing intolerance towards religious minority practices.[84] In contrast, the approach embraced by the Canadian Supreme Court was characterised by careful consideration of religious freedom and identities, alongside a judicial rationale that weighted freedom of religion or belief in light of public safety interests.[85] This concrete exercise of balancing resonates both with the legal language of fundamental rights and freedoms and with the foundation of a democracy based on religious pluralism.[86] It is also grounded in a context-specific analysis that focuses on 'the only, real, relevant'[87] legal question: whether the protection of public safety can validly limit the carrying of the *kirpan* as a manifestation of religious freedom in public and by observance.

Populist narratives have an ambivalent relationship with religious symbols. They may leverage them as identity markers to bolster consent and authority, or they may resist them to endorse majoritarian perspectives, potentially disregarding religious minority rights. This intricate dynamic is as challenging as it is elusive. Despite the inherent difficulties, effectively guarding judgements against the influence of judicial populism may be an achievable goal. The Canadian case shows that judicial decisions grounded in well-established legal principles, case law and precedents, and rigorous reasoning can provide a buffer against populist abuse of religious symbols. The Italian case shows that succumbing to abstract principles, if not 'legal intuitions', may have two negative externalities: in the short-term, it may increase the risk of undermining the universal scope of the right to religious freedom or belief; while in the long-term, it may deviate from the inclusive and pluralist constitutional conception of citizenry.[88]

84 Bernardi (n 24) 703.

85 Crawford (n 69) 179.

86 Morelli (n 3) 25.

87 Fabio Basile and Mariarosa Giannoccoli, 'Il Coltello Kirpan, i Valori Occidentali e gli Arcipelaghi Culturali Confliggenti: A Proposito di una Recente Sentenza della Cassazione' [2017] (3) *Diritto, Immigrazione e Cittadinanza* 1, 6.

88 On the relation between access to citizenship and religion see Tania Pagotto, 'Religion-based Boundaries: Restricting Pluralism through Symbolic Barriers' in Tania Pagotto, Joshua M Roose and GP Marcar (eds), *Security, Religion, and the Rule of Law: International Perspectives* (Taylor & Francis Limited, 2023).

Further Reading:

For analysis of the methods used in this chapter, see Chapter 15 – Section IV – subsection A *The Doctrinal Method*; C *The Functionalist Method*; D *The Analytical Method*; E *The Cultural method*; F *The Yardstick Method.*

For the author's rejoinder and reflection, see Appendix Section V.

For a comparative analysis based in Europe, see Chapter 9.

11 Of Missiles and Wedding Cakes: Utilising Human Dignity to Hold a Hohfeldian Lens in Comparative Jurisprudence

Neville Rochow KC[1]

I Introduction

This chapter offers different perspectives for the resolution of a perennial conflict between claims for liberty and equality.[2] The clashes between these claims have long posed a problem for common law courts and legislatures. The problem is poignantly illustrated in the contests between claims made under anti-discrimination laws and the claims for religious liberty as exceptions to those laws. A satisfactory solution has proved elusive. Instead of an organising principle, common law jurisdictions, including two discussed here, Australia[3] and the United States,[4] have developed a series of ad hoc rules through their courts and legislatures.

Common law courts, as exemplified here in the discussion of Australia and the United States, have lacked a tool such as human dignity in the resolution of rights disputes. Notoriously, Australia is one of the few Western jurisdictions not to have any constitutional or national legislative bill of rights.[5] Instead, it

1 Dr Neville Rochow KC Barrister and Adjunct Associate Professor Adelaide Law School.

2 For a brief overview on the Australian legislative and constitutional position, see Luke Beck, 'Why Are Religious Discrimination Laws Back in the News? And Where Did They Come from in the First Place?', *The Conversation*, 20 March 2024, https://theconversation.com/why-are-religious-discrimination-laws-back-in-the-news-and-where-did-they-come-from-in-the-first-place-226220.

3 Michael Quinlan, 'An Unholy Patchwork Quilt: The Inadequacy of Protections of Freedom of Religion in Australia', in Iain T Benson, Michael Quinlan and A Keith Thompson (eds), *Religious Freedom in Australia—A New Terra Nullius?* (Connor Court, 2019).

4 Frank S Ravitch, 'Be Careful What You Wish For: Why *Hobby Lobby* Weakens Religious Freedom' (2016) 55 *Brigham Young University Law Review* 55. See also Frank S Ravitch, *Freedom's Edge—Religious Freedom, Sexual Freedom, and the Future of America* (Cambridge University Press, 2016), chapter 1 for a discussion of *Masterpiece Cakeshop Ltd v Colorado Civil Rights Commission* 584 US ___ (2018).

5 Neville Rochow SC, 'Paying for Human Rights Before the Bill Comes: Towards a More Comprehensive Domestic Implementation of International Human Rights Norms in Australia' (University of Adelaide Law Research Paper No 2009-004 44, posted 11 Mar 2009, last revised 1 Feb 2015); Renae Barker, 'Freedom of Religion without a Bill of Rights: Australia's Peculiar Approach to Tackling Freedom of Religion and Other Human Rights Issues' in Paul Babie,

DOI: 10.4324/9781003397311-16

has developed a complicated patchwork under anti-discrimination legislation. As an alternative to this patchwork of laws and rules that have emerged, this chapter engages with the status of human dignity.

To provide a principled solution, the chapter examines how acknowledgement and instantiation of human dignity as an overarching constitutional principle can provide a standard by which courts, executives, and legislatures can rise above rule-bound contests to apply a set of universal principles that operate to reach just resolutions. Rather than applying rules that are confined to specific circumstances, it offers a set of principles, governed by the status of human dignity, that can operate generally in cases of rights claim conflict; and that same set of principles can operate specifically in the clashes involving claims for religious liberty and the claims for equality rights. Moreover, the chapter provides an analytical tool, a lens of deconstruction, useful for understanding what precisely courts are doing. That lens, developed by Wesley Hohfeld[6] and so often used in dissecting proprietary rights, has been honed by Joseph Singer for use in conflicts between anti-discrimination laws and religious liberty claims.[7] It is applied here to demonstrate the difference that invocation of human dignity can make.[8] The chapter will demonstrate that this analytical lens, applied to equality-libertarian conflicts, is well-suited to the deconstruction of the rights claims considered here in order to understand the correct norms to apply to the facts to achieve a dignified outcome.[9]

Neville Rochow and Brett Scharffs (eds), *Freedom of Religion or Belief: Creating Constitutional Space for Fundamental Freedoms* (Edward Elgar Publishing, 1 January 2020) 109–30. See also Andrew Byrnes, Hilary Charlesworth and Gabrielle McKinnon, *Bills of Rights in Australia*, (University of New South Wales Press, 2009) 229–40.

6 Wesley Newcomb Hohfeld, 'Fundamental Legal Conceptions as Applied in Judicial Reasoning' (1916) 26 *Yale Law Journal* 710 ('Fundamental Legal Conceptions'); Wesley Newcomb Hohfeld, 'Some Fundamental Legal Conceptions as Applied in Judicial Reasoning' (1913) 23 *Yale Law Journal* 16 ('Some Fundamental Legal Conceptions').

7 Joseph Singer, 'The Legal Rights Debate in Analytical Jurisprudence from Bentham to Hohfeld' [1982] (6) *Wisconsin Law Review* 975 ('The Legal Rights Debate'); Joseph Singer, *No Freedom without Regulation: The Hidden Lesson of the Subprime Crisis* (Yale University Press, 2015) ('*No Freedom without Regulation*'); Joseph Singer, 'Religious Liberty and Public Accommodations: What Would Hohfeld Say?' in Shyam Balganash, Ted Sichelman and Henry Smith (eds), *Wesley Hohfeld A Century Later: Edited Major Works, Select Personal Papers, and Original Commentaries* (Cambridge University Press, forthcoming), ('Religious Liberty & Public Accommodations').

8 Neville Rochow QC, 'Towards a Constitutional Spatial Theory for the Resolution of Conflicts in Rights and Liberties Claims' (2021) 29 *Michigan State International Law Review* 469.

9 Ibid. As to the application of norms to facts, see a discussion of Jerome Frank's legal realism (sometimes summarised as 'Rules x Facts = Decision') in Simon N Verdun-Jones, 'The Jurisprudence of Jerome N Frank: A Study in American Legal Realism', (1974) 7 *Sydney Law Review* 180–210; also discussed in Neville Grant Rochow, *Evidence,* Judicial Notice *and* Party Comment: *Principles for Ascertaining Facts Which Predicate Constitutional Validity* (Master of Laws Thesis, University of Adelaide, 1987). http://web4.library.adelaide.edu.au/theses/09LM/09lmr781.pdf.

The solutions offered in this chapter commence first with a workable definition of the type of "human dignity" under consideration, referred to here as *instrumental* dignity. Second, it considers a United States Supreme Court decision, *Masterpiece Cakeshop Ltd v Colorado Civil Rights Commission ('Masterpiece')*,[10] used here for comparative study. In the process of this analysis, utilising Hohfeld's methodology, *Masterpiece* is compared and contrasted with cases decided under dignitarian principles. The comparisons and contrasts demonstrate various ways in which the outcome of the case could (and should) have been different. Third, continuing the comparative process focused on in *Masterpiece*, the chapter discusses an often-overlooked common law principle, the "Innkeepers' Rule"; one that embodies dignitarian principles in the limited circumstance of public supply of goods and services. Using Hohfeldian analytics,[11] the chapter demonstrates how the Innkeepers' Rule should have been applied in reaching the *Masterpiece* decision, and how its application would have elevated the outcome from a strained invocation of the First Amendment to a dignified limitation of religious liberty in which the consumers, rather than the supplier of goods and services in public common, would and should have been successful. Next, the chapter considers other decisions that demonstrate how dignitarian principles change the outcome of cases in which rights claims conflict.

Lastly, the chapter suggests that the standards set by the status of human dignity, combined with the Hohfeldian analytic lens, are a useful tool set for common law lawyers and comparative lawyers alike. The chapter concludes that human dignity and its constitutional instantiation would provide a missing tool in the common law by which to determine rights claims disputes. Specifically with respect to cases involving claims of religious freedom competing with claims under an equality law, the chapter concludes that human dignity favours containment of individual exercise of private belief to the private sphere where public exercise would adversely affect the rights and freedoms of others. By adopting a Hohfeldian analysis, it can be seen more clearly, on a comparative basis, what courts are doing in their decision-making processes.

II Human Dignity

All human rights derive their legitimacy from the universal status of human dignity. Dignity provides the standard by which all humans enjoy their respective rights and freedoms. Human dignity also sets a boundary upon rights and freedoms. Consideration of it prevents unnecessary incursions upon the rights and freedoms of others. For the human rights project to progress in common law jurisdictions (and elsewhere), and for citizens of all nations to flourish,

10 *Masterpiece Cakeshop Ltd v Colorado Civil Rights Commission* 584 US ___ (2018).
11 Hohfeld, 'Fundamental Legal Conceptions' (n 5), Hohfeld, 'Some Fundamental Legal Conceptions' (n 5).

human dignity must be adopted and applied as an overarching constitutional principle.

Before demonstrating how human dignity, applied as a juridical standard, forms a critical element in resolution of the complex problem of competing rights and liberties claims, the concept of dignity itself must first be defined, and its context clarified.

There are three senses in which human dignity is used in modern human rights parlance:[12] the theological; the philosophical; and the instrumental. The three are quite distinct and have discrete applications. Problems arise from their conflation.[13] Clarity comes when they are distinguished. The instrumental conception is considered and defined first. The theological and philosophical conceptions are then compared.

12 See Michael Rosen, *Dignity: Its History and Meaning* (Harvard University Press, 2012); Francis Fukuyama, *Identity: The Demand for Dignity and the Politics of Resentment* (Profile Books, 2018); Donna Hicks, *Dignity: Its Essential Role in Resolving Conflict* (Yale University Press, 2011); Jeremy Waldron, *Dignity, Rank, and Rights* (Oxford University Press, 2012); George Kateb, *Human Dignity* (Oxford University Press, 2011); and Nicholas Aroney, 'The Rise and Fall of Human Dignity' (2021) 46 *Brigham Young University Law Review* 1211. In the last cited article, it can be seen that the survey of usages of 'human dignity' in its theological, philosophical, and instrumental applications is undertaken without distinction and leads to a promotion of the Catholic theological usages as superior to those in other contexts. As undertaken by Alex Deagon, 'The Symbolic Significance of God in the Australian Constitution', talkabout (Blog post, 30 November 2020) https://talkabout.iclrs.org/2020/11/30/symbolic-significance-of-god-in-the-australian-constitution/ ('The Symbolic Significance of God in the Australian Constitution'). See also Alex Deagon and Benjamin Saunders, 'Principles, Pragmatism and Power: Another Look at the Historical Context of Section 116' (2020) 43(3) *Melbourne University Law Review* 1; and Alex Deagon, 'Liberal Assumptions in Section 116 Cases and Implications for Religious Freedom' (2018) 46 *Federal Law Review* 113 ('Liberal Assumptions in Section 116 Cases').

13 For a recent description of human dignity, see Brett Scharffs and Ewelina Ochab, *An Introduction to the Punta del Este Declaration on Human Dignity for Everyone Everywhere* (Routledge 2023). The book introduces dignity in the following terms:

> *The Punta Del Este Declaration* simplifies and brings coherence to the concept of human dignity in 10 brief statements that capture the *many dimensions and aspects of human dignity* and the practical ways that human dignity is useful in the promotion of human rights. This book provides an overview of how the notion of human dignity has been used to *strengthen* human rights. It discusses how human dignity plays *many different roles in human rights discourse* and has the force to revitalise the human rights project; it is the *foundational principle* upon which the human rights project is built. But it is also the telos, or end goal, of human rights. At the same time, it is *an important evaluative mechanism* for assessing how well a country is doing in the implementation of human rights. (emphasis added).

Although it may appear as quibbling, this description critically fails to characterise human dignity as a *status* and to provide a definition that distinguishes the place of instrumental human dignity in contradistinction from its uses outside of the human rights project. These failures, though minor in their appearance, have been the source of much unnecessary debate and confusion.

A Instrumental Human Dignity as a Status

First, in the sense used here, "instrumental human dignity" is a *status*. It is immutable, universal, innate, and inviolable. This sense of its usage is recognised in Article 1 of the *German Constitution*, which instantiates dignity as the overarching constitutional principle:

> Dignity is a status is to be acknowledged and respected, in all circumstances whatsoever and without exception, by all governments, governmental instrumentalities, and their agencies, and, by all other human beings and by all legal persons of any form.[14]

The Article adopts the characterisation of "status". "Status", as quite distinct from a "right", "liberty", or "obligation", signifies a package or bundle of rights, liberties, and obligations that inhere in a particular legal circumstance. Jeremy Waldron refers to examples such as bankruptcy, infancy, royalty, being an alien, being a prisoner, being a member of the armed forces, and being married.[15] Other statuses include convict, employee, taxpayer, parent, testator, and citizen. Each status connotes settled legal conditions, placed into the package or bundle, sitting below the label and enjoyed or borne by the individual bearing the label. There is no need to inquire below the label because the legal conditions of a status are known and settled.

Second, the instrumental notion of "dignity", the status, as employed here, is a legal term intended to describe an organising principle in legal, constitutional, and human rights instruments for rights and freedoms that are vouchsafed by the instrument that invokes the status of dignity. As a status, it sits at the apex of human rights which derogate from it. Examples are found in the *German Constitution*, already cited, and in the preambles to the *Universal Declaration of Human Rights*,[16] the *International Covenant on Civil and*

14 *German Constitution* art 1. Author's translation.

15 Waldron (n 11) 40.

16 'Whereas recognition of the *inherent dignity* and of the equal and inalienable rights of all members of the human family is the foundation of freedom, justice and peace in the world,

'Whereas disregard and contempt for human rights have resulted in barbarous acts which have outraged the conscience of mankind, and the advent of a world in which human beings shall enjoy freedom of speech and belief and freedom from fear and want has been proclaimed as the highest aspiration of the common people,

'Whereas it is essential, if man is not to be compelled to have recourse, as a last resort, to rebellion against tyranny and oppression, that human rights should be protected by the rule of law,

'Whereas it is essential to promote the development of friendly relations between nations,

'Whereas the peoples of the United Nations have in the Charter *reaffirmed their faith in fundamental human rights, in the dignity and worth* of the human person and in the equal rights of men and women and have determined to promote social progress and better standards of life in larger freedom,

Political Rights,[17] and the *European Convention on Human Rights*.[18] In each instance of instrumental 'dignity', those rights and freedoms articulated in the balance of the document have their reference to and derivation from the universal status of human dignity.

'Whereas Member States have pledged themselves to achieve, in co-operation with the United Nations, the promotion of universal respect for and observance of human rights and fundamental freedoms,

'Whereas a common understanding of these rights and freedoms is of the greatest importance for the full realization of this pledge,

'Now, therefore,

'The General Assembly,

'Proclaims this Universal Declaration of Human Rights as a *common standard of achievement for all peoples and all nations*, to the end that every individual and every organ of society, keeping this Declaration constantly in mind, shall strive by teaching and education to promote respect for these rights and freedoms and by progressive measures, national and international, to secure their universal and effective recognition and observance, both among the peoples of Member States themselves and among the peoples of territories under their jurisdiction'. (emphasis added).

17 Preamble to the International Covenant on Civil and Political Rights:

'The States Parties to the present Covenant,

'Considering that, in accordance with the principles proclaimed in the Charter of the United Nations, *recognition of the inherent dignity and of the equal and inalienable rights of all members of the human family* is the foundation of freedom, justice and peace in the world,

Recognizing that these rights derive from the inherent dignity of the human person,...' (emphasis added).

18 'The Governments signatory hereto, being members of the Council

'of Europe,

'Considering the Universal Declaration of Human Rights

'proclaimed by the General Assembly of the United Nations on

'10th December 1948;

'Considering that this Declaration aims at securing the universal

'and effective recognition and observance of the Rights therein declared;

'Considering that the aim of the Council of Europe is the achievement of greater unity between its members and that one of the methods by which that aim is to be pursued is the maintenance and further realisation of Human Rights and Fundamental Freedoms;

'Reaffirming their profound belief in those fundamental freedoms which are the foundation of justice and peace in the world and are best maintained on the one hand by an effective political democracy and on the other by a common understanding and observance of the Human Rights upon which they depend;

'Being resolved, as the governments of European countries which are like-minded and have a common heritage of political traditions, ideals, freedom and the rule of law, to take the first steps for the collective enforcement of certain of the rights stated in the Universal Declaration,

'Affirming that the High Contracting Parties, in accordance with the principle of subsidiarity, have the primary responsibility to secure the rights and freedoms defined in this Convention and the Protocols thereto, and that in doing so they enjoy a margin of appreciation, subject to the supervisory jurisdiction of the European Court of Human Rights established by this Convention,

'Have agreed as follows: ...' (emphasis added).

Third, to have juristic efficacy, it must have sovereign constitutional force, enforceable by the courts with state's coercive force to ensure its efficacy. A part of this is that the courts must have power to declare non-conforming laws invalid and to make remedial orders when dignity is denied.

B The Definition of Instrumental Dignity

The difficulty in defining "dignity" is well-known.[19] Some of its invocations in preambles of human rights conventions, constitutions, and in scholarly discourse have been described as "a piece of decorative rhetoric".[20] Unthoughtful use of "dignity" is a notorious source of the apprehended ambiguity.[21] However, as Mary Ann Glendon has observed,[22] despite difficulty in definition, dignity has nevertheless played a critical role in the development of rights and freedoms. It is now so well-established as a central part of human rights and constitutional discourse that its use cannot be avoided.[23]

While Glendon is correct as to its prevalence, defence of the usage of the instrumental dignity can be far more robust; a defence can be propounded that readily withstands any attack to the effect that it is too vague and, therefore, not a useful juristic principle. There are many terms used in the common law and in statute that are inherently ambiguous until supplied with a definition and a context. Much like other terms that are difficult to define in the abstract, such as "justice", "rule of law", "independence", and "value", given a context, "dignity" is capable of operating as an organising principle and taking meaning from the purpose to which it is put.[24] Other examples of terms that are vague in isolation but have clarity in their contextual usages include

19 Mary Ann Glendon, *A World Made New: Eleanor Roosevelt and the Universal Declaration of Human Rights* (Random House, 2002); Stephan P Leher, *Dignity and Human Rights—Language, Philosophy, and Social Realizations* (Routledge, 2018); Christopher McCrudden, 'Human Dignity in Human Rights Interpretation' (2008) 19 *European Journal of International Law* 655; Doris Schroeder, 'How to Define Dignity and Its Place in Human Rights—A Philosopher's View', *The Conversation* (online, 9 August 2017) https://theconversation.com/how-to-define-dignity-and-its-place-in-human-rights-a-philosophers-view-81785; Doris Schroeder and AH Bani-Sadr, *Dignity in the 21st Century* (Springer, 2017).

20 Waldron (n 11) 26, 117–137.

21 Ibid. See also the following works cited by Waldron: Jeremy Waldron, 'Dignity and Rank' (2007) 48 *European Journal of Sociology* 201; Rosen (n 8); Kateb (n 11); McCrudden (n 18); Christopher McCrudden (ed), *Understanding Human Dignity* (Oxford University Press/British Academy, 2013); George Fletcher, 'Human Dignity as a Constitutional Value' (1984) 22 *University of Western Ontario* 178; Richard Rorty, *Contingency, Irony and Solidarity* (Cambridge University Press, 1989) 44–5 and 52–7. See also Fukuyama (n 11).

22 Mary Ann Glendon, 'The Bearable Lightness of Dignity' *First Things Magazine* 20 April, 2011 https://www.firstthings.com/article/2011/05/the-bearable-lightness-of-dignity.

23 Aharon Barak, *Human Dignity: The Constitutional Value and the Constitutional Right* (Cambridge University Press, 2015) 38–42, 114–35 and 156–9.

24 Ibid.

"equity",[25] "reasonable"[26] "fraudulent",[27] "misleading or deceptive",[28] and "unconscionable".[29] Dignity could yet be another such imprecise term *but for* the context, definition, and explanation, as, for example, provided here. Instrumental dignity, with the benefit of its contextual definition, would be, in no manner of understanding, a mere rhetorical flourish or a theoretical conception with no meaning or force behind it.

C Definition of Instrumental Human Dignity and Its Constitutional Recognition of Human Dignity as an Exercise of Sovereign Power

With an understanding of dignity's nature as a universal status that overarches all human rights, its definition and allocation of attributes becomes possible as summarised here:

1. Dignity is an immutable, universal, innate, and inviolable status of all humans that can be neither earned nor deprived;
2. Human dignity is the source of all guaranteed fundamental rights and freedoms;
3. Human dignity is the organising principle for any human rights framework;
4. Once instantiated, its constitutional role is to be acknowledged in all relevant constitutional, legislative, and procedural instruments to ensure that courts implement dignity as it is intended by each instrument;
5. Courts are, by declaration, to invalidate legislation that does not conform to its requirements and, in its application to any case, to subjugate all other constitutional, statutory, and common law norms, laws, and provisions to the principles necessary to permit its application; and
6. The status of dignity cannot be conferred or removed but must be recognised as an exercise of sovereign power of the state.

25 J D Heydon, M J Leeming and P G Turner, *Meagher, Gummow and Lehane's Equity: Doctrines and Remedies.*
(5th Edition, LexisNexis Butterworths 2014) chapter 1.

26 *Donoghue v Stevenson* [1932] AC 562.

27 *Derry v Peek* (1889) 14 App Cas 337; *Phillips v Brooks Ltd* [1919] 2 KB 243. See also the discussion in *Miller & Associates v BMW Australia* (2010) 241 CLR 357, 364 as per French CJ and Kiefel J (as her Honour then was known).

28 *Australian Consumer Law* s 18(1) provides: 'A person must not in trade or commerce, engage in conduct that is misleading or deceptive or is likely to mislead or deceive' ('*ACL*'). See also *Google Inc v Australian Competition and Consumer Commission* [2013] HCA 1; *Australian Competition and Consumer Commission v TPG Internet Pty Ltd* [2013] HCA 54; *Miller & Associates v BMW Australia* (2010) 241 CLR 357; *Murphy v Overton Investments Pty Ltd* (2004) 216 CLR 388; *Yorke v Lucas* (1985) 158 CLR 661; and *Parkdale Custom Built Furniture Pty Ltd v Puxu Pty Ltd* (1982) 149 CLR 191.

29 *ACL* s 20(1) provides: 'A person must not, in trade or commerce, engage in conduct that is unconscionable within the meaning of the unwritten law, from time to time'. See *Blomley v Ryan* (1954) 99 CLR 362; *Commercial Bank of Australia v Amadio* (1983) 151 CLR 447; and *Louth v Diprose* (1992) 175 CLR 621.

The constitutional recognition of the status of human dignity is critical to provide operational context. Consistent with constitutional principle, dignity should be recognised as a constitutional status to be enjoyed by all citizens once instantiated by an exercise of the state's sovereign power. It is not a status that the common law courts could merely invent or discover.[30] The necessary sovereignty is vested in the government by consent of the governed. It is instantiated to deliver on the promise to govern for their benefit, as accepted by constitutional theorists in Australia (Jeffrey Goldsworthy),[31] the United Kingdom (T R S Allan and Geoffrey Marshall),[32] and Canada (Peter Hogg,[33] Gérard Beaudoin, and Errol Mendes).[34]

The legal force and authority of the respective instruments recognising the status of dignity derive from having been constitutionally and legally instantiated by the relevant sovereign power and, internationally, by covenant among sovereign states.[35] The power and authority of the executive to initiate, legislatures to pass, and the courts to enforce constitutionally based laws cannot be questioned.[36] By exercise of this power and authority, the state delivers on its promise to use its agencies to enforce rights through adjudication by a court of competent jurisdiction under them.[37]

30 *Secretary, Department of Health and Community Services v JWB and SMB* (*Marion's Case*) [1992] HCA 15; (1992) 175 CLR 218.

31 Jeffrey Goldsworthy, *The Sovereignty of Parliament: History and Philosophy* (Oxford University Press, 2019).

32 Geoffrey Marshall, *Constitutional Theory* (Oxford University Press, 1971). See also Geoffrey Marshall, *Constitutional Conventions: The Rules and Forms of Political Accountability* (Oxford University Press, 1984).

33 Peter W Hogg, *Constitutional Law of Canada* (Thomson Canada Limited, 2005).

34 The Honourable Gérald-A. Beaudoin and Errol Mendes, *The Canadian Charter of Rights and Freedoms* (Carswell Thomson Professional Publishing, 3rd ed, 1996).

35 However, a basic law might be described, (such as a *Grundnorm* [Kelsen] or rule of recognition [Hart]), all legal philosophers in the modern era accept that in a liberal democratic society, sovereignty is captured in the constitution, behind which no instrument of government can go. Hans Kelsen tr Max Knight, *Pure Theory of Law*, (Lawbook Exchange, 2009); HLA Hart, *The Concept of Law* (Oxford University Press, 1961); Joseph Raz, *Practical Reason and Norms* (Oxford University Press, 2002); Joseph Raz, *The Authority of Law* (Oxford University Press, 2nd ed, 2009); Ronald Dworkin, *Taking Rights Seriously* (Duckworth, 8th ed, 1996); Ronald Dworkin, *Law's Empire* (Fontana Paperbacks, 1986). John Rawls, *Political Liberalism* (Columbia University Press, 2005). See also John Rawls, *A Theory of Justice* (The Belknap Press of Harvard University Press, 1999); John Rawls, *The Law of Peoples* (Harvard University Press, 1999); and John Rawls, *Justice as Fairness: A Restatement* (The Belknap Press of Harvard University Press, 2001).

36 Parliamentary Education Office, 'Separation of Powers: Parliament, Executive and Judiciary', Commonwealth Parliament of Australia https://peo.gov.au/understand-our-parliament/how-parliament-works/system-of-government/separation-of-powers-parliament-executive-and-judiciary.

37 Ibid. As to an implied nationhood power see *Davis v Commonwealth* (1988) 166 CLR 79. On sovereignty and its types, see also *Victoria v Commonwealth* (1975) 134 CLR 388 at 397 per Mason J (as his Honour then was known); Penelope Mathew, 'International Law and the

D Distinction of Instrumental Human Dignity from Uses of the Term "Dignity" in Theological and the Philosophical Contexts

There is a need to distinguish instrumental dignity from its usages in theology and philosophy. Their conflation with instrumental dignity produces analytical and historical errors.[38]

The theological usage could never be appropriate in the application of instrumental usage in the current context of constitutionalism and juristic development.[39] Theological notions of human dignity carry assumptions of the relationship between God and humankind. As George Kateb has pointed out quite clearly, the unsuitability of the theological usage, and certainly as employed by Christian commentators,[40] derives from assumptions regarding mankind, (the "created"), to God, (the "creator").[41] The Christian notion of that relationship involves notions of original sin and "fallen Man",[42] and the eschatological workout of fallen nature through Christ's atonement and redemption.[43] None of these doctrinal tenets can be readily assimilated into jurisprudential analysis of human dignity. The theological usage is riven with contingencies that deprive the status of its "immutable, universal, innate, and inviolable" nature. An assimilation of theological dignity with instrumental dignity would be contradictory. If undertaken, it would require so many caveats and qualifications as to render its invocation a greater problem to be solved than the one immediately at hand. An analysis invoking theological notions of dignity would be a futility.

While the philosophical conception of dignity is more closely aligned with the instrumental usage,[44] particularly as developed by Immanuel Kant,[45]

Protection of Human Rights in Australia: Recent Trends' (1995) 17 *Sydney Law Review* 177, 177–8; 181–2; 184–8; 192–3; 195; 200–1; and on parliamentary sovereignty under a written constitution, Goldsworthy (n 30) 2–9. See also M J Detmold, *Courts and Administrators: A Study in Jurisprudence* (Weidenfeld & Nicolson, 1989) 18–50, 157–72 and 204–7; Michael Detmold, 'The New Constitutional Law' (1994) 16(2) *Sydney Law Review* 228, 248.

38 Aroney (n 11).

39 As erroneously undertaken in Deagon 'The Symbolic Significance of God in the Australian Constitution' (n 11). See also Deagon and Saunders (n 11); and Deagon 'Liberal Assumptions in Section 116 Cases' (n 11) For an historical account on the issue, see Helen Irving, *To Constitute a Nation* (Cambridge University Press, 1999), 169–182.

40 Kateb (n 11), chapters 1 and 2.

41 Ibid.

42 Ibid.

43 Ibid.

44 Scott Cutler Shershow, *Deconstructing Dignity* (University of Chicago Press, 2013) ch 4; and Marián Palenčár, 'Some Remarks on the Concept and Intellectual History of Human Dignity' (2016) 26 *Human Affairs* 462; Jeremy Waldron, 'Is Dignity the Foundation of Human Rights?' in Rowan Cruft, S Matthew Liao, and Massimo Renzo (eds), *Philosophical Foundations of Human Rights* (Oxford University Press, 2015) ch 6.

45 Immanuel Kant, *Critique of Practical Reason: Revised Edition*, tr Mary Gregor (Cambridge University Press, 2015); Immanuel Kant, *Groundwork of the Metaphysics of Morals*, tr Mary Gregor and Jens Timmerman (eds) (Cambridge University Press, 2014); and Immanuel Kant,

it remains inappropriate to tie human dignity to any philosophical tradition, since the philosophical debate over dignity continues in parallel to the legal considerations of its place.[46] While dignity as conceived by Kant may, in many instances, appear compatible with instrumental use, the philosophical usage is neither designed, nor appropriate, for that use. Once embedded in an instrument, dignity needs no philosophical support. Its meaning derives from its context in the instrument to be applied in the case before the court.

III Masterpiece Cakeshop Ltd v Colorado Civil Rights Commission

Masterpiece,[47] a United States Supreme Court decision, exemplifies the errors that could have been avoided had an overarching constitutional status of human dignity been applied. The United States does not have human dignity as a part of its constitutionally entrenched Bill of Rights. Relevantly to *Masterpiece*, it was the Bill of Rights' First Amendment that had application, which provides:

> Congress shall make no law respecting an establishment of *religion, or prohibiting the free exercise thereof*; or abridging the freedom of speech, or of the press; or the right of the people peaceably to assemble, and to petition the Government for a redress of grievances. (emphasis added)

In *Masterpiece*, a Christian baker, Jack Phillips, refused to supply a wedding cake to a gay couple, Charlie Craig and David Mullins, on grounds that to do so would offend his religious belief that same-sex marriage was sinful. Baking

Critique of Judgment, tr Werner S Pluhar (Hackett Publishing Company, 1987). See also J B Schneewind (ed), *Moral Philosophy from Montaigne to Kant* (Cambridge University Press, 2003); J B Schneewind, *Essays on the History of Moral Philosophy* (Oxford University Press, 2010) Part V: On Kant; Jens Timmerman (ed), *Kant's Groundwork of the Metaphysics of Morals: A Critical Guide* (Cambridge University Press, 2009); Thomas E Hill, Jr, *Human Welfare and Moral Worth: Kantian Perspectives* (Oxford University Press, 2002); Paul Guyer, *Kant on Freedom, Law and Happiness* (Cambridge University Press, 2000); Hannah Arendt, *Lectures on Kant's Political Philosophy* (The University of Chicago Press, 1992); Michael Cholbi, *Understanding Kant's Ethics* (Cambridge University Press, 2016); Martha C Nussbaum, 'Kant and Stoic Cosmopolitanism' (1997) 5(1) *The Journal of Political Philosophy* 1, 1–25; Martha C Nussbaum, *The Cosmopolitan Tradition: A Noble but Flawed Ideal* (The Belknap Press of Harvard University Press, 2019) 64–96; and Jennifer K Uleman, *An Introduction to Kant's Moral Philosophy* (Cambridge University Press, 2010). Immanuel Kant, *Critique of Pure Reason*, tr Paul Guyer and Allen W Wood (Cambridge University Press, sixth printing, 2019) 157–62; See also Oliver Sensen, *Kant on Human Dignity* (Berlin/Boston: de Gruyter Verlag, 2011); Dieter and Elke Elisabath Schmidt 'E Kant's Ground-Thesis: On Dignity and Value in the Groundwork' (2018) 52 *Journal of Value Inquiry* 81 and works cited by the authors.

46 See the works cited in the previous note.

47 584 US ___ (2018).

and decorating the cake would indirectly involve him in celebration of the very thing that he conscientiously deprecated. Phillips insisted that dealing in the cake would be contrary to his First Amendment rights of religious liberty.

At first instance, before the Colorado Civil Rights Commission, Phillips' belief system was treated contemptuously. Bias against his religious defence was manifest in his treatment by the tribunal. Phillips ultimately won his appeal to the Supreme Court of the United States by a majority upholding his First Amendment claim. Phillips' refusal to deal was treated as an exercise of his religious liberty under the First Amendment's 'free exercise' clause.[48] He was not required to comply with the Colorado anti-discrimination law.

Phillips' conduct could only be justified under the long discredited "separate but equal" doctrine, found to be a fallacy in *Brown v Board of Education of Topeka*,[49] in which case the United States Supreme Court's decision overruled the *Plessy v Ferguson* doctrine. In addition to the ethical problem of failing to apply the principle of mutuality,[50] Phillips was not put to proof to establish that his belief was both sincere and consistent with professed Christian tenets. Had he been required to prove both of these matters, he would have, arguably, been confronted with several difficulties in the book from which he said he derived his beliefs. As examples, Lot, in Sodom, who dealt with the citizens of Sodom over a period of years despite his conscientious objection to their conduct.[51] In the Sermon on the Mount and teachings in going the extra mile,[52] requiring not only dealing with those to whom one has a conscientious objection, but to serve them beyond what is required by the law. Jesus enjoined the payment of Roman taxation, rendering unto Caesar that which is Caesar's, despite conscientious objection to payment of the tax due to conscientious objections to Roman occupation. Phillips would have to explain away the injunction from the Sermon on the Mount: "Do unto others as you would have them do unto you"; [53] and his acting contrary to the lesson in the parable of the Good Samaritan.[54]

48 For a discussion of claims of religious liberty in connection with cake making see Todd Marskell, 'Cake making and religious freedom', [2019] (Autumn) *Australian Bar News* 35.

49 *Plessy v Ferguson* 163 US 537 (1896). Overturned in *Brown v Board of Education of Topeka* 347 US 483 (1954).

50 See Nancy Sherman, *Making a Necessity of Virtue: Aristotle and Kant on Virtue* (Cambridge, 1997) 224–38; Dawn M Nothwehr, *Mutuality: A Formal Norm for Christian Social Ethics* (Wipf & Stock Publishers, 1998) 177 *et seq.*

51 Lot's story and his characterisation as a man favoured of God because of his righteousness appears throughout the *Book of Genesis*, chapters 11–14 and 19, including his extended sojourn in Sodom, an unrighteous city associated with the practice of sodomy and other practices considered evil in the sight of God.

52 Matthew 5:41 (KJV).

53 Matthew 7:12. 'Therefore all things whatsoever ye would those men should do to you: do ye even so to them: for this is the law and the prophets' (KJV).

54 Luke 10:25–37.

A Hohfeldian Analytics to Deconstruct Rights and Liberties Claims

The exceptional claim of the conscientious vendor ought to be a difficult one to make. Unlike any other member of the public to whom the law applies, the vendor claims in defence an unprovable and unverifiable belief to be an answer to the charge of unlawful discrimination. The defence asserts that the belief operates as an exculpation for what is otherwise a breach of a generally applying law forbidding discrimination in the marketplace. If a court were inclined to have regard to the problems created by permitting private conscientious disobedience to a law of general public operation, it would find several avenues open to it by which a claim for exemption could be refused. This is where competing rights need to be analysed and deconstructed.

Each of the substantive grounds open to a court in a case like *Masterpiece* is quite different in its legal and principled content. How, then, to compare the end results on each approach? Joseph Singer has shown that in cases such as *Masterpiece*,[55] when claims are analysed utilising the rights theory developed by Hohfeld, the nature of the respective claims can be better understood and compared on their merits by careful dissection of the claims.

The first matter to be considered is what are the *bundles* of rights and liberties enjoyed by the respective parties. "Bundle", as used by Hohfeld and Singer, is a metaphor to explain the composite nature of any supposed right or freedom. Through Hohfeld and Singer's lens, one sees religious freedom as a composite claim, comprised of various "jural relations". Singer and Hohfeld regard the conflicting claims to be conceptualised in their components.[56] Singer explains how, on Hohfeld's analysis, and using his vocabulary, claims made, and the choices available, are more complex than at first appears.[57] Singer[58] unpacks the conflict of claims in the *Masterpiece* case.[59] Missing from the Supreme Court decision-making process was the unpacking of what rights and obligations inhere in the operation of "public accommodations".[60] Just what jural relations comprise the bundle of "religious freedom" also needs to be analysed for their content and impact. Once audited for content and relationship to other bundles, religious freedom can be seen to be anything but monolithic.[61]

55 Singer, 'Religious Liberty and Public Accommodations' (n 6).

56 Hohfeld, 'Some Fundamental Legal Conceptions' (n 5); Hohfeld, 'Fundamental Legal Conceptions' (n 5).

57 Hohfeld, 'Some Fundamental Legal Conceptions' (n 5), 19 ('the tendency—and the fallacy—has been to treat the specific problem as if it were far less complex than it really is').

58 Ibid.

59 *Masterpiece* (n 9).

60 Ibid at 2–3.

61 Severability of rights is evident in Article 18(1) and (3) of the *ICCPR*, where belief and expression being discrete and severable rights. And in a case such as *Masterpiece*, the claim could and should be interrogated for its origins in the sacred text, binding upon the claimant as a believer, from which it is claimed to derive.

Table 11.1 Hohfeld's Table of Jural Relations

*Jural Correlatives**			
Right	Privilege	Power	Immunity
Duty	No-right	Liability	Disability
Jural Opposites**			
Right	Privilege	Power	Immunity
No-right	Duty	Disability	Liability

** Ibid.
* Hohfeld 'Fundamental Legal Conceptions' (n 5) 36, 65.

As mentioned previously, while Hohfeld's thought has proven particularly valuable in conceptualising property rights,[62] Singer extended Hohfeld's thought to an understanding of religionists' claims to liberty. Unpacking rights and freedoms in this way, it is possible to ask how, as a matter of conscience, there can be any right, whether religiously motivated or not, to discriminate in public market trade and commerce against another person.[63] It does not, on its face, suffice that it is claimed as a conscientious right to refuse to deal with persons of whose private conduct the religionist does not approve.[64] Something more is needed at common law; similarly to invoke a statutory or constitutional exemption.

Hohfeld and Singer tabulated the interrelationship of componentry of rights and liberties claims in the following form: see Table 11.1.

Thus, it is necessary, according to Hohfeld[65] and Singer,[66] to look past the labels of Phillips' claims of "religious liberty" and "conscientious objection" and examine the "bundle" of rights and privileges in issue. At the point of his refusal to deal, a set of potential jural relations and their opposites arose. Did Phillips have a "right" to refuse to deal? Did Craig and Mullins have the "privilege" to compel Phillips to accept a "duty" to supply goods and services equally to them? Or did Phillips enjoy an "immunity" under the First Amendment?

As to "jural correlatives", Hohfeld's theoretical analysis tells the arbiter of a rights claim where the coercive force of the state lies in any claims or transaction. A Hohfeldian *right* means a legal claim-right that has the coercive force

62 *Internet Encyclopaedia of Philosophy* (online at 24 September 2020) 'Property'. https://www.iep.utm.edu/prop-con/.

63 *Pichon and Sajous v France,* Application No. 49853/99 (2 October 2001) 191. https://www.echr.coe.int/Documents/Reports_Recueil_2001-X.pdf.

64 Singer, 'Religious Liberty and Public Accommodations', (n 6). See also *Christian Youth Camps Limited v Cobaw Community Health Service Limited* [2014] VSCA 75.

65 Ibid 36, 65.

66 Singer, 'Religious Liberty and Public Accommodations' (n 6).

of the state to support it.[67] This *right* amounts to legal protection from interference by another and prevents the withholding of assistance to exploit the claim-right.[68] The other who is not permitted to interfere, or is required to cooperate in the exploitation or realisation of the right, is under the correlative *duty* to do so.

A *privilege* is a liberty, or an *absence of a duty*, to abstain from any particular action. It is to be free of the constraints of duty owed to another.[69] A *power* is the ability to *alter* jural relations. It may be a power to enter a contract, gift property, or to receive profits. Its correlative is a *liability* on the part of another to bring the subject of that power to fruition. An *immunity* means that another has no power to change a legal position with respect to any entitlements falling within the immunity. The corresponding correlative, a *disability*, means a lack of power to compel a change in legal position.

This concept of an *immunity* is of particular application in determining the limits of state coercive power with respect to rights and freedoms conferred by a bill of rights.

On the Hohfeldian analysis of the kind conducted by Singer, the failure to consider all species of rights, liberties, privileges, and immunities had the effect of overlooking an important doctrine of the common law which should have placed the case outside of the operation of the First Amendment: the Innkeepers' Rule ('Rule').

B The Innkeepers' Rule: Hohfeld and Singer

The First Amendment's "free exercise" clause protects certain religious manifestations that have been held to fall within the words of the Amendment: "Congress shall make no law respecting an establishment of *religion or prohibiting the free exercise thereof*".[70] Not all claims to religious or conscientious liberties fall within the right to publicly manifest belief.[71] The result is that some matters of conscience may be held *privately*, but not manifested *publicly*. One reason for this is that not all laws that may limit public manifestation fall within the "free exercise" clause. The Rule is one such law that does not come within the "free exercise" clause because it is not a law made by Congress or any other legislature.[72] It is a common law rule. Certainly, it has been adopted by many legislatures as the basis for anti-discrimination laws. Those laws do not abolish the Rule. Even if those laws were to be invalidated, the Rule would remain as a common law rule, *not* made by Congress.

67 Ibid.
68 Ibid.
69 Ibid.
70 *United States Constitution* Amend. I (emphasis added).
71 That is, it must be a law passed *by Congress.*
72 See Singer, 'The Legal Rights Debate' (n 6).

This common law rule can be summarised simply, in the manner intended by Singer, reflecting the old English common law:

> A keeper of public accommodation is under a duty to provide food and lodging to all travellers who pay a reasonable price for the same.

Implicit in the Rule is its demarcation between public and private manifestations of conscience by an "innkeeper" in the provision of goods and services to the public. The Rule, based in English common law,[73] requires those who run any "public accommodation" to accept all prospective guests or consumers of their goods and services. An "accommodation" for the purpose of the Rule includes actual inns and hotels and extends to shopfront premises.[74] In the *post-bellum* United States, the Rule became a forerunner of and model for civil rights laws passed by Congress to ensure equality of treatment of all, regardless of their race.[75] Those laws notwithstanding, the Rule remains a part of the common law obligations placed upon "innkeepers".

The Rule is an exception to general rights in relation to real property such as freedom of contract and to exclude others from real property. Under the Rule, certain rights that might otherwise entitle a holder of an estate in land to refuse to deal with any person are abrogated. While at first blush this might appear highly irregular, the Rule is not unusual in its abrogation of rights that might otherwise accrue to an estate holder. There are many other laws that similarly restrict freedom of contract and full enjoyment of title to land. Examples include planning laws,[76] environmental regulations,[77] and competition laws.[78] Put in terms of packages or 'bundles of rights' to distinguish among liberty claims,[79] Singer (and Hohfeld),[80] find the right to refuse trade in goods and services to any person is *not* included in the larger bundle of rights enjoyed by the innkeeper or "accommodation" controller.[81] At common law,

73 See the history outlined for the Colorado equality law as the subject of the appeal in *Masterpiece* (n 9) 4–6, in the opinion of Kennedy J at 1 to 6 of his Honour's reasons.

74 Singer, 'Religious Liberty and Public Accommodations' (n 6) 4, 9–10.

75 Ibid. As to other contractual and tortious obligations and liabilities imposed upon innkeepers by the common law in relation guests and their chattels, see Theodore Plucknett, *A Concise History of the Common Law* (Liberty Fund, 6th ed, 2010) 480–1.

76 As an example, see the regime that regulates the development of land and improvement of fixtures under the South Australian *Planning, Development and Infrastructure Act 2016* (SA), See Australian Law Reform Commission, *Traditional Rights and Freedoms – Encroachments by the Commonwealth Laws* (ALRC Report 129, 2016) [20.96]–[20.131].

77 Ibid [20.96]–[20.131].

78 See, as an example, the Commonwealth of Australia essential facility access regime provided for in the *Competition and Consumer Act 2010 (Cth)*, Part IIIA.

79 See Isaiah Berlin, 'Two Concepts of Liberty', in Henry Hardy (ed), *Liberty* (Oxford University Press, 2016); and Singer, *No Freedom without Regulation* (n 6) ch 1.

80 Singer, *No Freedom without Regulation* (n 6) ch 1.

81 Singer, 'The Legal Rights Debate' (n 6).

the right to refuse to trade is just *not* part of the bundle of rights that inhere in the operation of a public accommodation. Any inclination that the "innkeeper" might privately harbour towards a consumer based upon any personal characteristic such as race, religion, gender, or sexuality, is subordinated to the obligation to trade and the right of the consumer not to be the subject of prejudicial treatment in respect of any personal attribute.

The Rule is obviously directed in its application to public vendors of goods and services. In that limited application, it produces dignitarian results collaterally. It prevents humiliating refusals of supply of goods and services based upon individual characteristics. The vendor's private beliefs about personal attributes of a consumer cannot be manifested in a publicly discriminatory manner. The human dignity of members of the public is preserved intact; the vendor remains free to maintain and manifest his or her beliefs in other ways that do not impose those beliefs upon others or detract from their rights and freedoms.

If the common law had been applied correctly, the First Amendment and its "free exercise" clause would have had no application. The Rule is a common law restriction upon rights of refusal and, thus, not a law made by Congress. The Supreme Court in *Masterpiece* failed to apply the common law rule. It incorrectly endorsed the public behaviour of Phillips as a First Amendment right that he did not possess.

But assuming the First Amendment *could* arguably have application, contrary to what has been argued at common law, was it correct as a matter of constitutional law to apply it; and was a dignitarian outcome still possible by an application of American constitutional principles?

Collaterally consistent with dignitarian reasoning, laws of general application are not readily overturned in favour of individual religious manifestations. Courts can, without reference to the principles of dignity, nevertheless achieve dignitarian outcomes by distinguishing private conscientious belief from the asserted right to publicly manifest that right where manifestation would be detrimental to the rights and freedoms of other or to the public good.

To illustrate, consider two cases in First Amendment jurisprudence that illustrate the private belief and public manifestation distinction and the need to uphold the public good that generally applicable laws achieve: *Reynolds v United States* ('*Reynolds*'),[82] and *Employment Division, Department of Human Resources of Oregon v Smith* ('*Smith*').[83]

82 98 U.S. 145 (1878)

83 Some 'compelling state interest' would need to be established: Stephen A. Siegel, 'The Origin of the Compelling State Interest Test and Strict Scrutiny' *The American Journal of Legal History* Vol. 48, No. 4 (Oct. 2006) 355–407.

C Of Polygamy and Peyote: Reynolds, Smith, Private Conscience, Public Manifestation, Laws of General Application, and Compelling Interests

In the religious conscience case regarding Mormon polygynous[84] practices, *Reynolds*,[85] the Supreme Court was clear in its reasons for refusal to extend "free exercise" protection. Despite the argument that plurality of wives was, under Mormon faith tenets, a theological prerequisite to salvation in the highest degrees of heaven, the Court rejected the argument; the practice of plural marriage was refused protection. Instead, the Court pronounced a distinction between private conscience and public practice. The Supreme Court held that despite a deeply held conscientious commitment to the practice of polygyny,[86] that commitment could only lawfully be held as a private *belief* under the *Morrill Anti-Bigamy Act* but could not be put into *practice*. The human dignity of prospective plural wives was preserved. The American public was spared the indignity of a barbaric practice. The Court upheld abolition of the public practice without abolishing the private belief.

After *Reynolds*,[87] the Supreme Court has generally refused to uphold "free exercise" claims in numerous contexts.[88] While it seemed to be the case that laws of general application that did not target a religion or its practices would be struck down only in peculiar circumstances,[89] it was unclear whether the Court would maintain its distinction between protection of belief and protection of actions.[90] In *Wisconsin v Yoder*,[91] the Court explained "that the First Amendment bars application of a neutral, generally applicable law to religiously motivated action" only in those cases involving "not the Free Exercise Clause alone, but the Free Exercise Clause in conjunction with other constitutional protections".

84 *Doctrine and Covenants* s 132: 15–21. For the (now) official of the plural wives practice from earliest days of the Latter-day Saint religion, see Gospel Topic Essays accessible at https://www.churchofjesuschrist.org/study/manual/gospel-topics-essays?lang=eng: 'Plural Marriage in the Church of Jesus Christ of Latter-day Saints'; 'Marriage between one man and one woman is the Lord's standing law of marriage'; 'Plural Marriage in Kirtland and Nauvoo'; 'Plural Marriage and Families in Early Utah'; The Manifesto and the End of Plural Marriage'. For more in-depth accounting of the practice, see Todd Compton, *In Sacred Loneliness: The Plural Wives of Joseph Smith* (Signature Books, 1997) and Fawn M Brodie, *No Man Knows My History: The Life of Joseph Smith, Mormon Prophet* (Knopf, 1945, rev. ed. 1971) 334–348; Appendix C, 457–488, 'The Plural Wives of Joseph Smith'.

85 98 U.S. 145 (1878).

86 That is, plural wives, as opposed to polygamy (plural spouses) and polyandry (plural husbands).

87 *Sherbert v Verner* 374 U.S. 398 (1963).

88 Ira C Lupu, 'Where Rights Begin: The Problem of Burdens on the Free Exercise of Religion' (1989) 102(5) *Harvard Law Review* 933.

89 Ibid.

90 Ibid.

91 406 U.S. 205 92 S. Ct. 1526; 32 L. Ed. 2d 15; 1972 U.S. LEXIS 144. Jeffrey Shulman, 'What Yoder Wrought: Religious Disparagement, Parental Alienation and the Best Interests of the Child', (2008) 53(1) *Villanova Law Review* 173.

Despite some earlier ambiguity as to the position under the 'free exercise' clause, the *Reynolds* distinction between belief and practice was revived in the 1990 decision of *Smith*.[92] Two Native American drug counsellors, Smith and Black, challenged the State of Oregon's refusal to pay them unemployment benefits. Smith and Black had been dismissed from their employment for use of the hallucinogenic peyote, imbibed as part of a religious ritual in the Native American Church. As their dismissal was for misconduct in employment, the benefits were not payable under Oregon law. They challenged the validity of that law under the 'free exercise' clause.

The Court rejected Smith's and Black's claims. The impugned law was generally applicable and only incidentally imposed a burden on religious practice. There was no compelling interest that required the making of any exception in favour of Smith and Black. Consistent with *Reynolds*,[93] the majority held that the "free exercise" clause protected religious belief, but that protection did not necessarily extend to protect religious practice unless the law in question had singled out religion for unfavourable treatment.[94]

D Of Wedding Cakes, Birth Control, and Missiles: Dignitarian Decisions of the European Courts

None of the United States Supreme Court's decisions considered were decided with human dignity as an overarching constitutional consideration. In contrast, the two European cases now considered were both decided under the requirement to consider human dignity. The first considered, *Pichon and Sajous v France*,[95] was a decision of the European Court of Human Rights. The second considered, *BVerfGE 87*,[96] was an earlier decision of the *Bundesverfassungsgericht* (German Federal Constitutional Court).[97]

In *Pichon and Sajous v France*,[98] the case considered applications made by two pharmacists who conscientiously refused to stock and sell contraceptives to the public, a refusal that would otherwise be contrary to French law. To do so, they contended, would offend their religious beliefs that considered the

92 *Employment Division, Department of Human Resources of Oregon v Smith*, 494 US 872 (1990). As to 'compelling interest', see Shulman (n 92) and *Sherbert v Verner* 374 U.S. 398 (1963).

93 494 U.S. at 878–890.

94 On whether and when a compelling interest could be established, see Michael W McConnell, 'Free Exercise Revisionism and the Smith Decision,' (1990) 57 *University of Chicago Law Review* 1109; Kathleen P Kelly, Abandoning the Compelling Interest Test in Free Exercise Cases: *Employment Division, Department of Human Resources v. Smith*, (1991) 40(4) *The Catholic University Law Review* 929.

95 Application No. 49853/99 (2 October 2001) 191 https://www.echr.coe.int/Documents/Reports_Recueil_2001-X.pdf.

96 *BVerfGE 87* (1992).

97 Federal Constitutional Court of Germany.

98 Application No. 49853/99 (2 October 2001) 191 https://www.echr.coe.int/Documents/Reports_Recueil_2001-X.pdf.

use of contraceptives to be sinful. In these respects, it can be seen, the refusal as vendors to sell contrary to their beliefs was analogous to Phillips' refusal to make the wedding cake for the homosexual couple in *Masterpiece*. The question was thus essentially the same as in *Masterpiece*: whether, as vendors, they were entitled to withhold the sale of goods pursuant to a conscientious exception to a generally applicable law.

To determine whether to permit their refusal to sell contraceptives to the public, the Court applied Article 9 of the *European Convention on Human Rights*, which provides:

> Everyone has the right to freedom of thought, conscience and religion; this right includes freedom to change his religion or belief and freedom, either alone or in community with others and in public or private, to manifest his religion or belief, in worship, teaching, practice and observance.[99]

The European Court refused the application. Applying Article 9, the Court held the view to be 'manifestly ill-founded'. The Court determined that it could not permit practice of the pharmacists' religious beliefs to take precedence over the pharmaceutical needs of members of the wider community.

In *BVerfGE 87*,[100] the *Bundesverfassungsgericht* considered, under Article 1 of the German Constitution, the constitutional validity of a law of the *Bundestag* (the German legislature). By the law, the *Bundestag* had conferred power upon the German Air Force to use lethal force in the interception of civilian passenger aircraft that had fallen under the control of hijacking terrorists. In such instances, the law gave the power to use such force; but confined its use to instances where it had become operationally necessary, with no feasible alternative. The *Bundestag* sought to permit a defence strategy with minimal harm, though civilian lives would be lost. But, in passing the law, it had determined the downing of a civilian aircraft, despite the consequent cost in lives, was appropriate and proportionate.

The Court disagreed and struck the law down. It held it was constitutionally invalid due to its inconsistency with Article 1 of the *German Constitution*. Applying Article 1, the Court observed:

> Human dignity is not only the individual dignity of every person, but also the dignity of the human being as a species. Everybody possesses

99 Sub-article (1). See also sub-article (2):

'Freedom to manifest one's religion or beliefs shall be subject only to such limitations as are prescribed by law and are necessary in a democratic society in the interests of public safety, for the protection of public order, health or morals, or for the protection of the rights and freedoms of others'.

100 BVerfGE 87 (1992).

> human dignity, regardless of [their] characteristics, achievements, or social status; those who cannot act in a meaningful way because of their physical or psychological condition also possess human dignity. It is not even forfeited by means of 'undignified' behaviour; it cannot be taken away from any human being.[101]

In both cases, it is clear that human dignity is not a mere individual consideration but has an important communitarian aspect. Under a human dignity requirement, a vendor such as Phillips in *Masterpiece*, could not assert his religious freedom at the expense of community interests in having the law applied to him. Assertion of a religious freedom right cannot be permitted to cause harm to others.

E Clubb: Human Dignity and Conflict with Other Constitutional Principles – Access Zones and Freedom of Political Expression

Recall that Australia does *not* have a constitutional bill of rights[102] and does not have human dignity as an overarching constitutional principle, the consideration is now of a legislative requirement to take human dignity into account. This is important since, as also mentioned, Australia has no clear system or set of principles by which to resolve disputes over anti-discrimination laws and the preservation of religious liberty where those laws impinge upon that liberty.[103] Closely allied to religious liberty is the claim of freedom of speech: the right to declare religious principles publicly, particularly when such declarations are coincidentally political complaints against liberal democratic laws, such as relating to abortion and the legal recognition of some sexual rights.[104]

As should by now be clear, the Australian Constitution differs from many other constitutions and from international human rights instruments in that it does not explicitly protect freedom of expression. Nevertheless, the Australian High Court has held an *implied* freedom of political communication does exist because it is an indispensable part of the system of representative and responsible government created by the Constitution. Unlike equivalents where there is an express right conferred, such as Article 19 in the *International Covenant on Civil and Political Rights* or the *First Amendment* to the American Constitution, this implied freedom operates negatively as a freedom from government restraint, rather than as an affirmative right conferred directly on individuals.

Despite its indispensability to the Australian federal government, an implied freedom under the current constitutional arrangement can be made to yield to

101 Ibid 209.
102 Rochow (4) note 8.
103 Quinlan (n 2).
104 Barker (n 4).

express statutory rights. In *Clubb v Edwards; Preston v Avery*, ('*Clubb*')[105] the High Court of Australia decided that the statutory requirement to consider dignity was an overarching consideration. It could, essentially, and as a matter of sovereignty, in appropriate cases, override an implied constitutional freedom of political expression.[106] The case involved two appeals, one Victorian and the other Tasmanian, both from convictions for breaches of prohibitions regarding communications made within abortion clinic "access zones". The Court unanimously dismissed both appeals. In both cases, the appellants failed in their challenges to the respective state laws. Both laws prohibited certain communications and activities in relation to abortions within "access zones" around abortion clinics. Both Clubb and Preston were Christians opposed to abortion and determined to discourage women from undergoing termination procedures. They asserted that their messages to the women were political in nature because they opposed legal abortions. In Clubb's case, the Court was required by the terms of the Victorian legislation to consider the meaning of and apply the concept of "dignity".

Under the *Public Health and Wellbeing Act 2008* (Vic) ('*PHWA*'), the prohibition is against certain communications within a radius of 150 metres from an abortion clinic. Section 185D of the *PHWA* prohibits a person from communicating in a manner able to be seen or heard by persons accessing or attempting to access premises at which abortions are provided if the communication is reasonably likely to cause distress or anxiety.

Clubb had been convicted under section 185D of the *PHWA*. She contended that section 185D impermissibly burdened her implied freedom of communication on governmental and political matters.[107] Both appellants challenged the respective laws under the tests for invalidity[108] laid down in

105 [2019] HCA 11.

106 See the summary and reasons for decision at the Court's website at http://www.hcourt.gov.au/assets/publications/judgment-summaries/2019/hca-11-2019-04-10.pdf. See also in the reasons of the Court.. In the Court's reasons, the plurality (Kiefel CJ, Bell and Keane JJ, with whom Nettle J agreed) expressed themselves in these terms at [51]:

> 'Generally speaking, to force upon another person a political message is inconsistent with the human dignity of that person. As Barak said, "[h]uman dignity regards a human being as an end, not as a means to achieve the ends of others". Within the present constitutional context, the protection of the dignity of the people of the Commonwealth, whose political sovereignty is the basis of the implied freedom, is a purpose readily seen to be compatible with the maintenance of the constitutionally prescribed system of representative and responsible government. Thus, when in *Lange* the Court declared that "each member of the Australian community has an interest in disseminating and receiving information, opinions and arguments concerning government and political matters that affect the people of Australia", there was no suggestion that any member of the Australian community may be obliged to receive such information, opinions and arguments'.

See [49]–[60], and [82]–[84] and Edelman J at [497].

107 Ibid.

108 See *Clubb v Edwards; Preston v Avery* [2019] HCA 11 at [4]–[5] where the reasons of Kiefel CJ, Bell and Keane JJ cite *McCloy v New South Wales* (2015) 257 CLR 178 at 193–195 [2]

Lange v Australian Broadcasting Corporation,[109] and as explained in *McCloy v New South Wales*,[110] and *Brown v Tasmania*.[111] All members of the Court made reference to 'dignity' in their reasons. It was in the reasons of the plurality, with whom Nettle J agreed, that "dignity" was examined in detail.

Section 185A of the *PHWA* has as its purpose "… [protection of] the safety and wellbeing and respect the privacy and dignity" of people accessing services and those employed to provide them.[112] Section 185C emphasised the object of 'dignity' by setting out principles that apply to Part 9A of the *PHWA*. Among those principles was the re-iteration that the medical services provided by the clinic were an entitlement provided by law,[113] that each "person's safety and wellbeing" needed to be protected,[114] and that there needed to be respect for "the person's *privacy and dignity*".[115]

The plurality referred to the *PHWA*'s Second Reading speech,[116] observing that privacy and dignity are closely linked.[117] Their Honours noted that the protection of dignity was an aspect of the purpose of the communication prohibition.[118] They cited with approval the extra-judicial writings of Aharon Barak, where he said:

> Most central of all human rights is the right to dignity. It is the source from which all other human rights are derived. Dignity unites the other human rights into a whole … [h]uman dignity regards a human being as an end, not as a means to achieve the ends of others.[119]

Their Honours held that the prohibition on communication within the access zone was consistent with the concept of dignity.[120] Later in the reasons, their Honours reiterated the sovereign competence of parliaments to pass laws to prevent communications that would offend dignity:

> A law calculated to maintain the dignity of members of the sovereign people by ensuring that they are not held captive by an uninvited

as modified by *Brown v Tasmania* (2017) 261 CLR 328 at 363–364 [104]. See also *Browne v Tasmania* (2017) 261 CLR 328 at 375-376 [155]–[156], 416 [277], 478 [481].

109 (1997) 189 CLR 520; [1997] HCA 25.

110 (2015) 257 CLR 178; [2015] HCA 34.

111 (2017) 261 CLR 328; [2017] HCA 43.

112 Emphasis added.

113 *Public Health and Wellbeing Amendment (Safe Access Zones) Act 2015* (Vic) s 185C(a).

114 Ibid s 185C(b)(i).

115 Ibid s 185C(b)(ii) (emphasis added).

116 *Clubb v Edwards; Preston v Avery* [2019] HCA 11 at [47]–[48].

117 Ibid.

118 Ibid.

119 Aharon Barak, *The Judge in a Democracy* (Princeton University Press, 2006), 86, cited in *Monis v The Queen* (2013) 249 CLR 92 at 182–183 [247].

120 *Clubb v Edwards; Preston v Avery* [2019] HCA 11 at [51].

political message accords with the political sovereignty which underpins the implied freedom.[121]

Thus, the extent of operation of the implied freedom had been limited by an overriding statutory requirement that dignity prevail as a consideration. Other than to describe it as a "right" rather than a "status" the use of "dignity" in the statute was interpreted in a manner that closely approximates the instrumental meaning discussed earlier in this chapter. Importantly for the purposes of current discussion, it was accorded juristic prevalence over the implied constitutional right. If the information would offend a recipient's dignity, they are not "obliged"[122] to receive it. The freedom to communicate does not include a reciprocal obligation on the part of the hearer to receive the message. There is no right to hold the intended recipient "captive".[123]

The decision was consistent with expressions found in instruments, such as Article 9 of the *European Convention on Human Rights*, that the freedom of expression of one's conscientious beliefs can be subject to such limitations as are prescribed by law that are necessary in a democratic society. Limitations on rights of conscientious objection and religious expression can include those that promote the protection of public order, health or morals, and the protection of the rights and freedoms of others.[124]

The place of "dignity" in the common law of Australian constitutional jurisprudence is, first, that when required by statute, if the terms of the provision require it, it will be applied by courts, even when to do so overrides an implied constitutional right. Second, this is the case because Australian parliaments have a sovereign right to protect the dignity of their citizens.

IV What Would Hohfeld Say?

It is apparent that the decision in *Masterpiece* was deficient in several respects. On any one of the alternative analyses considered, Phillips should have lost the appeal. His private beliefs should not have been carried into the marketplace at a cost to the consuming public. The offence caused to him by same-sex

121 *McCloy v New South Wales* (2015) 257 CLR 178 at 206-207 [42][45], 220–221 [93].

122 *Clubb v Edwards; Preston v Avery* [2019] HCA 11 at [60]; [78]; [82]; [98]–[99] and [101].

123 Ibid.

124 *The European Convention on Human Rights*, Article 9 provides for religious freedom with an express proviso to that effect:

1 *Everyone has the right to freedom of thought, conscience and religion; this right includes freedom to change his religion or belief and freedom, either alone or in community with others and in public or private, to manifest his religion or belief, in worship, teaching, practice and observance.*

2 *Freedom to manifest one's religion or beliefs shall be subject only to such limitations as are prescribed by law and are necessary in a democratic society in the interests of public safety, for the protection of public order, health or morals, or for the protection of the rights and freedoms of others.*

Table 11.2 Hohfeld's Table of Jural Relations (2)

*Jural Correlatives**			
Right	Privilege	Power	Immunity
Duty	No-right	Liability	Disability
Jural Opposites**			
Right	Privilege	Power	Immunity
No-right	Duty	Disability	Liability

** Ibid.
* Hohfeld "Fundamental Legal Conceptions" (n 5) 36, 65.

marriage as a personal religious tenet should have remained a private matter. Similarly, Craig's and Mullins' sexuality should have remained a private matter and not become the subject of Phillips' moral judgement and his public ostracism. Indeed, it was only chance that Phillips learned the sexuality of the couple. At best, the Supreme Court should certainly have acknowledged that Phillips was entitled to a fair hearing shorn of all indications of bias. The case could have been remitted to the Colorado Civil Rights Commission for a hearing according to law. However, in the end, Phillips would still have lost the case on any of the substantive grounds mentioned.

Adopting a Hohfeldian approach, rights and liberties are comprised in "bundles". Each bundle is unique in its composition to its particular circumstances. Singer unpacks the bundles of rights intended by the various usages of "liberty".[125] He argues that religious liberty in the context of "public accommodations" is distinct from its usage in other contexts where there is no duty to deal with consumers.[126] The freedom to act upon the religiously informed conscience is limited in the public sphere by obligations owed to the consuming public.

Public accommodations carry an historic legal obligation to serve the public. With this obligation running with the title, patrons have the privilege to enter the public accommodation and a power to compel the owner to provide them goods and services. The title "public accommodation" does *not* include the power to exclude or refuse to deal. The bundle of rights that run with the title to the typical home differs from the bundle of rights and obligations associated with a public accommodation.[127]

As mentioned, any bundle will break down into four different sets of jural relations and opposites as depicted in Hohfeld's table: rights; privileges;

125 Singer, *No Freedom without Regulation* (n 6) ch 1; Singer, 'Religious Liberty and Public Accommodations' (n 6).
126 Singer, 'Religious Liberty and Public Accommodations' (n 6) at 2–3.
127 Singer, 'Religious Liberty and Public Accommodations' (n 6) at 9.

immunities; and liabilities.[128] Recalling the tabulation discussed earlier, the task is to populate it with the components of each claim (Table 11.2).

The two parties' claims, described by Hohfeld[129] as "jural relations" are examined for their inherent validity and comparative strength. The claim must be closely audited and scrutinised for its claimed superiority over the purportedly suborned right. If rights or claims are validly claimed, the state (should and) will lend its coercive force; if the claim is invalid, the state will withhold its power to enforce. The relevant coercive power of the state is manifested through the orders of the court and the machinery for their enforcement.

The *Masterpiece* decision set no boundary to prevent vendors from making moral judgements, based in religious belief, on a consumer's worthiness to receive goods and services by reference to any personal attribute. The vendor is then free to enforce the moral judgement by refusal of goods and services. Phillips' moral judgement, in the *Masterpiece* case, was based upon sexuality. However, there is no reason why another religious tenet held by him would not dictate another judgement as a basis for discrimination. In Phillips' religious belief system, that could consistently extend to fornicators and adulterers. Perhaps another vendor's belief system would prevent baking cakes for events at which alcohol might be consumed. Yet another vendor's belief structure may forbid dealing with Jews;[130] or some vendors may refuse to deal with members of a dark-skinned race in the belief that they are marked to signify a curse from God.[131] It is necessary, therefore, to test the decision in *Masterpiece* for its principled consistency and correctness.

In his defence to the Colorado Civil Rights Commission's action to enforce the equality law in *Masterpiece*,[132] Phillips claimed that the First Amendment excused him from obedience to equality laws and permitted his refusal to provide goods and services to the same-sex couple.[133] As previously noted, there are good reasons to doubt the constitutional legitimacy of his claim. His religious conscientious objection to same-sex marriage, accepted as an untested fact, was claimed to be a "free exercise" of his religious beliefs. In Hohfeldian terms, he claimed an *immunity*.[134]

128 John Finnis, 'Some Professorial Fallacies about Rights' (1971) 4 *Adelaide Law Review* 377.

129 Hohfeld 'Fundamental Legal Conceptions' (n 5) 5–21 and 35–64. See also Albert Kocourek, 'Plurality of Advantage and Disadvantage in Jural Relations' (1920) 19(1) *Michigan Law Review* 47–61; Finnis (n 129) 378–82; and Arthur L Corbin, 'Jural Relations and Their Classification' (1920–1921) 30 *Yale Law Journal* 226–38.

130 See the online *Holocaust Encyclopedia* entry, 'The Boycott of Jewish Businesses' https://encyclopedia.ushmm.org/content/en/article/the-boycott-of-jewish-businesses

131 Matthew L Harris and Newell G Bringhurst, *The Mormon Church and Blacks: A Documentary History*. (University of Illinois Press, 2015).

132 *Masterpiece* (n 9).

133 Ibid, opinion of Kennedy J (for the Court) 3–4.

134 Ibid 18.

Phillips claimed a form of liberty that is an unrestrained conscientious licence to do whatever his beliefs required of him. Even if that asserted right were, for the purposes of argument only, to be accepted, a Hohfeldian approach would demonstrate that Phillips had "no-right" to refuse in exercise of that claimed liberty.[135] Hohfeld would demonstrate that by adopting either the Rule or by applying human dignity as an overarching principle. As Singer clearly demonstrates, under the Rule,[136] as the controller of a "public accommodation", the cake store, Phillips had no right to refuse supply of goods or services to any customer.[137]

As to the first, the common law and statutory origins of the Rule[138] were aimed at preventing racial and other prejudices preventing travellers from finding lodgings. The rationale of the Rule applies equally to race and to any other attribute that a traveller, or purchaser of goods and services, might possess. Phillips was an "innkeeper",[139] running an "accommodation", a publicly accessible retail space. He was, therefore, squarely within the Rule[140] and was thus obliged to set aside his conscientious objection and under a duty to deal with Craig and Mullins.[141] His bundle of religious liberty rights simply did *not* extend to a right to refuse to deal from public accommodations as an innkeeper. Even if a liberty of the kind Phillips claimed did exist, it was not among the rights that inured to him as an operator of a public accommodation. A right of refusal was simply not a component of the bundle of property rights he enjoyed as a public vendor, conscientious or otherwise. The freedom to contract and deal in his property and services as he saw fit had already been removed by the applicable rule under the Colorado statute. On any view, the law was generally applicable and there was no compelling reason to make any First Amendment carve-out because it just did not apply to the facts.

Equally, under dignitarian principles, there is no constitutional space in which an individual's religious liberty provides a right for a believer such as Phillips to put that belief into action discriminating among members of the public. When the human dignity of Phillips, Mullins, and Craig are all considered, there remains no constitutional immunity that inures to Phillips to diminish the dignity of others. The only freedom that Phillips could claim would be to act conscientiously, but then to accept the legal consequences.

It is the immunity box which becomes the fulcrum of decision-making in any rights claim conflict. If the Rule had been applied to the facts of *Masterpiece*, the immunity claimed by Phillips under the First Amendment

135 Singer, 'Religious Liberty and Public Accommodations'(n 6) 3–6.
136 Ibid 2–3.
137 *Masterpiece* (n 9), opinion of Kennedy J (for the Court) 4–6; Singer, 'Religious Liberty and Public Accommodations' (n 6) 4, 9–10.
138 *Masterpiece* (n 9), opinion of Kennedy J (for the Court) 4–6; Singer, 'Religious Liberty and Public Accommodations' (n 6) 4, 9–10.
139 Singer, 'Religious Liberty and Public Accommodations' (n 6) 3–6.
140 Ibid.
141 Ibid.

would be displaced. Introducing the Rule as the source of immunity precludes the First Amendment and reverses the result in *Masterpiece*. That is because once displaced, the effect of the First Amendment on rights, power, privilege, and liability are also simultaneously reversed. Jural correlatives and jural opposites all respond in the same precise way to the new common law immunity derived from the Rule, which had been omitted from consideration by the Court in *Masterpiece*. As appears from Table 11.3, the immunity Phillips

Table 11.3 Jural Correlatives*

Right: Craig and Mullins had the *right* to purchase Phillips' goods and services.	**Privilege**: Craig and Mullins had *no duty* to honour Phillips' private religious belief or to be submitted to his refusal to deal.**	**Power**: Craig and Mullins had *power* or ability to *alter* the jural relations by entering a contract for goods and services.	**Immunity**: Phillips' claim for immunity under the First Amendment fails because it has no application to the common law Innkeepers' Rule.
Duty: Phillips was under the correlative *duty* to supply Mullins and Craig goods and services.	**No-right**: If Phillips had enjoyed no right to right to impose discriminatory treatment.	**Liability**: If the claim is correct, Phillips had no liability.	**Disability**: The corresponding correlative *disability*, meant that because there was no immunity, Phillips lacked power to compel a change in legal position.
Jural Opposites***			
Right: Craig and Mullins had the right to goods and services.	**Privilege**: The jural relational duty to deal precluded the privilege of not dealing.	**Power**: Craig and Mullins had *power* to compel Phillips to deal.	**Immunity**: Phillips had no immunity under the First Amendment.
No-right: If Phillips had enjoyed had no right to impose discriminatory treatment.	**Duty**: Once the generally applying law had been found to fall outside the First Amendment, a duty to deal would follow.	**Disability**: Craig and Mullins were under no disability to insist upon Phillips dealing. Phillips was under a disability to refuse to deal.	**Liability:** Phillips was liable for his refusal to deal.

*** Ibid.

** Ibid.

* Hohfeld, "Fundamental Legal Conceptions" (n 5) 36, 65.

claimed was wrongly made and ought not to have afforded him any immunity whatsoever.

But the Rule is an isolated common law rule.[142] Its operation is confined to those circumstances involving public accommodations. What happens if another source of immunity is substituted? If it had been an application of the 'free exercise' clause as expressed by either *Reynolds* or *Smith*, the result would not alter from application of the Rule because in each case, the First Amendment would not provide Phillips immunity.

If dignity were introduced, from the examples of *Pichon and Sajous v France*,[143] and *BVerfGE 87*,[144] both decisions made under dignity as a constitutional principle, one would expect the same result as from the Rule. Taking the boxes in the table, the right, privilege, and power correlatives would be transformed in the same manner as with application of the Rule as the source of immunity because human dignity would not permit Phillips to behave as he did with impunity. It follows that the jural opposites would likewise change in the same manner as under the Rule as the source of immunity.

In Hohfeldian terms, the immunity box in *Clubb* would be in the following terms and operate to remove all other rights and liabilities that *Clubb* might claim:

Box 11.1

Immunity: Clubb's claim for immunity under the implied freedom of political speech fails because any such right is subjugated to the overarching principle of human dignity, even though the subjugation arises from a state law. Her refusal to observe the law with respect to the restriction zone does not fall within any constitutional freedom of political speech because the human dignity of those entering the zone for procedures overrides any such implied freedom. Her claimed liberty fails because it was:

- proscribed by the Victorian law, which law was necessary in a democratic society;
- in the protection of public order; and
- for the protection of the rights and freedoms of others.

142 Whereas human dignity is of general application in all cases. Refer to the cases cited and to an illustration in the context of employment, *Vera Egenberger v Evangelisches Werk für Diakonie und Entwicklung eV* (Judgment of the Court [Grand Chamber], C-414/16, ECLI:EU:C:2018:257, 17 April 2018).

143 Application No. 49853/99 (2 October 2001) 191 https://www.echr.coe.int/Documents/Reports_Recueil_2001-X.pdf.

144 BVerfGE 87 (1992).

Again, however, permutations of First Amendment jurisprudence are situational and highly technical in their application. But if the overarching constitutional principle were human dignity, the result is principled rather than situational. And human dignity is, or should be considered, by its nature, superior as a constitutional consideration to other constitutional principles. The immunity box, thus, changes, leaving the other boxes and the overall result to confine Phillips' religiously held prejudices in the private realm and not capable of being acted upon in the marketplace.

Box 11.2

Immunity: Phillips' claim for immunity under the First Amendment fails because any such right is subjugated to the overarching principle of human dignity. His refusal to deal does not fall within the religious liberty that derives from human dignity. His claimed liberty fails because it was:

- proscribed by the Colorado law, which law was necessary in a democratic society;
- in the protection of public; and
- for the protection of the rights and freedoms of others.

In contrast, *Masterpiece*, on the other hand, accorded no dignity to Mullins and Craig, the discriminated gay couple. The *Masterpiece* decision, to the extent that it invokes the First Amendment, opens the floodgates for vendors to ostracise on the sole basis that the vendor holds any belief that supports the refusal to deal.

In short, then, it can be concluded that the Rule and human dignity as an overarching constitutional principle would deliver a dignitarian outcome, whereas the actual decision in the Court in *Masterpiece* did not.

V Conclusion

On ordinary constitutional principles and applying the common law, the Supreme Court in *Masterpiece* should have found that, first, the Colorado anti-discrimination law was of general application and did not single out religious practices. Second, it should have found that there was no evidence that a refusal to deal was not an essential tenet of Phillips' Christian belief; rather it was an individual choice made by him, and for which First Amendment protection was not available, even if a conscientious one. Third, it should have found that Phillips was, at common law, as a controller of a public accommodation, under a duty to deal with all members of the public as part of the privilege of occupying that accommodation. Fourth, and in consequence of the foregoing, it should have found that Phillips' practice was outside of First Amendment protection; his belief could be held and given effect privately, but could not be practised as a refusal to deal in a public accommodation.

Human dignity operates as an overarching status. Had it been considered in *Masterpiece*, the result would have been the opposite of that reached by the Supreme Court, and its constitutional instantiation would provide a missing tool in the common law by which to determine rights claims disputes. In cases involving claims of religious freedom competing with claims under an equality law, human dignity favours containment of individual exercise of private belief to the private sphere where public exercise would adversely affect the rights and freedoms of others. By adopting a Hohfeldian analysis, it is clear, on a comparative basis, that courts decide cases more justly when human dignity is invoked. Such becomes clear from a comparative analysis utilising Hohfeldian theory. If adopted by courts and commentators, its use would limit the possibility of error.

Further Reading:

For analysis of the methods used in this chapter, see Chapter 15 – Section IV – subsection A *The Doctrinal Method*; C *The Functionalist Method*; D *The Analytical Method*; F *The Yardstick Method.*

For the author's rejoinder and reflection, see Appendix Section VI.

For another example of constitutional reference to human dignity, see Chapter 13.

12 Listening to the People? A Comparative Analysis of Parliamentary Committee Inquiries Concerning Freedom of Religious Belief in Australia and Scotland

Sarah Moulds[1]

I Introduction

This chapter explores how parliamentary committees engage with the public as part of their deliberative function with reference to two case studies from parliaments in Australia and Scotland relating to proposed laws that directly engage freedom of religion.[2] It introduces a four-step methodology that begins by considering the institutional context in which parliamentary committees undertake their inquiry work.[3] The second step identifies the engagement tools employed by parliamentary committees and evaluates these having regard to ten indicators of effective public parliamentary engagement,[4] which

1 Associate Professor of Law, Justice and Society Unit, University of South Australia.

2 The case studies used in this chapter relate to parliamentary committee inquiries undertaken in the Australian Parliament into the provisions of the *Religious Discrimination Bill 2021* (Cth), *Religious Discrimination (Consequential Amendments) Bill 2021* (Cth) and *Human Rights Legislation Amendment Bill 2021* (Cth) and parliamentary committee inquiries undertaken in the Scottish Parliament into the *Hate Crime and Public Order (Scotland) Bill 2021.*

3 This approach aligns with the strategies and methods advanced by scholars including Carolyn Evans and Simon Evans, 'Legislative Scrutiny Committees and Parliamentary Conceptions of Human Rights' [2006] *Public Law* 785; Meghan Benton and Meg Russell, 'Assessing the Impact of Parliamentary Oversight Committees: The Select Committees in the British House of Commons' (2013) 66 *Parliamentary Affairs* 772 ('Assessing the Impact'); and Malcolm Aldons, 'Problems with Parliamentary Committee Evaluation: Light at the End of the Tunnel?' (2003) 18(1) *Australasian Parliamentary Review* 79 ('Problems with Parliamentary Committee Evaluation'); Malcolm Aldons, 'Rating the Effectiveness of Parliamentary Committee Reports: The Methodology' (2000) 15(1) *Legislative Studies* 22 ('Rating the Effectiveness of Parliamentary Committee Reports').

4 These ten factors are identified in Cristina Leston-Bandeira, 'How Public Engagement Has Become a Must for Parliaments in Today's Democracies' (2022) 37(2) *Australasian Parliamentary Review* 8, 12–15. These ten factors draw upon the work of the Inter-Parliamentary Union, *Public Engagement in the Work of Parliament, Inter-Parliamentary Union and United Nations Development Programme* (Global Parliamentary Report, 2022) 8 ('the IPU Report')

DOI: 10.4324/9781003397311-17

include a focus on diversity of participation. The third step looks at parliamentary transcripts and reports to determine whether and how parliamentary committee inquiries influence the shape of the proposed law and the way it is debated inside and outside of parliament.[5] The final step uses this information to reflect on whether parliamentary committees provide effective deliberative forums for the discussion of human rights issues, including freedom of religious belief.

In this chapter, the term "freedom of religious belief" will be used as a shorthand term to refer to the internationally recognised right to freedom of thought, conscience, and religion, protected by the *International Covenant on Civil and Political Rights* ('*ICCPR*') and the *European Convention on Human Rights*.[6] Article 18 of the *ICCPR* describes this right as follows:

> Everyone shall have the right to freedom of thought, conscience and religion. This right shall include freedom to have or to adopt a religion or belief of his choice, and freedom, either individually or in community with others and in public or private, to manifest his religion or belief in worship, observance, practice and teaching.
>
> No one shall be subject to coercion which would impair his freedom to have or to adopt a religion or belief of his choice.
>
> Freedom to manifest one's religion or beliefs may be subject only to such limitations as are prescribed by law and are necessary to protect public safety, order, health, or morals or the fundamental rights and freedoms of others.
>
> The States Parties to the present Covenant undertake to have respect for the liberty of parents and, when applicable, legal guardians to ensure the religious and moral education of their children in conformity with their own convictions.

The methodology in this chapter is not focused on identifying specific priorities for law reform, or analysing the merits of the laws proposed in the case studies. Instead, it identifies which features of existing parliamentary committee systems could be used to improve the deliberative performance of parliaments, and which areas require further investment and reform. In this way it can also offer insights into how both lawmakers and community members

---

and 'Toolkit for Parliamentary Public Engagement' *International Parliamentary Engagement Network* (Web Page, 2021) https://ipen-network.org/ ('IPEN Toolkit').

5 Sarah Moulds, *Committees of Influence* (Springer, 2020) ch 10.

6 *International Covenant on Civil and Political Rights*, opened for signature 16 December 1966, [1980] ATS 23 Article 18; Council of Europe, *European Convention for the Protection of Human Rights and Fundamental Freedoms, as Amended by Protocols Nos. 11 and 14*, 4 November 1950, ETS 5 Article 9.

conceptualise of fundamental human rights, including freedom of religious belief, in different institutional contexts,[7] which can in turn help inform future efforts to improve legislative protections in Australian and Scotland. Before introducing the methodology in more detail, it is helpful to consider the role parliamentary committees play in facilitating parliament's deliberative and rights scrutiny functions, and some of the challenges associated with evaluating their performance in these conceptually complex, dynamic roles.[8]

A The Role of Parliamentary Committees in Facilitating a Deliberative Forum for Rights Scrutiny to Take Place

Parliamentary committees undertake many functions including scrutinising government expenditure and proposed legislation, reviewing procedural rules, and conducting thematic inquiries into policy issues referred to them by parliament.[9] Parliamentary committees are also responsible for alerting the parliament and the public to executive actions that unduly interfere with individual rights or freedoms or abrogate certain rule of law principles.[10] The parliaments considered in this chapter also rely heavily on the committee system to provide

7 These themes have been explored in detail by the work of Poulos and Barker, see Elenie Poulos, 'Three Discourses of Religious Freedom: How and Why Political Talk about Religious Freedom in Australia Has Changed' (2023) 14 *Religions* 669 ('Three Discourses of Religious Freedom'); Elenie Poulos, *The Politics of Belief: The Rise of Religious Freedom in Australia* (2020a, Sydney: Macquarie University) ('*The Politics of Belief*'); Elenie Poulos, 'The Power of Belief: Religious Freedom in Australian Parliamentary Debates on Same-Sex Marriage' (2020b) 55 *Australian Journal of Political Science* 1–19 ('Religious Freedom in Australian Parliamentary Debates on Same-Sex Marriage'); Renate Barker, 'The Place of the Child in Recent Australian Debate about Freedom of Religion and Belief' (2022) 11(6) *Laws* 83 ('The Place of the Child'); Renae Barker, *State and Religion: The Australian Story* (Routledge: London, 2019) ('*State and Religion*').

8 This includes challenges identified and explored by Scott Stephenson, *From Dialogue to Disagreement in Comparative Rights Constitutionalism* (Federation Press, 2016); Aldons, 'Problems with Parliamentary Committee Evaluation' (n 2), 81; Meghan Benton and Meg Russell, 'Assessing the Policy Impact of Parliament: Methodological Challenges and Possible Future Approaches' (Paper presented at the Public Service Association Legislative Studies Specialist Group Conference, London, United Kingdom, 24 June 2009) ('Assessing the Policy Impact'); Carolyn M Hendriks, Sue Regan and Adrian Kay, 'Participatory Adaptation in Contemporary Parliamentary Committees in Australia' (2019) 72(2) *Parliamentary Affairs* 267.

9 See, eg, David Monk, 'A Framework for Evaluating the Performance of Committees in Westminster Parliaments' (2010) 16 *Journal of Legislative Studies* 1; Laura Grenfell, 'An Australian Spectrum of Political Rights Scrutiny: 'Continuing to Lead by Example?'', (2015) 26(1) *Public Law Review*, 19–38; Gabrielle Appleby, Laura Grenfell and Alexander Reilly (eds), *Australian Public Law* (Oxford University Press, 2nd ed, 2014) 103–4.

10 See Brian Galligan, *Parliamentary Responsible Government and the Protection of Rights*, Parl Paper No 18 (1992); Brian Galligan, *Senate Committees – Can They Halt the Decline of Parliament*, Parl Paper No 12 (1990).

a forum for elected members to hear directly from the people they represent.[11] In this way, the committee system can also be described as a means of facilitating parliament's *deliberative function* by providing a forum for informed, reflective, and cooperative decision-making and policy development.[12]

Dalla-Pozza suggests that there are two primary ways in which parliamentary committees help the parliament to achieve its deliberative function.[13] One is by scrutinising laws and policies against certain rights-based criteria to help elucidate the "real world" impact and consequences of the proposal, beyond the political objectives prosecuted by the proponent of the bill or policy.[14] The other is through the practical capacity of committees to "reach out" to the community by inviting submissions and holding public hearings. This ensures that a wider range of interests are consulted[15] and provides what Odgers[16] and Marsh[17] have described as a chance for those with different perspectives or positions to find "common ground". This "reach out" activity is also described as a form of "public-parliamentary engagement" and is of central interest to the discussion in this chapter.[18]

B The Challenge of Measuring the Impact and Quality of the Work of Parliamentary Committees

The challenges associated with measuring the performance and impact of parliamentary committees has been recognised by scholars across the world.[19]

11 Elaine Thompson, 'The Senate and Representative Democracy' (Senate Brief No 10, Parliamentary Library, Parliament of Australia, 1998).

12 Graeme Orr and Ron Levy, *The Law of Deliberative Democracy* (Routledge, 2016) 22–23; Dominique Dalla-Pozza, 'The Conscience of Democracy? The Role of Australian Parliamentary Committees in Enacting Counter-Terrorism Laws' (Paper presented at the Australasian Law and Society Conference, Wollongong, December 2006).

13 Dalla-Pozza (n 11) 20–21. See also Dominique Dalla-Pozza, 'Promoting Deliberative Debate? The Submissions and Oral Evidence Provided to Australian Parliamentary Committees in the Creation of Counter-Terrorism Laws' (2008) 23(1) *Australasian Parliamentary Review* 39.

14 John Uhr, *Deliberative Democracy in Australia: The Changing Place of Parliament* (Cambridge University Press, 1998) 149–50.

15 Kelly Paxman, *Referral of Bills to Senate Committees: An Evaluation*, Parl Paper No 31 (1998) 76.

16 James Odgers, *Australian Senate Practice* (Commonwealth of Australia, 13th ed, 2012) 129.

17 Ian Marsh, *Can Senate Committees Contribute to Social Learning*, Parl Paper No 45 (2006) 1; See also Ian Marsh, 'Australia's Representation Gap: A Role for Parliamentary Committees?' (Speech delivered at the Department of the Senate Occasional Lecture Series, Parliament House, Canberra, 26 November 2004) ('Australia's Representation Gap').

18 IPU Report (n 3), 8.

19 See Aileen Kavanagh, 'The Joint Committee on Human Rights: A Hybrid Breed of Constitutional Watchdog' in Murray Hunt, Hayley Jane Hooper and Paul Yowell (eds), *Parliaments and Human Rights: Redressing the Democratic Deficit* (Hart Publishing, 2015) 111; Meghan Benton and Meg Russell, 'Assessing the Policy Impact' (n 7); Gareth Griffith, 'Parliament and Accountability: The Role of Parliamentary Oversight Committees' (Briefing Paper No 12/05, Parliamentary Library Research Service, New South Wales, 2005); Evans and Evans

This is because of their dynamic membership, functions and processes, and the politicised context in which they operate. As Webb and Roberts warn, it can be difficult to define precisely what a high-performing committee looks like and there is a risk that the assessor's approach will influence what a "good" committee means.[20]

In Westminster-inspired parliaments, these concerns are compounded by the dominance of executive government and the general reluctance of the "government of the day" to voluntarily submit itself to oversight and scrutiny, including by parliamentary committees.[21] This can lead to findings that parliamentary committees generally enjoy a low level of influence and generate few legislative amendments beyond those already contemplated by the government of the day.[22] It can also lead some to query the viability and desirably of measuring the impact of parliamentary committees at all.[23] However, it is possible to accept the reality of executive-dominated parliaments without being completely deterred from the task of investigating the impact that parliamentary committees have on the lawmaking process.[24] This can be achieved by specifically *factoring in* the executive-centric nature of the parliamentary landscape into any assessment framework,[25] for example, by adopting a multi-step approach that includes an explicit focus on institutional context, as offered in the methodology outlined in the following section.

The complexity of evaluating the deliberative work of parliamentary committees is also compounded by the challenges associated with testing the

---

(n 2); Michael C Tolley, 'Parliamentary Scrutiny of Rights in the United Kingdom: Assessing the Work of the Joint Committee on Human Rights' (2009) 44(1) *Australian Journal of Political Science* 41; J Smookler, 'Making a Difference? The Effectiveness of Pre-Legislative Scrutiny' (2006) 59 *Parliamentary Affairs* 522; John Uhr, 'Parliament and Public Deliberation: Evaluating the Performance of Parliament' (2001) 24 *University of New South Wales Law Journal* 708.

20 Philippa Webb and Kirsten Roberts, 'Effective Parliamentary Oversight of Human Rights: A Framework for Designing and Determining Effectiveness' (Paper presented at the Dickson Poon School of Law, King's College London, University of London, June 2014) 3.

21 Janet Hiebert, 'Governing Like Judges?' in Tom Campbell, K D Ewing and Adam Tomkins (eds), *The Legal Protection of Human Rights: Sceptical Essays* (Oxford University Press, 2011) 40, 41; Monk (n 8) 7. Cf Meghan Benton and Meg Russell, 'Does the Executive Dominate the Westminster Legislative Process? Six Reasons for Doubt' (2016) 69 Parliamentary Affairs 28. See also Benton and Russell, 'Assessing the Impact' (n 2).

22 George Willams and Daniel Reynolds, 'The Operation and Impact of Australia's Parliamentary Scrutiny Regime for Human Rights' (2016) 41(2) *Monash University Law Review* 469.

23 See, eg, Geoffrey Lindell, 'How (and Whether?) to Evaluate Parliamentary Committees – From a Lawyer's Perspective' (2005) August *About the House* 55.

24 Andrew Hindmoor, Phillip Larkin and Andrew Kenyon, 'Assessing the Influence of Select Committees in the UK: The Education and Skills Committee 1997–2005' (2009) 15(1) *Journal of Legislative Studies* 71.

25 Moulds (n 4). See also Tolley (n 18); Aldons, 'Problems with Parliamentary Committee Evaluation (n 2) 83–84; Benton and Russell, 'Assessing the Impact' (n 2).

effectiveness of public parliamentary engagement more broadly.[26] Many of these challenges have been explored by the Inter Parliamentary Union (IPU)[27] and considered by the International Parliamentary Engagement Network (IPEN) which has developed a practical template for evaluating public parliamentary engagement strategies across a range of institutional contexts.[28] These materials have been synthesised by Leston-Bandeira who identifies ten keys factors needed for effective public parliamentary engagement,[29] featured in Section II.

II The Methodology Adopted in This Chapter

The methodology employed in this chapter has four key steps, in addition to the important preliminary step of identifying relevant comparative case studies (discussed in the steps listed).

A Step 1: Institutional Context

The first step in any successful evaluation of the performance of parliamentary committees is to understand the institutional context in which such committees operate. This includes the constitutional context, the legislative competencies of the relevant legislature, the range of different parliamentary committees existing within a particular parliament and their different roles and functions. It can also include any relevant executive-led public consultations on policy matters or legislative proposals relevant to the work of the parliamentary committees being evaluated. One of the benefits of explicitly considering the institutional context of a particular parliamentary committee inquiry is to guard against some of the methodological challenges identified earlier, particularly those relating to the structural power dynamic occurring between the parliament and the executive, and within the executive itself.[30]

B Step 2: Identifying and Evaluating the Public Engagement Tools Used by the Parliamentary Committee

In order to assess the performance of parliamentary committees with respect to their deliberative function, it is necessary to identify and evaluate the tools and strategies these bodies employ when seeking to engage with the public. The suitability of these tools and strategies will depend on a range of factors

26 Christine Sheldon 'Closing the Gap: Establishing a 'Feedback Loop' for Effective Parliamentary Public Engagement' (2023) *Journal of Legislative Studies*, 1.
27 IPU Report (n 3).
28 IPEN Toolkit (n 3).
29 LestonBandeira (n 3).
30 Moulds (n 4).

including institutional context and the key attributes of the public or publics that the parliament is trying to reach.[31]

During a 2021 IPEN workshop on public engagement and parliaments, scholars and practitioners from around the world identified the following indicators of "good" public engagement: inclusivity; diversity of participation; empowering; flexible; meaningful; open and transparent; and collaborative.[32] These themes are also reflected in the findings of the IPU's *Global Parliamentary Report 2022*[33] which described effective engagement as being strategic, inclusive, participatory, innovative, and responsive.[34] Drawing on the work of the IPU and the IPEN, Leston-Bandeira has identified ten factors to ensure effective public engagement which provide a useful framework for evaluating the engagement tools utilised in the case studies considered in Table 12.1.[35]

C Step 3: Exploring the Impact of These Engagement Techniques on the Shape of the Proposed or Enacted Laws

The next step of the methodology is to consider what *impact* the parliamentary committee had on the shape of the proposed law and/or the way it was discussed inside and outside of the parliament. Assessing this type of impact is notoriously difficult, as it is impossible to establish a single causal factor to something as politically complex and dynamic as the introduction and passage of an amendment to a bill. For this reason, the purpose of this step in the methodology is not to categorically state that the work of the parliamentary committee "changed the law". Rather, it is designed to encourage consideration of parliamentary materials (such as transcripts of parliamentary debates, explanatory materials accompanying bills, and schedules of amendments) when looking for evidence of the impact or influence of parliamentary committee inquiries and the public engagement strategies they employ. Looking at these sources can be used to demonstrate what Aldons has described as the "power" or "influence" of the committee in its institutional context.[36]

31 See, eg, R Kennedy et al, 'Demographics and (Equal?) Voice: Assessing Participation in Online Deliberative Sessions' (2021) 69(1) *Political Studies*, 66–88; S Chambers and J Gastil 'Deliberation, Democracy, and the Digital Landscape' (2021) 69(1) *Political Studies* 3–6.

32 IPEN Toolkit (n 3).

33 IPU Report (n 3) Annex: Case Studies and Practical Guides.

34 Ibid 8.

35 Leston-Bandeira (n 3) 12–15. See also C Carman, 'The Process Is the Reality: Perceptions of Procedural Fairness and Participatory Democracy, (2010) 58(4) *Political Studies*, 731–51; Cristina Leston-Bandeira, 'Parliamentary Petitions and Public Engagement: an Empirical Analysis of the Role of E-petitions', (2019) 47(3) *Policy & Politics,* 415–436; C Leston-Bandeira and L Thompson, 'Integrating the View of the Public into the Formal Legislative Process: Public Reading Stage in the UK House of Commons', (2017) 23(4) *The Journal of Legislative Studies*, 508–528. This approach also aligns with the work of Sheldon (n 25).

36 Aldons, 'Problems with Parliamentary Committee Evaluation' (n 2) 81.

Table 12.1 Leston-Bandeira's Factors to Ensure Effective Public Engagement

Factor	*Indicator*
Accessibility Language and mechanisms used successfully conveys ideas to a diverse range of potential participants	Resources in multiple languages, styles, or formats
	Different modes of communication with different audiences
Reach of the Audience Actively seeking input from those not otherwise engaged with parliament as part of their work practice	Rates of participation
	Geographical diversity
Diversity of the Audience Facilitating participation beyond those already familiar with parliamentary processes and explicitly encouraging a diversity of views	Participation beyond the "usual suspects"
	Explicit encouragement for diverse groups to participate
Existing "Divides" Explicit efforts to understand and overcome existing political, social, economic, digital, or other divides	Practical barriers to diverse participation are identified and explicitly addressed
Diverse Communication Techniques A multiplicity of communication techniques have been employed	Evidence of multiple communication techniques eg text, audio, video, visual, infographics
Issue-led Rather than Process-led Recognition that ordinary people are more likely to engage with parliament because they care about an issue, not because they know how a process works	Evidence of procedural innovation or flexibility in response to issue-orientated engagement
Listening Rather than Broadcasting Institutional actors demonstrate active listening techniques and explicitly respond to ideas or input from others	Evidence of two-way communication where institutional actors respond to ideas or suggestions by other participants Opportunity to share lived experience Appropriate acknowledgement of inputs submitted
Closing the Feedback Loop Effective explanation of how inputs collected informed parliamentary business	Evidence of clear communication with participants about how their inputs informed parliamentary business
	Evidence that someone did listen, even if not to accommodate the exact demands made

(*Continued*)

Table 12.1 (Continued)

Factor	*Indicator*
Linking Engagement with Parliamentary Business Views of the participants are formally and actively linked to the process of considering the bill	Evidence of involvement or acknowledgement by diverse range of Members of Parliament
	Evidence that participant views are formally and actively linked to the process of considering the bill
Evaluation and Reporting of Activities Parliaments regularly seek feedback and report on engagement performance	Evidence of any internal reflection or reporting on the engagement activity

D Step 4: Reflecting on the Extent to which These Inquiries Provide an Effective Forum for Deliberating Human Rights Issues Arising from Proposed Legislation

The final step in the methodology uses the information collected to reflect on the extent to which parliamentary committee inquiries provide an effective forum for deliberating human rights issues, including freedom of religious belief. This step is interested in exploring whether the parliamentary committee's work demonstrates or helps to generate:

- a culture of understanding and respect for human rights among key participants (including those within government, parliament, and the broader community);
- a culture of understanding and respect for internationally recognised processes and concepts associated with "balancing" competing human rights, including concepts of proportionality;
- a broader public and parliamentary awareness of the need to protect and promote the rights of the most vulnerable members of the community and to guard against majoritarianism when it comes to legislative and policy design.[37]

This final step of the process invites critical reflection on how specific human rights are conceptualised within different political and public discourses. In this way it intersects with the work of Poulos[38] who has identified three major

37 This aligns with the approach adopted by Evans and Evans (n 2); George Williams and Lisa Burton, 'Australia's Exclusive Parliamentary Model of Rights Protection' (2013) 34(1) *Statute Law Review* 58; Stephenson (n 7).

38 See Barker, '*State and Religion*' (n 6); Barker, 'The Place of the Child' (n 6) and Poulos, 'Three Discourses of Religious Freedom' (n6); Poulos, '*The Politics of Belief*' (n 6) and Pou-

discourses of religious freedom in Australian public discourse emerging over three phases: "religious diversity", "balancing rights" and "freedom of belief".[39] These shifting discourses are evident in both the case studies considered in this chapter, where the predominant public and political conversation about "freedom of religious belief" shifts quickly from protecting religious minorities to preserving the rights of already privileged groups to manifest their "beliefs" in public without sanction.[40] As Poulos explains, this shift has occurred against the backdrop of increased international and domestic legal protections for the rights of other minority groups, including LGBTIQ+ groups, which have been interpreted by some as contrary to religious belief and an offence to the sensibilities of religious believers.[41] As Barker has explored, this has also manifested through the lens of children's rights, particularly when enhanced legal protections for LGBTIQ+ groups have intersected with the rights of religious schools to protect and promote their religious ethos in educational settings.[42] While it is beyond the scope of this chapter to provide a detailed analysis of these shifting discourses in the Scottish and Australian contexts, this step in the methodology offers a new tool for others to investigate changes in human rights discourse in the future.

III Applying the Methodology to the Case Studies

Two case studies have been chosen for this chapter. The first relates to parliamentary committee inquiries undertaken in the Australian Parliament into the provisions of the *Religious Discrimination Bill 2021*, the *Religious Discrimination (Consequential Amendments) Bill 2021*, and *Human Rights Legislation Amendment Bill 2021* (Religious Discrimination Bills package). The second relates to parliamentary committee inquiries undertaken in the Scottish Parliament into the *Hate Crime and Public Order (Scotland) Bill 2021* ('*Hate Crimes Bill*').

Undertaking a comparative law analysis between Scotland and Australia requires careful acknowledgement of their legal systems, historical backgrounds, and cultural variations.[43] Scotland operates under a mixed legal sys-

---

los, 'Religious Freedom in Australian Parliamentary Debates on Same-Sex Marriage' (n 6). See also D Gary, *Australian Soul: Religion and Spirituality in the 21st Century* (2006, Cambridge University Press); Elenie Poulos, 'Protecting Freedom/Protecting Privilege: Church Responses to Anti-discrimination Law Reform in Australia' (2018) 24 *Australian Journal of Human Rights*, 117–33.

39 Poulos, 'Three Discourses of Religious Freedom' (n 6) 674.

40 Ibid 682.

41 Ibid.

42 Barker, 'The Place of the Child' (n 6).

43 See, eg, A Watson, *Legal Transplants and the Frontiers of Legal Knowledge: Comparative and Historical Studies* (2014, Edinburgh University Press); G Bermann, et al, *Comparative Law: Problems and Prospects* (2011) 26(4) *American University International Law Review*, 935–968.

tem that combines elements of both common law and civil law, influenced by its historical connection to Roman law.[44] In contrast, Australia has a common law system, evolved in the context of its particular colonial history. Scotland's constitutional position within the United Kingdom and its evolving relationship with the European Union introduce intricacies when comparing legal frameworks.[45] Meanwhile, Australia's federal system enshrined in its written constitution, gives rise to distinct governance structures and legislative competencies.[46] These comparative challenges are explicitly acknowledged in Step 1 of the methodology, which has a sustained focus on the institutional context in which the case study inquiries took place.

Despite these institutional distinctions, the populations in Australia and Scotland share some important characteristics relevant to this study. For example, in both countries the largest religious group (comprising of between 30–40% of the population) identifies as Christian, however, in both countries around 40% of people identify as having no-religion and this cohort is growing.[47] The remainder of both populations is made up of those who self-identify with a minority faith such as Islam, Hinduism, Buddhism, or Judaism – and in Australia it is also important to acknowledge the percentage of the population who identify as First Nations peoples, or Aboriginal or Torres Strait Islander peoples, who have their own particular spiritual beliefs.

Parliaments in Scotland and Australia both have sophisticated committee systems, featuring both "standing" or "mandatory committees", and specialist or "select" committees that inquiry into proposed laws and policies. Both Scotland and Australia also have relatively comprehensive laws in place to provide legal protection for discrimination on the grounds of sex, gender, sexual orientation, and gender identity (although protections relating specifically to religious faith differ, as discussed following). These similarities enable sensible comparisons to be drawn, even if the institutional differences between the two jurisdictions warn against any "direct legal transplants" being made.[48]

44 For a detailed analysis of this history see J W Cairns, The Nature and History of Scots Law (2002, Edinburgh University Press); H L MacQueen and G Thomson, (eds) Studies in Scots Law Volume 1: A European Legal History (2006, Edinburgh University Press).

45 Ibid.

46 For further discussion see Appleby, Grenfell and Reilly (n 8) ch 4 'A Federal Commonwealth'.

47 Australian Bureau of Statistics, *2021 Census Shows Changes in Australia's Religious Diversity* (27 June 2022) https://www.abs.gov.au/media-centre/media-releases/2021-census-shows-changes-australias-religious-diversity; Scotland's Census, *Census Results: At a Glance – Religion* (last updated 2 August 2021) https://www.scotlandscensus.gov.uk/census-results/at-a-glance/religion/.

48 Watson (n 42); Stephenson (n 7).

A Australian Case Study: Parliamentary Committee Inquiries into the Religious Discrimination Bills Package

The Religious Discrimination Bills package 2021 was introduced in the Australian Parliament on 25 November 2021 by the Hon Scott Morrison MP, the then Prime Minister of Australia. The primary aims of this package of Bills were to:

- prohibit discrimination on the basis of a person's religious belief or activity in a range of areas of public life, including employment, education, access to premises, and the provision of goods, services and accommodation;
- establish general and specific exceptions from the prohibition of religious discrimination;
- provide that certain statements of belief do not constitute discrimination for the purposes of certain specified Commonwealth, state, or territory anti-discrimination laws; and
- establish the office of the Religious Discrimination Commissioner.

The Religious Discrimination Bills package was debated in the House of Representatives over the course of December 2021 and February 2022 and introduced into the Senate following an all-night sitting on 10 February. It was not debated in the Senate and lapsed (prior to enactment) at the end of the 46th Parliament on 25 July 2022.

Step 1: Institutional Context

The background to the introduction of this package is relevant to evaluating work of the parliamentary committees involved in scrutinising its contents. In 2017, the Australian government proposed a national postal survey on whether to amend the provisions of the *Marriage Act* to legalise same-sex marriage.[49] As the debate over marriage equality gained momentum, concerns were raised about how this reform might intersect with the rights and freedoms of individuals and institutions with religious objections to same-sex unions. Some argued that without adequate religious protections, individuals and religious organisations might face discrimination claims or legal challenges for upholding traditional views on marriage and sexuality.[50]

49 Amy Maguire, 'From Postal Survey to Parliament: How Australia Legalised Same-sex Marriage', *The Conversation*, online, 8 December 2017.

50 For discussion of some of these perspectives see Luke Beck, 'Marriage Equality/Inequality, Religion and the Constitution' on AUSPUBLAW (18 August 2016) https://auspublaw.org/blog/2016/08/marriage-equality/; Elaine Poulos, 'The Power of Belief: Religious Freedom in Australian Parliamentary Debates on Same-sex Marriage' (2020) 55(1) *Australian Journal of Political Science* 1–19.

In response, the then Prime Minister, the Hon Malcolm Turnbull MP, announced a wide-ranging review into religious freedom in Australia, to be conducted by an Expert Panel,[51] to examine and report on whether Australian law adequately protects the human right to freedom of religious belief.[52] The Expert Panel received around 15,620 written submissions and conducted around 90 consultation meetings with 180 individuals and groups.[53] It made 20 recommendations to enhance the protection of freedom of religious belief, both through legislative amendments to Commonwealth, state, and territory laws, and through non-legislative measures.[54] The Religious Discrimination Bills package formed part of the government's response to these recommendations.[55]

Prior to its introduction, the Religious Discrimination Bills package was subject to two exposure draft consultation processes conducted by the federal government. The first exposure draft consultation attracted over 6,000 submissions[56] and the second around 7,000.[57] The Bills were also informed by government-initiated round-table discussions and meetings with interested stakeholders such as LGBTIQA+ groups.[58]

Some of these public consultations occurred in the context of sustained media interest in the case of Israel Folau, a former professional rugby player who used social media posts to express religious views that were widely perceived as homophobic.[59] This led to his contract termination by Rugby Australia and a public debate about whether it was appropriate to limit or sanction the discriminatory comments of public figures, if they were made as part of a genuine expression of religious belief. A so-called "Folau clause" was included in the

51 Senate Standing Committee on Legal and Constitutional Affairs Legislation Committee, Parliament of Australia, *Inquiry into the Provisions of the Religious Discrimination Bill 2021 [Provisions]; Religious Discrimination (Consequential Amendments) Bill 2021 [Provisions] and Human Rights Legislation Amendment Bill 2021*, (4 February 2022), [1.29] ('the LCA Legislation Committee Report').

52 Ibid [1.30].

53 Expert Panel on Religious Freedom, *Religious Freedom Review* (2018) chaired by the Hon Philip Ruddock and comprising of Emeritus Professor Rosalind Croucher AM, the Hon Dr Annabelle Bennett AC SC, Father Frank Brennan SJ AO and Professor Nicholas Aroney.

54 LCA Legislation Committee Report, [1.31]. See also Expert Panel on Religious Freedom, *Religious Freedom Review*, 2018, 1–7.

55 LCA Legislation Committee Report, [1.31]. The religious discrimination bill seeks to implement recommendations 3, 15 and 19 of the Religious Freedom Review, while the human rights legislation bill would implement recommendations 3, 4 and 12.

56 LCA Legislation Committee Report, [1.33].

57 Ibid.

58 Attorney General's Department, *Submission 175*, 3.

59 Jack Anderson, 'Explainer: Does Rugby Australia Have Legal Grounds to Sack Israel Folau for Anti-gay Social Media Posts?' *The Conversation*, online, 30 April 2019.

draft *Religious Discrimination Bill 2021* that would make it clear that it was not unlawful to express a statement of religious belief, even if that belief was offensive or discriminatory to others. Early iterations also included conscientious objection provisions that would allow health practitioners to refuse to provide certain treatment on the basis of their personal religious beliefs and the ability for religious institutions to discriminate against staff on the basis of religion to maintain a "faith-based ethos".[60] Not all of these features of the proposed legislation were present in the Religious Discrimination Bills package when it was introduced into Parliament, however, a revised "statement of belief" provision was included that sought to override existing discrimination protections in prescribed state and territory laws.[61]

Before considering the specific inquiries undertaken by Australian parliamentary committees into these proposed laws, it is useful to recall the federal context in which they operate. The federal Parliament (referred to as the Australian Parliament) – where the Religious Discrimination Bills package was introduced and scrutinised – is bicameral and the host of the most sophisticated and powerful system of parliamentary committees in Australia, due to the political composition of the upper House, the Senate.[62] The Senate is sometimes described as "the House of Review" because its political makeup is often different to that of the House of Representatives, owing to proportionate representation of the states.[63] It is also important to note that the Australian Constitution does not contain a Bill of Rights, and there is no human rights legislation at the federal level. Instead, Australia relies upon a combination of constitutional limitations on legislative power,[64] specific legislative provisions (such as anti-discrimination laws)[65] and common law principles[66] to protect, promote, and balance the individual rights of its people.[67] This means that the rights-scrutiny work of different parliamentary committees becomes of central

60 Paul Karp, The Coalition's Religious Discrimination Bill: What's Changed and Can Doctors Refuse Treatment?, *The Guardian*, online, 11 December 2019.

61 *Religious Discrimination Bill 2021*, clause 12 (First Reading).

62 For further discussion see Appleby, Grenfell and Reilly (n 8) ch 4 'A Federal Commonwealth'.

63 Julie Debeljak and Laura Grenfell, 'Diverse Australian Landscapes of Law-Making and Human Rights: Contextualising Law-Making and Human Rights', in Julie Debeljak and Laura Grenfell (eds), *Law Making and Human Rights* (Thomson Reuters, Sydney, 2020), 1, 17.

64 See, eg, *Australian Constitution* s116, which places limits on the federal parliament's power to make laws with respect to religion. See also *Krygger v Williams* (1912) 15 CLR 336; *Adelaide Company of Jehovah's Witnesses v Commonwealth* (1943) 67 CLR 116; *Attorney General (Vic); Kruger v Commonwealth* (1997) 190 CLR 1 and *Williams v The Commonwealth* (2012) 248 CLR 156.

65 See, eg, *Race Discrimination Act 1975* (Cth); *Sex Discrimination Act 1984* (Cth).

66 For example, Australian common law recognises the 'principle of legality', which can be applied by the courts as a tool for interpreting ambiguous legislation (*Re Bolton; Ex parte Beane* 1987]) 162 CLR 514, 523; *Coco v The Queen* (1994) 179 CLR 427, 437 (Mason CJ, Brennan, Gaudron and McHugh JJ).

67 See Fergal Davis, 'Political Rights Review and Political Party Cohesion' (2016) 69 *Parliamentary Affairs* 213, 213–4.

importance to any inquiry into how internationally recognised human rights feature in Australian lawmaking processes.[68]

PARLIAMENTARY JOINT COMMITTEE ON HUMAN RIGHTS

As soon as it was introduced into the House of Representatives, the Religious Discrimination Bills package was referred to the Parliamentary Joint Committee on Human Rights (PJCHR) for inquiry and report. Under the *Human Rights (Parliamentary Scrutiny) Act 2011* ('*Parliamentary Scrutiny Act*') the PJCHR must examine Acts, Bills, and legislative instruments for compatibility with human rights and inquire into any matter relating to human rights which is referred to it by the Attorney-General.[69] The PJCHR is a *joint* committee, with members from both the House of Representatives and the Senate, with a government Chair with a casting vote.[70] The "human rights" referred to in the *Parliamentary Scrutiny Act* are those rights listed in seven core human rights conventions to which Australia is a party.[71]

Usually, the PJCHR sets out its concerns with respect to a bill in correspondence to the proponent Minister and allows the Minister to respond *before* the PJCHR tables its report. This "behind-closed-doors" exchange of correspondence between the committee and the proponent of the bill is seen by some as central to the human rights "dialogue" the PJCHR is tasked with creating.[72] However, unless proponent Ministers respond swiftly to the PJCHR's correspondence, this approach can leave the Parliament without the benefit of the PJCHR's analysis of a bill during the critical second reading stage.[73]

68 Laura Grenfell and Sarah Moulds, 'The Role of Committees in Rights Protection in Federal and State Parliaments in Australia' (2018) 41(1) *University of New South Wales Law Journal* 40.

69 *Human Rights (Parliamentary Scrutiny) Act 2011* (Cth) ss 4, 7 ('*Parliamentary Scrutiny Act*').

70 Ibid s 5.

71 Ibid s 3. These international treaties are: *International Convention on the Elimination of All Forms of Racial Discrimination*, *International Covenant on Economic, Social and Cultural Rights*, *International Covenant on Civil and Political Rights*, *Convention on the Elimination of All Forms of Discrimination against Women*, *Convention Against Torture and Other Cruel, Inhuman or Degrading Treatment or Punishment*, *Convention on the Rights of the Child*, *Convention on the Rights of Persons with Disabilities*.

72 See, eg, Parliamentary Joint Committee on Human Rights, Parliament of Australia, *Chair's Tabling Statement* (2016).

73 See, eg, Shawn Rajanayagam, 'Does Parliament Do Enough? Evaluating Statements of Compatibility under the Human Rights (Parliamentary Scrutiny) Act' (2015) 38(3) *University of New South Wales Law Journal* 1046; Adam Fletcher, *Australia's Human Rights Scrutiny Regime: Democratic Masterstroke or Mere Window Dressing?* (Melbourne University Press, 2018); Lisa Burton Crawford, 'The Human Rights (Parliamentary Scrutiny) Act 2011 (Cth): A Failed Human Rights Experiment?' in Matthew Groves, Janina Boughey and Dan Meagher (eds), *The Legal Protection of Rights in Australia* (Hart Publishing, 2019) 14.

Sometimes, the PJCHR will conduct public inquiries prior to issuing its report on a matter referred to it by the Parliament.[74] This is what happened with respect to the Religious Discrimination Bills package, which was referred to the PJCHR by the Attorney-General for inquiry and report by 4 February 2022. A public call for submissions was made and the PJCHR also invited 146 relevant stakeholders to make a submission.[75] The PJCHR also conducted an online survey comprised of ten questions relating to specific issues arising from the Bill. Survey participants could select "Yes" or "No" and provide further information to support their view. The PJCHR described the survey as follows in its report:

> [T]he committee received 48,107 responses. 39,808 participants chose to respond to the question of whether they supported the current version of the bill, of which 7,239 respondents (18.18 per cent) indicated that they did not support the bill and 32,569 (81.82 per cent) indicated support for the bill. … It is noted that some submitters questioned the accuracy of the survey. The most common criticism was that the wording of the questions in the survey swayed participants towards one answer over another. Further, some groups conducted their own survey or focus groups on the bill. For example, Equality Australia organised 'The People's Submission', which was signed by 6,108+ individuals and which contained a statement opposing the bill and set out a selection of personal stories and opinions.[76]

The PJCHR also held three public hearings in Canberra involving witnesses from a range of religious organisations, peak bodies and community groups, academics, legal experts, and the Attorney-General's Department.[77]

Despite the strong findings of the online survey, when reporting on the Religious Discrimination Bills package, the majority of the PJCHR concluded that:

> [t]he religious discrimination legislative package is, on the whole, a sensible and balanced approach to protect the right to freedom of religion. It reflects a tolerant and inclusive society that understands the importance of faith to a pluralist democracy, but does not seek to impose those beliefs on, or injure, others. The bills operate as a shield to protect those who genuinely, and in good faith, live their lives according to their religion, from being discriminated against on this basis. The committee considers

74 *Parliamentary Scrutiny Act* (n 68) s 7(c).

75 Parliamentary Joint Committee on Human Rights, Parliament of Australia, *Inquiry into Religious Discrimination Bill and Related Bills* (4 February 2022) [1.12] ('*PJCHR Report*').

76 Ibid [1.14] See also Appendix 4.

77 Ibid Appendix 2.

the bills provide adequate and appropriate safeguards to ensure that any limitation on rights are reasonable, necessary and proportionate.[78]

In making this finding, the PJCHR also noted that there are "a wide range of views on this important and difficult topic", and considered it important to "continue the conversation with the Australian people as to how to balance these rights".[79] The PJCHR also made a number of specific recommendations for amendments to the *Religious Discrimination Bill 2021*, including changes designed to narrow the scope of the proposed exemptions,[80] changes to tighten criteria relating to the exercise of delegated power,[81] and suggested additional information be included in explanatory material accompanying the Bill to clarify the scope of key provisions, including the "statement of belief" provision in clause 12.[82] Additional comments were provided by the Australian Labour members, and a dissenting report was issued by the Australian Greens, highlighting the strong opposition to key aspects of the Bills package as indicated in submissions and evidence provided to the PJCHR, and via the survey.

SENATE SCRUTINY OF BILLS COMMITTEE

The Religious Discrimination Bills package was also considered by the Senate Standing Committee on the Scrutiny of Bills (SSCSB). The SSCSB comprises six Senators, three nominated by the government and three members nominated by the opposition in consultation with any minor parties or independent

78 Ibid x and xi.
79 Ibid xii.
80 See, eg, ibid Recommendation 1, [3.88] which recommended that clause 14 be amended to require that in determining if a condition, requirement or practice imposed on a person resulted in indirect discrimination, the person who imposes, or proposes to impose, the condition, requirement or practice has the burden of proving it was reasonable.
81 See, eg, ibid Recommendation 4, [3.91] which recommended that Division 4 of Part 4 be amended to include a provision that the Australian Human Rights Commission and Attorney-General, in exercising powers under clauses 44 and 47, must include with the explanatory materials accompanying the instrument the following information: the Commission or Attorney-General's findings on material questions of facts in relation to the decision; the evidence on which those findings were based; the reasons for the decision and the fact that an application may be made to the Administrative Appeal Tribunal for a review of the decision.
82 See, e.g., ibid Recommendation 9, [6.135] which suggested that the government consider providing further explanation and examples with respect to clause 12 in the explanatory memorandum accompanying the *Religious Discrimination Bill 2021*, to provide greater clarity about what sort of statements or actions may, or may not, be considered to not constitute discrimination. Recommendation 3. Also including a legislative note in the *Religious Discrimination Bill 2021* that states that reasonable management action conducted within a reasonable manner will not constitute unlawful discrimination, and provide examples in the explanatory memorandum of the type of action that would likely constitute reasonable management action.

senators.[83] The SSCSB has a non-government Chair that enjoys a casting vote.[84] The SSCSB has a specific mandate to scrutinise every bill introduced into Parliament and consider whether bills or acts:

- trespass unduly on personal rights and liberties;
- make rights, liberties, or obligations unduly dependent upon insufficiently defined administrative powers;
- make rights, liberties, or obligations unduly dependent upon non-reviewable decisions;
- inappropriately delegate legislative powers; or
- insufficiently subject the exercise of legislative power to parliamentary scrutiny.

Like the PJCHR, the SSCSB employs a "dialogue model" in which the committee and ministers exchange formal correspondence which is then published in the committee's Digests and Reports.[85] This process occurred with respect to the Religious Discrimination Bills package, where the Committee "requested the Attorney-General's advice" on a number of specific questions, including why certain key aspects of the new laws, such as requirements for certain policies to be published by religious schools and the power to override certain state and territory laws, had been left to delegated legislation.[86] The Attorney-General responded by noting that the government had moved amendments to the *Religious Discrimination Bill 2021* to provide further clarity regarding what is required to be included in a publicly available policy and to ensure that the requirements for publicly available policies are consistent throughout the Bill.[87]

In its second Scrutiny Digest for 2022, the SSCSB welcomed the government amendments which set out further detail within the Bill as to what is required to be included within a publicly available policy and made no further comment on this matter, but continued to raise concerns about the extent to which the *Religious Discrimination Bill* left significant matters to delegated legislation, including the question of overriding state or territory laws in

83 Senate, Parliament of Australia, *Standing Order* 24 (amended 27 November 2019, 16 June 2021: with effect from 1 July 2021).

84 Senate Standing Committee for Scrutiny of Bills, Parliament of Australia, *Inquiry into the Future Direction and Role of the Scrutiny of Bills Committee* (2012) [2.15].

85 See, eg, Barney Cooney, 'Ten Years of Scrutiny' (Seminar to mark the tenth anniversary of the Senate Standing Committee for the Scrutiny of Bills, Canberra, 25 November 1991); Senate Standing Committee for Scrutiny of Bills, Parliament of Australia, *Inquiry into the Future Direction and Role of the Scrutiny of Bills Committee* (2012).

86 Senate Standing Committee for the Scrutiny of Bills, Parliament of Australia, *Scrutiny Digest No 18 of 2021* (1 December 2021).

87 See Senate Standing Committee for the Scrutiny of Bills, Parliament of Australia, *Scrutiny Digest No 2 of 2022* (18 March 2022) 102–108.

relation to employment by religious educational institutions and statements of belief.[88] The SSCSB also continued to raise concerns about the making of temporary exemptions to the general prohibition on religious discrimination and the scope of the minister's power to vary or revoke a temporary exemption.[89]

SENATE STANDING COMMITTEES ON LEGAL AND CONSTITUTIONAL AFFAIRS

When the Religious Discrimination Bills package was introduced into the Senate, it was scrutinised by the Senate Legal and Constitutional Affairs Legislation Committee (LCA Legislation Committee)[90] which has a government chair with a casting vote, along with five other members, at least one of which is required to be an independent or chosen by a minority party.[91] Other Senators can be appointed to the LCA Legislation Committee as substitutes for existing committee members or as "participating members" for particular inquiries.[92]

The LCA Legislation Committee has powers to conduct public inquiries into the bills referred to it by the Senate,[93] and can call for written submissions through media release or by directly approaching potentially interested parties to make submissions or appear to give oral evidence.[94] After the inquiry process is complete, the LCA Legislation Committee prepares a report to be tabled in the Senate, typically containing specific recommendations for amendments to the bill, as well as an overview of the key issues raised during the inquiry. The LCA Legislation Committee's reports regularly include dissenting or additional comments by opposition or minor party committee members.

88 Senate Standing Committee for the Scrutiny of Bills, Parliament of Australia, *Scrutiny Digest No 2 of 2022* (18 March 2022) 105, [2.117].
89 Senate Standing Committee for the Scrutiny of Bills, Parliament of Australia, *Scrutiny Digest No 2 of 2022* (18 March 2022) 107, [2.125].
90 Senate, Parliament of Australia, *Senate Standing Orders* 25 (1) (last amended 19 November 2002). Both LCA Committees have six members and contain at least one member nominated by minority parties and/or independent senators, *Senate Standing Orders* 25(5).
91 Senate, Parliament of Australia, *Senate Standing Orders* 25 (1) (last amended 19 November 2002) (10).
92 Senate, Parliament of Australia, *Senate Standing Orders* 25(7) (last amended 19 November 2002). The LCA Legislation Committee is responsible for consideration of bills referred to it by the Senate, estimates processes and departmental matters. The LCA References Committee deals with thematic or issues-based references from the Senate, which since 2008 generally do not include consideration of the provisions of particular bills. Senate, Parliament of Australia, *Senate Standing Orders* 25(2) (last amended 19 November 2002). Both LCA Committees receive guidance from the Senate about the focus of its inquiry and reporting times. This means that, in practice, it is the Senate Standing Committee for the Selection of Bills that determines the workload of the LCA Legislation Committee. Paxman (n 14) 76–8.
93 Senate, Parliament of Australia, *Senate Standing Orders* 25(1) (last amended 19 November 2002); Odgers (n 15) 491–3.
94 Sometimes described as the 'usual suspects', see, eg, Anthony Marinac, 'The Usual Suspects? Civil Society and Senate Committees' (Paper submitted for the Senate Baker Prize, 2003).

As soon as the Religious Discrimination Bills package was introduced into the Senate, it was referred to the LCA Legislation Committee for inquiry and report. The LCA Legislation Committee received 221 submissions, and five form letters (signed by a total of around 1,300 people) and held two public hearings in Canberra in January 2022.[95] Its detailed report included consideration of: the administrative details of the inquiry, background to the inquiry and the key provisions of the Bills; the need for a legal mechanism to protect against religious discrimination; issues pertaining to human rights and discrimination and the constitutionality of the Bills and their jurisdictional implications. The majority of the Committee recommended that the Bills be passed, subject to amending clauses 11 and 12 of the Bill which sought to "override" state and territory anti-discrimination laws to provide legal protections for those making "statements of belief". The majority recommended preserving the effect of these provisions, but amendment them to ensure that they were constitutionally sound.[96]

Step 2: What Types of Engagement Strategies Were Used?

Having gained a sense of the context in which the inquiries into the Religious Discrimination Bills package took place, the next step is to look carefully at the tools and strategies employed by those committees with reference to the factors indicating effective engagement identified in Table 12.2.

This analysis suggests that the engagement strategies undertaken by the parliamentary committees in the Australian case study were effective in terms of generating high rates of participation, and ensured a range of established religious organisations were included as witnesses in oral hearings. However, there is less evidence to suggest that these strategies included meaningful "two-way" engagement between submission makers and committee members, outside of a limited range of "usual suspects" whose suggestions for improvements to the Bill were actively considered and discussed in detail in committee reports. More novel engagement strategies, including the online survey, generated high levels of participation but did not appear to have a strong influence on positions adopted by committee members, which remained largely split along party-political lines.

95 LCA Legislation Committee Report, Appendix 1.

96 Additional comments were made by Australian Labor Members and Senate Andrew Bragg, and a Dissenting Report was provided by the Australian Greens, see LCA Legislation Committee Report, 99–133.

Table 12.2 Application of Leston-Bandeira's Factors to Religious Discrimination Bills

Nature of the Engagement Strategy or Strategies Employed	*Call for Written Submissions (LCA Legislation Committee + PJCHR)* *Invitation to Provide Written Submissions (LCA Legislation Committee + PJCHR)* *Invitation to Provide Oral Evidence Before the Committee at Public Hearings (LCA Legislation Committee + PJCHR)* *Public, Electronic Survey with Ten Questions (PJCHR only)*	
Factor	*Indicator*	*Evidence*
Accessibility	Resources in multiple languages, styles, or formats	Summary information and participation instructions provided on committee websites in plain English Websites included link to accessible online content No evidence of materials prepared for non-English-speaking participants
	Different modes of communication with different audiences	*Some evidence* Media release issued across various mediums (including social media) Inquiry "home page" was set up on committee website with links to the bill and other relevant material including the Explanatory Memorandum to the bill and the committee's terms of reference Proactive invitations issued to some potential submission makers Online survey provided for individuals to complete (PJCHR only)
Reach of the audience	Rates of participation	*Strong evidence* 221 submissions received, plus five form letters (engaging around 1,300 individuals) 56 witnesses called to give evidence across 2 days of hearings (LCA Legislation Committee) 205 submissions received, 48,107 responses to online survey, 3 public hearings held (PJCHR)
	Geographical diversity	*Some evidence* Submissions received from each Australian state and territory (capital city dominant), and some regional centres Witnesses from each Australian state and territory (capital city focused) Hearings conducted in person in Canberra but also via video conference

(*Continued*)

Table 12.2 (Continued)

Nature of the Engagement Strategy or Strategies Employed	*Call for Written Submissions (LCA Legislation Committee + PJCHR)* *Invitation to Provide Written Submissions (LCA Legislation Committee + PJCHR)* *Invitation to Provide Oral Evidence Before the Committee at Public Hearings (LCA Legislation Committee + PJCHR)* *Public, Electronic Survey with Ten Questions (PJCHR only)*	
Factor	*Indicator*	*Evidence*
Diversity of the audience	Participation beyond the "usual suspects"	*Limited evidence* Vast majority of submission makers and witnesses were from established religious organisations/institutions, well-resourced community organisations and peak bodies representing particular professions or service provision sectors Academics with legal backgrounds featured strongly in committee reports and recommendations
	Explicit encouragement for diverse groups to participate	*Some evidence* Proactive invitations issued to some potential submission makers Diversity of religious and non-religious groups reflected in witnesses providing evidence at hearings Online survey provided for individuals to complete (PJCHR only) Video conferencing available for oral hearings
Existing "divides"	Practical barriers to diverse participation are identified and explicitly addressed	*Some evidence* General information provided via the "committees" website Online survey provided for individuals to complete (PJCHR only) Video conferencing available for oral hearings for those in remote locations "Form" letters accepted (although distinguished from "substantive" submissions) Diversity of religious and non-religious groups reflected in invitation to witnesses to provide evidence at hearings

(*Continued*)

Table 12.2 (Continued)

Nature of the Engagement Strategy or Strategies Employed	*Call for Written Submissions (LCA Legislation Committee + PJCHR)* *Invitation to Provide Written Submissions (LCA Legislation Committee + PJCHR)* *Invitation to Provide Oral Evidence Before the Committee at Public Hearings (LCA Legislation Committee + PJCHR)* *Public, Electronic Survey with Ten Questions (PJCHR only)*	
Factor	*Indicator*	*Evidence*
Diverse communication techniques	Evidence of multiple communication techniques eg text, audio, video, visual, infographics	*Some evidence* Summary information and participation instructions provided on committee websites in plain English Websites included link to accessible online content Live broadcast of oral hearings Social media posts provided about upcoming hearings "Track this committee's" email updates available No evidence of materials prepared for non-English speaking participants
Issue-led rather than process-led	Evidence of procedural innovation or flexibility in response to issue-orientated engagement	*Some evidence* Proactive invitations issued to some potential submission makers Diversity of religious and non-religious groups reflected in invitation to witnesses to provide evidence at hearings Online survey provided for individuals to complete (PJCHR only) Video conferencing available for oral hearings
Listening rather than broadcasting	Evidence of two-way communication where institutional actors respond to ideas or suggestions by other participants	*Some evidence* Transcripts of committee proceedings suggest exchange of positions between members and submission makers, and opportunities for submission makers to comment on other submission maker's positions PJCHR Report includes outcomes of survey and provides some reflections on criticisms of survey Both PJCHR Report and LCA Committee Report include reference to submissions from wide range of submission makers

(*Continued*)

Table 12.2 (Continued)

Nature of the Engagement Strategy or Strategies Employed	*Call for Written Submissions (LCA Legislation Committee + PJCHR)* *Invitation to Provide Written Submissions (LCA Legislation Committee + PJCHR)* *Invitation to Provide Oral Evidence Before the Committee at Public Hearings (LCA Legislation Committee + PJCHR)* *Public, Electronic Survey with Ten Questions (PJCHR only)*	
Factor	*Indicator*	*Evidence*
	Opportunity to share lived experience	*Some evidence* Lived experience perspectives largely conveyed through written submissions, predominantly in the form of written submissions authored by religious organisations or community organisations Online survey provided some opportunity for respondents to include accounts of person experiences
	Appropriate acknowledgement of inputs submitted	*Strong evidence* Email acknowledgement at time of submission Submission makers notified of tabling/ publication of committee report Witnesses thanked during oral hearings Submission makers acknowledged in text of Committee report and in some parliamentary debates
Closing the feedback loop	Evidence of clear communication with participations about how their inputs informed parliamentary business	*Some evidence* General information provided via the committee's website More specific information provided to witnesses via correspondence ahead of hearings Some indication of how the information provided by submission makers informed the development of recommendations in committee reports
	Evidence that someone did listen, even if not to accommodate the exact demands made	*Some evidence – particularly for those participating in oral hearings* Suggestions/recommendations made by some submission makers extensively acknowledged and accepted Submission makers acknowledged in text of committee report and in some parliamentary debates

(*Continued*)

Table 12.2 (Continued)

Nature of the Engagement Strategy or Strategies Employed	*Call for Written Submissions (LCA Legislation Committee + PJCHR)* *Invitation to Provide Written Submissions (LCA Legislation Committee + PJCHR)* *Invitation to Provide Oral Evidence Before the Committee at Public Hearings (LCA Legislation Committee + PJCHR)* *Public, Electronic Survey with Ten Questions (PJCHR only)*	
Factor	*Indicator*	*Evidence*
Linking engagement with parliamentary business	Evidence of involvement or acknowledgement by diverse range of Members of Parliament	*Strong evidence* In addition to active participation by PJCHR and LCA Legislation Committee members, there was also engagement in the LCA Legislation Committee's inquiry by "participating members" (Senators Andrew Bragg and Deborah O'Neill)
	Evidence that participant views are formally and actively linked to the process of considering the bill	*Some evidence* Suggestions/recommendations made by some submission makers extensively acknowledged and accepted (eg Professor Twomey and Professor Aroney) Submission makers acknowledged in text of Committee report and in some parliamentary debates
Evaluation and reporting of activities	Evidence of any internal reflection or reporting on the engagement activity	*Limited evidence* PJCHR provided Annual Report which included reflection on this inquiry (eg PJCHR, Annual Report 2022, pp. 22–23)

Step 3: The Impact of These Engagement Techniques on the Shape of the Proposed Laws

Although it received lengthy debate in the House of Representatives, the Religious Discrimination Bills package was never passed by the Australian Parliament. It lapsed with the proroguing of the 46th Parliament on 25 July 2022 and the political discourse associated with the Bills package became publicly associated with the demise of the Morrison Coalition Government at the 2022 federal election. Despite this outcome, the deliberative work of the committees described previously had a discernible impact on content of the Bills and the relevant accompanying explanatory materials. For example, the recommendations made by the LCA Legislation Committee and PJCHR are reflected in the amendments that were moved by the shadow Attorney-General Mark Dreyfus MP, some of which were later reflected in the 22 amendments proposed by the government that were agreed to in the House of Representatives. The work of the SSCSB and the PJCHR also had an impact on the content of the Revised Explanatory Memorandum that was introduced to accompany the amended Religious Discrimination Bills package.[97]

The LCA Legislation Committee and the PJCHR were also specifically referred to in 31 of the 64 Second Reading Speeches made in the House of Representatives with respect to the Religious Discrimination Bills package, with many other speeches referring to the organisations or individuals that provided evidence to these committees during public hearings.[98] The work of parliamentary committees was also referred to in 258 media reports published during the period 25 November 2021 to 25 July 2022[99] and many more media reports included reference to the evidence given by witnesses and submission makers to the parliamentary committees tasked with inquiring into the bill,[100] particularly the voices of the "usual suspects" (legal academics, peak representative bodies, and established religious institutions), who already enjoyed political status vis-a-vis the key political party groupings of the day.'

When taken together, this suggests that the work of the parliamentary committees *did influence* the shape of the Religious Discrimination Bills package and the way these laws were debated. However, this influence appeared to *reinforce* rather than *challenge* the predominant political positioning on the Bills package that was already unfolding in Australia. As will be discussed further, while there is some evidence that the work of parliamentary committees did transcend these binary political positions (for example, by the SSCSB challenging the scope of delegated power provided to Ministers or the PJCHR documenting the accounts of religious minorities who experience discrimination on religious grounds), these aspects of the committee experience were largely "drowned out" by louder voices inside and outside Parliament.

97 Parliamentary Joint Committee on Human Rights, Parliament of Australia, *Annual Report 2021–2022* (2022).

98 Ibid [3.19].

99 The database used for this purpose was the Australia/New Zealand Reference Centre accessed through the University of Adelaide Library. This database is supported ProQuest and provides access to Australian and New Zealand newspapers, magazines, and radio and television transcripts. The time period set for these searches was 25 November 2021 to 25 July 2022, search terms used were 'religious discrimination bill' AND 'committee'.

100 See, eg, Melissa Coade, 'Religious Discrimination Bill Scratched for Now', *The Mandarin*, 11 February 2022; Kishor Napier-Raman, 'The Horror, the Horror: Weakened Morrison Faces Insurrection as Parliament Returns', *Crikey*, 7 February 2022; Jeanene Williams, 'Hasluck Candidate Jeanene Williams Dismayed at Religious Discrimination Report', *Out in Perth*, 5 February 2022; Luke Beck, 'As Parliament Returns for 2022, the Religious Discrimination Bill Is Still an Unholy Mess', *The Conversation*, 7 February 2022; Paul Karp, 'Labor Offers Conditional Backing to Coalition's Religious Discrimination Bill', *The Guardian*, 4 February 2022.

Step 4: Reflecting on the Extent to which These Inquiries Provide an Effective Forum for Deliberating Human Rights Issues Arising from Proposed Legislation

There are two ways to reflect on the extent to which these Australian parliamentary inquiries provide an effective forum for deliberating human rights issues in the context of the Religious Discrimination Bills package. On the one hand, the work of the three parliamentary committees involved in this case study illustrates the rights-enhancing potential of the complex system of parliamentary committees that exists at the federal level in Australia.[101] The contrasting but complementary nature of their respective functions and powers means that their combined efforts can give rise to relatively robust scrutiny of human rights concerns. For example, although SSCSB did not facilitate an effective deliberative forum for rights debate, the dialogue the SSCSB created with the Attorney-General elicited important new information and justifications for limiting freedom of religious belief that was utilised by other committees in the system. The SSCSB's "technical" approach to the application of rights-based criteria also provided a consistent reasoning structure for the PJCHR and the LCA Legislation Committee to utilise when seeking to process and prioritise the range of views it received into their reports on the package of Bills. Both the PJCHR and the LCA Legislation Committee included detailed references to the views of participants in their inquiries. This includes representatives from a broad range of organised religions in Australia (including religious minorities), as well as non-religious bodies and advocacy groups representing other impacted communities, including LGBTQIA+ communities.[102]

101 Moulds (n 4).

102 For example, the LCA Legislation Committee referred to the following submitters in the text of its report: Australian Catholic Bishops Conference (ACBC) [2.9]; Christian Schools Australia and Adventist Schools Australia [2.10]; Executive Council of Australian Jewry (ECAJ) [2.11], Presbyterian Church of Victoria (PCV) [2.12]; Institute for Civil Society [2.13]; Australian Muslim Advocacy Network (AMAN) [2.14]; Professor Nicholas Aroney, Professor of Constitutional Law at the University of Queensland and member of the Expert Panel on Religious Freedom [2.15]; PM Glynn Institute at the Australian Catholic University [2.19]; Australian Association of Christian Schools (AACS) [2.20]; Australian Christian Churches (ACC) [2.22]; Presbyterian Church of Australia (PCA) [2.23]; National Catholic Education Commission (NCEC) [2.24]; Australian Christian Lobby (ACL) [2.25]; Australian National Imams Council (ANIC) [2.26]; Australia/Israel Jewish Affairs Council (AIJAC) [2.27]; Dr Alex Deagon [2.28]; Dr Denis Dragovic [2.29]; Hillside Christian College [2.35]; Catholic Education Tasmania [2.39]; Dr Renae Barker [2.41]; Australian Christian Higher Education Alliance [2.42]; Lutheran Education Australia [2.48]; Associate Professor Mark Fowler [2.57]; Anglican Church Diocese of Sydney [2.71]; Bishop Mark Edwards [2.85]; Human Rights Law Alliance (HRLA) [3.12]; Adventist Schools Australia [3.14]; Karina Okotel, a law lecturer [3.15]; Australian Human Rights Commission [3.17]; Australian Discrimination Law Experts Group [3.18]; Professor Anne Twomey [3.24]; Hon Selena Uibo, Attorney-General and Minister for Justice in the Northern Territory Legislative Assembly [3.25]; Anglican Church of Australia, [3.26]; Equality Australia [3.27]; PIAC [3.32]; Victorian Government [3.31]; Equality Tasmania [3.33]; Venerable Akaliko, Board

On the other hand, is it possible to be more cynical about the extent to which these parliamentary committee inquiries were able to withstand the external political pressures that dominated the broader public discourse on the Religious Discrimination Bills package? As Poulos and Barker have explained,[103] this broader discourse was generally *not* focused on how to ensure the proposed new laws protected the rights of vulnerable religious minorities who had experienced comparatively high rates of discrimination, abuse, and exclusion.[104] Instead, this broader discourse morphed into what some have described as "culture wars" involving proponents of unlimited (or at least almost unlimited) free speech on the one side,[105] and those calling for increased protections for the rights of other minority groups, such as LGBITQ+ communities, and particularly transgender or gender diverse children and teachers, on the other.[106] As Barker observes:

> During the Second Reading debate on the failed *Religious Discrimination Bill* Greens party leader Adam Bandt argued 'no child in this country should have to wake up to headlines that say they are being traded off as political collateral ...' (Bandt 2022). Yet, this is exactly what has happened. As Poulos (2019) has observed, debate about freedom of religion in Australia has been framed as a clash of rights. This clash is particularly evident when the role and place of children in these debates are considered. The debate has descended, as Claydon (2022) noted, into a choice between 'protecting' children and [freedom of religious belief]. Yet, as Aly (2022) argued, equality should mean equality for all otherwise '[i]t's like having two children but only loving one of them'.[107]

Member, Buddhist Council of New South Wales [3.41]; Venerable Mettaji of the Australian Sangha Association [3.43]; Unions Tasmania [3.54]; Australian Industry Group (Ai Group) and the Australian Chamber of Commerce and Industry (ACCI) [3.55]; Australian Council of Trade Unions (ACTU) [3.56]; Professor Croucher [3.68]; Australian Lawyers Alliance [4.9]; Law Council of Australia [4.10]; and Wilberforce Foundation, [4.113].

103 Poulos, 'Three Discourses of Religious Freedom' (n 6); Barker, 'The Place of the Child' (n 6).

104 See Australian Human Rights Commission (AHRC), *Submission* 32, 1, 10–11.

105 See, eg, Peta Credlin, 'Free Speech Isn't Free' and Australians are 'Failing to Defend It' *Herald Sun, Melbourne* (online), 22 September 2020.

106 See, eg, Nicola Heath, 'Parents and Transgender Teachers React to Religious Discrimination Bill Debate' *ABC Radio National*, Broadcast and Online, 11 Feb 2022 at 5:46am, updated Fri 11 Feb 2022 at 3:12pm.

107 Barker, 'The Place of the Child' (n 6) 93, referring to: Commonwealth, *Parliamentary Debates*, House of Representatives, 9 February 2022, 142 (Adam Bandt); Elenie Poulos, 'Constructing the Problem of Religious Freedom: An Analysis of Australian Government Inquires into Religious Freedom (2019) 10 *Religions* 583; Commonwealth, *Parliamentary Debates*, House of Representatives, 9 February 2022, 251 (Sharon Claydon); Commonwealth, *Parliamentary Debates*, House of Representatives, 9 February 2022, 196 (Anne Aly).

While these themes were reflected in many submissions received by the parliamentary committees, and dominated second reading speeches made in the House of Representatives, it is not clear that they completely distracted the committees from their rights scrutiny tasks. For example, the transcripts and reports of both the PJCHR and the LCA Legislation Committee suggest that those involved in the preparation of the final reports were genuine in their attempts to honour the input provided by those with lived experience of discrimination on religious (and non-religious) grounds and set out these views with reference to human rights concepts.[108] The reports of the committees also reveal a strong focus on improving the technical aspects of the Religious Discrimination Bills package, including ensuring the constitutionality of the Bills. To this end, the written and oral submissions made by legal experts, in particular Professor Anne Twomey and Professor Aroney, dominated the recommendations made by the LCA Legislation Committee. This may not be surprising given the fact that Government Senator the Hon Sarah Henderson was Chair of the LCA Legislation Committee and had a strong interest in ensuring the constitutionality, and enactment, of the Bill. This can be contrasted with the approach taken by the SSCSB (non-government Chair) and PJCHR, which had a stronger focus on the scope of power delegated to Ministers and other members of the executive under the Religious Discrimination Bills package, including the potential for these powers to be used to broader exceptions to the provisions designed to prohibit religious discrimination.

When taken together, this case study suggests that the Australian parliamentary committee system has the *potential* to facilitate an effective forum for deliberating human rights issues, including freedom of religious belief, but remains vulnerable to external discourses on human rights, particularly when those discourses distort internationally recognised principles and concepts by forcing those who seek to engage in public debate into politically-orientated binaries. The fate of the Religious Discrimination Bills package suggests that in the end, broader political forced proved too powerful for meaningful deliberation to occur. As will be discussed further, the Scottish experience may offer some insights into how to guard against this vulnerability in the future.

B Scottish Case Study: Hate Crime and Public Order (Scotland) Bill

The *Hate Crime and Public Order (Scotland) Bill* ('*Hate Crime Bill*') was introduced into the Scottish Parliament on 23 April 2020 by the Cabinet Secretary for Justice, Humza Yousaf MSP. The Bill aimed to:

- consolidate existing hate crime legislation into one statute and modernise and extend current legislation by adding age as a characteristic in new provisions for aggravation of offences by prejudice;

108 LCA Legislation Committee Report [1.5].

- create new offences relating to stirring up hatred that apply to characteristics including age, disability, race, religion, sexual orientation, transgender identity, or variations in sex characteristics;
- update the definition of transgender identity including removing the term "intersexuality" and creating a separate category for variations in sex characteristics; and
- include a power to enable the characteristic of sex to be added at a later date.

The Bill also sought to abolish the common law offence of blasphemy.[109] The *Hate Crimes Bill* was passed on 11 March 2021[110] and became law on 23 April 2021.

Step 1: Institutional Context

Like the Australian case study, the pre-enactment history of the *Hate Crime Bill* is relevant to evaluating the parliamentary committees involved in scrutinising its provisions. The Bill's origins trace back to an independent review conducted by Lord Bracadale into hate crime legislation in Scotland in 2017.[111] In response to the publication of Lord Bracadale's report, the Scottish Government agreed to consolidate existing hate crime legislation into one single statute and commenced the work of consulting Scottish people about its scope.[112] The consultation also sought views on whether sectarianism should be included within this Bill and, if so, how sectarianism would be defined.[113]

109 Explanatory Notes, Hate Crime and Public Order (Scotland) Bill 2020, 2. https://www.parliament.scot/-/media/files/legislation/bills/current-bills/hate-crime-and-public-order-scotland-bill/introduced/explanatory-notes-hate-crime-and-public-order-scotland-bill.pdf. This document relates to the Hate Crime and Public Order (Scotland) Bill (SP Bill 67) as introduced in the Scottish Parliament on 23 April 2020.

110 The Bill was passed with 82 votes in favour, 32 votes against, and 4 abstentions. Parliament of Scotland, *Hate Crime and Public Order (Scotland) Bill* (2020) https://www.parliament.scot/bills-and-laws/bills/hate-crime-and-public-order-scotland-bill.

111 Justice Committee, Parliament of Scotland, *Hate Crime and Public Order (Scotland) Bill Stage 1 Report*, (10 December 2020), 9, [32] ('Justice Committee Stage 1 Report').

112 Ibid 9–10. On 14 November 2018 the Cabinet Secretary for Justice and Cabinet Secretary for Communities launched a public consultation on hate crime legislation in Scotland in response to recommendations made by Lord Bracadale, see *Independent Review of Hate Crime Legislation in Scotland: Final Report*, Scottish Government, 31 May 2018 https://www.gov.scot/publications/independent-review-hate-crime-legislation-scotland-final-report/.

113 Ibid 9, [41]. In parallel to Lord Bracadale's work, the Working Group on Defining Sectarianism in Scots Law had been developing its report *Final Report of the Working Group on Defining Sectarianism in Scots Law*, Scottish Government, November 2018 https://www.parliament.scot/-/media/files/legislation/bills/current-bills/hate-crime-and-public-order-scotland-bill/introduced/policy-memorandum-hate-crime-and-public-order-scotland-bill.pdf.

The consultation attracted 1,051 written responses from individuals and 108 from organisations, including faith groups and other organisations.[114] "Roadshows" were also held across Scotland involving around 400 individuals and organisations.[115] These public discussions took place against a backdrop of sustained media interest in the public comments of celebrity figures in the UK, including JK Rowling, the renowned author of the Harry Potter series, who questioned the validity of transgender identities and the importance of recognising gender diversity.[116] Concerns were also raised about the extent to which the proposals would unjustifiably infringe upon freedom of speech and freedom of religious belief in Scotland.[117]

These internationally protected human rights are also protected under domestic law in Scotland, due to its status as one of the "devolved" parliaments within the UK, and the modern Scottish Parliament has important historical origins which help to illustrate the institutional context in which it approaches the conduct of parliamentary committee inquiries into proposed laws engaging human rights, including freedom of religious belief.

The origins of the Scottish Parliament can be traced to the historic events surrounding the *Act of Union* in 1707,[118] and more recently the demand for a Scottish Parliament that resurfaced in the late 20th century, driven by a resurgence of Scottish nationalism and a desire for greater autonomy.[119] Following decades of unsuccessful attempts to review the structures of the UK Constitution and advance devolution,[120] the *Scotland Act 1998* was passed by the UK Parliament, and on 1 July 1999, the Scottish Parliament was officially reconvened. The *Scotland Act 1998* devolved certain legislative powers to the Scottish Parliament, granting it authority to legislate in areas such as health, education, and justice, and confirming that Scotland remains bound by the European Convention on Human Rights (ECHR), which is given domestic effect through the *Human Rights Act 1998* and the *Equality Act 2010*, both of which include specific protections prohibiting religious discrimination and protecting freedom of religious belief.[121]

114 Ibid 9, [41].

115 Ibid.

116 See, eg, Alona Ferber, 'Judith Butler on the Culture Wars, JK Rowling and Living in 'Anti-Intellectual Times'. *New Statesman* (22 September 2020).

117 See, eg, 'Why Is Scotland's Hate Crime Bill so Controversial?' *BBC News Online*, 15 December 2020.

118 For further discussion see T M Devine, *The Scottish Nation: A Modern History* (Penguin UK, 2000).

119 For further discussion see M Lynch, *Scotland: A New History* (Random House, 2002).

120 Parliament of Scotland, *History of the Scottish Parliament: The Path to Devolution* (2020) https://www.parliament.scot/about/history-of-the-scottish-parliament/the-path-to-devolution#topOfNav.

121 For example, the *Equality Act 2010* (UK) s 10 makes it unlawful to discriminate against someone because of religion or belief or because of a lack of religion or belief. The *Human Rights Act 1998* (UK) ss 6 and 13 provides that all public authorities and other bodies car-

Prior to the enactment of the *Scotland Act*, the Secretary of State for Scotland appointed a Consultative Steering Group comprising of major political parties in Scotland and other public groups and interest to develop proposals for how the new Parliament would operate. This Group produced a report entitled, "Shaping Scotland's Parliament" which became a blueprint for the Parliament's initial set of procedural Rules, and emphasised that parliamentary committees would play an important role in the new Parliament.[122] This is reflected in the procedural Rules governing the passage of legislation in the Scottish Parliament, which integrate committee scrutiny and review of proposed laws at key legislative stages (described as Stage 1, Stage 2, and Stage 3 debates on a bill).[123]

The Rules also establish a Parliamentary Bureau which assists in the identification of a "lead committee"[124] to coordinate parliamentary scrutiny of proposed new legislation and work collaboratively with any other committees whose remit may encompass the subject matter of the Bill.[125] The lead committee is usually one of the "all-purpose Committees" which combine the Westminster Select and Standing Committee roles.[126] The membership of these committees is based on proportional representation from each of the elected political parties.[127] The Scottish Parliament also has a "Convenors Group" that provides an informal forum where Committee Conveners can meet to discuss matters of mutual interest and to facilitate liaison between

rying out public functions, such as care services, have to act consistently with the *European Convention on Human Rights*. One of these rights, Article 9, protects freedom of thought, conscience and religion.

122 Parliament of Scotland, *History of the Scottish Parliament: Report of the Consultative Steering Group* (2020) https://www.parliament.scot/-/media/files/history/report_of_the_consultative_steering_group.pdf

123 Parliament of Scotland, *About the Scottish Parliament: Part 2: Stages of Bills – The General Rules* (2020) https://www.parliament.scot/about/how-parliament-works/parliament-rules-and-guidance/guidance-on-public-bills/part-2. See in particular, Rule 9.6.4, and Rule 9.6.3A.

124 Parliament of Scotland, Fact Sheet, *Scottish Parliament Committees: Current Committees, Remits and Membership* (14 July 2023) https://www.parliament.scot/-/media/files/spice/factsheets/parliamentary-business/scottish-parliament-committees-current-committees-remits-and-membership-updated-14-july-23.pdf.

125 Parliament of Scotland, *About the Scottish Parliament: Part 2: Stages of Bills – The General Rules* (2020) https://www.parliament.scot/about/how-parliament-works/parliament-rules-and-guidance/guidance-on-public-bills/part-2. Rule 9.6.1.

126 These Committees are empowered to conduct joint meetings and inquiries and incorporate a reporter (or 'rapporteur') to share with the Committee Convener the responsibility for supervising the progress of deliberations on a particular issue, drawing up the results of deliberations on the topic in question and preparing the Committee's report to the Plenary Chamber. Parliament of Scotland, *About the Scottish Parliament: Part 2: Stages of Bills – The General Rules* (2020) https://www.parliament.scot/about/how-parliament-works/parliament-rules-and-guidance/guidance-on-public-bills/part-2.

127 Parliament of Scotland, *About the Scottish Parliament: Chamber and Committees* (2020) https://www.parliament.scot/chamber-and-committees/committees/about-committees.

the Committees, the Parliamentary Bureau, and the Scottish Parliamentary Corporate Body.[128]

The lead committee generally enjoys broad discretion when it comes to determining how it will fulfil its scrutiny function. It can call for written evidence, as well as adopting a range of other methods of gathering evidence from those who are likely to have an interest in the Bill or be affected by its provisions. The lead committee will normally also take oral evidence from witnesses over a number of meetings. For any government bill, the relevant Minister or junior Minister and Scottish Government officials can also be called to give oral evidence on any matter for which the Scottish Government has general responsibility.[129] In exceptional circumstances, a committee may request the attendance of specific Ministers.[130]

JUSTICE COMMITTEE – LEAD COMMITTEE FOR THE HATE CRIME BILL

The Scottish Parliament's Justice Committee was identified as the "lead committee" for Stage 1 consideration of the *Hate Crimes Bill.*[131] It received an unprecedented number of written submissions, including over 2,000 in its first call for evidence and a further 276 as part of a time-restricted call for views on the proposed freedom of expression amendments. Five hearings were held in October and November 2020, involving witnesses from legal and police bodies, arts and media, faith and non-faith groups, race organisations, women's rights groups, and organisations representing listed hate crime characteristics including race, age, sexual orientation, disability, transgender identity, and

128 Ibid.

129 Such invitations may express a preference for the attendance of a particular Minister or Ministers, but it is for the Scottish Government to decide which Minister (or Ministers) is best placed to attend (according to responsibilities, experience and availability) and to decide whether officials should accompany the Minister(s) also for the purpose of giving oral evidence. Parliament of Scotland, *About the Scottish Parliament: Parliamentary Rules and Guidance: Protocol on the Handling of Committee Business* (2009) https://www.parliament.scot/about/how-parliament-works/parliament-rules-and-guidance/protocol-on-the-handling-of-committee-business.

130 Parliament of Scotland, *About the Scottish Parliament: Parliamentary Rules and Guidance: Protocol on the Handling of Committee Business* (2009) https://www.parliament.scot/about/how-parliament-works/parliament-rules-and-guidance/protocol-on-the-handling-of-committee-business.

131 A motion for a financial resolution in relation to the Bill was lodged in the name of Kate Forbes MSP, Cabinet Secretary for Finance. Under the Scottish Parliament's Rule 9.6.3(a), it is for the lead committee to report to the Parliament on the general principles of the Bill. This means it must take account of views submitted to it by any other committee. The lead committee is also required to report on the Financial Memorandum and Policy Memorandum, which accompany the Bill. The Justice Committee is responsible for considering and reporting on matters falling within the responsibility of the Cabinet Secretary for Justice, and functions of the Lord Advocate other than as head of the systems of criminal prosecution and investigation of deaths in Scotland.

variations in sex characteristics. The Justice Committee also commissioned independent research to assist with its inquiry.[132]

As the lead committee, the Justice Committee was also responsible for considering the work of the Delegated Powers and Law Reform Committee,[133] which reported its views on the Bill on 27 August 2020 and found that each of the delegated powers in the Bill were framed appropriately. The Finance and Constitution Committee also considered the *Hate Crimes Bill* and issued a call for evidence in June 2020. Six written submissions of evidence were received, however, once the Justice Committee was appointed the lead committee on the Bill, the Finance and Constitution Committee agreed to take no further action.

The Justice Committee published its unanimous Stage 1 Report on the *Hate Crimes Bill* on 10 December 2020.[134] It made a number of recommendations to the Scottish Government, including seeking clarification on what should constitute abusive behaviour; whether behaviour within the scope of stirring up offences should be required to have a public element even when taking place in a private dwelling; and whether freedom of expression provisions should be deepened and broadened to ensure compliance with Article 10 of the ECHR.[135] The Scottish Government responded on 14 December 2020,[136] indicating that the government intended to move amendments that addressed a number of the recommendations contained in the Justice Committee's Report.

In its Stage 1 Report, the Justice Committee also referred to concerns expressed by witnesses about the "chilling effect" of the proposed new offences on rights, including freedom of expression and freedom of religious belief, and drew attention to options suggested to the committee including the addition of a more specific reasonableness defence or a general requirement that the Bill be compatible with Articles 9 and 10 of the ECHR. In its response to

132 This was conducted by Professor Chalmers and Professor Leverick of the University of Glasgow to advise on approaches taken to hate crime laws in other jurisdictions. The Committee also considered research undertaken by Dr Hannah Bows of the University of Durham and the Scottish Parliament Information Centre. See Justice Committee Stage 1 Report (n 110) 5.

133 The Delegated Powers and Law Reform Committee normally considers the Delegated Powers Memorandum provided by the member in charge, and may also take evidence from officials and other interested parties. The Committee considers in particular: whether the delegation of powers proposed by the Bill is appropriate or whether any powers concern matters which should properly be the subject only of primary legislation; and if the delegation of powers is appropriate, whether the parliamentary control over exercise of the delegated power proposed in each case is suitable. *Public Bodies Act 2011* (UK), s 9.

134 Justice Committee Stage 1 Report (n 110).

135 Ibid [183]–[184].

136 Scottish Government Response to the Justice Committee's Inquiry into the *Hate Crime and Public Order (Scotland) Bill Stage 1 Report*, (14 December 2020), https://www.parliament.scot/S5_JusticeCommittee/Inquiries/20201214_Hate_Crime_Bill_SGResponse.pdf.

the Stage 1 Report, the Cabinet Secretary noted that he had considered the suggestion of a reasonableness defence but indicated that he did not "think it would be appropriate to place provision of this sort on the face of the Bill".[137] Stage 2 debate on the *Hate Crimes Bill* commenced in February 2021, facilitated by the Justice Committee, which met virtually and made use of virtual voting technology to confirm votes on proposed amendments to the Bill.[138]

In a departure from usual procedure, on 22 February 2021, the Justice Committee convened again to take evidence from a range of witnesses with respect to the amended *Hate Crimes Bill*, before the Stage 3 proceedings. The witnesses appearing before the Committee included the Cabinet Secretary and relevant government officials, as well as a range of community organisations, including faith-based and non-faith based groups.[139] The purpose of the Justice Committee meeting was to consider the proposed free speech amendments to the Bill. As the Convenor of the Committee explained:

> This is an unusual session, in that it is not principally driven by members' questions. We are here to listen rather than to speak, and we want to hear as much as possible from the guests whom we have invited. I reiterate my thanks to them for their time and for all the effort that has been poured in to help the committee to do its job as best as it can, to ensure that Parliament, if it passes the bill, passes the best possible bill.[140]

At the end of this special meeting of the Justice Committee, the Convenor expressed gratitude for all witnesses attending and observed that as a result of

137 Ibid [60].

138 Parliament of Scotland, Delegated Powers and Law Reform Committee, *Hate Crime and Public Order (Scotland) Bill: Stage 2*, (5 March 2021) https://digitalpublications.parliament.scot/Committees/Report/DPLR/2021/3/5/6c52201e-4726-41de-bfdb-7ab3501df64c#Annex-A [12]. Among the amendments made during the Stage 2 debate were the inclusion of revised delegated powers to enable Scottish Ministers to use regulations to add the characteristic of sex to the list of characteristics to the proposed new offence provisions in the Hate Crimes Bill. These amendments were considered to be unproblematic by the Delegated Powers and Law Reform Committee.

139 Parliament of Scotland, *Hate Crime and Public Order (Scotland) Bill: Evidence Taken Before Stage 3* (22 February 2021) https://www.parliament.scot/bills-and-laws/bills/hate-crime-and-public-order-scotland-bill#target3. (referred to as 'Justice Committee, *Evidence Taken Before Stage 3*'). Justice Committee, *Evidence Taken Before Stage 3*. Evidence was provided by Danny Boyle from Black and Ethnic Minority Infrastructure in Scotland; Michael Clancy from the Law Society of Scotland; Eilidh Dickson from Engender; Anthony Horan from the Catholic Parliamentary Office of the Bishops Conference of Scotland; Tim Hopkins from the Equality Network; Lucy Hunter Blackburn from Murray Blackburn Mackenzie; Becky Kaufmann from the Scottish Trans Alliance; Iain Smith from Inclusion Scotland; Susan Smith from For Women Scotland; Fraser Sutherland from the Humanist Society Scotland; Dr Andrew Tickell from Glasgow Caledonian University; and Kieran Turner from the Evangelical Alliance.

140 Ibid.

the suggestions and evidence provided to the Committee, the Bill "now looks very different indeed from the one that was introduced to Parliament a year or so ago".[141]

Stage 3 debate on the Bill commenced on 10 March 2021. Extensive reference was made to the evidence provided to the Justice Committee in its prior consideration of the Bill, and two amendments designed to strengthen protection of free speech were passed unanimously by MSPs.[142] The Stage 3 debate was also dominated by discussions as to the appropriateness of including "sex" as an attribute that could form part of the proposed new hate crime offences.[143] Amendments proposed by MSP Johann Lamont that sought to include "sex" as a protected attribute under the legislation were defeated. The Scottish Government instead committed to establishing a working group to look at whether misogynistic abuse should be a separate crime.[144]

Step 2: What Types of Engagement Strategies Were Used?

The public engagement strategies employed by the Justice Committee, as the lead committee responsible for facilitating scrutiny of the *Hate Crime Bill*, had three key components:

- call for views in response to specific questions;[145]
- oral hearings where witnesses could appear to give evidence to the Committee – conducted at Stage 1, Stage 2, and then again at a special meeting of the Committee immediately prior to the Stage 3 debate; and
- commission of research to assist the Committee in its deliberations on the Bill.

Having gained a sense of the context in which the inquiries into the *Hate Crime Bill* took place, the next step is to look carefully at the tools and strategies employed by those committees with reference to the factors indicating effective engagement identified in Table 12.3.

This analysis suggests that the engagement strategies undertaken by the Justice Committee in the Scottish case study were effective in terms of

141 Ibid.
142 Ibid.
143 Ibid.
144 'Why is Scotland's Hate Crime Bill so Controversial?' *BBC News Online*, 15 December 2020.
145 This call for views included questions such as: Do you think there is a need for this Bill and, if so, why? Are there alternatives to this legislation that would be effective, such as non-legislative measures, wider reforms to police or criminal justice procedures? Are there other provisions you would have liked to have seen in the Bill or other improvements that should have been made to the law on hate crime? See Parliament of Scotland, Justice Committee, *Hate Crime and Public Order (Scotland) Bill Call for Views* (2020) https://archive2021.parliament.scot/parliamentarybusiness/currentcommittees/115038.aspx.

Table 12.3 Application of Leston-Bandeira's Factors to Justice Committee's Inquiry into the Hate Crime Bill

Nature of the Engagement Strategy or Strategies Employed	*Call for Views with Specific Questions (Justice Committee + Finance Committee)* *Invitation to Provide Oral Evidence Before the Committee at Public Hearings (Justice Committee)* *Commission of Independent Academic Research*	
Factor	*Indicator*	*Evidence*
Accessibility	Resources in multiple languages, styles, or formats	*Strong Evidence* Easy read versions of materials relevant to the Bill Specific instructions for participation in committee inquiry Video version including one video with British Sign Language ("BSL")
	Different modes of communication with different audiences	*Strong Evidence* Easy read versions of materials relevant to the Bill Specific instructions for participation in committee inquiry Video version including one video with BSL
Reach of the audience	Rates of participation	*Strong Evidence* Unprecedented engagement with Justice Committee following call for views (eg around 2,000 responses received in response to Stage 1 call for views)
	Geographical diversity	*Moderate Evidence* Views received from individuals and organisations located in regional and metropolitan areas
Diversity of the audience	Participation beyond the "usual" suspects	*Moderate Evidence* Majority of views received came from individuals, however, organisations and representative bodies strongly represented in witnesses appearing before the Justice Committee
	Explicit encouragement for diverse groups to participate	*Moderate Evidence* Easy read versions of materials relevant to the Bill Specific instructions for participation in committee inquiry Video versions of supporting materials including one video with BSL Video conferencing/remote hearings used for Justice Committee hearings Content Accessibility Guidelines

(*Continued*)

Table 12.3 (Continued)

Nature of the Engagement Strategy or Strategies Employed	*Call for Views with Specific Questions (Justice Committee + Finance Committee)* *Invitation to Provide Oral Evidence Before the Committee at Public Hearings (Justice Committee)* *Commission of Independent Academic Research*	
Factor	*Indicator*	*Evidence*
Existing "divides"	Practical barriers to diverse participation are identified and explicitly addressed	*Moderate Evidence* Multiple languages used to communicate information across a range of different mediums Remote participation available for witnesses and MSPs materials including one video with BSL Accessible general information about participating in committee hearings including materials using BSL and materials produced in a range of languages
Diverse communication techniques	Evidence of multiple communication techniques eg text, audio, video, visual, infographics	*Strong Evidence* Easy read versions of materials relevant to the Bill Specific instructions for participation in committee inquiry Video version including one video with BSL Live broadcast of oral hearings Social media posts provided about upcoming hearings.
Issue-led rather than process-led	Evidence of procedural innovation or flexibility in response to issue-orientated engagement	*Moderate Evidence* Proactive invitations issued to some potential submission makers Diversity of religious and non-religious groups reflected in invitation to witnesses to provide evidence at hearings Specific questions included in call for views to encourage range of lived experiences to be shared Multiple examples of departure from 'standard procedure' to enable meaningful Committee-led interaction with proposed amendments

(*Continued*)

Table 12.3 (Continued)

Nature of the Engagement Strategy or Strategies Employed	*Call for Views with Specific Questions (Justice Committee + Finance Committee)* *Invitation to Provide Oral Evidence Before the Committee at Public Hearings (Justice Committee)* *Commission of Independent Academic Research*	
Factor	*Indicator*	*Evidence*
Listening rather than broadcasting	Evidence of two-way communication where institutional actors respond to ideas or suggestions by other participants	*Strong Evidence* Transcripts of committee proceedings suggest exchange of positions between members and submission makers, and opportunities for submission makers to comment on other submission makers' positions
	Opportunity to share lived experience	*Moderate Evidence* Transcripts of committee proceedings suggest some committee members demonstrating interest in lived experience – although many witnesses were from organisations/representative bodies Lived experience perspectives largely conveyed through response to call for views, which includes specific questions/prompts to include lived experience
	Appropriate acknowledgement of inputs submitted	*Strong Evidence* Submission makers receive email acknowledgement at time of submission Submission makers notified of tabling/publication of Committee report and of Committee hearings Witnesses thanked during oral hearings Submission makers acknowledged in text of Committee report and in parliamentary debates
Closing the feedback loop	Evidence of clear communication with participations about how their inputs informed parliamentary business	*Strong Evidence* General information provided via the Justice Committee website More specific information provided to witnesses via correspondence ahead of hearings Clear indication of how the information provided by submission makers informed the development of recommendations in committee reports

(*Continued*)

Table 12.3 (Continued)

Nature of the Engagement Strategy or Strategies Employed	*Call for Views with Specific Questions (Justice Committee + Finance Committee)* *Invitation to Provide Oral Evidence Before the Committee at Public Hearings (Justice Committee)* *Commission of Independent Academic Research*	
Factor	*Indicator*	*Evidence*
	Evidence that someone did listen, even if not to accommodate the exact demands made	*Strong Evidence* Most demands articulated during Justice Committee hearings were acknowledged by the Scottish Government and many were included in amendments to the Bill
Linking engagement with parliamentary business	Evidence of involvement or acknowledgement by diverse range of Members of Parliament	*Strong Evidence* Active participation by Justice Committee members and other MSPs including Cabinet Secretary and relevant departmental officials
	Evidence that participant views are formally and actively linked to the process of considering the Bill	*Strong Evidence* Suggestions/recommendations made by participants at committee hearings acknowledged and reflected in committee recommendations Submission makers acknowledged in text of Committee report and in parliamentary debates
Evaluation and reporting of activities	Evidence of any internal reflection or reporting on the engagement activity	*Some Evidence* Justice Committee provided Annual Report which included reflection on this inquiry ([17]–[21] Annual Report 2020–2021). Scottish Parliament includes general feedback avenues for participants in committee activities

generating high rates of participation and facilitating meaningful two-way engagement between proponent Minister, committee members, and witnesses. The engagement tools used by the Justice Committee also display a strong focus on accessibility – however, the types of witnesses engaging directly with the Justice Committee remain within the "usual suspects" category, with limited opportunity for those with lived experience of the harm of hate speech to speak directly with key decision-makers in the process.

Step 3: The Impact of These Engagement Techniques on the Shape of the Proposed Law

The passage of the *Hate Crime Bill* through the Scottish Parliament had some unusual elements that generated important opportunities for the Justice

Committee to influence the content of the enacted Bill. For example, even prior to the commencement of the Stage 1 inquiry, the Cabinet Secretary responsible for the *Hate Crime Bill* had indicated that the government intended to move amendments to tighten the scope key provisions and limit the potential chilling effect on freedom of expression and freedom of religious belief posed by the new offences.[146] These amendments were considered by the Justice Committee in its Stage 1 Report, which included further detailed suggestions about how to improve the Bill's compliance with human rights protected in the ECHR.[147] The recommendations and suggested changes proposed by the Justice Committee were also reflected in the Revised Explanatory Notes issued following the Stage 2 debate, and in the Supplementary Financial Memorandum and Revised Delegated Powers Memorandum.[148] The work of the Justice Committee was also referred to in 245 media reports published during the period 23 April 2020 to 23 April 2021.[149] Many more media reports included reference to the evidence given by witnesses and submission makers to the parliamentary committees tasked with inquiring into the Bill.[150]

Step 4: Reflecting on the Extent to which These Inquiries Provide an Effective Forum for Deliberating Human Rights Issues Arising from Proposed Legislation

The Justice Committee's public inquiry into the *Hate Crimes Bill* had many features that point to effective human rights deliberation, including meaningful engagement with both the community and the government of the day. In contrast to the Australian example, the Scottish case study included direct engagement between the Justice Committee and the proponent Minister (in this case the Cabinet Secretary), which facilitated an exchange of ideas and generated options for legislative amendments that could be tested in real time with government officials and key community organisations.

In fact, even before the Justice Committee had commenced its oral hearings into the Bill, the Scottish Government announced important amendments to the Bill that sought to strike a better balance between the competing human rights at play, suggesting that it had anticipated – at least to some

146 Ibid.

147 Justice Committee Stage 1 Report (n 110) [183]–[184].

148 Parliament of Scotland, *Hate Crime and Public Order (Scotland) Bill: Evidence Taken Before Stage 3* (22 February 2021) https://www.parliament.scot/bills-and-laws/bills/hate-crime-and-public-order-scotland-bill.

149 The database used for this purpose was the NewsBank Database accessed through the University of South Australia Library. Search terms used were: 'hate crime bill' AND 'committee', date range 23 April 2020 to 23 April 2021, sources searched were newspaper and web-only sources.

150 For example, a broader search using search terms 'hate crime bill' delivered 1,745 results. NewsBank Database accessed through the University of South Australia Library. Search terms used were: 'hate crime bill', date range 23 April 2020 to 23 April 2021, sources searched were newspaper and web-only sources.

extent – the significance of the work of the Committee, in the context of the broader public debate on key features of the *Hate Crimes Bill*. This trend of government-led amendments in response to the Justice Committee's deliberations continued throughout the passage of the Bill through Parliament.

The engagement strategies employed by the Justice Committee also displayed many of the key factors identified by Leston-Bandeira as indicators of effective public engagement. In particular, the way the Justice Committee was able to facilitate a direct dialogue between the proponent Minister and community organisations on the merits of proposed amendments demonstrated a capacity not just to *receive* views from the public, but also to actively explore ways to *implement* these views within the legal parameters set by the proposed legislation.

However, like the Australian case study, the Justice Committee's inquiry into the *Hate Crimes Bill* continued to display a preference for the views and involvement of the "usual suspects" (such as academics, legal representative bodies, and representatives from religious institutions), particularly when it comes to involvement in oral hearings and meetings. It is also important to note that some of the politically-orientated discourse that dominated the Australian experience was diffused in the Scottish example because of the pre-existence of legal provisions prohibiting religious discrimination, as well as provisions prohibiting discrimination on the grounds of sexual orientation and gender reassignment status.[151] Having said this, media commentary on the *Hate Crimes Bill* suggests some similarities with the "culture wars" playing out in the Australian context, particularly when it comes to those advancing the right to (almost unlimited) free speech and those seeking stronger protections against harmful or offensive public comments.[152] Like the Australian experience, the passage of the *Hate Crimes Bill* was highly dependent on the political appetite of the government of the day, but in the Scottish case study there is at least some evidence to suggest that important rights-enhancing legislative gains were made through the Committee process.

151 See, eg, *Equality Act 2010* (UK) ss 7, 10, 11 and 12.

152 See eg Shona Craven, 'Targetting of Cherry and Salmond has become obsessive', *The National* (online), 1 Nov 2021, 26; Editorial, 'Alba Party Supporters Have Two Choices: Capitulate or Fight Their Corner', *The National*, (online), 31 Oct 2021; Shona Craven, 'Dorries Shows Herself to Be Petty and Petulant', *The National*, (online), 26 Oct 2021, 24; Jane Cassidy, 'Lawyer Likens the SNP to Hitler's Nazi Party in Series of Tweets', *The National*, (online), 30 Dec 2020, 7; Drew Allan, 'No Wonder the Decent People of Scotland Are Keen to Be Free of this Callous Westminster Tory Government', *The Sunday Herald*, (online), 27 Dec 2020, 27; Caitlin Logan, 'Let's Focus on Real Cancel Culture, Not Has-beens in Search of Free Publicity', *The National*, 20 Dec 2020; Jane Cassidy, 'Yousaf Hits Out as Far-right Group Targets His Office', *The National*, (online), 16 Dec 2020, 2.

IV Conclusion: Are Parliamentary Committees Listening to the People?

The case studies discussed in this chapter demonstrate the complexities associated with seeking to evaluate the performance of inherently dynamic bodies such as parliamentary committees, and the challenges that arise from seeking to "balance" freedom of religious belief with other important rights and interests, such as protection from harm caused by "hate speech". These complexities stem from entrenched cultural and legal norms derived from the institutional context in which the parliamentary committees operate, as well as the dominance of executive decision-making that permeates modern democracies.

The case studies also remind us that parliamentary committees in Australia and Scotland have an institutional duty to undertake a deliberative function on behalf of the parliament and to preserve the rights of the people to communicate directly with those they elect to represent them.[153] This means embracing techniques that enable parliaments to reach beyond the well-resourced, politically-savvy "usual suspects" when it comes to engaging with the community on matters of public interest. This is critical in our diverse modern democracies where geographical location, socio-economic status, and diverse lived experiences can work to marginalise or isolate individuals or communities from the work of the parliament.

The methodology offered in this chapter documents the potential benefits of multi-committee scrutiny in both parliamentary systems, enabling technical human rights analysis to take place alongside inquiry-based engagement by committees with community members and experts. This helps facilitate meaningful two-way dialogue with proponent Ministers on legislative details and design options, as well as equipping external submission makers and witnesses with important insights into policy impacts and objectives that can be combined with the lived experiences of those "on the ground". The methodology also brings to the surface the important role "lead" committees play within these systems – whether formally allocated (such as in Scotland) or emerging on a more ad hoc basis (such as in Australia). Parliamentary committees that can directly engage proponent Ministers appear to be best placed to generate legislative amendments informed by people with lived experience that are also palatable to the executive government.

The methodology introduced also looks at *how* parliamentary committees attempt to engage with the broader community, and *who* they seek to engage with. Although neither case study achieved a "perfect score" when it comes to the indicators of effective public engagement, there are encouraging signs that both parliaments are aware of the need to create meaningful forums for individuals most likely to be impacted by proposed laws to share their views. The case studies also suggest that the Australian Parliament could benefit by

153 Thompson (n 10); Marsh, 'Australia's Representation Gap' (n 16).

learning from some of the Scottish Parliament's systems and practices. For example, the Australian Parliament could consider developing a suite of accessible resources for potential submission makers modelled on the Scottish Parliament's examples, which include video resources in BSL, and materials published in multiple languages. The Scottish Parliament's approach to calling for views with reference to specific questions could also be considered in the Australian context, in addition or as an alternative to online surveys. The Australian Parliament could also benefit from formally identifying a "lead committee" to coordinate public engagement activity with respect to parliamentary scrutiny of proposed legislation (although this is more complex in a bicameral system), and by looking to implement processes to facilitate direct engagement between committees, witnesses, and proponent Ministers during oral hearings (in addition to existing written correspondence "dialogues" conducted by the PJCHR and SSCSB). The broader legal frameworks in place in Scotland (such as the *Human Rights Act 1998* [UK]) also create incentives for all participants in the lawmaking system to consider whether any proposed laws unjustifiably abrogate internationally protected human rights. In addition, legislative processes within the Scottish Parliament integrate committee-facilitated debates in ways that help diffuse party-political dominated discourses, at least to some degree.

Although the Scottish Parliament emerges as having specific strengths in terms of both public engagement techniques and human rights scrutiny of proposed legislation, both case studies show that unless human rights concepts dominate broader public discourse on proposed laws, thoughtful debates about the best ways to protect the rights of vulnerable minorities (including religious minorities) can be highjacked in favour of politically-orientated binaries. Guarding against this risk demands political leadership as well as strong human rights literacy among the general public and the media. This is inherently difficult to generate and sustain, but can be achieved by welcoming previously excluded groups and communities into parliamentary processes and forums where competing human rights are considered and proportionality analysis applied. This is because when groups or individuals move from being "outsiders" to "valued contributors", they can begin the type of "engagement journey" Leston-Bandeira describes as being central to engendering trust in parliamentary processes,[154] even if they do not achieve the advocacy goals they initially set for themselves.

This is where the methodology introduced in this chapter has something important to offer. It helps identify how parliamentary committees in different jurisdictions might adjust their practices to bring more diverse voices into their public inquiries. It also brings into focus parliamentary committees' role

154 Cristina Leston-Bandeira, 'The Public Engagement Journey' *Centre for Democratic Politics* (Blog Post, 25 May 2021) https://cde.leeds.ac.uk/2021/03/24/the-public-engagement-journey/.

in fostering greater human rights literacy within and outside of the parliament. In this way, the methodology opens up new space from which to consider the shifts in rights discourse thoughtfully documented by Poulos and Barker,[155] and also assists parliaments to develop practical, contextualised approaches to meaningful public engagement.[156]

Further Reading:

For analysis of the methods used in this chapter, see Chapter 15 – Section IV – subsection C *The Functionalist Method*; D *The Analytical Method*; F *The Yardstick Method*.

For the author's rejoinder and reflection, see Appendix Section VII.

For another analysis involving Australia see Chapters 7, 8, 11, 13, and 14.

155 Poulos, 'Three Discourses of Religious Freedom' (n 6); Barker, 'The Place of the Child' (n 6).

156 Robert Foa et al, *The Global Satisfaction with Democracy Report 2020* (Report, January 2020) https://www.bennettinstitute.cam.ac.uk/publications/-global-satisfaction-democracy-report-2020/. See further Mark Evans and Gerry Stoker, *Saving Democracy* (Bloomsbury, 2021); Phil Parvin, 'Is Deliberative Democracy Feasible? Political Disengagement and Trust in Liberal Democratic States' (2015) 98(4) *The Monist*, 407.

13 Religion as Individual Affair and Constitutional Permissions in India-Gathering Comparative Perspective of Practicing It and Religious Mark on Body in Public Domain

Arvind P Bhanu[1] *and Sonia Sthapak*[2]

I Introduction

India, as a multi-faith country, organises itself in such a manner that the respect of all faiths forms part of the structural foundation of the country. These faiths, such as Hinduism, Islam, Christianity, Sikhism, Buddhism, and Jainism, each believes in unity in diversity. The expression "unity in diversity" is often used to describe India's cultural, linguistic, and religious diversity, which has contributed to the country's rich history. Various scholars, leaders, and philosophers have recognised this diversity as the foundation of "oneness".[3] Swami Vivekananda, a renowned spiritual leader and philosopher, believed that all religions hold fundamental truths and advocate for interfaith harmony and understanding.[4]

Mahatma Gandhi,[5] a great leader, came up with the view that India's diverse religious and cultural traditions co-existing was a key factor contributing to the nation's progress. Acknowledging the diverse character of Indian society, the framers of the Indian Constitution worked towards ensuring equality and social justice for all and envisioned a nation where diverse communities

1 Professor of Law and Research and Additional Director, Amity Law School, Amity University Noida, U.P., India and Adjunct Professor at ALS, University of Adelaide, Australia.
2 Associate Professor, Department of Education, University of Allahabad, Prayagraj, U.P., India.
3 *Tehseen S Poonawalla v Union of India* (2018) 9 SCC 501; *St. Stephen's College v University of Delhi* (1992) 1 SCC 558; *Sri Adi Visheshwara of Kashi Vishwanath Temple, Varanasi v State of UP* (1997) 4 SCC 606; *State of Karnataka v Dr Praveen Bhai Thogadia* (2004) 4 SCC 684; *State of Uttar Pradesh v Lalai Singh Yadav* (1976) 4 SCC 213.
4 Refer generally to his famous quote 'I am proud to belong to a nation which has sheltered the persecuted and the refugees of all religions and all nations of the earth' at the World Parliament of Religions at Chicago in 1893.
5 See Anthony J Parel, *Gandhi's Philosophy and the Quest for Harmony* (Cambridge University Press, 2006) 107.

DOI: 10.4324/9781003397311-18

could live harmoniously and participate in nation-building.[6] Legal scholars argue that the strength of India's independence struggle was the unity of all faiths, through which the goal of independence was achieved, and in turn setting the foundation for the recognition of secular principles by the Indian Constitution.[7] This is one element. However, every principle recognised in any country's constitutional framework is sourced from its past. In the words of Dr Radhakrishnan, former president of India:

> When India is said to be a secular state, it does not mean that we reject the reality of an unseen sprit or the relevance of the religion to life or that we exalt religion. It does not mean that secularism itself becomes a positive religion or that the State assumes divine prerogatives [...] We hold that not one religion should be given preferential status [...] This view of religious impartiality or comprehension and forbearance, has a prophetic role to play within the National and International life.[8]

The concept of secularism was not alien to the history of India. The rule of *Dharma*,[9] which was hardly different from the rule of law, constitutionalism, or limited government, was completely recognised throughout that history.[10] The Supreme Court of India has recognised secularism as part of the rule of law and the secular character of the Indian Constitution as part of its basic structure.[11] Thus, the ancient philosophical traditions, the influence of tolerant rulers, the vision of independence leaders, and the legal framework established by the Indian Constitution and the Supreme Court have contributed to the religious diversity in India.

II Constitutional Framework

The constitution of a country is a basic rulebook that establishes the system for how its government works and how its people are governed. Generally

6 Indian Constitution preamble: 'We, the People of India, having solemnly resolved to constitute India into a sovereign socialist secular democratic republic and to secure to all its citizens justice, liberty, equality and to promote among them all fraternity ...'

7 Tahir Mahmood, 'Professedly Secular v Conspicuously Communal', *The Hindu*, (1 May 2014).

8 Sarvepalli Radhakrishnan, *Recovery of Faith* (Hind Pocket Books, 1967) 184.

9 Rule of dharma means rule of righteousness: see V K Ahuja, *Krishna and Mediation* (National Law University and Judicial Academy Assam, 2023) 78; see also *Shri AS Narayana Deekshitulu v State of Andhra Pradesh* 1996 AIR 1765: 'Dharma is for the stability of the society, the maintenance of social order and the general well-being and progress of humankind. Whatever conduces to the fulfilment of these objects is Dharma; that is definite'. Chapter 69, Verse 58 *Karna Parva of the Mahabharata* – an ancient Indian epic.

10 Vedic age (Circa 3000–1000 BC).

11 *S R Bommai v Union of India* (1994) 3 SCC 1 ('*SR Bommai*'); see generally Paul T Babie and Arvind P Bhanu, 'The Form and Formation of Constitutionalism in India' (2022) 11(2) *Laws* 33 ('*Babie & Bhanu – Form*').

speaking, constitutions create three main parts of the government: the body that makes the laws (legislature), those who carry out and enforce the laws (executive), and the courts that decide if the laws are fair and how they should be interpreted (judiciary). Constitutions also state what powers each part of the government has, their responsibilities, and how they should work together. It is a higher law in the country and all other laws passed by legislatures are subject to it. The common components of a constitutional framework include a preamble, fundamental rights, separation of powers, structure of government, amendment processes, protection of minority rights and judicial review, along with any of the country's specific components. The issue in hand is to be examined through these elements of the constitutional framework in subsequent parts of the chapter.

At the very outset, the Preamble of the Indian Constitution, through the resolution of "We, the People of India …", commits to secure to all its citizens justice, liberty, equality, and fraternity.[12] These four commitments comprise the foundational structure of the Indian constitutional framework.[13] The Preamble does not contain the word "religion"[14] and nowhere except in *Commissioner, Hindu Religious Endowments* (1954),[15] is the term defined, but religion remains included by way of securing liberty to all. The Indian Constitution makes sure that every individual must have liberty of thought, expression, belief, faith, and worship. However, in the constitutional framework itself, it has been provisioned that no liberty is absolute.[16] Rather, it is subject to the restrictions which may be considered as constitutional permissions to enjoy those freedoms. To make freedom of religion more express, the Indian Constitution was amended by the 42nd Amendment Act 1976, with the word "secular" was added to the Preamble, declaring India as a "secular democratic republic".[17] However, it is an assessment of constitutional experts that the Indian republic was conceived and made secular from the very beginning.[18] Part III of the Indian Constitution provides various fundamental rights. Articles 25-28 (right to freedom of religion) are exclusively given to secure the freedom of religion. They are supplemented by other provisions

12 Indian Constitution preamble.

13 *Keshvananda Bharti v State of Kerala* AIR 1973 SC 1461.

14 Arvind P Bhanu, 'Faith, Food and Secularism: A Human Rights Approach' in V K Ahuja (ed), *Human Rights: Contemporary Issues – Festschrift in the Honour of Professor Upednra Baxi* (EBC Publishing, 2019) 373.

15 *Commissioner, Hindu Religious Endowments v Sri Lakshmindra Thirtha Swamiar of Sri Shirur Mutt* AIR 1954 SC 282 ('*Bhanu – Faith*').

16 *Acharya Maharajshri Narendra Prasadji v State of Gujrat* AIR 1974 SC 2098: 'No right in an organized society can be absolute' ('*Acharya*').

17 *S R Bommai v Union of India* (n 9): The word 'Secular' recognises the concept of secularism as manifested in the guarantee of freedom of religion as a fundamental right in the Constitution. Thus, secularism was as much part of the Constitution even before the word 'secular' was inserted in the preamble.

18 M P Singh, *V N Shukla's Constitution of India* (Eastern Book Company, 12th ed, 2013) A-23.

such as Articles 15(1)[19] and (2),[20] 16(2),[21] 29(2)[22], and 325,[23] which prohibit discrimination in different matters on the basis of religion; and Article 30,[24] which grants some special rights to religious minorities. Article 19 also supplements to the protection to the exercise of religious faith.[25] Article 32 itself is a fundamental right for constitutional remedies in cases of violation of freedom of religion.[26] It enables an individual to approach the Supreme Court directly for the enforcement of the freedom of religion.

It is notable that the constitutional framework of India ensures that no organ of the state is superior to the other. This is due to the harmonisation that the Indian Constitution has effected between Parliamentary sovereignty and the written Constitution through the provision of judicial review.[27] The Indian Constitution adopts a middle ground between the American system of judicial supremacy and the British principle of Parliamentary supremacy by endowing the judiciary with the power of declaring a law as unconstitutional if it is beyond the competence of the legislature as per the distribution of powers in the Constitution. As stated earlier, no fundamental right is absolute, as the grounds of restriction are given against the right itself in the Constitution and the subjection of state action to judicial review. The description of expressly given grounds of restriction[28] for exercise of fundamental rights not only adds a unique feature to the Indian constitutional framework in terms of various freedoms, but goes beyond that to state that unlike the unwritten British

19 Indian Constitution art 15(1): The State shall not discriminate against any citizen on grounds only of religion, race, caste, sex, place of birth, or any of them.

20 Ibid art 15(2): 'No citizen shall, on grounds only of religion, race, caste, sex, place of birth, or any of them, be subject to any disability, liability, restriction, or condition with regard to …'

21 Ibid art 16(2): 'No citizen shall, on grounds only of religion, race, caste, sex, descent, place of birth, residence, or any of them, be ineligible for, or discriminated against in respect of, any employment or office under the State'.

22 Ibid art 29(2): 'No citizen shall be denied admission into any educational institution maintained by the State or receiving aid out of State funds on grounds only of religion, race, caste, language or any of them'.

23 Ibid art 325: 'No person to be ineligible for inclusion in, or to claim to be included in a special, electoral roll-on grounds of religion, race, caste or sex'.

24 This Article makes provision for religious and linguistic minorities in India to establish and administer educational institutions of their choice. It contemplates that the minority communities should have the freedom to preserve and develop their own culture, language and religion through the medium of education.

25 Indian Constitution art 19(1)(a): All citizens shall have the right to freedom of speech and expression.

26 Ibid art 32: Remedies for enforcement of rights conferred by this Part III.

27 D D Basu, *Introduction to Constitution of India* (LexisNexis, 23rd ed, 2018) 43 ('*Basu 2018*').

28 See for detailed discussion, A V Dicey, *Introduction to the Study of the Law of the Constitution* (1885) at 86–95.

constitution,[29] the Indian Constitution determines the limitations on the fundamental rights.[30]

The amendment process is given in Article 368 of the Indian Constitution. Under this provision, the Indian Parliament may, in the exercise of its constituent powers, amend any provision of the Indian Constitution by following the procedure laid down within it. The amending power of the Indian Parliament is not absolute but is subject to the procedure laid down in Article 368 and the 'basic structure' theory – a substantive limitation developed by the full bench of the Supreme Court of India in *Keshavananda Bharati*.[31] As discussed previously, the combined effect of all these provisions, legislative developments, and judicial pronouncements of restrictions on the amending power of the Parliament of India means that, it goes without saying, the freedom of faiths that form part of the basic structure of the secular character of the Indian state is beyond the amending power of the Indian Constitution. The next element of the judicial review power in the constitutional framework in India makes the judiciary the independent guardian of the fundamental rights of the citizens.[32] Through the judicial review power, the courts (the High Courts and Supreme Court) interpret the Constitution and review the constitutionality of laws and government actions.[33] This ensures the protection of constitutional rights and ensures that laws and policies are in line with constitutional provisions. Thus, the framework of the Indian Constitution makes sure that India is a secular state, however, debate may continue on the nature of Indian secularism.[34] The Supreme Court has time and again held that secularism is an unamendable basic feature of the Indian Constitution.[35]

A Examining the Constitutional Safeguards and Permissions

A constitution, as a foundational document of a nation's law, precisely ensures all the rights that enable a human being to live with human dignity.[36] Part III of the Indian Constitution provides a code for all those rights and ensures their protection. It also takes an approach that enumerates certain rights expressly

29 Ibid: 'The Parliament is supreme and can do everything that is not naturally impossible'.

30 Granville Austin, *The Indian Constitution* (Oxford University Press, 1999).

31 *Keshavananda Bharati v State of Kerala* (n 11).

32 Indian Constitution art 13(1): 'All laws in force in the territory of India immediately before the commencement of this Constitution, in so far as they are inconsistent with the provisions of Part III, shall, to the extent of such inconsistency, be void. (2) The State shall not make any law which takes away or abridges the rights conferred by Part III and any law made in contravention of this clause shall, to the extent of the contravention, be void'.

33 Ibid.

34 Singh (n 16).

35 Ibid A-24.

36 *Francis Coralie Mullin v Administrator, Union Territory of Delhi* AIR 1981 SC 746: It was emphasised in this case that the right to life is not merely confined to the physical existence of a person but encompasses a life of dignity and respect.

in some provisions, with the remaining essential rights that are required to live with human dignity are covered under Article 21 of the Constitution.[37] The freedom of faith and belief has expressly been enumerated through Articles 25–28, which guarantee the freedom of individual and/or collective faith and belief. These provisions provide complete freedom of faith but not without limits. But what are those limits? The Constitution has specifically set the limits through its provisions (Articles 25–28) and judiciary by applying its "Essentiality Test".[38] Within that test, to enquire about a particular practice of a faith is to enquire about the permission of the Constitution to exercise the practice. However, before discussing the Essentiality Test in more detail shortly, it is necessary to say that in India the freedom of religion is a constitutionally monitored freedom.

Article 25,[39] without supporting the salient feature of the Constitution as a secular document,[40] nonetheless gives the fundamental right to each person to freedom of conscience and the right to freely profess, practise, and propagate religion.[41] This right is applicable to all persons, irrespective of their citizenship status, as long as they are within the territory of India. Non-citizens can claim the freedom of religion under Article 25, which protects their right to follow and practice their chosen religion without discrimination. Article 14 extends further protection against discrimination but to citizens only. In the context of religious freedom, non-citizens can claim equality before the law under Article 14 of the Indian Constitution, read with the freedom of religion guaranteed by Article 25. Article 14 asserts that the state shall not deny to any person equality before the law or the equal protection of the laws while within the territory of India. In the case of the protection of religious freedom, Article 14 is not limited to Indian citizens alone but extends to all persons within the territory of India, including non-citizens such as non-residents, refugees, or foreign visitors.[42]

37 *Indian Constitution* art 21: 'No person shall be deprived of his life or personal liberty except according to procedure established by law'.

38 *Commissioner, Hindu Religious Endowments, Madras v Sri Lakshmindra Thirtha Swamiar of Sri Shirur. Mutt Shirur* 1954 AIR 282: The court laid down the Essentiality Test to determine what constitutes an essential religious practice and what can be regulated by the State in the name of social welfare and public order ('*CHRE*').

39 Indian Constitution art 25: Freedom of conscience and free profession, practice and propagation of religion.

40 Paul T Babie and Arvind P Bhanu, 'Freedom of Religion and Belief in India and Australia: An Introductory Comparative Assessment of Two Federal Constitutional Democracies' (2018) 39(1) *Pace Law Review* ('*Babie & Bhanu – Freedom*').

41 Indian Constitution art 25(1): Subject to public order, morality and health and to the other provisions of this Part, all persons are equally entitled to freedom of conscience and the right freely to profess, practice and propagate religion.

42 *Rev Stainislaus v State of Madhya Pradesh* 1 (977 AIR 908, 1977 SCR (2) 611) ('*Rev Stanislaus*').

Articles 14, 15, and 16 collectively form a code of equality in the Indian Constitution. These articles are specifically dedicated to prohibiting discrimination based on certain grounds. For example, Article 15(1) prohibits discrimination on the grounds of religion among other grounds;[43] and similarly Article 16(2),[44] which ensures equal opportunity in matters of public employment, prohibits discrimination in employment based on religion among other grounds.[45] Article 14 covers all those types discrimination which are not expressly covered by Articles 15 and 16. Discrimination in this case means to make an adverse distinction by "distinguish[ing one] unfavourably from others".[46] The safeguard against discrimination in these articles is based on the ground that a person professes a particular religion.[47] Article 29(2) is a counterpart of the equality clause of Article 15.[48] This safeguards the interest of a minority against discrimination on the ground of religion – for example, in the matter of admission into any educational institution maintained or aided by the state.[49] The protection extended by this clause is an individual right given to the citizen as a citizen, rather than as a member of any particular community.[50] For example, if a section of people is identified as a religious minority, they have a right to establish and administer an educational institution of their choice.[51] D D Basu says "Though styled as a right, it is more in the nature of protection for minorities".[52] The Supreme Court holds that it is an additional protection which Article 30(1) grants to these religious minorities.[53]

Article 19 guarantees certain fundamental freedoms, such as the freedom of speech and expression, assembly, and association. These freedoms indirectly support the practice and expression of one's religious beliefs as protected under Article 25 of the Constitution. This article protects freedom of speech, with added protection for religious speech through its interplay with Articles 25–28. Religious speech, as opposed to free speech alone, is protected only if it is exercised in furtherance of the profession, propagation, and practice of the

43 Indian Constitution art 15(1).

44 Ibid art 16(2).

45 Ibid.

46 *Kathi R Rawat v State of Saurashtra* AIR 1952 AC 123.

47 *State of Rajasthan v Pratap Singh Thakur* AIR 1960 1208 (1210).

48 Indian Constitution art 29(2).

49 Ibid art 29(1): Any section of the citizens residing in the territory of India or any part thereof having a distinct language, script, or culture of its own shall have the right to conserve the same. After perusal of drafting committee (CAD) 1 November 1947, the word minority was substituted with 'Section of Citizens'.

50 D D Basu, *Shorter Constitution of India* (Lexis Nexis, 14th ed, 2011) 439 ('*Basu 2011*').

51 *National Commission for Minorities Act 1992* (India) s 2(c): 'minority' means a community notified by the Central Government of India. Based on religion, there are six notified religious minorities, namely, Muslims, Christians, Sikhs, Buddhists, Parsis and Jains. See also *TMA Pai Foundation v State of Karnataka* (2002) 8 SCCC 481.

52 *Basu 2018* (n 25) 495.

53 *PA Inamdar v State of Maharastra* AIR 2005 SC 3226 ('*PA Inamdar*').

religious beliefs falling within the protection of Articles 25–28. While Article 19 uses the word 'citizens', Article 25 provides that 'all persons are equally entitled to freedom of conscience and the right freely to profess, practise, and propagate religion'. The difference between the two protections – citizens versus all persons – results in differential treatment for speech alone, protected only for citizens, and religious speech, protected for all persons. In some instances, though, Article 19 may provide auxiliary protection for religious speech. This occurs where speech is not, in a strict sense, "religious" – that is, it is not for the propagation of one's beliefs – such as when a member of the Hindu tradition sings for God by chanting *mantras* or when a member of the Muslim tradition performs *Namaz*.[54]

Article 325 of the Indian Constitution gives the provision relating to voting rights of citizens.[55] It prohibits discrimination on the grounds of religion in matters of voting rights. It ensures that no person can be disqualified from voting or being a candidate in any election on the basis of their religion. It does not directly address religious practices or freedom of religion, but plays a crucial role in promoting equality and ensuring that religious discrimination does not interfere with the electoral process. In *Poudyal's* case, two judges in the minority opined that Article 325 is of crucial significance for maintaining the secular character of the Constitution. A contravention of this provision would have an adverse impact on the secular character of the republic that is a basic feature of the Constitution.[56]

B Analysing the Nature of Restrictions in Their Operation

As discussed earlier, Articles 25–28 are dedicated to managing the constitutional freedom of religion in consideration of four principles; justice, liberty, equality and fraternity, as enshrined in the Preamble of the Constitution. Article 25 of the Indian Constitution marks the beginning of a set of provisions that guarantee equality among all religions, promoting the principles of secularism. It primarily focuses on the practice of religious freedom by individuals. On the other hand, Article 26 places emphasis on the establishment and management of religious institutions. However, Article 25 can also extend its protection to instances where religious practices by individuals are conducted through institutions.[57]

While granting the permissions to individuals to profess, practice, and propagate the religion, Article 25(1) empowers the state to impose restrictions on the ground of public order, morality, and health and to the other provisions

54 Arvind P Bhanu, Paul T Babie and Gian-Luca Stirling, 'Protecting Religious Speech as Expressive Conduct in the Constitutions of Australia, United States and India', (2022) 100(1) *University of Detroit Mercy Law Review* 32–3.
55 Indian Constitution art 325.
56 See generally Babie & Bahnu – Form (n 9).
57 PM Bakshi, *The Constitution of India* (Universal Law Publishing, 15th ed, 2018) 86.

of Part III.[58] Article 19, as discussed previously, extends protection to religious expression when the coverage of Article 25 ends[59] though it still needs protection, but also serves the purpose of filtering the permissions. Article 19, being within Part III of the Indian Constitution, empowers the state to restrict individual freedoms to profess, practice, and propagate one's faith in the collective interest under clauses (2)–(6) of Article 19, and the rights guaranteed to other citizens by the different subclauses of Article 19(1).[60] The essence of these constitutional permissions is that individuals have the freedom to hold and express their beliefs. They can share their beliefs with others through their outward actions and also spread them based on their own judgement and conscience for the edification of others.[61] However, it is important to note that the government can impose certain limitations on these freedoms if it deems necessary to maintain public order, protect public health, or uphold moral standards. These principles are embedded in Article 25 and Article 26 of the Constitution.[62] In *State of Gujarat v Mirzapur Moti Kureshi Kassab Jamat*, the Court held that certain practices, even if carried out under the guise of religion, cannot be protected if they are contrary to public health or morality.[63]

C Public Order, Morality, and Health

The freedom of faith is not confined to matters of doctrine or belief but goes further, extending to external performances in pursuance of belief-like rituals, observances, ceremonies, and modes of worship, which are essential or integral parts of religion.[64] Since the freedom of faith belongs to every person, the freedom of one cannot encroach upon a similar freedom given to another person.[65] The responsibility to maintain public order rests on the state and the power of the legislature to make law on the subject is given under Schedule VII in List-II ('State List'). The meaning of "public order", listed as Entry-1 under the State List, is taken as the absence of violence and an orderly state of affairs in which citizens can peacefully pursue their normal avocation of life.[66]

58 Indian Constitution pt III: Part III is exclusively meant for describing various fundamental rights and nowhere other than this part in Indian legal system, the fundamental rights are given.

59 *P A Inamdar* (n 51) 33.

60 *Nrendra Prasadji, Acharya Maharajshri v State of Gujrat* AIR 1974 SC 2008, [25].

61 Basu 2011 (n 48) 471.

62 *N Adithyan v Tranvancore Devaswom Board* AIR 2002 SC 3538 ('*N Adithyan*').

63 *State of Gujarat v Mirzapur Moti Kureshi Kassab Jamat* (2005) 8 SCC 534.

64 *Acharya* (n 14): 'In addition to persons believing in religious faith, there are some forms of practicing religion by outward actions which are as much part of religion as faith itself'.

65 *Rev Stanislaus* (n 40) 166.

66 *Basudeva v Rex* AIR 1949 ALL. 513.

Anything that disturbs public tranquillity disturbs "public order".[67] In short, it refers to public peace, safety, and tranquillity.[68]

D D Basu[69] explains the concept of public order as different from "law and order" and the "security of State". Basu refers to three concentric circles. Law and order represent the largest circle, within which is the next circle representing the public order, and the smallest circle represents security of the state.[70] Absence of public order is an aggravated form of disturbance of public peace, which affects the general current of public life.[71] Public order is also one of the grounds in Article 19(2) to restrict the freedom of speech and expression.[72] There are several examples wherein the state has prohibited the profession, practice, and propagation of religion on the ground of public order, and the Court has approved such prohibitions. Practices like sacrificing a human being in the name of religion,[73] performing the *Tandava* dance by the *Ananda Margis* in public streets or places,[74] and performing prayers by using amplifiers or beating of drums that disturb old or infirm persons, students, or children having their sleep, have been held as valid prohibitions by the Indian courts. In *Ismail Faruqui*,[75] the Supreme Court, by majority, held that the state can, in exercise of its sovereign power, acquire places of worship like mosques, churches, and temples, which is independent of Article 300-A of the Constitution.[76]

As per the provisions of Article 25 and judicial observations, an individual's exercise of religious freedom should not infringe upon the fundamental rights of others. While everyone is entitled to enjoy their rights, it is essential that this enjoyment remains consistent with the rights of others. In cases where voluntary harmony among conflicting interests cannot be achieved through the free play of social forces, the state has a role to rectify the imbalance. The courts have emphasised that a specific fundamental right cannot exist in isolation but that it must co-exist harmoniously with the exercise of other fundamental

67 *Ramesh Thappar v State of Madras* (1960) SCJ 418, 423.

68 *Superintendent Central Prison, Fatehgarh v Ram Manohar* AIR 1960 SC 633, 639.

69 Indian Constitution art 29(2).

70 *Ram Manohar Lohia v State of Bihar* AIR 1996 SC 740.

71 *Bhupal Chandra Ghose v Arif Ali* AIR 1971 SC 2486.

72 Indian Constitution art 19(2): Nothing in subclause (a) of clause (1) of Article 19 shall affect the operation of any existing law, or prevent the State from making any law, in so far as such law imposes reasonable restrictions on the exercise of the right conferred by the said subclause in the interests of … public order […].

73 *Saifuddin Saheb, Sardar Syedna Taher v State of Bombay* AIR 1962 SC 853, 863.

74 The *Ananda Margis* believes that the Lord Shiva was the originator of *Tandava* dance and introduced it about 6,500 years back for physical, mental and spiritual upliftment of every human being. *Tandava* dance is to be performed with a skull, knife and *Trishul* (trident); see *Acharya* (n 14).

75 *Ismail Faruqui v Union of India* (1994) 6 SCC 360 ('*Ismail Faruqui*').

76 Indian Constitution art 300-A: No person shall be deprived of his property save by authority of Law.

rights by others. In addition to that, the state may exercise its power within reasonable and valid limits, considering the Directive Principles of State Policy in Part IV of the Constitution in the interest of social welfare as a whole.[77] In *Lily Thomas*, the Supreme Court observed that the freedom guaranteed under Article 25 of the Constitution is such freedom that does not encroach upon a similar freedom of the other persons.[78] On religious conversion, the Supreme Court observed in *Rev Stainislaus* that Article 25(1) of the Constitution guarantees freedom of conscience to every citizen, irrespective of their religious affiliation.[79] The Court stated that there is no fundamental right to convert another person to one's own religion and made a distinction between intentionally seeking to convert someone to one's religion, which encroaches upon the freedom of conscience guaranteed to all citizens, and the effort to transmit or spread the principles of one's religion, which does not. While individuals have the right to propagate their religion, intentionally converting another person to their religion goes against the principle of freedom of conscience that is guaranteed to all citizens in the country equally.

In the landmark judgement of *Bijoy Emmanuel*, the Supreme Court recognized Jehovah's Witnesses as a religious denomination.[80] The Court ruled that forcing a student who belongs to the Jehovah's Witnesses to participate in the singing of the national anthem, despite their genuine conscientious religious objection, would violate their right under Articles 19(1)(a) and 25(1) of the Indian Constitution. The right not to speak is also a fundamental right guaranteed under Article 19(1)(a). The Court took note of the practice followed by Jehovah's Witnesses in countries like England and the US, where they do not sing the national anthem but demonstrate respect by standing up when it is sung. The Court acknowledged that Jehovah's Witnesses hold a sincere and conscientious belief that their religion prohibits the singing of a national anthem:

> ... the question is not whether a particular religious belief or practice appeals to our region or sentiment but whether the belief is genuinely and conscientiously held as part of the profession or practice of religion. If the belief is genuinely and conscientiously held, it attracts the protection of Article 25 but subject, of course, to the inhibitions content therein.

77 M P Jain, *Indian Constitutional Law* (LexisNexis, 8th ed., 2018) 1206; see also *Acharya* (n 14): 'No right in an organized society can be absolute'.

78 *Lily Thomas v Union of India* AIR 2000 SC 1650, 1666.

79 *Rev Stainislaus* (n 40).

80 *Bijoe Emmanuel v State of Kerala* AIR 1987 SC 748: Three children belonging to the Jehovah's Witnesses. of the Christian Community were expelled from the school for refusing to sing the National Anthem ('*Bijoe*').

III Essentiality Test Doctrine

The other permission to religious practice requires passing the Essentiality Test. The Essentiality Test doctrine was propounded by the Supreme Court of India in the landmark case of *Sri Shirur Mutt*.[81] The object of the test is to examine whether a particular religious practice is an essential and integral part of a religion, as opposed to a mere peripheral or incidental practice. According to the ruling, only those religious practices that are considered essential to the religion are protected under Articles 25 and 26, and the state has the authority to regulate or restrict non-essential practices if they are deemed to be socially harmful or against public order, morality, or health, or the fundamental rights given in Part III of the Indian Constitution. However, this is notable in the context that the term "religion" is not defined in the Constitution, and it is understood that it is a term which is not susceptible to any precise definition.[82] In *Laksmindra*,[83] the Supreme Court has, however, given this term an expensive content as:

> Religion is certainly a matter of faith with individuals or communities, and it is not necessarily theistic. There are well known religions in India like Buddhism and Jainism which do not believe in God or in any intelligent first cause.

Further, in *P.M.A. Metropolitan*,[84] the Supreme Court has observed that:

> ... religion is the belief which binds spiritual nature of man to super-natural being. It includes worship, belief, faith, devotion etc. and extends to rituals. Religious right is the right of a person believing in a particular faith to practice it, preach it and profess it.

In subsequent cases,[85] the Supreme Court has noted down the manner in which the question of the Essentiality Test has to be performed for deciding the question:

> ... whether a given religious practice is an integral part of the religion or not[,] the test always would be whether it is regarded as such by the community following the religion or not. This question will always have to be decided by the Court and in doing so the Court may have

81 *CHRE* (n 36).
82 Jain (n 75) 1203.
83 *CHRE* (n 36) 290.
84 *PMA Metropolitan v Mohan Mar Marthoma* AIR 1995 SC 2001, 2026.
85 *Tilkayat Shri Govindlalji Maharaj v State of Rajasthan* AIR 1963 SC 1638; see also *CHRE* (n 40); *HH Srimad Perarulala ERJ Swami v State of Tamil Nadu* AIR 1972 SC 1586,1593; *AS Narayana v State of Andhra Pradesh* AIR 1996 SC 1765, 1792.

> to inquire whether the practice in question is religious in character and if it is, whether it can be regarded as an integral or essential part of the religion and the finding of the Court on such an issue will always depend upon the evidence adduced before it as to the conscience of the community and the tenets of its religion.

This Test requires that the practice which is considered under the Test is in consonance with public order, morality and not harmful to the health and respecting the basic rights of other person. The other angle from which to consider religious freedom has been discussed in relation to Article 44[86] in *John Vallatom v Union of India*.[87] The Court has observed that Article 25 guarantees religious freedom, whereas Article 44 divests religion from social relations and personal law. This has significantly been reflected in the recent and socially prominent case of *Shayara Bano*.[88] The Court, by applying the Essentiality Test, made it clear that any practice that is integral and essential to a religion is protected under Article 25, and that instant *triple talaq* (*talaq-e-biddat*)[89] is not found to be an essential religious practice. Among other cases, in *P M M Ibrahim v State of Kerala* the Court applied the essential practices doctrine to determine the rights of Muslim women to spousal maintenance.[90] At present, Article 44, which puts an obligation upon the state to secure for citizens a uniform civil code, is the subject matter of a public debate from a religious and state affairs point of view. In India, this is the comprehensive code of freedom of religion contained within Article 25–28 and the Essentiality Test doctrine). However, legal scholars raise questions on judicially determined religious practices that shall be discussed in later part of this section.

This Test has widely been used by the Indian courts to analyse the constitutional validity of various religious practices. Some examples include the offerings made by devotees at *Dargah*,[91] and their subsequent distribution among poor, not being regarded as essential religious practices of Islam,[92] performance of *Tandava* dance by *Anand Margis* in procession or public places as a non-essential religious rite,[93] the slaughtering of healthy cows on *Bakri Eid*[94]

86 Indian Constitution art 44: The State shall endeavour to secure for the citizens a uniform civil code throughout the territory of India.

87 *John Vallatom v Union of India* AIR 2003 SC 2902.

88 *Shayara Bano v Union of India* (2017) 9 SCC 1 ('*Shayara Bano*').

89 A practice in Islamic personal law where a husband can divorce his wife by uttering the word '*talaq*' thrice in one sitting.

90 *PMM Ibrahim v State of Kerala* AIR 1973 SC 106.

91 Dargah is a place of worship, pilgrimage, and reflection for Sufi devotees and Muslims in general.

92 *Durgah Committee, Ajmer v Syed Hussain Ali* 1961 AIR 1402 ('*Durgah Committee*').

93 *Acharya* (n 40).

94 *Bakri Eid* (Eid al-Adha or the Feast of Sacrifice) is a significant Islamic festival observed by Muslims worldwide.

day as a non-essential religious practice,[95] the appointment of a non-brahmin to perform *Puja* (worship) in temple as not contrary to the religious practice,[96] the use of loudspeakers for performing religious activities as not an essential practice,[97] performance of the ritual of *"Samadhi"* by Jains as not an essential practice,[98] a mosque not being an essential part of practice of religion of Islam as *Namaz* (prayer) can be offered anywhere,[99] practices with superstitious character and not having rational basis for being essential to religion not being protected,[100] and a recent case famously known as *Sabarimala Temple Entry* Case (2018), in which exclusion of women of a certain age group from entering the Sabarimala temple was not treated as an essential religious practice.[101]

The Indian courts, specifically the High Courts and Supreme Court, have played a pivotal role in determining the boundaries of religious practices and their compatibility with constitutional freedoms. Through a consistent application of the Essentiality Test doctrine, these courts have not only safeguarded an individual's right to religious belief and expression, but have also delved into administrative matters and issues of ownership in religious endowments. This separation of secular and non-secular aspects within religious activities is a testament to the doctrine's extensive influence.

Even in deeply personal aspects such as marriage, maintenance, and divorce, where certain practices are defended in the name of religion, the courts have utilised the Essentiality Test doctrine to scrutinise their constitutionality. This has led to a significant assertion: no matter how deeply entrenched a practice might be, it cannot survive if it contradicts the foundational principles of justice, liberty, equality, and fraternity enshrined in the Indian Constitution, reflecting the collective values of the nation.[102] An illustrative instance as cited above, is the landmark *Shirur Mutt* case, where the Supreme Court held that any religious practice, custom, or usage which is in violation of principles of justice, equity, and good conscience cannot endure.[103] Similarly, in the case of *Shayara Bano*, the Court confronted the issue of *triple talaq'* in the Muslim community.[104] While not explicitly invoking the term "Essentiality Test", the Court ruled that the practice could not be considered an integral part of the religion, as it ran contrary to the principles of justice, equity, and

95 *State of West Bengal v Ashutosh Lahiri* AIR 1995 SC 464.

96 *N Adithayan* (n 60).

97 *Church of God (Full Gospel) in India v KKR Majestic Colony Welfare Association* AIR 2000 SC 2773; see also *Moulana Mufti Sayeed Mohd. Noorur Rehman Barkariq v State of West Bengal* AIR 1999 Cal 15 ('*Moulana*').

98 *D P Joshi v State of Madhya Bharat* AIR 1955 SC 334.

99 *Ismail Faruqui* (n 73).

100 *State of West Bengal v Subodh Gopal Bose* AIR 1954 SC 92; see also *Durgah Committee* (n 90).

101 *Indian Young Lawyers Association v State of Kerala* AIR 2019 SC 1779 ('*IYLA*').

102 Indian Constitution preamble.

103 *Shri Sidheshwar Shaiwarya Dev v State of Madhya Pradesh* (1954) 2 SCR 1005.

104 *Shayara Bano* (n 86).

good conscience. This subtle application of the Essentiality Test doctrine, particularly evident in personal law cases, signifies its expansion and evolution. This journey extends back to the seminal case of *State of Bombay v Narasu Appa Mali* (1951), where the Bombay High Court established that personal laws, rooted in religious texts and traditions, are shielded from constitutional scrutiny under the protective umbrella of religious freedom enshrined in Article 25 of the Constitution.[105] However, later judgements of the Courts, such as *Shayara Bano*, exemplifies the doctrine's wide-ranging impact and its role in shaping India's legal landscape. In the recent case of *Aishat Shifa v State of Karnataka*, famously known as the *Hijab Ban Case*, the High Court of Karnataka, in applying the Essentiality Test, held that "...Wearing hijab should be simply a matter of choice. It may or may not be a matter of essential religious practice, but it still is, a matter of conscience, belief, expression".[106]

IV Question of the Test

Dr B R Ambedkar, while deliberating upon the importance of religious freedom and its implications in the Indian context, expressed himself that Religious beliefs in this Country are so broad that they encompass every aspect of life, from birth to death.[107] Further to his deliberation, he added that:

> There is nothing extraordinary in saying that we ought to strive hereafter to limit the definition of religion in such a manner that we shall not extend beyond beliefs and such rituals as may be connected with ceremonials which are essentially religious.[108]

The judiciary has treated it as the founding source of segregating those religious practices which are associated with the religion but are not integral parts of the faith. They are the extension of the faith, because followers are extending them and, at the same time, on their segregation, the basic structure of that faith is not dismantled. The state can interfere in such a domain to regulate the behaviour of the society by mechanism of law. It is pertinent to mention here that the issue is not "why segregation?", but "who segregates it?" There are scholars and legal experts who have expressed critical perspectives on the doctrine in various academic and legal forums:

105 *State of Bombay v Narasu Appa Mali* AIR 1952 Bom 84.

106 *Aishat Shifa v State of Karnataka* WP No. 2880 of 2022, decided on March 15, 2022 ('*Aishat Shifa*').

107 *S R Bommai vs Union of India,* 1994 AIR 1918, (the Court, while emphasising the need for a secular approach in governance, contextualized his articulation).

108 *Constituent Assembly Debates*, vol VII, 2 December 1948, 781, quoted in *Aishat Shifa* (n 104).

> The Supreme Court of India, through the creation and continued use of the essentiality test, has tried to reform religion by restricting the scope of this freedom. The judiciary has taken over the role of clergy in determining what essential and non-essential religious practices are.[109]

In addition to that, subjectivity in terms of interpretation to disassociate a religious practice relied by religious leaders and traditionalists is cause of concern for many critics to the doctrine. As such, it is argued that the Essentiality Test gives the judiciary excessive power to define and determine religious practices, potentially infringing on the autonomy of religious communities. The argument is that the Essentiality Test suffers from cultural bias, causing an interference in religious matters without adequate safeguards to stop potential misuse or misinterpretation by the judiciary which may lead to unintended restrictions on religious practices.

Coming back to the mooted question after all, who is to determine whether a particular practice is essential to religion or not? The deliberation in *Shirur Mutt* case itself acknowledges the fact that this question is to be determined by a religious denomination itself.[110] But their decision cannot be accepted as final, because the Constitution gives that power to the Court to determine, in case a question relating to religion comes on the ground that the state has interfered in the religious freedom of a person under Articles 25(1) or 26(b). The question naturally arises as to where the line is to be drawn between "what are matters of religion and what are not?"[111] Even after a practice is found to be an essential part of a religion, judicial scrutiny can be invoked if the state has transgressed the limitations permitted by the Constitution under Article 25 as on public order, morality, or health and the state's measure of social welfare. This indicates that on the basis of the judicial review power arising out of Article 25, the court is final arbitrator. Moreover, within every religion, there exist certain tenets of faith and belief, alongside practices that possess connections to religion yet essentially encompass economic, financial, and political aspects. Article 25 of the Constitution authorises the state to regulate such secular activities. It is the court which has to determine as and when such state regulation is challenged on the ground of religion – whether the relevant activities form an integral part of that religion, or a merely secular activity associated with religious practice. Hence, in India, the court has to determine a particular activity as secular, or a matter of religion and the validity of restrictions imposed by the state on the ground of the limitations provided under Article 25 of the Constitution.

109 Faizan Mustafa and Jagteshwar Singh Sohi, 'Freedom of Religion in India: Current Issues and Supreme Court Acting as Clergy' (2018) *BYU Law Review* 915.
110 *CHRE* (n 36); *Ratilal v State of Bombay* AIR 1954 SC 388 ('*Ratilal*').
111 Ibid.

With regard to essential practice finality, the weight of opinions is not less in favour of the religious community or denominations that they should decide what tenets or practices constitute religions. In various judgements, the courts have observed that a court is not competent in determining that a particular "belief or practice is not part of religion".[112] In the *Ratilal* case, it was said that "practices or performances of acts, in pursuance of religious belief are as much a part of religion as faith or belief in particular doctrines". No outside authority has any right to say that these are not essential parts of religion'.[113] In the *Jamshedji Cursetjee Tarachand* case,[114] the Court said that:

> If this is the belief of the community ... a secular judge is bound to accept that belief. It is not for him to sit in judgment on that belief. He has no right to interfere with the conscience of a donor who makes a gift in favour of what he believes to be in advancement of his religion and for the welfare of his community or of mankind, and say to him, *'You shall not do it'*.

In the *Bijoe Emmaanuel case*, it was held that the question is not whether a particular religious belief or practice appeals to our reason or sentiment, but whether the belief is genuinely and conscientiously held as part of profession or practice of religion.[115] Our personal views and reactions are irrelevant – so long as the belief is genuine and conscientiously held it attracts the protection of Article 25. Justice Gajendragadkar's words in *Govindlalji* are also in support. He said that "In deciding the question as to whether a given religious practice is an integral part of the religion or not the test always would be whether it is regarded as such by the community following the religion or not [...]".[116]

In the *Sabarimala Temple Entry Case*, Justice Indu Malhotra in her dissenting opinion said that the court should not be the authority to determine the essentiality of religious practices.[117] She argued that the court should exercise restraint in delving into questions of religious beliefs and practices, as it may lead to excessive judicial interference in matters of faith. She emphasised that the court should not be deciding what constitutes an essential religious

112 *Acharya* (n 14): Justice Lakshmanan observed what constitutes an essential part of a religion is primarily to be ascertained with reference to the doctrine of that religion itself and the Court cannot say that a belief or practice is not part of religion, relying on: *CHRE* (n 36) 1028; *Sardar Syedna Taher Saifuddin Saheb v State of Bombay* [1962] (Supp.2) SCR 496, 531–532; *Seshammal v State of Tamil Nadu* [1972] (2) SCC 11; *Ratilal* (n 108); *N Adithayan* (n 60).

113 *Ratilal* (n 108).

114 *Jamshedji Cursetjee Tarachand v Soonabai* ILR (1909) 33 Bom 122.

115 *Bijoe* (n 78).

116 *Govindlalji v State of Rajasthan* AIR 1963 SC 1638.

117 *IYLA* (n 99).

practice, stating "What constitutes an essential religious practice is for the religious community to decide". The same case has been referred to a larger nine-judge bench to reopen, among other issues, the issue of the validity of the Essentiality Test doctrine and the scope of interference by the judiciary in matters of religion.[118] D D Basu, in his book, while tracing back the process of determination of essential practice to the ancient times, said that "such questions had to be determined by the King or some representative of his, such as a *Kazi*,[119] which role is now performed by the Court in India as the judicial limb of the sovereign".[120]

V Comparative Perspective: International Examples

A Anti-Establishment Clauses

Beginning with the example of the United States, there are two clauses in the United States Constitution in relation to freedom of religion. One is the Establishment Clause and the other, the Free Exercise Clause. These two clauses are significantly independent but there may be some overlap in their application.[121] Both aim at the freedom of the individual, but their scope differs.[122]

The Establishment Clause reads: "Congress shall make no law respecting an establishment of religion or prohibiting the free exercise thereof".[123]

Similar to that discussed above, the free exercise of religion includes freedom of religious belief, freedom to practice, and to propagate religious beliefs. However, this freedom of outward religious practice or propagation is not free from restrictions if it is a threat to the public morals,[124] safety, peace or order,[125] comfort or convenience, or for the prevention of fraud.[126]

In Australia, there is provision for freedom of religion similar to the Establishment Clause under section 116[127] of the Australian Constitution.

118 6 February 2020 (First hearing of the case before nine-judge bench).

119 A religious judge or magistrate in Islamic legal tradition who has the authority to oversee and officiate various aspects of Islamic law.

120 D D Basu, *Commentary on the Constitution of India* (Lexis Nexis, 8th ed, 2008) 3485 ('*Basu 2008*').

121 *Welsh v US* (1970) 398 US 333, 373.

122 *Engel v Vitale* (1962) 370 US 421.

123 United States Constitution First Amend.

124 *Reynolds v US* (1879) 98 US 145 ('*Reynolds*').

125 *Sherbert v Vermer* (1963) 374 US 398 ('*Sherbert*'); *Thomas v Indiana Employment Security Review Board* (1981) 450 US 707.

126 *Cantwell v Connecticut* (1940) 310 US 296.

127 'The Commonwealth shall not make any law for establishing any religion, or for imposing any religious observance, or for prohibiting the free exercise of any religion, and no religious test shall be required as a qualification for any office or public trust under the Commonwealth'; see also *P A Inamdar* (n 51) at 6–7; *Krygger v Williams* (1912) 15 CLR 366, 369 (Griffith CJ).

The freedom of religion can be restricted on grounds similar to other jurisdictions like public safety and order, health, child welfare, national security and religious freedom as no defence to criminal law.[128] Section 2(a)[129] of the Canadian Charter confirms the freedom of religion, contemplating the object of such freedom as to safeguard the freedom of individual conscience and individual judgement essential to human worth and dignity.[130] Herein too, it is not an absolute freedom.[131] The Constitution of Ireland, through Article 44, outlines the relationship between the state and religion, and ensures a freedom of religion that may still be restricted on the grounds of public order and morality.[132] Similarly, the Indian Constitution in Article 25 expressly mentions the grounds of limitations[133] for state action, such as on the grounds of public order, morality, health and other fundamental rights, to restrict the profession, practice and propagation of religious belief. In all these countries, as well as Germany[134] and Japan,[135] religious belief and religious non-belief are equally protected, whereas there is no such protection to activities which are economic, commercial or political in their character, though they are associated with such belief. Further, no one can be disadvantaged by reason of adherence or non-adherence to a particular religious denomination[136] and the state can regulate the outward conduct of the religious belief. However, imposed restrictions are subject to judicial review.

The Establishment Clause in the United States Constitution has been interpreted as:

> Neither a State[137] nor the federal government can set up a Church. Neither can pass laws which aid one religion, aid all religions or prefer

128 *Adelaide Company of Jehovah's Witnesses Incorporated v Commonwealth* (1943) 67 CLR 116.

129 'Freedom of conscience and religion'.

130 *R v Big M Drug Mart Ltd* (1985) 1 SCR 295 (Canada).

131 Ibid.

132 Irish Constitution art 44(1): The State acknowledges that the homage of public worship is due to Almighty God. It shall hold His Name in reverence and shall respect and honor religion. (2) Freedom of conscience and the free profession and practice of religion are, subject to public order and morality, guaranteed to every citizen.

133 Indian Constitution art 25(1): Subject to public order, morality and health and to the other provisions of Part III of the Constitution.

134 German Constitution art 4(1): Freedom of faith and of conscience, and freedom to profess a religious or philosophical creed, shall be inviolable. (2) The undisturbed practice of religion shall be guaranteed. (3) No person shall be compelled against his conscience to render military service involving the use of arms. Details shall be regulated by a federal law.

135 Japanese Constitution art 20: Freedom of religion is guaranteed to all. No religious organization shall receive any privileges from the State, nor exercise any political authority. No person shall be compelled to take part in any religious act, celebration, rite, or practice. The State and its organs shall refrain from religious education or any other religious activity.

136 *Toracaso v Watkins* (1961) 367 US 488 ('*Toracaso*').

137 *Abington School District v Schempp* (1963) 374 US 203: the U.S. Supreme Court ruled that school-sponsored religious activities, such as reading Bible verses and reciting the Lord's Prayer in public schools, violated the Establishment Clause of the First Amendment.

> one religion over another. Neither can enforce nor influence a person to give to or remain away from Church against his will or force him to profess a belief or disbelief in any religion. No person can be punished for entertaining or professing religious beliefs or disbelieves, for church attendance or non-attendance. No tax in any amount large or small can be levied to support any religious activities or institutions whatever form they may adopt to teach or practice religion. Neither a State nor the federal government can openly or secretly participate in the affairs of any religious organizations or groups or vice-versa as observed by the Court in *Everson v Board of Education.*[138] Further, in this case it was emphasised that ... complete separation between the State and religion is best for the State and best for religion.[139]

Through earlier cases[140] in the United States, the Establishment Clause was seen as a wall of separation between church and state. However, with reference to later decisions, it was assessed that such a complete separation does not exist from the birth of the United States Constitution, nor it is contemplated by the Establishment Clause, since such rigid separation is absurd and impracticable,[141] and would defeat the purpose of the Establishment Clause by making the church and state adversaries to each other.[142] Further in *United States v Seeger*,[143] it was observed that there is no official church in the United States as there is in England. As no particular religion is entitled to get governmental support, the state cannot pick and choose among religious beliefs. India does not contribute to the consideration of separation of church and the state as it is seen in the United States. India has adopted the principle of secularism as arising from the freedom obtained through independence. It never means that the state is separate from religion, nor does it mean neutrality on the part of the state – rather, it establishes the secularity of the state.[144] The separation in the context of India should be construed in the light of the qualified freedom of religion. As H M Seervai notes, "India is [a] secular but not antireligious State".[145]

138 *Everson v Board of Education* (1947) 330 US 1, 59 ('*Everson*').
139 Ibid.
140 Ibid, *Reynolds* (n 122) 164.
141 *Lemon v Kurtzman* (1971) 403 US 602, 612 ('*Lemon*'): The Court established the *Lemon* Test to assess the constitutionality of government actions with respect to religion; see also *Lee v Weisman* (1992) 505 US 577.
142 *Zorach v Clauson* (1952) 343 US 306, 312, 314, (Douglas J).
143 *United States v Seeger* (1965) 380 US 163, 165.
144 Arvind P Bhanu, 'An Assessment of the Constitutional Space for Secularity and Equality in India' in Paul T Babie, Neville G Rochow QC and Brett G Scharffs (eds) (Edward Elgar Publishing, 2020) 320 ('*Bhanu – Assessment*').
145 HM Seervai, *Constitutional Law of India* (N M Tripathi Private Ltd, 3rd ed, 1983) 897.

B Free Exercise Clause

The US Supreme Court in *United States v Ballard*,[146] stating on the relationship of man to his God, said that:

> We are not at liberty to inquire into the truth of the appellant's religious beliefs. These are matters of faith, and they transcend our powers of thought and knowledge. Man's relation to his God is no concern of the State. He has been granted the right to worship as he pleased and to answer to no man for the variety of his religious views. To worship God in accordance with his own conscience or to entertain disbelief in any religion or the existence of God is his right. However, in the name of religious belief, one cannot be allowed to avoid the duties which every citizen owes to the Nation. But on the other side in the interest of national unity, compulsory salute cannot be imposed on those who object to it as a form of worship of a graven image.[147]

On this point, the approach of Indian Supreme Court in *Bijoe Emmanuel*[148] took a similar line, while holding that compelling a Jehovah's Witness student to join in singing of the national anthem despite their "genuine conscientious religious objection" would contravene the rights guaranteed by Articles 19(1)(a) and 25(1). Further, the Court also held that it violated Article 19(1)(a) to punish a student for not singing the national anthem when there is the negative right to remain silent, which is implied by the freedom of speech guaranteed by Article 19(1)(a). The case revolved around the conflict between the student's religious beliefs and the school's requirement to sing the national anthem.

The Court held[149] that that the government cannot inquire into the truth or falsity of religious beliefs, as it would violate the Free Exercise Clause of the First Amendment. In *Prince v Massachusetts*, the Court explained when a belief can be interfered with by the State.[150] The Court said that:

> Congress was deprived of all legislative power over mere opinion. But was left free to reach actions which were in violation of social duties or subversive of good order [...] Laws are made for the government of actions and while they cannot interfere with mere religious belief and opinions, they may with practices. Suppose that one believed that human sacrifices were a necessary part of their religious worship, would it be seriously contended that the civil government under which he lived

146 *United States v Ballard* (1940) 322 US 78 ('*Ballard*').
147 *State Board of Education v Barnette* (1943) 319 US 624 ('*Barnette*').
148 *Bijoe* (n 78).
149 *Ballard* (n 144).
150 *Prince v Massachusetts* (1944) 321 US 158.

> could not interfere to prevent a sacrifice? … To permit this would be to make the professed doctrines of religious belief superior to the law of the land, and in effect permit every citizen to become the law unto himself. Government could exist only in name under the such circumstances.

Hence, the observation of the Court that no religious belief can be allowed to defeat the objectives of the criminal law is the correct position in between mere religious belief and religious belief in practice.[151] Practices resulting from religious belief, like handling a live snake in the course of a church service,[152] polygamous marriage being prohibited by law, committing human sacrifices,[153] using peyote (an illegal drug) while claiming to be a part of a Native American church,[154] religious belief against one uniform day of rest for all workers,[155] and religious belief against the rule of compulsory high school education are not constitutionally permitted. In *Wallace*, it was observed by the Court that polygamy or bigamy can be prohibited and can be made a ground for disqualification of exercising political rights, notwithstanding the fact that it is in accordance with the creed of a religious body.[156] In India, through section 494[157] of the Indian Penal Code 1860, bigamous practice is prohibited. The constitutional validity of the offence of bigamy was challenged on the ground of religious belief in *Sarla Mudgal v Union of India*, the petitioner argued that the husband had converted to Islam and married again without obtaining a divorce from first marriages, which was permissible under Islamic law.[158] The Supreme Court, rejecting the argument, held that a Hindu husband converting to Islam solely for the purpose of contracting a second marriage without legally dissolving the first marriage would amount to a grave offence. On the other side, in the US case of *Larkin*, the Court declared unconstitutional a statute giving veto power to churches to issue liquor licenses to restaurants within five hundred feet of the church or a school.[159]

The Court said that "such delegation of power is amounting to effect of advancing religion and provides a significant symbolic benefit in the minds of some". Further, the state cannot force a person 'to profess a belief or disbelief in any religion' due to the constitutional protection to the faith. The US

151 *Bunn v N Carolina*, (1949) 336 US 942.

152 Ibid.

153 *Reynolds* (n 122); *Cleveland v US* (1946) 329 US 14.

154 *Employment Division, Department of Human Resources of Oregon v Smith* (1990) 494 US 872 ('*Smith*').

155 *Brannfield v Brown* (1961) 366 US 599.

156 *Wallace v Labrenz* (1952) 344 US 824; *George v US* (1966) 382 US 1010.

157 *Indian Penal Code* s 494: 'Whoever, having a husband or wife living, marries in any case in which such marriage is void by reason of it taking place during the life of such husband or wife, shall be punished with imprisonment of either description for a term which may extend to seven years, and shall also be liable to fine'.

158 *Sarla Mudgal v Union of India* 1995 AIR 1531.

159 *Larken v Grendel's Dew* (1982) 459 US 116.

Supreme Court in *Toracaso v Watkins* invalidated a provision in the Maryland Constitution requiring state officials to declare their belief in the existence of God.[160] In subsequent cases, the Court applied the *Toracaso* principle to invalidate statutes forcing a person to become a believer or disbeliever.

VI Judicial Treatise with Doctrines

As it is universally understood that every person desires one's spiritual well-being, the constitutions of different countries set out provisions granting freedom of belief. While entertaining their inner conscience, they may come out associated with what is not granted in the name of the freedom. The state, through the mechanism of law in these democratic countries, regulates the limitations set by their basic law of the land. To make sure that the state, through its legislative or executive action, cannot invade the domain, which is protected for spiritual well-being, the courts have propounded doctrines and applied them in finding whether a religious practice is associated with secular activities or it is an essential part of religion. As referred to previously, the Supreme Court of India, in 1954, developed the Essentiality Test. However, it is unexplained in India what the Court did from 1950 to 1954 to segregate the associated activities with religious practice.

Similarly, in the United States, for making "religious scrutiny" tests like the *Lemon* Test, also known as the "No Aid Test", and the *Sherbert/Yoder* Test were developed. The *Lemon* Test was developed by the Supreme Court in the case of *Lemon v Kurtzman* to check whether state action or law is aligned with a secular purpose or if promoting or endorsing religious beliefs or practices will result in an excessive entanglement between government and religion.[161] The *Sherbert/Yoder* Test is the result of the combination of two Supreme Court cases, *Sherbert v Verner*[162] and *Wisconsin v Yoder*.[163] This test is applied where the petitioner seeks exemptions from generally applicable laws or regulations due to their religious beliefs.[164] One more notable test known as the *Smith* Test is designed to protect the Free Exercise Clause and was established by the Supreme Court of United States in the case of *Employment Division v Smith* in 1990.[165] The *Lemon* Test, though not the first test, remained one of the most well-known and enduring tests to be applied by the courts in the United States. However, it has also been the subject of debate and criticism over the years, and its application by courts has varied, as has been seen in the case of the Essentiality Test in India. On the other side, it is contended that it provides a valuable framework for balancing religious freedom with the

160 *Toracaso* (n 134).
161 *Lemon* (n 139).
162 *Sherbert* (n 123).
163 *Wisconsin v Yoder* (1972) 406 US 205.
164 See *Frazee v Illinois Department of Employment Security* (1989) 498 US 829.
165 *Smith* (n 152).

separation of church and state. The *Sherbert/Yoder* Test and the *Smith* Test, which are applied to strike a balance between religious freedom and the government's interest in regulating various aspects of public life, have also been the subject of criticism and legal debate. However, it is not always so easy to decide if any particular matter falls under essential religious practice or is only a secular, commercial, or political activity which has come to associated with the religion.[166] *Bijoe Emmanuel*, as referred to earlier, was recognised by the Kerala High Court differently than from the Supreme Court, as no infringement of the right of children regarding religion on the ground that it is their fundamental duty to sing the national anthem and the school expulsion was upheld.[167]

The courts in the United States are not an exception to this view. In *Minersville School District v Gobitis*,[168] two children belonging to Jehovah's Witnesses were expelled from their school for refusing to salute the national flag as part of a daily exercise. Their defence was that saluting the flag is contrary to the injunction laid down in their holy scriptures. The US Supreme Court held that no infringement of their right to freedom of religion occurred, and that it was within the competence of the legislature to adopt appropriate means to evoke and foster a sentiment of national unity among the children in the school. However, within two years the Court retracted the view taken in that case and held that the action of the State, in making it compulsory for children in public schools to salute the national flag, violated their fundamental right of religion.[169] The US Supreme Court is constantly endeavouring to reconcile the Anti-Establishment and Free Exercise clauses. The Supreme Court in India too, though applying the Essentiality Test doctrine to come to a conclusion when a matter is challenged on the ground of religious freedom, is revisiting the Essentiality Test following a recent development in referring the *Sabarimala temple entry* case[170] issue to a seven-judge bench to enquire about, among other religious issues, the Essentiality Test doctrine, clearly indicating that a refinement, replacement, or renouncement (3 Rs) is being considered.

VII Display of Religious Marks in Public Space

Certainly, a person's relation through his conscience to his God is an individual and private affair. This spiritual well-being is recognised by the basic law of many countries. However, once the entertainment of one's conscience is allowed outwardly, the same law of the land must also take care of the liberty of others. In India, the US, Australia, Canada, and even the UK wherein

166 M P Singh (n 16) 262.
167 *Bijoe* (n 78).
168 *Minersville School District v Gobitis* (1940) 310 US 586.
169 *West Virginia State Board of Education v Barnette* (1942) 319 US 624.
170 *IYLA* (n 99).

there is no separation of church and state, every person has the freedom of conscience and profession of his own religion, and this freedom goes to the extent of propaganda for a non-religious society.[171] This is the manifestation and size of freedom of religion. However, the fact that it is a personal affair, individual freedom and individual spiritual well-being still invites the question whether public demonstrations of religious marks should be allowed. In India, during the Constituent Assembly debates, there was extensive discussion on the issue of religious freedom and the protection of individual rights, including the right to display religious marks on one's body. *Tazul Islam* proposed that an explanation should be added to prohibit the wearing of religious marks in public places.[172] However, his proposal was not accepted by the Assembly on the ground that India was a diverse country.[173] Article 25 of the Indian Constitution, in providing the freedom to profess one's religion, encompasses the right to display religious symbols and marks. The other provision supporting this is under Article 19, protecting freedom of expression, meaning the display of religious marks on one's body can be protected. In several cases, if any mark is an essential part of the religion, it has been allowed to be displayed on someone's body even in public places.[174] The validity of religious markings on the body is also determined with reference to the Essentiality Test, the validity of which is itself in doubt.

In the case of *Amnah Bint Basheer v Central Board of Secondary Education* (*CBSE*), the petitioner challenged the dress code prescribed by the CBSE for the National Eligibility cum Entrance Test (NEET). The dress code prohibited the wearing of headscarves, full-sleeved shirts, and other religious symbols. The petitioner argued that the dress code violated her right to freedom of religion under Article 25 of the Constitution. The Court held that the practice of wearing a *hijab* constitutes an essential religious practice and the petition was allowed. However, in *Fathima Thasneem v State of Kerala*, by the same High Court of Kerala on the same contention of protection, the *hijab* as a religious symbol in school held that the "collective rights" of an

171 *Bowman v Secular Society* (1917) AC 406.

172 A member of the Constituent Assembly of India and a member of the Bengal Legislative Assembly who represented the Muslim League.

173 *Constituent Assembly Debates*, 3 and 6 December 1948.

174 *Sardar Syedna Taher Saifuddin Saheb v State of Bombay* 1962 AIR 853: It was held that the wearing of a religious cap by a Muslim was an essential part of his religion and was protected under Article 25 of the Constitution; see also *Bijoe* (n 78): Kerala High Court held that the wearing of a religious symbol, such as a cross, was a part of the Christian religion and was protected under Article 25 of the Constitution; *Acharya* (n 14): Supreme Court held that the wearing of saffron robes by a Hindu monk was an essential part of his religion and was protected under Article 25 of the Constitution; *State of Punjab v Sodhi Sukhdev Singh* 1961 AIR 493: held that the wearing of a *kirpan* by a Sikh was an essential part of his religion and was protected under Article 25 of the Constitution; *Moulana* (n 95): Calcutta High Court upheld the right of Muslim students to wear religious marks, including headscarves, in educational institutions as an expression of their religious beliefs.

institution would be given primacy over the individual rights of the petitioner.[175] In a recent case, it was held that wearing the *hijab* was not an essential religious practice in Islam, and hence, was not allowed to be displayed on the body in school.[176] In *Aishat Shifa*, a two-judge bench of the Supreme Court delivered a split opinion upholding a state order that mandated a uniform for educational institutions, consequently banning the *hijab*. Writing for the Court, Justice Gupta affirmed the High Court's decision, while Justice Dhulia decided in favour of the appellants.[177] The case has been referred to a larger bench of the Supreme Court.[178]

Explanation-I to Article 25 of the Indian Constitution recognises rights of the followers of the Sikh religion to wear and carry on their persons *kirpan* (a sword) as an emblem of their religion.[179] No size and shape have been prescribed by the Sikh religion. It may be a sword of any size and shape, but that a Sikh is not allowed to possess an extra sword without license was judicially determined in 1952.[180] Thus, the displaying of an essential mark of one's religion on the body in public places is constitutionally protected. However, the school system is seen differently, with the final word of India's apex court pending, as the case has been referred to a larger bench as noted. The judicial approach in the United States in upholding the protection of religious markings on the body in public places if they are integrated in good faith with a person's religious beliefs and do not infringe the rights of others and are not injurious to public health, safety, or order, is not seemingly connected to any similar principle. The *Hobbs* ruling by the US Supreme Court is one of the examples wherein a Muslim prisoner argued that growing a beard was a necessary part of the practice of his religion.[181] Prohibiting him from growing a short beard in accordance with his religious beliefs has violated the *Religious Land Use and Institutionalized Persons Act* (RLUIPA). However, the Supreme Court in India in *Mohammed Zubair* did not accept the contention to maintain a beard as an essential practice of religion by a member of the Indian Air Force on the ground of Armed Forces discipline.[182] Similarly, in *Mohd. Farman*, the Allahabad High Court held that the maintaining of a beard by a member of a disciplined force may not be protected under Article 25 of the Indian Constitution.[183] There are many examples wherein the higher

175 *Fathima Thasneem v State of Kerala* [High Court of Karnataka, 4 December 2018].

176 *Resham v State of Karnataka* [High Court of Karnataka, 10 February 2022].

177 *Aishat Shifa* (n 104).

178 Referred to a larger bench on 13 October 2022.

179 The *kirpan* is a religious symbol of *Sikh* religion is similar to other religious symbols such as the Christian cross, the Jewish Star of David or the Muslim hijab, with one crucial exception: it is not optional; see also *Masud Alam v Commissioner of Police* AIR 1956 Cal. 9.

180 *R v Dhyan Singh* AIR 1952 ALL 53.

181 *Holt v Hobbs* 574 US 352.

182 *Mohammed Zubair Corporal No 781467-G v Union of India* AIR 2017 SC 107.

183 *Mohd Farman v State of UP* [2021] AIR (All) 2536.

and highest courts of the judiciary have not been on same page in respect of religious markings on the body in a public place. The reference to the Essentiality Test, along with the restrictions on the practice, are seen to have been applied before coming to the conclusion. Certainly, the words of Chief Justice Waite in *Reynolds* (1879) are quite relevant while looking for constitutional permissions to have religious markings on the body in public spaces: "Laws are made for the government of actions, and while they cannot interfere with mere religious belief and opinions, they may with practices".[184]

VIII Conclusion

The exploration of the intricate relationship between religion, individual rights, and constitutional provisions in India, coupled with a comparative analysis, has unveiled the multifaceted dimensions of religious freedom. This has become a focal point of constitutional concerns and has shaped the judicial approach to balancing the rights assigned to the individuals. While the Indian Constitution expressly provides the grounds for restrictions on religious freedom, the judiciary has had to develop its own tools to further refine the boundaries of religious freedom within the legal order. This comparative study has revealed that similar judicial efforts have also been made in other countries, reflecting a global discourse on religious freedom.

From the perspective of spiritual well-being, the protection of the relationship between an individual and their faith has been addressed in a positive manner. The secular principles upheld by the fundamental laws of various nations play a significant role in safeguarding the freedom of religion. As demonstrated in the examination in this chapter, the legal framework, commitment to secularism, and landmark judicial decisions provide a deeper understanding of how and when religion is treated as a personal matter subject to constitutional restrictions, especially when it extends into the public domain.

Analysing the delicate balance between individual religious freedom and the state's authority to regulate religious practices in the interest of public order, health, and morality, it becomes evident that India's Constitution, like those of other nations, strives to strike this equilibrium. The application of the Essentiality Test in determining the validity of religious practices stands out as a prominent example of this balance, evolving through significant judicial decisions. However, the questions of such judicial approaches to set boundaries for exercising religious faith demands scrutiny. Furthermore, the discussion delves into the permissions for, and implications of, displaying religious marks on the body in public spaces. This highlights the nuanced intersection of religious expression, individual rights, and societal norms. It underscores the importance of upholding fundamental rights while still acknowledging the necessity for reasonable restrictions to maintain harmony in a diverse society.

184 *Reynolds* (n 122).

This comprehensive examination of the interplay between religion, constitutional provisions, and individual freedoms underscores the importance of preserving the sanctity of the principles of justice, liberty, equality, and fraternity. As India and other nations continue to grapple with these complex issues, it becomes clear that the maintenance of these principles is paramount to achieving a harmonious and just society. We may close with the reflections of the former Chief Justice of the Supreme Court of India, Justice R C Lahoti, in his lecture on the occasion of Constitution Day in 2017, in which he made reference to the treatment of secular constitutions in religious thought. He quoted a verse from the *Shrimad Bhagavad Gita* as follows:

In *Shrimad Bhagavad Gita* Lord Krishna has said

Sarva dharmani parityajyam mamekam sharanam brajah.[185]

What this means is – do practice and profess your religion, yet surrender to Me as I am Religion of all religions. Adapting this *shloka* to our Constitution, it can be said – our Constitution is Religion of all religions and unconditional surrender to the command of the Constitution, rising above the narrow dogmas can resolve our several issues.[186]

This reflection sets out the idea that the Indian constitutional sense of the freedom of religion is based in the principle of unity in diversity[187] and in commitment to *justice, liberty, equality,* and *fraternity.*

Further Reading:

For analysis of the methods used in this chapter, see Chapter 15 - Section IV – subsection A *The Doctrinal Method*; F *The Yardstick Method.*

For the author's rejoinder and reflection, see Appendix Section VIII.

For chapters discussing the United States see, Chapters 6, 7, and 11.

185 AC Bhaktivedanta Swami Prabhupada, *Bhagavad Gita – As It Is* (Bhaktivedanta Book Trust, 2nd ed, 1986).

186 Justice RC Lahoti, 'Constitutional Values' (Speech, 26 November 2017); cited in Babie & Bahnu – Freedom (n 38).

187 Bhanu – Assessment (n 142) 338.

14 Grounded Theory in the Study of Religion: A Critical Appraisal to Socio-cultural Factors and Gender-Based Legislation in Brazil and Pakistan

Flavia Bellieni Zimmermann[1]

I Introduction

The assumption "from theory to empirical research", is questioned through a grounded theory episteme.[2] Initially developed by Glaser and Strass,[3] it is currently one of the most relevant approaches to qualitative research analysis. This methodology is a grassroots inductive process emerging as a response to the deductive twentieth century hypothesis-driven theories, allowing researchers to distance themselves from biases and epistemological preconceptions.[4] Grounded theory upholds the view that "concept and hypothesis should not precede the gathering of information".[5] Thus, the theoretical approaches of this chapter are investigated throughout the qualitative interviews, "rooting" them to social reality and observation. This qualitative research design allows for the testing of theories, making room for improvement, as well as for new theoretical frameworks to flourish. By providing greater freedom for academic exploration, grounded theory can be instrumental in improving gender empowerment legislation in traditional cultures, which are significantly influenced by religious views towards the family.

Through grounded theory, a method where results and new theory are forged through emerging new data, the chapter explores shortcomings from the legislation dealing with women in Brazil and Pakistan. The chapter looks critically at the role of honour and religion in gender relations, and how the nuance of these variables is not reflected in gender legislation when dealing with violence against women. Qualitative interviews with Brazilian and Pakistani women in Australia show that honour and religion are integral parts

1 Lecturer in Public Policy, School of Social and Political Sciences, the University of Melbourne; Adjunct Research Fellow, School of Social Sciences, the University of Western Australia.
2 Ibid.
3 Helen Heath and Sarah Cowley, 'Developing a Grounded Theory Approach: A Comparison of Glaser and Strauss' (2004) *International Journal of Nursing Studies* vol. 41, 2, 141–150.
4 Ibid.
5 Corbetta (n 1).

DOI: 10.4324/9781003397311-19

of their identities, although experienced across a spectrum. In the case of Brazil, honour and the role of religion are not reflected in legislation to protect women from violence. In the case of Pakistan, essentialising perspectives dismiss women's agency and views towards honour. Legislation endeavours to clamp down on honour killings, but does not acknowledge views towards honour and religion that are "moderate", which could be leveraged by state initiatives.

The chapter, firstly, explores Brazil's views towards honour and religion, and legislation dealing with violence towards women in Brazil and the crimes of femicides. The chapter then examines Pakistan's views towards honour and religion and state initiatives to address the endemic levels of honour-based violence, particularly so-called "honour killings". The third part of this chapter draws from 30 interviews conducted in Australia, using grounded theory as the main epistemological framework. Data results show new perspectives on honour and religion and how there is a spectrum as to how it shapes gender relations. The views of Brazilian and Pakistani women bridge the gap between current legislation addressing violence against women in both countries. The chapter demonstrates how the use of grounded theory, and conducting fieldwork "with no strings attached", can be instrumental in the study of law and religion and how to better frame legislation addressing traditional views towards gender, violence towards women, and women's empowerment.

II Brazil's and Pakistan's Histories, Populations, Religions, and Legislation – The Use of Grounded Theory as a Research Method Bridging the Gap between Culture, Society, and Law

This section provides an overview of Brazil's and Pakistan's histories, populations, and religious affiliations, with a brief discussion on the legislation addressing violence and the killings of women. Then the section outlines how this research, and the use of grounded theory, bridges the disconnection between Brazilian and Pakistani experiences of honour, religion, and gender, with the current legislation. It explains how this methodological approach paves the way for new legal approaches that can be more effective in the fight against violence against women.

A Brazil

Brazil was discovered by the Portuguese in 1500, with the period until 1815 regarded as Brazil's colonial period. In 1815, the Portuguese Royal family relocated the metropolis' centre of power to Rio de Janeiro during Europe's Napoleonic Wars, elevating Brazil to a kingdom in union with Portugal and

Algarves.[6] Brazil's independence from the Portuguese Crown was declared on 7 September 1822 by Don João VI's son, Prince Don Pedro I. The 1822–1889 period is known as Brazil's "Empire", with the Portuguese heirs remaining as heads of state under a constitutional monarchy.[7] Brazil's first Republican period started with the Republic's declaration in 1889, lasting until 1964. In 1964, Brazil's military staged a coup d'état, with this period of government ended in 1985. Since then, Brazil has been going through a "re-democratisation period". Brazil is a country with great ethnic diversity but has been marred by the mistreatment of its Indigenous peoples during the times of colonisation, as well as the ill-treatment of African slaves. From colonial times until the end of Brazil's 'Empire', there was no separation between church and state, with Catholicism being Brazil's official religion.[8] Brazil's colonisation and history goes some way towards an explanation of the current and acute social divides and different lived experiences based on class, social status, race, and region (in both urban and rural areas).

In the nineteenth century, Catholicism became the official religion of Brazil and was formally institutionalised into the country's political and social systems. Whilst this formality has eased greatly, Brazil still has one of the largest Christian populations in the world. According to the World Bank Data 2022,[9] Brazil has a population of over 212 million people. Data from the Pew Research Centre indicates Brazil as being the second largest Christian nation in the world with 175,770,000 believers, behind only the US.[10] Statistical data shows Brazil's religious composition with 54.2 per cent of Catholics, 20.5 per cent of Evangelicals (unspecified), 3.7 per cent of Pentecostal evangelists, 2.0 per cent of Afro-American cults (Umbanda), 0.8 per cent of Protestants, 0.7 per cent of Jehovah's Witnesses, 0.6 per cent of Adventists, 0.3 per cent believers without formal affiliation to any religion, 0.1 per cent Mormons, 2.8 per cent of other religions, 12.1 per cent no religion, 0.4 per cent agnostic, and "unsure about affiliation" at 0.9 per cent. A 2019 Datafolha survey indicates that over 80 per cent of the Brazilian population follows Christian beliefs, with 50 per cent being Catholics, 31 per cent Evangelicals, and only 10 per cent "without religion".[11]

6 Sérgio Buarque de Holanda and Pedro Moacyr Campos, *'História geral da civilização brasileira'* (Editora Bertrand, 1985).

7 Ibid.

8 Ibid.

9 World Bank Open Data, *Population Brazil* (Web Page, 26 May 2024) https://data.worldbank.org/indicator/SP.POP.TOTL.

10 Pew Research Centre. *Regional Distribution of Christians* (Web Page, 26 May 2024) https://www.pewresearch.org/religion/2011/12/19/global-christianity-regions/

11 Data Folha. *44% dos Evangélicos são ex-Catolicos* (Web Page, 26 May 2024) https://datafolha.folha.uol.com.br/opiniaopublica/2016/12/1845231-44-dos-evangelicos-sao-ex-catolicos.shtml.

Brazil, a former Portuguese colony, is a country following the codified Romano-Germanic civil law tradition and the civil law system. Therefore, it is a country relying on legal codes and legislation rather than legal precedents. Brazil's Law 11.340 from 07 August 2006, better known as "Lei Maria da Penha", is a key piece of legislation in the criminalisation of acts of violence towards women. Brazil's 1988 Constitution, in article 226, expanded fundamental rights to include the right of women to be treated equally before the law. Nonetheless, given cultural views towards the role of women and high levels of violence towards women, there was a need to also enact new legislation establishing legal mechanisms to prevent domestic and family violence. The "Lei Maria da Penha" was named after the life story of a pharmacist who suffered many years of domestic violence under the hands of her former husband.[12] He attempted to kill her, but she survived. The attempted murder left her paraplegic. Maria da Penha became an activist for women's rights in the fight against violence against women, denouncing the legal barriers women face to bring their aggressors to justice.[13] She became a relentless advocate for women's rights and lobbied for years to the Centre for Justice and International Law (CEJIL) and the Latin America and Caribbean Committee for the Defence of Women's Rights (CLADEM). In 1988, these international bodies referred her case to the Inter-American Commission of Human Rights of the Organization of the American States (OAS). The international pressure opened a window of opportunity for legal reforms in the prevention of violence towards women in Brazil.

The Maria da Penha Law creates mechanisms to prevent domestic and family violence against women and special domestic and family violence courts, establishing assistance for female victims of domestic violence.[14] The legislation guarantees that every woman, regardless of their class, race, ethnicity, sexual orientation, income, culture, educational level, age, or religion, will have their fundamental rights protected – which means to live a life which is free from violence, either physical or physiological.[15] The Maria da Penha Law aims to protect the conditions for women's exercise of their rights to life, security, health, food, education, housing, freedom, dignity, and respect within the family and community.

12 After surviving the first attempt of murder, Maria's former husband tried to electrocute her. The violence was also extended to their daughters. In 1994, she wrote a memoir called *I've Survived … to Tell My Story* where she tells the years of violence she and her daughters endured. See https://www.fundobrasil.org.br/blog/lei-maria-da-penha-historia-e-fatos-principais/.

13 Fundo Brasil. *Lei Maria da Penha* (Web Page 26 May 2024) https://www.fundobrasil.org.br/blog/lei-maria-da-penha-historia-e-fatos-principais/.

14 Casa Civil. *Constituicao Federativa do Brasil 1988* (Web Page 26 May 2024) http://www.planalto.gov.br/ccivil_03/Constituicao/Constituicao.htm#art226§8, Title I Fundamental Principles.

15 Ibid.

This legislation paved the way for Brazil's Lei do Feminicidio (Femicide Law), an important legislation tackling gender-based-violence. Former President Dilma Rousseff enacted Law 13.104 (Femicide Law) on 9 March 2015, amending Brazil's Criminal Code.[16] The Femicide Law created a new type of homicide classification (femicide), as an aggravating factor to the crime of murder.[17] According to the legislation, the crime of femicide is the killing of a woman because of their gender, and when it results from domestic violence.[18]

Yet Brazil is one of the most dangerous countries in the world for women, with the highest numbers of violence towards women – 14 women are physically assaulted per minute.[19] Brazil's annual Report of National Security 2023 indicates that the levels of violence against women and femicides increased 6.1 per cent compared to 2022.[20]

B Pakistan

Indian Muslim frustration with underrepresentation during British rule led to the creation of the state of Pakistan in 1947. British-trained lawyer, Muslim nationalist Mohammed Ali Jinnah, was the leading architect of Pakistan's fight for political rights and independence.[21] By evoking Indian Muslim rights of self-determination, Jinnah fought for an undivided Punjab and Bengal for Indian Muslims.[22] In 1947, the Pakistani state was established in the Muslim majority regions of Punjab and Bengal, in Western and East Pakistan. Though East Pakistan seceded after the third Indo-Pakistani War in 1971, forming the state of Bangladesh, Indian Muslim nationalism is an important factor in Pakistani identity formation. Scholarship discussing the genesis of Pakistan ascribes a central role to religion in relation to Indian Muslim nationalism.[23] More recent perspectives unravel a secularist view of Muslim nationalist aspira-

16 Casa Civil. *Lei 113104* (Web Page 26 May 2024) https://www.planalto.gov.br/ccivil_03/_ato2015-2018/2015/lei/l13104.htm art1, review of art121 Decree-Law (Executive Order) no. 2.848, de 7 December 1940 – Brazil's Penal Code.

17 Ibid.

18 Ibid.

19 Flavia Bellieni Zimmermann, 'Women's Empowerment and Equality in Brazil: One Step Forward and Two Steps Back?' (2024) *Australian Outlook* (online) https://www.internationalaffairs.org.au/australianoutlook/womens-empowerment-and-equality-in-brazil-one-step-forward-and-two-steps-back/.

20 Anuario Brasileiro de Seguranca Publica 2023 (Web Page, 27 May 2024) https://forumseguranca.org.br/wp-content/uploads/2023/07/anuario-2023.pdf. The original information, in Portuguese, was translated to English by the author.

21 Ayesha Jalal, *The Struggle for Pakistan: A Muslim Homeland and Global Politics*' (Harvard University Press, 2014), vol. 34/35 (4/1) ('*The Struggle for Pakistan*').

22 Ayesha Jalal, 'The Creation of Pakistan' (2017) *Oxford Research Encyclopedia of Asian History* 114.

23 Stephen P Cohen and Milind Thakar, 'The Idea of Pakistan' (2006) 5(2) *India Review* 233.

tions, with deep governance divides over representation in post-colonial India being the key drivers for the creation of an independent state.

According to the World Population Review 2021, Pakistan has a population of over 226 million people, with one of the highest birth rates in the world.[24] Pakistan is also a state suffering various security challenges,[25] including political extremism, secessionist, interfaith and intrafaith extremist violence, and ethnic tensions.[26] Even though it was created as a state for Muslims, Pakistan is characterised by diversity in its religious and ethnic composition. The leading religion is Islam, with Muslims making up 96.2 per cent of the population according to the 2017 census.[27] But the country also encompasses other religious minorities. Accordingly, Hindus comprise 1.6 per cent of the population, followed by Christians 1.59 per cent, "scheduled castes" 0.25 per cent, Ahmadis 0.22 per cent, and other minorities 0.07 per cent.[28] The main ethnic groups in Pakistan are Punjabis, Sindhis, Balochis, and Pashtuns in the Northwest Frontier and the formerly Federally Administered Tribal Areas, near the border with Afghanistan. Each ethnic group represents, respectively: Punjabis 44.7 per cent of the population, followed by Pashtuns 15.4 per cent, Sindhis 14.1 per cent, Sariakis 8.4 per cent, Muhajirs 7.6 per cent, Balochis 3.6 per cent, with 6.2 per cent representing other ethnic groups.[29]

Pakistan's legal system is influenced by the English common law system, based on legal precedents and Sharia law. It adapted its pre-1947 colonial law with amendments inspired in Islamic traditions. Legal scholars contest the compatibility of the system of precedent and common law doctrine with Islamic law, and Pakistan's Federal Sharia Courts.[30] Islamic law derives from two primary sources: the *Quran* and *Sunnah* (traditions based on the life and examples set by the Holy Prophet). Comprising these two sources together is what is known as Sharia law. According to Sharia law, there are two categories: penal offences such as *hadd* and *tazir*, and *qisas* and *diyyat* offences.[31] *Qisas* and *diyyat* defines the offence and punishment under Islamic terms in cases of

24 World Population Review. *Pakistan Population 2021* (Web Page, 26 May 2024) https://worldpopulationreview.com/countries/pakistan-population.

25 Salma Malik, 'Security Sector Reforms in Pakistan: Significance, Challenges and Impediments' (2018) 38(3) *Strategic Studies.* 1–21.

26 Saira Yamin and Salma Malik, Mapping Conflict Trends in Pakistan (United States Institute of Peace, 2014).

27 Pakistan Population and Housing Census 2017 (Web Page, 27 May 2024). https://ghdx.healthdata.org/record/pakistan-population-and-housing-census-2017

28 Pakistan Population and Housing Census 2017 (Web Page, 27 May 2024). https://ghdx.healthdata.org/record/pakistan-population-and-housing-census-2017.

29 World Atlas, *Ethnic Groups in Pakistan* (Web Page, 27 May 2024) https://www.worldatlas.com/articles/ethnic-groups-in-pakistan.html.

30 Muhammad Munir, 'Precedent in Islamic Law with Special Reference to the Federal Shariat Court and the Legal System in Pakistan' (2008) 1 *Islamic Studies* 445–482.

31 Maha Shafqat, 'Does the Concept of Qisas and Diyyat in Sharia Law Omit to Provide Justice for Victims of Honor Killings?' (LLM Thesis, University of London, 2024).

murder, homicide, or infliction of injury. [32]*Qisas* are the equal punishment for the crime of murder, and *diyyat* the financial compensation to the victims and their legal heirs – also known as "blood money".

During Pakistan's Islamisation process, introduced by former military dictator Zia-ul-Haq, the Supreme Court declared parts of the penal code "un-Islamic" due to the lack of mention to *qisas* and *diyyats.*[33] *Federation v Gul Hassan 1989* introduced *qisas* and *diyyat* to Pakistan's legal system. Many scholars dispute the right of retribution and *diyyat*'s payment of "blood money" as compatible with both Islamic law and Sharia law.[34] Only in 2004, as the result of many years of domestic and international lobbying by Pakistani women's groups, Pakistan's Penal Code (PPC) and Criminal Procedure Code (CrPC) were amended. These amendments included a definition of *karo kari* (honour killings) as murder with penal punishment.[35] Nonetheless, Pakistan's right of *qisas* and *diyyat* and the right to retribution continued to provide a legal loophole for honour killings against women and girls.

In 2016, international pressure against honour killings in Pakistan reached new heights after Pakistani film maker Sharmeen Obaid Chinoy won an Academy Award for the *Girl by the River* documentary, depicting honour killings in Pakistan. The assassination of Pakistani model and social media start Qandeel Balochi was another important turning point for new legislation tackling honour killings in the country.[36] Baloch was murdered by her brother for breaking traditional Pakistani gender norms and expectations of 'female piety'. Baloch is an interesting case study. She lived life on her own terms. Her case demonstrates that traditional views of honour and religion leading to violence are not restricted to those women with no access to resources and information and who live in remote areas of the country.[37] Balochi's case led Pakistan's Senate to pass an anti-honour-killing bill eliminating family rights to *qisas* and *diyyat* (right of pardon) for the murder of women "in the name of honour". The *Criminal Law Act (Amendment) Offences in the Name or Pretext of Honour 2016* addresses offences in the name of honour by amending the Pakistani Criminal Code's sections 290, 302, 309, 310, 338E, and 345.[38] These reforms included the *Fasad-fil-arz* concept, which is used to decide

32 Ibid.

33 Dawn, How to Get Away with Murder: Pakistan Edition (Web Page, 27 May 2024) https://www.dawn.com/news/1715680.

34 Shafqat (n 31).

35 Asif Khan and Ullah Maseeh, '*Judicial Patronage of Honor Killings' in Pakistan: The Supreme Court's Persistent Adherence to the Doctrine of Grave and Sudden Provocation'* (2022) SSRN Electronic Journal.

36 Dawn. *PM Nawaz Vows to Eradicate Honour Killings after the Oscar's Nod* (Web Page, 26 May 2024) https://www.dawn.com/news/1233168.

37 Ibid.

38 Criminal Law Act (Amendment) (Offences in the Name or Pretext of Honour) Act 2016.

the severity of punishment awarded to offences committed in the name of honour.[39]

Regardless of the change in legislation, Pakistan's levels of violence and the killings of women continue to rise. According to the Human Rights Commission in Pakistan, in 2019, 2020, and 2021, there were over 11,000 reported cases of rape and gang rape, with 4,000 murders of women and 1,000 cases of honour killings.[40]

C Women Interviewed

Drawing from 30 interviews with Brazilian and Pakistani women, this chapter discusses how their lived experiences of honour, religion, and gender are transmitted in Australia. The use of grounded theory, and freedom from other pre-existing theoretical frameworks, provided greater insight into their stories. According to data results, there are limitations in the legislation addressing violence against women in both countries. It fails to reflect the nuances of these women's lived experiences.

In this chapter I explore how their stories of honour and religion significantly shape their identities in Australia. Participants explained how each person has their own experience of honour and religion, elaborating how their experiences are predominantly positive and not associated, in any shape or form, with violence. Their experiences were classified as "moderate", and manifested through traditional notions of womanhood within the family, reconciled with women's agency, political activism, and the fight against violence towards women. In the perspective of participants, there are also "extreme" notions, which are characterised by female suppression, violence towards women, and honour killings. These women's experiences were dissociated from violence and oppression. However, their 'moderate' perspective has not been incorporated into either Brazil's or Pakistan's legislation, and policies in the prevention of violence towards women.

The lack of in-depth investigation and consultation with the main stakeholders, women, is reflected in the Brazilian legislation, which fails to incorporate the killings of women under the umbrella of honour-based violence, as well as addressing only "extreme" manifestations of honour, religion, and gender. The legislation protecting women from violence and addressing honour killings in Pakistan ignores the multidimensional aspects of honour, religion, and gender in the lived experiences of these women. This persistent institutional failure and the lack of nuance in legal and policy responses is manifested

39 Ibid.

40 The Nation. *Unfolding the Honour Killing Phenomenon in Pakistan* (Web Page, 27 May 2024) https://www.nation.com.pk/02-Jan-2024/unfolding-the-honour-killing-phenomenon-in-pakistan#:~:text=In%20the%20year%202023%20till,%2C%20Lahore%2C%20Sheikhupura%20and%20Kasur.

through the skyrocketing levels of violence and killings of women, both in Brazil and Pakistan.

In both case studies, legislation criminalises acts of violence and the killings of women, addressing "extreme" manifestations of honour and religion associated with female oppression and an absence of agency. The chapter brings a nuanced view of lived experiences of honour and religion. This chapter explains how "moderate" views towards honour, religion, and gender are associated with women's agency and can pave the way for new legal approaches. This new perspective contributes to future strategy in crime prevention and re-education programs to engage men in changing societal views towards women.

III Theoretical Framework Approaches to Data Analysis

The chapter draws from grounded theory, with data results being analysed as a means for providing greater understandings of traditional views towards gender and religion in legislation to protect women from violence in Brazil and Pakistan.

The main aim of the use of grounded theory in this study is to situate Brazilian and Pakistani women's lived experiences of honour and religion, and how these views are reflected (or not) in legislation addressing violence towards women. By applying grounded theory, I approach data from an inductive method, instructing a new framing of analysis, proposing a new perspective on how to deal with gender, honour, and religion in Brazil and Pakistan. Data results impact how we see legislation dealing with violence against women in Brazil and Pakistan, as not reaching out to real perception of honour and religion experienced in both countries.

A qualitative framework allows greater sensitivity and understanding towards participants.[41] Qualitative interviews open frames of reference, with emerging themes providing a platform to explore the stories and experience of the participants, demonstrating a comprehensive picture of traditional views of gender and the role of religion. In addition, qualitative individual interviews with open-ended questions provided greater flexibility for the interviewer and for the interviewees. This methodology allowed participants to reflect upon their lived experiences, and for the researcher to understand in greater depth the themes and nuances shaping their notions of honour, the interplay of honour and religion, and how these affect migrant women's lived experiences of gender in Australia.

The chapter's primary source of information is qualitative interviews. I conducted 30 interviews with migrant women living in Australia: 15 interviews with Brazilian (Christian) women and 15 interviews with Pakistani (Muslim) women. In the interviews with migrant Brazilian women, 14 were conducted

41 Corbetta (n 1).

in Portuguese,[42] and one was conducted in English, at Western Sydney University, Sydney, New South Wales. Interviews with Pakistani women were conducted in English.[43] Of these, five face-to-face interviews were conducted at the University of Western Australia, Perth. After the imposition of COVID-19 lockdowns, the remaining ten interviews were conducted remotely via WhatsApp video calls.

Interviews lasted, on average, between 60–90 minutes and were audiotaped. I also applied the technique of "deep hanging out" with participants, spending time with them before[44] or after the interviews. I explained to each interviewee that our conversations before or after the interviews would be incorporated into my field notes. This is regarded as a useful ethnographic technique in order to access politically sensitive information.[45] 'Deep hanging out' is also seen as a good strategy to break down any power imbalances between interviewer and interviewee. This is a suitable methodological approach to address possible power imbalances, which can be an issue when dealing with vulnerable communities such as migrant women. As explained by Walmsley, citing Ingold's experience with this technique:

> My personal reflection on this is that deep hanging out generated the most equal power dynamics of any research process I have ever taken part in, as it genuinely realised Ingold's call for anthropologists to immerse themselves in an environment of joint activity.[46]

Respondents were not identified in the research records but were instead given serial numbers to ensure de-identification, with each number corresponding to a culturally sensitive pseudonym. Interview discussions did not disclose information that could reveal the respondents' identities either in the text of interviews or in any publications arising out of the interviews. The respondents were asked to share notions of honour, lived experiences of honour, how honour shapes religion and gender identity, as well as the impact of honour on family life and gender relations in Australia.

All the data gathered during interviews was transcribed verbatim, coded, and analysed using NVivo software and thematic coding. The aim of this

42 Interviews conducted with Brazilian women in Portuguese have been translated by the author into English language, and I acknowledge that there could be information lost in translation.
43 Interviews conducted with Pakistani women in English language have been translated by the author into clear and grammatically correct English.
44 As 'ice-breaker' technique to connect at a deeper level with participants.
45 Brendan Ciarán Browne and Ruari-Santiago McBride, 'Politically Sensitive Encounters: Ethnography, Access, and the Benefits of 'Hanging Out' (2015) 11(1) *Qualitative Sociology Review* 34.
46 Ben Walmsley, 'Deep Hanging out in the Arts: An Anthropological Approach to Capturing Cultural Value' (2018) 24(2) *International Journal of Cultural Policy* 272.

research was to identify key words and develop an understanding of patterns and themes emerging from women's lived experiences of honour.

In this research I adopted the methodology of grounded theory and semi-structured interviews, given their greater flexibility for both to the interviewee and the interviewer. A malleable interview design assisted the researcher to make adaptations during interviews should difficulties be encountered, since the interviews dealt with a potentially sensitive topic. Thus, it was appropriate to allow room for adaptation and change. Interviews were non-standard, semi-structured, and with an interview guide rather than a schedule. This framework allowed those interviewed to talk about their lived experiences of honour, religion, and gender within their own frames of reference.

Another benefit of semi-structured open-ended questions is to avoid an overly formal setting. Overly formalising the interview would make it look transactional, mechanical, and empty of meaning. The researcher engaged with participants before the interview with informal "get-to-know-you", ice-breaker conversations. The pre-interview informal conversations put participants at ease, developing a connection with them, and creating bonds of trust. This allowed participants to feel safe and relaxed when sharing their stories.

There were several ethics considerations throughout the course of the research to minimise any potential risks to participants, including to protect the researcher. To minimise any potential risks, several strategies were developed. The research plan was assessed and approved by the University of Western Australia Human Research Ethics Committee by approval #: RA/4/20/4441. To mitigate risks to participants and maintain high standards of ethical research, a detailed plan was developed, describing possible risks to participants and strategies to mitigate these. With regard to consent from participants, a Participant Consent Form (PCF) was developed, as well as a Participant Information Form (PIF), providing information regarding research objectives and aims. In addition, two participant handouts were produced. The first handout provided a de-identification management plan, and the second one provided a risk management plan for participants.

The chapter looks at the nuances and influence of traditional views in gender relations. Through interview results, they are hybridised, shifting from "moderate" to "extreme" notions of honour and religion, and how they impact gender power relations. Migrant women taking part in the interviews predominantly hold "moderate" views. According to interview results, however, 'extreme' notions of honour consciousness and religion can also translate to the Brazilian and Pakistani communities in Australia. Although the women taking part in this survey did not report suffering violence, there were reports of women's suppression and violence against women.

Data results explain how migrant Brazilian women hold traditional views of the family (in this case as interpreted by Catholicism) through "cultural Christianity". In such case, honour and religion are key in shaping their identities but have not been regarded by legislators when addressing violence against women in Brazil. Although most participants were nominal Catholic

Christians, the respondents also included practicing Evangelicals and Roman Catholics, Spiritism Kardecist, and Spiritualist. All 15 Brazilian women interviewed were influenced by what is referred to as "cultural Christianity".[47] In interviews with 15 Pakistani Muslim women, however, they explicitly conflated their lived experiences of honour with religion (Islam) and the "values of Islam". The use of grounded theory in this comparative study breaks down essentialising perspectives towards South Asian communities, Muslims, and honour, and a monochromatic approach to honour-based violence in Pakistan.

The use of grounded theory allows innovative epistemological perspectives on legislation on gender and religion, challenging dominant legal perspectives addressing gender relations in traditional cultures. Legislation on violence against women in Brazil and Pakistan, regrettably, lack in sophistication. Grounded theory approaches provide data for a holistic framing of gender legislation, targeting more effectively the root causes of violence against women.

IV Brazil's Views Towards Honour, Religion, and Gender, and Legislation Addressing Violence against Women and Femicides

Brazil's Catholic views are key to understanding the interplay between traditional views of the family and Brazil's notions of womanhood. In Brazil, Christianity generally plays a central role in shaping institutions, views towards female honour, and notions of womanhood. But Catholicism is the Christian denomination with the greatest socio-cultural influence in Brazil.

Drawing from the Catechism of the Catholic Church, women and men are both endowed with fundamental rights. Women have the right to hold paid employment outside the home; however, their primary role is to work inside the family home and to ensure the functionality of domestic affairs.[48] The Catholic Church openly advocates for the equal protection of human rights of women and men but, at the same time, it stresses that it is more important that women work in the domestic sphere, with their focus on the greater good: their husbands and children.

In the words of John Paul II in the Encyclical *Familiaris Consortio*:[49]

> There is no doubt that the equal dignity and responsibility of men and women fully justify women's access to public tasks. On the other hand, the true advancement of women also requires that the values of their maternal and family role be clearly recognised in comparison with all

47 Wayne G Cogell 'Cultural Christianity: The Puritan Heritage' (2001) *International Congregational Journal* 2.

48 Catecismo da Igreja Católica (Web Page, 26 May 2024). https://www.vatican.va/archive/cathechism_po/index_new/prima-pagina-cic_po.html.

49 Paul II, John. *Encyclical Letter Familiaris Consortio* (Web Page 26 May 2024) https://www.vatican.va/content/john-paul-ii/en/apost_exhortations/documents/hf_jp-ii_exh_19811122_familiaris-consortio.html.

> other public tasks and with all other professions. Moreover, such tasks and professions must be integrated with each other if social and cultural evolution is to be truly and fully human (...). This will be more easily achieved if (...) a renewed 'theology of work' clarifies and deepens the meaning of work in the Christian life (...) the original and irreplaceable meaning of housework and raising children. (...) Therefore, the Church can and must help today's society, insistently asking that the work of women in the home be recognised by all and honoured in its irreplaceable value.

Brazil's socio-historic Catholic framing of notions of womanhood and family life permeates every single aspect of Brazilian society. This influences all Christians denominations, as well as non-Christian groups. Brazil's laicity in the first Republic is hotly contested in the literature, as in practical terms, the Catholic Church's influence and power continued mostly unquestioned.[50] Even in contemporary times, religious teachings in Brazil's public schools consolidate Christian Catholic values and white European privileges amongst future generations.[51]

The overwhelming socio-historical influence of Catholicism and Christianity in Brazil creates what is referred to as Brazil's "cultural Christianity".[52] I draw from the definition of "cultural religion" from Demerath III, as a common syndrome 'in which religion affords a sense of personal identity and continuity with the past even after participation in ritual and belief have lapsed'.[53] In Brazil's "cultural Christianity", traditional notions of womanhood and family life are seen as "honourable". These are strongly manifested in all Christian denominations in Brazil as well as in non-Christian groups.

In recent years, however, Brazil has been experiencing an Evangelical surge. According to a 2016 Datafolha survey, 44 per cent of Evangelicals are former Catholics.[54] Data from Brazil IBGE 2012 indicates 86.8 per cent of Brazilians identify as Christians, with 64.6 per cent of Catholics and 22.2 of Evangelicals.[55]

50 Fábio Carvalho Leite, 'O Laicismo e outros exageros sobre a Primeira República no Brasil' (2011) 31(1) *Religião e Sociedade* 32.

51 Da Silva Gonçalves, Wesley, *O ensino religioso nas escolas públicas: debate sobrea a inclusão das minorias e a representatividade de suas indentidades* (Web Page, 27 May 2024) https://educacaopublica.cecierj.edu.br/artigos/19/28/o-ensino-religioso-nas-escolas-publicas-debate-sobre-a-inclusao-das-minorias-e-a-representatividade-de-suas-identidades

52 Cogell (n 47).

53 N J Demerath III, 'The Rise of "Cultural Religion" in European Christianity: Learning from Poland, Northern Ireland, and Sweden' (2000) 47(1) *Social Compass* 127.

54 Data Folha. *44% dos Evangélicos são ex-Catolicos* (Web Page, 26 May 2024) https://datafolha.folha.uol.com.br/opiniaopublica/2016/12/1845231-44-dos-evangelicos-sao-ex-catolicos.shtml.

55 Instituto Brasileiro de Geografia e Estatística (IBGE) (2013). Distribuição Racial no Brazil (Web Page, 26 May 2024) https://biblioteca.ibge.gov.br/index.php/biblioteca-catalogo?view=detalhes&id=284235.

However, Catholicism is still the predominant Christian denomination in the country, with Brazil's ultra-conservative Evangelical movement the second largest Christian group.

Evangelical (Pentecostals and Neo-Pentecostals) views of honour, religion, and traditional views of the family have been framed through traditional Catholic views on notions of womanhood and family. Nonetheless, their interpretation of the Gospels is taken literally (religious fundamentalism). Evangelical interpretation of religious texts is predominantly focused on the individual, rather than drawing from institutional tradition. This results in stricter codes of conduct for women, predominantly supporting views of female submission to male "headship".[56] Such a perspective may increase the likelihood of domestic violence and femicides of Pentecostal women in Brazil.[57]

Since 2019 in Brazil, crimes of femicide, the murder of women *because* they are women, have been on the rise.[58] The condition of women and girls has deteriorated further during the COVID-19 crisis, with many girls over the age of 16 experiencing some form of violence during the pandemic.[59] Through epistemic disobedience lenses, this chapter explains that the elevated numbers of femicides and cases of violence against women in Brazil should be seen as a manifestation of 'extreme' notions of honour. Femicides and violence towards women in Brazil should be dealt with as honour-based violence (HBV).

Figures from the United Nations' 'The Violence Map: Homicides against Women in Brazil' are staggering.[60] In 2013 alone, 4,762 female murders were reported to Brazilian police authorities. Of those 4,762 reported female murders, 2,394 were perpetrated by a family member or partner, comprising 50.3 per cent of all female murders reported in that year.[61] This would translate into seven women being murdered every day at the hands of a family member or partner. Additionally, *the* Violence Map indicates that from those 2,394 female murders, 1,583 women were killed by their partners or ex-partners, comprising 33.3 per cent of all reported female murders.

The Violence Map shows that the homicide rate of white females in Brazil is on the decline since 2003 (2003–2013), from 3.6 per cent to 3.2 per cent

56 Nádson Araújo dos Santos, Wilton Petrus and Rosana Letícia Pugina, 'Sermões Evangélicos e Idealização Do Comportamento Feminino: Uma Análise Bakhtiniana Da Voz Do Terceiro No Discurso' (2021) 56(3) *Letras de hoje* 598.

57 Sandra Duarte de Souza and Claudia Poleti Oshiro, 'Mulheres Evangelicas e Violencia Domestica: O que o Poder Publico e a Igreja tem a ver com isso?' (2018) 16(2) *Caminhos (Goiânia, Brazil)* 203.

58 Fórum de Segurança Pública. *Visivel and Invisivel: A Vitimizacao das Mulheres no Brasil* (Web Page, 26 May 2024) https://forumseguranca.org.br/wp-content/uploads/2021/06/relatorio-visivel-e-invisivel-3ed-2021-v3.pdf.

59 Ibid.

60 Waiselfsiz, J J *O Mapa da Violência Contra as Mulheres no Brasil* (Web Page, 26 May 2024) https://flacso.org.br/files/2015/11/MapaViolencia_2015_mulheres.pdf.

61 Ibid.

for each 100,000 female murders, whereas the rates for black women and girls have increased from 4.5 per cent to 5.4 per cent for each 100,000 female murders, comprising a 19.5 per cent increase in the victimisation of black women and girls.[62] Proportionally to the Brazilian population in 2013, there were 66.7 per cent more murders of black women and girls' murders compared with the rates of white women's murders. Between 2003 and 2013, there was a 190.9 per cent increase in the victimisation of black women and girls. This report demonstrates how Brazilian women of African descent are hugely disadvantaged in Brazil, due to limited access to education, opportunities, and more broadly to the justice system and crime impunity more broadly, as well as to the socio-historical inequalities suffered by Brazil's African descendants.

However, when dealing with female oppression, violence towards women and the killings of women are not restricted to less developed areas, or to women who did not access education, or just to those of African and coloured descent. Brazil has one of the highest rates of violence towards women in the world. According to the Wilson Centre's Brazil Institute, Brazil is one of the most dangerous countries for women in the world, with the highest levels of gender-based violence and femicides in Latin America.[63]

Until 2021, the "honour defence" argument was invoked by defence lawyers throughout Brazil to acquit husbands who killed their wives in the name of honour. Between 1990 to 2016, approximately 58 cases have argued the honour defence to acquit husbands who killed their wives.[64] In most cases, the jury has acquitted husbands who killed their wives "in the name of honour",[65,66] with courts of appeal reversing the decisions of lower courts.[67] Nonetheless, there were at least three cases where the court of appeal confirmed the trial decision, acquitting husbands who killed their allegedly unfaithful wives.[68] Decisions confirming these trial verdicts were made by the São Paulo Justice Tribunal, Acres and from the Superior Justice Tribunal,[69] with a decision acquitting a husband for inflicting 'punches' to his partner for her marital infidelity. Only in 2021 did Brazil's *Supremo Tribunal Federal* (STF), the High Court which deals with constitutional matters, in a unanimous decision, rule

62 Ibid.

63 Wilson Centre Brazil Institute Infographics, *Fighting Gender-based Violence* (Web Page 28 June 2024) https://www.wilsoncenter.org/article/fighting-gender-based-violence-brazil

64 Margarita Danielle Ramos, 'Reflexões sobre o processo histórico-discursivo do uso da legítima defesa da honra no Brasil e a construção das mulheres' (2012) 20(1) *Estudos Feministas* 53.

65 Ibid.

66 Silvia Pimentel, Valéria Pandjiarjian, and Juliana Belloque. 'Legitima defesa de honra. Ilegítima impunidade de assassinos: um estudo crítico da legislação e jurisprudência da América Latina'. In Mariza Corrêa and Erica Renata de Souza (eds) *Vida em família: uma perspectiva comparativa sobre crimes de honra* (2006 Campina).

67 Ramos (n 64); Pimentel and Pandjiarjian, and Belloque (n 66).

68 Ibid.

69 Pimentel, Pandjiarjian and Belloque (n 66).

the "honour defence" unconstitutional. Justice Dias Toffoli sustained in his decision:

> [The honour defence] is a practice that cannot be sustained in the light of the 1988 Constitution, as it protects the dignity of the human person, the prohibition of discrimination and the right to equality and Lives injured and should not be transmitted in the course of the criminal proceedings in the pre-litigation and procedural phase under penalty of the nullity of the respective postulation act and the judgment, even if this is practised before the jury.[70]

The decision of Brazil's *STF* is welcomed, but confirms fears this jurisprudence, unless deemed unconstitutional, would continue in the Brazilian legal system. In his decision, Justice Toffoli acknowledged the endemic levels of violence towards women and femicides in Brazil.[71] Given the honour-violence nexus indicated by the literature in Section II, I argue that acts of gender violence towards women in Brazil are embedded in honour consciousness and these should be re-classified as HBV for policy purposes, crime prevention, and for victim support.

But why are the "honour defence" argument, as well as its jurisprudence, not classified as HBV? In Brazil, these crimes are classified as "crimes of passion".[72] Brazil's 'honour defence' argument and jurisprudence gives leeway to acts of violence towards women embedded in Brazil's cultural views towards honour. A legislative achievement includes the 2006 Maria da Penha Law, vanguard legislation protecting women from gender-based violence, and domestic violence. Yet, despite the advancement of formal rights of women, the "honour defence's" jurisprudence, until recently, was still a legal loophole used by defence teams in Brazil. In addition, the influence of honour and religion in Brazil's gender relations is not reflected in legislation to protect women from violence or in re-education programs against gendered violence. Violence towards women is regarded as gender-based violence and not honour-based violence, with the legislation criminalising femicides failing to address the complexity of such crimes in Brazilian society.

70 Jus Brasil. *Legítima defesa da honra é inconstitucional e viola o princípio da proteção da dignidade da pessoa humana, bem como, proteção a vida e igualdade de gênero* (Web Page, 26 May 2024) https://www.jusbrasil.com.br/noticias/legitima-defesa-da-honra-e-inconstitucional-e-viola-o-principio-da-dignidade-da-pessoa-humana-bem-como-protecao-a-vida-e-igualdade-de-genero/1182697368 (translated from Portuguese).

71 Ibid.

72 Luiza Nagib Eluf, *A paixão no banco dos réus* (Saraiva Educação SA, 2021).

V Pakistan's Views towards Honour, Religion, and Gender and Legislation Addressing Honour Killings

In the early years of the Pakistani state (1947–1977), there was state support towards women's movements. The first wave of Pakistani women's movements emerged with organisations such as the All-Pakistan Women's Association (APWA), created in 1949, by then-First Lady Begum Raana Liaquat Ali Khan, to work towards better economic and educational conditions for Pakistan's disadvantaged women.[73] APWA enjoyed government support throughout the country, with many government officials' wives heading local chapters. This organisation was well known for lobbying for Muslim family law reform and for greater female participation in politics and government agencies. In the Pakistani context, nonetheless, women's agency and political participation post-independence was a privilege enjoyed by upper-middle-class women, and operated within the constraints of Pakistani tradition and honour consciousness.

Early attempts towards female leadership roles in politics failed, due to consolidated views towards tradition, honour, religious, and male headship. Liaquat Ali Khan, during his re-election bid, did not shy away from lobbying together with Muslim clergy to extract a *fatwa*, ruling Fatima Jinnah's (the sister of Jinnah) candidacy "un-Islamic".[74] In Pakistan's early years, most women involved in the political process participated as the wives, daughters, and sisters of politicians; not by having a political platform in their own right. Women's agency operated within societal roles assigned to women and those engaging in the political process, and with organisations such as APWA, generally had connections with men in power – with many of them being the mothers, wives, sisters, or daughters of such men. In other words, their agency was limited to a support role, constrained within traditional boundaries of women as nurturers, and they were required to respect men's headship over the political process. Consequently, honour consciousness's traditional gender roles were not expunged from Pakistani Muslim women's political activism.

Pakistan's then-Prime Minister, Ayub Khan, introduced reforms such as the *Muslim Family Laws Ordinance of 1961*, thus increasing women's rights in marriage, divorce, maintenance, and child custody. These laws came into being through the active lobbying of women's groups such as APWA and the United Front for Women's Rights.[75] Pakistan's modernising agenda continued during the governing years of Zulifkar Ali Bhutto's Pakistani People's Party (PPP), increasing women's political participation and the protection of women's rights.

73 Farhat Haq, 'Women, Islam, and the State in Pakistan' (1996) 86(2) *The Muslim World* 158.

74 Khawar Mumtaz and Farida Shaheed, *Women of Pakistan: Two Steps Forward, One Step Back?* (Vanguard Books, 1987).

75 Ibid.

The first wave of Pakistani feminism emerged post-1977, during General Mohammad Ziaul Haq's dictatorship. This is a pivotal moment in Pakistan's history of women's rights, characterised by a period of political resistance and struggle. In his first speech, General Ziaul declared:

> Pakistan, which was created in the name of Islam, will continue to survive only if it stays with Islam. That is why I consider the introduction of an Islamic system as an essential prerequisite for the country.[76]

Islamising reforms during the Ziaul administration were radical, with a key promise of the regime being to widely implement Sharia (Islamic laws) in the country. Ziaul's Islamisation agenda had, as its main goal, the limitation of women's freedoms and political participation. During Ziaul's administration, state-led television censorship required women to wear headscarves and 'decent' clothing to go on air, with the federal government mandating the use of *chador* for all women employees.[77] Ziaul's rule envisaged the consolidation of traditional social norms, curbing women's agency in Pakistani society.

The most radical legal changes of the status of women, however, were with the *Hudood Ordinances of 1979* and the *1984 Law of Evidence* and *qisas* and *diyyat*. The *1979 Ordinances* encompasses crimes such as adultery (*zina*) and rape (*zina-bil-jabir*). The maximum penalty for the crime of adultery was stoning to death for married persons, and 100 lashes for unmarried individuals, requiring four Muslim male eyewitnesses, completely excluding women's witnesses from the legislation.[78] In 1984, the laws of *qisas* (retribution) and *diyyat* (financial compensation for murder) were ratified. According to this legislation, the *diyyat* for women would be half of that given to men, whereas women guilty of murder would have a punishment equal to that assigned for men.[79] But Ziaul's aggressive legislation led a group of professional women to create, in 1981, the Women's Action Forum (WAF). Although with only a limited number of members, and with an active base predominantly in the urban areas, this pressure group started a national debate on the unfairness of the new legislation which undermined women's status in Pakistan.[80] WAF was instrumental in delaying the implementation of the new legislation against women's equal treatment before the law, as well as blocking other laws.

The impact upon tradition, honour, and religion in Pakistani society is demonstrated by the high levels of violence towards women and honour killings, which are still experienced throughout Pakistani society. The motivation

76 Dawn. *Special Report: Darkness Descends 1977–1988* (Web Page, 27 May 2024) https://www.dawn.com/news/1364410.
77 Mumtaz and Shaheed (n 74).
78 Ibid.
79 Ibid.
80 Haq (n 73).

behind those crimes is embedded in honour consciousness and religious consciousness, with literal interpretations of the Qur'an and readings of Islam based in the cultural notion of *izzat.*

Honour killings are predominant in Pakistan's underdeveloped areas, such as Western Pakistan's Merged Areas. According to a study conducted by the Khyber Pakhtunkhwa government, with the support of the UNDP's Merged Areas Governance Project (MAGP), there are massive gender disparities in these areas, with women having no access to healthcare, employment opportunities, education, or ownership of assets.[81] This survey indicated that 86 per cent of women were traditional housewives, responsible for household chores, as well as having to perform extended hard labour, with 85 per cent of the women over the age of 15 responsible for fetching water for their families.[82] These factors contribute to 'extreme' views of honour consciousness and religious consciousness in Pakistan's remote areas, since women are not given a chance to challenge *izzat's* cultural norms through direct access to education, workforce participation, and an understanding of women's fundamental rights.

Human rights advocates contend that violence towards women in the name of honour, and honour killings, have been on the rise in the past 20 years. Most victims are women whose families oppose their social interaction with other men, or who are in marriages that are made against their will. According to the Aurat Foundation, in 2008, 8,548 incidents of HBV were reported in Pakistan's four provinces and in the capital Islamabad. In 2013, approximately 869 women died in honour-related attacks. In 2014, approximately 1,000 women died in honour-related crimes. In 2015, the Human Rights Commission of Pakistan reported 1,987 cases of honour killings: 1,096 females and 88 males, with at least 170 of these crimes against minors.[83] Further, these figures are only estimated numbers, since these crimes go vastly underreported. They are usually disguised as 'accidents', or are covered up by family members.[84]

As stated by Brad Adams, Executive Director of Human Rights Watch Asia Division:

> So-called honour killings have been a long-festering problem in Pakistan, and the recent escalating trend makes it clear they won't go away on

81 D E Shawar and B N Abda Khalid, 'Women in Politics: Critical Analysis of Government Policies for Gender Mainstreaming in Khyber Pakhtunkhwa (KP), Pakistan' (2021) *Linguistica Antverpiensia* 1.

82 Ibid.

83 United Nations Women. *The United Nations in Pakistan Urges Government Action to End 'Honour Killings'* (Web Page, 26 May 2024) https://asiapacific.unwomen.org/en/news-and-events/stories/2016/06/the-united-nations-in-pakistan-urges-government-action-to-end-honour-killings.

84 Ibid.

their own (…) The government needs to step up its prosecution of these horrific cases and send a message of zero tolerance.[85]

In 2004, as the result of many years of domestic and international lobbying by Pakistani women's groups, Pakistan's *Criminal Law Act* was amended, criminalising violence against women in the name of honour.[86] Nonetheless, Pakistan's right of *qisas* and *diyyat* continued to provide a legal loophole for honour killings against women and girls.[87] Despite Pakistan's move to criminalise honour killings, it continued to be a matter of concern as cases continued to rise throughout the country.[88] In 2016, the United Nations urged the Pakistani government to take immediate action against "honour killings", to ensure perpetrators would be brought to justice.

The *Criminal Law (Amendment) Offences in the Name of Pretext of Honour Act 2016* repealed the loophole which allowed perpetrators of honour crimes and honour killings to seek forgiveness by family members (the rights of *qisas* and *diyyat*) and being legally pardoned or receiving a light punishment. However, even with the amendment, Pakistani legislation has been traditionally lenient with regard to punishment for honour killings.[89] The new legislation did not alter Pakistan's *Criminal Code* which allowed family members to pardon the perpetrators of honour killings.

The work of NGOs, such as the Aurat Foundation, are of great significance in the fight for Pakistani women's rights, giving Pakistani women's issues a voice both domestically and internationally. Founded in 1986, the Aurat Foundation is committed to creating a widespread awareness of women's endowed universal human rights, fighting for equal treatment before the law and society, ensuring both men and women lead "their lives with dignity and respect".[90] With a head office in Islamabad and regional offices in the provincial capitals of Lahore, Karachi, Peshawar, Quetta, and Gilgit, the Aurat Foundation is known worldwide for its commitment in the fight for Pakistani

85 Human Rights Watch. *Pakistan Prosecute Rampant Honour Killing* (Web Page, 27 May 2024) https://www.hrw.org/news/2016/06/15/pakistan-prosecute-rampant-honor-killings#:~:text=%E2%80%9CSo%2Dcalled%20honor%20killings%20have,a%20message%20of%20zero%20tolerance.%E2%80%9D

86 Aleena Khan, 'Honour' Killings in Pakistan: Judicial and Legal Treatment of the Crime – A Feminist Perspective' (2020) (74) *LUMS Law Journal* 7.

87 Ibid.

88 United Nations Women. *The United Nations in Pakistan Urges Government Action to End 'Honour Killings'* (Web Page, 27 May 2024) https://asiapacific.unwomen.org/en/news-and-events/stories/2016/06/the-united-nations-in-pakistan-urges-government-action-to-end-honour-killings.

89 Dawn. '*PM Nawaz Vows to Eradicate Honour Killings after the Oscar's Nod*' (Web Page, 26 May 2024) https://www.dawn.com/news/1233168.

90 Aurat Publication and Information Centre Foundation. *Aurat March 2021* (Web Page, 26 May 2024) https://www.af.org.pk.

women's empowerment, engaging with all levels of society and at the grass roots level.[91]

Since 2018, the Aurat Foundation has promoted an annual march to raise awareness of women's rights in Pakistan. In 2021, the Aurat March conducted demonstrations in Karachi addressing patriarchal violence, in Lahore raising awareness of the current health crisis since COVID-19, and in Islamabad focusing on crisis care. Two organisers from the Karachi march tackling patriarchal violence stated:

> Our social media campaign, 'A–Z of Patriarchal Violence', highlights some specific tools that are used to perpetuate patriarchal violence, for example, acid attacks, enforced disappearances, discriminatory legislation against women and trans people, surveillance etc. …[92]

The foundation's front-line approach has been fundamental in the fight for women's protection against all types of violence and honour killings.

VI Grounded Theory and Semi-structured Data Analysis – Key Findings through Interviews with Migrant Brazilians and Pakistanis in Australia

Drawing from interviews with Brazilians in Sydney, New South Wales, participants 1, 2, 3, 4, 9, 5, 10, 11, 13, 14, and 15 during their interviews discussed how honour is, for them, 'a value' or 'morality'.

Participant 5 ('Alice'), for instance, defined honour in the following terms:

> [The word honour means] for me … its very linked to values, honour, and respect. In my opinion. And for example, trying to have a life, trying to do things based precisely on these values …

For other Brazilian women taking part in interviews, this is also a key variable in understanding how honour shapes their moral compass. For these women, honour is a concept 'inserted inside your head while you are growing up', as explained by participant 4 ('Maria Paula'). These concepts shape behaviour and has an impact upon gender power relations.

Likewise, Pakistani participants 1, 4, 5, 6, 9, 10, 12, 13, 14, and 15 discussed their lived experiences in depth, speaking of honour as "a value" and "morality" (related or not to Islam). In their interviews, honour as "a value" or "morality" is a key variable to understanding other participants' views of

91 Ibid.

92 Luavut Zahid, *Why Do Women March? A Look at the Aurat March 2021 Manifestos* (Web Page, 27 May 2024) https://images.dawn.com/news/1186695.

honour and how honour comprises an inherent part of their moral compass and their notions of right and wrong.

Nonetheless, Pakistani participants 1, 4, 6, 9, 13, and 14 explicitly connect honour with religion (Islam). For example, participant 14 ('Zara'), explicitly conflated honour consciousness with religion (Islam) in the following terms:

> [regarding honour] It's about everything. Honour is the most respected word for me. Because, you know, I told you, I am a Muslim. My Muslim concepts come from my religion. God gave us born rights to be honoured.

The lived experiences of honour and religion for both migrant Brazilian Christian women and migrant Pakistani Muslim women was consistently described as "something deep" and as a "value". For example, Brazilian participant 6 ('Diolinda') explained: "… and what you have most precious is your honour. For me is a very strong thing". Similarly, Pakistani participant 12 ('Shamaila'), reflected that honour is "… a very deep word … for me it surrounds everything".

Honour as a "value" is a key variable bringing meaning to their lived experiences of honour and religion. Although there are other underlying subthemes in their lived experiences of honour, 'honour as value' is a crucial feature shaping their views of the world. Family plays a central role in consolidating lived experiences of honour, religion, and gender, since honour is "something taught", which is then internalised in their ways of thinking through their upbringing in the family. As explained by Brazilian participant 13 ('Poliana'), honour is something learned ("I learned it from my mother"). Pakistani participant 8 ('Abida'), stated that the family raises you to "keep honour" ("I was raised in a manner where I kept the honour of my family").

The women taking part in interviews clarified that honour and religion are not experienced in the same way by all women living in either Brazil or Pakistan. During their interviews, women from both sample groups explained how their experiences are multilayered. Honour, based on their stories, is shaped by "where you come from", from the values taught by your parents, from your level of education, from the region where you were raised (small country cities in Brazil or rural Pakistan, for instance), socio-economic background, as well as parental views on religion.

For example, Brazilian participant 2 ('Clara') explained that notions of honour:

> … depends on the context. Because for me it is very personal. I think it depends very much on where you come from, what were the values that were given to you. Then it will determine to whether it is an honour for me, or what it is not an honour for you.

Pakistani participant 10 ('Hiba') tells how social class, and "where you come from"', shape your notions of honour and religion, with "extreme notions" (in the participant's own words) being prevalent for people who are "struggling" financially or are "ignorant", living in remote areas of Sindh province. As 'Hiba' explains:

> People who are – who are struggling for the basic needs, they're overpowered by people with resources, but still living in ignorance and the absence of law ... It's the concept of Karo-Kari and it's found in the backward parts of Sindh [province].

Participants from both sample groups agreed that there are "different" notions of honour and that each person has their own notion of honour. For example, Brazilian participant 3 ('Alana') discussed the subjectivity of "notions of honour", in her words: "For me [honour], it's not necessarily a cultural or religious thing. It's just a personal thing for me".

Pakistani participant 13 ('Naila') explains the "personal" character of honour, as follows: "Honour is very personal. It has to do with the way you conduct yourself, your beliefs, and your values. It is related to your family and the town you are from".

Most participants agreed that there is a degree of subjectivity in lived experiences of honour. In some interviews, participants discussed in detail how honour can be manifested in a "negative way" or as "something which horrifies me", or in an "extreme way". These I classify as "extreme" notions of honour and religion.

As explained by Brazilian participant 14 ('Laila'), who comes from the northeast region of Brazil, the region where you come from can influence "extreme" notions of honour and religion. This is manifested through women's lack of agency (accepting all types of behaviour from men), paving the way for abusive relationships. In her words:

> [My notions of honour] have been influenced by accepting abusive relationships. So not being aware that that relationship was being abusive. It's a society that kind of raised women to accept any behaviour from a man, not just any, not physical aggression, but going out without asking, and drinking, and hanging out with other women, and you will be the last one to know.

Now living in Australia, she distances herself from these 'extreme' notions of honour and religion.

Pakistani participant 2 ('Haniya') explained how Pakistan's "extreme" notions of honour are different from her own notions of honour ("moderate"), distancing herself from the "social other". These "extreme" notions of honour and religion are manifested by violence towards women and honour killings. In Haniya's words:

> So, you can go to that extreme level of some people killing the whole family, sometimes boys kill the whole family, like parents, if they are supporting their daughter, those kinds of things. It is very sad. So, this is extreme.

Women from both cohorts explained, however, how their lived experiences of honour and religion are predominantly "positive", or "something good". Brazilian Christian women and Pakistani Muslim women distanced themselves from those "othering" notions of honour consciousness regarded as "extreme". Extreme notions of honour are manifested through female subjection, interpartner oppression, lack of agency, violence towards women and honour killings. Women taking part in this study hold notions of honour that are predominantly "moderate", since they reconcile traditional notions of womanhood with women's agency, women's participation in the workforce and politics; they engage in political activism and in the fight against violence towards women.

Most migrant Brazilian Christian women discussed their lived experiences of honour in the light of traditional family values that were taught to them by their families, shaping their notions of womanhood. Although religion is not explicitly connected, their views of honour as a "value" and an "inherent" part of their notions of "right from wrong" are an inherent part of what was taught "by their parents". Brazilian women's lived experiences of honour are deeply influenced by the Catholic values of the family and traditional notions of womanhood, transmitted through Brazil's "cultural Christianity".

On the other hand, Pakistani Muslim migrant women's lived experiences of honour are explicitly connected with Islam, which informs their "moral code" and "value system", and "understanding from right and wrong". Pakistani participants discussed extensively the role played by Islam in Pakistan and "different" or "other" notions (regarded as "extreme") of honour consciousness. In their lived experiences of honour consciousness, they explicitly link it with Islam and religion (participants 1, 4, 6, 9, 13, 14). Pakistani Muslim women taking part in this survey also discussed how upbringing, the region where women come from, and levels of education influence religious views, distancing themselves from 'extreme views' which can lead to women's suppression, lack of women's rights, violence towards women, and honour killings. In the views of survey participants, such perspectives are not supported by Islam. In Pakistani Muslim women's lived experiences, "there is nothing giving as much as freedom as Islam give us as a woman, the empowerment, it's when I look or study in detail" (participant 7, 'Hiba').

In the light of the literature and the interview results, the key difference between their lived experiences of honour and religion is the result of the interplay of historical, religious, and cultural factors. Honour and religion in Brazil is the result of "whitening" colonial practices, which have played a part in the shaping of Brazilian women's lived experiences of gender. This chapter draws from Quijano's[93] episteme of "coloniality of power", and Lugones'[94] perspective of "coloniality of power", and the ways in which class and race impact women's lived experiences in Brazil. Brazil's "coloniality of power" highlights honour and religion's intersectional dimensions and the effects of race and class on Brazilian women's lived experiences of gender. Brazilian women, who may be practicing or non-practicing Christians, or even non-Christians, continue to be influenced by these notions of womanhood. Since they are so deeply embedded in Brazil's cultural fabric, these values are not explicitly linked to religion by participants (Catholicism or Christianity).

Notably, Pakistan's state formation is different from Brazil's, following a more secularist framework. Pakistan's partition from India in 1947 was triggered by Indian Muslim aspirations or greater and fairer representation in India's political system.[95] The influence of Indian Muslim identity in the creation of the Pakistani state is, however, hotly contested by the literature. Recent perspectives reveal a secularist view of Muslim nationalistic aspirations.[96] Consequently, Pakistan's secularist views of the state have shaped Pakistani Muslim women's lived experiences of honour consciousness and religious consciousness. According to interview results, Islam and Islamic values are highly influential at the level of the individual and for those women professing to be Muslim and practicing Islam.

In Pakistan's case, the South Asian notion of *izzat* is key in shaping Pakistani women's lived experience of honour. However, *izzat* is not confined simply to Muslims: it also affects the lives of Hindus and Sikhs alike.[97] Thus, Pakistani Muslim women's lived experiences of honour are influenced by the subcontinent's cultural notions of *izzat* and readings of Islam. These two variables can be manifested through "moderate"' or "extreme" notions of honour and religion.

There are readings of Islam embedded in cultural notions of *izzat*, establishing a distinction between honour and dignity. Honour and dignity can be seen as synonyms with Islamic texts or it can be argued they have different meanings.[98] This is a contested issue amongst Muslim scholars, with several neglecting the distinction between honour and dignity in the Qur'an. This school of thought reconciles Islamic texts with modern views of human dignity through the framing of universal human rights.[99] Pakistani women

93 Aníbal Quijano, 'Coloniality of Power and Eurocentrism in Latin America' (2000) 15(2) *International Sociology* 215.

94 Maria Lugones, 'Colonialidad y género' [2008] (9) *Tabula Rasa* 7.3.

95 Jalal, *The Struggle for Pakistan* (n 21).

96 Ayesha Jalal, *South Asia* (Encyclopaedia of Nationalism 2, 2000).

97 Aisha K Gill and Avtar Brah, 'Interrogating Cultural Narratives about 'Honour'-Based Violence' (2014) 21(1) *European Journal of Women's Studies* 72.

98 Hamid Andishan, 'Honour or Dignity? An Oversimplification in Islamic Human Rights' (2019) 20(4) *Human Rights Review* 461.

99 Ibid.

taking part in this survey had predominantly "moderate" notions of honour and religion. Women living in big cosmopolitan centres have more access to information and education. This increases their likelihood of accessing those Islamic teachings that reconcile notions of *izzat* with the universal protection of human rights, women's rights of agency, and political representation.

Significantly, both Brazilian Christian women and Pakistani Muslim women explained how honour and religion (in the case of Brazilians, through cultural Christianity) has been transmitted to them through the way they were brought up by their parents and by their parents' and family's "values" and "principles".

Interview results show how Brazilian and Pakistani women have their identities influenced by tradition, honour, and religion, and how these impact gender relations. In Australia, these continue to shape "moderate" and "extreme" notions, with "extreme" notions predominantly manifested in small cities or in Brazil's northeastern region. In Pakistani women's stories, honour and religion are taught by their parents and families and are deeply embedded in cultural notions of *izzat*. As a result, "moderate" or "extreme" notions of honour and religion have been reproduced within Pakistan's regions. Based on my research findings, in big city centres, for instance, 'moderate' notions are predominant, whereas in rural and less developed regions, "extreme" notions of honour and religion are more common. Data results show that Brazilian migrant women are significantly shaped by traditional notions of honour and religion and that Pakistani women experience tradition, honour, and religion in ways which depart from essentialising notions associated predominantly with honour killings. The data highlights how tradition, honour, and religion is experienced in a spectrum, which can be "moderate" (associated with female agency) or "extreme" (associated with female oppression and violence towards women). Such finding can be a breakthrough to legislation addressing violence towards women and female empowerment in these two tradition-based societies.

VII Conclusion

This chapter proposed a new perspective on how to study women and law, and how grounded theory, by providing greater freedom to the researcher and being an inductive method, provides new insight in women's experiences of honour, religion, and gender. Grounded theory, and a theoretical approach to data coding detached from existing theory, helps researchers to break down social and legal biases towards religious influences in gender relations and the condition of women. This methodology provides intellectual freedom for minority groups to challenge the predominant understanding of the literature and the leading influences shaping legislation. This chapter examined lived experiences of Brazilian and Pakistani women in Australia and how honour and religion have been perceived through Brazilian and Pakistani legislation through oversimplified lenses.

Through the use of grounded theory, open-ended interviews, and NVivo thematic coding with emerging data in both cohorts, interview results show that honour and religion are experienced on a spectrum of "moderate" and "extreme" – as expressed in participants' own words. Another important code is honour as part of Brazilian women's identities, as well as how religion shapes Brazilian society. The legislation, when dealing with violent crimes and violence towards Brazilian women, follows international guidelines on gender-based violence, not considering honour and religion as variables shaping gender relations in Brazil. Grounded theory, and the ability of having greater freedom from previous theories and scholarly assumptions, provides a window of opportunity for legislative chance in Brazil. Crimes against Brazilian women need to consider the impact of honour and religion in women's control and interpartner violence. The use of grounded theory with Pakistani women, and greater freedom to data analysis through thematic coding, shows a spectrum through which these women experience honour and religion in their lives. Pakistani legislation towards honour-based crimes should engage women with "moderate" notions of honour and religion in strategies to reach out to women living in remote areas in Pakistan, and in the promotion of prevention plans towards honour killings and violence towards women in Pakistan. This perspective breaks down unidimensional approaches to honour, religion, and violence. Women from this cohort are deeply influenced by honour and religious views and can be empowered and have agency. Brazil's legislation on violence towards women ought to consider its honour dimensions to have more effective results in prevention plans, re-education programs, and strategies to empower women.

Further Reading:

For analysis of the methods used in this chapter, see Chapter 15 – Section IV – subsection C *The Functionalist Method*; D *The Analytical Method*; E *The Cultural Method*.

For the author's rejoinder and reflection, see Appendix Section IX.

For another analysis taking a non-legal approach, see Chapter 5.

Part III

Critiquing Comparative Approaches

15 Comments on Comparative Methodology Used throughout the Book

Mohammad Rasmi Alumari,[1] *Camilla Baasch Andersen,*[2] *and Renae Barker*[3]

I Introduction and Aim

This chapter will non-critically analyse the comparative approaches employed in the preceding chapters and position them within the broader context of the literature on comparative epistemology and method. It will offer comments on the comparative approaches taken in the chapters and how they pursue the aims outlined in each chapter, without qualitatively assessing them, but rather examine their utility in context. We label this NON-critical as we are not judging the techniques as they are applied by the authors, nor setting out to perform a qualitative judgement on the methods in question. Such a pursuit would belie the fact that each comparatist – budding or seasoned – designs their own subjective method for each project, and would also be utterly pointless as well as overly judgemental. No. What we seek to do is to map where many of the known elements of each comparative approach are employed, what they are used for, and how they measure up to their goal as pursued by the author. The aim is to showcase how such elements/components of legal comparison measure up as applied to each objective. Overall, our goal is to inspire designs of comparative method for future comparatists and to open a broader debate about utility of each defined component in a context of multivalent transnational understanding, which we will explain following.

We have also tried to expand on how to design a yardstick for comparing, by laying out a grid and a colour system for differentiating the different comparative techniques (Section IV). Although arguably somewhat oversimplified, we hope this meta-approach to deliberate how to set up components to compare exemplifies a typical yardstick, or protocol, in setting up such an evaluation. After all, before we can effectively compare anything, we need to break down the individual elements we are comparing, to "measure" similarities and differences.

1 Assistant Professor, Faculty of Law, Mutah University, Jordan.
2 Professor, Law School, University of Western Australia.
3 Senior Lecturer, University of Western Australia Law School, Honorary Research Fellow Centre Muslim States and Societies.

DOI: 10.4324/9781003397311-21

Given the complexity comparative methodology, with all its subjective epistemology, elements and potential approaches and components, this exercise will never be exhaustive, nor does it purport to be. Moreover, although it never seeks to qualitatively rank the approaches, it remains a subjective exercise by the authors of this chapter, and even the authors of the papers we analyse may not agree. So, we have invited authors to comment on our analysis of their methods as we see them applied, and in places, the replies in rejoinders are enlightening, proving yet again what a colourful endeavour comparative method can be – these can be found in the Appendix to this volume.

Before we launch this comparison of comparative approaches, however, we must expand on our view of comparative methodology, protocols, and goals. We first illustrate some main points with a basic introduction to our perspectives in comparison, in a nutshell (Section II); then we explain our choice of main comparative tools, which also act as components chosen for this comparison of comparatists (Section III); and after our visual grid of techniques chosen, we engage in detail with selected authors and highlight what we make of their methods (Section IV). Rejoinders from authors are then available.

II Our Take on Legal Comparitive Method in a Nutshell

A Gandalf and Subjectivity

We are not the first to suggest that comparative legal analysis is effectively a toolbox with many components, where the author of the analysis must compose a bespoke approach before attempting the study. Vernon Palmer dubbed this subjective method composition a "sliding scale" of comparative analysis,[4] and Glanert exhorts that it is so subjective as to not be a method at all but an epistemology.[5] Foster and Andersen, in their writings (and teachings), label the composition of an individual and unique approach to a comparative study an "intermediary jurisprudence",[6] and Samuels writes of hermeneutic approaches[7] and broad legal roadmaps. We agree with all of this, but – although the taxonomical debate regarding the labelling of this discipline as

4 Vernon Valentine Palmer, 'From Lerotholi to Lando: Some Examples of Comparative Law Methodology' (Pt American Society of Comparative Law, Inc) (2005) 53(1) *The American Journal of Comparative Law* 261–90.

5 Simone Glanert, 'Method?' in P G Monateri (ed), *Methods of Comparative Law* (Edward Elgar, 2012).

6 See Renae Barker and Camilla Andersen 'What Is a Child? Developing and Testing the Methodology for Comparative Research on Legal Age Limits: The Australian Model Advancing an International Study' (2023) 49(2) *Monash University Law Review* 191–224; Nicholas H D Foster, Comparative Commercial Law: Rules or Context? in Esin Örücü and David Nelken (eds), *Comparative Law—A Handbook* (Hart Publishing, 2007).

7 Geoffrey Samuel, 'Taking Methods Seriously (Part One)' (2007) 2(1) *Journal of Comparative Law* 94–119; Geoffrey Samuel, 'Taking Methods Seriously (Part Two)' (2007) 2(2) *Journal of Comparative Law* 210–237.

having a "method" or an "epistemology" seems ongoing – we feel a need to simplify comparative analysis and make it more approachable in legal research, without too much theoretical engagement.[8] We would like to see it made more accessible, while avoiding certain pitfalls. The method of legal comparison is simply to compare what needs to be compared in pursuit of a goal – and the protocol or approach will depend on what the author wants to do with their analysis, as also evidenced by some of the chapters in Part I of this book. For example, Patrick (Chapter 1) outlines considerations for comparative law and religion projects generally while Erlings (Chapter 4) specifically examines the context of children noting the particular issues raised by religion.

Simply put, different projects and goals require different depths of analysis and angles of approach, or as Örücü puts it, the method of each writer will be informed by their own strategy.[9] Such a subjective approach inherently means that each comparative method for every paper and project does what it intends to do. To paraphrase using Gandalf from the Lord of the Rings: "A wizard is never late, nor is he early. He arrives precisely when he means to".[10] Similarly, a legal comparativist is never too superficial, nor are they too entrenched in method – they approach legal comparison precisely as they mean to. In other words, since the author of a legal comparative analysis should pursue a goal of depth and approach which suits their projects, their subjective goal and approach means they are never really wrong. In many cases authors may state this intention specifically, for example, Moulds (Chapter 12). However, in others it must be inferred from what they, in fact, do such as in Bellieni Zimmermann (Chapter 9). In this case we can infer that her intention was to use the cultural and legal landscape in Brazil and Pakistan to explain the views of honour held by (Australian) migrant women from these two countries. That is not to say that an author will not be critiqued for overlooking issues, cherry-picking examples, or not demonstrating sufficient cultural insight and skating the surface of functionalism – but if the goal was a one-sided comparison or a superficial first-glance analysis, then no one can say it is wrong. The trick to understanding that, is multivalence. Bhanu and Sthapack (Chapter 13) provide an example of a one-sided analysis, in this case focused on India. Here their approach is to demonstrate certain things about the Indian legal system via brief comparisons with features of other legal systems that the authors have identified as similar in some way.

8 A much more in-depth analysis of the protocols, legal comparative theory and the components of a simpler approach is forthcoming in The Journal of Comparative Law, see Mohammad Rasmi Alumari, Camilla Andersen and Jeanette Jensen 'Rethinking Comparative Method' (2025) 20(2) *Journal of Comparative Law* (forthcoming).

9 See David Nelken, 'Comparative Law and Comparative Legal Studies' in Esin Örücü and David Nelken (eds), *Comparative Law—A Handbook* (Hart Publishing, 2007), 48.

10 Fittingly, this quote was not in the Tolkien books but an addition to the more popular and accessible film. The quote is from 'The script for The Lord of the Rings: The Fellowship of the Ring' by Fran Walsh, Philippa Boyens and Peter Jackson (Newline Cinema, 2001).

B Multivalence and Superman

Legrand famously, and provocatively, wrote that comparison is, in fact, impossible as the multifaceted cultural understanding required of any one individual assessing and comparing two different legal systems would require two lifetimes; one lived in each.[11] Patrick (Chapter 1) makes a similar point regarding truly understanding religion. Legrand, as a great comparative scholar of note himself, who has – as far as we are aware – only lived one lifetime, disproves his own point across an illustrious career. But his point is to provoke, to humorously highlight the importance of cultural context in viewing law as a component in societies that will operate differently. And he is right – we cannot forget that law does not operate in a vacuum, but in a synergy of society and legal culture – the latter of which is nearly impossible to define if you have not lived in it. The same can be said for religious insight. But that does not make comparison impossible or without worth. As our colleague Nick Foster used to point out in the classroom, several decades ago when one of us had the privilege of teaching alongside him, we do not expect the comparative scholar to don a Superman cape, fasten his underwear on the outside, and perform the superhuman feat Legrand outlines. No. What we DO need to do is temper our expectations of what comparative legal analysis does. A multilayered scale of depth of insight and analysis. Because, as all lawyers increasingly work on transnational levels, the utility of comparative tools becomes clear to more and more legal disciplines. As Twining so succinctly puts it: "We are all comparativists now".[12]

Some will tell you that sociologists make better comparatists, as they are trained in methods and sensitivities which can render insight into different societies more nuanced.[13] If you have read Bellieni Zimmermann's Chapter 14 in this book, you will have noted the societal scientist's touch. Similarly, Shoval's (Chapter 5) background in philosophy gives him a different perspective and approach to comparison. And while we will not argue that point – or engage in the debate on whether law is even a social science[14] – we would posit

11 Pierre Legrand, 'How to Compare Now' (1996) 16(2) *Legal Studies*, 234.

12 W Twining, 'Globalisation and Comparative Law' Esin Örücü and David Nelken (eds), *Comparative Law—A Handbook* (Hart Publishing, 2007), 84. For a more nuanced view, see Wilson, for whom '(…) comparative law has, more often than not, been seen as an extension of the study of national law' and '[l]ooking at law from a comparative point of view (…) still remains a specialism (…) [and] [i]t cannot yet be said that it has become part and parcel of the orientation of law students or legal scholars, let alone legal practitioners'. See G Wilson 'Comparative Legal Scholarship' in M McConville and W Hong Chui (eds), *Research Methods for Law* (Edinburgh University Press, 2007) 87, 101.

13 If we were to point to one social scientist in particular who has demonstrated an inspiring method across comparative law, we might nominate the work of David Nelken, Distinguished Professor of Legal Institutions and Social Change, co-author and editor of Esin Örücü and David Nelken (eds), *Comparative Law—A Handbook* (Hart Publishing, 2007).

14 Geoffrey Samuel, 'Is Law Really a Social Science? A View from Comparative Law' (2024) 67(2) *The Cambridge Law Journal* 288–321.

that the lawyer is doing something a little different when comparing. Ideally, a good legal comparative analysis should be sensitive to societal contexts and legal culture, lest the lawyer fails to see how cases and legislation are truly applied locally. But we should temper expectations as to how this is done and how deeply this contextual understanding will run. We are but human – and different comparative projects will aim for and contribute different levels of depth and insight. They will have multivalent levels of in-depth understanding, and in turn, different levels of usefulness in contributing knowledge and perspectives. We have to accept the truth that we are not superheroes and that Legrand's perfect comparison is out of reach. But different levels of depth and insight will require different degrees of cultural perspective. Which then leads us to examine the sources of comparative legal culture.

C Kahn-Freund, Gods, and Quicksand – and More Superficiality

Legal culture is more or less undefinable. Which is not helpful, as it remains the most significant context for any insight into different cultures and legal systems. As Rene David put it 75 years ago: "Law cannot be understood without understanding the society governed by it, and in ignorance of patterns of behaviour, of thought and of feeling among the members of that society".[15]

We can attempt to define legal culture by isolating specific components of most societies where it is evident that there has been an influence on the development in legal understanding/evolution (such as politics, finance, history, anthropology, geography, and of course, religion et cetera, et cetera) but the list would be endless and still not exhaustive. And this never-ending list of potentially relevant facets of law is even more frightening to the lawyer as it is so interdisciplinary; a thing which we lawyers are often wary of – (albeit not so much in the contexts of law and religion, where sociology is not so alien as evidenced by the backgrounds of many of our chapter authors). We could also define legal culture as those aspects of culture that have had an effect on law and legal interpretation and applications. But, frankly, that seems too wide to be of any use, and how would lawyers define culture? In social science, Nelken analyses the utility of the term "legal culture" in depth and uses Friedmans "internal" and "external" concepts of legal culture to advance a more pragmatic model of dissimilar legal models to define idiosyncrasies.[16] But this still does not help us define legal culture – and if one of our times' most preeminent social scientists engaged in legal change cannot do it, we would hesitate to try. So, as Fakete also points out, we need a more careful use of the term for

15 Rene David, *Traité* élémentaire de droit civil comparé, (Librairie générale de droit et de jurisprudence, 1950) 17 (translation by Nick Foster).

16 David Nelken, 'Using the Concept of Legal Culture' (2004) 29 *Australian Journal of Legal Philosophy* 1–26.

it to be constructive.[17] And therein lies the rub. Different legal cultures may be affected by factors which are not overtly relevant in others – and all legal culture is so entrenched in local customs and societies that insight is difficult, as Legrand and our superhero analogy pointed out. But embracing the fact that any comparison may be useful on a multivalent scale, what then should a comparative scholar look at?

The answer is: that depends. And going back to our point about Gandalf and wizards, it depends entirely on what the author intended. The WHY drives the HOW, in a seemingly endless contextual societal well of choices.

Noted comparativist Otto Kahn-Freund may have said it best, in his famous quote, nearly 60 years ago:

> … on the professor of comparative law the gods bestowed the most dangerous of all their gifts, the gift of freedom.[18]

While this dangerous gift can be intimidating, especially in the light of the transdisciplinary onus placed on the comparativist, it can also be seen as liberating if we keep our multivalence and our right to be subjective in mind. Husa wrote an insightful blog on the topic, likening the comparativists' attempt at proper interdisciplinary method to the task of Sisyphus,[19] but he also concluded that it is not quite that hopeless.

Yes, the choices can be overwhelming. As can the difficulty in mapping the relationships between societal events, infrastructures, and rules – not unlike chaos theory.[20] However, we can avoid the veritable quicksand swamp by making decisions guided by our goals. As far back as 1949, F H Lawson forgave any superficiality this might entail, by eloquently stating: "Now, in a sense, a comparative lawyer is bound to be superficial; he would soon lose himself in the sands of scholarship".[21]

D In Closing – Our Approach/Perspective Bias

Based on the previous paragraphs, in teaching the subject to students we break it down in order to simplify and exemplify legal comparative methods. We advance a subjective approach, which we label the intermediary jurisprudence,

17 Balazs Fekete, 'Inconsistencies in the Use of Legal Culture in Comparative Legal Studies' (2018) 25(1) *Maastricht Journal of European and Comparative Law* 551–564. Note that we like his call to arms over the utility of the term, but question his conclusion as we believe some degree of legal cultural context is always needed.

18 Otto Kahn Freund, *Comparative Law as an Academic Subject* (Clarendon Press, 1965) 40–41.

19 Jaakko Husa 'Interdisciplinary Comparative Law – a Sisyphean task?', *British Association of Comparative Law* (blog post, 24 June 2022) https://british-association-comparative-law.org/2022/06/24/interdisciplinary-comparative-law-a-sisyphean-task-by-jaakko-husa/.

20 See the section on chaos theory and comparison in Alumari, Andersen & Jensen (n 5).

21 F H Lawson, 'The Field of Comparative Law' (1949) 61 *Judicial Review* 16, 26.

composed of whatever it takes to shed light on the goal of the analysis. We advise specific steps and introduce students to some of the main tools they can choose from and remind them of their duty to carefully structure their analysis into components or parts that can be used to look at both (or all) jurisdictions involved. To actually COMPARE and not summarise two separate legal systems without having designed a yardstick for comparison. We also advise students to declare any perspective bias – which this exposition of our method is meant to represent as a meta example.

It is with this lens and the tools set out following that we have attempted to compare the comparisons in this book. Where a chapter does not fit our approach, usually because it is, in itself, methodological and not an applied comparison, we have left it out – these are primarily chapters from Part I of the volume.

Set out, then, is a "Readers Digest" look at the elements of our basic comparative tool box and a look at how we identified methods in the chapters in this volume.

III Readers Digest Version of the Toolbox as We See It

Next we set out some of the most significant tools which we have observed in this book and beyond, that can be combined and blended to provide the bespoke method needed for an "intermediary jurisprudence" allowing a sound comparison. These are by no means the only tools available to the prospective comparativist, we would argue, however, that they provide a repetitive sample which is a useful starting place:

- The Doctrinal Method
- The Historical Method
- The Functional Method
- The Analytical Method
- The Cultural Method
- The Yardstick

We stress that none of these methods are better off on their own – they thrive in the company of each other, and thus some of them inherently overlap. We will return to them after presenting our assessment of the chapters in this book, when we offer our view of how they were employed by the authors (who will comment in the rejoinders in the Appendix on whether they feel we have hit the mark in identifying their approach). The goal is to allow the reader to absorb some of the more complex comparative legal methodological theory in a less complex format, and then consider our forensic explorations into what others have done. We hope this allows inspiration for further future use of comparative legal methodology in the field of law and religion.

A The Doctrinal Method

The doctrinal method is the most common method applied in legal studies and may be defined as "a detailed and highly technical commentary upon, and systematic exposition of, the context of legal doctrine".[22] It entails "analysing legal rules and decisions, clarifying ambiguities within rules, structuring them in a logical and coherent manner and describing their interrelationships".[23] To this end, it focusses on the collection and organisation of data from primary and secondary sources, including case law, statutes, and law in books, in order to identify the underlying system and aims to obtain a general understanding of a legal system in terms of its applicable rules.[24] For these reasons, it is also referred to as the descriptive or "black letter law"' method. And we begin here, as it is likely to be the one most familiar to the legal scholar and very much where our skills sets are at home.

The doctrinal method, generally, perceives law as a body of rules,[25] and, therefore, considers social, political, and moral factors to be of marginal relevance at best for legal analysis.[26] As Vick puts it,

> In its purest form, 'black-letter' research aims to understand the law from no more than a thorough examination of a finite and relatively fixed universe of authoritative texts consisting of cases, statutes and other primary sources, the relative importance of which depends on the legal tradition and system within which the legal researcher operates.[27]

Because the doctrinal method "ignores" the societal context of legal rules,[28] Salter and Mason believed that it is too formalistic and inadequate and, thus, that the results of such comparisons are misleading.[29] The doctrinal method would be more useful if it considered law in terms of its cultural, historical, and political contexts.[30] These contexts are important in a comparative study to explain law as a final product comprising several factors. Thus, the doctrinal

22 Michael Salter and Julie Mason, *Writing Law Dissertations: An Introduction and Guide to the Conduct of Legal Research* (Pearson, 2007) 49.

23 Reza Banakar, 'Having One's Cake and Eating It: The Paradox of Contextualisation in Socio-Legal Research' (2011) 7(4) *International Journal of Law in Context* 487–503, 487; Glanert (n 2) 68.

24 Banakar (n 20) 487–503.

25 Roger Cotterrell, *Law's Community: Legal Theory in Sociological Perspective* (Clarendon Press, 1995) 50–3.

26 Terry Hutchinson, 'Doctrinal Research, Researching the Jury' in Dawn Watkins and Mandy Burton (eds), *Research Methods in Law* (Routledge, 2nd ed, 2018) 21.

27 Douglas W Vick, 'Interdisciplinarity and the Discipline of Law' (2004) 31(2) *Journal of Law and Society* 163–93, 178.

28 Cotterrell (n 22) 50–3.

29 Salter and Mason (n 19) 99–108.

30 Esin Örücü, 'Developing Comparative Law' in Esin Örücü and David Nelken (eds) *Comparative Law: A Handbook.* (Hart 2007) 43–65, 57.

method combined with the historical and/or cultural methods will offer a better understanding of the legal systems being compared. We have noticed, as is evident in Section IV of this chapter, that much to our delight, black letter doctrinal research with limited societal context does not seem to be as common in the field of law and religion as we have seen in other areas (most notably international commercial contexts). We hazard a guess on why this is – as you will see later.

While the criticism of the doctrinal method is valid, it is indispensable to a comparative study.[31] The doctrinal method is "the main supplier of concepts, categories and criteria",[32] and also a staple component in the lawyers' wheelhouse. Thus, although the doctrinal method is inadequate on its own, it is necessary to include in a comparative study. For example, the historical method is necessary to address the shortcomings of the doctrinal method, but the use of the former depends largely on the data gathered by the latter.[33]

B The Historical Method

The historical method focuses on understanding the historical development of the legal rules being compared. The historical context helps to explain contemporary law,[34] as one must understand its historical origin to understand law.[35] In fact, Jaakko Husa claimed that the use of the historical method is inescapable:

> Nevertheless, as soon as the comparatist exceeds the narrow limits of black letter law, historical context(s) become highly relevant. There are two places where legal history actually comes into play. First, understanding the sources is easier if there is knowledge of the legal historical context of those sources. Second, legal historical knowledge is of quintessential significance since it is virtually impossible to explain observations without knowledge of legal history. We need to look at the research

31 John C Reitz, 'How to Do Comparative Law (Symposium: New Directions in Comparative Law)' (1998) 46(4) *American Journal of Comparative Law* 617, 630, 619; John Wightman, *Contract: A Critical Commentary* (Pluto Press, 1996) 11.

32 P Westerman, 'Open or Autonomous? The Debate on Legal Methodology as a Reflection of the Debate on Law' in M Van Hoecke (ed), *Methodologies of Legal Research: Which Kind of Method for What Kind of Discipline?* (Hart Publishing, 2011) 94.

33 Jörg Fedtke, The Method and Culture of Comparative Law: Essays in Honour of Marc Van Hoecke (2016) 4(2) *Comparative Legal History* 255–9.

34 Rodolfo Sacco, 'Legal Formants: A Dynamic Approach to Comparative Law (Part 2)' (1991) 39(2) *American Journal of Comparative Law* 343–401, 384.

35 George Mousourakis, 'Legal Transplants and Legal Development: A Jurisprudential and Comparative Law Approach' (2013) 54(3) *Acta Juridica Hungarica* 219.

> process of comparative law in order to get a clearer picture concerning where to place legal historical knowledge in comparative law.[36]

The historical method seeks to understand and explain the factors that have contributed to the formation of the targeted legal rules.[37] It focuses on the roots of the law instead of the existing body of rules. Thus, it is important to understand the differences between legal systems. The historical method also opens up the opportunity to treat two different time periods of the same jurisdiction as different for the purposes of comparison. Opening up new ways to understand one's own jurisdiction using comparative approaches without the need to go beyond the borders (metaphorical and literal) of your own state. Barker and Clarke (Chapter 2) propose this approach as one way to use models of state-religion relationships in their chapter in Part I of this volume.

However, as with the doctrinal method, the historical method is more effective when it is combined with other methods, in particular, the functional method because it can help explain differences that are not rooted in doctrinal thinking.[38]

C The Functional Method

There is no universal definition of the functional method,[39] which can be attributed to the many variations of functional methods in literature.[40] Overall, however, we like the definition offered by Butler and Saidov, which covers all subcategories of functionalism in comparative legal analysis:

> the investigation of legal means and methods for the resolution of similar or identical social and legal problems by different legal systems.[41]

36 Jaakko Husa, 'Developing Legal System, Legal Transplants and Path Dependence: Reflections on the Rule of Law' (2018) 6(2) *The Chinese Journal of Comparative Law* 129–50, 132.

37 Mark Van Hoecke, 'Methodology of Comparative Legal Research' (Pt Boom Juridische Uitgevers) (2015) *Law and Method*, 17.

38 Martin Löhnig, 'Comparative Law and Legal History: A Few Words about Comparative Legal History' in Maurice Adams and Dirk Heirbaut (eds), *The Method and Culture of Comparative Law: Essays in Honour of Mark Van Hoecke* (Hart Publishing, 1st ed, 2014) 113–20, 114.

39 John J Macionis and Linda M Gerber, *Sociology, Seventh Canadian Edition with MySocLab* (Pearson Education Canada, 7 ed, 2010) 14; Ralf Michaels, 'The Functional Method of Comparative Law' in Mathias Reimann and Reinhard Zimmermann (eds), *The Oxford Handbook of Comparative Law* (Oxford University Press, 2006) 344–5.

40 According to Ralf Michaels, 'one can distinguish at least seven different concepts of functionalism across disciplines: (1) finalism … (2) adaptionism … (3) classical (Durkheimian) functionalism … (4) instrumentalism … (5) refined functionalism … (6) epistemological functionalism … and (7) equivalence functionalism … Largely oblivious of incompatibilities, functionalist comparative law (8) uses all of these'. Michaels (n 36) 342.

41 William Elliott Butler and A Kh Saidov, *Comparative Law* (Wildy, Simmonds & Hill, 2003) 33.

The focus here is on MEANS and METHOD, and thus, ultimately, on EFFECT. The functional method views society as a living organism that gradually evolves and therefore focuses mainly on analysing the mutual relationship between phenomena, in order to identify the latent functions of legal rules.[42] Instead of focusing on the formulation of law, like the doctrinal method, the functional method highlights the role of law as a component of a complex system and compares legal rules according to their effect.[43] Thus, the functional method focuses on case law as the practical outcomes of law.[44] A common outcome or function enables comparison of different legal rules. As Michaels argued, "legal and non-legal [rules], even doctrinally different ones, are comparable if they are functionally equivalent, if they fulfil similar functions in different legal systems".[45]

The functional method can be used for three different purposes. First, it can be used to understand the legal rules being compared in light of their functional relation to society, which is referred to as the "epistemological function".[46] Defining this function may require a lot of groundwork in developing a yardstick for determining what law accomplishes in different systems and may rely heavily on social science, finance, biology, or whatever specific societal issues the author has in focus. For example, a comparison on fishery prohibition across very different legal systems may need to develop an epistemological yardstick of functional effects – ie, has a fish species been protected? Does it work? Is it law or biology? Et cetera et cetera.[47]

Secondly, it can be used to determine the "better" law,[48] which is referred to as "the evaluative function".[49] We caution here against normative qualifiers which stand on their own – defining what a better law represents, with outcomes and perspectives, would seem to be essential.

Finally, the functional method can be used to determine comparable rules or what has to be compared with what.[50]

The functional method has been criticised for not paying sufficient attention to the influence of historical, cultural, and political factors surrounding the law that could have affected its formation and legal cultural contexts.

42 Roscoe Pound, 'Law in the Books and Law in Action' (1910) 44 *American Law Review*, 12.

43 Jaakko Husa, 'Functional Method in Comparative Law – Much Ado about Nothing?' (2013) 2(1) *European Property Law Journal* 4–21, 12.

44 Michaels (n 36) 342.

45 Ibid.

46 Ibid.

47 See for example Erika Techera, 'Advancing a Sustainable Blue Economy – Case Study: Fisheries Governance in the Indian Ocean' in Simone Borg, Felicity G Attard and Patricia M Vella de Fremeaux (eds), *Research Handbook on Ocean Governance Law* (Edward Elgar, 2023) 283–294.

48 Nelken, 'Using the Concept of Legal Culture' (n 13) 26.

49 Michaels (n 36) 363.

50 K Zweigert, 'Methodological Problems in Comparative Law' (1972) 7(4) *Israel Law Review* 465, 467.

Again, a consideration of these factors is essential for effective comparison.[51] Since a valuable comparative study must seek to understand law as it acts in real life, which can be achieved by determining the relevant values of its society, both the analytical and cultural methods are required to supplement the functional method.[52] Then again, there is a strong relationship between the functional method's epistemological function and the other comparative methods because it is important to identify relevant "functionally equivalent" sources and data.[53] The term "functional equivalence" can be defined as "a term in the target legal system designating a concept or institution, the function of which is the same as that in the source legal system",[54] although they may not be equivalent in name.

One approach to addressing the critique of the alleged superficiality of (some) applications of functional method is the development of the term "Neo-Functional",[55] as a label to ensure that the contextual societal and cultural factors are not divorced form the expressions of the functions of law in cases etc. See "The Cultural Method".

Regardless of any previous critique of functionalism as a method, we will champion it happily. First of all, because functionalist approaches have matured to allow better contextualisation and insight into influences of legal culture – whether labelled neo-functionalist or not. But secondly, because as outlined earlier, we have to accept the multivalent usefulness of comparative analysis – even a more superficial effect-based analysis may be helpful and provide insight and value.

D The Analytical Method

The analytical method focuses on legal and non-legal terms used in legal contexts by comparing the meaning of those concepts in different jurisdictions.[56] In addition to clarifying the meaning and use of legal terms in different contexts,[57] it can be used to identify relevant cases. Relevant case law is often identified by using the concept in question as the search term. The analytical method is essential because "[t]he marriage of the comparative and analytical processes is what ensures continuity of the comparative legal scholarship; it is

51 Husa, 'Developing Legal System' (n 33).
52 Reitz (n 28).
53 Michaels (n 36) 364.
54 Marcela Müllerová Shiflett, 'Functional Equivalence and Its Role in Legal Translation' (2020) 3 *English Matters III*, 29.
55 Esin Örücü, 'What Is a Mixed Legal System: Exclusion or Expansion?' (2008) 12(1) *Electronic Journal of Comparative*, 52.
56 Caslav Pejovic, 'Civil Law and Common Law: Two Different Paths Leading to the Same Goal' (2001) 32(3) *Victoria University of Wellington Law Review* 817–851, 817.
57 Nelken, 'Comparative Law and Comparative Legal Studies' (n 6) 28.

what allows later researchers to build on previous models and findings".[58] Like the other methods, this method relies on both primary and secondary sources, and conceptual analysis of law "lies at the heart of 'black letter law' and is the basis upon which legal scholarship is built", which demonstrates the strong relationship between the analytical method and the doctrinal method.

Similarly, there is a fundamental relationship between the analytical and cultural methods. As argued earlier, context is essential for the vast majority of comparative legal methods, particularly, the analytical method, which must consider cultural context to understand the meaning of legal terms.[59] This is especially important where the comparison involves translation:

> [I]s not easy. We need to be extremely careful here. We cannot assume that an idea or word will translate perfectly from one culture to another. We must recognise the meaning of the idea or word in its own culture, explain its underlying cultural context and then translate that meaning as best we can to another legal culture, whether our own or a different, foreign culture. Translation calls upon us to explain the underlying context of the culture in which the idea or word is found. It requires understanding the multiple semiotic systems and linguistic contexts that situate ideas and then determining how to adjust and transfer over that particular worldview into that of another. If we do this well, translation can be a bridge to connect cultures.[60]

Thus, the cultural method may also be crucial to determine the comparable rules. In turn, this means that the functional method needs the analytical method as well. To understand semiotic systems and linguistic contexts, the use of the analytical method to search for 'functional equivalence' of terms becomes crucial.

E The Cultural Method

The cultural method is both one of the most important and one of the most controversial methods. Again, there is not one cultural method but many, three of which are the most popular. Like the historical method, the first one deals with culture as a possible explanation for variations in law. The

58 Hamid Harasani, 'Islamic Law as a Comparable Model in Comparative Legal Research' (2014) 3(2) *Global Journal of Comparative Law* 186–202, 189.

59 Rene David, *Major Legal Systems in the World Today: An Introduction to the Comparative Study of Law* (Stevens, 3rd ed, 1985) 361.

60 Edward J Eberle, 'The Method and Role of Comparative Law' (2009) 8(3) *Washington University Global Studies Law Review* 451, 459. See also Müllerová Shiflett (n 51) 29.

second utilises law to explain culture, and the third considers law as culture.[61] Thus, the difference between these methods stems from the goals they seek to achieve. For example, if a study aims to explain the cultural changes that occurred in a particular society within a specific period, then it makes sense to consider law as an influencing factor. However, if the purpose of a study is to examine the factual differences between two legal systems regarding the same matter, then it would be more appropriate to consider law as an expression of culture. It should be noted that comparative legal culture does not have a specific method to be followed, and there is some overlap with the historical and analytical methods.

We would suggest that, essentially, all sound contextual legal comparative analysis – even if being multivalently superficial – needs to contextualise the law or legal phenomenon in the society in which it belongs to SOME degree. The degree of this context will depend on the extent to which the author has decided that legal cultural context is relevant. So, as per our outline of approach in Section II, we cannot really say an analysis is wrong if it chooses to be superficial and divorced from the reality of its societal contexts, but it may be misleading if the applied law in context deviates from any presumptions made by the author. So it is in this pitfall that methods like functionalism often get accused of being insufficient – hence the notion of neo-functionalism, which combines functional approaches with cultural method or context.

F The Yardstick

Most comparisons have to develop some sort of system for measuring a function, doctrine, rule, or historical development in law in order to compare a legal phenomenon in one jurisdiction against another or several others. We label this the metaphorical "yardstick" for comparison, and as ever, it needs to be developed or adapted by the author to fulfil a specific function in the comparison. As an inherent part of any analytical approach, it nonetheless deserves its own category.

The yardstick serves a dual purpose in this context. Firstly, it aids in comprehending the intended legal rule within its specific legal framework. This involves grasping the significance of the legal rule within the system and understanding its connection to the societal culture. Such comprehension is vital for assessing the rule's effectiveness. Secondly, it is crucial for determining the relevant factors to consider when comparing two legal systems, particularly when there are significant cultural disparities between the systems being compared.

This is to say, that in order to avoid the misunderstandings of foreign legal systems, which usually leads to misleading results, the comparatist should rely

61 Abigail C. Saguy and Forrest Stuart, 'Culture and Law: Beyond a Paradigm of Cause and Effect' (2008) 619(1) *The Annals of the American Academy of Political and Social Science* 149–164, 149.

on objective criteria that developed out of deep understanding of the roots of a legal rule. These criteria include historical context, cultural context, religious influences, ... etc.

Certainly, developing a yardstick necessitates a profound understanding of the specific rule in question and the legal framework to which it pertains. It also requires a precise definition of the comparison's objective. It is important to recognise that what may effectively serve one study's purpose may not necessarily serve another's. For instance, if a comparatist aims to propose an improved solution for a legal system, the applicable yardstick will differ from the one used to assess how two legal systems might adopt and interpret the same rule differently.

IV Comparing the Comparative Chapters

What we have noted in this volume has been both intriguing and enlightening regarding the use of comparative methodology, especially in the context of religion. This section concentrates on a forensic examination of the methods applied in the chapters of Part II of this book, using our definitions of the selected methods as outlined in Section II herein. The first five chapters of Part I, which focus more on methodology–designing, are not the primary focus of this section, but we will nonetheless look briefly at their contributions to methodology.

In the following paragraphs, we set out a meta-approach to measuring the chapters using our own yardstick of these methods, in a meta-cognitive recognition of the power of visuals in demonstrating comparative approaches. We laid out the chosen chapters for comparison of method into the grid with the components, using a simple black, grey, and white system for visually communicating how reliant we felt each author was on each component. Following this, we comment on each of the components and respective authors who gave us cause for comment.

However, this does not mean that the methods we are highlighting were the only methods used in the chapters attributed to them, but the most obvious ones. It also does not mean that the chapters in Part I in this book did not adopt the selected methods listed, but it means that those methods were used for a purpose other than comparing legal systems or simply used to develop a general understanding of the use of the comparative methodology; as the focus of chapters in Part I is dedicated to exploring how methodologies in law and religion should be designed, spanning five chapters that offer different perspectives in specific areas. The consensus among the authors, in our opinion, is that no one methodology is valid for all legal studies, even within a relatively small area in comparison to comparative law in general, such as law and religion. This is to say, that each researcher must identify the methodology that works for their research question.

Let us first run through the contributions in Part I. For instance, Patrick (Chapter 1) contributes to the general understanding of the comparative methodology by justifying Reitz's principles to the law-religion studies. The author achieved that by adopting the doctrinal and the analytical methods to develop a framework that highlights both similarities and differences between law and religion as normative structures in the society. Barker and Clarke (Chapter 2) use a mix of doctrinal, historical, analytical, and functional methods to provide a comprehensive framework for understanding state-religion relationships. This can help comparatists in avoiding the quicksand surrounding this area. Likewise, Amin Al-Astewani (Chapter 3) outlines a multistage methodology that aims to understand legal context and the political context, analysing theoretical foundations including the functionality of legal terms and institutions, and evaluating practical utility. To this end, he adopted a methodology combining doctrinal, historical, functional, and analytical methods to explore legal pluralism in the UK. Erlings (Chapter 4) focuses on establishing a theoretical framework for comparing legal-religion studies involving children. The chapter employs cultural and doctrinal methods along with the analytical method. Finally, Shoval (Chapter 5) discusses methodologies for interpreting religious texts, particularly the Bible, drawing parallels to legal text analysis, using doctrinal, analytical, and functional methods to emphasise the importance of cultural and historical contexts in understanding religious texts. These are all great illustrations of the unique composition and perspective on comparative method, as it generally applies to law and religion.

As foreshadowed previously, however, it is in the application of method in Part II where we can best analyse methodology in action. Table 15.1 sets out our assessment of the comparative approaches used by the authors in Part II of this book using a simple black, grey, and white system to visually communicate how reliant we felt each author was on the comparative approaches in our meta-yardstick.

A The Doctrinal Method

Commenting on doctrinal approaches and how they are applied is not normally necessary, as this is what lawyers rely most on. However, we have a general comment on this method specifically in this book. We noticed early on, as alluded to in Section III of this chapter, that much to our delight, black letter doctrinal research with limited societal context does not seem to be as common in the field of law and religion as we have seen in other areas (most notably international commercial contexts). We hazard a guess on why this is, and frankly, we are not surprised.

Different areas of legal study will inevitably consider themselves (fallacy or not) more or less connected to legal culture. For example, Kahn-Freund famously said of commercial law that it was "culture-free",[62] a misstatement

62 Otto Kahn-Freund, 'On Uses and Misuses of Comparative Law' (1974) 37 *Modern Law Review* 1. The authors argue that, in context, what is meant is that commercial law is comparatively more culture-free than other disciplines in law.

Table 15.1 Comparative Methods/Approaches Used by Authors in Part II of This Book

Chapter No.	*Author*	*Method / Approach*					
		Doctrinal	*Historical*	*Functional*	*Analytical*	*Cultural*	*Yardstick*
6	*Watson*						
7	*Babie*						
8	*Barker and Andersen*						
9	*van der Schyff*						
10	*Pagotto*						
11	*Rochow*						
12	*Moulds*						
13	*Bhanu and Sthapak*						
14	*Zimmermann*						

that these authors, two of whom are commercial legal scholars, can assure you is incorrect, and most certainly not what Kahn-Freund meant. What IS true, however, is that the link between commercial law and society and culture is not as obvious for commercial law as it is in other fields of law; the prime example being law and religion.

As Patrick (Chapter 1) reminds us, with reference to Barker,[63] the fine line between law and religion necessitates a more sensitive and less black letter law approach. We concluded in Section III that for a field of legal study so enmeshed in culture, society, and beliefs, we would not expect a purely legal doctrinal approach to be workable. Yet, as demonstrated by Bhanu and Sthapak (Chapter 13) who manage to compose a very useful analysis of a strongly doctrinal area of law and religion, using the legal benchmarks as comparators in themselves. We are reminded of the multivalence of comparative study, this contribution serves to illustrate that comparative analysis in law can come in many guises.

Bhanu and Sthapak's approach is to first set out key features of the Indian legal system before identifying similar features in other legal systems. While they make comparisons to a number of jurisdictions including, for example, Australia, their primary point of comparison is the United States. Indeed, we would observe that the United States is often chosen as a jurisdiction for comparison in law and religion. Within this book, for example, Watson (Chapter 6), Babie (Chapter 7), and Rochow (Chapter 11) all include the United States in their analysis. The reasons for this frequent reference to the Unites States are beyond the scope of our discussion but interesting to note in the context of the selection of jurisdictions. However, the selection of the jurisdictions included in any comparative analysis is an important step in the design of the research and will be largely influenced by what the author intends to do, or in other words, their purpose. Here, the selection of the United States as one of the comparators serves the purpose Bhanu and Sthapak, and they, therefore, like Gandalf, arrive where they intend to arrive when they intend to get there.

More broadly what we saw across the field in this volume were chapters that developed some clear doctrinal analysis, as lawyers must,[64] but very rarely on its own and all with very clear analytical or contextual approaches, with yardsticks or intermediary jurisprudential identification of what was being compared.

One example is Al-Astewani (Chapter 3), who defines and analyses the utility of legal pluralism as a conceptual approach and explores the legal status of British Sharia Tribunals. It is not a comparative law analysis as such, but it provides essential context for a comparative topic. While mainly doctrinal, it also adopts an analytical method, which focuses on legal and non-legal terms

63 Renae Barker, *State and Religion: The Australian Story* (Routledge, 2019).

64 See for example Watson (Chapter 6), Babie (Chapter 7), van der Schyff (Chapter 9), Pagotto (Chapter 10) and Rochow (Chapter 11).

used in legal contexts by comparing the meaning of those concepts in different legal systems.

Watson (Chapter 6) used the doctrinal method to elucidate the legal doctrines that govern state support for religious education in the United States and Canada. The findings from his application of the doctrinal method provided the theoretical framework for the application of other methods used in the chapter. It served both as a descriptive approach and as a tool to outline the jurisprudence surrounding state aid for religious schools in the two countries considered in the analysis.

Another example is van der Schyff (Chapter 9), who utilised the doctrinal method to delineate the case study, facilitating an understanding of the research problem's origins and identification of pertinent factors, before compiling the elements needed for the composition of the method of comparison and the yardstick. This doctrinal approach was complemented by the historical method, a combination often deemed essential in such endeavours. To avoid the misleading results, the author correctly established the fundamental differences between ECHR and CJEU's by employing the functional method.

Al-Astewani (Chapter 3) also takes an initially doctrinal approach, which is complemented by other methods that suit different aims. He uses the doctrinal method to describe the main ideas on which he based his argument, in particular, legal pluralism as explained by Griffiths and its relationship with Ehrlich's theory of living law. As is often seen, he also adopted the historical method in order to better contextualise the background of legal pluralism. The analytical method is also employed to characterise the differences between legal pluralism and Ehrlich's theory of living law. It also used the law in context method to illustrate how the British court dealt with the Sharia law in the UK. However, this chapter could potentially be criticised for not applying sufficient cultural context to the functional rules, as it does not distinguish clearly between the British Muslims and Muslims from other nationalities living in the UK – a potentially very significant distinction to some of the points made. This can serve to illustrate why doctrinal approaches – even when complemented by others – can sometimes be broadly criticised for not offering vital context. We must always, however, remember the multiplicity of utility; others can add different nuances.

B The Historical Method

As noted, we often see the doctrinal method complemented by the historical method. Together, they tend to create more depth to a perspective. This is particularly evident in the analysis from both Watson (Chapter 6) and Babie (Chapter 7). Indeed, both apply the historical method in the context of government funding of education using the Unites States as one of their comparators. This provides an interesting opportunity to examine how two different authors approach ostensibly similar topics using similar methods, yet produce two very different analyses. In the context for a book all about method, we seized this opportunity and invited both Watson and Babie to comment on each other's approach as you will have seen in Chapters 6.1 and 7.1.

Turning to the two chapters, Watson (Chapter 6) employed the historical method to establish and trace the development of historical and social facts that ultimately influenced the ideology upon which the constitutions of both America and Canada were based. In this chapter, the historical method aids the author in understanding the differences between the compared legal systems, highlighting the relationship between their constitutions and the societal doctrines and thoughts that influenced them.

Babie (Chapter 7) has composed a very interesting approach which also helps to highlight aspects of the historical method. To evaluate his methodology, we need a better understanding of his aim. He seems guided by Alan Watson in his understanding of comparative methodology and transplant theory,[65] in his endeavours to establish relationships between the compared legal system, in order to determine who copied from whom, then use the older text to explain the similarities between the legal systems. While interesting from a historical perspective, this indirectly overlooks the functional theory by not incorporating political and social contexts, which differentiate these historical societies. In other words, Babie uses the legal transplant theory of legal historian Alan Watson to justify the usage of the American court interpretations. He then employs a doctrinal method to extract a yardstick based on the understanding of the American court and interpretation to help Australia in understanding their own constitution. In doing this, he also employs an asymmetrical approach to the law in context method (as interpreted by the court), with a predominantly American perspective. Now, such an approach is clearly dominated by one cultural perspective – so we return to the question of aim. Because, as Babie illustrates, there is value in seeing a set of Australian legal rules through the eyes of another legal system. This chapter thus also helps to highlight the subjectivity of the comparative method, as AIM will drive the choice of approach.

C The Functionalist Method

Generally, the functional method can be used to understand the legal rules being compared in the light of their functional relation to society, which is referred to as the "epistemological function",[66] determine the "better" law,[67] which is referred to as "the evaluative function", and to decide comparable rules or what has to be compared with what.[68]

65 Alan Watson, 'Legal Transplants: An Approach to Comparative Law' (1975) 27(4) *Stanford Law Review* 1208.

66 Michaels (n 36) 372.

67 Nelken, 'Comparative Law and Comparative Legal Studies' (n 6) 27.

68 Zweigert (n 47) 467.

Four of the authors in Part II of the book have employed the functional method in their chapters: Babie (Chapter 7), van der Schyff (Chapter 9), Pagotto (Chapter 10), and Rochow (Chapter 11). Functionalism also indirectly played a role Moulds (Chapter 12), as the author relied on research based on the functional method.

Babie (Chapter 7) relies on the functional method to determine the constitutional comparable rules in Australia and the US. The use of the functional method in the context of the chapter was for the purpose of establishing the relationship between the legal systems being compared. Likewise, van der Schyff (Chapter 9) employed the functional method to establish the relationships between CFR and ECHR. In those two chapters, the use of the functional method served the purpose of highlighting the fingerprints of legal transplant between the legal systems being compared, and it was necessarily to combine it with the historical context, as both authors did. Such methods played a vital role in the context of those chapters to determine their scopes as well as to select the relevant materials.

Rochow (Chapter 11) employed the functional method, among others, to define human dignity as an overarching status and a missing tool in the common law by which to determine rights claims disputes. The functional method was employed alongside the doctrinal method and the analytical method, which is based on Hohfeldian analysis.

Finally, Pagotto (Chapter 10) employed the functional method to assess the targeted rules and the courts' responses to the conflict involving the kirpan. After employing the doctrinal method to define the research question and its scope, and using analytical methods to clarify relevant terminology, she then needed to evaluate the findings of those methods and demonstrate the societal function of these rules. In this sense, both the "epistemological function" and the "evaluative function" were applied at various points throughout the chapter. The first helped illustrate the conflict surrounding the kirpan from both the perspective of its adherents and those opposed to it. It raised the question of whether the court should classify it as a religious practice to be protected or as a weapon to be banned. The functional method was required to address this question effectively. In simple terms, the functional method was employed in this chapter to highlight how culture can play a role in interpreting law and characterising factual situations such as the kirpan.

D The Analytical Method

The use of the analytical method in a comparative study is mostly unavoidable. Especially if the researcher deals with legal and non-legal concepts in a legal context. This is not only relevant to a comparative study but in order to understand the legal rules being compared in their own legal systems. It helps the researcher to avoid interpreting legal text according to their own understanding, which may be very different from the real one. Babie (Chapter 7) employed the analytical method to interpret the American understanding of

the constitutional text being compared or suggested to a better understanding of the Australian text. However, this method might be confused with the law in the context method as both might rely on case law to understand a legal rule; however, the difference between them, in our opinion, might be in the goal that the research may try to achieve. The analytical method is more in line with comparative methodology as it offers a better understanding of the targeted concepts in their own legal systems.

van der Schyff (Chapter 9) employs the analytical method to determine the meaning (which determines the scope) of the targeted legal rules in both CFR and ECHR. He used this method as a tool to compare the understanding of the right in both jurisdictions, which helped him to determine the relevant factors that he may need to consider further in his research. Thus, the role of the analytical method was twofold; it helped in determining the scope of the targeted rules, as well as in determining what aspects were relevant to compare those two legal systems.

Pagotto (Chapter 10) used the analytical method to define practical terms such as kirpan; this definition was necessarily to determine the source of the legal debate surrounding this issue and, thus, determine the scope of the study in general. This usage of the analytical was unavoidable in the context of her research because, without defining those terms, it was impossible to structure the debate in a logical manner. However, the usage of the analytical method for such a purpose can only be possible when combining it with the cultural method.

Rochow (Chapter 11) employed the analytical method in order to establish his argument. According to him, the determination of the meaning of human dignity was essential to his analysis and eventual argument. In such cases, the analytical method not only plays a role in defining the legal and non-legal concept, but also in illustrating the reasons behind the term's complexity. The author needed to combine the analytical method with the historical and functional methods in order to deal with the protracted debate on the definition of one of main terms which was key to his overall analysis.

Moulds (Chapter 12) employed the analytical method in her chapter to avoid any disagreement on the legal concept around which she built her argument, that is the freedom of religious belief. In such a context, the analytical method appears as if it is part of the doctrinal method since the authors themselves did not use it to define the legal concept. However, that does not change the fact that using the analytical method, regardless of whether its usage was direct or indirect, serves the same purpose; that is, to define the legal and non-legal concepts used in a legal context, which is supposed to offer a better understanding of the legal rules, and thus offer the foundations foundations upon which the comparatist will build their hypothesis, argument, and conclusions.

Zimmermann's (Chapter 14) background as a sociologist influences the methodology employed in her analysis. Sociology and law approach social and legal issues differently, so integrating these perspectives enriches our understanding of social problems and enhances our chances to address them effectively. In this case, the author's goal was not to compare the laws of different countries but to explore, from a sociological standpoint, how the concept of honour linked to religion impacted violence against immigrant women from different countries. Her chapter demonstrates how analysing complex societal phenomena or understanding the religious-legal framework in shaping societal views often necessitates interdisciplinary approaches. She employed the analytical method to allocate her research question in its social, political, and legal contexts; and to define some central terminology in her study such as "honour".

E The Cultural Method

Most comparative methods will have to have incorporated an element of cultural assessment or comparison in order to highlight the influence or effects of culture – or perhaps to explain the lack of significance of culture in a given area.

Watson (Chapter 6) employed the cultural method in various parts of his chapter to explore, analyse, and elucidate the differences between American and Canadian approaches to religious freedom, particularly in the context of public funding for religious schools. By using the cultural method, Watson explained significant contrasts between the two legal systems, providing insights that explain the discrepancies in how each of those countries handles public funding for religious schools.

Pagotto (Chapter 10) has a very clear focus on cultural differentiation. She initially introduces the two jurisdictions (Italy and Canada) being compared, by mapping them in the traditional "legal families" of common law and civil law and describing specific differences between them. In a cultural context, this could be labelled as "cultural structuralism" and although it is a simple categorisation, it provides an overview and basic understanding of the jurisdictions being compared. In her analysis, she focuses on the similarities and differences of judicial orientations and approaches, rather than the institutional elements characterising Italian and Canadian legal orders, so her structural comparison is more cultural than institutional/formal.

By focusing on the practical outcomes of law, and therefore its functional relation to society, Pagotto merges her cultural approach with the functional method to compare how two secular courts respond to demands for religious accommodation and requests for court intervention (wearing of the kirpan as a case study). She also uses the cultural method to explain variations in approach to balance safeguarding religious observance and ensuring public safety, in particular by considering the influence of judicial populism (if that can be considered culture). She draws the line in utilising a cultural method, however, as using the two cultures to explain the different judicial approaches. Rather, she describes the different legal bases upon which decisions were made, and therefore relies mainly on the doctrinal method to explain and "understand the rationale of each judgement". While she does analyse her findings from a cultural perspective, this is not an analytical method in a comparative sense, although the section on how freedom of religion is balanced with public safely in the two jurisdictions approaches it. To us, this chapter is a great example of cultural method in action, done sensitively and with respect of its own limitations.

Zimmermann (Chapter 14) employs the cultural method in order to define the roots of the issue being dealt with. The use of the cultural method in this chapter aligns with the findings of comparative law scholars who have spent decades examining the relationship between law and culture: the role of the culture not only in shaping the law but also its role in influencing its interpretations and, thus, the social behaviour in general.

F The Yardstick Method

In more recent comparative methodology, there has been a marked increase in result-oriented writing that develops specific parameters or yardsticks to allow a legal phenomenon to be "measured or weighed" across similar factors. However, as an inherent part of an analytical approach and the protocol of comparing, the most challenging step is often determining HOW to isolate individual components that can be used in two or more jurisdictions to measure and compare legal phenomena.

This book has shown many chapters developing such yardsticks, all with different underlying methods, and all as part of a more complex structure and intermediary jurisprudence. And the variety is fascinating.

From a yardstick based on the Charter of Fundamental Rights of the European Union ('CFR') (van der Schyff Chapter 9), to a complex yardstick of evaluating human dignity societally (Rochow Chapter 11). One uses constitutionality of public funding of religious schools as a yardstick (Watson Chapter 6), while another measures the American perspective of Australian constitutional elements (Babie Chapter 7). Another chapter has developed ten indicators of effective public parliamentary engagement (Moulds Chapter 12), yet another measures how secular courts respond to demands for religious accommodation and requests for court intervention, and the wearing of the kirpan (Pagotto Chapter 10). We also have a chapter applying the secular aspects associated with religious practice, the Essentiality Test and restrictive mechanisms to faith and religious practice (Bhanu and Sthapak Chapter 13). All of these varied mechanisms for facilitating a comparison offer insight into the significance of varied perspectives of the author, and ultimately highlight the aim of the analysis in the revelation of their perspective.

Barker and Andersen (Chapter 8) construct a very detailed "traffic light" system that attempts a pragmatic approach at weighing identified elements of children's rights, in an attempt to identify how these can be measured. They focus on developing a yardstick for measuring and comparing rights, with a neo-functional contextual analysis of where and how each legal aspect operates. Historical and doctrinal methods are applied in tandem. It is worth noting, as the authors do, that this chapter could not be written until after a separate piece of research substantiating the legitimacy of comparative ages of children and theories around children's rights had been completed and published elsewhere. It is, thus, a good example of scaffolding comparative work in order to facilitate future comparison.

One of the clearest examples we found of an accessible methodology in doing just that was Moulds' (Chapter 12) approach. Essentially, Moulds follows a bespoke approach advancing clear yardsticks for benchmarking, measuring, and describing the freedom of speech in religious beliefs in various systems. By using the functional factors identified by Leston-Bandeir, she takes an effective shortcut in establishing these parameters (the table in her method section). She is making a clear yardstick to use in evaluating the essential components in transnationally identified values and functions of the freedom of speech in a religious context. By enveloping cultural factors in the reception of the influences, she tailors a more neo-functional approach, incorporating both structural and institutional differences that challenge the study. Taking a functional stance to the effect of parliamentary initiatives renders her analysis more effective in pursuing her goal, than other hermeneutic methods would. To sum up: by looking at impact, using power and influence, she tailors her method to her analysis and goal with a neo-functional yardstick of comparison, making her results clear and able to illustrate several main points (her Steps 2 and 3).

V Conclusion and Final Reflections

Conducting a comparative study in law and religion is rarely straightforward and it is only manageable with the right methodologies based on a comprehensive understanding of the methods of comparative law. The methodology in such a complex area reflects the question of how the research should be done. There is no single definitive method, as the choice depends on various factors, leading to a need for diverse approaches. Moreover, the selection of methods is subjective and can vary from one researcher to another. In other words, if two researchers were given the same research question, each would likely use a different methodology. This variability arises because the approach to answering the 'how' question depends significantly on the researcher's perspective and objectives. Similarly, when using Google Maps, the directions we receive to reach a destination vary based on our starting point – illustrating how the answer to "how to get there" is context-dependent.

There is no universal comparative methodology capable of answering all research questions, even within the narrower scope of law and religion compared to comparative law more broadly. However, the methods discussed in this chapter, along with other available methods, can be effectively used to design a research approach, provided one understands their application and usage.

Appendix

Author Rejoinders and Reflections

I Esther Erlings[1]

Reading the comments chapter, I was captivated by the argument for subjectivity. Giving it some thought, I was reminded of my first encounter with common law and decisions that seemed wholly subjective exercises of judges offering their personal opinions. I later understood that common law judgements are informed by guiding principles, though the content of these may develop over time as society evolves. Perhaps, comparative analysis is like a common law judgement; guided by principles, but always seeking to provide a tailored response.

A related aspect was the emphasis on the fact that we are "but human" and cannot be expected to produce miracles. We are "but human", but because we are human, we have the power of communication. As also suggested by the authors, it is crucial that researchers clearly convey what they are trying to achieve and how. Ambitious projects are often costly, and we can appreciate good scholarship of a humbler nature but the communication of intentions remains key.

The authors further reject the idea that comparative research necessitates such a deep understanding of culture that comparing two legal systems requires two lifetimes; one lived in each. I could not find Legrand's quote, but, even so, there is nothing to say that the two lifetimes cannot be of different people. Multiple lifetimes of understanding can come together when researchers collaborate, and that may also be the future of comparative research in law and religion.

Finally, though not further discussed, it is interesting to see that the editors have aligned my contribution with doctrinal, cultural, and analytical methods. This probably reflects my view on comparative research well, as I believe that the three underlying concepts serve as the hallmarks of good comparative work – a deep understanding of the law, with keen cultural awareness, combined in thorough analysis.

1 Senior Lecturer in Law, Macquarie University.

II Matt Watson[2]

I am grateful to the editors for this very illuminating and thoughtful chapter, which does an excellent job of, firstly, exploring the essence of the comparativist project in legal scholarship; secondly, laying out the main methodological tools of the trade; and, thirdly, synthesising and analysing many of the chapters so as to tease out the particular methods the various authors employed. The picture that emerges is one in which a fascinating array of methods are on display across the authors' works, with no two authors relying on precisely the same methods, in the same proportions.

All of this, of course, is in keeping with the editors' underlying normative claim about method in comparative legal research (with which I quite agree): the only "right" way to go about doing good comparative legal research is to "compare what needs to be compared" in order to "shed light on the goal of the analysis". A bespoke approach is, therefore, not indulgent; it is imperative.

I further agree with the editors' suggestion that my chapter employs chiefly the doctrinal, historical, and cultural methods, with a sprinkling of the yardstick method operating in the background. In keeping with the editors' exhortations to be self-conscious about method, and with their claim that in comparative legal scholarship the doctrinal method is often best combined with other approaches, I deliberately set out to employ a methodology that went beyond mere doctrinal analysis by explicitly situating doctrinal differences within a historical and cultural framework.

III P T Babie[3]

Perhaps the most refreshing characteristic of Alumari, Andersen, and Barker's "Comments on Comparative Methodology Used throughout the Book" is simply that it allows the contributors, and the comparative approaches they adopt, to speak for themselves, allowing "each comparativist – budding or seasoned – [to] design their own subjective method for [their] project". With that in mind, and with Alumari, Andersen, and Barker as my guides, I was fascinated by the breadth and depth of approaches that can be used to study law and religion.

In the case of my own contribution, I was intrigued to find that there is so much more to be found in my methodology than I had identified. Perhaps most importantly, what Alumari, Andersen, and Barker reveal, constructively, for my own approach—and, indeed, for all authors in this volume—is not so much what my chapter does but what it does not do. In light of their analysis, I can see clear room for development of my approach using a more culturally informed methodology which "incorporate[s] an element of cultural

2 Lecturer, T C Beirne School of Law, University of Queensland.

3 Bonython Chair in Law and Professor of Law, Adelaide Law School, The University of Adelaide, Australia.

assessment or comparison in order to highlight the influence or effects of culture or perhaps to explain the lack of significance of culture". From that perspective, my analysis of the religion clauses of the Australian Constitution would clearly benefit from a broader engagement with the cultural sources of those clauses, as well as the way in which contemporary culture influences how those clauses are understood in modern Australia. This is something that would give greater valence to an understanding of, at least partially, the American origin story of the Australian religion clauses.

Still, in relation to my own method, I do hope that Alumari, Andersen, and Barker are right that because we are human, and "since the author of a legal comparative analysis should pursue a goal of depth and approach which suits their projects, their subjective goal, and approach means they are never really wrong"! Even if that is not true as concerns my comparative methodology, it gives me comfort that what I have attempted to do nonetheless makes a contribution to the rich diversity of approaches brought together in this volume.

IV Renae Barker[4]

Writing a rejoinder to a chapter in which one is a co-author presents a unique challenge, but it also offers an opportunity to engage critically with the analysis offered by fellow scholars. In this case, the analysis provided by Alamaric, Anderson, and Barker on the comparative methodologies used in our chapter was both thoughtful and illuminating. As the legal expert on law and religion, I found the classification of comparative methodologies insightful. I would argue that legal academics, particularly in doctrinal fields, are not often accustomed to explicitly outlining their methodologies.

Given that this chapter was intended for inclusion in a book about methodology, we were unusually conscious of methodology in undertaking our research. For example, rather than taking a more traditional doctrinal approach to case analysis, we employed an emergent thematic approach. We sought to uncover underlying themes rather than focus solely on deriving legal rules from case law. This thematic comparison allowed us to delve into the principles guiding judicial decisions, particularly in areas where the evolving capacities of minors are at stake, in an attempt to understand if the judicial reasoning in the jurisdictions under consideration were compatible with one another.

Unsurprisingly, given Andersen champions this method, our approach aligned with the yardstick method, as highlighted by the authors of the analysis. However, as highlighted by Alamaric, Anderson, and Barker, other methods of comparison found their way into our research as well. Some consciously, others unconsciously. It is hard retrospectively to go back and determine how

4 Senior Lecturer, Law School, University of Western Australia, Honorary Research Fellow Centre for Muslim States and Societies.

much of those that found their way into our research unconsciously were there via deliberate choice and how much osmosis played a role. However, I feel this highlights the need for volumes like this, in raising awareness and familiarity with different methodological (or epistemological) approaches, that it is possible for more diverse approaches to find their way into research.

V Tania Pagotto[5]

The chapter by Alumari, Andersen, and Barker offers a clear and valuable guide for future scholarship in comparative law and religion. Its thorough analysis identifies and describes six methods that are applied in the essays of this collection: doctrinal, historical, cultural, functional, analytical, and yardstick method.

Perhaps surprisingly, after the deep description of the five methods or techniques adopted, they also state that "a legal comparativist is never too superficial, nor are they too entrenched in method [...]. In other words, since the author of a legal comparative analysis should pursue a goal of depth and approach which suits their projects, their subjective goal and approach means they are never really wrong".

What could help to make a comparative analysis (in law and religion) truly successful, then?

As Rodolfo Sacco noted in his famous article "Legal Formants: A Dynamic Approach to Comparative Law": "the scholar has no other power than the one that comes from his capacity to persuade. He is, after all, a professor and an author, roles that multiply his chances of influencing the law by force of persuasion".[6]

It is crucial that legal comparativists clearly justify the methods they decide to use in their analysis. Doing so not only establishes credibility and authority in the research, but also ensures an intellectually rigorous and transparent approach, contributing to the integrity of the comparative process.

VI N G Rochow KC[7]

This work has provided a new and much needed perspective in the area of law and religion. It was only a few decades ago that "Law and Religion" was barely regarded as a legal discipline in its own right; and, indeed, it was considered by many with a degree of suspicion. That is no longer the case. Indeed, it is far from it. Its interfaces with constitutional law, discrimination law, and human

5 Post-doctoral Research Fellow in Law and Religion, School of Law, University of Milan-Bicocca.

6 Rodolfo Sacco, *Legal Formants: A Dynamic Approach to Comparative Law* (Installment II of II) (1992) 39(2) *The American Journal of Comparative Law* 343–401, 349.

7 Dr Neville Rochow KC Barrister and Adjunct Associate Professor, Adelaide Law School.

rights, to name but a few other disciplines, are well-established. As an area of legal academic discipline, it is now entrenched. And this work is a testament to the dimensions that are to be explored.

For me, as a lawyer with a foot in both camps, so to speak, the practice and the theory of law, the editors were patient to accommodate my idiosyncrasies. Their vision is broader than I at first appreciated. Somehow, the methodology adopted by one accustomed to developing arguments for courts has found a place among those approaches adopted by academic experts in the field. It is this refreshing acceptance of a diversity of methodological approaches that makes the work a valuable exercise and a worthy contribution to law and religion.

In the final analysis, while the law invites unending philosophical questions, both the theoretician and the practitioner meet as allies in pursuing the rights of individual and standing, often, as the last bulwark against state power. It is only by encouraging the widest range of methodological approaches to problems that the citizenry whose interests the law and lawyers serve, that the best outcomes can be achieved for individuals, the citizenry generally, and for promotion of the rule of law. This book should be seen as a contribution to those noble ends.

VII Sarah Moulds[8]

I have benefited greatly from the clear and thought-provoking methodological summary offered by Alumari, Andersen, and Barker's "Comments on Comparative Methodology Used throughout the Book". Having not previously sought to categorise my own methods with reference to the frameworks outlined in these comments, I have gained new insights into the strengths and weaknesses of my own analytical standpoint and that of others. I am delighted to see that I am not the only researcher that is attracted to a "hybrid" model that combines elements of the "analytical method" with other approaches such as the "doctrinal method" and aptly named "yardstick method". I like the idea of "hedging my analytical bets", so to speak!

Alumari, Andersen, and Barker's insights have also enabled me to see both the benefits and potential vulnerabilities of the benchmarking approach that is familiar to me and to the scholars that have influenced my thinking including Leston-Bandeira. I am often attracted to these methodological "benchmarks" because they promise a pathway out of what can seem like an intractably complex task of "evaluating" dynamic political institutions like parliaments. However, by showcasing the merits of other approaches – including the "cultural method" and the "functional method" – I am now inspired to take time to traverse more rugged terrain, particularly when confronted with epistemological challenges like evaluating policy and legislative response to religious

8 Associate Professor of Law, Justice and Society Unit, University of South Australia.

belief. While I remain a "recovering doctrinal scholar" at heart, I look forward to articulating more explicitly an additional fulsome spectrum of methodological influences in my research and legislative analysis in the future.

VIII Arvind P Bhanu[9] and Sonia Sthapak[10]

Doctrinal methodology used for setting stage and application of comparative tools for analysing the issue in order to examine the complex interplay between religious freedom, limitations, and permitted freedoms has properly been taken up by the editors (Alumari, Andersen, and Barker's "Comments on Comparative Methodology …"). Adding their methodological extractions as a new chapter is a great step followed by seeking response and rejoinder. Freedom of conscience within the framework of principle of secularism, we – Bhanu and Sthapak (Chapter 13) – have strategically chosen a fully comparative approach to examine the limitations of this freedom, the diverse patterns of such limitations, and the interplay between secularism and constitutional frameworks. The authors' assumption that internal conscience should be comparatively tested against external practices, while simultaneously assessing its validity in the external world, aligns with state-specific constitutional provisions. This functional testing approach has been a part of the research approach. The Essentiality Test, a tool employed in this analysis, raises pertinent questions not only about the sources and capabilities of those conducting the test but also about its adaptability to various contexts. The project's comparative approach to measuring permissions has been a research strategy that the editors may appreciate. To evaluate the adequacy, inadequacy, and prohibitions imposed on external permissions as tested in the research, the authors have effectively combined doctrinal and comparative methodologies, mirroring the approach taken by the commentators. Appreciably, the response and rejoinder chapter can provide an opportunity for the authors to engage with the comments and feedback received.

IX Flavia Bellieni Zimmermann[11]

The chapter that discusses grounded theory through a legal-comparative method draws from an inductive social research method to understand Brazilian and Pakistani women's subjectivity and interactions between subjectivity, social norms, and law. This epistemological approach provides a framework to understand the intersections between law and religion in Brazil and

9 Professor of Law and Research and Additional Director, Amity Law School, Amity University Noida, U.P., India, and Adjunct Professor at ALS, University of Adelaide, Australia.

10 Associate Professor, Department of Education, University of Allahabad, Prayagraj, U.P., India.

11 Lecturer in Public Policy, School of Social and Political Sciences, University of Melbourne. Adjunct Research Fellow, School of Social Sciences, University of Western Australia.

Pakistan. This grassroots methodological approach distances itself from previous Western-centric epistemological and scholarly biases, providing insight into the views of women from the Global South. The discussion, and data collected through this social research method, sets the scene for a reflection on the impact of societal views towards honour and religion in gender-based laws in these two non-Western countries. Brazilian and Pakistani women interviewed for this comparative-legal analysis are representative of diverse views within these two migrant communities, living in Sydney, New South Wales, and Perth, Western Australia. Although social research methods (and grounded theory) focus on the subjectivity of participants, which can be the object of critique and claims of "overlooking issues and cherry-picking examples", such claims bypass the rigors of NVivo coding and techniques of "rooting" themes inherent of this social research method. The legal-comparative analysis I conduct in the chapter showcases the multivalence of these women's experiences of honour and religion, and their intersecting views, and how these religious perceptions are translated into legislation. The insight from grounded theory lays down a framework for an in-depth understanding of the role of religion in gender-based laws in honour-based countries such as Brazil and Pakistan, which differs significantly from Western representations.

X Gerhard van der Schyff[12]

With this edited volume, Alumari, Andersen, and Barker have achieved four remarkable and interrelated things. First, they have shown that the comparativist cannot cover all the research methods conceivable for their research. Of all the chapters the editors have scrutinised, none addresses all the six methods they distinguish, namely the doctrinal, historical, functional, analytical, cultural, and yardstick approaches. Nor is this necessary for meaningful research either. Second, the volume shows what is necessary to conduct research, namely that authors should think about what they want to achieve with their research and decide how best to approach it methodologically. In other words, research ambitions require a considered approach. Third, the volume provides evidence for the proposition that meaningful research is likely to require the use of more than one method. Designing research is not a matter of simply choosing one method, but of combining methods to varying degrees. All research is essentially blended or mixed-method enterprises. And fourth, the volume achieved something new, namely the combination of a focus on method and content in the context of law and religion. While many studies focus on one or the other, this work not only presents varied content but also provides food for thought on how the content is or could be constructed.

12 Associate Professor, Department of Public Law and Governance, Law School, Tilburg University, The Netherlands.

Index

Note: Page numbers in **bold** reference tables.

FSC
www.fsc.org
MIX
Papier | Fördert
gute Waldnutzung
FSC® C083411

Kolibri 360 GmbH
Ferdinand-Jühlke-Straße 7
99095 Erfurt, Deutschland
produktsicherheit@kolibri360.de